MEMORY AND SUGGESTIBILITY IN THE FORENSIC INTERVIEW

MEMORY AND SUGGESTIBILITY IN THE FORENSIC INTERVIEW

Edited by

Mitchell L. Eisen
California State University, Los Angeles

Jodi A. Quas
University of California, Irvine

Gail S. Goodman
University of California, Davis

Routledge
Taylor & Francis Group

LONDON AND NEW YORK

First published 2002 by
Lawrence Erlbaum Associates, Inc.

Published 2014 by Routledge
2 Park Square, Milton Park, Abingdon, Oxfordshire OX14 4RN
711 Third Avenue, New York, NY 10017

Routledge is an imprint of the Taylor & Francis Group, an informa business

Cover design by Kathryn Houghtaling Lacey

Library of Congress Cataloging-in-Publication Data

Memory and suggestibility in the forensic interview / edited by
   Mitchell L. Eisen, Jodi A. Quas, Gail S. Goodman.
      p.   cm.
   Includes bibliographical references and indexes.
   ISBN 978-0-8058-3080-4 (hbk)
   ISBN 978-1-138-00316-3 (pbk)

   1. Eisen, Mitchell L.   II. Quas, Jodi A.   III. Goodman, Gail S.
HV8073 .M39   2000
363.25'4 – dc21   00-060978
                                                    CIP

Contents

II Stress, Trauma, and Individual Differences

III Adults in the Forensic Interview Context

IV Children in the Forensic Interview Context

Preface

Our goals in developing this book were straightforward. We wanted to provide researchers and practitioners with a review of state-of-the-art research and thinking on memory and suggestibility in the forensic context. We wanted the chapters to cover the exciting domains of both child and adult eyewitness testimony. And, importantly, we wanted to bring together a distinguished group of psychologists representing diverse points of view and diverse backgrounds to write chapters in their areas of expertise. Thanks to the contributors—and much to our delight—all of these goals have been achieved.

As will be evident to readers, the study of memory and suggestibility in the forensic interview has much to offer both scientists and practitioners. For scientists, it elucidates the nature of memory—its malleability and strengths—as well as the mechanisms that underlie its complex workings and development. For practitioners, it has the potential to educate interviewers of all sorts (e.g., law enforcement personnel, social workers, teachers, medical professionals, attorneys, judges, and "even" parents) about how to obtain the most accurate and credible information from children and adults. Clearly, the book will be of interest to researchers and practitioners spanning a broad range of disciplines. It will also serve as a useful overview for legal scholars and students of psychology and law who wish to gain insight into current debates and empirical findings.

Although the book is relatively balanced in its coverage of the child and adult eyewitness literatures, for several reasons (e.g., the complexities of interviewing children), there are a few more chapters on children than adults. Further, there is at times some inevitable overlap in the ideas and topics discussed by the different authors. We allowed the authors flexibility in structuring their chapters, and we declined to impose our opinions or feelings on the viewpoints presented. As a result, the book presents a particularly rich and realistic portrayal of empirical research on children's and adults' mnemonic capabilities, susceptibility to suggestions and false memories, and eyewitness capabilities.

The chapters in the book are divided into four parts: General Principles and Basic Processes; Stress, Trauma, and Individual Differences; Adults in the Forensic Interview Context; and Children in the Forensic Interview Context. The chapters in Part I, General Principles and Basic Processes, present an overview of basic mnemonic processes that should be considered when evaluating memory and suggestibility. In chapter 1, Roediger and Gallo discuss important principles of memory in adults by focusing on factors that affect encoding, storage, and retrieval of information. Ornstein and Haden take a similar approach in chapter 2 and review memory development, particularly how children's memory can be altered during the encoding, storage, and retrieval phases of memory. The basic information reviewed in chapters 1 and 2 applies to forensic contexts, as well as other contexts. These chapters are critical for the broad understanding of human memory on which evaluations of eyewitness reports must depend.

The next two chapters focus on principles associated with memory distortion. Chapter 3 concerns an extreme form of suggestibility—being subject to false memory creation. Hyman and Loftus describe fundamental mechanisms necessarily involved in false memory reports and provide examples of empirical research that illustrate the mechanisms in operation. Saywitz and Lyon (chapter 4) propose that suggestibility research in children can be seen as lying on a continuum. At one end of the continuum are suggestibility studies that expose children's vulnerabilities. At the other end are studies that test strategies to promote children's optimal performance. Evaluating prior research along this continuum reveals valuable, practical information about how and how not to question child witnesses to obtain the most accurate and complete accounts possible. In the final chapter in Part I, Brigham (chapter 5) presents an up-to-date overview of the face-identification literature. Brigham's review covers theoretical debates regarding the ontogeny of face identification, adults' and children's cross-racial identification, and practical issues of relevance to forensic interviewing. Combined, the five chapters in Part I constitute a foundation for a basic understanding of children's and adults' eyewitness memory and for an appreciation of the important information conveyed in subsequent chapters.

In Part II of the book, Stress, Trauma, and Individual Differences, the chapters address the influence on memory of the stress associated with events and the characteristics associated with individuals. Chapters 6, 7, and 8 focus on the role of stress and trauma in affecting memory. First, Engelberg and Christianson present case illustrations of individuals' memory (or lack thereof) for distressing and oftentimes traumatic personal experiences. They also discuss how memory processes and coping mechanisms may account for the sometimes unique, surprising characteristics of memory for traumatic events. Second, Pezdek and Taylor (chapter 7) present a compelling argument that memory for stressful events operates in the same manner and abides by the same rules as memory for nonstressful events. Third, Dalenberg, Hyland, and Cuevas (chapter 8) describe circumstances under which fantastic elements in eyewitness memory reports may be associated with true (rather than false) allegations of abuse. The authors present preliminary evidence in support of this fascinating claim.

Chapters 9 and 10, by Eisen, Winograd, and Qin, and by Pipe and Salmon, concern the problem of individual differences in memory and suggestibility, one that has received growing attention in recent years. Eisen, Winograd, and Qin offer a new organizational framework for the adult individual-difference literature by articulating how the relations between suggestibility and individual-difference factors, primarily personality characteristics, are dependent on the type of suggestibility research paradigm employed. Pipe and Salmon review recent evidence concerning sources of variability in children's memory and suggestibility, including memory for stressful events. They discuss both cognitive and social-personality factors that are associated with individual differences in children's performance as well as exciting new directions in this emerging area of research.

The three chapters that form Part III, Adults in the Forensic Interview Context, attest to the power of the interview context in affecting memory accuracy. Fisher, Brennan, and McCauley (chapter 11) describe the Cognitive Interview (CI), a questioning technique designed to facilitate recall of personal experiences. The authors review recent studies that uncover beneficial effects of the CI in combating suggestibility in real forensic interviews as well as in the laboratory. In contrast to the emphasis of the Fisher et al. chapter on methods that can augment the amount of mnemonic information provided in a forensic interview, that of the next two chapters is on how certain questioning methods may give rise to gross distortions in memory. Lynn, Neuschatz, and Fite (chapter 12) discuss important limitations to the use of hypnosis as a mnemonic aid because of the possible unreliability of the information gleaned. The authors take this argument one step further and describe how information obtained after hypnosis should also be considered suspect. In chapter 13, Shobe and Kihlstrom assert that many of the processes believed to underlie suggestibility in interrogative settings are also evident in some therapeutic contexts, where they can potentiate false memories of abuse. In all, the three chapters present a much-needed clarification of factors associated with interviewing contexts that can enhance or diminish the quality of information provided by adults.

Part IV, Children in the Forensic Interview Context, parallels Part III. For children, as for adults, some factors associated with the forensic context enhance memory performance, and other factors diminish it. Furthermore, these influences may well depend on age. In the first chapter of this part, Fivush, Peterson, and Schwarzmueller (chapter 14) summarize research on the impact on children's memory performance of repeated questions, both within and across interviews; lengthy delays; and suggestive questions. They conclude with practical information about the hazards of certain questioning strategies on children's report accuracy. Next, Poole and Lindsay (chapter 15) outline general conclusions regarding children's suggestibility, and, equally important, exceptions to these general conclusions. They further demonstrate how a Bayesian analysis, a type of probability model, can be applied to forensic decision making to identify likelihood ratios for true and false reports of abuse. Everson and Boat (chapter 16) highlight the findings and limitations of several influential studies of the use of props and anatomical dolls in forensic interviews with children. They also discuss promising new directions in the use of mnemonic aids, such as drawings, to augment recall. Sternberg, Lamb, Esplin, Orbach, and Hershkowitz (chapter 17) describe the development of their cutting-edge structured-interview protocol, designed to increase the amount of correct narrative information children provide in forensic contexts and reduce children's errors. Sternberg et al. also present recent data from their laboratory demonstrating the use of the protocol in actual forensic interviews with child abuse victims. Finally, in chapter 18, Davis and Bottoms discuss the role of interviewer demeanor in affecting children's memory and suggestibility. Specifically, they review prior research that has revealed benefits of interviewers behaving in a supportive rather than nonsupportive manner during an interview, particularly an improvement in older children's ability to resist false suggestions. Davis and Bottoms then discuss one possible mechanism (perceived self-efficacy) that may underlie the observed benefits and present preliminary evidence from their laboratory confirming the mechanism's importance. Together the chapters in Part IV highlight the many issues that need to be considered when questioning the child witness.

It is imperative to acknowledge the efforts of numerous people who contributed to the completion of this book. Since it was first conceived, all three editors worked long hours to make the book a success. But, many others helped as well. We would like to express our gratitude to Susan Milmoe and the editing staff at Lawrence Erlbaum Associates; to our colleague Barbara Boat; and to a number of graduate students, specifically, Kristen Alexander, Robin Edelstein, Simona Ghetti, Allison Redlich, Jennifer Schaaf, and Juliana Raskauskas. Finally, and perhaps most importantly, we thank our families for their support throughout our endeavor.

The diverse topics, viewpoints, and approaches presented in this book reveal the complexity of studying eyewitness memory. We hope readers will appreciate this complexity as well as appreciate the tremendous efforts made by scientists to advance our knowledge of memory and suggestibility in the forensic interview.

—Jodi A. Quas
—Gail S. Goodman
—Mitchell L. Eisen

I

---

*GENERAL PRINCIPLES
AND BASIC PROCESSES*

Processes Affecting Accuracy and Distortion in Memory: An Overview

Henry L. Roediger, III
David A. Gallo
Washington University

The empirical study of human memory is 115 years old, dating from Ebbinghaus's (1885/1964) pioneering investigations. Throughout most of the history of the study of memory, investigators focused on factors that affect accurate remembering: repetition of information, spacing of repetitions, retention interval, types of material, retrieval cues, and dozens more. Researchers have usually assessed accurate responding on memory tests or they have measured *forgetting*, typically defined as omissions of response on tests as a function of delay. Researchers rarely provided systematic investigations of various errors in memory, although a few early studies examined errors (see Roediger, 1996; Schacter, 1995, for the history of memory distortion research). It has only been relatively recently (since about 1970) that experimental psychologists began the systematic investigation of errors of memory. We may refer to *memory illusions* as occurring when people remember events quite differently from the way they originally happened or, in the most dramatic case, remembering events that never happened at all (Roediger, 1996). The goal of this chapter is to provide a brief overview of factors affecting both veridical and illusory memories that may be relevant for forensic purposes.

We choose as our object of understanding a person's encoding, storage, and retrieval of an event. Each term in the previous sentence needs elaboration. The term *event* is ambiguous and may refer to simple events (studying a list of words or pictures, or even the study of a single word or picture in a list) or complex ones, such as witnessing an armed robbery.

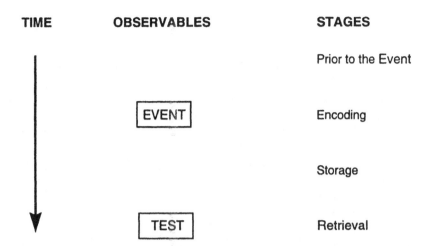

FIG. 1.1.   The four stages of the learning–memory process that are relevant
to understanding how an event is remembered. Although factors occurring
at each stage can influence later remembering, only the event in question
and the response to retrieval query (test) can actually be observed. Note that
these stages are theoretically useful, but difficult to separate in experiments.

No matter what the scope or complexity of an event, however, the description of memory for it can be usefully separated into encoding of the
event (its original perception and acquisition), its retention over time due
to some change in the nervous system that can be called memory storage,
and its later retrieval in response to some query.

Figure 1.1 provides the organizational theme of this chapter. We examine the retention of events in terms of (a) factors occurring before the event
in question, (b) factors operating during encoding of the event, (c) processes occurring after the event that might alter its retention, and finally (d)
processes operating during retrieval of the event. Some factors operating
at each stage may enhance memory for the event, whereas others may
hamper future retrieval and increase the likelihood of erroneous retrieval.
Our goal in writing this chapter is not to be exhaustive—we could not
be—but to highlight some salient points at each stage in the learning-
memory process that should be kept in mind when considering the forensic issues of memory.

FACTORS OCCURRING PRIOR TO THE EVENT

It might seem odd to consider factors that operate prior to the occurrence
of an event as affecting its later retention, but in fact such prior factors can
be critical. Even if several people experience "the same" event, they will
interpret it differently depending on their prior experiences. Each person

perceives an event with different backgrounds and proclivities. Each of us has had different experiences and likewise has different attitudes, knowledge, dispositions, and biases. Bartlett (1932) captured these differences in background knowledge with the term *schemata*, which are mental structures that organize our past experiences. Bartlett argued that memory is affected by how well (or poorly) we can encode new experiences in terms of schemata developed from our past experiences.

Bartlett (1932) conducted some casual experiments requiring English college students to remember a Native American folktale, "The War of the Ghosts." Because this story, filled with supernatural elements, was unlike the typical stories or experiences of his students, their schemata were not sufficiently developed for remembering the story. The students inserted systematic errors into their recalls of the story, making it more like a fairytale in its retelling. They had adapted the story to their own schemata. In general, past knowledge can distort memory by providing us with a set of categories into which we try to pigeonhole our new experiences, whether or not they fit.

Past experience can also enhance retention. If new information fits well with prior knowledge or schemata, retention of the information is generally better than when information does not fit. This point is aptly demonstrated in the psychological literature; people who are experts in some domain usually remember new information about that domain better than other people with less background knowledge. In these instances, background knowledge allows us to organize and make sense of incoming information. More prosaically, memory for material that is organized meaningfully is better remembered than when the same material is presented in a scrambled and less meaningful manner.

Consider a thought experiment: Two groups of subjects are asked to remember a long string of digits in order, after it is read once at the rate of one second per digit. Try it yourself by covering up the page after reading these digits and recalling them: 1, 4, 9, 1, 6, 2, 5, 3, 6, 4, 9, 6, 4, 8, 1. In our hypothetical experiment, one group would be tested as you were and they would not remember the series well, getting perhaps seven or so digits correct. Another group, however, would be instructed before they read the digits that the numbers would represent the squares of the numbers 1 to 9 (1 squared is 1, 2 squared is 4, etc.). For this group, the same list would be read, but recall would be perfect. The two groups experienced "the same event" being read to them, but in one case relevant knowledge (the schema for the digits) had been activated prior to study, whereas in the other case it had not. Again, retention is usually better when material can be interpreted in terms of relevant prior knowledge.

Exposure to prior material can also interfere with new learning and retention (Underwood, 1957). Consider the case in which you might have to remember details of a crime scene over long periods of time. If you have seen many crime scenes because you are a police detective, it might be difficult to remember the current scene because of interference from many crime scenes that you previously observed and studied. The process of similar events becoming confused in memory is referred to as *interference*. When prior events are confused with memory for a more recent event, it is called *proactive interference* (we discuss other types of interference later). Proactive interference in memory for an event is generally weak immediately after the event is experienced, but increases over time. To return to the case of the police detective who visits many crime scenes, she might have good retention for the most recent crime immediately after she studied it. But, if queried weeks later, the many prior crime scenes might provoke interference in her memory for the particular scene of interest. In general, the more closely the events in memory resemble one another, the more difficult it is to remember the details of one particular event without interference from the others.

Background characteristics of a person can also affect how well he or she retains events. In general, young children usually remember events less well than older children or adults, whereas older adults remember more poorly than young adults. Relative to young adults, both children and older adults are also more susceptible to interference effects. Memories from early in life, typically before the ages of 3 to 4, are often unreliable. The terms *infantile amnesia* or *childhood amnesia* refer to the notion that people generally recall little or nothing from this early period of life once they reach adulthood. However, children are clearly learning during these early years; the difficulty is consciously recollecting the information later (see Howe & Courage, 1993, for a review). Other people showing signs of profound amnesia are those who have suffered brain injuries (strokes, closed head injuries, damage from neurosurgery to remove tumors, etc.). Some debilitating neurological diseases (e.g., Alzheimer's disease) and other psychiatric illnesses (schizophrenia) can impair memory. Depressed people also generally show declines in memory.

Other personality characteristics can also affect retention. For example, some evidence suggests that a measure of how "spacy" people are predicts the occurrence of false memories in several paradigms. The measure is called the Dissociative Experiences Scale (DES), and it asks people to estimate how often they have experiences such as "listening to someone talk and they suddenly realize that they did not hear part or all of what was said," or "not being sure whether things that they remember happening really did happen or whether they just dreamed them" (Bernstein & Putnam, 1986). People who score high on this test tend to be more susceptible to false memories (Hyman & Billings, 1998; Winograd, Peluso, & Glover, 1998).

This section described some background factors that individuals bring to events that are relevant to accuracy and distortions in remembering. However, the statements in this section tell only part of the story. In order to influence memory, these background factors must affect how people encode, retain, or retrieve events. We return to some of these variables later.

THE ENCODING, STORAGE, AND RETRIEVAL FRAMEWORK

The remainder of this chapter is organized around the standard encoding–storage–retrieval conception of memory (Melton, 1963). As previously noted, encoding refers to the initial registration of information—its perception and the immediate postperceptual processing. *Retention* or *storage* refers to the maintenance of information over time, once it has been encoded. *Retrieval* refers to the utilization of stored information. When performance on a memory test reflects accurate responding—a person successfully remembers some past event—an inference can be made that all three stages were intact.

Although this three-stage conception of the learning–memory process is logically sound, in actual practice it is problematic for two reasons (Roediger & Guynn, 1996). First, it is difficult to separate the processes of encoding and storage. When does encoding end and storage or retention begin? Similarly, when forgetting occurs (response omission), or when there is an error of commission—a false memory—it is difficult to determine where the problem occurred. Was the information miscoded? Did processes operating during the retention interval produce interference, thereby causing the information to be misremembered? Or, was the information never encoded in the first place, and wrongly reconstructed during retrieval?

A second problem is that all three stages of the learning-memory process are intertwined and depend on each other. Encoding is an obvious prerequisite to storage, except in unusual cases. In addition, how information is encoded and stored determines what cues will be effective in its later retrieval (Tulving, 1974). It is important to note, however, that encoding and storage alone do not guarantee that information will be remembered. Retrieval is the critical process that must occur in order to convert latent information into a conscious experience (Roediger, 2000; Tulving, 1983).

Despite these caveats, we used this encoding–storage–retrieval framework for simplicity. We discuss a number of variables that can be manipulated during study (encoding), retention interval, and later test or retrieval query.

ENCODING FACTORS

The distinction between perceiving and remembering is often blurry, as the two processes overlap. When does perceiving and encoding end and retention and memory begin? The answer is arbitrary. Phenomena such as *iconic* and *echoic memory* — lingering sensory representations in the visual and auditory systems, respectively — reveal the fine line dividing perceiving and remembering. If events happen so rapidly that they cannot be accurately perceived and encoded, then they cannot be remembered later. Usually these events would not be considered forgotten because the concept of forgetting presupposes that the events were encoded and potentially could be remembered at some point in the future. However, it is not necessary for an event to be presented to the senses to be remembered. For instance, when dealing with errors of memory, it is possible for people to remember events that did not actually occur (e.g., Roediger & McDermott, 1995), a point that we discuss later. These events might have been internally generated by the rememberer — they could have been imagined or constructed — but were never actually experienced.

The perceptual world is vast. Try another thought experiment. Walk outside and survey a busy scene. Now close your eyes quickly and try to recall as much as you can. You probably found that you could not remember much of the detailed information that was before your eyes. If you did poorly on such a test when trying to recall immediately after the experience, think how much worse you would do after a long interval. One tactic lawyers sometimes use to discredit eyewitnesses of a crime is to produce a picture of the crime scene so that the judge and jury can see it, but the witness cannot. Then the lawyer asks the witness about details of the scene, usually resulting in a poor description. This demonstration appears to show poor retention on the witness' part, but the test is unreasonable. Although the judge and jury can pick out the details of a picture and may wonder why they are not recalled by the witness, virtually no one could pass such a test. Our minds are not capable of making complete records of events; rather, we encode features selectively. Even when we remember events reasonably well, we do not come close to remembering all the fine details that are part of the event. We are not like video recorders, faithfully taking in and storing all the details in a scene.

A key concept necessary in understanding processes occurring early in acquisition is coding, or recoding (Miller, 1956): We do not remember events as they happened, but rather as our minds have coded them. Think back to the hypothetical experiment. Two groups would try to remember the digit string 1, 4, 9, 1, 6, and so on. Both groups would see the same events, the 15 digits, but one group would code it as "squares of 1 to 9," whereas the other group would probably code it in a less meaningful manner, and hence would remember it less effectively.

As previously noted, past experience and knowledge can prompt different people to encode "the same experience" in different ways. Bartlett (1932) relied on "the old and familiar illustration of the landscape artist, the naturalist, and the geologist who walk in the country together. The one is said to notice the beauty of scenery, the other details of flora and fauna, and the third the formation of soils and rock. In this case, no doubt, the stimuli, being selected in each instance from what is present, are different for each observer, and obviously the records made in recall are different also" (p. 4). Many years later, Underwood (1963) captured this idea by distinguishing between the *nominal* and *functional* stimuli in learning and memory. A nominal stimulus is the complex event as it exists in the world; a functional stimulus is that part of the nominal stimulus that is coded and may (potentially) be remembered. Because the environment provides a complex array of information, coding is selective: Only some features are encoded for later retention.

The idea that different perspectives can lead to different coding of events was demonstrated in a famous experiment by Hastorf and Cantril (1954). They capitalized on a rivalry between two colleges and their favorite football teams. The event that motivated their study was a particularly acrimonious football game in which Dartmouth played against an undefeated Princeton team. The game was marred by fights, penalties, and injured players (including Princeton's star, Dick Kazmaier, who had just been featured on the cover of *Time* magazine). Princeton won, but a debate swirled for weeks over which team was responsible for the game's roughness, with students at each school blaming the opposing team. This polarized student opinion led Hastorf and Cantril (1954) to their experiment. They asked students at each school to watch a film of the game and judge the number of penalties that each team committed. The results are indicated in Fig. 1.2.

As noted in the figure, the Dartmouth students counted 4.3 infractions committed by their own team and 4.4 by the Princeton team. This outcome was in accord with the general belief of the Dartmouth students that the game had been rough but fair, and the Dartmouth team was not out to wound the Princeton star. On the other hand, the Princeton students judged the Dartmouth team to have committed 9.8 penalties, compared to only 4.2 for the Princeton team. This confirmed their belief that Dartmouth's players had resorted to dirty play to stay competitive with Princeton, which was (according to a writer for the *Daily Princetonian*)

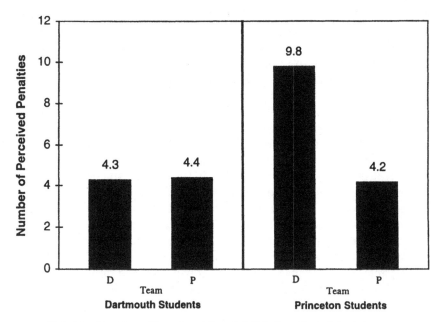

FIG. 1.2.   Data from Hastorf and Cantril (1954). Even though both groups watched the same game, the Princeton students reported more than twice as many penalties committed by the Dartmouth team than did the Dartmouth students.

"obviously the better team." Background attitudes shaped perceptions in this case and, surely, if Princeton and Dartmouth students had their memories tested, their recollections of the game would have been consistent with their different perceptions.

Obviously, a false perception typically results in a false memory. But some cases can be tricky to classify. Consider an experiment reported by Roediger and McDermott (1995). They presented adults with lists of words such as *door, glass, pane, shade, ledge, sill, house, open, curtain, frame, view, breeze, sash, screen,* and *shutter.* Participants were asked to recall the words in any order immediately after hearing them and admonished not to guess. After studying and recalling many lists, the adults took a recognition test that included both items from the study lists and items not from the lists (i.e., lures or distracters). Their task was to differentiate between words that had been presented on the original list (studied, or "old" words) and words that were not on the list (nonstudied, or "new" words). In addition, for words deemed "old" or studied, participants were further asked to make remember/know judgments (Tulving, 1985). For this decision, they were asked if they recognized the word because they could remember its actual occurrence on the study list or rather because they knew that the word was in the list, but could not actually remember any details about its occurrence.

There is interest in this paradigm because it provokes remarkably high levels of false recall and false recognition. The list of words presented above was derived from associates of the word *window*, but that word did not appear on the list. The data from the immediate recall test are shown in Fig. 1.3. These data form a serial position curve, plotting the probability of correctly recalling a word (on the ordinate) as a function of the word's position in the list (on the abscissa). Data were averaged over many lists and many participants. Note that items studied at the beginning of the list were recalled better than those studied in the middle (the primacy effect), as were items studied at the end of the list (the recency effect). Primacy and recency effects occur often in memory tests with various kinds of study materials. However, for present purposes the most interesting finding (represented by the dashed line) was the probability of recalling words like *window* as in the list although they were not actually presented. Participants recalled *window* as though it had occurred on the list; in fact, recall of such critical items was higher than that for words that were presented in the middle of the list.

Recognition is sometimes assumed to be a more sensitive test than recall in assessing stored information. However, like recall, the recognition re-

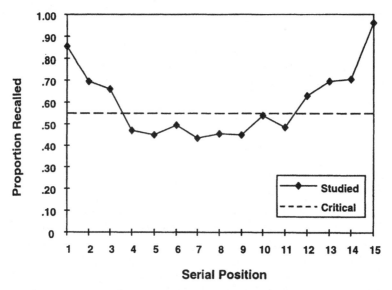

FIG. 1.3. Free recall data from Roediger and McDermott (1995), Experiment 2. The probability of falsely recalling the nonpresented critical items (e.g., *window*) was at least as high as the probability of correctly recalling the items from the middle of the list.

sults shown in Fig. 1.4 show a robust memory illusion. Participants claimed to recognize the critical lures like *window* at high rates, similar to those of the studied items. In addition, they claimed to "remember" the moment of occurrence of words like *window* at about the same rates as for the studied items, as shown in the black part of the bars in Fig. 1.4. The data in Figs. 1.3 and 1.4 reveal a powerful memory illusion occurring in a straightforward paradigm: People recall, recognize, and remember the occurrence of events (words appearing in a list) that objectively never happened.

Why does this illusion occur? One idea is that during study of the list, the word *window* might (consciously or unconsciously) have been activated as an *implicit associative response* to hearing the related words (Roediger, Balota, & Watson, 2001; Underwood, 1965). Basically, participants inferred the word, even though it was not presented, and then falsely recollected that it was presented. Like perceptual illusions, this memory illusion is difficult to modify. Although instructing adults about the nature of the illusion and then testing them with the lists causes a dampening of the illusion, people still falsely recall and recognize nonpresented words at a high rate (Gallo, Roberts, & Seamon, 1997; McDermott & Roediger, 1998). Although it is difficult to argue that the illusion in the Roediger–McDermott paradigm represents an encoding error exclusively, at least some evidence points to this conclusion (McDer-

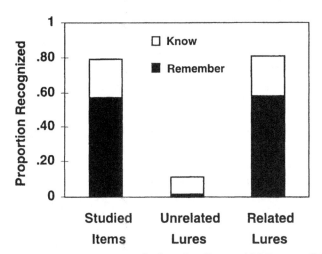

FIG. 1.4. Recognition test results from Roediger and McDermott (1995), Experiment 2. The related lures were falsely recognized as often as the studied words were correctly recognized, while recognition of unrelated lures was relatively low. Note that participants reported "remembering" the related lures about as often as they reported "remembering" items they had actually studied.

mott, 1997; Roediger et al., 2000; see Roediger, McDermott, & Robinson, 1998, for a review).

The general implication of these results for understanding truth and distortion in memory is that humans are inference machines — we make inferences in order to understand the world around us. We do not remember just the literal information in a message (e.g., the words in the list), but also what is implied (*window*). Research on retention of prose agrees that inferences can be remembered as having been explicitly stated (e.g., Brewer, 1977; Owens, Bower, & Black, 1979). Inferences are useful and the ability to derive them reflects human intelligence. However, especially in legal contexts, remembering events that were only inferred as actually having happened can be problematic, to say the least.

Although most of the foregoing has concentrated on errors people might make in encoding, experimental psychologists have spent much of the last century exploring encoding factors that enhance retention (although, to repeat, these variables may also affect retrieval processes). In the next paragraphs we provide a terse review of some of the most powerful encoding variables that affect performance on recall and recognition tests. These are standard measures of conscious recollection used in memory research. Each generalization provided is based on dozens and sometimes hundreds of studies. We cite only one reference that both documents the point and provides a useful starting place to examine the literature. Further, each statement carries an *e ceteris paribus* clause with it — all other things being equal — because in most cases there is an extreme circumstance that might invalidate the generalization. Nonetheless, the following statements are generally true.

Meaningful material is better remembered than less meaningful information, as previously noted. Similarly, organized material is more easily remembered than disorganized material (e.g., Marks & Miller, 1964). Pictures and highly concrete information are better remembered than words or abstract information (e.g., Paivio, 1986). Information presented slowly is better retained than information presented quickly (e.g., Glanzer & Cunitz, 1966). Material that receives a person's full attention is better retained than material that is presented under conditions of distraction (e.g., Fisk & Schneider, 1984). Repeated information is better retained than information presented only once, and the benefit of a repetition usually increases with the amount of time between the two presentations (Melton, 1970). Repetitions beyond two will continue to increase retention, although with diminishing returns (Challis & Sidhu, 1993). If conditions are conducive and enable people to reflect on the meaning of information when it is presented, they will remember it better than if attention is directed toward less meaningful aspects of the information (Craik & Tulving, 1975). Similarly, if people actively generate or interact with material, they generally remember better than if it is passively acquired (Jacoby, 1978; Slamecka & Graf, 1978). For example, people remember the word *cold* better if they generate it from the clue "opposite of hot" than if they just read the word *cold*.

Another powerful variable aiding retention is distinctiveness: Unusual or distinctive events are better remembered than more mundane and usual events (Hunt & McDaniel, 1993). Similarly (and perhaps for the same reason), emotional events are often easily remembered — the death of a loved one, a national crisis, or other salient and powerful events. In fact, such events are sometimes said to create "flashbulb memories," a phrase referring to the idea that people often believe they remember even fine details of highly emotional events as though they had been caught in a photographic flash (Brown & Kulik, 1977). However, some studies show that the strong impression of accuracy in flashbulb memories is not entirely warranted (Neisser & Harsch, 1992), even though memories for these events are probably better than for any reasonable set of control events.

Of course, many other encoding variables affect retention besides the ones described in the preceding paragraphs. In considering factors that can lead to poor retention, simply take the opposite of these factors. For example, meaningless information is difficult to encode and harder to accurately remember. This is also the case for information that is presented rapidly, under massed presentation conditions, or processed in a superficial manner. In addition, if the event is ordinary, or does not stand out, it will be more poorly remembered than a distinctive event.

This section focused on factors that strongly affect memory. We included them here because the manipulations provoking these effects usually occur during original learning. However, to reiterate, storage and retrieval must also be involved and are critical in producing the previously discussed effects. In the next section, we discuss factors that operate during the retention interval.

BETWEEN ENCODING AND RETRIEVAL

In studies of memory, the time between original encoding and later retrieval is referred to as the *retention interval*. As previously noted, providing a dividing line between the end of encoding and the beginning of the retention interval is somewhat arbitrary. However, it is clear that processes operating after encoding can greatly affect memory for an event.

One such process is *memory consolidation*, the idea that memory traces for an event may become stronger after the event is over. At the beginning of the 20th century, Müller and Pilzecker (1900) hypothesized that neural processes created by the perception of events perseverate after the event. At first the perseveration is labile and easily changed, but over time this perseveration of neural activity (consolidation) creates lasting neural traces. Hebb (1949) argued for two processes in consolidation. The first (labile) phase was identified with short-term memory and the more permanent condition with long-term memory. The primary evidence for such consolidation processes is found in studies of *retrograde amnesia*, a term that refers to forgetting events that occurred prior to some type of brain injury. For example, if someone is involved in an automobile accident and is rendered unconscious, he or she is unlikely to remember events that happened just prior to the accident (retrograde amnesia) and perhaps even for a few hours after the accident (anterograde amnesia). The prior events may have been in a labile state when the injury occurred and were not permanently consolidated. Over time the recollection of some events (those most distant in time from the injury) might be recovered, although events immediately surrounding the crash itself may not be. The severity of the amnesia is determined by the nature of the brain injury.

Memory for an event may also be altered during the retention interval by psychological means. *Retroactive interference* refers to the interfering effects of new events on prior events. If you park your car in slightly different places every day on your way to work, try to remember where you parked it 1 week ago. Assuming you have been to your place of work steadily during the previous week, you will probably find this a difficult task. The various places you parked every day during the past week would exert retroactive interference on your ability to remember where you had parked a week ago. If you had not been to work in the past week, the task would have been considerably easier. Again, as was the case with proactive interference, the more similar the events are to the critical event, the greater the interfering effect.

Loftus, Miller, and Burns (1978) showed how information occurring after a witnessed event can distort recollection of the event. In their experiments, adults viewed pictures of 30 colored slides depicting an automobile accident resulting from a car that failed to yield the right of way and caused a collision. A critical detail manipulated in one of the slides was whether a stop sign or a yield sign was present at the intersection. (Across participants, each sign occurred equally often). Participants were later asked a series of questions about the slides. One group was not asked about the sign (the control group), another group was asked "Did the car pass the red Datsun while it was stopped at the stop sign?", and a third group was asked this same question with "at the yield sign" instead. These questions provided information that was either consistent or inconsistent (misleading) with respect to the actual scene witnessed earlier. During a delay, participants completed a task unrelated to the experiment and next a memory test was given. One item on the test addressed the original type of sign that had appeared at the intersection (Was there a stop or a yield sign?). The results were straightforward: Adults who were given consistent information had better retention of the slides (70% correct) relative to the control group, which was given the information only once (63% correct). However, the most dramatic finding was the effect of the misinformation; responding in this condition was only 43% correct. Loftus et al.'s (1978) interpretation of this finding was that the misinformation caused adults to recode their memories for the original event so that they now included the erroneous sign.

In general, information given later about a witnessed event can mold and alter our retention of the event. If the following information is accurate, our memories may improve; if the information is inaccurate or misleading, we may nonetheless incorporate it into our recollections of the past. This misinformation effect, as it has come to be called, is a type of retroactive interference that has been often studied in the laboratory, and abundant literature employs the paradigm (see Ayers & Reder, 1998; Loftus, 1991, for reviews). The implications for the accuracy of eyewitness testimony are profound: Questions or statements occurring after an event can alter eyewitness accounts.

Another type of retroactive interference, *imagination inflation* (Garry, Manning, Loftus, & Sherman, 1996), refers to the finding that if people are asked to imagine events, they sometimes begin to believe they actually occurred. Garry et al. (1996) gave adults a Life Events Inventory that asked if particular events had ever occurred during the person's childhood ("Did you ever break a window with your hand?"). The adults were asked to imagine participating in half of the unlikely events. The other half were considered control items, and the adults were not asked to imagine them. Questions during the imagination session were intended to provoke vivid visual imagery. Later, participants were again asked to fill out the Life Events Inventory (they were told the first ones had been lost). On the retest, items that had been imagined during the intervening interval were judged as more likely to have occurred during childhood than items not imagined. Imagining the event inflated participants' confidence that it had actually occurred.

Of course, a counterargument is that imagining might have actually provoked memories of events similar to the one being tested, so perhaps the increase in confidence indicated a more accurate rather than a less accurate recollection of childhood events. Because testing childhood memories does not permit a researcher to know what events actually occurred during childhood, either interpretation of the Garry et al. (1996) results can be accepted (although we believe their interpretation is the correct one).

Goff and Roediger (1998) developed a laboratory paradigm that eliminates this interpretive problem. Action events, such as "Break the toothpick" or "Pick up the toy car," were used. Sometimes adults heard the command, sometimes they heard the command and imagined performing it, and on other occasions they heard the command and actually performed the task (using toys placed in front of them at the appropriate time by the experimenter). Later, the adults were engaged in an imagination session and were asked to imagine performing tasks when given the commands (some they had already heard, some were new). The question examined was whether imagining events would make people remember that they had actually performed them. When they were tested, results indicated that imagining actions prompted adults to report that they had actually performed them in the original session, even though they never had. Further, the more times the adults were required to imagine, the more likely they were to remember performing the action.

Similar results have been obtained from questioning participants repeatedly. Ceci, Loftus, Leichtman, and Bruck (1994) interviewed children ages 3 to 6 and asked them if they had ever experienced events that were implausible and would probably have been easily remembered if actually experienced. For example, children were asked if they had ever ridden in a hot air balloon. At the first interview, the children usually responded that this had not happened. (Parents had agreed that the events had not happened to the children.) However, the researchers continued interviewing the children every week for up to 10 weeks. About 25% of the children began to have "memories" for the events and, after repeated queries, some of the recollections became full of details. Some children appeared convinced by these new memories. A plausible mechanism for the development of these memories is imagination. Each time the child was asked about the event, he or she might have briefly imagined it. In response to a later query, the child may have confused imagined events with real events and reported the imagined events as real. Once again, the implications for testimony in forensic settings are profound. If repeated questioning encourages witnesses to imagine events, the witnesses may begin to remember the events as having actually occurred.

We have not mentioned the most commonly studied factor during the retention interval: time. Ebbinghaus (1885/1964) first plotted the relation between time and retention and obtained a logarithmic function, shown in Fig. 1.5. At first retention decreases rapidly but then levels off at long delays. This function is general and has been found across many different situations and types of material (Rubin & Wenzel, 1996).

The factors previously discussed focus on forgetting or errors induced during the retention interval. Can memories be improved by postevent processing? Yes. One way, as mentioned, is repetition of the event or some aspects of it. Another way is through retrieval of the event. Many studies have demonstrated *the testing effect*: If people's accurate recollections of

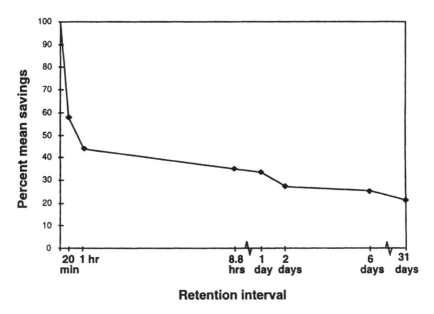

FIG. 1.5. A graph of Ebbinghaus's (1885/1964) famous forgetting function. Ebbinghaus learned material perfectly and measured how long it took him to do so. At later points in time he relearned the material and measured how much less time it took for relearning (the percent savings measure). The idea is that the better the memory for the original material, the greater the savings in relearning. Similarly, the less savings in relearning the material, the more forgetting he displayed. The graph plots retention (measured as savings) as a function of time since original learning. Note that the loss of information from memory (percent savings) is steep immediately after original learning, but becomes more gradual over time.

events are tested, they will remember the events better on future occasions than if they had not been tested. This benefit may be comparable to consolidation or reprocessing of the material. However, one proviso is that the testing effect can also enhance false memories: If someone recalls or recognizes an event incorrectly, that false recollection is also fixed into memory and more likely to reoccur on later tests (McDermott, 1996; Roediger, Jacoby, & McDermott, 1996; Schooler, Gerhard, & Loftus, 1986).

In summary, factors occurring during the retention interval that can have a negative impact on retrieval of an event include neurological trauma, retroactive interference arising from similar events, misleading information, imagining events that did not happen, and the presentation of questions about events that did not happen. However, postevent processing that encourages consolidation or accurate review or recollection of the prior events can improve later retrieval. We turn now to factors operating during retrieval.

RETRIEVAL PROCESSES

Retrieval has been called the key process in understanding memory (Roediger, 2000; Tulving, 1991) and research abounds on this topic (see Roediger & Guynn, 1996, for a review). Throughout most of the history of memory research, the retrieval stage was taken for granted. That is, researchers were concerned about processes of acquiring, storing, and retaining information, with an implicit assumption that if these processes were intact, memory would be good. The idea that forgetting or distortion—two common errors in memory—could be due to problems at retrieval was generally not accepted (although Bartlett's, 1932, work represents an exception). However, the retrieval stage is critical in many ways.

One important consideration is the form of the retrieval query: How is memory to be assessed? Psychologists have created many tests for measuring retention. Some of the primary measures are free recall (recalling information in any order in response to general queries), serial recall (retrieving information in order of presentation, such as one would a telephone number), cued recall (prompting recollection with various cues that can differ in many ways), and recognition (a type of cued response procedure in which various alternatives, including the correct one, are presented, and the rememberer picks the one that seems correct). There are several variants on each of these procedures.

Perhaps the primary conclusion to be drawn from work on retrieval processes is that whether a person remembers an event depends on how memory is assessed. Information that appears forgotten when measured by one type of test (such as free recall) may be expressed on a different test, such as when people are given powerful retrieval cues (Tulving & Pearlstone, 1966). Even more surprising is when the opposite occurs. Sometimes people fail to recollect a past event, even when the event itself is provided as a cue on a recognition test. However, when given a different cue, they will be able to recall the event which they could not previously recognize (Tulving & Thomson, 1973). Consider the following example: Are the names Bell and Ross surnames of famous people? If you answered no, then try again with the cues Alexander Graham _____ and Betsy _____. Something unfamiliar with one cue (even when the cue is a copy of the to-be-remembered information), can be perfectly retrievable with a different cue (Muter, 1978).

Free recall, by definition, occurs when the fewest cues are provided (and the ones that are provided are general). A sample test of free recall would be naming all the people with whom you went to high school, in any order. Free recall often produces limited estimates of what one knows. In the previous example, providing pictures from your high school yearbook to serve as cues for people's names would probably produce retrieval of more names than would free recall. The nature of retrieval cues is the critical determinant of retrieval. The important point for forensic purposes is that no single test is a perfectly reliable indicator of "what is remembered." Different tests can provide divergent answers to this question.

What determines the effectiveness of cues? The guiding ideas of the *encoding specificity principle* (Tulving & Thomson, 1973) and the *principle of transfer appropriate processing* (Bransford, Franks, Morris, & Stein, 1979) provide a means to determine cue effectiveness. In general, the encoding specificity principle states that the more a retrieval cue matches (or overlaps or reinstantiates) the way an experience was initially encoded, the more effective it is in provoking a memory for the experience. Pictures provide good cues for the names of high school classmates, in the previous example. As we discussed, during encoding not all features of an event can be coded; coding is selective. Similarly, particular features of a retrieval query or cue are used when a person tries to retrieve information. Cues are effective to the degree that the features of the cue used during the test match those of the encoded experience.

Let us consider an experiment to illustrate the point. Barclay, Bransford, Franks, McCarrell, and Nitsch (1974) presented adults with sentences to remember and later tested them in a cued recall paradigm. Across groups of participants, the sentences used the same nouns, but embedded them in different contexts. For example, different groups received either *The man tuned the piano* or *The man lifted the piano*. These sentence contexts were intended to create different encodings for the word *piano*, either as something that plays music or something that is heavy. The general idea is that the same concept (*piano*) can afford multiple features to be encoded. Later, participants' memory for the sentences was tested by the presentation of cues such as "something heavy" or "something that makes a nice sound." The authors found that when participants were tested with an appropriate cue (e.g., *something heavy* after encoding the sentence about the man lifting the piano), recall of the sentence was much greater than when participants were cued with the other phrase (*something that makes a beautiful sound*, in this instance). This experiment illustrates the encoding specificity principle in action: Cues that tap the encoded meaning produce greater retrieval than those that do not.

The principle of transfer appropriate processing captures much the same idea as the encoding specificity principle, but broadens it by stating that performance on tests assessing memory will benefit to the extent that the information processing demands of the test are similar to those which occurred during study. The greater the similarity, the greater the transfer of information from study to test.

Other evidence supports the broad conclusions of the encoding specificity hypothesis and the transfer appropriate processing principle (Roediger & Guynn, 1996; Tulving, 1983). One example is the phenomenon of *state-dependent retrieval*. Briefly, drugs such as alcohol and marijuana usually have a negative effect on memory. If people are even mildly intoxicated when exposed to information, they may recall the information less efficiently on a test when they are sober than if they were sober when the information was initially presented. This drug-induced amnesia has often been attributed to encoding and storage failures. However, retrieval differences also appear to be part of the problem. Consider an experiment reported by Eich, Weingartner, Stillman, and Gillin (1975). They tested army recruits in four different conditions. On the first day, subjects smoked cigarettes that either contained THC (the active ingredient in marijuana) or did not (a placebo condition). Next, they were asked to learn a list of 48 words. The words were compiled from 24 categories and two words were presented from each category (e.g., Birds: thrush, flamingo). A day later recruits returned to the laboratory and smoked another cigarette; again, for half the recruits the cigarette contained THC, and for half it did not. After waiting for the drug to take effect, recruits were instructed to recall the list. First, they were prompted to engage in free recall (recall the words presented yesterday in any order) and on a second try they were given a cued recall test. During this attempt they were given the 24 category names and asked to recall words belonging to the categories.

The results from the four conditions of Eich et al.'s (1975) experiment are shown in Table 1.1. Examining free recall first, note that participants in the drug–placebo condition showed the poorest recall—6.7 words recalled—substantially worse than participants in the placebo–placebo condition. Poor retention commonly results from using drugs during study. Note, however, that in the drug–drug condition recall was greater than in the drug–placebo condition. This is the state-dependent retrieval effect—reinstituting the same pharmacological state at test as prevailed during study leads to an improvement in performance. Of course, it would be wrong to reach the general conclusion that marijuana improves recall, be-

TABLE 1.1
State-Dependent Retrieval

Condition		Test Type	
Study	Test	Free Recall	Cued Recall
Placebo	Placebo	11.5	24.0
Placebo	Drug	9.9	23.7
Drug	Placebo	6.7	22.6
Drug	Drug	10.5	22.3

Note. Data from Eich, Weingartner, Stillman, and Gillin (1975). Number of words correctly recalled out of 48.

cause performance is still worse in the drug–drug condition than in the placebo–placebo condition. In addition, giving marijuana during either study or test impaired free recall. In accordance with the encoding specificity principle, when the "state" cues at test match those during encoding, recall is enhanced. For forensic purposes, the useful point is that drugs have a harmful effect on memory.

Many experiments have confirmed state-dependent retrieval findings in free recall. However, the effect is often not observed in cued recall or recognition experiments (Eich, 1980, 1989). From the right side of Table 1.1, it is apparent that marijuana had a slightly harmful effect on cued recall, but the state-dependent retrieval effect disappeared. Why? One idea is the "state cues" are relatively weak and can be overshadowed by more powerful retrieval cues. Participants relied on the category names to cue recall, and the effect of these cues eliminated the effect of the weaker state cues. Note that cued recall was much better than free recall in the Eich et al. (1975) experiment, because the category name cues matched the meaningful way the information was encoded.

Although retrieval cues can provide access to information that could not be retrieved under free recall conditions, memory recovery can occur in other conditions. For example, if people attempt to repeatedly retrieve information, they will often come up with more information on a later test than on an earlier test. Recall of memories on a later test that could not be recalled on an earlier test has been termed *reminiscence* (Ballard, 1913; Roediger & Thorpe, 1978). When overall performance improves — the total number of memories increases on a second test when compared to a first test — the phenomenon is referred to as *hypermnesia* (Erdelyi & Becker, 1974). Such "recovered memories" are not uncommon when people repeatedly retrieve information (see Roediger & Challis, 1989, for a review), but repeated retrieval can also lead to the development of false memories as well as accurate memories (see Roediger, McDermott, & Goff, 1997, for a review). An important point for forensic purposes is that recovery of memories on a later test does not necessarily mean that the seemingly forgotten event was "repressed." Recovery of memories on repeated tests is a perfectly normal occurrence that is obtained in most situations.

Hypnosis is sometimes assumed to aid memory retrieval and dramatic anecdotes demonstrate the point. However, systematic laboratory experiments have failed to find evidence that hypnosis improves memory retrieval (Smith, 1983). As noted by Lynn, Neuschatz, and Fite (chap. 12, this volume), if anything, hypnosis may lead to creation of false memories because the methods used during hypnosis often encourage people to free associate and to generate material without closely monitoring its source. The generated material may then function as misinformation that can distort retention of the original events (e.g., see Roediger, Wheeler, & Rajaram, 1993).

In general, confusions among sources of information can lead to illusions of memory. Johnson, Hashtroudi, and Lindsay (1993) formulated a source monitoring framework to enable understanding of factors that account for confusions about sources of information. For example, when events are close together in time, or similar in modality of presentation, in location, and in other ways, they are more easily confused. Thus, for example, if a witness to a crime is shown pictures of possible suspects soon after the crime and then tested again in a line-up a few weeks later, he might erroneously identify one of the suspects in the line-up as having been the culprit in the crime. The suspect would seem familiar from the photos witnessed earlier, and this familiarity might be misattributed to having seen the person at the crime scene, a process called *unconscious transference* (see Jacoby, Kelley, & Dywan, 1989).

Cues are powerful determinants of memory retrieval, and the way a retrieval query is worded can help determine the quality of the memory elicited. Consider an experiment by Loftus and Palmer (1974). They asked adults to watch a videotape of an automobile accident in which one car was driving by an intersection, and a second car, failing to stop or to yield, drove into the first car. Later the adults were given a long questionnaire that contained the question: "How fast were the two cars going when they contacted each other?" Other groups answered the same question about speed but with the verb changed to *hit, bumped, collided,* or *smashed.* The estimate of speed given by the different groups who received the slightly different questions is shown in Fig. 1.6. People who had read the question with *contacted* as the verb estimated the speed at an average of 32 miles per hour (mph). When the question was given with *smashed* the speed estimate increased to 41 mph. How a question is asked helps determine the answer that is given. If the speed limit had been 30 mph, a police officer asking a witness a question and using *contacted* or *hit* as the verb might conclude that no speeding occurred; however, an officer using *collided* or *smashed* might conclude that the cars were speeding.

As noted previously, the testing of memory is not a neutral event but can affect later retention. However, not all effects are negative ones, as shown in research on the testing effect reviewed earlier. If a person recalls information correctly on a first test, then it is more likely to be recalled accurately on a later test than if the first test had never occurred (e.g., McDaniel & Masson, 1985; Spitzer, 1939; Wheeler & Roediger, 1992). In agreement with the principle of transfer appropriate processing, retrieval of information once provides good practice (and positive transfer) for retrieving the information later.

Geiselman, Fisher, and their colleagues have developed a procedure called the cognitive interview. They incorporated several techniques determined to be efficient in prompting retrieval and have shown that it pro-

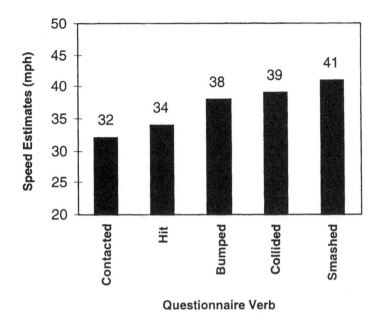

FIG. 1.6. Average speed estimates from the different groups of subjects in Loftus and Palmer's (1974) experiment. Although all the subjects observed the same accident, their estimates of the speed of the cars varied depending on the verb used in one item in the questionnaire.

duces better retrieval than typical interviewing strategies (Geiselman, Fisher, Mackinnon, & Holland, 1985). These techniques include trying to provide good cues, asking people to retrieve from different perspectives, asking them to retrieve sequences of events in different orders, and so on.

The critical question that psychologists (and many others) would like to answer is "Is there a way, long after encoding has occurred, to create conditions in which people will accurately recall events without being led into distortion and error?" The quest is a difficult one, because at the time of retrieval the encoding conditions and retention conditions have already passed. Only retrieval conditions can be manipulated. The cognitive interview is a first attempt to address this issue and to elicit more information from witnesses and others, but it is still in the stage of development (see Fisher, Brennan, & McCauley, chap. 11, this volume).

SUMMARY

This chapter provides a selective overview of factors affecting both veridical and illusory memories. If one considers memory for a single event and the factors that affect its retention, these can be classified as occurring (a) prior to the event, (b) during encoding of the event, (c) during the retention interval between encoding the event and being queried about it, and (d) during the retrieval process. For each of these four categories, some factors increase the probability of successful retrieval of the event and others can lead to forgetting of the event or distortions in its retrieval. Our overview of such factors was illustrative rather than exhaustive. However, we tried to touch on important variables whose understanding is critical for forensic purposes. Schacter (1996) has described human memory as having a "fragile power." The system is powerful, for we can learn and retain new events all our lives and often remember them quite well. On the other hand, the system is fragile, because forgetting and distortions in memory can be brought about easily. This chapter sketched many of the factors responsible for both the power and fragility of remembering events of our lives.

REFERENCES

Ayers, M. S., & Reder, L. M. (1998). A theoretical review of the misinformation effect: Predictions from an activation-based model. *Psychonomic Bulletin & Review, 5*, 1–21.

Ballard, P. B. (1913). Oblivescence and reminiscence. *British Journal of Psychology Monograph Supplements, 1*, 1–82.

Barclay, J. R., Bransford, J. D., Franks, J. J., McCarrell, N. S., & Nitsch, K. (1974). Comprehension and semantic flexibility. *Journal of Verbal Learning and Verbal Behavior, 13*, 471–482.

Bartlett, F. C. (1932). *Remembering: A study in experimental and social psychology.* Cambridge, England: Cambridge University Press.

Bernstein, E. M., & Putnam, F. W. (1986). Development, reliability, and validity of a dissociation scale. *The Journal of Nervous and Mental Disease, 174*, 727–735.

Bransford, J. D., Franks, J. J., Morris, C. D., & Stein, B. S. (1979). Some general constraints on learning and memory research. In L. S. Cermak & F. I. M. Craik (Eds.), *Levels of processing in human memory* (pp. 331–354). Hillsdale, NJ: Lawrence Erlbaum Associates.

Brewer, W. F. (1977). Memory for the pragmatic implications of sentences. *Memory & Cognition, 5*, 673–678.

Brown, R., & Kulik, J. (1977). Flashbulb memories. *Cognition, 5*, 73–99.

Ceci, S. J., Loftus, E. F., Leichtman, M. D., & Bruck, M. (1994). The role of source misattributions in the creation of false beliefs among preschoolers. *International Journal of Clinical and Experimental Hypnosis, 42*, 304–320.

Challis, B. H., & Sidhu, R. (1993). Dissociative effect of massed repetition on implicit and explicit measures of memory. *Journal of Experimental Psychology: Learning, Memory, and Cognition, 19*, 115–127.

Craik, F. I. M., & Tulving, E. (1975). Depth of processing and the retention of words in episodic memory. *Journal of Experimental Psychology: General, 104*, 268–294.

Ebbinghaus, H. (1964). *Memory: A contribution to experimental psychology* (H. A. Ruger & C. E. Bussenius, Trans.). New York: Dover. (Original work published 1885)

Eich, J. E. (1980). The cue-dependent nature of state-dependent retrieval. *Memory & Cognition, 8*, 157–173.

Eich, J. E. (1989). Theoretical issues in state-dependent memory. In H. L. Roediger & F. I. M. Craik (Eds.), *Varieties of memory and consciousness: Essays in honour of Endel Tulving* (pp. 331–354). Hillsdale, NJ: Lawrence Erlbaum Associates.

Eich, J. E., Weingartner, H., Stillman, R. C., & Gillin, J. C. (1975). State dependent accessibility of retrieval cues in the retention of a categorized list. *Journal of Verbal Learning and Verbal Behavior, 14*, 408–417.

Erdelyi, M. H., & Becker, J. (1974). Hypermnesia for pictures: Incremental memory for pictures but not for words in multiple recall trials. *Cognitive Psychology, 6*, 159–171.

Fisk, A. D., & Schneider, W. (1984). Memory as a function of attention, level of processing, and automatization. *Journal of Experimental Psychology: Learning, Memory, and Cognition, 10*, 181–197.

Gallo, D. A., Roberts, M. J., & Seamon, J. G. (1997). Remembering words not presented in lists: Can we avoid creating false memories? *Psychonomic Bulletin & Review, 4*, 271–276.

Garry, M., Manning, C. G., Loftus, E. F., & Sherman, S. J. (1996). Imagination inflation: Imagining a childhood event inflates confidence that it occurred. *Psychonomic Bulletin & Review, 3*, 208–214.

Geiselman, R. E., Fisher, R. P., MacKinnon, D. P., & Holland, H. L. (1985). Eyewitness memory enhancement in the police interview: Cognitive retrieval mnemonics versus hypnosis. *Journal of Applied Psychology, 70*, 401–412.

Glanzer, M., & Cunitz, A. R. (1966). Two storage mechanisms in free recall. *Journal of Verbal Learning and Verbal Behavior, 5*, 351–360.

Goff, L. M., & Roediger, H. L. (1998). Imagination inflation for action events: Repeated imaginings lead to illusory recollections. *Memory & Cognition, 26*, 20–33.

Hastorf, A. H., & Cantril, H. (1954). They saw a game: A case study. *Journal of Abnormal and Social Psychology, 49*, 129–134.

Hebb, D. O. (1949). *The organization of behavior.* New York: Wiley.

Howe, M. L., & Courage, M. L. (1993). On resolving the enigma of infantile amnesia. *Psychological Bulletin, 113*, 305–326.

Hunt, R. R., & McDaniel, M. A. (1993). The enigma of organization and distinctiveness. *Journal of Memory and Language, 32*, 421–445.

Hyman, I. E., & Billings, F. J. (1998). Individual differences and the creation of false childhood memories. *Memory, 6*, 1–20.

Jacoby, L. L. (1978). On interpreting the effects of repetition: Solving a problem versus remembering a solution. *Journal of Verbal Learning and Verbal Behavior, 17*, 649–667.

Jacoby, L. L., Kelley, C. M., & Dywan, J. (1989). Memory attributions. In H. L. Roediger & F. I. M. Craik (Eds.), *Varieties of memory and consciousness: Essays in honour of Endel Tulving* (pp. 391–422). Hillsdale, NJ: Lawrence Erlbaum Associates.

Johnson, M. K., Hashtroudi, S., & Lindsay, D. S. (1993). Source monitoring. *Psychological Bulletin, 114*, 3–28.

Loftus, E. F. (1991). Made in memory: Distortions in recollection after misleading information. In G. H. Bower (Ed.), *The psychology of learning and motivation* (Vol. 27, pp. 187–215). San Diego, CA: Academic Press.

Loftus, E. F., Miller, D. G., & Burns, H. J. (1978). Semantic integration of verbal information into a visual memory. *Journal of Experimental Psychology: Human Learning and Memory, 4*, 19–31.

Loftus, E. F., & Palmer, J. C. (1974). Reconstruction of automobile destruction: An example of the interaction between language and memory. *Journal of Verbal Learning and Verbal Behavior, 13*, 585–589.

Marks, L. E., & Miller, G. A. (1964). The role of semantic and syntactic constraints in the memorization of English sentences. *Journal of Verbal Learning and Verbal Behavior, 3*, 1–5.

McDaniel, M. A., & Masson, M. E. (1985). Altering memory representations through retrieval. *Journal of Experimental Psychology: Learning, Memory, and Cognition, 11*, 371–385.

McDermott, K. B. (1996). The persistence of false memories in list recall. *Journal of Memory and Language, 35*, 212–230.

McDermott, K. B. (1997). Priming on perceptual implicit memory tests can be achieved through presentation of associates. *Psychonomic Bulletin & Review, 4*, 582–586.

McDermott, K. B., & Roediger, H. L. (1998). Attempting to avoid illusory memories: Robust false recognition of associates persists under conditions of explicit warnings and immediate testing. *Journal of Memory and Language, 39*, 508–520.

Melton, A. W. (1963). Implications of short-term memory for a general theory of memory. *Journal of Verbal Learning and Verbal Behavior, 2*, 1–21.

Melton, A. W. (1970). The situation with respect to the spacing of repetitions and memory. *Journal of Verbal Learning and Verbal Behavior, 9*, 596–606.

Miller, G. A. (1956). The magical number seven, plus or minus two: Some limits on our capacity for processing information. *Psychological Review, 63*, 81–96.

Müller, G. E., & Pilzecker, A. (1900). Experimentelle Beitrage zur Lehre vom Gedachtniss [Experimental contributions to the theory of memory]. *Zeitschrift für Psychologie, 1*, 1–288.

Muter, P. (1978). Recognition failure of recallable words in semantic memory. *Memory & Cognition, 6*, 9–12.

Neisser, U., & Harsch, N. (1992). Phantom flashbulbs: False recollections of hearing the news about *Challenger*. In E. Winograd & U. Neisser (Eds.), *Affect and accuracy in recall: Studies of "flashbulb memories"* (pp. 9–31). Cambridge, England: Cambridge University Press.

Owens, J., Bower, G. H., & Black, J. B. (1979). The "soap opera" effect in story recall. *Memory & Cognition, 7*, 185–191.

Paivio, A. (1986). *Mental representations: A dual coding approach*. New York: Oxford University Press.

Roediger, H. L. (1996). Memory illusions. *Journal of Memory and Language, 35*, 76–100.

Roediger, H. L. (2000). Why retrieval is the key process in understanding human memory. In E. Tulving (Ed.), *Memory, consciousness and the brain: The Tallinn conference* (pp. 52–75). Philadelphia, PA: Psychology Press.

Roediger, H. L., Balota, P. A., & Watson, J. M. (2001). Spreading activation and the arousal of false memories. In H. L. Roediger, J. S. Nairne, I. Neath, & A. M. Surprenant (Eds.), *The nature of remembering: Essays in honor of Robert G. Crowder* (pp. 95–115). Washington, DC: American Psychological Association.

Roediger, H. L., & Challis, B. H. (1989). Hypermnesia: Improvements in recall with repeated testing. In C. Izawa (Ed.), *Current issues in cognitive processes: The Tulane–Floweree symposium on cognition* (pp. 175–179). Hillsdale, NJ: Lawrence Erlbaum Associates.

Roediger, H. L., & Guynn, M. J. (1996). Retrieval processes. In E. L. Bjork & R. A. Bjork (Eds.), *Memory* (pp. 197–236). San Diego, CA: Academic Press.

Roediger, H. L., Jacoby, D. J., & McDermott, K. B. (1996). Misinformation effects in recall: Creating false memories through repeated retrieval. *Journal of Memory and Language, 35*, 300–318.

Roediger, H. L., & McDermott, K. B. (1995). Creating false memories: Remembering words not presented in lists. *Journal of Experimental Psychology: Learning, Memory, and Cognition, 21*, 803–814.

Roediger, H. L., McDermott, K. B., & Goff, L. M. (1997). Recovery of true and false memories: Paradoxical effects of repeated testing. In M. A. Conway (Ed.), *Recovered memories and false memories* (pp. 118–149). Oxford, England: Oxford University Press.

Roediger, H. L., McDermott, K. B., & Robinson, K. J. (1998). The role of associative processes in creating false memories. In M. A. Conway, S. E. Gathercole, & C. Cornoldi (Eds.), *Theories of memory II* (pp. 187–245). Hove, Sussex, England: Psychological Press.

Roediger, H. L., & Thorpe, L. A. (1978). The role of recall time in producing hypermnesia. *Memory & Cognition, 6*, 296–305.

Roediger, H. L., Wheeler, M. A., & Rajaram, S. (1993). Remembering, knowing, and reconstructing the past. In D. L. Medin (Ed.), *The psychology of learning and motivation* (pp. 97–133). San Diego, CA: Academic Press.

Rubin, D. C., & Wenzel, A. E. (1996). One hundred years of forgetting: A quantitative description of retention. *Psychological Review, 103,* 734–760.

Schacter, D. L. (1995). Memory distortion: History and current status. In D. L. Schacter, J. T. Coyle, G. D. Fischbach, M. M. Mesulam, & L. E. Sullivan (Eds.), *Memory distortion* (pp. 1–43). Cambridge, MA: Harvard University Press.

Schacter, D. L. (1996). *Searching for memory.* New York: Basic Books.

Schooler, J. W., Gerhard, D., & Loftus, E. F. (1986). Qualities of the unreal. *Journal of Experimental Psychology: Learning, Memory, and Cognition, 12,* 171–181.

Slamecka, N. J., & Graf, P. (1978). The generation effect: Delineation of a phenomenon. *Journal of Experimental Psychology: Human Learning and Memory, 4,* 592–604.

Smith, M. C. (1983). Hypnotic memory enhancement of eyewitnesses: Does it work? *Psychological Bulletin, 94,* 387–407.

Spitzer, H. F. (1939). Studies in retention. *Journal of Educational Psychology, 30,* 641–656.

Tulving, E. (1974). Cue-dependent forgetting. *American Scientist, 62,* 74–82.

Tulving, E. (1983). *Elements of episodic memory.* Oxford, England: Clarendon Press.

Tulving, E. (1985). Memory and consciousness. *Canadian Psychologist, 26,* 1–12.

Tulving, E. (1991). Interview. *Journal of Cognitive Neuroscience, 3,* 89–94.

Tulving, E., & Pearlstone, Z. (1966). Availability versus accessibility of information in memory for words. *Journal of Verbal Learning and Verbal Behavior, 5,* 381–391.

Tulving, E., & Thomson, D. M. (1973). Encoding specificity and retrieval processes in episodic memory. *Psychological Review, 80,* 359–380.

Underwood, B. J. (1957). Interference and forgetting. *Psychological Review, 64,* 49–60.

Underwood, B. J. (1963). Stimulus selection in verbal learning. In C. N. Cofer & B. S. Musgrave (Eds.), *Verbal behavior and learning: Problems and processes* (pp. 33–48). New York: McGraw-Hill.

Underwood, B. J. (1965). False recognition produced by implicit verbal responses. *Journal of Experimental Psychology, 70,* 122–129.

Wheeler, M. A., & Roediger, H. L. (1992). Disparate effects of repeated testing: Reconciling Ballard's (1913) and Bartlett's (1932) results. *Psychological Science, 3,* 240–245.

Winograd, E., Peluso, J., & Glover, T. A. (1998). Individual differences in susceptibility to memory illusions. *Applied Cognitive Psychology, 12,* S5–S27.

The Development of Memory: Toward an Understanding of Children's Testimony

Peter A. Ornstein
University of North Carolina at Chapel Hill

Catherine A. Haden
Loyola University of Chicago

Over the last 20 years, there has been a dramatic increase in research on children's memory (Schneider & Bjorklund, 1998). A substantial corpus of work now documents the surprising mnemonic competence of infants (e.g., Bauer, 1995; Diamond, 1995; Meltzoff, 1988a; Rovee-Collier, 1995) and preschoolers (e.g., Baker-Ward, Gordon, Ornstein, Larus, & Clubb, 1993; Baker-Ward, Ornstein, & Holden, 1984; Fivush & Hudson, 1990; Goodman, Rudy, Bottoms, & Aman, 1990; Perris, Myers, & Clifton, 1990), at least under some conditions. The literature also indicates the presence of substantial age differences in many aspects of memory performance. For example, developmental changes are routinely observed in the degree of detail reflected in children's reports (e.g., Fivush & Hamond, 1990), the amount of forgetting observed (Brainerd, Kingma, & Howe, 1985; Brainerd, Reyna, Howe, & Kingma, 1990), and the deployment and effectiveness of deliberate strategies for remembering (Bjorklund, 1990; Ornstein, Baker-Ward, & Naus, 1988). The surprising sophistication of young children's memory, on the one hand, and clear age-related differences in performance, on the other, represent two themes that characterize our current understanding of the development of memory.

These themes are also of considerable relevance to any discussion of children's abilities to provide accurate testimony in legal situations. Children cannot be expected to report accurate information in a legal context if they are unable to remember what happened (and did not happen) to them. It therefore becomes especially important to understand what children of different ages can remember about salient events over relatively long delay intervals, as a function of the types of questions that are posed by interviewers. This characterization requires that we focus on a wide range of factors—both cognitive and social—that affect the encoding, storage, retrieval, and reporting of information. A detailed analysis of the flow of information is essential because children of varying ages who experience what is nominally the same event may end up providing dramatically contrasting reports. Under some conditions, children may have comparable amounts of information available to them in memory storage, but they may differ considerably in their abilities to search and retrieve the information, their skills in providing verbal (narrative) accounts, and/ or their motivation to comply with the requests of an interviewer. In contrast, under other conditions, children may focus on different aspects of the event and thus end up with differing representations established in memory. Admittedly, the resulting picture of children's changing memory skills is quite complex, but interviewers must understand these realities if they are to develop protocols that will maximize children's recall, in terms of both amount and accuracy.

With these issues of application in mind, in this chapter we provide a selective overview of research on children's memory and its development. Our treatment of the literature is built upon our commitment to a developmental orientation and is guided by our use of an informal framework for discussing the flow of information within the developing memory system. Before we introduce the framework, we spell out the implications of our developmental perspective. We then illustrate the framework and focus especially on ways in which memory representations may differ, both initially and over time.

DEVELOPMENTAL ORIENTATION

From our perspective, age-related differences in basic cognitive functioning have profound implications for understanding the flow of information within the memory system. For example, developmental changes in prior knowledge about events that are being experienced, in the strength and organization of underlying representations in memory, and in fundamental information processing skills can all influence what can be remembered and reported (Ornstein, Larus, & Clubb, 1991). Because memory begins with understanding an event as it is being experienced, it is of the utmost importance to know something about how a child makes sense of an experience as it takes place. Indeed, it is the child's construal of an experience that sets the stage for the establishment of a memory representation and thus later retention. Moreover, age differences in understanding and the constructive processes that are involved in comprehension can lead to dramatically different representations being established.

We also need to emphasize that memory representations are not static entities. Although representations are established as events are experienced, they may change dramatically over time, in part as a result of decay, and in part as a consequence of conversations, exposure to various media, and other intervening experiences (e.g., Ceci & Bruck, 1993; Howe, Courage, & Bryant-Brown, 1993). Because of the dynamic nature of memory representations, it is especially important to determine the degree to which a child who has experienced an event discusses it with parents and others, resulting in embellishment and reinterpretation over time. The influence of intervening activities may be particularly critical over long intervals during which memory traces undergo a process of decay (Baker-Ward, Ornstein, & Principe, 1997). It is also necessary to keep in mind the ways in which cognitive changes over extended delays may impact remembering. For example, as children's basic knowledge and understanding of events being remembered changes as a result of instruction or experience, their memories may shift in the direction of the newer understanding (Greenhoot, 2000; Ross, 1989). In the extreme, because of the fundamental changes in thinking that take place from the preschool years to adolescence, it may be difficult for a teenager to recover memories of early experiences that have not been influenced by current understanding (Ornstein, Ceci, & Loftus, 1998).

A FRAMEWORK FOR EXAMINING MEMORY

This developmental perspective fits well with an informal information processing framework that we have used to examine children's memory for salient, personally experienced events (Ornstein, 1995; Ornstein, Baker-Ward, Gordon, & Merritt, 1997a; Ornstein et al., 1991). Consistent with Loftus and Davies' (1984) analysis, the framework reflects the assumption that remembering is determined by a series of factors that influence the flow of information within the developing memory system. For example, we assume that memory for an event is determined by factors such as prior knowledge and expectations, the quality of the initial representation of the event that is established, the nature of experiences that take place prior to an assessment of remembering, and the types of cues that are used to elicit remembering. We have discussed these and other variables in terms of four general themes about memory: (1) Not everything gets into memory; (2) what gets into memory may vary in strength; (3) the status of information in memory changes over time; and (4) retrieval is not perfect.

In addition to organizing the literature on memory development, this framework enables us to discuss those aspects of memory that are most relevant to a consideration of age-related differences in children's abilities to provide evidence in legal situations. For example, because stress experienced during an event can influence the deployment of attention and the encoding of information, it can have an impact—for better or for worse—on later recall. In contrast, stress during an interview by a police officer, social worker, or attorney can affect the retrieval and reporting of information. Moreover, prior knowledge about events being experienced can affect the encoding of information, changes in the underlying representation, and the accuracy and completeness of recall (e.g., Chi & Ceci, 1987; Ornstein, Shapiro, Clubb, Follmer, & Baker-Ward, 1997b). It is also the case that this framework can facilitate our understanding of situations in which individuals believe that they are recalling a specific personal experience, but, in fact, they may be remembering an event that never really happened.

USING THE FRAMEWORK TO EXAMINE CHILDREN'S MEMORY

We now turn to a selective overview of the literature, making use of our framework to discuss many of the factors that affect the flow of information within the developing memory system. In this discussion, we introduce the four themes previously mentioned, commenting briefly on each. We then devote more attention to the first and third themes, those indicating that not everything that is experienced is entered into memory and that the status of information in memory changes over time. Although each of the themes is relevant to a developmental analysis of remembering, these two themes speak to the nature of the information available in memory and seem particularly important for understanding children's abilities to provide accurate testimony.

Theme 1: Not Everything Gets Into Memory

In the legal context, interviewers—parents, social workers, lawyers, or judges—ask children to retrieve details about previously experienced events. Yet not all presumed problems of remembering reflect difficulties with retrieval. Indeed, some things may not be remembered because they were not encoded and represented in memory in the first place. Because of the fundamental limitations of the human cognitive system, some incoming information is selected for subsequent processing and is attended to, whereas other information is excluded. Moreover, there is ample evidence that this selectivity takes place at the outset and that not everything that is experienced is routed to permanent memory (e.g., Broadbent, 1958; Nickerson & Adams, 1979). From this point of view, it is necessary to first ask how remembered events were encoded initially and then represented in memory.

As we see it, encoding begins with attentional deployment, which in turn is influenced by factors such as the stress experienced as an event unfolds and one's understanding of the situation. Concerning the effects of stress, consider, for example, Merritt, Ornstein, and Spicker's (1994) study of children's memory for the details of a voiding cystourethrogram (VCUG), a radiological procedure involving urinary bladder catheterization. Demonstrating the interfering effects of stress, at least under some conditions, Merritt et al. observed that children's abilities to remember this invasive procedure were negatively correlated with the stress experienced during the VCUG. It seems likely that the stressful nature of these medical procedures interfered with the children's attention and led to reduced encoding. Nevertheless, we recognize that under some conditions, stress during an event can lead to increased vigilance and information seeking, thereby resulting in enhanced encoding (see Ornstein, Merritt, & Baker-Ward, 1995).

Concerning the influence of comprehension, as already suggested, evidence indicates that perhaps the most important determinant of encoding is the extent to which an event is understood as it unfolds (Chi & Ceci, 1987; Ornstein & Naus, 1985). When children can make sense of what they are experiencing, they are able to attend more fully to the key features of the event and thus to encode them more completely than would otherwise be the case (Ornstein et al., 1997b). Moreover, there is substantial agreement that understanding can be driven by endogenous influences that are "within" the individual, such as prior knowledge and expectation (Ornstein et al., 1997b). For example, what a child already knows about a routine medical checkup can seriously influence the extent to which individual features of a specific physical examination are coded and placed in memory (Clubb, Nida, Merritt, & Ornstein, 1993). Importantly, understanding can also be fostered by exogenous influences, such as adult–child interchanges that help children to make sense of what is being experienced. For example, new "knowledge" that is acquired during the experience about the details of the VCUG procedure discussed earlier can facilitate understanding of the event (Principe, Myers, Furtado, Merritt, & Ornstein, 1996). In a similar manner, mother–child conversations during a novel experience can affect understanding, increasing encoding and subsequent remembering (Haden, Ornstein, Eckerman, & Didow, in press).

Theme 2: What Gets Into Memory May Vary in Strength

Assuming that an event has been encoded and stored in memory, several factors can influence the strength and organization of the resulting representation and the ease with which information may later be retrieved. Although there is no direct indicator of the status of any underlying memory representation, it seems likely that the amount of support needed to elicit recall can be used as a proxy measure. Indeed, we expect that strong and coherently organized traces may be readily retrieved, even in response to minimal cueing and prompting by an interviewer. In contrast, weak and loosely organized traces may be more difficult to retrieve and may require the provision of greater supports. For example, it seems likely that strong traces can be recovered in response to open-ended questions (e.g., "What happened this morning?"), whereas weak traces will require more direct questions (e.g., "Did the man have black hair?").

With increases in age there are substantial changes in a range of basic information processing skills (e.g., speed of encoding), in the flexible use of a repertoire of mnemonic strategies, and in basic knowledge about the world (e.g., Ornstein et al., 1988; Schneider & Pressley, 1997). These developmental changes are linked to corresponding differences in the efficiency of information acquisition, and as a consequence, older children routinely acquire more information from comparable exposure to a particular event than do younger children (e.g., Brainerd et al., 1985). Accordingly, after similar exposure to an event, older children would be expected to have stronger memory traces than younger individuals, other things being equal. These differences, moreover, seem consistent with the age-related trends that we have observed in our studies of children's memory for salient medical experiences (Ornstein, 1995; Ornstein et al., 1997a). For example, Baker-Ward et al. (1993) found that 7-year-olds were better able to provide information about a recently experienced physical examination in response to open-ended probes than were younger children, who, in turn, were highly dependent on the specific questions posed by the interviewer.

These findings, and others from our research program and the work of others (e.g., Dent & Stephenson, 1979), are consistent with a view of age-related changes in the nature of children's underlying representations. Alternatively, however, it may be the case that there are minimal or no developmental changes in memory trace strength and organization. Indeed, it is possible that the elevated performance of older children can be attributed to other factors, such as age-related differences in children's skills in retrieving information, in using narrative forms to discuss what is remembered, and in understanding the social dynamics of the interview situation (Ornstein et al., 1991). To explore this possibility, we provided children with extensive retrieval supports and permitted them to act out the details of recent checkups (Greenhoot, Ornstein, Gordon, & Baker-Ward, 1999), and we used a recognition-based interview protocol (Geddie, Myers, & Ornstein, 1994). Nonetheless, these efforts did not result in an elimination of age differences in children's reports of their experiences, and the hypothesis that age differences may operate largely at the level of encoding remains viable.

Theme 3: The Status of Information in Memory Changes

Once in the memory system, the status of information about an experience can be altered dramatically during the time period between an event and a later report of it. In addition to the passage of time, a wide variety of intervening events can have a strong impact on the integrity of the underlying representation in memory, and these influences may vary as a function of age.

A number of variables contribute to the changing nature of memory representations. Without reinstating experiences, the strength of a memory trace decreases over time, and the traces of younger children, initially weaker than those of older children, may undergo more rapid decay (e.g., Brainerd et al., 1985). As such, even without interfering experiences, time per se may be associated with increased difficulty in remembering, especially for younger children. In addition, just as preexisting knowledge can influence the encoding of information, it can also affect the status of information in memory. Especially over time, memory for earlier events can be changed substantially and reinterpreted in terms of current knowledge (Bartlett, 1932). These types of constructive processes also operate when details of an earlier experience seem to fade over time and general knowledge serves to fill in the gaps. As an example, consider a study in which we (Ornstein et al., 1998) demonstrated that as memory for the details of a specific physical examination fades, children tend to incorporate information from their generic knowledge of visits to the doctor into their reports.

What happens after an event has been experienced can also have a profound impact on the strength and organization of the memory representation. On the positive side, repeated discussion and partial repetitions of an event may serve to maintain it in memory (e.g., Poole & White, 1993; Rovee-Collier & Shyi, 1992). Thus, conversations about an experience may serve to maintain it in memory, but it must be emphasized that there is always the chance that some aspects of the interaction may lead to distortions in the representation. This possibility leads to the negative side, namely, that some intervening experiences can have a profoundly negative impact on remembering (e.g., Ceci & Bruck, 1993; Ceci, Ross, & Toglia, 1987; Loftus, 1979). Indeed, a considerable amount of evidence suggests that exposure to inconsistent postevent information can alter reports of previously experienced events, although there has been controversy concerning the mechanisms underlying these misinformation effects (e.g., Berkerian & Bowers, 1983; McCloskey & Zaragoza, 1985). Nonetheless, there seems to be an emerging consensus (e.g., Ceci & Bruck, 1993; Loftus & Hoffman, 1989; Tversky & Tuchin, 1989) that suggestibility induced by misleading postevent information may reflect both socially driven acceptance of misinformation and memory modifications. Finally, it should be added that under some conditions, a single intervening event may reinforce some aspects of an earlier experience, while at the same time interfering with other aspects of the activity (Principe, Ornstein, Baker-Ward, & Gordon, 2000).

Theme 4: Retrieval Is Not Perfect

The final step in remembering involves the retrieval and reporting of information in storage. Putting aside the serious issue of whether the underlying representations have been changed over the course of the delay interval, it is nonetheless the case that not everything in memory can be retrieved at all times. This retrieval problem may be particularly acute for young children, and it certainly contributes to age differences in remembering—and to the need for interviewers to supplement open-ended with specific forms of questions—that have been reported frequently in the literature (e.g., Ornstein, 1995; Schneider & Bjorklund, 1998). Moreover, for a variety of reasons (e.g., fear of embarrassment), not everything that is retrieved by a child may be reported in the context of an interview. In addition, what a child "remembers" and reports may not always have been retrieved from the event representation in memory. As already indicated, constructive processes that are driven by knowledge and expectation may operate to fill in the gaps in what can be accessed from memory (Ornstein et al., 1998). Also under some conditions, a child's report may be based on confusions between a personal experience and an alternative "source" of information, such as another person's account and information from the media (Johnson, Hashtroudi, & Lindsay, 1993).

With children, some retrieval problems may arise from communication failures and an imperfect understanding of the nature of the recall task (Donaldson, 1978; Ornstein, 1995). Because children's performance on cognitive tasks can be influenced strongly by their understanding of what is required, effective communication between the child and interviewer is critical. This communication clearly depends on factors such as language comprehension and shared assumptions about the nature of the memory interview, such as the importance of providing as complete an account as possible (Ornstein et al., 1991). In addition, various components of the social dynamic between child and interviewer can have a dramatic impact on a child's report of information available in memory. For example, children's reports may become increasingly problematic if an interviewer creates a stressful atmosphere by employing an aggressive and misleading style of questioning (see Clarke-Stewart, Thompson, & Lepore, 1989; Peters, 1997).

Other difficulties may reflect young children's lack of mastery of the narrative conventions of the culture (Mandler, 1991; Ornstein, 1995), a concern that has led to the exploration of interview protocols with reduced verbal demands. To illustrate, in our research on children's memory for medical experiences, we (Geddie et al., 1994) developed a recognition-based interview protocol (i.e., one involving only "yes" and "no" responses) but failed to observe any improvement in young children's performance. We (Gordon et al., 1993) also found that providing 3-year-olds with dolls as props for remembering does not improve their performance, an observation that is consistent with recent work by DeLoache and Marzolf (1995). In a final attempt to provide a more supportive context for retrieval, we (Greenhoot et al., 1999) examined the extent to which young children's memory performance might be enhanced if they were given access to both dolls and medical props and encouraged to act out the details of recent physical examination. Although this enactment procedure did facilitate 3-year-olds' recall, it also resulted in an unacceptable increase in errors (see also Steward et al., 1996). To date neither we nor any other research group has been successful in developing alternative interview protocols to facilitate preschool-aged children's retrieval and reporting.

EXTENDED ENCODING

Each of these four themes is clearly relevant to an understanding of young children's abilities to provide accurate testimony in a forensic context. Information may not be revealed in an interview because it was not entered into memory in the first place (Theme 1), or because the resulting memory representation was too weak or fragmented (Theme 2), or because the status of the representation changed over the course of an extended delay interval (Theme 3), or because of difficulties with retrieval (Theme 4). Of these themes, however, perhaps the most fundamental are Themes 1 and 3. Indeed, a thorough consideration of young children's testimony must rely on an understanding of the status of the information in memory that is potentially available for retrieval.

Accordingly, we now focus in greater depth on the encoding and establishment of representations in memory, as well as on their fate over long delay intervals. In the following sections, we emphasize the dramatic impact of knowledge on encoding and the establishment of a representation, as well as its continuing influence on the representation over time, as relevant new knowledge is added into memory. We recognize that some knowledge is endogenous in that it is brought to the situation by the child. Indeed, what is already known enables a child to make inferences about an ongoing experience that facilitate comprehension and the establishment of a coherent representation in memory. Other knowledge can be characterized as exogenous in that it is either provided for the child by adults (or older children) or jointly constructed in the context of interaction. These external forces that guide children's understanding and encoding are often critical in shaping comprehension, particularly when an event is novel or ambiguous. Importantly, we also recognize that knowledge can be a double-edged sword in that it can both facilitate and distort memory.

This perspective leads us to argue that the processes involved in encoding an experience must be viewed as being extended in time, often beyond the duration of the event itself. Events that are personally meaningful do not have a finite ending point, as children (and adults, for that matter) often ruminate for an extended period of time on their meaning and consequences. Moreover, depending on the nature of an experience, adult–child dialogues often continue for hours, days, and even years. As we see it, this extended within-the-child rumination and adult–child conversation must have serious implications for the status of the memory representation.

Initial Encoding

In this section, we consider knowledge-driven processes that operate as an event is experienced to determine initial encoding and the establishment of a representation in memory. We first illustrate the impact of prior knowledge that the child brings to the situation, making the assumption that this knowledge affects comprehension of the experience, influences the deployment of attention as the event unfolds, and contributes to the initial encoding in memory. We then consider cases in which the child does not have much a priori knowledge of the events being experienced but nonetheless acquires some understanding on the basis of information provided by adults. Finally, we explore the related situation in which knowledge about the event being experienced is derived from ongoing interactions with an adult.

Prior Knowledge. Abundant evidence attests to the impact of knowledge on encoding and subsequent memory (Bjorklund, 1985; Chi & Ceci, 1987; Ornstein & Naus, 1985). As already indicated, prior knowledge enables individuals to make sense out of the events that they experience, and this comprehension is essential for effective registration in memory. For example, studies that examine the development of expertise in specific domains (e.g., chess, soccer) have indicated repeatedly that the highly organized and accessible knowledge of experts enables them to encode and remember domain-related information more effectively than novices (e.g., Chi, 1978; Schneider, Körkel, & Weinert, 1989). In a similar manner, children's generalized event representations or "scripts" (Nelson, 1986) for frequently occurring events (e.g., bedtime rituals, trips to a restaurant) affect their understanding and later memory of specific instances of these events (e.g., Farrar & Goodman, 1990). More generally, a considerable body of evidence suggests that children's initial expectations about events, generated in part by their scripts, can affect perception and interpretation and consequently influence what gets into memory (Nelson, 1986).

One illustration of the impact of prior knowledge can be seen in our program of work on children's memory for the details of specific pediatric checkups (see, e.g., Baker-Ward et al., 1993; Ornstein, 1995). In our studies, we routinely observe age-related changes between 3 and 7 years of age in children's initial recall and retention over time. Recognizing that variations in children's knowledge about aspects of the physical examination could have affected their recall of the experience, Clubb et al. (1993) carried out a study to gather normative data about what children know about routine visits to the doctor. Clubb et al. used an interview protocol that focused on general knowledge and interviewed 5-year-olds about their understanding of what goes on during a regular checkup. They then pooled the children's responses into open-ended questions about the physical examination and formed "knowledge" scores for each feature of the office visit (e.g., heart check, urine specimen). These knowledge scores were based on the proportion of children in the normative sample who nominated each component of the checkup in response to the interviewer's general probes.

Armed with these knowledge scores, which can be viewed as reflecting variability in the 5-year-olds' understanding of the specific examination features, Clubb et al. (1993) then reanalyzed the recall protocols of the 5-year-olds who had been studied by Baker-Ward et al. (1993). In contrast to Baker-Ward et al., who reported their data in terms of the mean levels of performance for the 3-, 5-, and 7-year-olds in their sample, Clubb et al. changed the unit of analysis from the individual child to the individual examination feature. In this way, they were able to compute "memory scores" for the 5-year-olds for each component of the office visit at each recall assessment. Paralleling the knowledge scores, these new memory scores represented the proportion of 5-year-olds in the Baker-Ward et al. study who recalled each component of the checkup in response to open-ended probes.

Figure 2.1 illustrates the considerable variability in both knowledge and immediate recall for specific features of the checkup. For example, when asked open-ended questions about what happens during a checkup, receiving a prize and getting a shot were features most nominated by the sample, and checking the wrist and walking forward were features nominated least often. Similarly, receiving a prize and having a blood test (with finger sticks) were well remembered, whereas checks of the feet and elbows were remembered so poorly that one could question whether these features had been encoded and represented in memory. Most interestingly, the data displayed in Fig. 2.1 also indicate a linear relation ($r = .68$, $p < .01$) between the knowledge and recall scores, with increases in knowledge being associated with corresponding increases in memory performance. These data and analyses reported by Clubb et al. (1993) and Ornstein et al. (1997b) suggest strongly that what a child knows about a medical exam can seriously affect the extent to which component features of the checkup are coded and placed in memory.[1]

It is also important to note that the effects of prior knowledge on encoding are not restricted to language-based assessments of memory. Indeed, the use of elicited imitation paradigms indicates that by the middle of the second year of life infants' nonverbal recall of action sequences is already guided by their knowledge of the temporal and causal structure of events in the world (Bauer, 1995). In elicited imitation, a researcher models an action or sequence of actions that are associated with a specific object or objects. After a delay interval, the props are given to the child, and the spontaneous production of the previously modeled actions is understood to be indicative of recall of the event. Using this procedure, Meltzoff (1988a, 1998b) has shown that single, novel, object-specified actions can be reproduced by 9-month-olds after a delay of 24 hours, and that 14-month-olds can remember the actions for up to 1 week. In addition, Bauer and her colleagues (see Bauer, 1995, for a review) have demonstrated that 13-month-olds are capable of ordered recall of multiple-action sequences over delays of 1 week, and that older toddlers can retain temporal order information for up to a year (see also McDonough & Mandler, 1994; Meltzoff, 1995).

---

[1]We recognize that there is no direct readout of the status of an underlying representation, but we suggest that memory performance immediately after an event has been experienced can be taken as a proxy measure of what has been encoded (Baker-Ward et al., 1997). Moreover, our intent in presenting the Clubb et al. (1993) data is to suggest that prior knowledge can have a strong impact on encoding and therefore on the nature of the representation that is constructed. We also recognize, of course, that knowledge is important at all stages of information processing. As such, we discuss its subsequent influence on the status of the representation in memory storage and on processes associated with retrieval and reporting. However, even though knowledge has a continuing effect on memory, extending beyond the interpretation and encoding of an ongoing event, it may be particularly significant in the construction of the initial representation.

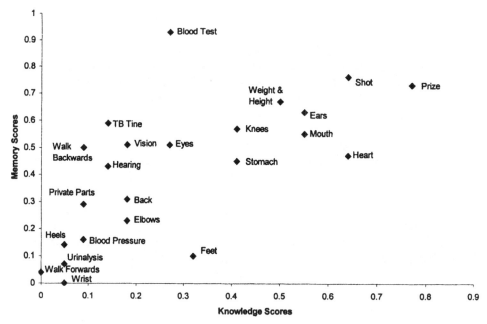

FIG. 2.1. Scatter plot of 5-year-olds' knowledge and immediate memory scores. Reprinted from *Cognitive Development, 8,* P. A. Clubb, R. Nida, K. Merritt, and P. A. Ornstein, "Visiting the Doctor: Children's Knowledge and Memory," pp. 361–372. Copyright © 1993, with permission of Elsevier Science.

Against this background of impressive nonverbal memory perform-ance, it is particularly interesting to observe that children as young as 13 months old can make use of their knowledge of the world to better re-member structured, as opposed to unstructured action sequences. Con-sider, for example, studies in which Bauer and her collaborators (Bauer & Dow, 1994; Bauer & Hertsgaard, 1993) compared children's abilities to re-member three different types of action sequences: familiar sequences (e.g., putting a bear in a bed, covering it with a blanket, and reading it a story), novel sequences that involved some built-in "enabling" relation (e.g., making a rattle by putting a ball into one cup, covering it with another cup, and shaking), and novel–arbitrary sequences that do not require an invariant temporal order (e.g., making a party hat by putting a balloon on the top, putting a headband around the cone, and putting a sticker on the front). The children's superior production of the familiar and novel–en-abling action sequences, in contrast to the novel–arbitrary sequences, rep-resents an early demonstration of the impact of prior knowledge on event comprehension, encoding, and remembering.

Newly Acquired Knowledge. Long-standing prior knowledge may not be necessary for encoding and subsequent retention, as long as "new" knowledge can be provided to facilitate understanding of an event that is being experienced. Consider, for example, Bransford and Johnson's (1972) classic demonstration of the dramatic impact of new knowledge on comprehension and encoding. In their study, adults who were presented with a complex passage that made little sense without an accompanying picture were essentially unable to understand and recall it, but control participants who were provided with the picture had no difficulty understanding and remembering the passage.

In our laboratory, we recently carried out a similar exploration by studying the impact of medically relevant information on children's recall of a stressful and unfamiliar medical procedure. More specifically, Principe et al. (1996) reanalyzed data collected by Merritt et al. (1994) in their VCUG study to examine the extent to which naturally occurring variation in the information provided was associated with recall. As previously discussed, the VCUG involved urinary bladder catheterization, and Principe et al. (1996) classified the radiological technologist's talk during each child's procedure as representing a "procedural narrative" if it provided the child with an account containing three central components of the VCUG. The three components were (a) a description of the catheter and its insertion, (b) mention of contrast fluid going through the catheter, and (c) a description of the filling of the child's bladder with this fluid. From our perspective, children receiving the procedural narrative would be better able than others to understand what was happening to them in this difficult radiological procedure.

Principe et al. had access to the videotaped records of 21 of the 3- to 7-year-olds who took part in the Merritt et al. (1994) study. Analysis of these tapes indicated that 13 of the children met the procedural narrative criteria. That is, these children were judged to have been given sufficient information about the VCUG procedure to be included in a Procedural Narrative Provided group. Admittedly, among these children, some received the narrative just prior to catheterization, whereas others were given the information as the event was in progress. Nonetheless, it seems likely that all of the children in this group were given enough information to understand the VCUG as it was unfolding. In contrast, the remaining eight children did not receive this information about the VCUG procedure and were placed in a Procedural Narrative Omitted group. Interestingly, the groups differed substantially in their initial and delayed recall. Immediately after the VCUG, in contrast to the children in the Procedural Narrative Omitted group, those in the Procedural Narrative Provided group displayed higher levels of total recall (.97 vs. .81 proportion of the features recalled) and recall in response to open-ended questions (.60 vs. .22). The difference between the two conditions increased somewhat over a 6-week delay interval in terms of both total recall (.97 vs. .67) and open-ended re-call (.51 vs. .13).[2]

Although the assignment of children to these two conditions was clearly done on a post hoc basis, subsequent analyses revealed that the differences in recall could not be attributed to either age or levels of stress. As such, the group differences in recall are consistent with the view that the greater knowledge conveyed by the procedural narrative enhanced the encoding of this stressful and unfamiliar radiological procedure.

Obtaining Knowledge Through Conversational Interactions

Children can also obtain knowledge about unfamiliar events through conversations with adults as these experiences are taking place. Indeed, a consensus view holds that narration contributes in an important manner to children's understanding of their personal experiences (e.g., Fivush & Haden, 1997; Nelson, 1996). From our perspective (see also Fivush, Pipe, Murachver, & Reese, 1997; Nelson, 1996), language-based interactions during an event have the potential to influence the encoding and subsequent recovery of information. Although adult–child narratives about ongoing experiences have not been explored as thoroughly as conversations about past events (e.g., Fivush & Haden, 1997; Reese, Haden, & Fivush, 1993), it seems likely that talk during an event serves to focus children's attention on salient components and to increase their understanding of it. These conversations are thought to result in the establishment of a richly detailed and organized representation of the experience.

In partial support of this point of view, consider the groundbreaking work by Tessler and Nelson (1994). In one study, a small sample of mothers and their 3-year-old children were observed as they visited the American Museum of Natural History in New York. When interviewed about the features of the museum trip 1 week later, only the objects that had been jointly talked about by both the mother and child during the event were recalled, suggesting the important role of adult–child talk during an event in focusing children's attention. In a second study, 4-year-olds were recorded during a picture-taking walk with their mothers through an unfamiliar neighborhood. Here again, the children did not recall aspects of their experience that had not been talked about during the event. Even more interesting, however, was Tessler and Nelson's observation that

---

[2]It should be noted that overall levels of recall are lower in Principe et al.'s (1996) reanalysis of the Merritt et al. (1994) data than in the original report because of the use of a subset of the sample and a decision to recode the data to conform to scoring procedures that are currently employed in our laboratory.

mothers who frequently connected the ongoing event to previous experiences had children who later recalled more of the pictures they had taken,
and remembered more about the activity, in contrast to children of mothers
who did not adopt this narrative "style" during the encoding of the event.

In our laboratory, we have also explored the linkages between mother–
child narrative interaction during specified events and children's subsequent memory of these experiences. In the context of a short-term longitudinal study of children from 2.5 to 3.5 years of age, Haden et al. (in press)
observed mothers and their children interact as they engaged in a specially constructed experience at three time points across the year. Within
the confines of each family's living room, the mother–child dyads took
part in a pretend camping adventure at 30 months, a birdwatching activity at 36 months, and the "opening" of an ice cream store at 42 months. To
illustrate the nature of these events, the camping activity began with the
mothers and children loading backpacks with various food items (e.g.,
hotdogs, hamburgers, sodas) in preparation for their trip. They then hiked
to a fishing pond where there was a fishing rod and net to use in catching
the fish. After fishing, the dyads continued on to a campsite where there
was a sleeping bag, along with a grill, pots, and utensils to use in cooking
and eating the food. The birdwatching and ice cream store events were
similarly structured, so that each activity was composed of a number of
component features.

Because these interactions were videotaped, we had a precise record of
how each mother–child pair nonverbally and verbally interacted with each
feature as the events unfolded. Moreover, we could link mother– child talk
about the events as they were ongoing to assessments of remembering that
were obtained in interviews carried out by examiners after delays of 1 day
and 3 weeks. These interviews were hierarchically structured and included
general open-ended questions (e.g., "Tell me about the camping trip that
you had with your mom."), followed by more specific open-ended questions (e.g., "What kind of food did you pack up?", "What did you put the
food in?"), and, finally, yes–no type probes (e.g., "Did you pack hotdogs?").

Given our interest in relating interaction during these activities to children's event recall, a critical first step was to characterize mother–child
behaviors directed toward specific features of each event. To do so, we developed a coding system to reliably score both mother and child nonverbal and verbal behaviors directed toward prespecified features. Nonverbal behaviors included pointing to a feature, touching a feature (e.g.,
patting, tossing, dumping), manipulating a feature (e.g., manually exploring, showing), and functionally using a feature (e.g., putting the pan on
the grill). Verbal behaviors included calling attention to a feature, requesting the name of a feature, naming a feature, or offering elaborative detail
about a feature (e.g., "The fire's hot."). Thus, for each feature we recorded

whether or not it had been engaged nonverbally and/or verbally, and if these behaviors were displayed by the mother only, the child only, or by both the mother and the child jointly.

Table 2.1 summarizes the results of this approach to characterizing mother and child engagement with the features of the three events. As can be seen, for each of four types of nonverbal behavior (mother–child joint, mother-only, child-only, no), we tallied the extent to which each of four patterns of verbal interaction (mother–child joint, mother-only, child-only, no) was observed. Inspection of Table 2.1 indicates that most of the features that were interacted with in some way were jointly engaged nonverbally by the mother and child. Mothers and children touched, manipulated and/or functionally used approximately 70% (or 18) of the total features engaged during the camping activity, 63% (or 15) of the total features engaged during birdwatching, and 78% (or 25) of the total features engaged during the ice cream store event. Moreover, it is apparent in the table that within each nonverbal behavior type, the majority of features

TABLE 2.1
Mean Number of Features Engaged Nonverbally
and Verbally During the Activities

Engagement	Activity					
	Camping		Birdwatching		Ice Cream Shop	
Joint Nonverbal						
Joint Verbal	8.48	(3.17)	8.48	(3.89)	13.10	(4.24)
Mother-Only Verbal	6.81	(2.87)	5.81	(3.63)	8.29	(3.89)
Child-Only Verbal	0.38	(0.74)	0.10	(0.30)	1.05	(1.43)
No Verbal	2.10	(1.61)	0.86	(0.85)	2.67	(2.01)
Mother Nonverbal						
Joint Verbal	0.81	(1.03)	1.52	(1.36)	0.95	(1.02)
Mother-Only Verbal	1.33	(1.46)	1.62	(1.77)	1.29	(1.06)
Child-Only Verbal	0.05	(0.22)	–		0.05	(0.22)
No Verbal	1.00	(1.05)	0.95	(0.97)	0.81	(1.03)
Child Nonverbal						
Joint Verbal	1.19	(1.89)	2.38	(2.54)	2.05	(1.86)
Mother-Only Verbal	1.24	(0.89)	1.10	(1.76)	0.90	(1.22)
Child-Only Verbal	0.05	(0.22)	0.14	(0.36)	0.14	(0.36)
No Verbal	0.43	(0.87)	0.48	(0.81)	0.57	(0.87)
No Nonverbal						
Joint Verbal	0.67	(0.97)	0.24	(0.54)	0.05	(0.22)
Mother-Only Verbal	0.86	(0.91)	0.43	(0.60)	0.14	(0.36)
Child-Only Verbal	–		–		–	
Total Present Features	25.38	(1.86)	24.10	(1.18)	32.05	(2.11)

Note. Standard deviations are in parentheses. From Haden et al. (2001). Adapted with permission of Society for Research in Child Development.

were either jointly talked about by the mother and child (approximately 49% across the three events), or were talked about only by the mother (approximately 37%).

A critical set of analyses enabled us to examine how these patterns of engagement with the events were related to the children's recall. Given that the majority of features that were interacted with during the events were jointly handled by both the mother and the child, the "base" for these analyses was the subset of features that had been jointly engaged nonverbally as the event unfolded. Differences in recall of these jointly handled features were then examined as a function of the type of talk directed toward these features during the events (e.g., joint-verbal, mother-verbal, no-verbal).[3] The results of these analyses for the 1-day (upper panel) and 3-week (lower panel) interviews are summarized in Fig. 2.2. For each event, we plotted the percentage of features recalled of those that were jointly handled and jointly discussed (solid bars), jointly handled and talked about only by the mother (striped bars), and jointly handled and not discussed (white bars). It should be noted that memory for features that were jointly engaged nonverbally but talked about only by the child (joint nonverbal–child verbal) is not illustrated, due to the small number of features fitting this category. Inspection of Fig. 2.2 indicates the dramatic effect of joint talk during the event on the information the children provided in response to general, open-ended questions of the interviewers. As can be seen, those features of the camping, birdwatching, and ice cream activities that were handled and discussed by both the mother and child were better recalled than features that were jointly handled but talked about only by the mother, which, in turn, were better recalled than those features not discussed. This pattern was observed at both memory interviews for each of the activities, with some indication of a drop in recall over the 3-week delay interval for features that had been jointly handled but only discussed by the mother.

In summary, these data indicate that children as young as 2.5 years of age are able to benefit from conversations about events in the here-and-now. Joint-talk between mothers and children about aspects of an event as it is unfolding is associated strongly with children's open-ended recall as much as 3 weeks later. These findings, as well as those of Tessler and Nelson (1994), reinforce our view that mother–child interaction as an event unfolds may facilitate children's understanding of the experience and

---

[3]At one level, this analysis of the features that had been jointly manipulated can be viewed as a prototype of other analyses of the recall of features manipulated by either of the members of each mother–child dyad. However, it should be indicated that not only were there fewer features that fell into these other nonverbal categories, but also that some dyads actually had no features included in the other nonverbal categories. As a consequence, these families would have to be removed from these analyses, thus reducing the sample size.

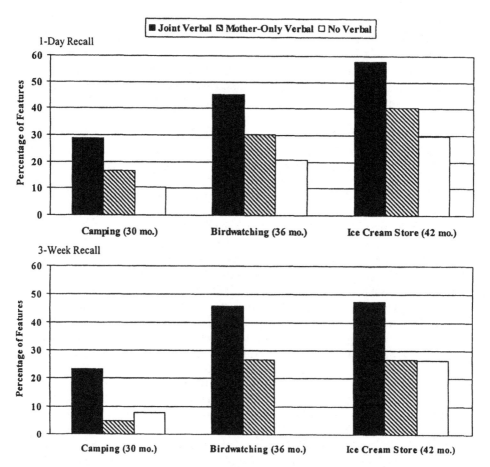

FIG. 2.2. Proportions of features of the camping, birdwatching, and ice cream store events remembered in response to open-ended questions at the 1-day and 3-week interviews, as a function of the type of talk directed toward jointly handled features (Haden et al., 2001; adapted with permission of Society for Research in Child Development).

serve to organize the resulting representation. For example, by naming component features of an ongoing event, a mother may focus her child's attention on various aspects of the situation that are particularly salient. And if this naming is followed by verbal elaboration, a more enriched representation may be established. In this way, mothers and children who are experiencing an event together may come to construct the event in a way that makes it more accessible in the future. We also recognize that the amount of help from a parent that children need in interpreting a situation may vary considerably as a function of the event that is being remembered. In our (relatively unfamiliar) camping, birdwatching and ice cream shop activities, joint mother–child attention in two modalities, linguistic and manipulative, seemed necessary for optimal remembering, but in more familiar situations, this may not be necessary, as the child's prior knowledge may be sufficient for encoding and remembering. In general, we would expect that there would be a developmental progression in children's understanding of experiences such that with increases in age, they may be able to attend to salient features more on their own, with less maternal involvement. Thus, over time, children may require less support from their mothers for the encoding process.

These findings also have at least two implications for understanding children's statements in legal settings. First, given the extent to which mothers' conversations with their children may help them to frame the situation and thus the resulting representation, interviewers must recognize that some aspects of children's reports about relatively unfamiliar or ambiguous situations may be influenced significantly by the interpretations of adults. The Haden et al. (in press) data attest most directly to the impact of adults' efforts to structure ongoing experiences, but, in a similar fashion, conversations about past events also have dramatic effects on children's remembering (e.g., Haden, Haine, & Fivush, 1997; Reese et al., 1993). Second, interviewers in forensic settings must also recognize that their own extended conversations with child witnesses have the potential to affect the children's understanding and subsequent reports.

Changes in the Representation Over Time

Although the encoding processes previously discussed lead to the establishment of representations in memory, these traces cannot be viewed as stable entities. It must be recognized that memory traces weaken over time and can be affected by a range of intervening experiences, experiences that can serve to either support or interfere with accurate remembering. In this section, the focus is not on the effects of time per se (see Ornstein et al., 1997a), but rather, because of its clear forensic relevance, we emphasize the impact of intervening experiences. Although we identify some events that have a positive or reinstating impact on remembering (see Campbell & Jaynes, 1966; Fivush & Hamond, 1989; Rovee-Collier & Shyi, 1992), most of our attention is devoted to intervening events that can distort memory. We do so because a large body of literature indicates that exposure to both inconsistent postevent information and to misleading, suggestive styles of interviewing can reduce the accuracy of children's reports (see Ceci & Bruck, 1995). Admittedly, as suggested, there has been considerable debate concerning the extent to which an underlying representation is altered following exposure to misleading information (e.g., Loftus, 1979; McCloskey & Zaragoza, 1985), but there is general agreement that suggestibility effects can reflect both socially motivated acceptance of misinformation and actual modification of memory traces (Loftus & Hoffman, 1989; Ornstein et al., 1991; Tversky & Tuchin, 1989).

It should also be emphasized that our consideration of events that intervene between a specific experience and a later memory interview includes the operation of both external and internal forces. In addition to obvious exogenous, external factors, we also explore the impact of events that take place within the individual, such as constructive processes that are driven by general knowledge. This treatment of endogenous process also requires that we discuss the complicating factor of changes over time in underlying knowledge.

Positive and Negative Effects of Varied Intervening Experiences.   In the context of our program of research on children's memory for the details of pediatric checkups, Principe et al. (2000) examined systematically the impact of a set of varied postevent experiences. We were particularly interested in the extent to which some intervening experiences might serve to maintain memory over time, whereas others would likely interfere with long-term retention.

The 3- and 5-year-olds who took part in this study were each interviewed both immediately and 12 weeks after a routine physical examination. The children differed, however, in the experiences that were provided for them midway through the delay interval. Approximately 6 weeks after the checkup, one group of children at each age level received a complete interview about their visit to the doctor, whereas a second group returned to the pediatrician's office, and a third group watched a videotape of another child receiving a checkup. It was expected that having an additional interview about the checkup would facilitate recall at 12 weeks because it essentially reinstated the children's memory for most of the features of the physical examination. In contrast, returning to the doctor's office was expected to reinstate the context of the checkup, but not to activate representations of the specific features of the examination. Moreover, mixed effects were expected for the videotape manipulation. Facilitation was expected because this unique video included the basic features of a routine physical examination. In contrast, however, interference was also anticipated because the tape had been designed to include a few medical procedures that had not been a part of the children's checkups. Principe et al. evaluated these possible effects by comparing the 12-week recall of three experimental groups with a control group that was not seen during the delay interval.

Consistent with expectations, the results displayed in Fig. 2.3 indicate mixed mnemonic consequences for the contrasting intervening experiences. The first bar in the top and bottom panels of Fig. 2.3 indicates the mean level of recall in response to open-ended questions at the initial inter-

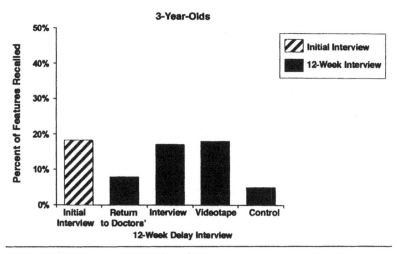

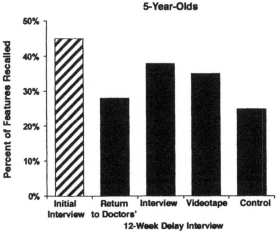

FIG. 2.3.   Percents of features of the physical examination remembered in response to open-ended questions at the immediate and 12-week interviews, as a function of age and experimental group. From "The Effects of Intervening Experiences on Children's Memory for a Physical Examination," by G. F. Principe, P. A. Ornstein, L. Baker-Ward, and B. N. Gordon, *Applied Cognitive Psychology, 14,* pp. 59–80. Copyright © 2000 by John Wiley & Sons, Ltd. Reproduced with permission.

view for the 3- and 5-year-olds, respectively. The remaining bars at each age level indicate the proportion of features of the physical examination recalled at the open-ended level by the four groups at the 12-week interview. As can be seen, with reference to the control condition, the children at both age levels showed elevated recall, or evidenced less forgetting, if they had been interviewed 6 weeks after their checkups, or if they had viewed the specially prepared video. Although final recall was somewhat elevated for the children who had returned to the doctor's office during the delay interval, the improvement was not statistically significant, and these children did not seem to differ from those in the control condition.

The data indicate that some of the intervening experiences seem to serve a reinstating function and to facilitate recall after a long delay. However, a somewhat different picture emerges when we examine the children's responses to questions about activities that had not been included in the physical examinations. The 3-year-olds' responses to these "absent feature" questions were relatively unaffected by any of the intervening experiences. In contrast, the 5-year-olds who viewed the video midway through the delay interval evidenced a significant reduction in the percentage of correct rejections, that is, in their abilities to say "no" to questions about things that simply did not happen during checkups. Indeed, the performance of these children declined to the 50% rate of correct denials that would be expected on the basis of chance alone, although the performance of the other 5-year-olds was good (approximately 81% correct denials), especially given the long delay.

These findings clearly indicate that young children's delayed recall can be influenced by the intervening events that they experience. It is especially interesting that the same experience (i.e., viewing the video) can have both positive and negative effects on children's remembering, and that the impact may vary as a function of age. It seems likely that the 5-year-olds who viewed the video were confused as to the "sources" of their information, as these children made some spontaneous intrusions in their open-ended recall of features that had been included on the video but not in their actual physical examinations. Although we cannot know for sure, the data suggest that the passage of time and exposure to the video altered the memory representations of the 5-year-olds in this condition. In contrast, it is difficult to know how to interpret the performance of the 3-year-olds. Receiving an additional interview and viewing the video did facilitate their recall, but there were no differential effects in response to absent feature questions. However, because these young children tended to respond at chance levels on these probes, as is often the case with their responses to yes–no questions after delays (see, e.g., Baker-Ward et al., 1993), it was impossible to determine if the intervening experiences had a negative influence on the accuracy of their reports.

Filling in the Gaps: Positive and Negative Effects of Knowledge

In addition to the clear impact of "external" events on delayed remembering, it is important to emphasize that some intervening events are "internal" in that they may take place within the individual. Typically, these endogenous factors involve the interplay between episodic and semantic memory in that memory representations (episodic) may be modified as a result of contact with underlying knowledge structures (semantic). For example, memory for a specific event may be modified over time because of the operation of knowledge-driven constructive processes that serve to fill in gaps in memory. Importantly, these processes seem more likely to occur with increases in the delay interval, as children come to make knowledge-based inferences and guesses to fill in missing information. Of course, if the information that is being remembered is consistent with the underlying knowledge, recall appears to be facilitated by the generation of correct inferences. An interesting illustration of this type of facilitative memory modification can be seen in Myles-Worsely, Cromer, and Dodd's (1986) demonstration that over increasing delays, children become more likely to incorporate information from their general scripts for the school day into their accounts of a specific day at preschool. In contrast, sometimes these knowledge-driven processes can lead to errors in recall, such as omissions or distortions of information that is inconsistent with prior knowledge, or intrusions of information that is incorrect, but nonetheless consistent with knowledge.

As suggested, knowledge can be a double-edged sword, and a recent study in our laboratory carried out by Ornstein et al. (1998) can serve to illustrate both the positive and negative influences of prior knowledge. A sample of 4- and 6-year-olds received a mock physical examination that was administered by a licensed pediatrician. The examination was constructed by omitting some highly expected medical features (e.g., listening to the heart), while including other typical features as well as a number of unexpected, atypical medical procedures (e.g., measuring head circumference). Each mock checkup included two types of Present (i.e., administered) features: Present-Typical and Present-Atypical. The children's recall of these expected and unexpected features was assessed immediately and after a 12-week delay. At each assessment, the children were also probed about two types of Absent features that had not been included in the mock examination: those that might have been expected on the basis of their scripts or knowledge about physicians' routines (Absent-Typical), and those that had not been expected (Absent-Atypical).

Consistent with expectations, the children's reports of the mock physical examination were clearly supported by their prior knowledge and expectations. At both assessments, the 4- and 6-year-olds showed enhanced recall of Present-Typical features, in contrast to Present-Atypical features. In addition, there was less forgetting of Present-Typical than the Present-Atypical Features over the course of the delay interval. Perhaps more importantly, however, the children's knowledge-based expectations also led them to make serious errors, particularly after 12 weeks. These errors in remembering seemed to reflect some confusion between the children's memory representations for the mock checkup and their general scripts for what usually happens during a visit to the doctor. One index of this confusion brought about by the children's general knowledge can be seen in the usually high levels of spontaneous intrusions at the 12-week assessment of Typical (and hence expected), but not Atypical, medical features that had not been included in their checkups. Surprisingly, 42% of the 4-year-olds and 72% of the 6-year-olds made at least one such intrusion, rates that are far higher than those observed in our other medical studies (e.g., Baker-Ward et al., 1993). The children's responses to direct (yes–no) questions about medical procedures not included in the mock examination provide additional evidence of these knowledge-based errors. For example, as can be seen in Fig. 2.4, correct denials (i.e., "no" responses) were high when the children were questioned about Atypical features, but at chance levels when they were probed about Typical features. This pattern of data is consistent with the view that as children's memory for the details of the mock physical faded over time, they filled in the gaps on the basis of their general medical knowledge.

Changes in Underlying Knowledge and Understanding. As we have seen, knowledge operates at many points in the flow of information within the memory system. Prior knowledge affects initial interpretation

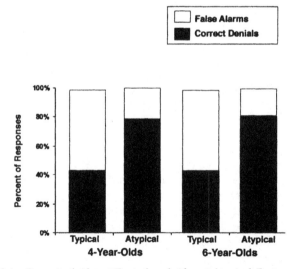

FIG. 2.4. Percent of Absent-Typical and Absent-Atypical Feature questions to which children responded with correct denials and false alarms by age, at the 12-week interview. From "Children's Knowledge, Expectation, and Long-Term Retention," by P. A. Ornstein, K. A. Merritt, L. Baker-Ward, E. Furtado, B. N. Gordon, and G. F. Principe, *Applied Cognitive Psychology*, 12, pp. 387–405. Copyright © 1998 by John Wiley & Sons, Ltd. Reproduced with permission.

and the establishment of a memory representation, but it can also contribute to changes in that representation. Moreover, knowledge-driven constructive processes can support the accurate recall of some aspects of an experience, while at the same time interfering with memory for other components of the experience. However, all of these demonstrations of the impact of knowledge are based on the view that one's understanding remains constant over time, and it is important to ask what happens if knowledge itself undergoes change. Moreover, because of the significant changes in basic knowledge and understanding of the world that take place across the childhood years (and over the time intervals often involved in legal cases), it is very important to consider the impact of changing knowledge on memory representations that themselves are in the process of decay. In his treatment of this complex matter, Ross (1989) suggested that changes in knowledge can engender constructive processes that lead to a reworking of earlier memories in ways that are consistent with current understanding. In support of this view, Ross (1989) presented a series of studies that demonstrate the ways in which current knowledge, beliefs, and attitudes can operate to shape adults' recollections of earlier experiences.

To examine the degree to which changes in children's knowledge could bias their later recollections, Greenhoot (2000) carried out dissertation research in our laboratory in which 5- and 6-year-olds were asked to recall the details of a fictional child's behavior that was depicted in a series of stories. These stories described ambiguous events. The behavior of the protagonist could be interpreted in a variety of ways, and the participants' knowledge about the child was manipulated both before and after they were read the stories. Consider, for example, the issue of how to interpret a scene in one of the stories in which another child's toy is broken while the protagonist was in close proximity. Should this incident be viewed as an accident or as a deliberate action on the part of the protagonist? To manipulate the children's interpretation of this (and other) ambiguous events, Greenhoot provided each participant with one of three different types of social information about the protagonist's personality and general behavioral characteristics. Some children were told that the protagonist was prosocially oriented (Positive), whereas others were informed that he or she was a bully (Negative), and others were given no relevant information (Neutral).

As might be expected, recall was highly constructive in that the children often went far beyond the literal information that was provided in the story. Indeed, their reports were filled with "errors" in the form of inferences, distortions, and intrusions that were consistent with the social knowledge provided to them. Thus, for example, children who had been told that the protagonist was a bully were more likely than their peers to "remember" hostile behaviors, whereas those who had been given positive information tended to "recall" prosocial behaviors. By demonstrating these effects of prior knowledge on remembering (and misremembering), Greenhoot could then determine the impact of a second knowledge manipulation. One week after the children first recalled the stories, they were presented with additional information about the social motives of the protagonist, and for some of them the new information was consistent with the earlier impressions of the protagonist, whereas for others it was inconsistent. Because the types of social information given in the two knowledge manipulations were crossed, there were six conditions: Positive-Positive, Positive-Negative, Negative-Positive, Negative-Negative, Neutral-Positive, Neutral-Negative.

To examine the impact of this second knowledge manipulation, the children's memory for the original stories was again assessed. Feature-by-feature comparisons of the recall from the first to the second assessments provide evidence that they reconstructed their reports of the stories on the basis of their newly acquired knowledge. Greenhoot identified within-subject revisions in the recall of specific story features and classified them as Positive when the protagonist's behavior was remembered positively over time, or negative when it was recalled in a negative fashion over time. For each child, memory revision scores were calculated as the difference between the overall rates of positive and negative revisions. The group data displayed in Fig. 2.5 reveal that the overall patterns of change in recall over time were consistent with the second manipulation of knowledge about the protagonist. Thus, when changes were made in children's recollections of specific acts that had been depicted in the stories,

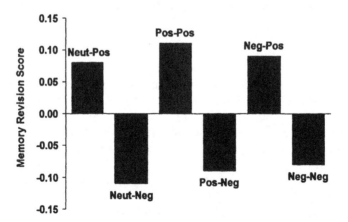

FIG. 2.5.   Memory revision scores, as a function of knowledge group. Neut = neutral; Pos = positive; Neg = negative (Greenhoot, 2000; adapted with permission of Society for Research in Child Development).

they were in the positive direction for children given positive information in the second knowledge manipulation, and in the negative direction for children given negative information.

Greenhoot's (2000) data indicate that, over time, changes in underlying knowledge result in reconstructive modifications of children's memory representations. These data—and those of Ross (1989)—go beyond the demonstrations of knowledge-driven processes presented throughout this chapter. Knowledge certainly does operate to fill in the gaps of what can be remembered, as was shown by Ornstein et al. (1998), but when knowledge changes over time, the result can be a restructuring of memory on the basis of current understanding.

CONCLUDING REMARKS

Our analysis of the development of memory has serious implications for researchers concerned with cognitive development. For example, it is of critical importance to explore more thoroughly the ways in which discussions within the family context will operate to modify representations in memory, and it is essential to develop more precise methodologies for assessing the status of these representations. This analysis also has implications for an understanding of children's abilities to provide accurate testimony. From our perspective, interviewers in a legal setting must focus their attention on the nature of children's (changing) understanding of the events that are being discussed, and they must recognize the myriad of factors that contribute to that understanding. And researchers on children's testimony need to explore the implications of the dynamic nature of the underlying representation for the construction and use of new protocols for interviewing children.

We close by emphasizing the importance of a developmental analysis for considerations of children's testimony. Early research on children as witnesses (e.g., Ceci, Ross, & Toglia, 1987; Goodman, 1984) was strongly influenced by then-current work in cognitive psychology, such as Loftus' (1979) pioneering research on the mnemonic consequences of exposure to misinformation. Much has certainly been learned since then, and researchers on children's testimony have clearly made a difference in the real world in the lives of children and families (Ceci & Bruck, 1995; Goodman & Bottoms, 1993; Poole & Lamb, 1998). As we see it, however, an understanding of children's memory requires a much greater focus on developmental issues than has been the case to date. Our hope, then, is that the next generation of research on children's testimony will capitalize on emerging perspectives in developmental psychology.

ACKNOWLEDGMENTS

Preparation of this chapter was supported in part by grants HD 32114 and MH 52429 from the U.S. Public Health Service.

REFERENCES

Baker-Ward, L., Gordon, B. N., Ornstein, P. A., Larus, D., & Clubb, P. A. (1993). Young children's long-term retention of a pediatric examination. *Child Development, 64,* 1519–1533.

Baker-Ward, L., Ornstein, P. A., & Holden, D. J. (1984). The expression of memorization in early childhood. *Journal of Experimental Child Psychology, 37,* 555–575.

Baker-Ward, L., Ornstein, P. A., & Principe, G. F. A. (1997). Revealing the representation: Evidence from children's reports of events. In P. van den Broek, P. Bauer, & T. Bourg (Eds.), *Developmental spans in event comprehension and representation: Bridging fictional and actual events* (pp. 79–110). Mahwah, NJ: Lawrence Erlbaum Associates.

Bartlett, F. C. (1932). *Remembering: A study in experimental and social psychology.* New York: Cambridge University Press.

Bauer, P. J. (1995). Recalling past events: From infancy to early childhood. In R. Vasta (Ed.), *Annals of child development* (Vol. 11, pp. 25–71). London: Kingsley.

Bauer, P. J., & Dow, G. A. A. (1994). Episodic memory in 16- and 20-month-old children: Specifics are generalized but not forgotten. *Developmental Psychology, 30,* 403–417.

Bauer, P. J., & Hertsgaard, L. A. (1993). Increasing steps in recall of events: Factors facilitating immediate and long-term memory in 13.5- and 16.5-month-old children. *Child Development, 64,* 1204–1223.

Berkerian, D. A., & Bowers, J. M. (1983). Eyewitness testimony: Were we misled? *Journal of Experimental Psychology: Learning, Memory, and Cognition, 9,* 139–145.

Bjorklund, D. F. (1985). The role of conceptual knowledge in the development of organization in children's memory. In C. J. Brainerd & M. Pressley (Eds.), *Basic processes in memory development: Progress in cognitive development research* (pp. 103–142). New York: Springer-Verlag.

Bjorklund, D. F. (Ed.). (1990). *Children's strategies: Contemporary views of cognitive development.* Hillsdale, NJ: Lawrence Erlbaum Associates.

Brainerd, C. J., Kingma, J., & Howe, M. L. (1985). On the development of forgetting. *Child Development, 56,* 1103–1119.

Brainerd, C. J., Reyna, V. F., Howe, M. L., & Kingma, J. (1990). The development of forgetting and reminiscence. *Monographs of the Society for Research in Child Development, 55*(3–4, Whole No. 222).

Bransford, J. D., & Johnson, M. K. (1972). Contextual prerequisites for understanding: Some investigations of comprehension and recall. *Journal of Verbal Learning and Verbal Behavior, 11,* 717–726.

Broadbent, D. E. (1958). *Perception and communication.* London: Pergamon Press.

Campbell, B. A., & Jaynes, J. (1966). Reinstatement. *Psychological Review, 73,* 478–480.

Ceci, S. J., & Bruck, M. (1993). The suggestibility of the child witness: A historical review and synthesis. *Psychological Bulletin, 113,* 403–439.

Ceci, S. J., & Bruck, M. (1995). *Jeopardy in the courtroom: A scientific analysis of children's testimony.* Washington, DC: American Psychological Association.

Ceci, S. J., Ross D., & Toglia, M. (1987). Age differences in suggestibility: Psycholegal implications. *Journal of Experimental Psychology: General, 117,* 38–49.

Chi, M. T. H. (1978). Knowledge structure and memory development. In R. Siegler (Ed.), *Children's thinking: What develops?* Hillsdale, NJ: Lawrence Erlbaum Associates.

Chi, M. T. H., & Ceci, C. J. (1987). Content knowledge: Its role, representation, and restructuring in memory development. In H. W. Reese (Ed.), *Advances in child development and behavior* (Vol. 20, pp. 91–142). Orlando, FL: Academic Press.

Clarke-Stewart, A., Thompson, W., & Lepore, S. (1989, May). *Manipulating children's interpretations through interrogation.* Paper presented at the Biennial Meeting of the Society for Research in Child Development, Kansas City, MO.

Clubb, P. A., Nida, R., Merritt, K., & Ornstein, P. A. (1993). Visiting the doctor: Children's knowledge and memory. *Cognitive Development, 8,* 361–372.

DeLoache, J. S., & Marzolf, D. P. (1995). The use of dolls to interview young children. *Journal of Experimental Child Psychology, 6,* 155–173.

Dent, H. R., & Stephenson, G. M. (1979). An experimental study of the effectiveness of differential techniques of questioning child witnesses. *British Journal of Social and Clinical Psychology, 18,* 41–51.

Diamond, A. (1995). Evidence of robust recognition memory in early life when assessed by reaching behavior. *Journal of Experimental Child Behavior, 59,* 419–456.

Donaldson, M. (1978). *Children's minds.* London: Croom Helm.

Farrar, M. J., & Goodman, G. S. (1990). Developmental differences in the relation between script and episodic memory: Do they exist? In R. Fivush & J. A. Hudson (Eds.), *Knowing and remembering in young children.* Cambridge, England: Cambridge University Press.

Fivush, R., Pipe, M.-E., Murachver, T., & Reese, E. (1997). Events spoken and unspoken: Implications of language and memory development for the recovered memory debate. In M. Conway (Ed.), *Recovered memories and false memories.* New York: Oxford University Press.

Fivush, R., & Hamond, N. R. (1990). Autobiographical memory across the preschool years: Toward reconceptualizing childhood amnesia. In R. Fivush & J. A. Hudson (Eds.), *Knowing and remembering in young children.* Cambridge, England: Cambridge University Press.

Fivush, R., & Hudson, J. A. (Eds.). (1990). *Knowing and remembering in young children.* Cambridge, England: Cambridge University Press.

Fivush, R., & Haden, C. A. (1997). Narrating and representing experience: Preschoolers' developing autobiographical recounts. In P. van den Broek, P. J. Bauer, & T. Bourg (Eds.), *Developmental spans in event comprehension and representation: Bridging fictional and actual events* (pp. 169–198). Mahwah, NJ: Lawrence Erlbaum Associates.

Geddie, L., Myers, J. T., & Ornstein, P. A. (1994, April). Children's memory of a physical examination: A comparison of recall and recognition assessment protocols. In B. N. Gordon (Chair), *Young children's accounts of medical and dental examinations: Remembering and reporting personal experiences.* Conference on Human Development, Pittsburgh, PA.

Goodman, G. S. (1984). Children's testimony in historical perspective. *Journal of Social Issues, 40,* 9–31.

Goodman, G. S., & Bottoms, B. L. (Eds.). (1993). *Child victims, child witnesses: Understanding and improving testimony.* New York: Guilford Press.

Goodman, G. S., Rudy, L., Bottoms, B. L., & Aman, C. (1990). Children's concerns and memory: Issues of ecological validity in the study of children's eyewitness testimony. In R. Fivush & J. Hudson (Eds.), *Knowing and remembering in young children* (pp. 249–284). New York: Cambridge University Press.

Gordon, B. N., Ornstein, P. A., Nida, R. E., Follmer, A., Crenshaw, M. C., & Albert, G. F. (1993). Does the use of dolls facilitate children's memory of visits to the doctor? *Applied Cognitive Psychology, 7,* 459–474.

Greenhoot, A. F. (2000). Remembering and understanding: The effects of changes in underlying knowledge on children's recollections. *Child Development, 71,* 1309–1328.

Greenhoot, A. F., Ornstein, P. A., Gordon, B. N., & Baker-Ward, L. (1999). Acting out the details of a pediatric check-up: The impact of interview condition and behavioral style on children's memory reports. *Child Development, 70,* 363–380.

Haden, C. A., Haine, R. A., & Fivush, R. (1997). Developing narrative structure in parent–child reminiscing across the preschool years. *Developmental Psychology, 33,* 295–307.

Haden, C. A., Ornstein, P. A., Eckerman, C. O., & Didow, S. (2001). Mother–child conversational interactions as events unfold: Linkages to subsequent remembering. *Child Development, 72*(4).

Howe, M. L., Courage, M. L., & Bryant-Brown, L. (1993). Reinstating preschoolers' memories. *Developmental Psychology, 29,* 854–869.

Johnson, M. K., Hashtroudi, S., & Lindsay, S. D. (1993). Source monitoring. *Psychological Bulletin, 114,* 3–28.

Loftus, E. F. (1979). *Eyewitness testimony.* Cambridge, MA: Harvard University Press.

Loftus, E. F., & Davies, G. M. (1984). Distortions in the memory of children. *Journal of Social Issues, 40,* 51–68.

Loftus, E. F., & Hoffman, H. G. (1989). Misinformation and memory: The creation of new memories. *Journal of Experimental Psychology: General, 118,* 100–104.

Mandler, J. M. (1991, April). *Discussion.* In N. L. Stein & P. A. Ornstein (Chairs), *The development of autobiographical memory for stressful and emotional events.* Society for Research in Child Development, Seattle, WA.

McCloskey, M., & Zaragoza, M. (1985). Misleading postevent information and memory for events: Arguments and evidence against the memory impairment hypotheses. *Journal of Experimental Psychology: General, 114,* 3–18.

McDonough, L., & Mandler, J. M. (1994). Very long term recall in infants: Infantile amnesia reconsidered. *Memory, 2,* 339–352.

Meltzoff, A. N. (1988a). Infant imitation after a 1-week delay: Long-term memory for novel acts and multiple stimuli. *Developmental Psychology, 24,* 470–476.

Meltzoff, A. N. (1988b). Infant imitation and memory: Nine-month-olds in immediate and deferred tests. *Child Development, 59,* 217–225.

Meltzoff, A. N. (1995). What infant memory tells us about infantile amnesia: Long-term recall and deferred imitation. *Journal of Experimental Child Psychology, 59,* 497–515.

Merritt, K. A., Ornstein, P. A., & Spicker, B. (1994). Children's memory for a salient medical procedure: Implications for testimony. *Pediatrics, 94,* 17–23.

Myles-Worsley, M., Cromer, C., & Dodd, D. (1986). Children's preschool script reconstruction: Reliance on general knowledge as memory fades. *Developmental Psychology, 22,* 22–30.

Nelson, K. (1986). *Event knowledge: Structure and function in development.* Hillsdale, NJ: Lawrence Erlbaum Associates.

Nelson, K. (1996). *Language in cognitive development: Emergence of the mediated mind.* Cambridge, England: Cambridge University Press.

Nickerson, R. S., & Adams, M. J. (1979). Long-term memory for a common object. *Cognitive Psychology, 11,* 287–307.

Ornstein, P. A. (1995). Children's long-term retention of salient personal experiences. *Journal of Traumatic Stress, 8,* 581–605.

Ornstein, P. A., Baker-Ward, L., & Naus, M. J. (1988). The development of mnemonic skill. In F. E. Weinert & M. Perlmutter (Eds.), *Memory development: Universal changes and individual differences* (pp. 67–91). Hillsdale, NJ: Lawrence Erlbaum Associates.

Ornstein, P. A., Baker-Ward, L., Gordon, B. N., & Merritt, K. A. (1997a). Children's memory for medical experiences: Implications for testimony. *Applied Cognitive Psychology, 11,* S87–S104.

Ornstein, P. A., Ceci, C. J., & Loftus, E. F. (1998). Adult recollections of childhood abuse: Cognitive and developmental perspectives. *Psychology, Public Policy, and Law, 4,* 1025–1051.

Ornstein, P. A., Larus, D., & Clubb, P. A. (1991). Understanding children's testimony: Implications of research on the development of memory. In R. Vasta (Ed.), *Annals of child development* (Vol. 8, pp. 145–176). London: Kingsley.

Ornstein, P. A., Merritt, K. A., & Baker-Ward, L. (1995, July). Children's recollections of medical experiences: Exploring the linkage between stress and memory. In J. Parker (Chair), *Eyewitness memory: Effects of stress and arousal upon children's memories.* Society for Applied Research in Memory and Cognition, Vancouver, Canada.

Ornstein, P. A., Merritt, K. A., Baker-Ward, L., Furtado, E., Gordon, B. N., & Principe, G. F. (1998). Children's knowledge, expectation, and long-term retention. *Applied Cognitive Psychology, 12*, 387–405.

Ornstein, P. A., & Naus, M. J. (1985). Effects of the knowledge base on children's memory strategies. In H. W. Reese (Ed.), *Advances in child development and behavior* (Vol. 19, pp. 113–148). Orlando, FL: Academic Press.

Ornstein, P. A., Shapiro, L. B., Clubb, P. A., Follmer, A., & Baker-Ward, L. (1997b). The influence of prior knowledge on children's memory for salient medical experiences. In N. L. Stein, P. A. Ornstein, B. Tversky, & C. Brainerd (Eds.), *Memory for everyday and emotional events* (pp. 83–112). Mahwah, NJ: Lawrence Erlbaum Associates.

Perris, E. E., Meyers, N. A., & Clifton, R. K. (1990). Long-term memory for a single infancy experience. *Child Development, 61*, 1797–1807.

Peters, D. P. (1997). Stress, arousal, and children's eyewitness memory. In N. L. Stein, P. A. Ornstein, B. Tversky, & C. Brainerd (Eds.), *Memory for everyday and emotional events* (pp. 351–370). Mahwah, NJ: Lawrence Erlbaum Associates.

Poole, D. A., & Lamb, M. E. (1998). *Investigative interviews of children: A guide for helping professionals.* Washington, DC: American Psychological Association.

Poole, D., & White, L. (1993). Two years later: Effects of question repetition and retention interval on the eyewitness testimony of children and adults. *Developmental Psychology, 29*, 844–853.

Principe, G. F., Myers, J. T., Furtado, E. A., Merritt, K. A., & Ornstein, P. A. (1996, March). The relation between procedural information and young children's recall of an invasive medical procedure. In L. Baker-Ward (Chair), *The role of individual differences in young children's reports of salient personal experiences.* Symposium presented at the biennial meetings of the Conference on Human Development. Birmingham, AL.

Principe, G. F., Ornstein, P. A., Baker-Ward, L., & Gordon, B. N. (2000). The effects of intervening experiences on children's memory for a physical examination. *Applied Cognitive Psychology, 14*, 59–80.

Reese, E., Haden, C. A., & Fivush, R. (1993). Mother–child conversations about the past: Relationships of style and memory over time. *Cognitive Development, 8*, 403–430.

Ross, M. (1989). Relation of implicit theories to the construction of personal histories. *Psychological Review, 96*, 341–357.

Rovee-Collier, C. K. (1995). Time windows in cognitive development. *Developmental Psychology, 31*, 147–169.

Rovee-Collier, C. K., & Shyi, G. C. W. (1992). A functional and cognitive analysis of infant long-term retention. In C. J. Brainerd, M. L. Howe, & V. F. Reyna (Eds.), *The development of long-term retention* (pp. 3–55). New York: Springer-Verlag.

Schneider, W., & Bjorklund, D. F. (1998). Memory. In W. Damon (Series Ed.) & D. Kuhn & R. S. Siegler (Vol. Eds.), *Handbook of child psychology: Vol. 2. Cognition, perception, and language* (5th ed., pp. 467–521). New York: Wiley.

Schneider, W., Körkel, J., & Weinert, F. E. (1989). Domain-specific knowledge and memory performance: A comparison of high- and low-aptitude children. *Journal of Educational Psychology, 81*, 306–312.

Schneider, W., & Pressley, W. (1997). *Memory development between two and twenty* (2nd ed.). Mahwah, NJ: Lawrence Erlbaum Associates.

Steward, M. S., Steward, D. S., Farquhar, L., Myers, J. E. B., Reinhart, M., Welker, J., Joye, N., Driskill, J., & Morgan, J. (1996). Interviewing young children about body touch and handling. *Monographs of the Society for Research in Child Development, 61*(4, Serial No. 248), pp. 1–203.

Tessler, M., & Nelson, K. (1994). Making memories: The influence of joint encoding on later recall. *Consciousness and Cognition, 3,* 307–326.

Tversky, B., & Tuchin, M. (1989). A reconciliation of the evidence on eyewitness testimony: Comments on McCloskey and Zaragoza. *Journal of Experimental Psychology: General, 118,* 86–91.

False Childhood Memories and Eyewitness Memory Errors

Ira E. Hyman, Jr.
Western Washington University

Elizabeth F. Loftus
University of Washington

After discussing false childhood memories in an undergraduate class, one of us (IH) was approached by a young woman (whom we'll call Sarah) who said, "I think that may have happened to me." In further conversation, Sarah explained that she entered therapy for an eating disorder and had been told, early in the course of treatment, that she most likely had been sexually abused as a child. She was also told that she could not expect her eating disorder to improve until she recovered her repressed memories. After 4 months of repeated questioning, group therapy focused on abuse stories, and hypnosis-like relaxation to aid in memory recovery, she eventually recovered an instance of childhood sexual abuse. Because this did not cure her eating disorder, she was told that there must be more repressed memories, possibly involving other perpetrators. She ended treatment at that center and received help from a different therapist who did not focus on child abuse. When she described her experience, she expressed concern about her memory. Was the memory a true memory that had been forgotten and recovered? Was the memory a false memory created in response to the intense demands and suggestions she experienced?

The controversy over recovered and false memories can be considered related to the problem of eyewitness memory. Is a witness's report reliable? Can people make errors in memory? Can they identify the wrong person? Can they create an entirely false memory? What factors contribute to reliable memory? What factors cause erroneous recall?

In many respects, eyewitness memory can be viewed as an application of basic research in human memory. Many of the same issues are addressed: for example, the role of emotion in memory or how retention interval influences memory. The interaction of basic and applied research is, however, bidirectional. Applied research occasionally documents new problems for basic research. Eyewitness memory research has provided such issues. For example, does postevent misleading information result in the replacement of the original memory, or is the misinformation effect better explained as a source memory failure (Ayers & Reder, 1998; Belli, 1989; Lindsay, 1990; McCloskey & Zaragoza, 1985; Zaragoza & Lane, 1994; Zaragoza & Mitchell, 1996)? In addition, eyewitness memory research has often reminded basic researchers of the importance of social processes in understanding human memory. More recently, applied memory researchers have been concerned with the possibility that people can create entire false memories.

In this chapter, we review research on false childhood memories, pointing out how it is an outgrowth of traditional research on eyewitness memory errors. We then discuss processes involved in the creation of false childhood memories and describe various research programs that are investigating these processes. In conclusion, we describe what this line of research tells us not only about eyewitness memory, but also of autobiographical memory more generally.

FALSE CHILDHOOD MEMORIES

Memory researchers have shown that remembering almost always involves a constructive process—whether the person is remembering a word list (Deese, 1959; Roediger & McDermott, 1995), a story (Bartlett, 1932), a song (Hyman & Rubin, 1990; Rubin, 1995), or a personal experience (Barclay & DeCooke, 1988; Neisser, 1982). Memory construction is guided both by internal schematic knowledge and by external suggestions. Using the classic misinformation paradigm, Loftus and her colleagues (see Loftus, 1991, 1992) showed people an event, provided neutral or misleading postevent information, and observed poorer memory performance following the misleading information. Often, the misleading information would affect not only the particular aspect of the event, but also show how the entire memory was reconstructed based on the new understanding of the event (Loftus & Palmer, 1974).

Applying this research on memory errors to the creation of false childhood memories is, however, difficult for several reasons. First, research on the misinformation effect demonstrates that people can change an aspect of their memory for an event that happened. Misinformation studies often involve the participant as an observer, not as an actor. In addition, the events studied in misinformation research are generally not emotional, although there are some studies that involve emotional events. One of the most stunning examples of the pliability of memory for highly upsetting events comes from a study of Dutch citizens who tried to recall the crash of an El Al Boeing 747 into an apartment building in Amsterdam (Crombag, Wagenaar, & Van Koppen, 1996). Although film crews rushed to the scene and quickly filmed the fire and rescue of survivors from the building, there was no film of the crash. Nonetheless, when people were asked to recall the crash 10 months later and asked leading questions, 66% claimed to have seen TV film of the crashing plane.

Still, most misinformation studies concern memory change of features of unemotional events that do not involve the self as a participant. In thinking about the relation between the misinformation studies and false memories of child sexual abuse, certain factors must be kept in mind. Creating a false memory of child abuse would involve the construction of an entire event rather than changing an aspect of an event. If someone creates a memory of childhood sexual abuse, such an event would be emotional and would involve the self as a central character. These differences could easily prompt one to conclude that the creation of false childhood memories is at least unlikely, if not impossible. Thus the research question became: Will people create entire false memories of an emotional event that involves the self?

When studying the creation of false childhood memories, the researchers' goal was to extend the exploration of memory errors. Most researchers generated similar methodologies to suggest to participants a complete memory that involved the self and that was somewhat emotional, although never traumatic (Ceci, Huffman, Smith, & Loftus, 1994; Ceci, Loftus, Leichtman, & Bruck, 1994; Hyman & Billings, 1998; Hyman, Husband, & Billings, 1995; Hyman & Pentland, 1996; Loftus & Pickrell, 1995). The research methodology was an outgrowth of misinformation studies and research investigating the ability of adults to recall early childhood experiences (e.g., Usher & Neisser, 1993). In most paradigms, researchers requested information from family members about events that occurred during the participant's childhood. Then, the participant was asked to recall these true events. In addition, the participant was asked about a false event—an event that the researchers were fairly sure did not happen to the participant. During a series of interviews, the false event was presented as if it were a true event that was obtained from the initial family solicitation. The participants were usually interviewed repeatedly about both the true and false events and told that their memories would improve over time. Although there is an interest in memory for the true experiences, the most important result is how the participants responded to the false event—Do the participants come to believe that the event took place sometime during their childhood?

For example, Hyman et al. (1995) used this methodology in a study investigating college students' childhood memories. First, the researchers visited an introductory psychology class and asked the students for permission to mail a questionnaire to their parents. The students were told that the researchers were interested in how well people could recall childhood experiences and therefore needed information from parents about what had happened. The researchers obtained descriptions of true childhood events from the parent surveys. When the parents returned the questionnaires, the researchers asked the introductory psychology students to participate in a series of interviews investigating their memory for early childhood experiences. The students were told that the researchers were interested in how completely and accurately they could recall childhood. In each of three interviews (separated by 1 day), the students were asked to remember several true events and one false event. For all true events and the false event, the interviewer provided the students with a basic description (including age, event, a few actions, other people involved, and a location) and asked the students what they remembered about the event. One of the false events used was called the punch bowl event: When you were 6 years old, you were at the wedding of a friend of the family, you were running around with some other kids at the reception, and you bumped into the table the punch bowl was sitting on and spilled punch on the parents of the bride. All of the false events used were self-involving and would have been somewhat emotional at the time of the event, although none were traumatic events.

The participants recalled a majority of the true events in the first interview and remembered even more of the true events over time. There are at least two ways to explain the increased recall of the true events. First, by thinking about the events over a period of time, the students provided themselves with additional memory cues that led to the recollection of previously unretrieved memories. Second, the participants created, rather than recalled, memories that matched the cues provided in the interviews. We cannot say whether this recovery of memory for the true experience represents actual memories or the creation of memories.

Regarding the false events, none of the participants remembered the false event on its initial presentation. However, by the third interview, 25% of the students remembered the event. Six students reported memories that were clear and included the critical information (such as turning over the punch bowl) as well as consistent elaborations (such as their parents being upset). Five of the reports were less clear; the students included little of the critical suggested information although they elaborated in a consistent fashion. Two of the students created clear images, but they were not sure if they were remembering or simply imagining the events that had been suggested to them. Although Hyman et al. used only college students in their study, other studies using various populations (e.g., preschool children, adults, teenagers) and different false events have found similar results (Ceci, Huffman, et al., 1994; Ceci, Loftus, et al., 1994; Loftus & Pickrell, 1995; Pezdek, Finger, & Hodge, 1997).

The proportion of individuals who create false childhood memories depends on the research method used. Using a similar methodology, Hyman and Pentland (1996) asked college students to imagine and describe any events, whether true or false, that they could not remember. They speculated that imagining events would cause people to construct clearer images and narratives that they would later confuse with personal memories. By the third interview, nearly 40% of the college students remembered spilling the punch bowl.

False childhood memory research has successfully extended the previous work on memory suggestibility. Not only will people alter aspects on an event in response to suggestions, but they will also create entire events. The created events involve the self and are at least mildly emotional.

Nonetheless, questions of generalizability still remain. Spilling a punch bowl at a wedding or being lost in a mall is not the same as being sexually abused. Currently, no researcher has attempted to have participants create memories of being sexually abused. For ethical reasons, it is unlikely that anyone ever will; if a memory impacts one's self-concept and family relationships whether it is true or false, then experimentally inducing such memories would be atrocious. This makes generalizing to sexual abuse memories difficult, but it is not impossible. Real-world cases often provide dramatic evidence that individuals can create false memories of a great variety of events. Recovered memory cases of alien abductions and satanic ritual abuse suggest that a variety of false memories can be created. Because in most of these cases the events cannot be true, but are nonetheless traumatic, evidence for the creation of false traumatic memories is substantiated. Although many examples could be provided, a single one will suffice to support the point.

In the mid-1980s, Nadean Cool, a nurse's aide in Wisconsin, sought therapy from a psychiatrist to help her cope with her reaction to a traumatic event. During therapy, the psychiatrist used hypnosis and other suggestive techniques to reveal buried memories of abuse that Cool had allegedly experienced. In the process, Cool became convinced that she had repressed memories of being in a satanic cult, eating babies, being raped, having sex with animals, and being forced to watch the murder of her 8-year-old friend. She began to believe that she had over 120 personalities—children, adults, angels, and even a duck. She was repeatedly urged to believe that these events had occurred. The psychiatrist also performed exorcisms on her; one lasted for 5 hours and included the sprinkling of holy water and screams for Satan to leave Cool's body. Such cases demonstrate the extreme experiences that people "remember" in response to repeated suggestions. How do people believe such unlikely things as being forced to eat babies or watch the murder of a friend?

THREE PROCESSES INVOLVED IN MEMORY CREATION

Three processes are involved in the creation of false childhood memories: *plausibility judgments, image and narrative construction,* and *source monitoring judgments* (Hyman & Kleinknecht, 1999). First, an individual judges the plausibility of a the suggested event: Is the event something that the person believes could have happened to them? For example, some participants in the research by Hyman and his colleagues (Hyman & Billings, 1998; Hyman et al., 1995; Hyman & Pentland, 1996) did not create memories of spilling a punch bowl at a wedding because they believed that they had never attended a wedding as child. They refused to accept the event as a plausible personal experience. Plausibility is a judgment that people make based on various types of information.

Various factors influence plausibility judgments, including: the source of a suggestion, an individual's belief about the general frequency of the event, whether the individual has experienced similar events, the connections made between the event and various aspects of the individual's current state, the ease with which the event comes to mind. In addition, there are several methods for suggesting to an individual that an event is generally, and individually, plausible. Event plausibility can be stated directly (25% of adults were sexually abused), tied to a particular characteristic that an individual may possess (the majority of people with that problem were abused as children), tied to an individual's personality (many people like you were abused), or implied by social groupings (you are like the people in this group and they were all abused).

Once someone believes that an event is personally plausible, that person still must construct a memory: an image with a narrative. People can believe, or even know, that an event occurred, without having a memory of the event. Since Bartlett (1932), researchers have studied memory construction. Memory is not like videotape—people do not simply retrieve a memory and replay the experience. Instead, people construct a memory by combining schematic knowledge from various sources with personal experiences, suggestions, and current demands. All memories are constructions.

Even when people believe an event is plausible and construct an image of the event, they still may not think that their knowledge is a personal memory. For example, all of the participants in the imagery condition of Hyman and Pentland's (1996) study constructed an image of spilling the punch bowl at a wedding and described that image in a narrative. Many, however, did not claim the image as a memory; instead, they correctly attributed the source of the image to a creation in response to the suggestion. In contrast, others made a source monitoring error: They claimed the constructed images as a personal memory. This illustrates the final process involved in creating a false memory. In addition to accepting an event as plausible and constructing a memory, people must make a source monitoring error—they must claim the false memory as a personal memory. Many studies have shown that people experience difficulties remembering the source of information they have learned (see Johnson, Hastroudi, & Lindsay, 1993). In addition, source misattributions have been suggested as a primary cause of the misinformation effect—people remember the misleading postevent information and incorrectly attributed the information to the original event (e.g., Zaragoza & Lane, 1994).

Although the processes of plausibility judgment, memory construction, and source monitoring error may occur in a linear fashion and be dependent on the preceding step, we suspect that the processes are somewhat interactive. For example, producing a clear image may influence one's assessment of the plausibility of an event having occurred (Garry, Manning, Loftus, & Sherman, 1996). It may be more accurate to claim that all three processes are necessary for false memory creation but that the processes are somewhat independent because different situational factors and individual differences may influence each process. False memory research can be interpreted in terms of this general framework of plausibility judgments, image and narrative construction, and source monitoring errors. We use the framework to integrate many of these findings and provide information about how people make plausibility judgments and how source monitoring errors occur in autobiographical memories.

Plausibility Judgments

In order for someone to create a false memory, that person must first accept the suggested event as plausible. Pezdek et al. (1997) documented the role of the event in plausibility judgments. They suspected that events that were similar to scripts from an individual's childhood would more likely be adopted as personal memories. In their first experiment, the researchers suggested false events that either did or did not match the religious background of their participants. The participants were either Catholic or Jewish. Thus, the false events were variations of Shabbat dinners and

Communion services. In agreement with their predictions, they found that individuals were more likely to create memories for events that matched their religious background than for events that did not (i.e., for a Catholic, the event involving Communion as opposed to the event involving Shabbat). In a second experiment, Pezdek and colleagues suggested a plausible event (being lost in a mall) and a less plausible event (receiving an enema). They argued that people have script knowledge of being lost that makes the event more easily accepted and created. They found that people have a greater tendency to create a memory of being lost than a memory of receiving an enema. In both cases, Pezdek et al. argued that plausible events are more likely to result in false memories.

Plausibility is not, however, simply a matter of the event. Plausibility judgments also depend on whether the event matches an individual's expectancy for a class of experiences. People rate the likelihood of events differently. For instance, most people think abduction by extraterrestrials is unlikely. Others may consider such an event relatively common. For example, Spanos, Cross, Dickson, and DuBreuil (1993) looked for personality factors to explain the difference between people who claimed to have had encounters with UFOs and individuals who did not claim such experiences. They found that belief in alien visitations was the primary variable that differentiated people who claimed such memories from individuals who did not. Knowledge and beliefs about the frequency of an event influence plausibility judgments. Knowledge and beliefs about the frequency of childhood abuse can influence individuals' judgments of how plausible an abuse experience is for them. In today's society sexual abuse is widely discussed and suggestions are made that many people have experienced child abuse.

Not only will people judge plausibility based on personal experiences and beliefs about the general frequency of events, but it is also possible to manipulate people's plausibility judgments. Kelley, Amodio, and Lindsay (1996) provided people with false feedback as a means of manipulating plausibility judgments and creating false memories. They gave participants a series of tests that were supposedly designed to assess innate handedness: whether someone was truly right- or left-handed. All participants were right-handed, and the tests were not actually constructed to provide information on native handedness. Nonetheless, Kelley et al. told some individuals that, based on the test results, they most likely were born left-handed. Other individuals were told that their test results indicated that they were right-handed. People believed this feedback even though the researchers told the participants that the tests were only preliminary. Kelly et al. suggested that the people try to remember times when they had been shaped to use their right hand rather than their left hand. A few days later, individuals who were given the false feedback that they were born left-handed remembered many more instances of hand-use shaping than those who were told that they were right-handed. Loftus (1997) reported a similar investigation in which she and her colleagues suggested to individuals that, based on test results of their visual abilities, the hospital most likely had hung colorful mobiles over their cribs when they were newborns. After time, many individuals claimed to remember seeing such a mobile over their crib—a memory that cannot be true given memory and visual development.

Similarly, Hyman, Chesley, and Thoelke (1997) used a Barnum-type methodology to provide false feedback and manipulate plausibility judgments of childhood experiences. The goal was to provide reasons for people to believe that certain events were likely to have occurred to them. Hyman et al. accomplished this by connecting rare childhood events to bogus personality feedback. In classic investigations of the Barnum effect, individuals took a personality test and were provided feedback supposedly based on the test. The feedback was not, however, based on the personality test. Instead, all participants received identical feedback containing statements that were vague and generally socially desirable and positive. The typical finding was that most individuals rated the resulting personality description as describing them.

Hyman et al.'s research on plausibility judgments began as a Barnum-type study. They administered two personality tests in a large introductory psychology class. The students were told that the researchers were investigating the relation between personality and autobiographical memory. One week later all students were provided with a packet containing their "individual" feedback and a followup questionnaire on autobiographical memory. The individualized feedback was bogus—all students were provided with the same personality description. The students were asked to read their personality description and rate how well it described them. After the students rated the personality description, they were asked to respond to the autobiographical memory questionnaire: This was the extension they added to the standard Barnum methodology. All students were told that the autobiographical memory questionnaire included some events that were likely to have happened to them, and other events that were unlikely to have happened to them based on their personality type. The students rated each event on a 7-point scale ranging from 1 (*did not happen*) to 7 (*did happen*).

Generally, the students rated the personality description as a good fit. Although there was an overall tendency for individuals to rate the events the researchers told them were likely as more plausible than the events they stated were unlikely, the effect was more profound for individuals who accepted the personality description. Individuals who rated the description as a better characterization of themselves rated the events they

were told were more likely to have occurred as more plausible. Those individuals who accepted the self-description also rated as more plausible
the events that were tied to that self-description. In the Kelley et al. (1996)
and Hyman et al. (1997) studies, event plausibility judgments were manipulated by connecting childhood events to false personality feedback.
Thus, plausibility judgments are assumed to be based on personal script
knowledge of the event, general beliefs about the frequency of events, and
connections of the suggested events to an individual's personality characteristics, whether the personality feedback is true or false.

In an extensive series of studies, Loftus and her colleagues investigated
other methods of affecting plausibility judgments. Previously, researchers
have shown that imagining a possible future event can increase a person's
judgment of the likelihood that the event will occur (Carroll, 1978; Gregory, Cialdini, & Carpenter, 1982; Sherman, Cialdini, Schwartzman, &
Reynolds, 1985). Imagining the event makes it come to mind with greater
fluency in subsequent tasks. In many judgments, the ease with which an
event comes to mind determines the judgment (Jacoby, Woloshyn, &
Kelley, 1989; Tversky & Kahneman, 1973). Subsequently, Garry, Manning,
Loftus, and Sherman (1996) wondered if imagining an event would have
the same effect on plausibility judgments for past events.

Garry et al. (1996) used the Life Events Inventory (LEI) to rate whether
or not a series of childhood events had happened to a group of college students. The participants were asked to rate each event using a Likert scale
ranging from 1 (*definitely did not happen*) to 8 (*definitely did happen*). This rating is a reflection of many possible sources of knowledge. A person can
rate the event as definitely having occurred if they remember it, if they
know about the event from other sources but do not remember it, or if
they have some other reason for believing the event occurred. In a separate experimental session, participants were asked to imagine possible
childhood events including events presented on the LEI. Participants
were asked to complete the LEI again. The results demonstrated how imaging affected ratings for events that participants previously rated as
likely did not happen (a rating of 4 and below on the 8-point scale).

It was hypothesized that when participants imagined childhood events
that they had previously rated as unlikely, the act of imagining would increase fluency for the events. Therefore, when the events were considered
while completing the LEI, the events would come to mind more easily.
This fluency would prompt people to inflate their ratings of the possibility
that the event occurred. Garry et al. (1996) observed that individuals who
imagined unlikely events were more likely to increase their ratings for
those events than those who did not imagine the previously unlikely
events. Imagining an event can affect fluency and increase plausibility
judgments.

Using this method, Loftus and her colleagues explored a variety of manipulations that affect plausibility judgments, and in some cases contribute to the creation of childhood memories. For example, Pickrell and Loftus (1999) investigated if plausibility judgments are affected by participants reading examples of an experience. If estimates of plausibility, or ratings of whether participants think the event happened to them, are based on the ease with which the event comes to mind, then any additional recent experience with the event should inflate plausibility ratings. Pickrell and Loftus found that individuals who read examples of childhood events rated the events as more likely to have occurred than did individuals who did not read event examples.

Mazzoni and Loftus (Mazzoni & Loftus, 1998; Mazzoni, Loftus, Seitz, & Lynn, 1999) studied the effects of dream interpretation on event plausibility ratings. First, participants completed a LEI. Next, the individuals participated in an apparently separate experiment involving dream interpretation. Regardless of the dream scenario that the individuals reported as part of the experiment, they were told that the dream indicated a critical childhood experience (such as being lost or being harassed by a bully). Later, the participants filled out another LEI, which included a critical item of being lost or harassed by a bully. Again, plausibility ratings on the LEI were inflated—the participants' belief that the experience had happened to them increased after the dream interpretation session. In addition, the researchers asked the participants to report any particular memories that they had of the disclosed experiences. Nearly half of the participants who experienced the dream interpretation reported actual experiences in agreement with the suggested experience. The dream interpretation not only affected plausibility estimates, but also resulted in complete memory creation for some individuals.

As Pezdek et al. (1997) argued, plausibility is a crucial factor in the creation of false childhood memories. Pezdek et al. argued for a narrow definition of plausibility related to an individual's script knowledge for an event based on personal experience. In contrast, Hyman and Kleinknecht (1999) argued that plausibility is a judgment that people make based on a variety of information. Therefore, plausibility judgments are affected by beliefs about event likelihood (Spanos et al., 1993), by making connections to an individual's understanding of self (Kelley et al., 1996; Hyman et al., 1997), by the availability of the event, which is influenced by imagining and reading about the event (Garry et al., 1996; Pickrell & Loftus, 1999), and by dream interpretation (Mazzoni et al., 1999). Undoubtedly, other factors also influence how people make judgments about event plausibility.

By themselves, manipulations of plausibility judgments may lead to the creation of false memories (e.g., Mazzoni et al., 1999). Often, however, people can accept that an event is plausible, that it is likely to have happened to them, without actually remembering the event. The second step in the creation of memories is the construction of a memory — an image with a narrative. Once individuals create an image and narrative, they still must make an additional judgment error — they must claim the constructed memory as a personal memory. In the next section we focus on research related to source monitoring errors in autobiographical memories.

Source Monitoring Errors

People make a variety of source monitoring decisions about the contents of their memory. Some decisions focus on discriminating among external sources of information: trying to remember who told you a joke, whether you learned a piece of news from the newspaper or from television, or trying to remember what class covered which topic. Other source monitoring decisions focus on discriminating between internal and external sources of thoughts and images: Was that something I did or did I only imagine it, dream it, or plan to do it? Discriminating the source of an image and narrative created in response to a suggestion can be difficult. A person must decide if the event is a personal memory. Internal and external sources are not mutually exclusive: The individual may continue to recall hearing about the event from the interviewer, but may also decide that the event is also remembered.

Johnson and her colleagues (Johnson, Foley, Suengas, & Raye, 1988; Johnson, Hastroudi, & Lindsay, 1993) have argued that source decisions are made based on the qualities of a memory. When memories are clear and contain an abundance of sensory information, the implication is that the sensory information could only be due to recollections of the original experience. People often claim that such a memory is a personal recollection. In contrast, if the contents of a memory are vague, include minimal sensory information, and contain a lot of information based on thought processes and reasoning, then people frequently decide that the experience is not a remembered event.

In an attempt to investigate how people make source monitoring decisions, Johnson et al. (1988) asked participants to remember a childhood experience and imagine a childhood experience. The participants rated both their memory and their image according to scaled questions. Several questions focused on the sensory qualities of the memory. Johnson et al. found that participants rated remembered events as more clear on the sensory characteristics questions than events that they imagined. The results indicated that people rely on phenomenological memory characteristics to decide if they remember something or if they only imagined it. The decision process is only reliable to the extent that the sensory characteristics are the result of directly experiencing an event. If the sensory characteristics can be introduced by other means, then the decision process can lead to erroneous source monitoring decisions.

Based on Johnson's source monitoring theory (Johnson et al., 1988; Johnson et al., 1993), Hyman, Gilstrap, Decker, and Wilkinson (1998) investigated how people make source judgments about autobiographical knowledge. The researchers relied on the remember–know distinction suggested by Tulving (1985). Some autobiographical experiences are remembered personally—when the events come to mind, they give an impression of reexperiencing and they are accepted as a personal memory. In contrast, for other autobiographical experiences, one knows the event happened, but does not personally remember it—the events come to mind with the feeling of nonpersonal knowledge. For example, you may remember taking a family vacation or you may simply know that the event occurred based on pictures, family stories, or souvenirs. The remember–know distinction has been frequently used in word list studies (Conway & Dewhurst, 1995; Donaldson, 1996; Gardiner & Java, 1991; Rajaram, 1993, 1996; Yonelinas & Jacoby, 1995), but only infrequently in studies of autobiographical memory (e.g., Conway, Collins, Gathercole, & Anderson, 1996).

Hyman et al. (1998) reasoned that the remember–know decision can be considered a source monitoring decision—is the source of autobiographical knowledge personal memory or external sources such as pictures or family stories. They asked people to briefly describe a childhood event they remembered and one they knew but did not remember. The participants then rated the remember and know events on several dimensions, based on the same questions used by Johnson et al. (1988). As predicted by source monitoring theory, the events that people claimed to remember were rated as having more sensory detail and emotion. The remember–know judgment for autobiographical experiences can therefore be viewed as a type of source monitoring decision.

In their second and third experiments, Hyman et al. (1998) found that source judgments could be manipulated. They asked people to describe a childhood event that they knew occurred but did not remember. Next, the participants were asked to elaborate on the sensory details and their emotional response to the event. They predicted that people would elaborate on sensory information associated with the recollection. Furthermore, when they considered the elaborated recollection, they would use their typical decision process of assuming that recollections with more sensory information are more likely to be personal memories. Hyman et al. found that people who imagined and described their images made ratings of their recollections as further from know and closer to remember than individuals who did not imagine their experiences. Hyman et al. concluded that source decisions are not absolute judgments based on particular settings for sensory information, but instead are relative judgments based on how clear people think their memories should be.

Goff and Roediger (1998) used a different methodology but similarly found that imagining experiences results in source monitoring errors. They asked participants to perform several simple tasks in the first session of the experiment. They also asked participants to imagine performing some simple tasks. In addition, they varied how many times participants imagined the experiences. They found that with repeated imaginings, people became more likely to claim that they had actually performed the action rather than simply imagined it (see Roediger & Gallo, chap. 1, this volume).

The self may also affect source monitoring judgments. The more the self is involved in a memory, the more likely people will claim the memory as a personal recollection—as something they remember having occurred. Conway and Dewhurst (1995) found that this was the case when people remembered a word list. Other researchers (Barclay & DeCooke, 1988; Conway et al., 1996) reported that the similarity of distracter events to events typically experienced by the self results in false claims of remembering distracter items in diary studies of autobiographical memory. In addition, studies of the creation of false childhood memories have found that individuals who tie false events to self-knowledge are more likely eventually to create false memories than are individuals who do not connect false events to self-knowledge (Hyman & Billings, 1998; Hyman et al., 1995). Various social factors in the remembering context may also affect source monitoring decisions.

Plausibility judgment, memory construction, and source monitoring judgment provide a framework for integrating many of the research findings on false childhood memory creation. In addition, this framework may eventually aid in understanding the individual differences associated with the tendency to create false childhood memories (e.g., Hyman & Billings, 1998; Wilkinson & Hyman, 1998). It is not yet clear if plausibility judgments and source judgments are two separate decisions. Because they are both affected by similar variables such as forming mental images, they may reflect a continuum of claiming an event as a personal experience. In the beginning, there is no recognition of the event as being about the self. Next, there is a recognition that the event occurred to the self (the individual may know the event occurred, but does not remember the experience). Finally, the person claims the event as a personal memory. Future research should investigate if there are differences in experimental factors and individual differences related to the various judgments.

COMPARISONS OF TRUE AND FALSE MEMORIES

One implication of the source monitoring perspective is that it may be possible for a person to discriminate true from false memories. Although memory characteristics associated with both true and false memories may overlap, in general there may be differences between them. If people attend to the relevant characteristics, they may learn to accurately distinguish true from false memories.

Several researchers investigated differences in ratings of the characteristics associated with true and false memories. For example, both Norman and Schacter (1997) and Mather, Henkel, and Johnson (1997) studied the characteristics associated with true and false memories of words from a word list. Participants were given lists of words semantically related to a nonpresented word—the critical lure (Deese, 1959; Roediger & McDermott, 1995). These types of lists reliably result in high levels of false recognition for the critical lure. Norman and Schacter (1997) and Mather et al. (1997) asked participants to rate their recollections for the true words and for the false critical lure. In general, the critical lure memories had lower ratings on many sensory characteristics.

Johnson et al. (1997) used a similar methodology to investigate the possible differences in patterns of brain activation when individuals accurately recognized true items and falsely recognized critical lures. They found evidence for differences in brain activation when the types of items were grouped—that is, if the participants were presented with sets of true items, critical lures, and distracter items at test. When the items were intermixed, however, they found no differences in brain activation between accurately recognizing true items and falsely recognizing critical lures. The findings on discriminating between true and false memories of words are mixed.

Other researchers have investigated discriminations of true and false memories of autobiographical experiences. Conway et al. (1996) used a diary method to study false autobiographical memories. Two participants kept records of daily experiences for several weeks. In addition, the participants wrote down things that did not occur, and an experimenter created false events based on the structure of the participants' lives. On a recognition test, the participants identified many of the false events as personal experiences. Compared to the true events, however, the participants were less likely to claim remembering the false events. Instead the participants more frequently reported guessing that the false events were true and claiming to know, without remembering, that the events happened.

In their investigation of false childhood memories, Pezdek et al. (1997) studied the descriptions that participants constructed of the true events and the false event. They found that people provided shorter and less detailed descriptions of the false events. Both of these findings suggest that false memories may be less detailed and therefore discriminable through various source monitoring judgments—such as the remember-know judgment.

Hyman and Pentland (1996) also examined ratings of true and false memories in their investigation of false childhood memories. They, however, made one additional important comparison. Like others (Conway et al., 1996; Pezdek et al., 1997), they found that when false memories were compared to childhood experiences that people were able to remember in the first and subsequent interviews, the false events were rated lower on measures of sensory qualities. The additional comparison made was to recovered memories. In their study, participants occasionally failed to remember a true event in the first interview and then claimed to remember the event in subsequent interviews. Ratings of these recovered true memories indicated less sensory clear memories than the true memories that the participants recalled in the first and subsequent interviews. More importantly, there was no discernible difference between the recovered and false memories. This distinction may be important in the recovered memory versus false memory controversy.

The results of studies investigating the discrimination of true from false memories are mixed. In some cases memories are rated differently and in others the differences are harder to discern. The comparisons that are used are crucial. When false memories are compared to memories that people have always had, the false memories appear less clear. When false memories are compared to recovered memories, however, no differences are apparent. The comparison of false to recovered memories is critical for applied concerns. Hyman (1999) argued that discriminating true from false autobiographical memories may be difficult for people to do. In general, people believe their memories. Furthermore, they seldom receive reliable feedback on the veracity of their recollections. There are not external records for most personal experiences. The external records that exist are often other people's recollections. Without feedback, people may not learn which autobiographical memories are reliable and which are not. If people receive reliable feedback, they may learn to differentiate between true and false memories.

CONCLUSION

The research of false childhood memories has extended the work on eyewitness memory errors. In response to suggestion, people not only change features of events, but they also create complete memories of self-involving, emotional events. Clearly, the contexts in which people are asked to remember their childhoods will sometimes lead to erroneous recall. False memories are created when events are made plausible, when people are encouraged to construct images and narratives, and when people erroneously claim the source to be a personal memory.

In many interview contexts, false events are made plausible. Authors of popular press books identify personality characteristics and psychological problems that are indicative of certain childhood experiences. Therapists may provide similar feedback. Individuals may participate in groups that share current characteristics and childhood experiences — such groups imply that new members also share the same experiences. In addition, hearing stories and imagining experiences increases the availability of such ideas and the subjective plausibility of experiences. Through a variety of channels, false events are made to appear plausible.

Once people accept the plausibility of a false event or a misleading suggestion, they construct a new image and narrative that includes the erroneous information. In false childhood memories, many activities encourage the construction of false narratives. For example, when people make connections between the self and the false event, the constructive process begins. When they later consider the false event, they construct an event that combines both the suggested information with general self-knowledge to create a new memory (Hyman & Billings, 1998; Hyman et al., 1995). Other activities, such as imagining the experience and journaling can also lead to the construction of the false memories. A crucial aspect of this construction is the impact of the false suggestion on other aspects of the event. Many studies of false childhood memories have found that participants elaborate on suggested events. These elaborations are consistent with the false event, but are most likely a reflection of an individual's general event knowledge and personal experiences. False memories extend beyond the simple implantation of the suggested event.

Once an individual has constructed a memory of a plausible childhood event, that person must still claim the memory as a personal recollection. The more effort that an individual devotes to developing the image, the more likely the individual is to eventually claim the image is remembered (Goff & Roediger, 1998; Hyman et al., 1998; Hyman & Pentland, 1996). In addition, there are probably social factors that influence the source monitoring decision.

At the least, the research on false childhood memories demonstrates how memory errors can be introduced via misleading suggestions. Moreover, these three processes of plausibility judgments, memory construction, and source judgments can be applied to traditional studies of eyewitness suggestibility. For over two decades now, researchers have been concerned with the underlying explanation of misinformation acceptance: Does the misinformation replace the original information in memory, or do people lose track of the source of the misinformation and claim the misinformation was part of the original experience? The growing emphasis has been on source monitoring explanations for the misinformation effect. This emphasis, although helpful in explaining the misinformation effect, has overlooked other aspects of eyewitness suggestibility.

For example, in traditional investigations of suggestibility in eyewitness memory, plausibility was not investigated. The false suggestions are implicitly, and sometimes explicitly, designed to be plausible: not too many false suggestions, not too large of suggestions, use a reliable source, and so on. How people judge the plausibility of misleading information is not well understood. A few studies have shown that the source of misleading suggestions affects the rate of errors (Dodd & Bradsaw, 1980; Greene, Flynn, & Loftus, 1982). This could be because the source influences whether people accept the suggestions as plausible.

Most recent investigations have focused on whether people include the specific suggestion in their recollection. This will miss the constructive aspect of human memory. If false information becomes part of a memory, then it should influence other aspects of the memory when the memory is reconstructed. Loftus and Palmer (1974) demonstrated this possibility in memories of an automobile accident. People's understanding of the severity of a car accident was altered by the way they asked how fast the cars were going. They asked some people "how fast when they hit each other," whereas they asked others "how fast when they smashed into each other." The verb change affected estimates of speed and can be described as a typical misinformation effect. In a subsequent interview, Loftus and Palmer asked if the participants recalled seeing broken glass (there was none). Those who were asked about smashing cars more often recalled seeing broken glass. The changed understanding of speed affected other aspects of the event when it was eventually reconstructed. If researchers focus only on the critical suggested item, by following source monitoring theory, then they will miss the overall reconstructive nature of human memory.

Research on false childhood memories is also important for understanding autobiographical memory. People accept misleading suggestions and construct false childhood memories because autobiographical memory is generally constructive. In many ways, "life is an ongoing misinformation experiment" (Hyman & Pentland, 1996). People are constantly encountering others' views of experiences. Through conversation, people share their memories. In the midst of this exchange of memories, people may adopt information from other individuals into their own memories (Hyman, 1999). Furthermore, two individuals may interpret a remembered event in very different ways. Over time, one individual may adopt another's interpretation. In addition, some of our memories could be stories that we have heard told many times and that we now believe we remember. This may lead to the creation of entire experiences. The past is an ongoing creation—a construction built with our memories and the current social context.

To the extent that the self is defined in terms of our memories (Greenwald, 1980; James, 1890; Neisser, 1988), the self is also malleable. One way we understand ourselves is through the narrative we tell about the past. When this narrative is altered, the self is altered as well (Oakes & Hyman, in press). The person who discovers a traumatic memory in therapy may develop a new understanding of the past. For the effect on the self-concept, it doesn't matter if the memory is true or false — the self may change in either case. Sarah, the woman who disclosed her experience with recovered memories in response to a class discussion, is an unfortunate example. She found that her understanding of her past, her self, and her relationships with her family were altered by the recovered memories of abuse. Unfortunately, she can not differentiate whether the memories are true or if the memories are false.

REFERENCES

Ayers, M. S., & Reder, L. M. (1998). A theoretical review of the misinformation effect: Predictions from an activation-based memory model. *Psychonomic Bulletin & Review, 5*, 1–21.

Barclay, C. R., & DeCooke, P. A. (1988). Ordinary everyday memories: Some of the things of which selves are made. In U. Neisser & E. Winograd (Eds.), *Remembering reconsidered: Ecological and traditional approaches to the study of memory* (pp. 91–125). New York: Cambridge.

Bartlett, F. C. (1932). *Remembering: A study in experimental and social psychology.* Cambridge, England: Cambridge University Press.

Belli, R. F. (1989). Influences of misleading postevent information: Misinformation interference and acceptance. *Journal of Experimental Psychology: General, 118*, 72–85.

Carroll, J. S. (1978). The effect of imagining an event on expectations for the event: An interpretation in terms of the availability heuristic. *Journal of Personality & Social Psychology, 36*, 1501–1511.

Ceci, S. J., Huffman, M. L. C., Smith, E., & Loftus, E. F. (1994). Repeatedly thinking about non-events. *Consciousness and Cognition, 3*, 388–407.

Ceci, S. J., Loftus, E. F., Leichtman, M. D., & Bruck, M. (1994). The possible role of source misattributions in the creation of false beliefs among preschoolers. *International Journal of Clinical and Experimental Hypnosis, 42*, 304–320.

Conway, M. A., Collins, A. F., Gathercole, S. E., & Anderson, S. J. (1996). Recollections of true and false autobiographical memories. *Journal of Experimental Psychology: General, 25*, 69–95.

Conway, M. A., & Dewhurst, S. A. (1995). The self and recollective experience. *Applied Cognitive Psychology, 9*, 1–19.

Crombag, H. F. M., Wagenaar, W. A., & Van Koppen, P. J. (1996). Crashing memories and the problem of source monitoring. *Applied Cognitive Psychology, 10*, 95–104.

Deese, J. (1959). On the prediction of occurrence of particular verbal intrusions in immediate recall. *Journal of Experimental Psychology, 58*, 17–22.

Dodd, D. H., & Bradshaw, J. M. (1980). Leading questions and memory: Some pragmatic constraints. *Journal of Verbal Learning & Verbal Behavior, 19*, 695–704.

Donaldson, W. (1996). The role of decision processes in remembering and knowing. *Memory & Cognition, 24*, 523–533.

Gardiner, J. M., & Java, R. I. (1991). Forgetting in recognition memory with and without recollective experience. *Memory & Cognition, 19*, 617–623.

Garry, M., Manning, C. G., Loftus, E. F., & Sherman, S. J. (1996). Imagination inflation: Imaging a childhood event inflates confidence that it occurred. *Psychonomic Bulletin & Review, 3,* 208–214.

Goff, L. M., & Roediger, H. L., III (1998). Imagination inflation for action events: Repeated imaginings lead to illusory recognition. *Memory & Cognition, 26,* 20–33.

Greene, E., Flynn, M. S., & Loftus, E. F. (1982). Inducing resistance to misleading information. *Journal of Verbal Learning & Verbal Behavior, 21,* 207–219.

Greenwald, A. G. (1980). The totalitarian ego: Fabrication and revision of personal history. *American Psychologist, 35,* 603–618.

Gregory, W. L., Cialdini, R. B., & Carpenter, K. M. (1982). Self-relevant scenarios as mediators of likelihood estimates and compliance: Does imagining make it so? *Journal of Personality & Social Psychology, 43,* 88–99.

Hyman, I. E., Jr. (1999). Creating false autobiographical memories: Why people believe their memory errors. In E. Winograd, R. Fivush, & W. Hirst (Eds.), *Ecological approaches to cognition: Essays in honor of Ulric Neisser* (pp. 229–252). Mahwah, NJ: Lawrence Erlbaum Associates.

Hyman, I. E., Jr., & Billings, F. J. (1998). Individual differences and the creation of false childhood memories. *Memory, 6,* 1–20.

Hyman, I. E., Jr., Chesley, C. A., & Thoelke, R. S. (1997, November). *False memories: False personality feedback affects plausibility judgments.* Paper presented at the meeting of the Psychonomic Society. Philadelphia.

Hyman, I. E., Jr., Gilstrap, L. L., Decker, K., & Wilkinson, C. (1998). Manipulating remember and know judgments of autobiographical memories: An investigation of false memory creation. *Applied Cognitive Psychology, 12,* 371–386.

Hyman, I. E. Jr., Husband, T. H., & Billings, F. J. (1995). False memories of childhood experiences. *Applied Cognitive Psychology, 9,* 181–197.

Hyman, I. E. Jr., & Kleinknecht, E. E. (1999). False childhood memories: Research, theory, and applications. In L. M. Williams & V. L. Banyard (Eds.), *Trauma and memory.* Thousand Oaks, CA: Sage.

Hyman, I. E., Jr., & Pentland, J. (1996). The role of mental imagery in the creation of false childhood memories. *Journal of Memory and Language, 35,* 101–117.

Hyman, I. E., Jr., & Rubin, D. C. (1990). Memorabeatlia: A naturalistic study of long-term memory. *Memory & Cognition, 18,* 205–214.

Jacoby, L. L., Woloshyn, V., & Kelley, C. M. (1989). Becoming famous without being recognized: Unconscious influences of memory produced by dividing attention. *Journal of Experimental Psychology: General, 118,* 115–125.

James, W. (1890). *Principles of psychology.* New York: Holt.

Johnson, M. K., Foley, M. A., Suengas, A. G., & Raye, C. L. (1988). Phenomenal characteristics of memories for perceived and imagined autobiographical events. *Journal of Experimental Psychology: General, 117,* 371–376.

Johnson, M. K., Hastroudi, S., & Lindsay, D. S. (1993). Source monitoring. *Psychological Bulletin, 114,* 3–28.

Johnson, M. K., Nolde, S. F., Mather, M., Kounios, J., Schacter, D. L., & Curran, T. (1997). The similarity of brain activity associated with true and false recognition memory depends on test format. *Psychological Science, 8,* 250–257.

Kelley, C., Amodio, D., & Lindsay, D. S. (1996, July). *The effects of "diagnosis" and memory work on memories of handedness shaping.* Paper presented at the International Conference on Memory, Padua, Italy.

Lindsay, D. S. (1990). Misleading suggestions can impair eyewitnesses' ability to remember event details. *Journal of Experimental Psychology: Learning, Memory, & Cognition, 16,* 1077–1083.

Loftus, E. F. (1991). Made in memory: Distortions of recollection after misleading informa-tion. In G. Bower (Ed.), *Psychology of learning and motivation* (Vol. 27, pp. 187–215). New York: Academic Press.

Loftus, E. F. (1992). When a lie becomes memory's truth. *Current Directions in Psychological Science, 1*, 121–123.

Loftus, E. F. (1997). Dispatch from the (un)civil memory wars. In J. D. Read & D. S. Lindsay (Eds.), *Recollections of trauma: Scientific evidence and clinical practice* (pp. 171–198). New York: Plenum.

Loftus, E. F., & Palmer, J. C. (1974). Reconstruction of automobile destruction: An example of the interaction between language and memory. *Journal of Verbal Learning and Verbal Be-havior, 13*, 585–589.

Loftus, E. F., & Pickrell, J. E. (1995). The formation of false memories. *Psychiatric Annals, 25*, 720–725.

Mather, M., Henkel, L. A., & Johnson, M. K. (1997). Evaluating characteristics of false memo-ries: Remember/know judgments and memory characteristics questionnaire compared. *Memory & Cognition, 25*, 826–837.

Mazzoni, G. A. L., & Loftus, E. F. (1998). Dreaming, believing, and remembering. In J. DeRivera & T. R. Sarbin (Eds.), *Believed-in imagings* (pp. 145–156). Washington, DC: American Psychological Association.

Mazzoni, G. A. L., Loftus, E. F., Seitz, A., & Lynn, S. J. (1999). Changing beliefs and memories through dream interpretation. *Applied Cognitive Psychology, 13*, 125–144.

McCloskey, M., & Zaragoza, M. (1985). Misleading postevent information and memory for events: Arguments and evidence against the memory impairment hypothesis. *Journal of Experimental Psychology: General, 114*, 3–18.

Neisser, U. (1982). John Dean's memory: A case study. In U. Neisser (Ed.), *Memory observed: Remembering in natural contexts* (pp. 139–159). San Francisco: Freeman.

Neisser, U. (1988). Five kinds of self-knowledge. *Philosophical Psychology, 1*, 35–59.

Norman, K. A., & Schacter, D. L. (1997). False recognition in younger and older adults: Ex-ploring the characteristics of illusory memories. *Memory & Cognition, 25*, 838–848.

Oakes, M. A., & Hyman, I. E., Jr. (in press). The role of the self in false memory creation. *Jour-nal of Aggression, Maltreatment, and Trauma.*

Pezdek, K., Finger, K., & Hodge, D. (1997). Planting false childhood memories: The role of event plausibility. *Psychological Science, 8*, 437–441.

Pickrell, J. E., & Loftus, E. F. (1999, July). *Multiple examples can change beliefs about the past.* Pa-per presented at Society for Applied Research in Memory and Cognition, Boulder, CO.

Rajaram, S. (1993). Remembering and knowing: Two means of access to the personal past. *Memory & Cognition, 21*, 89–102.

Rajaram, S. (1996). Perceptual effects on remembering: Recollective processes in picture rec-ognition memory. *Journal of Experimental Psychology: Learning, Memory, and Cognition, 22*, 365–377.

Roediger, H. L., III, & McDermott, K. B. (1995). Creating false memories: Remembering words not presented in lists. *Journal of Experimental Psychology: Learning, Memory, and Cog-nition, 24*, 803–814.

Rubin, D. C. (1995). *Memory in oral traditions.* New York: Oxford University Press.

Sherman, S. J., Cialdini, R. B., Schwartzman, D. F., & Reynolds, K. D. (1985). Imagining can heighten or lower the perceived likelihood of contracting a disease: The mediating effect of ease of imagery. *Personality & Social Psychology Bulletin, 11*, 118–127.

Spanos, N. P., Cross, P. A., Dickson, K., & DuBreuil, S. C. (1993). Close encounters: An exami-nation of UFO experiences. *Journal of Abnormal Psychology, 102*, 624–632.

Tulving, E. (1985). Memory and consciousness. *Canadian Psychology, 26*, 1–12.

Tversky, A., & Kahneman, D. (1973). Availability: A heuristic for judging frequency and probability. *Cognitive Psychology, 5*, 207–232.

Usher, J. A., & Neisser, U. (1993). Childhood amnesia and the beginning of memory for four early life events. *Journal of Experimental Psychology: General, 122,* 155–165.

Wilkinson, C., & Hyman, I. E., Jr. (1998). Individual differences related to two types of memory errors: Word lists may not generalize to autobiographical memory. *Applied Cognitive Psychology, 12,* S29–S46.

Yonelinas, A. P., & Jacoby, L. L. (1995). The relation between remembering and knowing as bases for recognition: Effects of size congruency. *Journal of Memory and Language, 34,* 622–643.

Zaragoza, M. S., & Lane, S. M. (1994). Source misattributions and the suggestibility of eyewitness memory. *Journal of Experimental Psychology: Learning, Memory, & Cognition, 20,* 934–945.

Zaragoza, M. S., & Mitchell, K. J. (1996). Repeated exposure to suggestion and the creation of false memories. *Psychological Science, 7,* 294–300.

4

Coming to Grips With
Children's Suggestibility

Karen J. Saywitz
University of California, Los Angeles – School of Medicine

Thomas D. Lyon
University of Southern California – School of Law

When children are asked to describe what they have seen, heard, or experienced, they bring their limitations along with their capabilities to the task. Adults who rely on children's answers must come to grips with the imperfections and inadequacies, as well as the merits and utility, of children's reports. Some research findings appear to condemn children's reports, others champion their competencies. One way to understand this inconsistency is to align the studies along a continuum.

At one end of the continuum, researchers seek to understand the effects of combining multiple, suggestive techniques into a single protocol that is often repeated over several interviews with very young children between the ages of 3 and 5. These paradigms illustrate the very young child's social, cognitive, and memory deficiencies. In the worst case scenarios, preschool children are repeatedly questioned in an accusatory context with highly misleading and suppositional questions, peer pressure, and selective reinforcement. These scenarios are thought to resemble the highly publicized preschool molestation cases that occasionally headline the newspapers. Often there is persistent questioning about fictitious events despite children's denials. Predictably, these studies find the most dramatic and disconcerting suggestibility effects. Their results have enlightened practitioners and policymakers regarding the dangers of certain techniques, many of which can be avoided without much loss of valuable information.

At the other end of the continuum are studies that seek to understand how to promote children's optimal performance. Relying on techniques that maximize independent reporting by elementary school-aged children, these studies highlight how accurate and meaningful older children's reports can be under the best of circumstances. The emphasis is on open-ended and direct, nonleading questions about the central aspects of experienced events. Also at this end of the continuum are studies designed to test techniques thought to improve children's reports. Results reveal some areas of malleability, indicating the potential for improving children's resistance to suggestion. Results also underscore the limits on modifying children's performance.

In between these two endpoints are studies highlighting the complexity of the interview process and the interacting factors that contribute to children's suggestibility and resistance. This is where practitioners out in the field often function, in between the worst and best case scenarios. They try to balance the need to avoid distortion with the need to elicit as much trustworthy detailed information as necessary for immediate decision making.

In this chapter, we explore findings from both ends of the continuum. First, we summarize results of the basic research on the developmental limitations that contribute to children's suggestibility. Then, we examine conditions for maximizing and minimizing suggestibility effects. Our goal is to create a review that is useful to researchers planning future studies and to practitioners making case-by-case decisions.

DEVELOPMENTAL DIFFERENCES AND
THE SUGGESTIBILITY OF YOUNG CHILDREN

Basic research in developmental psychology has revealed three factors affecting young children that make them particularly vulnerable to suggestive interviewing. First, young children find free recall considerably more difficult than cued-recall and recognition. This makes it challenging to elicit information from young children without asking specific questions designed to assist retrieval. Second, young children are particularly deferential to adults' beliefs. Adults may convey their own view of events to children through the questions they ask. Third, young children have special difficulty when identifying the sources of their beliefs. A child who has experienced an event and has received false information about that event may subsequently confuse memories of the event with memories of the false information. In combination, these characteristics increase the risk that suggestive interviewing techniques will elicit false reports. Recent studies have produced some dramatic suggestibility effects. The research cautions that interviewing preschool children is problematic, and it suggests ways in which interviews could be less suggestive.

An understanding of these basic ideas about children's cognitive and social development, however, also cautions against the wholesale application of suggestibility research to investigative interviews in real cases of child abuse. If younger children are much more suggestible than older children, older children are much less suggestible than younger children. It is therefore hazardous to generalize too quickly from research on preschool children to school-age children. The fact that children are generally deferential to adults emphasizes the danger of telling (rather than asking) young children what occurred, either through coaching or asking questions that presuppose the suggested information. Finally, children's source monitoring difficulties highlight the distinctive suggestiveness of questions that encourage children to form mental pictures of nonevents. Although some real-world questioning reflects recent research techniques, and thus exploits preschool children's greatest vulnerabilities, both real-world questioning and research must be scrutinized closely before concluding that a child's testimony in a particular case has been tainted.

Young Children's Recall Is Deficient

To remember information, one must be able to encode, retain, and retrieve that information. Not surprisingly, young children often encode less information than older children, and retain less information over time (Brainerd, Reyna, Howe, & Kingma, 1990; Howe, 1991). Particularly striking, however, is young children's difficulty with retrieval. Recognition is easier than free recall because recognition tasks facilitate retrieval. Basic research in developmental psychology has established that young children are able to recognize much that they cannot recall, and their free recall is less complete than older children's (Jones, Swift, & Johnson, 1988; List, 1986; Todd & Perlmutter, 1980). In a series of studies examining children's memories for pediatric examinations, Ornstein and his colleagues found that "it was necessary to rely more fully on yes–no, specific probes when dealing with the 3-year-olds, because these children generated relatively little information in response to the open-ended questions" (Ornstein, Gordon, & Larus, 1992, p. 58; see also Baker-Ward, Gordon, Ornstein, Larus, & Clubb, 1993; Gordon, Ornstein, Clubb, Nida, & Baker-Ward, 1991; Ornstein, Baker-Ward, Myers, Principe, & Gordon, 1995).

Young children's responses to free recall questions may be incomplete for nonmnemonic reasons as well. Like adults, children's productive vocabulary lags behind their receptive vocabulary (Flavell, Miller, & Miller, 1993), making it difficult for them to describe events in response to free recall questions but possible for them to understand recognition questions about those events. Children may have particular difficulty in describing sexual experiences, given their limited sexual vocabulary (Schor & Sivan, 1989). If the topic is embarrassing or frightening, children may be reluctant to disclose information (Lyon, 1999). Finally, young children may not understand what information is important or expected, again requiring more guidance from the interviewer (Fivush, 1993).

Although recognition questions increase the completeness of reports, they reduce accuracy, and preschool children err at a much higher rate than older children (Brady, Poole, Warren, & Jones, 1999; Garven, Wood, Malpass, & Shaw, 1998; Ornstein, Baker-Ward, Myers, Principe, & Gordon, 1995; Peterson & Biggs, 1997; Poole & Lindsay, 1996, 1997). On a recognition task, the interviewer provides the information and the witness merely verifies whether the statement is true or false. This type of question increases the risk that the witness will answer "yes, that happened," when the witness is not sure whether the event occurred or not. Moreover, recognition questions may suggest to the witness what the interviewer believes. If the witness trusts the interviewer, the suggestions may become part of the witness' narrative of the event.

Young Children Trust Adults' Knowledge

Young children may not appreciate that adult interviewers do not know the answers to their questions. During the preschool years, children acquire a great deal of understanding about the way in which knowledge and beliefs are acquired (Flavell & Miller, 1998). Although 3-year-old children recognize that perception and knowledge are related, they appear to lack an appreciation of the necessity of perception when attributing knowledge (Montgomery & Miller, 1997). Other factors, such as the status and desires of the individual, may influence young children's decisions about whether an individual knows some fact (Lyon, 1994; Montgomery & Miller, 1997; Pillow & Weed, 1997; Weed, 1991). Preschool children are also acquiring an understanding that some beliefs are true and others false, and that one can hold a belief with more or less certainty (Moore & Furrow, 1991).

However, one fact about knowledge is well understood at an early age: Adults know more than children (Taylor, Cartwright, & Bowden, 1991). This fact, coupled with their limited understanding of whether and why others know things, increases young children's susceptibility to suggestive questioning by adults. Preschool children are more suggestible when questioned by an adult than when questioned by a child (Ceci, Ross, & Toglia, 1987). Older children are less susceptible to the status of adults as questioners; Kwock and Winer (1986) found that third graders, but not sixth graders, were more susceptible to the misleading implications of questions asked by adults rather than by peers.

As an interviewer moves beyond free recall in questioning a young child, he or she risks suggesting to the child what the interviewer believes occurred, and young children are particularly likely to accept the suggestion as true. To obtain complete but also accurate reports from young children, interviewers must carefully monitor their questions to elicit more of what the child remembers without imposing the interviewer's beliefs.

Young Children Find It Difficult to Identify the Sources of Their Beliefs

It is bad enough for a child to provide false information by acquiescing to a suggestive question; it is worse for that child to accept the false information as true and to incorporate it into her subsequent memory for the event. The danger that suggested information will be incorporated into the child's memory is raised if the child cannot distinguish between memory of the original event and memory of the suggestive questions.

Related to preschool children's growing awareness of how knowledge in general is acquired is a developing ability to identify the sources of their own beliefs. Memory for the sources of one's beliefs is known as *source monitoring*, and a number of researchers have found dramatic age differences in preschool children's source monitoring abilities as assessed through simple tasks. For example, Gopnik and Graf (1988) showed 3- to 5-year-olds drawers with various objects inside, and either told the child what was inside, showed the child the contents, or gave the child a clue as to the contents. Immediately afterwards, the researchers confirmed that the child knew the contents, and then asked the child to identify how he or she knew. Whereas 5-year-olds were almost 100% correct in identifying the correct source of their knowledge, 3-year-olds rated barely above chance.

Other researchers have found similarly dramatic age differences among preschool children on elementary source monitoring tasks (O'Neill & Gopnik, 1991; Woolley & Bruell, 1995). Although some studies have found age differences in source monitoring among older children (Ackil & Zaragoza, 1995; Foley & Johnson, 1985; Lindsay, Johnson, & Kwon, 1991), "developmental differences in source monitoring appear and disappear as a function of the difficulty of the discrimination subjects have to make" (Ackil & Zaragoza, 1995, p. 79). Researchers can construct extremely difficult tasks that confuse even the brightest child, and source monitoring errors contribute to the suggestibility of adults as well as children (e.g., Zaragoza & Lane, 1994). Nevertheless, young children's source monitoring errors are the most profound.

Several studies have documented relations between individual children's source monitoring abilities and suggestibility (Leichtman & Morse,

1997; Welch-Ross, in press; Welch-Ross, Decidue, & Miller, 1997). Young children's difficulty in identifying the sources of their beliefs may make them vulnerable to false beliefs induced by suggestive questioning.

Implications of Developmental Differences for Suggestibility Research

At first blush, a review of the basics of developmental differences in memory and understanding of the origins of knowledge paints a depressing picture of young children's capacity as witnesses. Young preschool children have difficulty with simple tasks, making their performance as eyewitnesses a daunting prospect. Asking a free recall question of a 3-year-old may yield little or no useful information. Moving to a specific question can suggest details to the impressionable and deferential young child. Subsequent interviewers may hear more about what previous interviewers asked than about what the child actually remembers.

However, children develop quickly. The developmental differences between 3-year-olds and 5-year-olds and between preschoolers and older children may be cause for alarm when questioning the very young child, but cause for cautious optimism when questioning a school-age child. Furthermore, the interviewer who is aware of preschool children's special vulnerabilities is armed with knowledge that can help to avoid the serious mistakes in interviewing emulated by the most popular suggestibility research. Finally, a good understanding of the basic factors underlying preschool children's difficulties enables the professional to identify differences between her less-than-perfect interviews and the interviews used by suggestibility researchers.

MAXIMIZING SUGGESTIBILITY EFFECTS

Accentuating Young Children's Deference to Adult Knowledge

Because young children are often less than forthcoming when asked for free recall, an interviewer may be forced to ask more specific questions in order to make necessary decisions about safety and protection in a given case. Young children's lack of understanding of the origins of knowledge and the uncertainty of beliefs, however, obligates the interviewer to think twice before asking specific questions that too often elicit guessing and deference to the adult's suppositions.

Close attention to the types of questions asked in child eyewitness research reveals a promising middle ground between free recall and recognition. Several studies with young children have found that interviewers can move to open-ended wh- questions and increase the completeness of reports without decreasing accuracy (Hamond & Fivush, 1991; Hudson, 1990; Poole & Lindsay, 1995). "Open-ended" questions ask for a narrative (or multiword) response. Wh- questions begin with *who, what, where, when, why,* and *how.* Wh- questions avoid implying that the interviewer prefers a particular response and make it easier for the child to respond "I don't know" (Peterson, Dowden, & Tobin, in press). Furthermore, although repeating yes–no questions may suggest to the child that her first answer was incorrect, researchers have found that one can repeat wh- questions within an interview (Poole & White, 1991, 1993) and across repeated interviews (see reviews in Fivush & Schwarzmueller, 1995; Lyon, in press; Poole & White, 1995) without decreasing the accuracy of young children's reports.

When interviewers are given biased information about an event and left to formulate their own questions, they tend to ask yes–no questions for which the desired response is *yes* (White, Leichtman, & Ceci, 1997). These questions will be suggestive to the extent that young children exhibit a tendency to respond *yes.* Although some research has found that young children tend to respond *yes* to yes–no questions (Fay, 1975; Peterson, Dowden, & Tobin, in press), several studies have failed to find consistent *yes* biases (Brady, Poole, Warren, & Jones, 1999; Clubb & Follmer, 1993, described in Baker-Ward, Ornstein, Gordon, Follmer, & Clubb, 1995), and in a study examining children's memory for traumatic injury and its aftermath, Peterson and Biggs (1997) found what appeared to be a *no* bias among younger children. Moreover, children are more accurate in responding to yes–no questions when the questions concern central details (Peterson & Bell, 1996), when the questions regard actions rather than descriptions of clothes or objects (Peterson, Dowden, & Tobin, in press), and when asked about details that violate their expectations regarding scripted events (Ornstein et al., 1995).

However, there are ways of making recognition questions more suggestive. Recognition questions can be phrased as tag questions (e.g., "He hurt you, *didn't he?"*). Tag questions change recognition questions into statements that are followed by requests for affirmation, making clear the interviewer's beliefs. Tag questions disproportionately impair younger children's performance (Cassel, Roebers, & Bjorklund, 1996; Greenstock & Pipe, 1996). Recognition questions can also be phrased as negative term questions (e.g., *"Didn't* he hurt you?" in which "didn't" is the negative term). Studies comprised of both children and adults have found that negative term questions increase error (Binet, 1900, as reported in Whipple, 1915; Lippmann & Wendriner, 1906, as reported in Bruck, Ceci, & Hembrooke, 1998; Loftus & Zanni, 1975; but see Dale, Loftus, & Rathbun, 1978).

Suppositional questions are considered to be even worse. Information is presumed without an opportunity to affirm or deny (e.g., "When he hurt you, was he happy or mad?"). A subtle form of suppositional question involves using a definite rather than an indefinite article (e.g., "Did you see *the* stop sign" vs. "Did you see *a* stop sign"), which has been shown to influence 4-year-old children's responses (Dale, Loftus, & Rathbun, 1978).

The most often cited suggestibility studies rely on tag questions, negative term questions, and suppositional questions to elicit false reports. Lepore and Sesco (1994) found that repeating yes–no questions about potentially sexual activities did not elicit errors among 4- to 6-year-old children, but labeling every action as *bad* and asking suppositional, tag, and negative term questions resulted in false narratives that were subsequently repeated in response to yes–no questions.

In a study of 3- to 4-year-olds' memories for a visit to their school by Sam Stone (Leichtman & Ceci, 1995), four suggestive interviews were employed, comprised of forced-choice suppositional questions (e.g., "Did Sam Stone rip the book with his hands, or did he use scissors?") that not only told participants that Sam Stone had committed misdeeds that never occurred but assisted the preschool children in developing elaborated narratives of how he had done so.

In another study, Bruck and her colleagues (Bruck, Ceci, Francouer, & Barr, 1995) examined efforts to convince 4- and 5-year-olds that someone other than their pediatrician had given them a shot 11 months previously. The researchers employed two suggestive interviews including forced-choice suppositional questions like those used in the Sam Stone study (e.g., "When Laurie [the RA] gave you the shot, was your mom or your dad with you?"). Other aspects of the interviews were more blunt. The interviewer told the child that the research assistant "gives kids their shots. She gave you your shot. Laurie said that she remembered when she gave you your shot . . ." The interviewer thus asserted the suggested information as a rule, as a specific fact, and as a fact remembered by the alleged actor.

Suggestibility studies such as these demonstrate that young children are vulnerable to suppositional questions, tag questions, and negative term questions. These types of questions clearly convey the adults' interpretation of events to the impressionable young child. On the other hand, open-ended, wh- questions may present few dangers, and yes–no questions fall in between, depending on wording and context. Yes–no questions increase error, and these errors will increase over time, if only because memory decays. However, yes–no questions vary in suggestiveness. If cautiously phrased, yes–no questions need not necessarily imply a particular view of the facts ("You said Bill was there, *did he talk to you? What did he say?*"). Dramatic demonstrations of false narratives have relied on much more coercive questioning techniques.

Increasing Young Children's Source Monitoring Difficulties

Suggestibility studies producing large effects have often capitalized on young children's vulnerability to source monitoring errors. One effective method for increasing source confusion is to elicit visualization of the suggested event (Hyman & Pentland, 1996). Ceci, Loftus, Leichtman, and Bruck (1994) repeatedly told 3- to 6-year-old children that fictitious events had occurred and assisted them in forming mental images of the events, including details regarding what they were wearing, who they were with, and how they would have felt. Children's false assents increased over the course of 11 interviews. In contrast, Ceci, Huffman, Smith, and Loftus (1994) told 3- to 6-year-old children that some of the queried events had occurred, and simply asked them to "think real hard" about each event. Children's false assents did not increase over time.[1] More recently, Bruck, Hembrooke, and Ceci (1997) have elicited elaborate false narratives from preschool children describing a man coming to their school and stealing food through multiple interviews using "peer pressure, visualization techniques, repeating misinformation, and selective reinforcement" (p. 204).

Other techniques in suggestibility research may have similarly increased children's source monitoring errors. In the Sam Stone study (Leichtman & Ceci, 1995), children were presented with physical evidence of Sam's fictitious misdeeds in the first two interviews: They were shown a ripped book and a soiled teddy bear. In Bruck and colleagues' inoculation study (Bruck et al., 1995), the suggestive interviewers pointed to pictures of the research assistant and the pediatrician when misidentifying who had performed the various checkup procedures.

A series of studies by Poole and Lindsay (1995, 1996, 1997) directly examined young children's ability to monitor their sources of information about a science demonstration. Their research is worthy of careful examination because it highlights the importance of considering both how source monitoring errors are created and the magnitude of age differences in source-monitoring performance.

In the original study (Poole & Lindsay, 1995), 3- to 4-year-olds played with "Mr. Science," who conducted four demonstrations. Three months after the visit, each child's parents read a storybook to the child about the visit, once per day, for 3 consecutive days. The book used the child's name throughout, contained accurate contextual information about the child's visit (e.g., the building within which the visit occurred), and described

---

[1]Curiously, a large percentage of children falsely assented to fictitious events in the first interview, which may have been attributable to the fact that the interviewer read a statement about the event off a card and then asked the child whether that event had ever occurred.

four demonstrations, two that had occurred and two that had not. All children were falsely told in the stories that Mr. Science had wiped their faces with a wet wipe that "tasted yucky." Although the parents were informed that the stories included demonstrations that had not occurred, they were not told what their child had experienced. One day after the third reading of the suggestive story, children were interviewed about their visit to Mr. Science.

The researchers found that suggested material from the stories appeared in the children's reports at high rates. Almost half of the children reported a suggested event in response to the open-ended questions, and answered *yes* to 82% of the yes–no questions about the suggested events. Half of the children responded *yes* when asked if Mr. Science put something yucky in their mouth. Moreover, children performed poorly on source monitoring questions that explicitly asked if they had experienced the events and whether they appeared in the stories.

Although some commentators have referred to the stories in the Mr. Science study as "subtle suggestions" (Ceci & Bruck, 1995, p. 218), several aspects of the study made the manipulation particularly suggestive. First, the suggestions were presented in the form of statements rather than questions. The researchers emphasized that "parents did not explicitly tell the children that the suggested events had occurred" (Poole & Lindsay, 1995, p. 132), yet the descriptions parents read explicitly referred to the child as experiencing nonevents (e.g., "Mr. Science wiped [child's name]'s hands and face with a wet wipe"), and placed the nonevents in a context that indicated the other details were accurate. Second, the interview took place shortly after the last repetition of the suggestive story, and 3 months after the actual event, so that memories of the false information would be more accessible than memories of the event. Third, children who denied that events had occurred were nevertheless asked to provide details, which may have suggested over the course of questioning that the interviewer was asking about the stories rather than the event. Indeed, the authors warned that "the children's spontaneous comments during the interview, and their responses to informal questioning after the interview, indicated that in some cases they could discriminate source but were confused about the intent of the interview or did not interpret the questions as requiring a distinction between information from different sources" (Poole & Lindsay, 1995, p. 145).

Given young children's difficulty in making simple source monitoring judgments, it is notable that the subjects in Poole and Lindsay's (1995) original study were 3 to 4 years of age. If children believed that the story was accurately depicting their visit to Mr. Science, they would have difficulty in subsequently identifying if their beliefs about what occurred were based on the event or the story. In their follow-up work, Poole and

Lindsay (1996, 1997) examined older children's ability to discriminate between events that actually occurred and events in the stories, and if the children's errors persisted in a subsequent interview. Studying 3- to 8-year-old children ($N = 114$), the researchers used the same procedure as in the original study, except that they added an additional interview, which occurred 1 month after the suggestive stories and 4 months after the original event.

There were vast age differences in the children's ability to identify the sources of their knowledge about Mr. Science when asked yes–no questions. As in the original study, the 3- to 4-year-olds claimed, both in the first interview following the stories and at the 1-month follow-up interview, that just over half of the suggested events had actually occurred. At both interviews, the 5- to 6-year-olds erred at about half the rate as the younger children, and the 7- to 8-year-olds erred at half the rate of the 5- to 6-year-olds. On the question regarding putting something yucky in the child's mouth, almost half of the 3- to 4-year-olds claimed, at both the initial and follow-up interviews, that it actually occurred. In contrast, 13% of the 7- to 8-year-olds asserted this belief at the first interview, and only 3% at the follow-up interview. The authors concluded that "[t]here was a marked age trend in children's ability to identify the book as the source of a nonexperienced event they had previously reported" (Poole & Lindsay, 1997).

With respect to free recall, Poole and Lindsay (1997, 1998) emphasized the lack of age differences in children's tendency to report false details. However, although the absolute number of false details did not decrease with age, there was a linear decrease with age in the proportion of free recall that was suggested by the stories. Whereas up to 20% of the 3- to 4-year-olds' free recall was suggested material, it comprised only 6% of the 8-year-olds' recall. In the 1-month follow-up interview, up to 16% of the 3- to 4-year-olds' recall was suggested material, compared to 2% of the 8-year-olds' recall. The reason that the older children produced as many suggested details as younger children, is that their free recall was much better overall; indeed, the 8-year-olds' free recall contained about seven times as many details as the 3- to 4-year-olds'. Despite the repetition of the suggestive stories, only the 3- to 4-year-olds' recall accuracy fell below 90% in the first interview following the stories and in the 1-month follow-up interview.

The Mr. Science studies document serious difficulties among very young children in identifying sources of information, and prove that young children can be prompted to provide narratives about personally experienced events containing large amounts of false information. At the same time, the studies reiterate important distinctions between telling children that false events have occurred and asking children about such events. Moreover, they support the conclusion that there are considerable age differences in vulnerability to suggestive interviewing. Finally, the studies indicate how interviewers might attempt to reduce suggestiveness, an issue we discuss next.

REDUCING CHILDREN'S SUGGESTIBILITY

In the remainder of this chapter, we review investigations of the conditions under which suggestibility effects might be minimized. First, we examine interventions designed to facilitate independent reporting and free recall, thus reducing the need for leading follow-up questions later. Next, we examine ways to decrease children's deference to adult knowledge by avoiding and rewording suggestive questions, as well as warning children to anticipate misleading questions, and not to expect help answering questions from adults. Then attempts to reduce children's perceptions of the status differential between children and adults are reviewed. Next, ideas for reducing source monitoring errors are discussed. Finally, efforts to increase children's awareness of the unique task demands of the forensic context are reviewed. The research begins to illuminate the conditions under which certain procedures are beneficial, ineffective, or detrimental.

Maximizing Free Recall

Supplying Retrieval Strategies.   As children mature they show increasing ability to generate and use retrieval strategies to help them search their own memories more independently, efficiently, and fully (see Schneider & Pressley, 1989, for a review). Younger children often fail to generate retrieval strategies even though they are capable of using the strategies when supplied externally. Moreover, children often fail to use strategies successfully because they do not know when and how to apply the strategies they generate (Flavell, 1981).

Two experimental interviewing techniques were developed based on the premise that adults can help children to generate and/or employ retrieval strategies during the forensic interview. In studies of the revised cognitive interview, children were asked to retell a staged event several times, once after context reinstatement, once in reverse order, and once from a perspective other than their own (Fisher & McCauley, 1995; Saywitz, Geiselman, & Bornstein, 1992). These strategies were designed to help the child find alternate routes to activate additional details in memory (Tulving, 1974). Studies have revealed positive results (Fisher, Brennan, & McCauley, chap. 11, this volume; Fisher & McCauley, 1995; Saywitz et al., 1992) when comparing the cognitive interview to standard interview techniques (better recall without increased error), or no differences when compared to a group receiving motivating instructions (Memon, Cronin, Eaves, & Bull, 1996, Experiment 2). A number of researchers found certain components of the interview, such as the change perspective task, difficult for children and recommend that it be reserved for adults until there is further study of its effects with children (Fisher & McCauley, 1995; Saywitz & Geiselman, 1998).

Another interview technique, narrative elaboration, utilizes pictorial prompts as retrieval aids to remind children to report the kind of information and the level of detail that might not be reported spontaneously (Saywitz & Snyder, 1996; Saywitz, Snyder, & Lamphear, 1996). Before the interview, children practice using four picture cards to remind themselves to report about categories of information represented by a drawing on each card: the participants, setting, actions, and conversations. After free recall, children are shown each card and asked, "Does this card remind you to tell something else?" In three separate studies of interviews about staged events, children, 4 to 5 and 7 to 11 years of age, responded to the cards with additional accurate details, and without increased error in comparison to control groups (Dorado & Saywitz, in press; Saywitz & Snyder, 1996; Saywitz et al., 1996).

These studies suggest that school-age children can benefit from being provided with retrieval strategies during forensic-type interviews about experienced events. However, we do not yet completely understand the effects of these retrieval strategies when children who deny experiencing a certain fictitious event are further questioned about it with suggestive questions, despite their denials (Camparo et al., 1999). Moreover, even when there is physical evidence that the events in question have occurred, the additional detail children report is not error free. As productivity increases, individual children make errors they would not otherwise have made, even if the majority of the new information is accurate. We do not know whether such errors can be minimized by simple efforts, such as warning children not to speculate. The necessary studies are still to be conducted; however, supplying children with nonbiased retrieval strategies appears to be a promising avenue for future research.

Practice Exercises. One approach for improving free recall is the use of practice recall tasks prior to questioning children about the events under investigation (Lamb, Sternberg, & Esplin, 1995; Saywitz et al., 1996; Yuille, Hunter, Joffe, & Zaparniuk, 1993). The purpose of the practice is to model the format of the interview to insure that children understand what is expected of them—independent production of as much, or little, information as they recall with the least use of specific questions.

Several studies have included conditions in which children are asked to practice remembering past events before they take a memory test for a staged event. Generally researchers extoll the benefits of practice (Dorado & Saywitz, in press; Lamb et al., 1994, 1995; McCauley & Fisher, 1996; Memon et al., 1996; Saywitz et al., 1992, Experiment 2; Saywitz & Snyder, 1996; Saywitz, Snyder, & Nathanson, 1999; Sternberg et al., 1997). Despite the enthusiasm with which practice narratives have been received by researchers, there has been little research comparing the efficacy of different practice tasks for the forensic interview. In some protocols (e.g., stepwise interview), children are asked to describe one or more remote prior life events (e.g., birthday party, field trip, or doctor visit). Other studies have used "here and now" descriptions of the room followed by recall of recent events, such as what a child did from the time she awoke to the time she arrived at the interviewer's office (Dorado & Saywitz, in press), or routine events like how she brushes her teeth (McCauley & Fisher, 1996). Others have used a social interaction contrived by the interviewer as a practice event. In one case an interviewer feigned losing and searching for a favorite pen (Dorado & Saywitz, in press); in another case a waiting room incident with a confederate was used (Saywitz et al., 1992).[2] To establish practical guidelines, studies comparing the utility of these practice tasks are still needed, but findings thus far are encouraging.

Completeness Instructions. Studies have shown that instructing adults to be more complete fosters better free recall (Geiselman, 1988). In numerous studies, instructions, warnings, and clarifications have also improved children's performance (e.g., Lovett & Pillow, 1995). Several researchers have included completeness instructions in their paradigms (McCauley & Fisher, 1996; Saywitz, Goodman, Nicholas, & Moan, 1991; Saywitz et al., 1992; Sternberg, Lamb, Esplin, & Baradaran, 1999). Several of the most widely used clinical protocols recommend such instructions. The stepwise interview suggests stating: "The more you tell me about what happened, the more I will understand what happened." (Yuille et al., 1993). However, instructions that promote completeness have also been criticized for fear that they promote speculation, fostering the perception that more is better.

In one study, instructions were independently assessed (i.e., "Tell as much as you can remember about what really happened, even the little things, without guessing or making anything up.") with no measurable benefit or liability when presented once, in the beginning of the interview, with school-age children (Saywitz & Snyder, 1996). Yet, given that the insufficiency of children's free recall is a central problem for interviewers, there remains a need to investigate the conditions under which such in-

---

[2]The advantage of a contrived event to which the interviewer is privy is that the interviewer can provide feedback, correct mistakes, and caution children not to guess.

structions (along with warnings not to speculate) might be useful or deleterious in the recall of staged and fictitious events.

Reducing Deference to Adult Knowledge

Structuring the Questions.   The research reviewed indicates that interviewer presuppositions can be conveyed to impressionable young children
through questions. One response by practitioners and researchers has been
the notion that interview questions should be structured to begin with
open-ended questions that are typically referred to as nonleading (e.g., "Is
there something I can help you with today?"; e.g., Bull, 1995; Lamb, Sternberg, & Esplin, 1995; Sternberg et al., 1999). Interviewers are cautioned to
phrase additional questions in the most nonleading form possible, progressing towards more specific questions with caution. The protocol designed by Lamb and his colleagues is the most well researched of this type,
especially with actual child witnesses (Sternberg et al., 1999; Sternberg et
al., 1997).

Avoiding Suggestive Questions.   The research reviewed in the first
half of this chapter portrayed questions along a continuum of suggestiveness. Questions with the greatest power of suggestion include accusatory
questions, tag questions, negative term insertion questions, and suppositional questions (as defined on pp. 91–92 of this chapter). Studies indicate that interviewers can reduce suggestibility effects by avoiding these
question types altogether.

Rewording Suggestive Questions.   The research reviewed also suggests that wh- questions are far less potent vehicles for suggestion than
the other question types mentioned, although studies have not fully explored whether interviews limited to wh- questions would be sufficient
for decision making in most cases. Future research on the utility of wh-
questions could be pivotal for establishing practical guidelines. In the
meantime, however, suggestibility effects are likely to be further reduced
by rephrasing yes–no and multiple-choice questions into wh- form whenever possible (e.g., "Did he hit you?" becomes "*What* did he do with his
hands?"; "You said he wore a jacket, was it *red or blue*?" becomes "You
said he wore a jacket, *what* color was it?").
    As previously discussed, if yes–no questions are deemed necessary,
thoughtful wording is required, for instance, tag, negative term insertion,
and suppositional questions can be avoided with minimal loss of valuable
information. Answers to yes–no questions are less accurate but more complete, children's accuracy on yes–no questions substantially improves
with age, and accuracy is higher on questions regarding central details.
Therefore, asking older children yes–no questions about central informa-

tion may not increase error rates and these question types should continue to be investigated, especially with regard to recall for falsely suggested events.

No Help Instructions. As a way of reducing children's deference to adult knowledge, researchers have studied the effects of informing children that the adult is not knowledgeable and cannot help the child answer the question. In one study, 4- and 5-year-olds instructed not to expect help answering questions made fewer errors than children not so instructed (Mulder & Vrij, 1996). An effort to combine this instruction with other techniques in two studies of older children (8- to 10-year-olds) also showed positive results in recall for staged events (e.g, Saywitz & Moan-Hardie, 1994; Saywitz et al., 1999). In one study, 4- to 8-year-olds who were informed that the interviewer did not remember the stimulus story well were only half as susceptible to misinformation as children who were told the interviewer knew the story "real well" (Toglia, Ross, Ceci, & Hembrooke, 1992).

Additional research would be useful to test whether children's perceptions of adult authority status do in fact change as a result of instructions. However, the research thus far is promising. With increased understanding that the child is the expert about what happened, not the adult, there is a better chance that children will orient interviewers more fully, spontaneously providing the details necessary for someone with little prior information. Comments implying the interviewer already knows what happened ("Your mom told me. . . .") imply the child only need convey partial information, increasing the need for follow-up questions that invite suggestion.

Warnings. Another factor contributing to children's suggestibility is the interviewer's tendency to repeat questions and the child's tendency to change her answer in deference to the adult, perhaps assuming that the first answer was unacceptable (e.g., Fivush & Schwarzmueller, 1995). Sometimes repetition may occur because children's responses are vague or meager, necessitating clarification and returning to a previous point. Other instances may be due to interviewer forgetfulness. In an effort to reduce the adverse effects of repeated questions, researchers have warned 5- and 7-year-olds that some questions might be repeated. In one study this warning had no effect (Memon & Vartoukian, 1996). However, the authors speculated that the warning's failure could be due to the fact that it was general and presented only once (before free recall). They suggested future studies to test warning children immediately before specific questions are asked. In addition, children may need to be given a rationale for why the interviewer might need to repeat the question (e.g., "I would like to ask you this question again because I am confused. This does not mean you need to change your answer. Just tell what you really remember."). To date, however, there is no evidence that children change their behavior in response to warnings about repeated questions.

Similarly, researchers have tried to curb the adverse effects of leading questions by warning children that some questions might mislead. Researchers have suggested to children that questions might be tricky (Warren, Hulse-Trotter, & Tubbs, 1991) or that the interviewer might put her guess into the question but could not know what really happened if she were not present (Saywitz & Moan-Hardie, Experiment 2, 1994). Results showed a reduction (not elimination) of suggestibility effects, suggesting that warning school-age children about misleading questions may be one promising method of curtailing the adverse side effects of specific questions with older children.

Interviewer Demeanor. The interviewer's demeanor can convey support or intimidation. Interviewers are often criticized for going too far in either direction. The argument is made that excessive support invites acquiescence to leading questions out of a desire to please; too much intimidation causes similar results, but out of fear. However, the available studies indicate that moderate support leads to greater resistance, not acquiescence, to misleading questions.

In one study, 3-year-olds demonstrated better memory and greater resistance to suggestion in a supportive social atmosphere than in a neutral one (Goodman, Bottoms, Schwartz-Kenney, & Rudy, 1991). In two other studies, social support in the form of rapport development, relaxed body language, eye contact, smiles, and general emotional approval, given without regard for the accuracy or inaccuracy of children's responses, was compared to an intimidating environment, low in social support, where there was no attempt to establish rapport, little eye contact or smiling, and a formal body posture was adopted (Carter, Bottoms, & Levine, 1996; Davis & Bottoms, 1998). Social support was associated with greater resistance to misleading questions even for 5- and 7-year-olds, although support had no effect on free recall or responses to questions about abuse. (Abuse-related questions were answered quite accurately in both conditions.) The authors speculated that children in the supportive condition felt "less anxious, more empowered, and in turn, less intimated and better able to resist misleading questions" (Carter et al., 1996, p. 351).

We have much to learn about the best methods for conveying support free of bias and suggestion. For example, an interviewer can be supportive by recognizing a child's effort without endorsing the truth of a child's allegations (e.g., "Thank you for trying so hard to listen carefully and tell me what you have heard or seen."). Continued study of the effects of demeanor on children's willingness or ability to talk about genuine painful, unpleasant experiences may be key to reducing the use of leading questions as a way of extracting information from reluctant children. Further research is needed to elucidate the effects of demeanor on reports of fictitious events suggested to children.

Rapport Development. There is little research on the effects of time spent developing rapport before the interview. Yet most research paradigms and interview protocols involve some effort in this endeavor (e.g., Lamb et al., 1995; Sternberg et al., 1999). Interviewers are often cautioned that too little or too much rapport development is deleterious, but some illusive, poorly defined level of rapport is optimal. The experimental literature is practically silent on this fundamental question.

Greater rapport could lower children's perceptions of the interviewer's authority status and facilitate the assertiveness necessary to resist and contradict the interviewer's suggestions (i.e., telling the adult his or her assumption is wrong). If rapport leads to greater trust, it might facilitate discovery of both genuine victimization and false allegation. Greater rapport might help the child overcome reluctance due to shame, self-consciousness, embarrassment, and mistrust. Or, when the potential for coaching is high, greater rapport might promote honesty and disclosure of information related to manipulation of the child's statement.

Studies of maltreated children suggest they are at heightened risk for interpersonal problems when relating to interviewers. These children often experience decreased feelings of safety and trust in new situations and/or they possess disorganized attachment patterns from early experiences of maltreatment, neglect, and multiple placements that influence future interactions (Aber, Allen, Carlson, & Cicchetti, 1989; Barnett, Ganiban, & Cicchetti, 1992; Cicchetti, 1987; Cicchetti & Toth, 1995; Crittenden, 1985; Egeland & Sroufe, 1981; Eltz, Shirk, & Sarlin, 1995; Shirk, 1988). Therefore, there seems to be added reason to study the effects of rapport on memory and suggestibility within this population.

Addressing Source Monitoring Error

As discussed in the first half of this chapter, certain techniques blur the line between original events and postevent information, exacerbating suggestibility. Studies have demonstrated the problems of adults telling, rather than asking, young children, and the problems of adults confronting young children with physical evidence of fictitious events, especially when combined with selective reinforcement, peer pressure, and repetition. If these procedures are avoided, the potential for distortion in young children's reports is diminished.

It is not unreasonable to hypothesize that older children might benefit from efforts to help them distinguish among sources of information at the end of the interview. Researchers have found considerable age effects in source monitoring among children 5 years of age and over because they were significantly better able than children 4 years of age and younger to say "no" to events that did not occur but were suggested to them by their parents. Similarly, children older than 5 years of age were better able to identify their parents' suggestion as the source of their memory for a nonexperienced event than younger children (Poole & Lindsay, 1997). In addition, the researchers speculated that some of the errors were due to children's misunderstanding that they were to report knowledge rather than direct memory of the events.

These data introduce the possibility that children 5 years of age and older might benefit from efforts to help them distinguish between whether they personally experienced an event (saw or felt something) or whether they heard about a plausible event from some other source (parent, previous interviewer) by using source monitoring questions at the end of the interview. Similarly, it may be useful to give older children explicit instructions regarding the task under investigation, that is, report only what they personally saw, heard, and felt, not information from other sources. More research is necessary to determine the value of such interventions, but findings to date suggest it is an avenue worth pursuing.

Imagery.   Studies with young children suggest that when they are repeatedly asked to visualize the details of experiencing a fictitious event, their reports can become contaminated (Ceci, Huffman, et al., 1994; Ceci, Loftus, et al., 1994). When instructed to repeatedly visualize an event, preschoolers may become confused and lose the ability to distinguish the source of their memory — the original event or the suggested and imagined event. Conversely, researchers also have found that some people spontaneously visualize during recall as a way to enhance retrieval. Probing a witness' image of the event can elicit further information (e.g., Bekerian, Dennett, Hill, & Hitchcock, 1992).

Studies of imagery instructions show complex results. There is some evidence that imagery effects may be positive for certain aspects of events but not others (Suengas & Johnson, 1995). Studies have not examined the effects of imagery instructions in conjunction with methods to help children clarify the source of the information. Additional research is needed to sort out the effects of imagery instructions if used only once, or only for certain aspects of the image, with effective warnings, and with fictitious events.[3] The extent to which visualization leads to errors likely depends on the age of the child and whether the interviewer provides false details for the child to visualize.

Increasing Awareness of Task Demands

Given young children's fragmented and limited knowledge of the legal system, and their lack of experience, it is not surprising that they are unaware of many of the implicit demands of the forensic interview. Armed with greater awareness of the task demands, children may be less suggestible and more reliable. Greater awareness might be achieved through explicit instructions prior to the interview.

Preinterview Instructions. Sometimes interviewers instruct children in ways that increase children's awareness of the imperative for witnesses to tell the truth (e.g., "Tell the truth. Do not make anything up. Do not guess."). The protocol developed by Lamb and his colleagues calls for a "truth–lie ceremony" at the beginning of the interview that allows children to demonstrate their understanding of the difference between telling the truth and lying (Sternberg et al., 1999). In one study, Huffman, Warren, and Larson (1999) found positive effects on recall when interviewers engaged young children in an extended discussion of the meaning of lying prior to an interview about a staged event.[4] After discussing truthtelling and lying with the interviewer, children may have become a bit more careful in their reporting. Saywitz and Moan-Hardie (1994) found positive effects of an intervention that included reading a short story to school-age children prior to the interview. The story demonstrated the pitfalls of providing false information to authority figures by acquiescence to

---

[3]Context reinstatement is a well documented memory aid with adults (e.g., Tulving & Thomson, 1973) that has been incorporated into the cognitive interview (Fisher & Geiselman, 1992). It is important to distinguish between the context reinstatement task used in studies of the cognitive interview and the kinds of visualization instructions that have been employed in studies findings dramatic suggestibility effects. In the revised cognitive interview, older children (not preschoolers) are instructed to "picture" the environment of the event in their minds as a way of reinstating the original context before giving free recall for the event (e.g., "Close your eyes and draw a picture in your head, like a video, of what the room looked like." McCauley & Fisher, 1996). The use of this technique as a component of the cognitive interview has not led to an increase in error among school-age children in comparison to control groups (McCauley & Fisher, 1995; Memon et al., 1996; Saywitz et al., 1992).

[4]Larson (1999) was unable to replicate the finding that the extended truth–lie discussion was superior to standard truth–lie discussion that simulate the type of inquiry typical in an investigation. Rather, Larson found that children participating in a standard truth–lie discussion performed better than children participating in an extended truth–lie discussion. However, Larson did not include a control group with no discussion of truth-telling and lying, hence it is unclear whether standard truth–lie discussion improves recall performance.

adult suggestion. It was followed by discussion of the reasons for and against acquiescence by the child in the story. A third study found positive effects of asking 5- and 6-year-olds to promise to tell the truth (Lyon & Dorado, 1999). While waiting for an experimenter to return, children were greeted by a confederate who engaged them in play with an attractive toy, and then told them that they might get in trouble if anyone knew they had played. When directly asked by the experimenter whether they had played with the toy, most children denied doing so, but when another group of children were first asked to promise to tell the truth, most admitting playing.

Findings to date support the value of informing children of their truth-telling obligations. Still, future research is needed to determine the best methods of discussing issues of truth-telling and lying with children of various ages and to determine the effects when secrets or threats not to tell are involved. Moreover, these methods should not confuse children or adversely influence the credibility of children who have difficulty engaging in truth–lie conversations.

Some researchers have suggested that another potentially helpful instruction might include one that promotes children's motivation and effort (e.g., "Do your best; try your hardest."). Children may not always recognize that the forensic interview is a situation demanding high levels of motivation and effort. Impulsive or careless answering might heighten rates of acquiescence. In fact, children who have experienced traumatic events and losses may show symptoms of depression or posttraumatic stress, which could include indifference, hopelessness, helplessness, fatigue, avoidance, and poor concentration, that could affect effort and motivation. They may benefit more from these instructions than other children. On the other hand, instructions that increase effort could also promote speculation.

Compared with a no-instructions scenario, motivating instructions appeared to be associated with more complete free recall of a staged event for both preschoolers and school-age children (Dorado & Saywitz, in press; Saywitz & Snyder, 1996; Saywitz et al., 1996). However, we were unable to find systematic studies of the effects of motivating instructions when children were asked to elaborate on fictitious events or when they were asked suggestive questions. Hence further study is warranted to understand the drawbacks as well as benefits of such instructions.

When adults are instructed that "I don't know" is an acceptable response, they make fewer mistakes than when they do not receive these instructions (Warnick & Sanders, 1980). Children may not realize that admitting lack of knowledge is an acceptable, or even desirable, response in the forensic interview. Initially, Moston (1987) examined the effects of giving children explicit permission to say "I don't know" before a memory interview, but found no effects. Reexamining this question more recently, three sets of researchers increased 4- through 10-year-olds' use of "I don't know" in response to misleading and unanswerable questions. These researchers reminded children of the instruction during the interview, and/or gave children practice and feedback answering unanswerable questions with "I don't know" (Howie & O'Neill, 1996; Mulder & Vrij, 1996; Saywitz & Moan-Hardie, 1994, Experiment 1).

Unfortunately, however, the children in these studies did not discriminate well among question types, and correct responses to some types of questions diminished in favor of the "I don't know" response, albeit errors did not increase. Perhaps, children became more cautious about guessing, even in situations where they would have been correct. Hence, the value of suggesting to children that they admit lack of knowledge was limited by this unintended side effect.

One follow-up study with school-age children reveals a possibility for eliminating the problem (Saywitz & Moan-Hardie, 1994, Experiment II). Researchers added a warning ("If you don't know the answer, say you do not know, *but if you know the answer, tell the answer.*") that was repeated with feedback throughout a series of practice questions. In this study, the unintended side effect was eliminated with older children. (There were no preschoolers in the study.) However, other variables were manipulated as well, requiring further research on this question.

FUTURE DIRECTIONS

A productive agenda for applied research acknowledges the limitations of children's testimony at the same time that it seeks to promote children's abilities to the greatest extent possible. Revisiting our proposed continuum, the research reviewed in the first half of this chapter identifies factors that produce and exacerbate young children's suggestibility. Findings warn us to distinguish carefully between telling children that false events have occurred and asking them about events. Results underscore the dangers of tag, negative term insertion, and suppositional questions. Studies distinguish between the serious vulnerabilities of 3- to 5-year-olds and the diminished suggestibility effects with older children.

In the second half of this chapter, the research reviewed investigates conditions hypothesized to ameliorate suggestibility effects. Although a number of procedures appear to be promising mechanisms for minimizing suggestibility, their pitfalls have yet to be fully examined, and some procedures need to be avoided altogether under certain conditions. Reducing suggestibility will be a complicated and multidimensional issue with continued research to revise and refine, to eradicate unwanted side effects, and to test effects when fictitious events are suggested to children.

What guidance does the existing research offer interviewers who seek to eliminate distortion and concurrently elicit as much trustworthy information possible? Despite recent advances, research dictates that practical decisions in the field will still be made on the basis of imperfect information. Practitioners can not cede these difficult decisions to researchers in laboratories. In each case, interviewers need to weigh the merits and drawbacks of the options available to them at a given point in time. This may involve balancing the sufficiency of information obtained by free recall, the need for additional information, and the costs of additional error in a given situation. Decisions will depend not only on research findings, but also situational factors (e.g., corroborating evidence, risk of imminent danger). Logistical, fiscal, historical, social, and ethical considerations are also important. To promote more fully informed decisions, the decision-making process itself may need to become a target of systematic investigation in the next generation of research. Ultimately, questions regarding the definition of "proper" and "improper" interviewing techniques will be answered by researchers, practitioners, and policymakers who combine efforts to understand both sides of children's suggestibility.

REFERENCES

Aber, J., Allen, J., Carlson, V., & Cicchetti, D. (1989). The effects of maltreatment on development during early childhood: Recent studies and their theoretical, clinical, and policy implications. In D. Cicchetti & V. Carlson (Eds.), *Child maltreatment: Theory and research on the causes and consequences of child abuse and neglect* (pp. 579–619). New York: Cambridge University Press.

Ackil, J. K., & Zaragoza, M. S. (1995). Developmental differences in eyewitness suggestibility and memory for source. *Journal of Experimental Child Psychology, 60,* 57–83.

Baker-Ward, L., Gordon, B. N., Ornstein, P. A., Larus, D. M., & Clubb, P. A. (1993). Young children's long-term retention of a pediatric examination. *Child Development, 64,* 1519–1533.

Baker-Ward, L., Ornstein, P. A., Gordon, B. N., Follmer, A., & Clubb, P. A. (1995). How shall a thing be coded? Implications of the use of alternative procedures for scoring children's verbal reports. In M. S. Zaragoza, J. R. Graham, G. C. N. Hall, R. Hirschman, & Y. S. Ben-Porath (Eds.), *Memory and testimony in the child witness* (pp. 61–85). Newbury Park, CA: Sage.

Barnett, D., Ganiban, J., & Cicchetti, D. (1992). *Temperament and behavior of youngsters with disorganized attachments: A longitudinal study.* Paper presented at the International Conference on Infant Studies, Miami, FL.

Bekerian, D. A., Dennett, J. L., Hill, K., & Hitchcock, R. (1992). Effects of detailed imagery on simulated witness recall. In F. Losel, D. Bender, & T. Bliesener (Eds.), *Psychology and law: International perspectives* (pp. 302–308). Berlin, Germany: de Gruyter.

Brady, M. S., Poole, D. A., Warren, A. R., & Jones, H. R. (1999). Young children's responses to yes–no questions: Patterns and problems. *Applied Developmental Science, 3,* 47–57.

Brainerd, C. J., Reyna, V. F., Howe, M. L., & Kingma, J. (1990). Development of forgetting and reminiscence. *Monographs of the Society for Research in Child Development, 55*(3–4, Serial No. 222).

Bruck, M., Ceci, S. J., Francouer, E., & Barr, R. (1995). "I hardly cried when I got my shot!": Influencing children's reports about a visit to their pediatrician. *Child Development, 66,* 193–208.

Bruck, M., Ceci, S. J., & Hembrooke, H. (1998). Reliability and credibility of young children's reports: From research to policy and practice. *American Psychologist, 53,* 136–151.

Bruck, M., Hembrooke, H., & Ceci, S. J. (1997). Children's reports of pleasant and unpleasant events. In D. Read & S. Lindsay (Eds.), *Recollections of trauma: Scientific research and clinical practice* (pp. 199–213). New York: Plenum.

Bull, R. (1995). Innovative techniques for the questioning of child witnesses, especially those who are young and those with learning disability. In M. Zaragoza, G. Graham, G. Hall, R. Hirschman, & T. Ben-Porath (Eds.), *Memory and testimony in the child witness* (pp. 179–194). Thousand Oaks, CA: Sage.

Camparo, L. B., Wagner, J., Saywitz, K. J., Jawad, M., Fregoso-Graciano, N. Brown, A., & Medina, C. (1999, April). *Interviewing children about real and fictitious events: Revisiting the narrative elaboration procedure.* Paper presented at the biennial convention of the Society for Research on Child Development, Albuquerque, NM.

Carter, C., Bottoms, B. L., & Levine, M. (1996). Linguistic and socioemotional influences on the accuracy of children's reports. *Law and Human Behavior, 20,* 335–358.

Cassel, W. S., Roebers, C. E. M., & Bjorklund, D. F. (1996). Developmental patterns of eyewitness responses to repeated and increasingly suggestive questions. *Journal of Experimental Child Psychology, 61,* 116–133.

Ceci, S. J., & Bruck, M. (1995). *Jeopardy in the courtroom: A scientific analysis of children's testimony.* Washington, DC: American Psychological Association.

Ceci, S. J., Huffman, M. L. C., Smith, E., & Loftus, E. (1994). Repeatedly thinking about a nonevent: Source misattributions among preschoolers. *Consciousness and Cognition, 3,* 388–407.

Ceci, S. J., Loftus, E. F., Leichtman, M. D., & Bruck, M. (1994). The possible role of source misattribution in the creation of false beliefs among preschoolers. *International Journal of Clinical and Experimental Hypnosis, 62,* 304–320.

Ceci, S. J., Ross, D. F., & Toglia, M. P. (1987). Age differences in suggestibility: Narrowing the uncertainties. In S. Ceci, M. P. Toglia, & D. F. Ross (Eds.), *Children's eyewitness memory.* New York: Springer-Verlag.

Cicchetti, D. (1987). Developmental psychopathology in infancy: Illustrations from the study of maltreated youngsters. *Journal of Consulting and Clinical Psychology, 55,* 837–845.

Cicchetti, D., & Toth, S. (1995). Child maltreatment and attachment organization: Implications for intervention. In S. Goldberg, R. Muir, & J. Kerr (Eds.), *Attachment theory: Social, developmental, and clinical perspectives* (pp. 279–308). Hillsdale, NJ: The Analytic Press.

Clubb, P. A., & Follmer, A. (1993, April). *Children's memory for a physical examination: Patterns of retention over a 12 week interval.* Poster presented at the biennial meeting of the Society for Research in Child Development, New Orleans, LA.

Crittenden, P. M. (1985). Maltreated infants: Vulnerability and resilience. *Journal of Child Psychology and Psychiatry Allied Disciplines, 26,* 85–96.

Dale, P. S., Loftus, E. F., & Rathbun, L. (1978). The influence of the form of the question on the eyewitness testimony of preschool children. *Journal of Psycholinguistic Research, 7,* 269–277.

Davis, S. L., & Bottoms, B. L. (March, 1998). Effects of social support on children's eyewitness reports. In B. L. Bottoms & J. A. Quas (Chairs), *Situational and individual sources of variability in children's suggestibility and false memories.* Symposium conducted at the meetings of the American Psychology-Law Society, Redondo Beach, CA.

Dorado, J. S. D., & Saywitz, K. (in press). Interviewing preschoolers: Test of an innovative technique. *Journal of Clinical Child Psychology*.

Egeland, B., & Sroufe, A. (1981). Attachment and early maltreatment. *Child Development, 52*(1), 44–52.

Eltz, M. J., Shirk, S. R., & Sarlin, N. (1995). Alliance formation and treatment outcome among maltreated adolescents. *Child Abuse and Neglect, 19*(4), 419–431.

Fay, W. H. (1975). Occurrence of children's echoic responses according to interlocutory question types. *Journal of Speech and Hearing Research, 18*, 336–345.

Fisher, R., & Geiselman, R. E. (1992). *Memory enhancing techniques for investigative interviewing: The cognitive interview*. Springfield, IL: Thomas.

Fisher, R., & McCauley, M. (1995). Improving eyewitness testimony with the cognitive interview. In M. Zaragoza, J. Graham, G. Hall, R. Hirschman, & Y. Ben-Porath (Eds.), *Memory and testimony in the child witness* (pp. 141–159). Thousand Oaks, CA: Sage.

Fivush, R. (1993). Developmental perspectives on autobiographical recall. In G. S. Goodman & B. L. Bottoms (Eds.), *Child victims, child witnesses: Understanding and improving testimony* (pp. 1–24). New York: Guilford.

Fivush, R., & Schwarzmueller, A. (1995). Say it once again: Effects of repeated questions on children's event recall. *Journal of Traumatic Stress, 8*, 555–580.

Flavell, J. (1981). Cognitive monitoring. In W. Dickson (Ed.), *Children's oral communication skills* (pp. 35–59). New York: Academic.

Flavell, J. H., & Miller, P. H. (1998). Social cognition. In W. Damon (Series Ed.) & D. Kuhn & R. S. Siegler (Vol. Eds.), *Handbook of child psychology: Vol. 2. Cognition, perception, and language* (5th ed., pp. 851–898). New York: Wiley.

Flavell, J. H., Miller, P. M., & Miller, S. A. (1993). *Cognitive development* (3rd ed.). Englewood Cliffs, NJ: Prentice-Hall.

Foley, M. A., & Johnson, M. K. (1985). Confusions between memories for performed and imagined actions. *Child Development, 56*, 1437–1446.

Garven, S., Wood, J. M., Malpass, R. S., & Shaw, J. S. (1998). More than suggestion: The effect of interviewing techniques from the McMartin preschool case. *Journal of Applied Psychology, 83*, 347–359.

Geiselman, R. E. (1988). Improving memory through mental reinstatement of context. In G. M. Davies & D. M. Thomson (Eds.), *Memory in context: Context in memory*. Chichester, England: Wiley.

Goodman, G., Bottoms, B. L., Rudy, L., & Schwartz-Kenney, B. M. (1991). Children's testimony about a stressful event: Improving children's reports. *Journal of Narrative and Life History, 1*, 69–99.

Gopnik, A., & Graf, P. (1988). Knowing how you know: Young children's ability to identify and remember the sources of their beliefs. *Child Development, 59*, 1366–1371.

Gordon, B. N., Ornstein, P. A., Clubb, P. A., Nida, R. E., & Baker-Ward, L. E. (1991, October). *Visiting the pediatrician: Long-term retention and forgetting*. Paper presented at the annual meeting of the Psychonomic Society, San Francisco.

Greenstock, G., & Pipe, M. E. (1996). Interviewing children about past events: The influence of peer support and misleading questions. *Child Abuse and Neglect, 20*, 69–80.

Hamond, N. R., & Fivush, R. (1991). Memories of Mickey Mouse: Young children recount their trip to Disney World. *Cognitive Development, 6*, 433–448.

Howe, M. L. (1991). Misleading children's story recall: Forgetting and reminiscence of the facts. *Developmental Psychology, 27*, 746–762.

Howie, P., & O'Neill, A. (1996, September). *Monitoring and reporting lack of knowledge: Developmental changes in the ability to say "I don't know" when appropriate*. Paper presented at the annual conference of the Australian Psychological Society, Sydney.

Hudson, J. A. (1990). Constructive processing in children's event memory. *Developmental Psychology, 26*, 180–187.

Huffman, M. L., Warren, A., & Larson, S. (1999). Discussing truth and lies in interviews with children: Whether, why, and how? *Applied Developmental Science, 3,* 6–15.

Hyman, I. E., & Pentland, J. (1996). The role of mental imagery in the creation of false childhood memories. *Journal of Memory and Language, 35,* 101–117.

Jones, D. C., Swift, D. J., & Johnson, M. A. (1988). Nondeliberate memory for a novel event among preschoolers. *Developmental Psychology, 24,* 641–645.

Kwock, M. S., & Winer, G. A. (1986). Overcoming leading questions: Effects of psychosocial task variables. *Journal of Educational Psychology, 78,* 289–293.

Lamb, M., Sternberg, K., & Esplin, P. (1994). Factors influencing the reliability and validity of statements made by young victims of sexual maltreatment. *Journal of Applied Developmental Psychology, 15,* 255–280.

Lamb, M., Sternberg, K., & Esplin, P. (1995). Making children into competent witnesses: Reactions to the Amicus Brief in re: Michaels. *Psychology, Public Policy and Law, 1,* 438–449.

Larson, S. M. (1999, June). *Another look at truth–lie discussions: Do they improve preschoolers' testimony?* Paper presented at the annual meeting of the American Psychological Society, Denver, CO.

Leichtman, M. D., & Ceci, S. J. (1995). The effects of stereotypes and suggestions on preschoolers' reports. *Developmental Psychology, 31,* 568–578.

Leichtman, M. D., & Morse, M. B. (1997, April). *Individual differences in preschooler's suggestibility: Identifying the source.* Paper presented at the biennial meeting of the Society for Research in Child Development, Washington, DC.

Lepore, S. J., & Sesco, B. (1994). Distorting children's reports and interpretations of events through suggestion. *Journal of Applied Psychology, 79,* 108–120.

Lindsay, D. S., Johnson, M. K., & Kwon, P. (1991). Developmental changes in memory for source monitoring. *Journal of Experimental Child Psychology, 52,* 297–318.

List, J. A. (1986). Age and schematic differences in the reliability of eyewitness testimony. *Developmental Psychology, 22,* 50–57.

Loftus, E. F., & Zanni, G. (1975). Eyewitness testimony: The influence of the wording of a question. *Bulletin of the Psychonomic Society, 5,* 86–88.

Lovett, S., & Pillow, B. (1995). Development of the ability to distinguish between comprehension and memory: Evidence for strategy selection tasks. *Journal of Educational Psychology, 87*(4), 523–536.

Lyon, T. D. (1994). Young children's understanding of desire and knowledge (Doctoral dissertation, Stanford University, 1994). *Dissertation Abstracts International, 54*(12-B), 6478.

Lyon, T. D. (1999). The new wave in children's suggestibility research: A critique. *Cornell Law Review, 84,* 1004–1087.

Lyon, T. D. (in press). *Questioning children: The effects of suggestive and repeated questioning.* Thousand Oaks, CA: Sage.

Lyon, T. D., & Dorado, J. S. (1999, June). *Does the oath matter? Motivating maltreated children to tell the truth.* Paper presented at the annual meeting of the American Psychological Society, Denver, CO.

McCauley, M. R., & Fisher, R. P. (1995). Facilitating children's eyewitness recall with the revised cognitive interview. *Journal of Applied Psychology, 80*(4), 510–516.

McCauley, M. R., & Fisher, R. P. (1996). Enhancing children's eyewitness testimony with the cognitive interview. In G. Davies, S. Lloyd-Bostock, M. McMuran, & C. Wilson (1996), *Psychology, law and criminal justice: International developments in research and practice* (pp. 127–134). New York: DeGruyter.

Memon, A., Cronin, O., Eaves, R., & Bull, R. (1996). An empirical test of the mnemonic components of the cognitive interview. In G. Davies, S. Lloyd-Bostock, M. McMuran, & C. Wilson (Eds.), *Psychology, law and criminal justice: International developments in research and practice* (pp. 135–145). New York: DeGruyter.

Memon, A., & Vartoukian, R. (1996). The effects of repeated questioning on young children's eyewitness testimony. *British Journal of Psychology, 87,* 403–415.

Montgomery, D. E., & Miller, S. A. (1997). Young children's attributions of knowledge when speaker intent and listener access conflict. *British Journal of Developmental Psychology, 15,* 159–175.

Moore, C., & Furrow, D. (1991). The development of the language of belief: The expression of relative certainty. In D. Frye & C. Moore (Eds.), *Children's theories of mind: Mental states and social understanding* (pp. 173–193). Hillsdale, NJ: Lawrence Erlbaum Associates.

Moston, S. (1987). The suggestibility of children in interview studies. *First Language, 7,* 67–78.

Mulder, M., & Vrij, A. (1996). Explaining conversations rules to children: An intervention study to facilitate children's accurate responses. *Child Abuse and Neglect, 10(7),* 623–631.

O'Neill, D. K., & Gopnik, A. (1991). Young children's ability to identify the sources of their beliefs. *Developmental Psychology, 27,* 390–397.

Ornstein, P. A., Baker-Ward, L., Myers, J., Principe, G. F., & Gordon, B. N. (1995). Young children's long-term retention of medical experiences: Implications for testimony. In F. E. Weinert & W. Schneider (Eds.), *Memory performance and competencies: Issues in growth and development* (pp. 349–371). Mahwah, NJ: Lawrence Erlbaum Associates.

Ornstein, P. A., Gordon, B. N., & Larus, D. M. (1992). Children's memory for a personally experienced event: Implications for testimony. *Applied Cognitive Psychology, 6,* 49–60.

Peterson, C., & Bell, M. (1996). Children's memory for traumatic injury. *Child Development, 67,* 3045–3070.

Peterson, C., & Biggs, M. (1997). Interviewing children about trauma: Problems with "specific" questions. *Journal of Traumatic Stress, 10,* 279–290.

Peterson, C., Dowden, C., & Tobin, J. (In press). Interviewing preschoolers: Comparisons of yes–no and wh- questions. *Law and Human Behavior.*

Pillow, B. H., & Weed, S. T. (1997). Preschool children's use of information about age and perceptual access to infer another person's knowledge. *Journal of Genetic Psychology, 158,* 365–376.

Poole, D. A., & Lindsay, D. S. (1995). Interviewing preschoolers: Effects of nonsuggestive techniques, parental coaching, and leading questions on reports of nonexperienced events. *Journal of Experimental Child Psychology, 60,* 129–154.

Poole, D. A., & Lindsay, D. S. (1996, June). *Effects of parental suggestions, interviewing techniques, and age on young children's event reports.* Paper presented at the NATO Advanced Study Institute, Recollections of Trauma, Port de Bourgenay, France.

Poole, D. A., & Lindsay, D. S. (1997, April). *Misinformation from parents and children's source monitoring: Implications for testimony.* Paper presented at the biennial meeting of the Society for Research in Child Development, Washington, DC.

Poole, D. A., & Lindsay, D. S. (1998). Assessing the accuracy of young children's reports: Lessons from the investigation of child sexual abuse. *Applied and Preventive Psychology, 7,* 1–26.

Poole, D. A., & White, L. T. (1991). Effects of question repetition on the eyewitness testimony of children and adults. *Developmental Psychology, 27,* 975–986.

Poole, D. A., & White, L. T. (1993). Two years later: Effects of question repetition and retention interval on the eyewitness memory of children and adults. *Developmental Psychology, 29,* 844–853.

Poole, D. A., & White, L. T. (1995). Tell me again and again: Stability and change in the repeated testimony of children and adults. In M. S. Zaragoza, J. R. Graham, G. C. N. Hall, R. Hirschman, & Y. S. Ben-Porath (Eds.), *Memory and testimony in the child witness* (pp. 24–43). Thousand Oaks, CA: Sage.

Saywitz, K. J., & Geiselman, E. (1998). Interviewing the child witness: Maximizing completeness and minimizing error. In S. Lynn & K. McConkey (Eds.), *Truth in memory* (pp. 190–223). New York: Guilford.

Saywitz, K. J., Geiselman, R. E., & Bornstein, G. (1992). Effects of cognitive interviewing and practice on children's recall performance. *Journal of Applied Psychology, 77*(5), 744–756.

Saywitz, K. J., Goodman, G. S., Nicholas, E., & Moan, S. (1991). Children's memories of a physical examination involving genital touch: Implications for reports of child sexual abuse. *Journal of Consulting and Clinical Psychology, 59*, 682–691.

Saywitz, K. J., & Moan-Hardie, S. (1994). Reducing the potential for distortion of childhood memories. *Consciousness and Cognition, 3*, 257–293.

Saywitz, K. J., & Snyder, L. (1996). Narrative elaboration: Test of a new procedure for interviewing children. *Journal of Consulting and Clinical Psychology, 64*, 1347–1357.

Saywitz, K. J., Snyder, L., & Lamphear, V. (1996). Helping children tell when happened: Follow-up study of the narrative elaboration procedure. *Child Maltreatment, 1*, 200–212.

Saywitz, K. J., Snyder, L., & Nathanson, R. (1999). Facilitating the communicative competence of the child witness. *Applied Developmental Science, 3*, 58–68.

Schneider, W., & Pressley, M. (1989). *Memory development between 2 and 20.* New York: Springer-Verlag.

Schor, D. P., & Sivan, A. B. (1989). Interpreting children's labels for sex-related body parts of anatomically explicit dolls. *Child Abuse and Neglect, 13*, 523–531.

Shirk, S. R. (1988). The interpersonal legacy of physical abuse in children. *Childhood and Adolescence*, 57–81.

Sternberg, K. J., Lamb, M. E., Esplin, P. W., & Baradaran, L. P. (1999). Using a scripted protocol in investigative interviews: A pilot study. *Applied Developmental Science, 3*, 70–76.

Sternberg, K. J., Lamb, M. E., Hershkowitz, I., Yudilevitch, L., Orbach, Y., Esplin, P. W., & Hovav, M. (1997). Effects of introductory style on children's abilities to describe experiences of sexual abuse. *Child Abuse and Neglect, 21*, 1133–1146.

Suengas, A., & Johnson, M. (1995). Qualitative effects of rehearsal on memories for perceived and imagined complex events. *Journal of Experimental Psychology: General, 117*, 377–389.

Taylor, M., Cartwright, B. S., & Bowden, T. (1991). Perspective-taking and theory of mind: Do children predict interpretive diversity as a function of differentiation in observers' knowledge? *Child Development, 62*, 1334–1351.

Todd, C. M., & Perlmutter, M. (1980). Reality recalled by preschool children. In W. Damon (Series Ed.) & M. Perlmutter (Vol. Ed.), *New directions for child development: No. 10. Children's memory* (pp. 69–85). San Francisco: Jossey-Bass.

Toglia, M. P., Ross, D. F., Ceci, S. J., & Hembrooke, H. (1992). The suggestibility of children's memory: A social-psychological and cognitive interpretation. In M. L. Howe, C. J. Brainerd, & V. F. Reyna (Eds.), *Development of long-term retention* (pp. 217–241). New York: Springer-Verlag.

Tulving, E. (1974). Cue-dependent forgetting. *American Scientist, 62*, 74–82.

Tulving, E., & Thomson, D. M. (1973). Encoding specificity and retrieval processes in episodic memory. *Psychological Review, 80*, 352–373.

Warnick, D., & Sanders, G. (1980). Why do eyewitnesses make so many mistakes? *Journal of Applied Social Psychology, 10*, 362–367.

Warren, A., Hulse-Trotter, K., & Tubbs, E. (1991). Inducing resistance to suggestibility in children. *Law and Human Behavior, 15*, 273–285.

Weed, S. T. (1991). *The roles of perceptual access and age-of-observer in young children's attributions of knowledge.* Unpublished master's thesis, University of Pittsburgh.

Welch-Ross, M. K. (in press). Preschoolers' understanding of mind: Implications for suggestibility. *Cognitive Development.*

Welch-Ross, M. K., Decidue, K., & Miller, S. A. (1997). Young children's understanding of conflicting mental representations predicts suggestibility. *Developmental Psychology, 33*, 43–53.

Whipple, G. M. (1915). *Manual of mental and physical tests: Part 2. Complex processes* (2nd ed.). Baltimore, MD: Warwick & York.

White, T. L., Leichtman, M. D., & Ceci, S. J. (1997). The good, the bad, and the ugly: Accuracy, inaccuracy, and elaboration in preschoolers' reports about a past event. *Applied Cognitive Psychology, 11,* S37–S54.

Woolley, J. D., & Bruell, M. J. (1995, February). *Young children's awareness of the origins of their mental representations.* Poster presented at Current Directions in Theories of Mind Research, Eugene, OR.

Yuille, J., Hunter, R., Joffe, R., & Zaparniuk, J. (1993). Interviewing children in sexual abuse cases. In G. S. Goodman & B. L. Bottoms (Eds.), *Child victims, child witnesses* (pp. 95–116). New York: Guilford.

Zaragoza, M. S., & Lane, S. (1994). Source misattributions and the suggestibility of eyewitness memory. *Journal of Experimental Psychology: Learning, Memory, and Cognition, 20,* 934–945.

5

Face Identification: Basic Processes and Developmental Changes

John C. Brigham
Florida State University

Learning to differentiate between faces is one of the most important tasks attempted by a very young child. This learning constitutes a critical aspect of cognitive and social development. As Goldstein (1983) noted, "The face is the most important visual stimulus in our lives, probably from the first few hours after birth, definitely after the first few weeks" (p. 249). A person's ability to describe or recognize faces accurately can be a critical forensic factor when the person has witnessed a crime or been the victim of actions (e.g., physical abuse, sexual abuse) by a stranger. Knowledge about how children and adults perceive faces, how accurately they identify and describe them, and an awareness of factors (such as race/ethnicity) that may affect this accuracy, can be important for evaluating the facial descriptions and identifications that people may give during interviews.

Beginning at approximately the time of Charles Darwin (1872/1965), scientists have been intrigued by the way in which our ability to discriminate among faces, and to identify the emotions they portray, develops in infancy and childhood. However, empirical research using faces as stimuli has accelerated considerably since the 1970s. In part, this may be a consequence of an increased emphasis on face recognition memory, stimulated by concerns about the psychological and forensic issues surrounding the vagaries of eyewitness identifications (e.g., Brigham, Wasserman, & Meissner, 1999; Cutler & Penrod, 1995; Ross, Read, & Toglia, 1994; Sporer, Malpass, & Koehnken, 1996; Wells & Loftus, 1984). Furthermore, as children's memory reports and identifications are increasingly involved in legal proceedings, interest in developmental trends in perception and memory has expanded (e.g., Ceci & Bruck, 1995; Ceci, Leitchman, & Putnik, 1992; Dent & Flin, 1992; Doris, 1991; White, Leichtman, & Ceci, 1997).

This chapter first reviews psychological theory and research related to the development of face recognition from childhood to adulthood. Next, the way in which being asked to describe a face in detail may actually interfere with one's ability to recognize that face is described. Finally, the effect of race on memory for faces is discussed. The "own-race bias," wherein both Whites and African Americans generally perform more poorly at recognizing faces of other race persons, has recently been the focus of theorizing and research, although there is still much to learn about its origin.

IS FACE RECOGNITION AN INNATE PROCESS
OR A LEARNED SKILL?

There are two major theoretical perspectives that describe how face recognition develops during childhood. One is the *modularity hypothesis*, the idea that face recognition is "special," a unique process mediated by a separate face–specific "module" in the brain that is biologically endowed and relatively unaffected by experience. In contrast, the *skill (or expertise) hypothesis* asserts that the recognition of faces is not a unique process but instead occurs in the same way that other objects are recognized. Both hypotheses assert that face recognition will improve during childhood; however, the reasons are different. The modularity hypothesis attributes improvement to the maturation of the face-recognition module, and the skill theory attributes improvement with age to extensive experience with faces. Forensically, these theories have different implications for face recognition (e.g., identifications from lineups) of children. If face recognition is an innate skill, perhaps the experiences of the child are not relevant to the likelihood that an accurate identification decision will be made. In contrast, if face recognition is a learned skill, then the amount of experience that the child has had in recognizing the faces of strangers could be important for determining how much confidence one should have in the accuracy of the child's identification decision.

The Possible Existence of a Unique Face-Processing
"Module"

Some scientists have proposed that face recognition is a unique perceptual/cognitive process involving a face-specific "module" in the brain. A module has been defined as a mandatory, domain-specific, hardwired input system that performs innately determined operations (Fodor, 1983). There are two ways in which modularity can be conceived: (a) as the existence of a specific part of the brain (a processing system) that processes faces in a way similar to other systems (*specificity*), or (b) in terms of a process of recognizing faces that is qualitatively different than recognizing other stimuli (*uniqueness*; Hay & Young, 1982). These concepts are theoretically independent of one another, and both have been invoked as evidence for modularity (Tanaka & Gauthier, 1997).

Face Memory as a Learned Skill

In contrast to the modularity hypothesis, other researchers have asserted that facial processing represents an area of *skilled memory*, in which individuals gradually acquire knowledge and expertise in discriminating particular members from a class of stimuli (e.g., Tanaka & Gauthier, 1997). Certain strategies may be developed that enable individuals to manage and catalog the vast number of faces seen each day. One strategy involves the "chunking" of individual features of the face into a holistic pattern (Fallshore & Schooler, 1995; Tanaka & Farah, 1993). The mechanism of chunking has been shown to produce significant increases in memory for stimuli in a wide range of skilled areas, including chess (Chase & Simon, 1973), digit strings (Chase & Ericsson, 1982), and basketball (Allard & Burnett, 1985). Also referred to as configural processing, this cognitive encoding strategy for facial memory is discussed later in more detail. An additional assumption made by the skill hypothesis involves individuals' ability to accrue extensive memory systems for the storage and access of previously viewed faces.

INNATE VERSUS LEARNED: THE RESEARCH EVIDENCE

Four main issues have been raised in analyses of whether face recognition is better seen as an innate ability or as a learned skill (Nachson, 1995; Tanaka & Gauthier, 1997). They are: (a) empirical findings indicating that a preference for faces may be innate, (b) empirical evidence that there are cortical cells that respond specifically to faces, (c) findings that face recognition is disproportionally impaired by inversion, and (d) the existence of a face-specific neuropsychological deficit—*prosopagnosia* (also known as *face agnosia*), a disorder that results from cerebral injury and involves the inability to recognize familiar faces (e.g., see Bruyer, 1989). Research evidence on each of these points is briefly reviewed.

Infants' Preference for Faces

It is well known that infants perceive faces as compelling stimuli, and early research (e.g., Fantz, 1961) showed that infants preferred to look at human faces more than other stimuli, such as a bull's eye, colored circles, or newsprint. Recognition is important for the development of attachment between infants and their caregivers (Bowlby, 1969). Fantz's findings implied that infants are born with some form of pattern vision, supporting the view of Zuckerman and Rock (1957), who argued that "perceptual organization must occur before experience . . . can exert any influence" (p. 294). Subsequent findings have questioned this assumption, however. Studies of infant vision have shown that 1-month-old infants can obtain only limited visual information from observing a face: the outer contour as defined by the hairline, and vague darker areas in the region of the mouth and eyes (Souther & Banks, 1979). Other studies have shown an "externality effect," a preference for attending to the boundaries of stimuli, in the first 2 months of life (e.g., Bushnell, Gerry, & Burt, 1983). Further, Maurer and Barrera (1981) demonstrated that whereas 1-month-old infants looked with equal interest at intact and scrambled schematic faces, 2-month-olds looked longer at the face-like configuration. Other work has suggested that a preference for face-like configurations is first visible at 4 months of age (Haaf, 1977; Haaf, Smith, & Smitty, 1983). Analyzed together, this body of findings suggests that infants do not respond differentially to faces until they are at least 2 months old, which is in contrast to the assertion that there are innate perceptual preferences for faces or face-like stimuli.

However, other work supports the existence of innate perceptual preferences. At a conceptual level, it has been asserted that because recognizing others is of vital importance to people, "it makes sense to postulate a selective evolutionary pressure to evolve neural mechanisms specifically for the recognition of faces" (Nachson, 1995, p. 257). Goren, Sarty, and Wu (1975) found that newborn infants (median age 9 min) showed more interest in a moving schematic face pattern, as measured by head and eye movements, than in scrambled "faces" or a blank head outline.

Cortical Cells That Respond Specifically to Faces

The existence of cortical cells that respond specifically to faces has been supported by the discovery of neurons in the monkey's visual cortex that respond predominantly to faces (Leonard, Rolls, Wilson, & Baylis, 1985; Rolls, 1992; Rolls, Baylis, & Leonard, 1989). Each neuron does not respond only to one face. Instead, each neuron has a different pattern of responses across a set of faces. The recordings in these studies are made primarily with nonhuman primates because the temporal lobe, the site of this processing, is more developed than in nonprimates (Rolls, 1992). It has been found that the neurons respond to human faces as well as monkey faces, and to facial photographs as well as live faces. The response of these neurons did not change when faces were presented sideways or inverted, or when size was changed or color was modified (Damasio, 1989). Evidence indicates that some of these neuron responses were altered by experience so that new stimuli became incorporated in the neural network (Rolls, 1992). When components of faces (e.g., mouth, eyes) are presented in isolation, different neurons respond to various components. It has also been found that some neurons are specialized for face recognition and for the decoding of facial expressions (Rolls, 1992).

Effects of Facial Inversion

The third set of findings that support the modularity hypothesis involve the effects of facial inversion. Generally, faces are recognized more easily than any other class of stimuli that are as similar to one another in their configuration. But, turn them upside down (invert them), and faces become harder to distinguish than other classes of inverted stimuli such as airplanes, stick figures, and houses. This effect was first reported in a series of studies by Yin (1969, 1970, 1978). Scapinello and Yarmey (1970) reported a similar pattern of results. Yin argued that the unique reversal of recognition accuracy for faces, from best upright to worst inverted, indicated that face recognition was the product of a system distinct from the one used for recognizing other types of visual stimuli. Yin suggested that neural specialization had evolved to support a process specific to human faces.

Subsequent research, however, has questioned Yin's explanation of these findings. In several experiments Diamond and Carey (1986) showed that the inversion effect found for faces was not unique, but was apparently due to expertise with the stimulus materials. When people are experienced in perceiving stimuli, such as human faces, inverting those stimuli causes a major disruption in encoding. They found that expert dog breeders showed the same inversion effect for dog faces (for the breed for which each was an expert) that people show for human faces. Diamond and Carey argued that experts, people who are accustomed to discriminating between highly similar objects from the same class (e.g., human faces, or dog faces from a single breed for dog breeders), rely on extracting "second-order relational features" in order to make these complex discriminations. This process is most disrupted by inversion. They posited that faces are processed by utilizing a holistic strategy, rather than a piecemeal strategy that examines distinctive features of the stimulus object. When an expert's normal processing strategy for a class of objects (e.g., a holistic strategy for faces) is disrupted by inversion, face recognition is at a particular disadvantage because the holistic strategy works poorly for inverted objects.

Therefore, what first seemed to be a face-specific effect instead appears to be an "expertise-specific effect" (Cohen-Levine, 1989; Nachson, 1995). It is also true, however, that face recognition appears "special" because it involves more configural processing than what is necessary for the recognition of other objects (Tanaka & Farah, 1993).

Prosopagnosia

The fourth set of research findings cited as supporting the modularity position is derived from the study of clinical cases of *prosopagnosia*, the inability to recognize familiar faces as the result of brain injury. This disorder is generally correlated with bilateral lesions located either in the inferior occipital region or anteriorly in the temporal region of the brain (Damasio, Tranel, & Damasio, 1990). Prosopagnosic persons may be unable to recognize faces of friends, family members, or even their own face in a mirror, though they may be able to recognize others on the basis of gait, clothing, voice, or context (Bruyer, 1989). Because the ability to recognize other visual objects and words remains relatively intact, this pattern implies that face recognition constitutes a special, unique system that can be damaged in isolation.

However, in-depth study of prosopagnosia has revealed problems in recognizing other classes of objects as well (Bruyer, 1989; Damasio, Damasio, & van Hoesen, 1982; Ellis, 1975). Damasio, Tranel, and Damasio (1990) noted that these patients have consistently demonstrated difficulty in identifying unique stimuli viewed previously from a group of objects that share certain configural properties (e.g., houses, cars, pets, articles of clothing). Hence, from the standpoint of the skill hypothesis, it might be argued that prosopagnosia involves a disruption in individuals' ability to interpret configural information leading to recognition of unique items (Damasio et al., 1990). Studies measuring subtle "covert identification responses" (either cognitive responses or psychophysiological autonomic identification responses) have found that prosopagnosics may show subtle recognition response patterns when observing familiar faces, even though they appear unable to recognize them (Bauer, 1984; Bruyer et al., 1983; Tranel & Damasio, 1985).

Several cases have been described, notably by Bruyer et al. (1983) and DeRenzi (1986), that appear to be instances of the "pure" syndrome, in which the only perceptual deficit was for face recognition. Ellis and Young (1989) asserted that, "for the moment we are inclined to accept that prosopagnosia can occur in a form undiluted enough to warrant the view that it is a distinct cognitive deficit which could only arise from the existence of a cognitive system containing functional components specific to face recognition" (p. 14). Addressing this same issue, Bruyer (1989) observed that, "All that can be said at this time is that the question is still open" (p. 455).

DEVELOPMENT OF FACE RECOGNITION ACROSS CHILDHOOD

Qualitative and Quantitative Changes During Childhood

Analyses of the development of children's face recognition skills have generally focused on the encoding stage of the process; the period when facial information is acquired and coded for storage. Carey, Diamond, and Woods (1980) defined encoding as "the dual process of forming a representation of a face and storing that representation in memory" (p. 257). Thus, encoding is a blanket term that encompasses attention, selective perception, translation into mnemonic code, and registration of this representation into a storage system (Flin & Dziurawiec, 1989). Previously, it was generally assumed that age differences in recognition memory occur specifically in the encoding process, rather than in the subsequent stages of memory (such as forgetting), but recent research (e.g., Brainerd & Reyna, 1995) indicates that forgetting rates also decline with increasing age.

The two major perspectives of developmental changes in encoding have focused on: (a) *qualitative* changes in processing information, that is, different encoding processes that might be used by children of different ages, and (b) *quantitative* changes, wherein older children are able to encode more information. The research findings relevant to the possibility of a qualitative shift in information processing for recognition of faces are discussed first.

It has been well established that children's ability to recognize faces of unfamiliar people improves with age (e.g., Carey & Diamond, 1977; Chance, Turner, & Goldstein, 1982; Ellis & Flin, 1990). As noted earlier, this could be attributed to the maturation of a face-specific module or to the development of a skill through experience. Recognition accuracy has also been shown to increase with age when adolescents were compared to adults (e.g., Ellis, Shepherd, & Bruce, 1973; Saltz & Sigel, 1967). Studies also show that adults are better at recognizing adult faces than child or infant faces (Chance, Goldstein, & Anderson, 1986; McKelvie, 1981). These findings imply that studies using adults' faces as stimuli may have, as a consequence, overestimated the age differences in face recognition ability (Chung & Thomson, 1995).

Children's Eyewitness Identification

Of particular importance for the forensic context is research on children's abilities to recognize faces in photographic lineups. This area of research is directly relevant to the forensic context because law enforcement officials often use photo lineups in their attempts to arrest and prosecute perpetrators. Reviews by Davies (1993, 1996) of the child eyewitness identification literature are available, and thus the current description will be brief.

The typical procedure used in identification studies is for children first to be exposed to a stranger for a limited period of time (e.g., 10 min.). The exposure may be through direct experience in a "victim" role (e.g., the child is touched by a confederate during a play session; the child receives an inoculation by a doctor) or direct or indirect experience in a "bystander witness" role (e.g., the child views, either in person or via videotape, a staged theft). Then, after a delay (e.g., minutes, weeks, months), the child is asked to identify the stranger from an array of photographs of similar-looking individuals. Usually the identification takes place in the context of an experiment rather than in the context of a mock forensic investigation. That is, typically a researcher, rather than a real or pretend police officer, administers the lineup, and there is no implication that someone did anything wrong (but see Honts, Devitt, Tye, Peters, & Vondergeest, 1995; Tobey & Goodman, 1992, for exceptions). Some studies only involved target-present lineups that included a picture of the stranger; other studies added target-absent lineups that did not include a picture of the stranger.

Overall, results from these studies indicate that children of approximately 5 to 6 years of age perform about as well on target-present lineups as adults (e.g., Goodman & Reed, 1986; Parker & Carranza, 1989). These results contrast with those from traditional studies of face recognition in which adult performance is not reached until children are around 12 years of age (Chance & Goldstein, 1984). However, in the photo identification studies, younger children (e.g., 3-year-olds) make more errors than older children and adults, even when the target person is present in the array (Goodman & Reed, 1986). Importantly, age differences are more pronounced when target-absent lineups are utilized. In this case, even adolescents (e.g., 12- to 13-year-olds) tend to make more false alarms (point to an "innocent" person) than adults (see Pozzulo & Lindsay, 1998, for a meta-analysis).

There has been limited research on children's abilities to identify familiar persons, which is an important issue in certain types of legal cases, such as child sexual abuse cases where assaults by known persons occur more frequently than assaults by strangers. A study by Lewis, Wilkins, Baker, and Woobey (1995) indicated that 3-year-olds had difficulty even when asked to identify their own fathers in a photo lineup. Part of young children's inaccuracy may result from not understanding the identification task. Attempts to train children to be more accurate have been only partially successful, and the success obtained has been limited to older children (Goodman, Bottoms, Schwartz-Kenney, & Rudy, 1991; Parker & Ryan, 1993).

Is There a "Dip" in Face Recognition Performance in Early Adolescence?

The development of face recognition performance across age may not follow a smooth, monotonic curve. Several studies, beginning with an unpublished study by Carey and Diamond that was cited in Carey (1978), have found a temporary dip in performance around the ages of 11 to 14 (Carey et al., 1980; Diamond, Carey, & Back, 1983; Flin, 1980, 1983). Similar dips in performance at these ages have been reported for recognition memory of other visual stimuli (Flin, 1985), for voice recognition accuracy (Mann, Diamond, & Carey, 1979), and for problem-solving tasks involving memory (Somerville & Wellman, 1979). But the research evidence is not entirely consistent. In a thorough review, Chung and Thomson (1995) noted that three experiments had reported a significant drop in performance in the course of development, six showed a small, nonsignificant decrement in performance, and two studies found a plateau rather than an actual decline in performance. This inconsistency in the research findings raises the question of whether the occurrence of a developmental dip is a genuine and reliable phenomenon.

What could cause this decline or plateau? Proposed explanations have focused on either *maturational/neuropsychological development* or on *cognitive/information processing factors*. One possibility is that the dip is caused by physiological changes associated with maturation of the brain (e.g., Carey, 1978; Carey et al., 1980; Diamond et al., 1983). Another possibility is that maturational events associated with the onset of puberty, such as hormonal changes, might temporarily disrupt face encoding processes. Current evidence does not support these maturational hypotheses, however (e.g., see Chung & Thomson, 1995). For example, because the onset of puberty occurs earlier in girls than in boys, one would expect that if maturational factors determine the timing of the dip in face recognition performance, the dip should occur earlier in girls than in boys. This prediction has not been borne out by the data, however (Carey et al., 1980, 1983; Diamond et al., 1983; Flin, 1980).

An interaction between maturational and social factors has also been postulated as an explanation for the dip. Soppe (1986) suggested that young adolescents' awareness of their own puberty-induced physiognomic changes might cause them to attend to aspects of others' faces that are not useful for recognition. Alternatively, Soppe proposed that during puberty opposite-sex faces gain erotic meaning, which might interfere with face encoding. However, contrary to these speculations, the dip does not appear to be specific to the indirect effect of maturation on face recognition.

Different Facial Encoding Processes

Cognitive explanations proposed for the age-related dip in performance have focused on a possible shift in encoding strategy. Several researchers have argued that, before age 10, children encode and recognize faces via a *featural* encoding strategy (also known as *piecemeal* encoding) that focuses on isolated, salient features of individual faces (Carey, 1981; Carey et al., 1980; Chung & Thomson, 1995; Thomson, 1986; 1989). Older children, in contrast, utilize *configural* information relative to the global appearance of a face (also known as *holistic* encoding) taking into consideration the relationship between various facial features (e.g., "close-set eyes on a round face"). For featural encoding, as age and experience increase, children are able to scan faces in a more systematic and organized manner, thereby encoding additional relevant features. The dip in performance around age 10 could be due to difficulties in making the shift from the earlier featural encoding strategy to the utilization of configural information. From this perspective, the dip may represent a "growth error" that occurs when the child changes from one cognitive strategy to another, potentially more effective strategy. During the transitional period the child stops using the old strategy but is not yet proficient in the new strategy, resulting in a temporary decline in performance. Despite the wide appeal of this hypothesis, however, Chung and Thomson (1995) asserted that the available research findings do not provide enough support for the encoding shift hypothesis.

The existence of a dip appears somewhat similar to what has been termed the *intermediate effect* in studies of the development of expertise (e.g., see Patel, Arocha, & Kaufman, 1994; Schmidt & Boshuizen, 1993). Studies of the development of expertise in complex tasks, such as making medical diagnoses, have found temporary plateaus or dips in performance that are associated with acquiring new skills or knowledge. "The intermediate effect is not a one-time phenomenon, rather, it occurs repeatedly at strategic points in a student's or physician's training that follow periods in which large bodies of new knowledge or complex skills are acquired. These periods are followed by intervals in which there is a decrement in performance until a new level of mastery is achieved" (Patel et al., 1994, p. 228). Hence, if learning to use prototypes or configural information is conceptualized as learning a new skill, a dip could be considered an instance of the intermediate effect.

Other researchers have argued, however, that there is not an age-related shift from one strategy to the other. Studies indicate that young children do not engage in a qualitatively different kind of process for recognizing faces than do older children and adults (e.g., Baenninger, 1994). Rather, older children and adults are simply able to encode more information of all types than younger children (Flin, 1985; Flin & Dziurawiec, 1989; Thomson, 1986). Several reviews (Baenninger, 1994; Chung & Thomson, 1995; Flin & Dziurawiec, 1989) concluded that the most parsimonious explanation of the accumulated findings is that the manner of encoding facial information does not change with age; older children simply encode more facial information of all types, featural and configural.

A further distinction has been proposed by Thomson and his colleagues, who have distinguished between two kinds of configural encoding, a sort of perceptual "global matching" process that is based on feelings of familiarity, and a cognitive process that analyzes subtle and complex relationships between individual features. This cognitive process is important for the recognition of faces that share the same basic configuration. Thomson (1989) proposed that the first type of configural encoding may be hardwired (i.e., automatic and represented by a module) and thus would make little contribution to developmental differences in face recognition performance. In contrast, a more cognitive kind of configural processing, the ability to discriminate between individual members of a class of stimuli that share a common configuration (i.e., faces), should improve as experience with the class of stimuli accumulates with age (see also Carey, 1992).

Chung and Thomson (1995) proposed that this distinction between two kinds of configural processing can resolve, at least partly, an apparent contradiction between two sets of findings—that infants within the first year of life encode configural information from faces (Fagan, 1979; Gibson, 1969) but that children under 10 years of age appear unable to use such information (e.g., Carey & Diamond, 1977; Diamond & Carey, 1977). These two sets of findings could represent the influence of (a) the automatic, perceptual type of configural encoding that is hardwired, and (b) the fact that the efficiency of both featural encoding and the more cognitive type of configural processing increases with age and experience.

What Is the Forensic Significance of a Possible Age-Related Dip?

Given that a dip in face recognition performance around ages 10 to 14 has been observed in several studies, though not in others, what is the possible forensic significance of this phenomenon? If we assume its genuineness as a general effect, is the dip consistent enough and of sufficient magnitude to have forensic relevance? To put it another way, should people who work with children's face-recognition responses, such as child protection workers, police interviewers, and attorneys, be told that identifications made by children 10 to 14 years old are substantially more likely to be incorrect than identifications made by somewhat younger children or by older persons? Is this effect consistent and substantial enough that it should be communicated to triers of fact (jurors, judges) in cases that involve disputed identifications made by a child 10 to 14 years of age? It appears that current research data are not consistent enough to provide a clear-cut answer to this question. This is an area where additional research would be particularly valuable.

When Interviewing May Interfere With Face Identification Memory

If a child or adult has been victimized by a stranger, initial forensic interviews may focus on getting as complete a description as possible of the perpetrator. Although this is obviously important for directing the search for the criminal, it may have a downside as well. Research indicates that being encouraged to describe a face may interfere with one's ability to identify that face from a lineup. This phenomenon, known as *verbal overshadowing*, was first identified in a series of six experiments by Schooler and Engstler-Schooler (1990). Their results consistently indicated that adults asked to provide a description of a target person, prior to identification, were significantly less accurate in subsequent identifications than were individuals who did not attempt a description.

Since this initial set of studies, similar results have been found for facial memory (e.g., Dodson, Johnson, & Schooler, 1997; Fallshore & Schooler, 1995; Ryan & Schooler, in press) and have been extended to other domains involving perceptual expertise (e.g., wine tasting, Melcher & Schooler, 1996). It has been proposed that there are three possible main factors that contribute to the effect: *modality mismatch* (the notion of competing verbal vs. nonverbal representations), *availability* (the assumption that the visual representation remains available in memory), and *recoding interference* (the notion that overshadowing effects occur because a nonveridical verbal trace of the target is created and later recalled).

Inconsistent Findings Regarding Verbal Overshadowing

Although numerous studies have found the verbal overshadowing effect, there have been a number of studies in which it has not occurred. Indeed, some studies have demonstrated positive effects of verbal description, rehearsal, and elaboration on later recognition of faces (Chance & Goldstein,

1976; Mauldin & Laughery, 1981; McKelvie, 1976; Read, 1979; Wogalter, 1991, 1996; Yu & Geiselman, 1993).

What can account for these divergent findings? Schooler, Ryan, and Reder (1996) suggested that failures to find the effect may have resulted from variations in either: (a) the encoding processes in which participants spontaneously engaged, or (b) the degree of interference generated by the description task. Whereas the first point suggests the notion of a process/modality mismatch (i.e., holistic/visual vs. featural/verbal processing of faces), the second possibility is consistent with the *recoding interference* interpretation. This approach suggests that verbal overshadowing may be dependent upon demand characteristics of the description task itself.

Researchers across a variety of domains recently began investigating such effects by systematically varying the nature of the initial recall task. Within the verbal overshadowing domain, Finger and Pezdek (1999) were interested in whether the Cognitive Interview (CI; Fisher & Geiselman, 1992; see also Fisher et al., chap. 11, this volume), an interview procedure believed to elicit more verbal descriptions and critical information about a crime incident, would produce a verbal overshadowing effect when compared to a Standard Interview (SI) procedure. When obtaining a facial description of the perpetrator was made central to the interview, Finger and Pezdek found that the CI markedly impaired recognition memory, to a level below that of the SI procedure. Finger and Pezdek found that individuals who misidentified the target produced significantly more correct and incorrect details. This finding suggests that the representation created when individuals generated a description of the target did not resemble the perceptual representation in memory.

Research in other domains has analogously noted the influence of an initial retrieval task on later identification and recall, a paradigm quite similar to that used in verbal overshadowing studies. With regard to facial memory, previous studies have demonstrated that faces are quite susceptible to the impact of postevent misinformation (Lindsay, 1990; Lindsay & Johnson, 1989; Loftus, 1975) provided either by the experimenter or in the context of a description ostensibly generated by another individual. In addition, several studies (Brown, Deffenbacher, & Sturgill, 1977; Fleet, Brigham, & Bothwell, 1987; Gorenstein & Ellsworth, 1981) have demonstrated that when individuals were forced to select an incorrect foil on an initial identification task, they were more likely to incorrectly identify the same foil on a later recognition test, despite the addition of the target face on the final identification task.

Studies investigating the effects of *retrieval-induced interference* have illustrated that lowering individuals' response criterion on an initial test, thereby forcing them to generate incorrect responses, increases the likelihood that memory errors will occur in subsequent attempts at recall

(Roediger, Wheeler, & Rajaram, 1993). To see if this process might account for the inconsistent findings on verbal overshadowing, Meissner, Brigham, and Kelley (in press) varied the instructions given in a facial description task. Some participants were instructed to be cautious in listing characteristics of the face they had seen, and some were encouraged to list as many characteristics as they could, even if some might represent guesses. A third group was simply asked to list as many characteristics as they could remember. As hypothesized, a verbal overshadowing effect was found only for the second group, those who were encouraged to use a loose response criterion. These respondents listed more incorrect characteristics than those in the other two groups, and we suggested that the generation of incorrect items interfered with their ability later to recognize the face they had seen. Consistent with this finding, a meta-analysis across 15 studies by Meissner and Brigham (in press) found that instructions that exhort people to give very full descriptions (which may include more incorrect information) are most likely to produce the verbal overshadowing effect.

Forensic Relevance of the Verbal Overshadowing Effect

Research findings to date suggest that asking for a description can be a significant detriment in people's ability to identify a face, via verbal overshadowing, if the person is encouraged to guess or is urged to provide more information than he or she did spontaneously. In contrast, if people are allowed to provide only as much descriptive information as they prefer to, then it seems unlikely that verbal overshadowing is a major factor. It should be stressed that most of this research has been conducted with adults, and it remains to be seen if the process occurs in the same way for children. Nevertheless, an awareness of the possibility of this effect, and knowledge that it is most likely to occur when people are encouraged to "stretch" their descriptions, may be valuable information for interviewers or those who analyze interview responses.

THE EFFECT OF RACE ON FACIAL RECOGNITION MEMORY

The "Own-Race Bias"

"They all look alike to me." This oft-heard statement describes an important factor affecting facial recognition accuracy — an interaction between the race of perceiver and the race of the person observed. The *own-race bias* (or other-race effect, or cross-racial identification effect, or differential recognition effect, as it has been variously labeled) refers to the finding that recognition memory tends to be better for faces of one's own race than for faces of other races.

Since the mid-1970s, a host of studies have investigated this phenomenon as it applies to face recognition, generally in relation to African Americans and Whites. Summarizing this research, a meta-analysis of 14 samples of Whites and African Americans found evidence of a reliable own-race bias effect (ORB), accounting for 11% of the variance in face recognition performance of African Americans and 10% of the variance of face recognition performance in Whites (Bothwell, Brigham, & Malpass, 1989). A significant degree of ORB was visible in roughly 80% of the samples that we reviewed. A subsequent meta-analysis by Anthony, Copper, and Mullen (1992) of 15 studies that involved 22 separate hypothesis tests found evidence of a significant weak-to-moderate tendency for participants to show the ORB. There was a trend in their analysis for the effect to be stronger among White respondents. Finally, a recent meta-analysis of 39 studies involving almost 5,000 participants (Meissner & Brigham, 2000) found that the ORB accounted for 15% of the variance across the studies. The ORB occurred most strongly for "false alarm" responses, the incorrect memory that a face had been seen before when it had not been. Such false alarm errors were over 1.5 times as frequent for other-race faces than for own-race faces (e.g., see Barkowitz & Brigham, 1982; Slone, Brigham, & Meissner, 2000). In a recent review, Chance and Goldstein (1996, p. 171) observed that, "The number of studies that have replicated the other-race effect is impressive. Few psychological findings are so easy to duplicate." Two surveys of research "experts" in this area found that most endorsed the importance and reliability of this effect (Kassin, Ellsworth, & Smith, 1989; Yarmey & Jones, 1983).

Possible Causes of the Own-Race Bias

Brigham and Malpass (1985) outlined four reasons that might account for the ORB effect. These were: (a) possible group differences in the inherent recognizably of faces of particular races, (b) the influence of ethnocentric attitudes, (c) the experience/contact hypothesis (a variant of the skill/expertise position discussed earlier), and (d) differential cognitive processes. They noted that there was no empirical evidence supporting the first point, and little evidence supporting the second possibility, that ethnocentric attitudes may cause the ORB. One could speculate that negative attitudes toward another race could lead people to cease processing a face once it has been categorized as belonging to the disliked group (Brigham & Malpass, 1985). Further, one could speculate that negative intergroup attitudes could motivate one to avoid contact with members of the disliked group, or to limit contact to superficial interactions, thereby constraining the opportunity to develop expertise in distinguishing between other-race faces (Chance & Goldstein, 1996). However, research to date has failed to find a substantial relationship between facial recognition accuracy and attitudes toward the group whose faces are identified (e.g., Brigham & Barkowitz, 1978; Platz & Hosch, 1988; Slone et al., in press). Several studies in our lab have, however, found a predicted relationship between negative attitudes toward a group and less self-reported contact with members of the disliked group (Brigham, 1993; Slone et al., in press), as more prejudiced Whites and African Americans generally reported less interracial contact both in the past and in present-day interactions than did less prejudiced persons. The final two reasons enumerated by Brigham and Malpass (1985), experience/contact and differential cognitive processing, are discussed later.

It has been widely assumed that one's degree of experience with other-race persons can affect the likelihood that the ORB will occur. In 1914, Feingold asserted that it is "well known that, all other things being equal, individuals of a given race are distinguishable from each other in proportion to our familiarity, to our contact with the race as a whole" (p. 50). Many contemporary researchers have also endorsed this race-specific skill or expertise hypothesis (e.g., Brigham & Malpass, 1985; Chance & Goldstein, 1996; Ng & Lindsay, 1994). But until recently, there has been little theoretical attention devoted to explaining why the ORB should be related to cross-race experience and/or expertise.

The prediction that experience will affect the ORB is suggested by empirical work on the beneficial attitudinal effects of equal-status contact (e.g., Allport, 1954; Amir, 1969; Cook, 1969). Research findings have led some observers to hypothesize that people who have a greater degree of interracial contact would be less likely to show an own-race bias in face recognition. However, studies have provided only mixed empirical support for the hypothesis. Some studies have found that people who report greater levels of other-race contact are less likely to show an own-race bias in face recognition (e.g., Brigham, Maass, Snyder, & Spaulding, 1982; Carroo, 1986, 1987), whereas some studies have found no apparent relationship (Brigham & Barkowitz, 1978; Malpass & Kravitz, 1969; Ng & Lindsay, 1994; Slone et al., 2000). Still others have found mixed results within the same study (Chiroro & Valentine, 1995; Platz & Hosch, 1988). It seems apparent that either the theoretical grounds for predicting a relationship between contact/experience and face recognition accuracy are not adequately specified, or that our methods for empirically assessing the quantity and/or quality of contact or experience with other-race persons are not adequate.

Cognitive Processes That May Be Involved in the Own-Race Bias

We know little about the cognitive mechanisms through which a reduction in ORB due to experience or expertise might occur. At a general level, it could be hypothesized that increased contact leads to more experience in processing other-group faces, thereby increasing one's expertise in making such discriminations. One could also speculate that increased contact might reduce the perceived complexity of previously unfamiliar classes of stimuli, such as other-race faces (Goldstein & Chance, 1971), or that it might convince people that stereotypical responses to other-race faces are not useful and thus instigate the search for more individuating characteristics. Alternatively, one could predict that increased levels of contact make it more likely that one's social rewards and punishments are dependent on correctly distinguishing among other-race persons with whom one has contact, presumably increasing one's motivation to remember faces of other-race persons accurately (Malpass, 1990).

It is important to stress that almost all of the investigations of the own-race bias were conducted with adults. At present, we do not know whether the ORB occurs in children as well; nor do we know whether ability to recognize faces of other-race children or adults develops at the same rate as the ability to recognize same-race others. If experience plays a key role in face-recognition ability, as has been suggested from several theoretical perspectives, would those young children who have had virtually no interactions with other-race persons show a particularly strong ORB in face recognition? Alternatively, would the overall contribution of experience to recognition memory be less in younger children, who have fewer experiences overall, meaning that the ORB will be small or absent in their memory performance? These are important issues, and the paucity of relevant research data is surprising.

An early candidate for a cognitive process that might affect the ORB was differential depth of processing for faces of own- and other-races. Researchers proposed that same-race faces would be cognitively processed at a deeper level, leading to better subsequent recognition (Chance & Goldstein, 1981). However, research findings have not generally supported this hypothesis. Several studies that attempted to manipulate the depth of processing via instructions to make superficial (e.g., size of facial features; racial classification) or deep (e.g., friendliness or intelligence) judgments did not find that deeper-processing instructions significantly affected the own-race bias (Chance & Goldstein, 1981; Devine & Malpass, 1985; Sporer, 1991). The most consistent finding appears to be that shallow-processing instructions impair memory for all faces, regardless of race (Chance & Goldstein, 1996).

As noted earlier, studies have suggested that the cognitive processing of faces may involve two or more cognitive processes: attention to individual facial features (featural processing), and attention to the configural relations between features and general information about face shape (configural or holistic processing). There is considerable evidence that configural processing of faces is associated with perceptual expertise, and it can be argued that people are generally more experienced (have more expertise) in distinguishing between same-race faces than between other-race faces. A model of representation of faces that accounts for the cross-race effect is provided by the *multidimensional space model* of Valentine and his colleagues (Valentine, 1991; Valentine & Endo, 1992). This model proposes that faces are encoded as locations (points, nodes) in a multidimensional space. Representations are distributed from a central exemplar with respect to their typical or distinctive aspects. Familiar individual faces are represented as points (nodes) and face categories (such as race) are represented as different clusters or "clouds" of points (Levin, 1996). When identifying a previously seen face, the nearest and therefore most active node will be chosen as the correct one for that face. Representations of other-race faces are more densely clustered in the multidimensional space because the dimensions of the space are most appropriate for own-race faces. Recognition is thus impaired for other-race faces because an other-race face activates many neighboring nodes in the dense cluster of representations for other-race faces. The model also predicts that people will show equivalent sensitivity to distinctive information in own and other-race faces. Although there is some early support for the validity of this model (e.g., Chiroro & Valentine, 1995), its overall applicability and accuracy is still undetermined.

There is another finding about race and faces that appears somewhat paradoxical. When asked to categorize each of a series of faces by race, Whites are able to categorize African American faces faster than White faces. Hence, for this task, performance on other-race faces is superior to that for own-race faces. Levin (1996) compared three possible explanations for this effect: Valentine's *multidimensional space model*, an *interference hypothesis* which suggests that expertise-based configural coding of faces interferes with coding by race, and a *race-feature hypothesis* that asserts that race is coded directly for other-race faces, while same-race faces are coded by non-race-specifying information. Levin's results supported the race-feature hypothesis for White perceivers. He also pointed out that this effect should only operate when the other race is a numerical minority (e.g., African American in American society) where categorization by race and one or two additional features would usually be effective for later recognition. Hence, African American perceivers should not show the effect, that is, they should not categorize White faces faster than African American faces.

Forensic Implications of the Own-Race Bias

Studies with adults have consistently found that own-race identifications are more likely to be accurate than identifications of other-race persons. But what does the research tell us about interviews with children? The first implication is that one should place more confidence in a child's positive identification of a person of the child's own race than when the child identifies someone of a different race. But it should be noted that almost all of the relevant research has been carried out with adult participants. Although there is no obvious reason to suspect that the effect would not also be applicable to children, relevant research that analyzes children's responses would be most valuable.

One thing that is not known, for children or for adults, is whether there is an own-race bias for descriptions, as well as identifications. If a witness is describing a person of his or her own race, is that description more likely to be accurate than a description of an other-race person would be? This might seem to be a logical extension of the own-race bias in recognition, but it may not be so simple. Description memory, unlike recognition memory, may benefit from featural encoding processing. And there is reason to believe that cognitive processing of other-race faces is more likely to involve featural processing than is the processing of same-race faces. If so, this could produce better descriptions of other-race faces than of same-race faces, because descriptions mainly involve features. This is purely conjecture at this point, because the pertinent research to address this possibility has not yet been conducted.

CONCLUSION

This chapter has reviewed basic processes in face recognition accuracy, as well as evidence about the way recognizing faces develops across childhood and into adolescence and adulthood. The issue of whether face recognition involves a unique, special, hard-wired face module system remains hotly debated by researchers, though the evidence for the existence of such modules seems increasingly strong. The consistency and magnitude of a possible dip in face recognition ability between the ages of 10 to 14 remains a controversial and unsettled issue. Also unsettled is the practical question of whether the dip is sufficiently large and universal that it should be taken into account by interviewers and others who deal with young people's face-recognition reports.

Awareness of the possibility that forcing more detailed descriptions of a stranger can interfere with subsequent memory for the stranger's face may have important implications for the way in which interviews are conducted.

Race and ethnicity may significantly affect memory for faces. The own-race bias in recognition accuracy has been widely observed and empirically documented, although the cause of this effect remains difficult to determine. Many important issues remain to be resolved regarding the ways that ethnicity may influence how well we recognize faces, and why ethnicity has the impact that it does.

REFERENCES

Allard, F., & Burnett, N. (1985). Skill in sport. *Canadian Journal of Psychology, 39*, 294–312.

Allport, G. W. (1954). *The nature of prejudice.* Reading, MA: Addison-Wesley.

Amir, Y. (1969). Contact hypothesis in ethnic relations. *Psychological Bulletin, 41*, 753–767.

Anthony, T., Copper, C., & Mullen, B. (1992). Cross-racial identification: A social cognitive integration. *Personality and Social Psychological Bulletin, 18*, 296–301.

Baenninger, M. A. (1994). The development of face recognition: Featural or configural processing? *Journal of Experimental Child Psychology, 57*, 377–396.

Barkowitz, P., & Brigham, J. C. (1982). Recognition of faces: Own-race bias, incentive, and time delay. *Journal of Applied Social Psychology, 12*, 255–268.

Bauer, R. M. (1984). Autonomic recognition of names and faces in prosopagnosia: A neurophysiological application of the Guilty Knowledge Test. *Neuropsychologia, 22*, 457–469.

Bothwell, R. K., Brigham, J. C., & Malpass, R. S. (1989). Cross-racial identification. *Personality and Social Psychology Bulletin, 15*, 19–25.

Bowlby, J. (1969). *Attachment and loss: Vol. 1. Attachment.* New York: Basic Books.

Brainerd, C. J., & Reyna, V. F. (1995). Learning rate, learning opportunities, and the development of forgetting. *Developmental Psychology, 31*, 251–262.

Brigham, J. C. (1989). Disputed eyewitness identifications: Can experts help? *The Champion, 8*(5), 10–18.

Brigham, J. C. (1993). College students' racial attitudes. *Journal of Applied Social Psychology, 23*, 1933–1967.

Brigham, J. C., & Barkowitz, P. (1978). Do "They all look alike?": The effect of race, sex, experience, and attitudes on the ability to recognize faces. *Journal of Applied Social Psychology, 8*, 384–386.

Brigham, J. C., Maass, A., Snyder. L. D., & Spaulding, K. (1982). Accuracy of eyewitness identification in a field setting. *Journal of Personality and Social Psychology, 42*, 673–681.

Brigham, J. C., & Malpass, R. S. (1985). The role of experience and contact in the recognition of faces of own- and other-race persons. *Journal of Social Issues, 41*, 139–155.

Brigham, J. C., Wasserman, A. W., & Meissner, C. A. (1999). Disputed eyewitness evidence: Important legal and scientific issues. *Court Review, 36*(2), 12–25.

Brown, E., Deffenbacher, K., & Sturgill, W. (1977). Memory for faces and the circumstances of encounter. *Journal of Applied Psychology, 62*, 311–318.

Bruyer, R. (1989). Disorders of face processing. In A. W. Young & H. D. Ellis (Eds.), *Handbook of research of face processing* (pp. 437–473). Amsterdam: Elsevier.

Bruyer, R., Laterre, C., Seron, X., Feyereisen, P., Strypstien, E., Pierrard, E., & Rectem, D. (1983). A case of prosopagnosia with some preserved covert remembrance of familiar faces. *Brain and Cognition, 2*, 257–284.

Bushnell, I. W. R., Gerry, G., & Burt, K. (1983). The externality effect in neonates. *Infant Behavior and Development, 6*, 151–156.

Carey, S. (1978). A case study: Face recognition. In E. Walker (Ed.), *Explorations in the biology of language*. Montgomery, VT: Bradford Books.

Carey, S. (1981). The development of face perception: In G. Davies, H. Ellis, & J. Shepherd (Eds.), *Perceiving and remembering faces* (pp. 9-38). New York: Academic.

Carey, S. (1992). Becoming a face expert. *Philosophical Transactions of the Royal Society of London, 3335*, 95-103.

Carey, S., & Diamond, R. (1977). From piecemeal to configurational representation of faces. *Science, 195*, 312-314.

Carey, S., Diamond, R., & Woods, B. (1980). The development of face recognition—A maturational component? *Developmental Psychology, 16*, 257-269.

Carroo, A. W. (1986). Other race face recognition: A comparison of Black American and African participants. *Perceptual and Motor Skills, 62*, 135-138.

Carroo, A. W. (1987). Recognition of faces as a function of race, attitudes and reported cross-racial friendships. *Perceptual and Motor Skills, 64*, 319-325.

Ceci, S. J., & Bruck, M. (1995). *Jeopardy in the courtroom: A scientific analysis of children's testimony*. Washington, DC: American Psychological Association.

Ceci, S. J., Leichtman, M. D., & Putnick, M. (Eds.). (1992). *Cognitive and social factors in early deception*. Hillsdale, NJ: Lawrence Erlbaum Associates.

Chance, J., & Goldstein, A. G. (1976). Recognition of faces and verbal labels. *Bulletin of the Psychonomic Society, 7*, 384-386.

Chance, J. E., & Goldstein, A. G. (1981). Depth of processing in response to own-race and other-race faces. *Personality and Social Psychology Bulletin, 7*, 475-480.

Chance, J. E., & Goldstein, A. G. (1996). The other-race effect and eyewitness identification. In S. L. Sporer, R. S. Malpass, & G. Koehnken (Eds.), *Psychological issues in eyewitness identification* (pp. 153-176). Mahwah, NJ: Lawrence Erlbaum Associates.

Chance, J. E., Goldstein, A. G., & Anderson, B. (1986). Recognition memory for infant faces: An analog of the other-race effect. *Bulletin of the Psychonomic Society, 24*, 257-260.

Chance, J. E., Turner, A. L., & Goldstein, A. G. (1982). Development of face recognition for own- and other-race faces. *Journal of Psychology, 112*, 29-37.

Chase, W. G., & Ericsson, K. A. (1982). Skill and working memory. In G. H. Bower (Ed.), *Psychology of learning and motivation* (Vol. 16, pp. 1-58). New York: Academic.

Chase, W. G., & Simon, H. A. (1973). Perception in chess. *Cognitive Psychology, 4*, 55-81.

Chiroro, P., & Valentine, T. (1995). An investigation of the contact hypothesis of the own-race bias in face recognition. *Quarterly Journal of Experimental Psychology, 48A*, 879-894.

Chung, M. S., & Thomson, D. (1995). Development of face recognition. *British Journal of Psychology, 86*, 55-87.

Cohen-Levine, S. (1989). The question of faces: Special is in the brain of the beholder. In A. W. Young & H. D. Ellis (Eds.), *Handbook of research on face processing* (pp. 37-48). Amsterdam: Elsevier.

Cook, S. W. (1969). Motives in a conceptual analysis of attitude-related behavior. In W. J. Arnold & D. Levine (Eds.), *Nebraska Symposium on Motivation*. Lincoln: University of Nebraska Press.

Cutler, B. L., & Penrod, S. D. (1995). *Mistaken identification: The eyewitness, psychology, and the law*. Cambridge, MA: Cambridge University Press.

Damasio, A. R. (1989). Neural mechanisms. In A. W. Young & H. D. Ellis (Eds.), *Handbook of research on face processing* (pp. 405-425). Amsterdam: Elsevier.

Damasio, A. R., Damasio, H., & van Hoeson, G. W. (1982). Prosopagnosia: Anatomic basis and behavioral mechanisms. *Neurology, 32*, 331-341.

Damasio, A. R., Tranel, D., & Damasio, H. (1990). Face agnosia and the neural substrates of memory. *Annual Review of Neuroscience, 13*, 89-109.

Darwin, C. (1965). *The expression of emotion in man and animals*. Chicago: University of Chicago Press. (Original work published 1872)

Davies, G. M. (1993). Children's memory for other people: An integrative review. In C. A. Nelson (Ed.), *Memory and affect in development: Minnesota symposium on child psychology* (Vol. 26, pp. 123–157). Hillsdale, NJ: Lawrence Erlbaum Associates.

Davies, G. M. (1996). Children's identification evidence. In S. L. Sporer, R. M. Malpass, & G. Koehnken (Eds.), *Psychological issues in eyewitness identification* (pp. 233–258). Mahwah, NJ: Lawrence Erlbaum Associates.

Dent, H., & Flin, R. (1992). *Children as witnesses*. New York: Wiley.

DeRenzi, E. (1986). Current issues in prosopagnosia. In H. D. Ellis, M. A. Jeeves, F. Newcombe, & A. Young (Eds.), *Aspects of face processing* (pp. 243–252). Dordrecht, Netherlands: Nijhoff.

Devine, P. G., & Malpass, R. S. (1985). Orienting strategies in differential face recognition. *Personality and Social Psychology Bulletin, 11*, 33–40.

Diamond, R., & Carey, S. (1977). Developmental changes in the representation of faces. *Journal of Experimental Child Psychology, 23*, 1–22.

Diamond, R., & Carey, S. (1986). Why faces and are not special: An effect of expertise. *Journal of Experimental Psychology: General, 115*, 107–117.

Diamond, R., Carey, S., & Back, K. J. (1983). Genetic influences on the development of spatial skills during early adolescence. *Cognition, 13*, 167–185.

Dodson, C. S., Johnson, M. K., & Schooler, J. W. (1997). The verbal overshadowing effect: Why descriptions impair face recognition. *Memory and Cognition, 25*(2), 129–139.

Doris, J. L. (Ed.). (1991). *The suggestibility of children's recollections*. Washington, DC: American Psychological Association.

Ellis, H. D. (1975). Recognizing faces. *British Journal of Psychology, 66*, 409–426.

Ellis, H. D., & Flin, R. H. (1990). Encoding and storage effects in 7-year-olds' and 10-year-olds' memory for faces. *British Journal of Developmental Psychology, 8*, 77–92.

Ellis, H. D., Shepherd, J., & Bruce, A. (1973). The effects of age and sex upon adolescents' recognition of faces. *Journal of Genetic Psychology, 123*, 173–174.

Ellis, H. D., & Young, A. W. (1989). Are faces special? In A. W. Young & H. D. Ellis (Eds.), *Handbook of research on face processing* (pp. 1–26). Amsterdam: Elsevier.

Fagan, J. F. (1979). The origins of facial pattern recognition. In M. Burnstein & W. Kessen (Eds.), *Psychological developmental from infancy* (pp. 83–113). Hillsdale, NJ: Lawrence Erlbaum Associates.

Fallshore, M., & Schooler, J. W. (1995). The verbal vulnerability of perceptual expertise. *Journal of Experimental Psychology: Learning, Memory, and Cognition, 21*, 1608–1623.

Fantz, R. L. (1961). A method for studying depth perception in infants under six months of age. *Psychological Record, 11*, 27–32.

Feingold, G. A. (1914). The influence of environment on the identification of persons and things. *Journal of Criminal Law and Political Science, 5*, 39–51.

Finger, K., & Pezdek, K. (1999). The effect of verbal description on face identification accuracy: "Release from verbal overshadowing." *Journal of Applied Psychology, 84*, 340–348.

Fisher, R. P., & Geiselman, R. E. (1992). *Memory-enhancing techniques for investigative interviewing*. Springfield, IL: Charles C. Thomas.

Fleet, M. L., Brigham, J. C., & Bothwell, R. S. (1987). The effects of choosing on the confidence-accuracy relationship in eyewitness identifications. *Journal of Applied Social Psychology, 17*, 171–187.

Flin, R. H. (1980). Age effects in children's memory for unfamiliar faces. *Developmental Psychology, 16*, 373–374.

Flin, R. H. (1983). *The development of face recognition*. Unpublished doctoral dissertation, University of Aberdeen, Scotland.

Flin, R. H. (1985). Development of face recognition: An encoding switch? *British Journal of Psychology, 76*, 123–124.

Flin, R. H., & Dziurawiec, S. (1989). Developmental factors in face processing. In A. W. Young & H. D. Ellis (Eds.), *Handbook of research on face processing* (pp. 335–378). Amsterdam: Elsevier.

Fodor, J. (1983). *The modularity of the mind.* Cambridge, MA: MIT Press.

Gibson, E. J. (1969). *Principles of perceptual learning and development.* New York: Appleton-Century-Crofts.

Goldstein, A. G. (1983). Behavioral scientists' fascination with faces. *Journal of Nonverbal Behavior, 7,* 223–255.

Goldstein, A. G., & Chance, J. E. (1971). Visual recognition of complex configurations. *Perception and Psychophysics, 9,* 237–241.

Goodman, G. S., Bottoms, B. L., Schwartz-Kenney, B., & Rudy, L. (1991). Children's memory for a stressful event: Improving children's reports. *Journal of Narrative and Life History, 1,* 69–99.

Goodman, G. S., & Reed, R. S. (1986). Age differences in eyewitness testimony. *Law and Human Behavior, 10,* 317–332.

Goren, C. C., Sarty, M., & Wu, D. Y. K. (1975). Visual following and pattern discrimination of face-like stimuli by newborn infants. *Pediatrics, 56,* 544–549.

Gorenstein, G., & Ellsworth, P. (1981). Effect of choosing an incorrect photograph on a later identification by an eyewitness. *Journal of Applied Psychology, 65,* 616–622.

Haaf, R. (1977). Visual response to complex face-like patterns by 15- and 20-week old infants. *Developmental Psychology, 13,* 77–78.

Haaf, R., Smith, P., & Smitty, S. (1983). Infant responses to face-like patterns under fixed-trial and infant-control procedures. *Child Development, 54,* 172–177.

Hay, D. C., & Young, A. W. (1982). The human face. In A. W. Ellis (Ed.), *Normality and pathology in cognitive functions* (pp. 173–202). New York: Academic.

Honts, C., Devitt, M., Tye, M., Peters, D., & Vondergeest, L. (1995, April). *Credibility assessments with children.* Paper presented at the Society for Research in Child Development Meeting, Indianapolis, IN.

Kassin, S., Ellsworth, D. C., & Smith, V. C. (1989). The "general acceptance" of psychological research on eyewitness testimony: A survey of the experts. *American Psychologist, 44,* 1089–1098.

Leonard, C. M., Rolls, E. T., Wilson, F. A. W., & Baylis, G. C. (1985). Neurons in the amygdala of the monkey with responses selective for faces. *Behavioral Brain Research, 15,* 159–176.

Levin, D. (1996). Classifying faces by race: The structure of face categories. *Journal of Experimental Psychology: Learning, Memory, and Cognition, 22,* 1364–1382.

Lewis, C., Wilkins, R., Baker, L., & Woobey, A. (1995). "Is this man your daddy?" Suggestibility in children's eyewitness identification of a family member. *Child Abuse and Neglect, 19,* 739–744.

Lindsay, D. S. (1990). Misleading suggestions can impair eyewitnesses' ability to remember event details. *Journal of Experimental Psychology: Learning, Memory, and Cognition, 16,* 1077–1083.

Lindsay, D. S., & Johnson, M. K. (1989). Misleading suggestibility and memory for source. *Memory and Cognition, 17,* 349–358.

Loftus, E. F. (1975). Leading questions and the eyewitness report. *Cognitive Psychology, 7,* 560–572.

Malpass, R. S. (1990). An excursion into utilitarian analyses, with side trips. *Behavior Science Research, 24,* 1–15.

Malpass, R. S., & Kravitz, J. (1969). Recognition of faces of own and other race. *Journal of Personality and Social Psychology, 13,* 330–334.

Mann, V. A., Diamond, R., & Carey, S. (1979). Development of voice recognition: Parallels with face recognition. *Journal of Experimental Psychology, 27,* 153–165.

Mauldin, M. A., & Laughery, K. R. (1981). Composite production effects on subsequent facial recognition. *Journal of Applied Psychology, 66*, 351–357.

Maurer, D., & Barrera, M. (1981). Infants' perception of natural and distorted arrangements of a schematic face. *Child Development, 52*, 196–202.

McKelvie, S. J. (1976). The effects of verbal labeling on recognition memory for schematic faces. *Quarterly Journal of Experimental Psychology, 28*, 459–474.

McKelvie, S. J. (1981). Sex differences in memory for faces. *Journal of Psychology, 107*, 109–125.

Meissner, C. A., & Brigham, J. C. (in press). Thirty years of investigating the own-race bias in memory for faces: A meta-analytic review. *Psychology, Public Policy, and Law.*

Meissner, C. A., & Brigham, J. C. (in press). A meta-analysis of the verbal overshadowing effect in face recognition. *Applied Cognitive Psychology.*

Meissner, C. A., Brigham, J. C., & Kelley, C. M. (in press). The influence of retrieval processes in verbal overshadowing. *Memory and Cognition.*

Melcher, J. M., & Schooler, J. W. (1996). The misremembrance of wines past: Verbal and perceptual expertise differentially mediate verbal overshadowing of taste memory. *Journal of Memory and Language, 35*, 231–245.

Nachson, I. (1995). On the modularity of face recognition: The riddle of domain specificity. *Journal of Clinical and Experimental Neuropsychology, 17*, 256–275.

Ng, W., & Lindsay, R. C. L. (1994). Cross-race facial recognition: Failure of the contact hypothesis. *Journal of Cross-Cultural Psychology, 25*, 217–232.

Parker, J., & Carranza, L. (1989). Eyewitness testimony of children in target-present and target-absent lineups. *Law and Human Behavior, 13*, 133–149.

Parker, J. F., & Ryan, V. (1993). An attempt to reduce guessing behavior in children's and adults' eyewitness identifications. *Law and Human Behavior, 17*, 11–26.

Patel, V. L., Arocha, J. F., & Kaufman, D. R. (1994). Diagnostic reasoning and medical expertise. *The Psychology of Learning and Motivation, 31*, 187–252.

Platz, S. J., & Hosch, H. M. (1988). Cross-racial/ethnic eyewitness identification: A field study. *Journal of Applied Social Psychology, 18*, 972–984.

Pozzulo, J. D., & Lindsay, R. C. L. (1992). Identification accuracy in children versus adults: A meta-analysis. *Law and Human Behavior, 22*, 549–571.

Pozzulo, J. D., & Lindsay, R. C. L. (1998). Identification accuracy of children versus adults: A meta-analysis. *Law and Human Behavior, 22*, 549–570.

Read, J. D. (1979). Rehearsal and recognition of human faces. *American Journal of Psychology, 92*, 71–85.

Roediger, H. L., Wheeler, M. A., & Rajaram, S. (1993). Remembering, knowing, and reconstructing the past. In D. L. Medin (Ed.), *The psychology of learning and motivation: Advances in research and theory* (pp. 97–134). San Diego: Academic.

Rolls, E. T. (1992). The processing of face information in the primate temporal lobe. In V. Bruce & M. Burton (Eds.), *Processing images of faces* (pp. 41–68). Norwood, NJ: Ablex.

Rolls, E. T., Baylis, G. C., & Leonard, C. M. (1989). Role of low and high spatial frequencies in the face-selective responses of neurons in the cortex in the superior temporal sulcus. *Vision Research, 25*, 1021–1035.

Ross, D. F., Read, D. J., & Toglia, M. P. (1994). *Adult eyewitness testimony: Current trends and developments.* New York: Cambridge University Press.

Ryan, R. S., & Schooler, J. W. (1998). Whom do words hurt? Individual differences in susceptibility to verbal overshadowing. *Applied Cognitive Psychology, 12*, 105–126.

Saltz, E., & Sigel, I. E. (1967). Concept overdiscrimation in children. *Journal of Experimental Psychology, 73*, 1–18.

Scapinello, K. F., & Yarmey, A. D. (1970). The role of familiarity and orientation in immediate and delayed recognition of pictorial stimuli. *Psychonomic Science, 21*, 329–331.

Schmidt, H. G., & Boshuizen, H. P. A. (1993). On the origin of intermediate effects in clinical case recall. *Memory and Cognition, 21*, 338–351.

Schooler, J. W., & Engstler-Schooler, T. Y. (1990). Verbal overshadowing of visual memories: Some things are better left unsaid. *Cognitive Psychology, 22,* 36–71.

Schooler, J. W., Fiore, S. M., & Brandimonte, M. A. (1997). At a loss from words: Verbal over-shadowing of perceptual memories. In D. Medin (Ed.), *The psychology of learning and motivation* (pp. 293–334). San Diego: Academic.

Schooler, J. W., Ryan, R. S., & Reder, L. M. (1996). The costs and benefits of verbalization. In D. Hermann, M. Johnson, C. McEvoy, C. Hertzog, & P. Hertel (Eds.), *Basic and applied memory: New findings* (pp. 51–65). Mahwah, NJ: Lawrence Erlbaum Associates.

Slone, A., Brigham, J. C., & Meissner, C. A. (2000). The "own-race bias": An effect in search of a cause. *Basic and Applied Social Psychology, 22,* 71–84.

Somerville, S. C., & Wellman, H. M. (1979). The development of understanding as an indirect memory strategy. *Journal of Experimental Child Psychology, 27,* 71–86.

Soppe, H. (1986). Children's recognition of unfamiliar faces: Developments and determinants. *International Journal of Behavioral Development, 9,* 219–233.

Souther, A. F., & Banks, M. S. (1979, March). *The human face: A view from the infant's eye.* Paper presented at the meeting of the Society for Research in Child Development, San Francisco.

Sporer, S. L. (1991). Deep–Deeper–Deepest? Encoding strategies and the recognition of human faces. *Journal of Experimental Psychology: Learning, Memory and Cognition, 17,* 323–333.

Sporer, S. L., Malpass, R. S., & Koehnken, G. (Eds.). (1996). *Psychological issues in eyewitness identification.* Mahwah, NJ: Lawrence Erlbaum Associates.

Tanaka, J. W., & Farah, M. J. (1993). Parts and wholes in face recognition. *Quarterly Journal of Experimental Psychology, 46,* 225–245.

Tanaka, J., & Gauthier, I. (1997). Expertise in object and face recognition. In R. G. Goldstone, D. L. Medin, & P. Schyns (Eds.), *Perceptual mechanisms of learning* (Vol. 36, pp. 83–125). San Diego: Academic.

Thomson, D. M. (1986). Face recognition: More than a feeling of a familiarity? In H. D. Ellis, M. A. Jeeves, F. Newcombe, & A. Young (Eds.), *Aspects of face processing* (pp. 391–399). Amsterdam: Elsevier.

Thomson, D. M. (1989). Issues posed by developmental research. In A. W. Young & H. D. Ellis (Eds.), *Handbook of research on face processing* (pp. 391–399). Amsterdam: Elsevier.

Tobey, A., & Goodman, G. S. (1992). Children's eyewitness memory: Effects of participation and forensic context. *Child Abuse and Neglect, 16,* 779–796.

Tranel, D., & Damasio, A. R. (1985). Knowledge without awareness: An autonomic index of facial recognition by prosopagnosics. *Science, 228,* 1453–1454.

Valentine, T. (1991). A unified account of the effects of distinctiveness, inversion and race in face recognition. *Quarterly Journal of Experimental Psychology, 43A,* 161–204.

Valentine, T., & Endo, M. (1992). Towards an exemplar model of face processing: The effects of race and distinctiveness. *Quarterly Journal of Experimental Psychology, 44A,* 671–703.

Wells, G. L., & Loftus, E. F. (1984). *Eyewitness testimony: Psychological perspectives.* Cambridge, England: Cambridge University Press.

White, T. L., Leichtman, M. D., & Ceci, S. J. (1997). The good, the bad, and the ugly: Accuracy, inaccuracy, and elaboration in preschoolers' reports about a past event. *Applied Cognitive Psychology, 11,* S37–S54.

Wogalter, M. S. (1991). Effects of post-exposure description and imaging on subsequent face recognition performance. *Proceedings of the Human Factors Society, 35,* 575–579.

Wogalter, M. S. (1996). Describing faces from memory: Accuracy and effects on subsequent recognition performance. *Proceedings of the Human Factors and Ergonomics Society, 40,* 536–540.

Yarmey, A. D., & Jones, H. P. T. (1983). Is the psychology of eyewitness identification a matter of common sense? In S. M. Lloyd & B. R. Clifford (Eds.), *Evaluating witness evidence* (pp. 13–40). New York: Wiley.

Yin, R. K. (1969). Looking at upside-down faces. *Journal of Experimental Psychology, 81,* 141–145.

Yin, R. K. (1970). Face recognition by brain injured patients: A dissociable ability? *Neuropsychologia, 8,* 395–402.

Yin, R. K. (1978). Face perception: A review of experiments with infants, normal adults, and brain-injured persons. In R. Held, H. W. Leibovitz, & H. L. Tueber (Eds.), *Handbook of sensory physiology: Vol. VIII. Perception* (pp. 593–608). New York: Springer-Verlag.

Yu, C. J., & Geiselman, R. E. (1993). Effects of constructing Identi-kit composites on photospread identification performance. *Criminal Justice and Behavior, 20,* 280–292.

Zuckerman, C. B., & Rock, I. (1957). A re-appraisal of the roles of past experience and innate organizing processes in visual perception. *Psychological Bulletin, 54,* 269–296.

II

STRESS, TRAUMA, AND INDIVIDUAL DIFFERENCES

6

Stress, Trauma, and Memory

Elisabeth Engelberg
Sven-Åke Christianson
Stockholm University, Sweden

Since the early 1900s there has been interest in how stress generally and trauma in particular affect individuals' well-being. There has also been interest in the role of both stress and trauma in affecting memory, since the 1990s, in relation to questions about the reliability of eywitnesses. Considerable theorizing about, and numerous scientific and case studies concerning how well individuals remember and recount personally experienced stressful events has resulted. It is not the intent of this chapter to provide an extensive overview of scientific research and theory on relations between stress and memory (see Christianson, 1992). Rather, our intent is to discuss clinical findings concerning trauma and memory that are in need of explanation and to link clinical observation to research and theory in cognitive psychology. We acknowledge the need for continued scientific research to clarify the mechanisms involved. Our hope is that this chapter will help encourage further research regarding the role of stress and trauma in affecting memory.

The chapter is organized as follows: We first review the basic principles uncovered in studies of the relations between emotion and memory. Second, we describe case examples of individuals' reactions to and memory for extremely stressful, traumatic events. Third, we describe the relation between emotional distress and dissociation, and explore how the latter principle may relate to memory. We discuss the potential role of context-dependent retrieval fourth, and other factors associated with the retrieval process fifth. Sixth, and finally, we review the importance of carrying out

143

a proper interview for a more comprehensive retrieval of the traumatic event. In drawing attention to these areas, the chapter provides a realistic portrayal of the way in which victims of trauma appear to remember such experiences.

AFFECT, AROUSAL, AND SELECTIVE PROCESSING

Two general issues are important to consider when evaluating emotions and memory. These include selective attention to emotion-congruent information and selective attention to emotion-eliciting information. Each is discussed in turn.

Research on different factors influencing memory has shown interesting effects of affect-congruent processing at the stages of encoding and retrieval (e.g., Bower, 1981; Isen, Shalker, Clark, & Carp, 1987; Mogg, Mathews, & Weinman, 1987). In one study, adults completed the Beck Depression Inventory, a widely used, self-report questionnaire that measures depression. The adults were asked to rate to what extent each of a series of positive or negative adjectives was descriptive of themselves. At a later session, they were asked to recall the adjectives and then recognize them from a larger set of positive and negative items. Results showed that individuals with high scores on the Beck Depression Inventory had a bias to encode information with negative associations (Zuroff, Colussy, & Wielgus, 1983). Other studies that have employed similar designs reveal similar types of biases, for instance, an encoding bias among clinically anxious patients for anxiety-relevant adjectives (Greenberg & Beck, 1989) and panic-disordered patients for threat-related words (McNally, Foa, & Donnell, 1989).

Bower (1981) reported that negative information is preferentially processed in an emotion congruent fashion when negative moods are induced. Adults were hypnotized into a happy or a sad mood and then asked to read a story about two men. One of the men was described as a happy and sucessful individual, and the other as a sad person with many problems in life. After reading the story, participants were asked with whom they had identified the most, and their answers were congruent with the valence of the hypnotically induced mood. Further, during a recall test the following day, participants previously hypnotized into a happy mood remembered approximately half of the facts pertaining to both characters. Thus, they did not exhibit a bias toward either individual. In contrast, participants previously hypnotized into a sad mood remembered almost exclusively the facts pertaining to the sad character of the story. This result suggests that we, to some extent, are predisposed to memorize negatively valenced emotional information, especially when that information is consistent with our own feeling state. Indeed, research has similarly shown that an angry face in a crowd of neutral looking faces is perceived faster than a happy looking one (Hansen & Hansen, 1988), and that pictures with blood or physical injuries are retained in memory better than neutral pictures (e.g., Öhman, Dimberg, & Esteves, 1989). Together, the studies show that depression and the inducement of sadness may alter cognitive processsing in a congruent manner and that exposure to aversive or threatening stimuli may even alter moods into an arousal-like state.

Research on the effects of arousal on memory has, however, uncovered mixed results. Although a few studies have shown no differential effects of arousal (e.g., Hosch & Bothwell, 1990), most findings reveal either a decremental or enhancing effect on memory performance. A negative effect of arousal has been demonstrated with regard to retrograde or anterograde amnesia for information not related to the gist of the event or the critical target (e.g., Christianson & Nilsson, 1984; Loftus & Burns, 1982). Studies that include an emotion-laden or divergent stimulus, such as a loud sound or a nude or injured person, presented in a series of neutral and homogoneous items, strongly suggest that anterograde and retrograde amnesias are caused by heightened attention and processing allocated to unique items at the expense of other information (e.g., Detterman, 1975; Kramer, Buckhout, Widerman, & Tusche, 1991). These studies may indicate a problem of initial retrieval, as inhibitory effects of this kind have been shown to recede with recognition. By contrast, studies more specifically focused on memory of details that pertain to the gist or the critical target have shown that arousal enhances recall (e.g., Christianson & Loftus, 1987). In laboratory studies, a rather consistent pattern of encoding and memory under emotional stress has been revealed (e.g., Christianson, 1984; Christianson & Loftus, 1990, 1991; Heuer & Reisberg, 1990, 1992; Kebeck & Lohaus, 1986). Specifically, details that are central or critical to the cause of the stress are better retained in memory than details that are peripheral or noncritical. There is, in other words, a preponderance for remembering the details that gave rise to the emotional reactions and thoughts during the event. Heightened arousal focuses attention automatically to emotion-laden details which are therefore more thoroughly processed than are details in the periphery of attentional resources (cf. Easterbrook, 1959). The encoding of emotion-laden detail information will not, however, be enhanced in cases in which arousal arises by means of manipulation that is independent of (i.e., unrelated to) the content of the to-be-remembered stimuli (e.g., Christianson & Mjörndal, 1985; Christianson, Nilsson, Mjörndal, Perris, & Tjellden, 1986). Nonetheless, because emotion-laden details are most often intrinsically related to emotional stress experienced during the event, arousal should be positively related to recall of details of crimes and other emotionally stressful experiences.

Children and adults alike have shown the same pattern of enhanced memory retention for central details. In one study of children's memory for a medical checkup, children received either a vaccination on their arm or a pretend tattoo sticker placed on the same location. After 3 or 4 days, children were questioned about what had happened during the checkup. Children who received the inoculation remembered more central detail information, whereas children who received the tatoo remembered more peripheral details (Goodman, Hepps, & Reed, 1986; but see Vandermaas, Hess, & Baker-Ward, 1993). In a study by Maass and Kohnken (1989), the effect of exposure to a syringe and the possible threat of an injection was investigated in adults as a parallel to the phenomenon of *weapon focusing* (e.g., Cutler, Penrod, & Martens, 1987; Loftus, Loftus, & Messo, 1987). Adults were approached by the experimenter who either had a syringe or a pen in her hand. Results showed that recall of details of the experimenter's hand was better among adults exposed to the syringe than adults exposed the pen. The difference was even larger when adults exposed to the syringe were told that they might get an injection.

Outside the laboratory, what may be perceived as central or critical details of a stressful real-life event is of course less evident. However, recurrent details imbued with special traumatic meaning are usually revealed in play and drawings when children process a trauma. A clinical interpretation of symbolic activity of this kind is that it may reflect what is considered central, that is, the critical details of the trauma, to a child who experiences such an event. For instance, a boy who saw a jet of water eviscerate his younger sister, constantly played with yarn by stretching it and tying it between pieces of furniture (Terr, 1990). The yarn may have been reminiscent of intestines that he had seen. Another boy, who saw his mother being killed with a two-pronged pitchfork, drew two-pronged buildings and abstract images (Nader & Pynoos, 1990). As suggested by Wessel and Merckelbach (1994), it may be possible that the retention of central detail accounts for the reexperiencing of traumatic symptoms often found in individuals diagnosed with posttraumatic stress disorder (PTSD).

INFLUENCE OF EMOTIONAL TRAUMA ON MEMORY

The acute reaction to overwhelming, shocking, or life-threatening situations consists of an extreme state of arousal. For instance, a boy described his reactions to witnessing his father being gunned down: "It was awful, my heart hurt, it was beating so loud" (Pynoos & Eth, 1986). During hyperarousal, the sequence of events is perceived and processed differently than during less stressful events. Many people report having perceived the passage of time as slowing down, and although some remember a narrowed field of vision, most remember the other senses to have sharpened remarkably. A policeman who had just been shot at and taken cover, recalled that he was so vigilant at that instance that "I think I would have heard an ant cross the floor" (Karlsson & Christianson, 1999).

Reactions to traumatic stress give rise to a different processing of the experience as compared to instances of heightened arousal. Such processing could be described along the theories that Pierre Janet (1893) postulated. According to Janet, traumatic experience is not primarily encoded as an episodic memory among patients with hysteria, but rather fragments of the experience are stored at a somatic level. Memories of a trauma can, therefore, be expressed through behavioral symptoms, affective reactions, and reexperiencing of visual or other perceptual details from the original traumatic event (van der Kolk & van der Hart, 1989). One of Janet's case studies may serve as an example of the type of memory retention that he had been able to observe. Friends of the husband of an older woman rang the doorbell in the middle of night. When she opened the door, her husband was sitting on the doorstep, and his friends then told her as a joke that he was dead. She could not recall the incident, but "froze with terror" every time she passed through the front door (Janet, 1893, as cited in Tobias et al., 1992). Her reaction may also represent an instance of Pavlovian defensive conditioning: Despite the door being a rather innocuous stimulus, it nevertheless became associated with feelings of horror.

Memories established through defensive or fear conditioning are rapidly acquired by experiencing an event in which the individual could not control the situation and lacked sufficient resources to cope with the episode. Although the reason for such reactions has yet to be elucidated fully and may lie beyond conscious awareness, there is documentation suggesting that traumatic symptoms may be evoked during conscious recollection of the trauma-eliciting event. A contemporary example describes a woman who, soon after the 6th birthday of her daughter, suddenly suffered from pain in her lower back. After some time, she realized that her father had started abusing her sexually soon after she herself had turned 6 years old (Terr, 1994). Another example is provided by one of the few survivors in the 1994 ferry tragedy on the Baltic Sea, where more than 800 passengers drowned. A year after surviving the ferry catastrophe, a young woman attended a ballet performance. Suddenly she felt as if she could not breathe and went out into the lobby where she fainted. After regaining consciousness, she realized that some of the dance movements with floating hands had reminded her of all the hands above the water surface of those passengers who did not make it to the life rafts. A third example is of a man who had been a passenger on board a crashing airplane (e.g., Dyregrov, 1992). He sensed a strong smell of gasoline the moment after the plane hit the ground. Despite the crash having happened many years ago, the memory of that odor often overwhelms him when he drives a car.

These anecdotal examples of conditioned fear responses may be interpretable in light of neurobiological research on nonhuman animals. Conditioned responses triggered by trauma-related perceptual stimuli have been observed in studies suggesting that synapses and neurons around the amygdoloid complex and part of the hypothalamus exhibit a certain plasticity during classical conditioning (e.g., Clugnet & LeDoux, 1990; Teyler & DiScenna, 1987). This specific form of plasticity is believed to consist of a modification of neural activity in the circuits that relay sensory information to the amygdala through acoustic or visual thalamic and cortical areas. As a result, different patterns of neural activity are established and then initiated on later exposure to previously conditioned sensory-specific stimuli. The execution of the conditioned response may also be possible because of motor-specific modifications in the hypothalamus. This modified activity in certain synapses may take place in the amygdala during two temporally overlapping inputs and may constitute a mechanism for associative emotional memories to be established through classical conditioning (LeDoux, 1991, 1996; Rogan, Staubli, & LeDoux, 1997). This putative neurobiological circumstance may, for instance, account for the particular occasions when a brutally gang-raped woman would reexperience the same anxiety, shaking, and palpitations as during the rape. The affective reactions would overcome her only when she encountered people of the same ethnic backgrond as the perpertrators, although she was usually preoccupied with ruminating about the assault in her thoughts (Hartman & Burgess, 1993). It is also possible that a projection route relays some sensory information from the thalamus directly to the amygdala, instead of first projecting the information through the cortex, instigating an emotional or behavioral reaction that is not dependent on conscious awareness of the episode that gave rise to the neural circuits that established the projection route (LeDoux, 1992). Further research is needed to elucidate the neurobiological mechanisms that underlie conscious and unconscious responses following trauma.

EMOTIONAL STRESS AND DISSOCIATIVE REACTIONS

Dissociation is believed to result from extreme stress experienced during an event, such as a crime, but also from multiple incidents of trauma and unbearable violations of integrity. Shame, guilt, and grief may overwhelm one's coping ability, and not being able to consciously remember a trauma may serve as a protective measure, limiting conscious thoughts about an experience that are difficult to deal with or confront. It has also been hypothesized that degrees of dissociation exist that stand in proportion to the level of psychic pain considered tolerable by an individual. Thus, dissociation can range from a conscious act of denial to unconscious processes leading to psychogenic forms of amnesia (e.g., Kopelman, Christensen, Puffett, & Stanhope, 1994; Putnam, 1997).

Although more research is needed to specify, more precisely, the conditions that lead to dissociation, including the mechanisms underlying the phenomenon, several case examples appear consistent with the general notion of dissociation. Adolescents who as children were involved in the production of pornography persistently denied to the police that they had actually been part of it. One of the girls could spontaneously tell the police that she remembered playing with other children, but she had no recollection of adults being present, her picture being taken, or that someone recorded her on film. The police finally showed her a photo portraying herself as a young child in an explicit sexual act with the perpertrator. Her only response was that her hair had looked like a real mess; she refused to say anything further (Svedin & Back, 1996). By focusing on nonthreatening details, she may have actively inhibited memories, feelings, and thoughts associated with the abuse. Although we again stress that scientific research is needed, it is possible that, in cases of repeated and longstanding aversive or overwhelming experiences, the individual may develop dissociative behaviors that include storage of such events outside of what is considered conscious awareness. Thus, despite the range of associations to the emotional context being restricted at a conscious level, suppression of emotion-eliciting information intrinsically related to the stressful event may be a further necessary step to block traumatic memories. Traumatic memories would then become difficult to retrieve because few links exist to other memory information. Further, because only a few links exist, intrusive emotions and thoughts may be prevented from surfacing. Such a phenomenon is illustrated by a former victim of incest when talking about the return of memories of abuse in the following way: "This memory—it's only been back in my consciousness for a year, so it's very close to my feelings. Some of the other memories that came back to me almost feel as if they're out-of-body—beyond my feelings. But this one, I just can't defend against it" (Terr, 1994, p. 116).

Clinical observations of dissociative phenomena suggest that cognitive factors may prompt these types of reactions. For instance, although the individual is unable to recount the emotional experience verbally, she may still exhibit nonverbal indications that the event is retained in memory. Such indications may be seen through emotional reactions and behavioral reenactments that, unlike verbal memories, are beyond conscious control. A traumatized person suffering from psychogenic amnesia may, for instance, experience anxiety and nausea when exposed to trauma-related stimuli (cf. Christianson & Nilsson, 1989). Also, it may not be unusual for exposure to seemingly harmless details pertaining to a previously unrecallable period of life to trigger reactions that will eventually lead to conscious recollection of the blocked memories. In one case report, an elderly man who claimed he had no idea of his personal identity or previous life history was recognized by a neighbor who had once lived next door. He was then accompanied to the apartment where somebody else now lived; still the man had no recollection of the apartment or the neighbor. A week later the man suddenly recalled that he had lost his memory following the death of his wife to whom he had been very attached (Domb & Beaman, 1991). The apartment, which presumably was associated with an emotionally gratifying time in the man's life, may have triggered an affective link that bridged a gap to the episodic memory that was blocked (cf. Erdelyi & Goldberg, 1979).

Another often reported circumstance indicating the importance of cognitive factors (e.g., links among different memories) underlying dissociative tendencies concerns the kind of memory fragments usually available during dissociative reactions as compared to organic amnesia. In organic amnesia, for instance as caused by head trauma, memory fragments tend to appear as a random assortment of details from the time of the evoking event. There are few clear temporal and causal links between the emerging memories. In contrast, there is logical and temporal order in the fragments that are remembered about a trauma. It is simply the unpleasant information that is selectively excluded. As an example, a man lapsed into fugue state at the time of the funeral of a close relative and could only remember a few fragments. After recovery, he described these fragments as pertaining to the happiest moments of his life (Schachter, Wang, Tulving, & Freedman, 1982).

It has been hypothesized that dissociative reactions may be motivated by the inability to assimilate and accomodate stressful or traumatic experiences into the schemata of the individual, insofar as the individual's schemata do not include representations of the self as being a victim of such trauma or information regarding how to interpret traumatic life events. A trauma's disorganizing effect on cognitive processing may cause self perceptions or schemata to be altered due to an attempt to reconcile the experience with an individual's self-image and outlook on life. This may result in a loss of memory for the stressful event only, or perhaps a loss of personal identity and previous life history (Horowitz & Reidbord, 1992). Such loss is commonly referred to as *psychogenic amnesia* and constitutes the extreme form of a dissociative reaction because full amnesia enables an individual to block out entirely threatening or unbearable experiences. In the latter case, it is no longer a matter of deliberately applying a strategy to render certain memories less accessible to consciousness. It is instead an extreme defense reaction that is automatically activated by the immense and cumbersome emotional stress and that temporarily hampers mechanisms for retrieval of all information related to one's self history.

CONTEXT-DEPENDENT RETRIEVAL CUES, MEMORY SYSTEMS, AND SELF-REFERENT KNOWLEDGE

The effectiveness of context-dependent retrieval cues is evident when evaluating individuals' memory for stressful and traumatic events. Context-dependent retrieval occurs when some circumstance that was present during a to-be-remembered event later cues memory of the event. Thus, retrieval can be triggered by circumstances that bear some relevance to the circumstances of the to-be-remembered event. One victim of repeated childhood molestation offers an example. The first time he recalled the previously unrecalled episodes, he experienced a sudden return of memories of three different instances as a child lying naked on the bathroom floor. These memories returned on a hot and humid day, which probably was the same sort of humidity that may have been present in a slightly steamy bathroom (Terr, 1994). Another example of context-dependent cues triggering the return of memory consists of a woman who suffered from psychogenic amnesia following a rape that occurred a few months earlier while she was jogging. She was jogging for the first time since the assault in a different area and caught sight of a pile of bricks. The bricks cued memory of her running on a path covered with crushed bricks during a frantic attempt to escape the rapist (Christianson & Nilsson, 1989). As suggested by these case studies, it may not necessarily be the same or a highly similar physical environment that serves as the context-dependent memory cue. Sensory associations (visual, auditory, tactile, and olfactory) may equally serve as context-dependent retrieval cues.

Several studies on trauma patients have, however, shown that these types of sensory cues may lead to behavioral responses suggestive of memory, whether or not the same cues lead to conscious, verbal recall of the episode. A case study of a woman who had been sitting in her car when another driver bumped into her from the rear offers an example. Fortunately, she had no other injuries than a concussion and bruising on her forehead. She had, however, mentioned that she had heard car tires breaking right before the impact, and that she, in that second, had felt convinced she would die. For a long time after the accident, she suffered from panic attacks whenever she heard the sound of tires squealing (de L Horne, 1993). Another woman who had been assaulted and raped in her home avoided taking the subway because the smell in the underground area reminded her of the rapists and made her nauseous (McMurran, 1988).

The occurrence of context-dependent retrieval, and the effectiveness of sensory cues as well as physical cues, may be explained, in part, by considering that different types of memory exist. On the basis of empirical findings, Johnson and colleagues envision sensory retrieval cues as mediated by nonverbal, so called "perceptual subsystems" of the brain, that stem from early evolution of humans (Johnson, Kim, & Risse, 1985; Johnson & Multhaup, 1992). These can be contrasted with later developing "reflective subsystems." In a slightly different classification of memory, Squire (1995) suggested that there is an implication that emotional aspects of an event may be stored separately from other aspects of an event (e.g., factual, self-referent information) at a nondeclarative or procedural level, and memory of these emotional aspects may then be expressed through behavior. Other researchers have proposed dual representations of autobiographical events. Conway (1992) has, for instance, proposed that representations consist of a "phenomenological record" containing online phenomenal experiences of specific events, on the one hand, and "thematic knowledge" containing more semantic or abstract knowledge about the events in the personal history of an individual, on the other hand. Brewin, Dalgleish, and Joseph (1996; see also Brewin, 1989) have specifically focused on trauma in their theoretical distinction between "situationally accessible knowledge" and "verbally accessible knowledge." The former indeliberately triggers emotional responses, as originally conditioned, in situations where some aspects may be reminiscent of the traumatic event. These aspects may well include sensory cues. This situationally-accessible knowledge is not available to consciousness or verbal recall. In contrast, "verbally accessible knowledge" consists of generic knowledge that enables an individual to appraise the implications of the traumatic event from both a personal and a general point of view. Finally, Tulving and others have made distinctions between *implicit* and *explicit memory*. Implicit memory consists of learned behaviors and responses, does not operate at a conscious level, and is expressed through behaviors and actions. By contrast, explicit memory includes deliberate, conscious recall of events and information.

Event memory could thus be regarded as organized at multiple levels, and, various types of information contained in those levels may be differently accessible depending on the retrieval cues. The following case studies, one about a girl who had not yet developed an episodic memory system, the other about a woman whose episodic memory was blocked, may provide useful examples. In the first case, an 18-month-old girl had a fishbone stuck in her throat, which had to be removed by a physician. After the incident, the girl refused to eat fish and would only reluctantly have her throat examined. At the age of 2 years and 1 month, that is, 7 months after the incident, she could identify the physician from a series of photos, but she could not explicitly recall the incident (Howe, Courage, & Peterson, 1994). In the other case, a former rape victim was at a medical clinic due to a sore throat. Although the woman had no conscious recollection of the assault, when the doctor pressed down her tongue to examine it, she suddenly pushed him away, cried hysterically, and left the clinic. At home, she still could not understand her own behavior at the clinic, but she was compelled to dial a phone number. She reached the policeman who explained to her that he had investigated her rape 3 years earlier (Hartman & Burgess, 1993). As she supposedly had called the police immediately after the assault, the affective reaction experienced at the clinic may have reactivated this behavior.

These two cases demonstrate, of course, conditioned reactions, but also suggest memory on some levels, but lack of memory on others. In other words, there appeared to be dissociations between different levels of memory (cf. Graf & Schacter, 1985; Schacter, 1987). The lack of conscious recollection was to some extent compensated by implicit retrieval in both cases of event information in the form of emotional and behavioral reactions. Implicit memory may have been automatically activated by external stimuli, such as contextual components of the past event that were accessed by means of perceptual and tactile, trauma-related cues. For the episodic memory representation to be cued, however, it would have been necessary to retrieve contextual information that by definition was self-referent, thus pointing to "the central role played by the self in the reexperienced past: In episodic remembering the remembered is always an observer or a participant in the mentally recreated earlier real-life happenings" (Tulving, 1987, p. 72). In the case of the 18-month-old girl, her sense of self was not yet fully developed, and thus the incident with the fishbone may not have been encoded as an episodic memory. In the case of the woman at the medical clinic, the rape may have carried too heavy an implication for her integrity and ultimately her individual sense of self. She may have blocked episodic memory of the rape event. In any case, for both the young girl and the woman, because the connection to the self could not be made at retrieval (see Kihlstrom, 1995), episodic memory was inaccessible.

A third example also demonstrates both the dissociation between types of memory as well as the importance of self-referent encoding for retention and the effectivenes of context cues. An Italian woman suffered *semantic memory* deficit following encephalitis (DeRenzi, Liotti, & Nichelli,

1987). Semantic memory consists of general and personal knowledge that is not related to memory of specific events and experiences. Memory of specific events and personal experiences is referred to as episodic memory. Despite the woman's loss of semantic memory, her episodic memory was still intact. Thus, she could not recall figures of great significance in the history of Italy, such as Mussolini. The few public events she could recall were those that seemed to be associated with some personal significance. For instance, she remembered the nuclear accident in Chernobyl because this disaster meant that she had not been able to eat the vegetables that she had grown in her garden.

Interestingly, it is possible that events that have implications for the individual's sense of self, including stressful events, may promote elaborative rehearsal that would then facilitate memory in the long run. Heuer (1987) argued that the recall pattern for emotional events centers around the causes of the evoked emotions. This circumstance prompts the individual to personalize a narrative account around the critical elements of the experience. There is a natural correspondence between a person's feelings and the emotion-eliciting information in emotionally arousing situations. Neutral situations do not normally elicit feelings that are intrinsic to information about the event. Elaboration, such as thinking about and reacting to details in the emotion-provoking sequence of events, will promote memory for the core information, or the gist of the event.

RETRIEVING EVENT INFORMATION

Once a memory has been cued, several factors can influence the type and amount of information that is actually retreieved. For example, research conducted during the 1990s has revealed an ability to retrieve event information without actually retrieving an episodic memory of the event itself. As discussed previously, sensory cues may trigger retrieval of implicit memory (see Schacter, 1987), and implicit memory may be useful in providing important, behaviorally based event information. In one case, police needed to know exactly how far the perpertrator had run into the woods before catching up with his victim. When the police first posed the question to the perpertrator, his answer was about 100 meters. He was later brought to a similar area where the crime had been commited, and he was now instructed to walk or run the same distance as he could recall it. With this implicit retrieval attempt, that was as close to the circumstances for encoding as possible, the perpertrator instead moved 300 meters through the woods, and the longer distance was corroborated by forensic findings at the crime scene (Christianson, 1996).

Feelings and emotion cues may also facilitate retrieval. For example, a negative emotional reaction like fear, disgust, or anger, may cue a person to remember the negative or upsetting details of a previous experience. A recent study of the effects of activating event memory by cueing associated emotions was carried out using preschool children between the ages of 2.5 and 6.5 years old (Liwag & Stein, 1995). Parents were interviewed about a recent event that had made their child either happy, sad, angry, or afraid. Each child was interviewed about the event in one of four conditions. In the first condition, the child was only asked to tell the experimenter about the event that she or he had experienced. In the second condition, the child was also asked "What did you think?," "What did you do?," and "What did you feel?" In the third condition, an instruction was added to make a face corresponding to the emotion that the child had experienced at the time of the event. To the fourth condition, yet another instruction was added. The child was also asked to act out the scene and to show, with the whole body, how he or she had felt at the time. Results showed that children in the fourth condition provided the most nonverbal cues and remembered significantly more about the event than children in any of the other conditions. Further, children in the fourth condition not only recalled more details that were directly related to the specific event, but they also mentioned other related types of incidents. For instance, a boy who was interviewed about his visit to the dentist also recalled the time when his brother had been taken to the hospital. Instructions or interviewing techniques that aim at recreating feelings or emotions experienced at the time of the event facilitate retrieval of more detailed information. The emotional cues may activate event information stored at different levels of memory, and the retrieval process may then take place by increasing the number of links in memory associated with the representation of the specific event.

The principle of using emotions to increase links in memory can also be seen in some studies of adults' memory for emotional events. For instance, Engelberg and Christianson (2000) assessed adults' recall of unpleasant information using the Cognitive Interview (CI) technique (Fisher & Geiselman, 1992; see also Fisher, Brennan, & McCauley, chap. 11, this volume). Specifically, participants were shown a 10-minute unpleasant and violent film clip and were then asked to rate their emotional reactions. After 6 weeks, one group of participants was asked to rate emotional reactions experienced at the film event and to recall somewhat detailed information about the event depicted in the film clip. Another group of participants was however first asked to recall the film event by means of instructions based on some of the principles of the CI. These instructions were aimed at assisting participants to mentally recreate the circumstances of the event and their own physical and emotional state at the time, and also to recall the film clip from different points in the sequence of events. Participants in the CI condition recalled their previously reported unpleasant emotion more accurately and also remembered the event information more correctly than participants who had not received the CI instructions. Thus, a wise retrieval strategy may be to ask questions about the emotions that had been experienced to aid in retrieval or to ask about details that evoked emotions. Such event information usually consists of the critical or central details and tends to be readily available to recall, possibly unlike peripheral details, which may involve more cuing.

Care must also be taken to allow sufficient time for an individual to recall all unique characteristics of a particular event before trying to retrieve details that are not immediately accessible. In applying the principles of the CI, plenty of time is allowed to recreate the circumstances surrounding an event, including time to recreate the emotional feelings associated with the event. This may facilitate eventual recall of peripheral details of the to-be-remembered event. Further, as has been suggested earlier in this chapter, nonverbal information pertaining to body movements and sensory perception (sights, colors, sounds, olfactory, and gustatory details, etc.), may not only take time to access in memory, but also require different types of memory cues, ranging from sensory-motor, to verbal, to emotional cues.

Once a person has recounted what is remembered most clearly, the person will eventually be able to recall more details, as, for instance, shown in studies on hypermnesia (net gain in memory when memory of certain information is tested repeatedly; see Payne, 1987, for a review). In a study by Scrivner and Safer (1988), subjects were presented with a videotape depicting a burglary in which three people were shot and killed. Subjects' memory was then tested during four consecutive recall tests within 48 hours. Results showed that details presented before, during, and after watching the videotape were more accurately recalled with repeated testing. According to one clinical perspective, in the case of a very stressful or traumatic real-life event, the most distressing and upsetting details may surface in conscious awareness only after a number of recall attempts. Traumatized persons may be reluctant to recollect due to fear of overpowering emotion or even painful sensations, and even though they finally break through a first barrier, aspects of the trauma may still remain hidden. In some cases, it may take months and even years before the entire experience of trauma is fully recollected.

Several studies identify the beneficial effects on mental health of talking about an emotionally stressful or traumatic event. For instance, in one study, university students who had experienced a traumatic event before 17 years of age were randomly assigned to two groups (Pennebaker, 1988). Participants in one of these groups went every day for 4 consecutive days to a special room where they spent 20 minutes writing about the trauma. They were asked to write down everything that crossed their mind about the trauma during those 20 minutes and were informed that they would not receive any feedback. Subjects in the other group were asked to write about something neutral of their own choice. During 6 months after the last day of writing, all subjects were followed up with regard to study results and physical health. Those who had written about the traumatic event were more succesful in their studies and had fewer visits to the health center. Although not specifically a goal of the study, by writing or talking about a trauma, the participants may have begun to understand the event more clearly and subsequently to remember the event in greater detail than they would have otherwise.

In fact, some trauma victims describe their experiences as a "big black mess" or a "thick soup," and recounting the event therefore gives them a possiblity to chunk the trauma into more manageable components that are easier to grasp, analyze, and process. The presumed reason for this possibility is that writing or recounting a stressful or traumatic event entails a processing of the experience that activates links to other memories. This in turn facilitates an assimilation of the trauma into the individual's schemata for viewing themself and the world in general. A certain category of traumatized persons may have great difficulty in assimilating displaced memories of the experience and thereby in reconstructing a more comprehensive sense of self-representation. In these cases, many clinicians let the person talk about his or her experience in the third person, that is, as if it happened to someone else, and as if he or she had been merely an observer. This procedure does not always yield a detailed description, but it is a suitable first attempt at recall, for example, with victims of rape or sexual abuse for whom shock, shame, and violated integrity bar any sharing of the most intimate details of their traumata.

THE ROLE OF THE INTERVIEWER

Thus far, this chapter has focused on the ability of individuals to retrieve emotionally distressing information. As we have reviewed, explanations for poor recall of such information include first, how the distressing information is organized and stored in memory, which may render some details less accessible than others. Additionally, poor recall may occur as a result of a motivation on the part of the individual to block out memories associated with unbearable psychic pain. Yet, as we have also reviewed, the retrieval context and type of retrieval cues can influence the degree to which distressing information can be recalled. The interviewer, including his or her behavior, is an important component of the retrieval context that cannot be overlooked.

There is a wealth of clinical expertise on how to help traumatized individuals overcome difficulties and readjust following traumatic experiences. Such techniques are equally valuable and applicable for an interviewer outside the clinical realm. Foremost, an interviewee has to be provided with an atmosphere of safety and reassurance. In doing so, adults and children alike may be more willing to confront the trauma in memory and to tell about it in a more consistent and complete fashion. Repeatedly traumatized children, however, may still be held back by poor self-confidence, fear, and a lack of trust in others. They may subsequently shy away from discussion of trauma, thus making their disclosures appear incoherent at times. An adult who was a victim of incest said that "the shame was so overwhelming that the abuse could not be spoken about, no less revisited in my thoughts." One traumatized boy told the police that the reason he had told them so little during the initial interrogations, was that "I had to repair myself, before being able to talk about it" (Svedin & Back, 1996). Many formerly abused children have claimed that they overcame their reluctance to tell about their traumata because they were fortunate enough to be interrogated by 1 or more people who had the strength to hear them out, and most of all believed in them.

Once traumatized adults and children begin to communicate about their ordeals, the interviewer may have to deal with his or her own difficulty in listening to real-life stories that may challenge her or his schemata or outlook on life and the world in general. For instance, the belief that there is a general consensus that children should be provided with love, care, and protection may be threatened and shattered by information that demonstrates how children's dependence on an adult is taken advantage of, in order to exploit, abuse, and degrade these children. This sort of confrontation with a cruel side to reality may evoke emotional reactions, a troubled mind, and a feeling of inadequacy to help on the part of an interviewer. Listening to stories of trauma victims may also trigger memories of negative experiences in an interviewer's life. The interviewer may therefore avoid asking certain necessary questions to avoid reexperiencing awkward feelings. Traumatized individuals, especially adults, may be sensitive to the reactions of others on disclosure and may quickly resume reluctance to share traumatic experiences when others are less than fully supportive. Or perhaps worse, while listening, the interviewer may put inappropriate interpretations of the trauma into the mind of the traumatized individual, which of course may distort the veracity of what the traumatized person has actually recounted (see Hyman & Loftus, chap. 3, this volume). These difficulties may be overcome if the interviewer acquires proper knowledge and training to deal with traumatized persons.

CONCLUDING REMARKS

Over the years the literature has revealed numerous inconsistencies concerning the degree to which emotional events are well or poorly retained in memory. Despite the discrepancies, there are also points of commonality across studies using different methodological approaches. These common points should be useful in guiding our interpretations of speculative judgments and scientific facts. As stated by Christianson, Goodman, and Loftus (1992) in a discussion of the use of pychologists as expert witnesses in court proceedings, "Even if the experts do not resolve issues such as the impact of postevent information or of stress on memory for the jury, at least they provided the background necessary for the jury to begin to evaluate the potential impact of these factors on eyewitness memory" (p. 237). We concur with these points, and we would like to see continued research efforts designed to understand the degree to which individuals can and cannot recall traumatic experiences, and the conditions that lead to their enhanced or poor memories.

REFERENCES

Bower, G. H. (1981). Mood and memory. *American Psychologist, 36*, 129–148.

Brewin, C. R. (1989). Cognitive change processes in psychotherapy. *Psychological Review, 96*, 379–394.

Brewin, C. R., Dalgleish, T., & Joseph, S. (1996). A dual representation theory of posttraumatic stress disorder. *Psychological Review, 103*, 670–686.

Christianson, S.-Å. (1984). The relationship between induced emotional arousal and amnesia. *Scandinavian Journal of Psychology, 25*, 147–160.

Christianson, S.-Å. (1992). *The handbook of emotion and memory: Research and theory.* Hillsdale, NJ: Lawrence Erlbaum Associates.

Christianson, S.-Å. (1996). *Rättspsykologi: Den forensiska psykologin i Sverige – en kunskapsöversikt* [Forensic psychology in Sweden: An overview]. Centraltryckeriet, Borås: Natur och Kultur.

Christianson, S.-Å., Goodman, J., & Loftus, E. F. (1992). Eyewitness memory for stressful events: Methodological quanderies and ethical dilemmas. In S.-Å. Christianson (Ed.), *The handbook of emotion and memory: Research and theory* (pp. 217–241). Hillsdale, NJ: Lawrence Erlbaum Associates.

Christianson, S.-Å., & Loftus, E. F. (1987). Memory for traumatic events. *Applied Cognitive Psychology, 1*, 225–239.

Christianson, S.-Å., & Loftus, E. F. (1990). Some characteristics of people's traumatic memories. *Bulletin of the Psychonomic Society, 28*, 195–198.

Christianson, S.-Å., & Mjörndal, T. (1985). Adrenalin, emotional arousal, and memory. *Scandinavian Journal of Psychology, 26*, 237–248.

Christianson, S.-Å., & Nilsson, L.-G. (1984). Functional amnesia as induced by a psychological trauma. *Memory and Cognition, 12*, 142–155.

Christianson, S.-Å., & Nilsson, L.-G. (1989). Hysterical amnesia: A case of aversively motivated isolation of memory. In T. Archer & L.-G. Nilsson (Eds.), *Aversion, avoidance, and anxiety: Perspectives on aversively motivated behavior* (pp. 289–310). Hillsdale, NJ: Lawrence Erlbaum Associates.

Christianson, S.-Å., Nilsson, L.-G., Mjörndal, T., Perris, C., & Tjelldén, G. (1986). Psychological versus physiological determinants of emotional arousal and its relationship to laboratory amnesia. *Scandinavian Journal of Psychology, 27,* 301–312.

Clugnet, M. C., & LeDoux, J. E. (1990). Synaptic plasticity in fear conditioning circuits: Induction of LTP in the lateral nucleus of the amygdala by stimulation of the medial geniculate body. *Journal of Neuroscience, 10,* 2818–2824.

Conway, M. A. (1992). A structural model of autobiographical memory. In M. A. Conway, D. C. Rubin, H. Spinnler, & W. A. Wagenaar (Eds.), *Theoretical perspectives on autobiographical memory* (pp. 167–194). Dordrecht, Netherlands: Kluwer.

Cutler, B. L., Penrod, S. D., & Martens, T. K. (1987). The reliability of eyewitness identification: The role of system and estimator variables. *Law and Human Behavior, 11,* 233–258.

Damasio, A. R. (1994). *Descartes' error: Emotion, reason and the human brain.* Chatham, Kent, England: Mackays.

de L Horne, D. (1993). Traumatic stress reactions to motor vehicle accidents. In J. P. Wilson & B. Raphael (Eds.), *International handbook of traumatic stress syndromes* (pp. 499–506). New York: Plenum.

De Renzi, E., Liotti, M., & Nichelli, N. (1987). Semantic amnesia with preservation of autobiographical memory. A case report. *Cortex, 23,* 575–597.

Detterman, D. K. (1975). The von Restorff effect and induced amnesia: Production by manipulation of sound intensity. *Journal of Experimental Psychology: Human Learning and Memory, 1,* 614–628.

Domb, Y., & Beaman, K. (1991). Mr. X—A case of amnesia. *British Journal of Psychiatry, 158,* 423–425.

Dyregrov, A. (1992). *Katastrofpsykology.* Lund, Sweden: Studentlitteratur.

Easterbrook, J. A. (1959). The effect of emotion on cue utilization and the organization of behavior. *Psychological Review, 66,* 183–201.

Engelberg, E., & Christianson, S.-Å. (2000). Recall of unpleasant emotion using the memory-enhancing principles. *Psychology, Crime, and Law, 6,* 99–112.

Erdelyi, M. H., & Goldberg, B. (1979). Let's not sweep repression under the rug: Toward a cognitive psychology of repression. In J. F. Kihlstrom & F. J. Evans (Eds.), *Functional disorders of memory* (pp. 355–402). Hillsdale, NJ: Lawrence Erlbaum Associates.

Fisher, R. P., & Geiselman, R. E. (1992). *Memory-enhancing techniques for investigative interviewing.* Springfield, IL: Charles C. Thomas.

Goodman, G., Hepps, D. H., & Reed, R. S. (1986). The child victim's testimony. In A. Haralamic (Ed.), *New issues for child advocates.* Phoenix: Arizona Council of Attorneys for Children.

Goodman, G., Quas, J. A., Batterman-Faunce, J. M., Riddlesberger, M. M., & Kuhn, J. (1996). Predictors of accurate and inaccurate memories of traumatic events experienced in childhood. In K. Pedzek & W. P. Banks (Eds.), *The recovered memory/false memory debate* (pp. 3–28). San Diego: Academic Press.

Graf, P., & Schacter, D. L. (1985). Implicit and explicit memory for new associations in normal and amnesic subjects. *Journal of Experimental Psychology: Learning, Memory, and Cognition, 11,* 501–518.

Greenberg, M. S., & Beck, A. T. (1989). Depression versus anxiety: A test of the content-specificity hypothesis. *Journal of Abnormal Psychology, 98,* 9–13.

Hansen, C. H., & Hansen, R. D. (1988). Finding the face in the crowd: An anger superiority effect. *Journal of Personality and Social Psychology, 54,* 917–924.

Hartman, C. R., & Burgess, A. W. (1993). Treatment of victims of rape trauma. In J. P. Wilson & B. Raphael (Eds.), *International handbook of traumatic stress syndromes* (pp. 507–516). New York: Plenum.

Heuer, F. (1987). *Remembering detail: The role of emotion in long-term memory.* Unpublished doctoral dissertation, New School for Social Research, New York.

Heuer, F., & Reisberg, D. (1990). Vivid memories of emotional events: The accuracy of remembered minutiae. *Memory and Cognition, 18,* 496–506.

Heuer, F., & Reisberg, D. (1992). Emotion, arousal, and memory for detail. In S.-Å. Christianson (Ed.), *The handbook of emotion and memory: Research and theory* (pp. 151–180). Hillsdale, NJ: Lawrence Erlbaum Associates.

Horowitz, M. J., & Reidbord, S. P. (1992). Memory, emotion, and response to trauma. In S.-Å. Christianson (Ed.), *Handbook of emotion and memory: Research and theory* (pp. 343–358). Hillsdale, NJ: Lawrence Erlbaum Associates.

Hosch, H. M., & Bothwell, R. K. (1990). Arousal, description, and identification accuracy of victims and bystanders. *Journal of Social Behavior and Personality, 5,* 481–488.

Howe, M. L., Courage, M. L., & Peterson, C. (1994). How can I remember when "I" wasn't there: Long-term retention of traumatic experiences and emergence of the cognitive self. *Consciousness and Cognition, 3,* 327–354.

Isen, A. M., Shalker, T. E., Clark, M., & Carp, L. (1987). Affect, accessibility of material in memory and behavior: A cognitive loop. *Journal of Personality and Social Psychology, 36,* 1–12.

Janet, P. (1893). Continuous amnesia. *Revue Generale des Sciences, 4,* 167–179.

Johnson, M. K., Kim, J. K., & Risse, G. (1985). Do alcoholic Korsakoff's syndrome patients acquire affective reactions? *Journal of Experimental Psychology: Learning, Memory, and Cognition, 11,* 22–36.

Johnson, M. K., & Multhaup, K. S. (1992). Emotion and MEM. In S.-Å Christianson (Ed.), *The handbook of emotion and memory: Research and theory* (pp. 67–92). Hillsdale, NJ: Lawrence Erlbaum Associates.

Johnson, M. K., Nolde, S. F., & De Leornadis, D. M. (1996). Emotional focus and source monitoring. *Journal of Memory and Language, 35,* 461–462.

Karlsson, I., & Christianson, S.-Å. (1999). *Polisers minnen av traumatiska upplevelser i tjänsten.* Unpublished manuscript.

Kebeck, G., & Lohaus, A. (1986). Effect of emotional arousal on free recall of complex material. *Perceptual and Motor Skills, 63,* 461–462.

Kihlstrom, J. F. (1995). Memory and consciousness: An appreciation of claparéde and recognition et moïtè. *Consciousness and Cognition, 4,* 379–386.

Kopelman, M. D., Christensen, H., Puffett, A., & Stanhope, N. (1994). The great escape: A neurospsychological study of psychogenic amensia. *Neuropsychologia, 32,* 675–691.

Kramer, T. H., Buckhout, R., Fox, P., Widman, E., & Tusche, B. (1991). Effects of stress on recall. *Applied Cognitive Psychology, 5,* 483–488.

LeDoux, J. E. (1991). Systems and synapses of emotional memory. In L. Squire, N. M. Weinberger, G. Lynch, & J. L. McGaugh (Eds.), *Memory: Organization and locus of change* (pp. 205–216). New York: Oxford University Press.

LeDoux, J. E. (1992). Emotion as memory: Anatomical systems underlying indelible neural traces. In S.-Å. Christianson (Ed.), *The handbook of emotion and memory: Research and theory* (pp. 269–288). Hillsdale, NJ: Lawrence Erlbaum Associates.

LeDoux, J. E. (1996). *The emotional brain: The mysterious underpinnings of emotional life.* New York: Simon & Schuster.

Liwag, M., & Stein, N. (1995). Children's memory for emotional events: The importance of emotion-related retrieval cues. *Journal of Experimental Child Psychology, 60,* 2–31.

Loftus, E. F., & Burns, T. E. (1982). Mental shock can produce retrograde amnesia. *Memory and Cognition, 10,* 318–323.

Loftus, E. F., Loftus, G. R., & Messo, J. (1987). Some facts about "weapon focus." *Law and Human Behavior, 11,* 55–62.

Maass, A., & Kohnken, G. (1989). Eyewitness identificiation: Simulating the "weapon effect." *Law and Human Behavior, 13,* 397–408.

McMurran, K. (1988, November 14). Memoir of a brief time in hell. *People Weekly,* 154–160.

McNally, R. J., Foa, E. B., & Donnell, C. D. (1989). Memory bias for anxiety information in patients with panic disorder. *Cognition and Emotion, 3,* 27–44.

Mogg, K., Mathews, A., & Weinman, J. (1987). Memory bias in cinical anxiety. *Journal of Abnormal Psychology, 96,* 94–98.

Nader, K., & Pynoos, R. S. (1990). Drawing and play in the diagnosis and assessment of childhood post-traumatic stress syndromes. In C. Schaeffer (Ed.), *Play, diagnosis, and assessment* (pp. 375–389). New York: Wiley.

Öhman, A., Dimberg, U., & Esteves, F. (1989). Preattentive activation of aversive emotions. In T. Archer & L.-G. Nilsson (Eds.), *Aversion, avoidance, and anxiety* (pp. 169–193). Hillsdale, NJ: Lawrence Erlbaum Associates.

Payne, D. G. (1987). Hypermnesia and reminiscence in recall: A historical and empirical review. *Psychological Bulletin, 101,* 5–27.

Pennebaker, J. W. (1988). Confiding traumatic experiences and health. In S. Fisher & J. Reason (Eds.), *Handbook of life stress, cognition, and health* (pp. 669–682). Chichester, England: Wiley.

Pennebaker, J. W. (1997). Writing about emotional experiences as a therapeutic process. *Psychological Science, 8,* 162–166.

Putnam, F. W. (1997). *Dissociation in children and adolescents: A developmental perspective.* New York: Guilford.

Pynoos, R., & Eth, S. (1986). Witness to violence: The child interview. *Journal of the American Academy of Child Psychiatry, 25,* 306–319.

Rogan, M. T., Staubli, U. V., & LeDoux, J. E. (1997). Fear conditioning induces associative long-term potentiation in the amygdala. *Nature, 11,* 604–607.

Schacter, D. L. (1987). Implicit memory: History and current status. *Journal of Experimental Psychology: Learning, Memory, and Cognition, 13,* 501–518.

Schacter, D. L., Wang, P. L., Tulving, E., & Freedman, M. (1982). Functional retrograde amnesia: a quantitative case study. *Neuropsychologia, 20,* 523–532.

Scrivner, E., & Safer, M. A. (1988). Eyewitnesses show hypermnesia for details about a violent event. *Journal of Applied Psychology, 73,* 371–377.

Squire, L. (1995). Biological foundations of accuracy and inaccuracy in memory. In D. L. Schacter (Ed.), *Memory distortions: How minds, brains, and societies reconstruct the past* (pp. 197–225). Cambridge, MA: Harvard University Press.

Svedin, S., & Back, M. (1996). *Barn som inte berättar: Om att utnyttjas i barnpornografi.* Scandbook, Falun: Rädda Barnen.

Terr, L. (1990). *Too scared to cry: Psychic trauma in childhood.* New York: Harper & Row.

Terr, L. (1994). *Unchained memories.* New York: Basic Books.

Teyler, T. J., & DiScenna, P. (1987). Long-term potentiation. *Annual Review of Neuroscience, 10,* 131–161.

Tobias, B. A., Kihlstrom, J. F., & Schacter, D. L. (1992). Emotion and implicit memory. In S.-Å. Christianson (Ed.), *The handbook of emotion and memory: Research and theory* (pp. 67–92). Hillsdale, NJ: Lawrence Erlbaum Associates.

Tulving, E. (1987). Multiple memory systems and consciousness. *Human Neurobiology, 6,* 67–80.

van der Kolk, B. A., & van der Hart, O. (1989). Pierre Janet and the breakdown of adaptation in psychological trauma. *American Journal of Psychiatry, 146,* 1530–1540.

Vandermaas, M. O., Hess, T. M., & Baker-Ward, L. (1992). Does anxiety affect children's reports of memory for a stressful event? *Journal of Applied Psychology, 7,* 109–128.

Wessel, I., & Merckelbach, H. (1994). Characteristics of traumatic memories in normal subjects. *Behavioural and Cognitive Psychotherapy, 22,* 315–324.

Yuille, J. C., & Tollestrup, P. A. (1992). In S.-Å Christianson (Ed.), *The handbook of emotion and memory: Research and theory* (pp. 201–216). Hillsdale, NJ: Lawrence Erlbaum Associates.

Zuroff, D. C., Colussy, S. A., & Wielgus, M. S. (1983). Selective memory and depression: A cautionary note concerning response bias. *Cognitive Therapy and Research,* 223–232.

7

Memory for Traumatic Events in Children and Adults

Kathy Pezdek
Jennifer Taylor
Claremont Graduate University

> *If we stop remembering, we stop being.*
>
> —Elie Wiesel (1985)

One of the major tenets of psychotherapy is the principle that traumatic experiences have long-term effects on individuals (Freud, 1915/1957). Few clinical psychologists, trauma researchers, or victims of trauma question this principle. As an impressive example of this, Elie Wiesel, Nobel Laureate and holocaust survivor of Auschwitz and Buchenwald, has devoted his life to the importance of preserving the traumatic memories of human history. Recently, however, cognitive psychologists have begun to explore a different aspect of the trauma, that is, the accuracy of memories for traumatic events. Without doubting that traumatic events have long-term effects, these researchers seek to understand if memory for traumatic events functions similarly to memory for nontraumatic events, and if these two types of memories have similar characteristics. Understanding the nature of memory for traumatic events is important because it provides a basis from which to evaluate the veracity of individuals' traumatic recollections. This intriguing notion, that although traumatic events might have a significant long-term effect on an individual, the individual may not retain an extensive veridical memory for the original traumatic event, is the focus of this chapter.

Researchers have addressed a different situation involving memory for traumatic events. This occurs when an individual has no access to his or her memory following a traumatic event. This phenomenon is known as *dissociative* or *retrograde amnesia* (two forms of psychogenic amnesia) and is associated with the recent debates regarding the repression and subsequent recovery of traumatic memories (for summaries of this issue, see Loftus, 1993; Pezdek, 1994; Pezdek & Banks, 1996). In a recent discussion, Arrigo and Pezdek (1998) presented six classes of events (in addition to childhood sexual abuse) that have been documented as sources of psychogenic amnesia. However, in this chapter neither amnesia for traumatic events nor posttraumatic stress disorder (PTSD) symptoms are discussed.

This chapter addresses situations in which individuals do have at least some access to their memory for a traumatic event and can recall aspects of the event. Whether this memory is likely to be accurate and whether it shares features with memory for nontraumatic events are discussed. If similar processes operate on memory for traumatic and nontraumatic events, then the wealth of research currently available on everyday memory for nontraumatic events should apply to memory for traumatic events as well. If not, new memory models need to be developed to address memory for traumatic events.

In this chapter, research and case studies on memory for salient traumatic events are presented. This is not intended to be a comprehensive review of the literature on this topic. Rather, we present a representative sample of the more recent research on memory for salient traumatic events. The studies discussed concern incidents in which a traumatic event is remembered, and researchers have assessed characteristics of memory for the event. Although this chapter primarily addresses children's memories for traumatic events, several important studies that involve adults' memories are also included. The inclusion of adult studies as well as studies of children allows a broader treatment of the question, "Are memories for traumatic events similar to normal nontraumatic memories?"

The first set of studies discussed addresses memory for medical procedures. As a point of comparison, we begin with a discussion of several studies that involve memory for routine medical procedures that although anxiety arousing, do not qualify as truly traumatic. This is followed by a discussion of research on memory for traumatic medical procedures. Subsequent sections present research on memory for disasters, violent events, and childhood sexual abuse. We conclude with a discussion of the lessons that can be gleaned from the research on memory for such a wide range of salient traumatic events. These lessons focus on the question: Does memory for traumatic events follow the same cognitive principles as memory for distinctive nontraumatic events?

MEMORY FOR ROUTINE MEDICAL PROCEDURES

Motivated by an interest in studying children's memory for salient events that occur in the course of everyday lives, Baker-Ward, Gordon, Ornstein, Larus, and Clubb (1993) examined the recall of 3-, 5-, and 7-year-old children for a well-child checkup. The children were tested either immediately after the procedure, or 1, 3, or 6 weeks later. The physicians and nurses completed a checklist for each child against which each child's subsequent memory was compared. Although recall accuracy was impressive in the initial interview (the percentage of the features of the physical examination recalled was 75.1% for 3-year-olds, 82.2% for 5-year-olds, and 92.2% for 7-year-olds), the recall differences between each age group were significant. Also, with increasing time delay, the expected forgetting of features from physical examination occurred, with the forgetting rate significantly higher for the 3-year-olds than for children in the two older groups. In terms of children's responses to questions about features that were not actually part of the physical exam, the overall false alarm rate was well below chance; however, the 3-year-olds were significantly more likely to false alarm to these features (probability of a false alarm in the initial test condition = .24) than were the 5-year-olds (.06) and 7-year-olds (.09).

Children's memory for a physical examination that included a more stressful feature was examined in four experiments reported by Goodman, Hirschman, Hepps, and Rudy (1991). In this study, children were videotaped at a health clinic during a physical examination that included venipuncture or an inoculation. A control group participated in the same procedure at the same clinic, but without the venipuncture or inoculation. Children ranged in age from 3 to 7 years old. After delays as short as 2 to 3 days, or as long as 1 year later, free-recall and specific and misleading questions were used to assess children's memory for the person who administered the examination, the room where it was given, and the actions that were involved. The amount of information freely recalled was not voluminous (mean number of units recalled was about 3 to 4 across the four experiments); however recall output was accurate (recall of inaccurate details was rare at any age). Although the amount and accuracy of recall did not differ by age, older children answered specific and misleading questions more accurately than younger children. To examine the effect of stress on memory, research assistants observed the child during the exam and rated the child's stress levels at various time points. Overall, stress levels were not significantly correlated with memory performance, except for children who exhibited high levels of stress. These children recalled more information and resisted suggestive questions more frequently than children who were observed to have experienced lower levels of stress.

Saywitz, Goodman, Nicholas, and Moan (1991) conducted a similar investigation of children's memory for a medical examination, but in their study, for half of the 5- and 7-year-old children, the procedure included an embarrassing and salient feature, an external genital/anal exam. One week or 1 month later, the children's memories were tested. Surprisingly, of the 36 children in the genital/anal condition, 28 (77.8%) did not mention the genital touching in an open-ended free recall test, and 30 children (83%) did not demonstrate genital/anal touching even when an anatomically detailed doll was provided to assist recall. Only when the interviewer pointed to the vaginal/anal area of the doll and asked, "Did the doctor touch you here?" did all but five of the children (86.1 %) finally disclose the experience. A different group of 36 children received a physical examination for scoliosis that did not include anal/genital touching. Only three children in this condition (8%) falsely reported genital/anal touching, even when the leading question previously mentioned was asked.

The finding that 86% of the children in the anal/genital touching condition eventually responded "yes" to the leading question, compared to only 8% of the children in the comparison condition who made false reports, suggests that when a child's physical examination included an embarrassing and salient feature (in this case, anal/genital touching), this feature was likely to be stored in memory. However, the finding that so few children spontaneously recalled this particular aspect of the physical examination even when an anatomically detailed doll was present suggests that this feature was not likely to be accessible to recall without prompting. Alternatively, perhaps children could access this information in memory but did not report the anal/genital touching because they were embarrassed to do so. Although it is not possible to differentiate between these two interpretations of the results, it is nonetheless clear that this salient feature of the medical examination was not omitted from memory.

While the results of Saywitz et al. (1991) may seem surprising, these findings are consistent with the schema-based notion of memory. For example, Brewer and Treyens (1981) asked participants to wait in a graduate student's office that included some items that were strongly associated with an office (desk, chairs, typewriter—remember, it was 1981!) and some items that were weakly associated with an office (wine bottle, skull, picnic basket). When participants were later asked to recall everything they could remember from the office, the strongly associated items were more likely to be recalled; few participants recalled the weakly associated items. This is exactly what would be predicted if participants were using their "office schema" to guide subsequent recall. According to this framework, although anal/genital touching may be a relatively more anxiety arousing aspect of a physical exam, it is nonetheless a weakly associated feature of children's schema for visiting a doctor's office as it is not frequently included in a routine doctor's visit. Thus, although this feature is likely to be retained in memory, it is less likely to be cued by children's schema for a doctor's visit, and is less likely to be recalled. This finding, along with relevant results from studies that follow, provides an argument for why unprompted recall would not be expected to be an effective memory assessment tool in real-world interviews of children.

The schema-based notion of memory can account for why unusual aspects of a routine event may not be recalled. However, what do we know about people's memory for events about which they do not have a well-developed schema—events about which they have no previous knowledge? Although children develop schemas for the frequently experienced routine events in their life (Nelson, 1986) as well as for traumatic events to which they have repeated exposure, such as cancer treatments (Bearison & Pacifici, 1989), most traumatic events, such as medical emergencies, accidents, and natural disasters, occur infrequently.

MEMORY FOR TRAUMATIC MEDICAL PROCEDURES

A number of researchers have investigated children's memory for an invasive medical procedure known as Voiding Cystourethrogram Fluoroscopy (VCUG). This procedure is used to identify "reflux," a precursor to kidney failure and other urinary tract problems. The VCUG procedure is of particular interest to memory researchers because the procedure involves painful, forced genital contact, and thus presents a physical approximation to sexual assault of a child. In one study of children's memory for the VCUG experience, Merritt, Ornstein, and Spicker (1994) assessed children 41 to 87 months of age. Although a small minority of the children had experienced the VCUG procedure before, none had experienced the VCUG within the previous year. Three major results of this study contrast with results of the parallel studies that have assessed children's memory for routine medical procedures. First, recall of the 21 features of the VCUG was notably high. In an immediately memory test, children correctly recalled 65% of the features in response to open-ended questions, and an additional 23% in response to yes–no questions. The correct rejection rate for features not in the VCUG procedure was also high in both the immediate test ($p = .94$) and 6 weeks later ($p = .93$). Second, there was relatively little forgetting between the initial test session and a 6-week follow-up (60% correct recall in response to open-ended questions and an additional 23% in response to yes–no questions). Third, total recall was only modestly correlated with age ($r = .40, p < .06$); however, this may be a result of the restricted range in the recall output. Although it is difficult to compare the results of studies assessing memory for different events using different test items, nonetheless, these results suggest that children remembered the VCUG procedure better, and not worse, than routine medical procedures.

Goodman, Quas, Batterman-Faunce, Riddlesberger, and Kuhn (1996) specifically probed factors that relate to the accuracy of children's recall for the VCUG procedure. Forty-six children, ranging in age from 3 to 10, were tested on their memory for the VCUG between 6 and 27 days after the procedure. Consistent with previous studies, age differences in memory resulted; 3- to 4-year-old children recalled less, answered fewer questions correctly, and made more commission and omission errors than the older children. Also consistent with previous research, in this case research concerning the social construction of autobiographical memory (see, e.g., Nelson, 1993; Tessler & Nelson, 1996), Goodman et al. reported significant relations between several aspects of mothers' interactions with their child and children's subsequent memory for the VCUG procedure. Children whose mothers did not sympathetically talk with them or physically comfort them after the procedure recalled significantly more incorrect information in free recall and made significantly more commission errors to misleading questions. Children whose mothers did not discuss or explain the VCUG procedure to their child also made more commission errors to misleading questions. These important findings suggest interpersonal factors that mediate the accuracy of memory for traumatic events.

In the sample studied by Goodman et al. (1996), 63% of the children (n = 29) had received only one VCUG procedure in their life, 17% ($n = 8$) had received two VCUGs and 20% ($n = 9$) had received more than two VCUGS. Given that repeated experience with an event increases schema development for the event, it is particularly interesting to examine memory accuracy as a function of previous experience. The main effect of number of VCUGs was not significant on any of the memory measures, including amount and accuracy of free recall and accuracy of responses to specific and misleading questions. However, it would not be expected that children would develop schematized memory for an event that had been experienced only once or twice, and few of the children, only 20%, had experienced the VCUG more than two previous times. Also, the VCUG procedure is not repeated on children within a short time interval, so perhaps the memory for this procedure is more gradually schematized than is memory for procedures that are repeated within shorter time intervals such as treatments for cancer (Bearison & Pacifici, 1989).

In a similar study by Pipe et al. (1997), memory for the VCUG procedure was assessed following longer delays. Children ranging in age at the time of the VCUG from 29 months to 95 months were interviewed at delay intervals ranging from 9 months to 69 months. Compared to the children who were 4 years of age or older when they underwent the VCUG, children who were younger than 4 at the time of the VCUG were less likely to remember the procedure and were less accurate in their recall. In addition, the delay between the VCUG and the memory interview did not predict children's memory. This is one of the few studies that has assessed children's memory for a traumatic medical procedure over delay intervals of more than 6 weeks, and the results suggest that little additional information is lost from memory during the longer delay intervals.

Another study that compared children's recall for a traumatic event over long delays is that of Howe, Courage, and Peterson (1996). In this program of research, children's memory was assessed for accidents that led to emergency room treatment. These were naturally occurring traumatic events and as such, they occurred one time only and prior conversations with parents were precluded. Parents of 25 children brought to an emergency room for treatment were interviewed by the experimenter. The children ranged in age from 17 months to 66 months old. Immediately following treatment, children and their parents were interviewed about the events surrounding the incident. The interview consisted of free recall followed by a standardized cued-recall segment. Approximately 6 months later, the children were interviewed a second time using the same procedure.

Two major results followed from this research. First, because the age range of the children in this study was greater than that in previous studies, the results of this study can be used to assess the predictions of infantile amnesia. Howe et al. (1996) reported that children under 24 months of age at the time of the incident were not able to provide coherent accounts of what happened, using either free-recall or cued-recall techniques. These younger children remembered that they had been involved in an accident, and they could recall some of the global features of this accident. However, their narrative accounts were fragmented and incomplete. The researchers interpreted this result as evidence that the development of a concept of self is prerequisite to accurate autobiographical memory, and because a concept of self is not in place until approximately 24 months of age, this is the age at which accurate accounts of autobiographical memory begin to be evident.

The second major finding in the study by Howe et al. (1996) is that, for children older than 24 months of age, recall accuracy was quite high and commission errors were rare, even when prompts were used in open-ended cued recall. Further, although cued and free recall of peripheral details declined over the 6 month course of the study, memory for central details did not significantly decline over time.

In a separate report of the children just described, Howe, Courage, and Peterson (1995) examined changes in the rate of intrusion errors over time as a function of the children's age at the time of the accident. This comparison is of interest because although it has been reported in other studies that intrusion errors increase with the length of the retention interval

(Flin, Boon, Knox, & Bull, 1992; Poole & White, 1993), this relationship has rarely been examined developmentally and has rarely included preschool age children. Further, it is important to examine the rate of spontaneous *intrusion errors* that occur in the absence of misleading or suggestive circumstances. Intrusion errors were defined in this study as recall of details from a different traumatic event, and thus reflect children's confusion between events that are semantically and affectively related. Overall, intrusion rates in this study were higher in the 6 month test than in the immediate test, but this difference was significant only for the youngest age group (M = 30 months), and not for the other two age groups (M = 36 months and 48 months). This finding suggests that children's tendency to confuse two traumatic events with the passage of time is of concern primarily for preschool children younger than 3 years of age.

MEMORY FOR DISASTERS

Memory for natural disasters was extensively studied after Hurricane Andrew, a devastating storm that struck the Florida coast on August 24, 1992. Bahrick, Parker, Fivush, and Levitt (in press) interviewed 3- and 4-year-old children about their experiences during the hurricane between 2 and 6 months after the event. Children's recall for the hurricane was detailed and highly accurate. By comparison, in a study conducted by Hamond and Fivush (1990), children recalled significantly more information about Hurricane Andrew (about 100 correct propositions) than comparable aged children who recalled a family visit to Disneyland (about 40 correct propositions). In addition, 4-year-olds recalled more correct information than 3-year-olds, and children's memory did not linearly vary as a function the retention interval; the children who were interviewed 6 months after the hurricane did not recall less than those interviewed 2 months after the hurricane. However, in this study, children who experienced more objective damage from the hurricane, in terms of damage to their home, recalled less than did children who experienced less severe damage.

Memory for the personal consequences of a natural disaster has also been studied by Neisser et al. (1996). In this study, adults' memory for the 1989 Loma Prieta earthquake was assessed immediately following the earthquake and 1½ years later. Of primary interest in this study was a comparison of recall by participants in San Francisco and Santa Cruz at the time of the earthquake (the direct experience groups) with those in Atlanta at the time of the earthquake (the observers). The California participants, who experienced the earthquake directly, remembered significantly more information 1½ years later than those who heard about the earthquake indirectly. Further, within the San Francisco and Santa Cruz samples, memory was also tested for how participants learned about the collapse of the upper deck of the Bay Bridge, an event that was widely reported on the news, but not directly observed by any of the participants. Memory for the details of how they learned about the collapse of the bridge was more poorly retained after 1½ years delay than were similar details for directly experienced aspects of the earthquake.

A similar comparison was made in a study by Terr et al. (1996) of children's memory for the Challenger explosion on January 28, 1986. Memory for this disaster was assessed in two groups of children. The high involvement group included 8- and 15-year-old children from Concord, New Hampshire, where Christa McAuliffe had taught prior to joining the Challenger crew. The low involvement group included age-matched children from a control school in Porterville, California. In terms of both the quality of memory for the explosion itself, and memory for the personal experiences of the participant on hearing of the explosion, performance was significantly better in the high involvement group than in the low involvement group, both in 1986 and 1 year later.

These results are similar to the findings reported by Yuille and Cutshall (1986) in a case study of eyewitness memory of an actual crime. In this study, 13 adults who were eyewitnesses to a shooting incident were interviewed shortly afterward by police officers and 4 to 5 months later by the researchers. Witness accounts showed little decline in accuracy over the 5-month delay interval, and witnesses more involved in the incident remembered more accurate information than those less involved. The 5 eyewitnesses with the highest involvement in the shooting had direct contact with either the thief, the storeowner who eventually shot the perpetrator, or a weapon used in the shooting.

Together, these results assessing memory for upsetting or traumatic events, along with similar findings by Rudy and Goodman (1991) assessing memory for a nontraumatic event, suggest that participation in an event produces better memory for the event than indirectly observing the event. One interpretation of this finding is that people have better constructed narratives for events that they directly experience than for events that they only learn about second hand, and memories are better preserved if they are coherent and well structured. Also, the recall of specific features of an event is more likely to cue related features of that event if the features are stored in a well-structured form in memory.

These results also highlight the need to differentiater in the research between the personal salience of or involvement in an event and the extent to which the event is truly traumatic. Although Terr et al. (1996) and Neisser et al. (1996) reported that personally salient events were better remembered than less salient events, the results of Bahrick et al. (in press) suggest that, for events that more closely approximate traumatic ones, memory correlates negatively with degree of trauma—the greater the destruction to a child's own home, the less he or she recalled about Hurricane Andrew. Clearly additional research is necessary to clarify this issue by focusing on research that involves truly traumatic events and not simply upsetting events. In the next section, research is discussed that considers memory for traumatic events.

MEMORY FOR VIOLENT EVENTS

Several researchers interested in memory for personally salient events have studied memories for violent events. To begin with an extreme case, Wagenaar and Groeneweg (1990) studied memories of 78 survivors of a Nazi concentration camp. In this study, the researchers compared transcripts of interviews with the survivors at two points in time regarding their experiences in Camp Erika. The first interviews were collected between 1943 and 1948. The second interviews were collected between 1984 and 1987 in connection with the trial of Marinus De Rijke for Nazi war crimes. The survivors were in their mid-20s during their stay in Camp Erika and in their mid-60s when interviewed the second time.

The major results involved the quality of retention over the 40-year period of study. Although most of the survivors could recognize a picture of De Rijke taken in the camp, and they remembered the date on which they entered the camp, De Rijke's name, and their camp registration number, there were many notable voids in memory. Three of the survivors who described in their early interview how they had been maltreated or tortured by De Rijke, could not remember his name 40 years later. Forty-two percent of the survivors (5 out of 12) who had not seen De Rijke's picture on television during the intervening years since 1947 could not recognize a photograph of him taken in the camp. Some survivors forgot and even denied ever having remembered observing other extreme incidents including being tortured and maltreated by De Rijke themselves and watching fellow prisoners being maltreated until they died by drowning, flogging, or beating.

The results of Wagenaar and Groeneweg (1990) make it clear that memories for extreme traumatic events are not impervious to forgetting, even forgetting of salient and disturbing aspects of the experience. Although these findings might be attributed to aging effects, as people at the time of the second interview were in their mid-60s, other interpretations of these results seem more compelling. For example, it is well established that active attempts to inhibit retrieval of information from memory can reduce access to that information (Anderson, Bjork, & Bjork, 1994). This phenomenon is known as *retrieval induced forgetting*. Because it is likely that Nazi concentration camp survivors did not want to continue to think about their concentration camp experiences and relive these events in their memory, they may have actively attempted to inhibit retrieval of this information, and just "not go there" in their memory. This might explain why memory for even highly salient aspects of their concentration camp experience were not accessible to some survivors 40 years after their release from the camp.

But what about memory for a single, time-limited traumatic event that is violent or devastating? One such incident has been extensively studied by Lenore Terr. This is the kidnapping for 24 hours of 26 school children from their school bus on July 15, 1976 in Chowchilla, California. Terr compared the children's memory for the event immediately after the incident in addition to 1 and 5 years later. The major finding was that the children retained accurate memory for the gist of the incident over the 1-year (Terr, 1979) and 5-year delays (Terr, 1983). There were some consistent patterns of memory inaccuracy, although these tended to involve peripheral information such as the date, time, and duration of the event. These results are consistent with findings reported by Howe, Courage, and Peterson (1996) and support the position that, as with memory for normal events, memory for the peripheral details of traumatic events is more likely to be forgotten over time than is the gist of these memories.

Other single-occurrence violent traumatic events that have been studied include witnessing the homicide of a parent (Pynoos & Eth, 1984) and surviving a sniper attack at school (Pynoos & Nader, 1989). Children studied by Pynoos and Eth (1984) ranged from preschoolers to adolescents. The researchers initially interviewed each child within a few weeks of the murder and compared these accounts with the event as reported throughout the criminal proceedings. Although Pynoos and Eth (1984) reported little empirical data and primarily focused on children's affective reactions to having observed their parent's death, some conclusions regarding memory were noted. The authors reported, "We believe that parental homicide leaves indelible, highly accurate, and detailed visual images" (p. 95). And further, "These children focus on the central action and disregard other details. For example, in one of his accounts, one 3-year-old boy repeated the phrase, 'Daddy squished mommy's neck.' " (p. 92).

Pynoos and Nader (1989) interviewed children who had survived a violent attack. A sniper shot repeated rounds of ammunition at children on a playground at their elementary school. Two people were killed and 14 were injured. The siege lasted for several hours. The major finding was that children who were most endangered during the incident later reported themselves as farther away from deceased or injured persons and somehow safer and more protected than they had actually been. On the other hand, children who were least threatened later reported that they had been closer to the danger and at greater risk than they had been. This reconstructive nature of memory has been well documented in other arenas involving memory for nontraumatic events (see, e.g., the early work of Bartlett, 1932).

MEMORY FOR CHILDHOOD SEXUAL ABUSE

Although numerous studies have examined children's memory for sexual abuse, in only a few of these studies has it been possible to compare memory for the abusive incident with corroborating evidence of what actually happened. However, two prospective studies on memory for sexual abuse have been conducted. In the first, Williams (1994) studied 129 women who in childhood had participated in a study on the immediate consequences of sexual abuse. Detailed medical records documented the abuse. Seventeen years after the abuse, when Williams interviewed them, 38% of these women reported no memory for the target sexually abusive event, despite the fact that more than half of these women reported details of other abusive incidents or other personal and embarrassing events. Further, there was no difference in the rate of not remembering the target abusive event between individuals who were 3 years old or younger as compared with those who were 4 to 6 years of age at the time of the abuse.

Similar findings were reported by Widom and Morris (1997) and Widom and Shepard (1996) from a prospective study of 726 people who had been physically abused, sexually abused, or neglected when they were less than 11 years old. Court records validated the abuse history in each case. A control group was also included. Twenty years later, the researchers interviewed the people regarding their memory for the target events. Only 63% of the individuals who had been sexually abused in childhood reported having had at least one sexual experience before the age of 12. Thus, 37% of the individuals did not appear to remember the target sexually abusive event. Regarding the individuals who had been severely physically abused in childhood, only 60% reported memory for physical abuse when assessed using the Very Severe Violence subscale and 92% reported memory for physical abuse when assessed using the Minor Violence subscale. Although neither Williams (1994), Widom and Morris (1997), nor Widom and Shepard (1996) assessed the accuracy of the specific details in the interview responses they gathered, it is clear that sexual abuse occurring before the age of 12, and to lesser extent physical abuse, is under-reported, at least in part due to the inaccessibility of the resulting memories.

A different experimental approach was utilized in a recent study by Bidrose and Goodman (2000) to study children's memory for documented incidents of sexual abuse. This study took advantage of police records that were available as a result of a situation that occurred in New Zealand. In this case, the police were informed that a man was prostituting young girls. The police located four of the girls; one was age 7, and three were age 12 when the incidents began. Following extensive police interviews of the girls, the police obtained a warrant and searched the alleged perpetrator's home. They located hundreds of photographs and several hundred audiotapes recording sexual acts between the girls and various men. The girl's allegations could then be compared with the photographic and audiotaped evidence.

Of the 246 allegations that were reported in hearings or police interviews, 194 (78.9%) were supported by available evidence and 52 (21.1%) were not supported. More specifically, of the 160 allegations that specifically involved sexual acts, 137 (85.6%) were supported by available evidence. The rate of unsupported allegations could reflect commission errors by the girls, or perhaps the absence of audiotapes or photographs of the encounters. In addition, the researchers reported that many of the audiotapes were difficult to code because they contained unidentifiable sexual activity and involved more than one of the girls. Computed differently, there was evidence for 318 different sexual acts involving the girls, and allegations were made for 194 of these (61%). The remaining 124 (39%) acts were omitted from the girls' reports of what happened. In addition, there were three events that were denied to have occurred, even though the evidence documented their occurrence. These findings suggest an impressive memory for the details of multiple incidents of childhood sexual abuse spanning as much as a 2-year period of time for one of the girls.

Together, these studies suggest that the details of sexual acts that are still part of one's current and ongoing life are likely to be accessible to memory with a high rate of accuracy. However, although adults' memories for childhood sexual abuse are often accurate, they are less likely to be accessible to conscious recollection than are memories for less traumatic events.

CONCLUSIONS: ARE MEMORIES FOR TRAUMATIC EVENTS SIMILAR TO MORE NORMAL MEMORIES?

Although some people portray memory for traumatic events as unusually accurate and highly detailed (see, e.g., Pynoos & Eth, 1984, & Terr, 1988), most of the research reviewed here characterizes memory for traumatic events as generally correct, although by no means perfect, and in many ways similar to memory for more normal nontraumatic events. Based on the research on memory for traumatic events reviewed in this chapter, it is apparent that many characteristics of memory for nontraumatic events apply to memory for traumatic events as well. Thus, when individuals are interviewed about traumatic events, their reported memories are expected to exhibit many of the same qualities as memories for nontraumatic events, and many of the cognitive processes that operate on memory for more normal events apply as well. What are some of these processes?

First, in the research on memory for nontraumatic events, it is well documented that unique or distinctive events are better retained in memory than are nondistinct events. This effect was perhaps first cited by Koffka (1935), in reference to the dissertation results of von Restorff. The *von Restorff effect* refers to the finding that in a list of unrelated words, the distinctive items (i.e., those not semantically related to other words in the list) are learned faster and retained longer than the other items. Although an explanation of this effect has plagued cognitive psychologists (see, e.g., Hunt & McDaniel, 1993), nonetheless, the effect seems to be a robust one. Brewer (1988), for example, reported in an autobiographical memory study that infrequent events and those that occurred in infrequent locations were best recalled.

Disregarding the incidents for which some individuals exhibit amnesia for a hightly traumatic event, the uniqueness effect would explain why events that are wholly unusual or distinctive, such as the traumatic events discussed in this chapter, are predicted to be more accurately retained in memory and subsequently more accessible than more normal nontraumatic events. However, this is a precarious finding because within the context of a particular event, the distinctive features are sometimes weakly associated with the event schema, and as such are less likely to be accessible. This is consistent with reports by Saywitz et al. (1989) regarding memory for the features of a medical examination that involved anal/genital touching and Brewer and Treyens (1981) regarding memory for consistent versus inconsistent items in an office.

A second principle that applies to memory for traumatic and nontraumatic events is the finding that memory for traumatic events is not impervious to the effects of temporal delay that characterize forgetting in normal memory. In most of the studies reported here, with the passage of time the accuracy of recall decreased and the tendency to false alarm to suggested items increased. However, although it is difficult to directly compare forgetting rates for traumatic and nontraumatic events, it appears that the rate of forgetting traumatic events is less steep than the rate of forgetting nontraumatic events. For example, Merritt et al. (1994) reported minimal forgetting of the 21 features of the VCUG procedure between the initial test session and a 6-week follow-up. Likewise, Pipe et al. (1997) tested memory for the VCUG procedure at delay intervals ranging from 9 to 69 months and reported similar low forgetting rates in the short and long delay conditions. One interpretation of this result is based on a finding known as *Jost's Law* (Jost, 1897). According to Jost's Law, the greater the strength of information in memory, the more slowly the memory will decline over time. Thus, because the memory strength for traumatic events is generally greater than the memory strength for nontraumatic events, traumatic events are expected to be forgotten more slowly.

This relationship can also be observed in the results reported by Neisser et al. (1996). When people were tested on their memory for the Loma Prieta earthquake, details of how they learned about the collapse of the Bay Bridge (an event not directly experienced by these individuals) were more likely to be forgotten after 1½ years than were similar details for directly experienced aspects of the earthquake. Because the memory strength for directly experienced events is greater than the memory strength for events not directly experienced, directly experienced events should be more resistant to forgetting over time.

The finding that traumatic events are ordinarily retained at higher levels of memory strength than are nontraumatic events has been related to the effects of adrenaline and related hormones (see McGaugh, 1992, for a review). However, although elevated levels of adrenaline enhance memory, the dose-response curve is an inverted U-shaped function predicted by the Yerkes-Dodson law (Gold, 1987). Accordingly, although moderate levels of adrenaline do enhance memory, when very high levels of adrenaline are released, such as by extreme levels of arousal, memory suffers relative to memory following more modest levels of activation.

A third principle that applies to memory for traumatic and nontraumatic events is the finding that memories for traumatic events show age-related patterns similar to those for memories for nontraumatic events. These age-related patterns show that generally the accuracy of memory and the amount of detail in memory increases with age during childhood. In addition, although the rate of false alarms and commission errors for features of traumatic events is generally low, preschool-age children are more likely to false alarm to information suggested by experimenters than are older children. However, in a number of the reported studies (see, e.g., Pipe et al., 1997) the accuracy of memory did not vary with age. Jost's Law may also apply here. If the memory strength for traumatic events is generally greater than the memory strength for nontraumatic events, then memory for traumatic events should be less likely to decline with decreasing age, and age differences in memory for traumatic events would be less consistent.

A fourth principle that applies to memory for traumatic and non-traumatic events is the finding that the gist of an event is retained in memory more accurately than the peripheral details, and memory for the peripheral details is more likely to decline with the passage of time than is memory for gist. For example, in a study of survivors of a Nazi concentration camp, Wagenaar and Groeneweg (1990) reported that memory for the gist of daily life in the camps remained more accurate (although not flawless) over the 40-year period of the study than did memory for some of the peripheral details of the experience. Similarly, Terr reported accurate gist memory by the children kidnapped from Chowchilla despite less memory and less accurate memory for peripheral details after 1 year (Terr, 1979) and 5 years (Terr, 1983). Also, Howe et al. (1996) reported that, for the children in their study who were older than 24 months of age at the time of a medical emergency, although cued and free recall of peripheral details declined over 6 months, memory for central details did not significantly decline. These findings suggest that memory for both traumatic and nontraumatic events is hierarchically organized with features higher in the hierarchy more likely to resist forgetting with the passage of time.

There is another lesson to be learned from the review of the research on memory for traumatic events that has implications for forensic interviewing. Across several of the studies discussed, unprompted recall was not found to be an effective interview tool. For example, Saywitz et al. (1991) reported that of the 36 children interviewed regarding their memory for a medical examination that involved genital/anal touching, 28 did not mention the genital touching in an open-ended free recall test, and 30 children did not demonstrate genital/anal touching even when an anatomically detailed doll was provided. However, when the interviewer pointed to the genital/anal area of the doll and asked, "Did the doctor touch you here?" all but five of the children disclosed the experience. Although it is possible that the children simply did not report the genital/anal touching because they were embarrassed, an alternative interpretation of this finding is that the genital/anal touching was an unusual feature of a medical examination, and unusual features are not likely to be recalled without prompts or cues.

Further, it is important to note that prompts or cues were not reported to significantly increase the number of commission errors in the studies reviewed. Saywitz et al. (1989) reported that in a different group of 36 children who received a physical examination for scoliosis that did not include anal/genital touching, only three children falsely reported genital/anal touching, even when the leading question previously mentioned was asked. Also, Howe (1996), reported that the use of prompts in open-ended cued recall did not increase the number of commission errors in children interviewed about a medical emergency. The use of additional prompts, however, needs to be differentiated from the use of props, such as dolls, to facilitate memory. These types of cues have been found to increase errors in children's reports under some circumstances, such as those in which leading questions accompany the props' presentation. For an extended discussion of the use of props, such as dolls, see Everson and Boat (chap. 16, this volume).

In conclusion, although some individuals can be amnesiac for some traumatic events, when traumatic events are remembered, these memories are generally accurate and exhibit many of the characteristics of memories for distinctive nontraumatic events. This suggests that special memory mechanisms may not be needed to account for memory for the traumatic events that are remembered. Thus, although traumatic events are likely to have a significant long-term effect on an individual, memory for traumatic events appears to follow the same cognitive principles as memory for distinctive nontraumatic events.

REFERENCES

Anderson, M. C., Bjork, R. A., & Bjork, E. L. (1994). Remembering can cause forgetting: Retrieval dynamics in long-term memory. *Journal of Experimental Psychology: Learning, Memory, and Cognition, 20,* 1063–1087.

Arrigo, J. M., & Pezdek, K. (1998). Lessons from the study of psychogenic amnesia. *Current Directions in Psychological Science, 6,* 148–152.

Bahrick, L. E., Parker, J. F., Fivush, R., & Levitt, M. (in press). The effects of stress on young children's memory for a natural disaster. *Journal of Experimental Psychology: Applied.*

Baker-Ward, L., Gordon, B. N., Ornstein, P. A., Larus, D. M., & Clubb, P. A. (1993). Young children's long-term retention of a pediatric examination. *Child Development, 64,* 1519–1533.

Bartlett, F. C. (1932). *Remembering.* New York: Cambridge University Press.

Bearison, D. J., & Pacifici, C. (1989). Children's event knowledge for cancer treatment. *Journal of Applied and Developmental Psychology, 10,* 469–486.

Bidrose, S., & Goodman, G. S. (2000). Testimony and evidence: A scientific case study of memory for child sexual abuse. *Applied Cognitive Psychology, 14,* 197–213.

Brewer, W. F. (1988). Memory for randomly sampled autobiographical events. In U. Neisser & E. Winograd (Eds.), *Remembering reconsidered: Ecological and traditional approaches to the study of memory* (pp. 21–90). New York: Cambridge University Press.

Brewer, W. F., & Treyens, J. C. (1981). Role of schemata in memory for places. *Cognitive Psychology, 13,* 207–230.

Flin, T., Boon, J., Knox, A., & Bull, R. (1992). The effect of a five-month delay on children's and adults' eyewitness memory. *British Journal of Psychology, 83,* 323–336.

Freud, S. (1957). Repression. In J. Strachey (Ed.), *The standard edition of the complete psychological works of Sigmund Freud* (Vol. 14). London: Hogarth. (Original work published 1915)

Gold, P. E. (1987). Sweet memories. *American Psychologist, 75,* 151–155.

Goodman, G. S., Hirschman, J. E., Hepps, D., & Rudy, L. (1991). Children's memory for stressful events. *Merrill-Palmer Quarterly, 37,* 109–158.

Goodman, G. S., Quas, J. A., Batterman-Faunce, J. M., Riddlesberger, M. M., & Kuhn, J. (1996). Predictors of accurate and inaccurate memories of traumatic events experienced in childhood. In K. Pezdek & W. P. Banks (Eds.), *The recovered memory/false memory debate* (pp. 3–28). San Diego: Academic.

Hamond, N. R., & Fivush, R. (1990). Memories of Mickey Mouse: Young children recount their trip to Disneyland. *Cognitive Development, 6,* 433–448.

Howe, M. L., Courage, M. L., & Peterson, C. (1995). Intrusions in preschoolers' recall of traumatic childhood events. *Psychonomic Bulletin and Review, 2,* 130–134.

Howe, M. L., Courage, M. L., & Peterson, C. (1996). How can I remember when "I" wasn't there: Long-term retention of traumatic experiences and emergence of the cognitive self. In K. Pezdek & W. P. Banks (Eds.), *The recovered memory/false memory debate* (pp. 121–149). San Diego: Academic.

Hunt, R. R., & McDaniel, M. A. (1993). The enigma of organization and distinctiveness. *Journal of Memory and Language, 32,* 421–445.

Jost, A. (1897). Die Assoziationsfestigkeit in ihrer Abbangigkeit von der Verteilung der Wiederholungen. *Zeitschrift fur Psychologie, 14,* 436–473.

Koffka, K. (1935). *Principles of Gestalt psychology.* New York: Harcourt, Brace.

Loftus, E. (1993). The reality of repressed memory. *American Psychologist, 48,* 518–537.

McGaugh, J. L. (1992). Affect, neuromodulatory systems, and memory storage. In S.-A. Christianson (Ed.), *The handbook of emotion and memory* (pp. 245–268). Hillsdale, NJ: Lawrence Erlbaum Associates.

Merritt, K. A., Ornstein, P. A., & Spicker, B. (1994). Children's memory for a salient medical procedure: Implications for testimony. *Pediatrics, 94,* 17–23.

Neisser, U., Winograd, E., Bergman, E. T., Schreiber, C. A., Palmer, S. E., & Weldon, M. S. (1996). Remembering the earthquake: Direct experience vs. hearing the news. *Memory, 4,* 337–357.

Nelson, K. (1986). *Event memory.* Hillsdale, NJ: Lawrence Erlbaum Associates.

Nelson, K. A. (1993). The psychological and social origins of autobiographical memory. *Psychological Science, 4,* 7–14.

Pezdek, K. (1994). The illusion of illusory memory. *Applied Cognitive Psychology, 8,* 339–350.

Pezdek, K., & Banks, W. P. (Eds.). (1996). *The recovered memory/false memory debate.* San Diego: Academic.

Pipe, M.-E., Goodman, G. S., Quas, J., Bidrose, S., Ablin, D., & Craw, S. (1997). Remembering early experiences during childhood. In J. D. Read & D. S. Lindsay (Eds.), *Recollections of trauma: Scientific evidence and clinical practice* (pp. 417–423). New York: Plenum.

Poole, D. A., & White, L. T. (1993). Two years later: Effects of question repetition and retention interval on eyewitness testimony of children and adults. *Developmental Psychology, 29,* 844–853.

Pynoos, R. S., & Eth, S. (1984). The child as witness to homicide. *Journal of Social Issues, 40,* 87–108.

Pynoos, R. S., & Nader, K. (1989). Children's memory and proximity to violence. *Journal of the American Academy of Child and Adolescent Psychiatry, 28,* 236–241.

Rudy, L., & Goodman, G. S. (1991). Effects of participation on children's reports: Implications for children's testimony. *Developmental Psychology, 27,* 527–538.

Saywitz, K., Goodman, G. S., Nicholas, E., & Moan, S. F. (1991). Children's memories of physical examinations involving genital touch: Implications for reports of child sexual abuse. *Journal of Consulting and Clinical Psychology, 59,* 682–691.

Terr, L. (1979). Children of Chowchilla: A study of psychic trauma. *Psychoanalytic Study of the Child, 34,* 547–623.

Terr, L. (1983). Chowchilla revisited: The effects of psychic trauma four years after a schoolbus kidnapping. *American Journal of Psychiatry, 140,* 1543–1550.

Terr, L. (1988). What happens to early memories of trauma? A study of twenty children under age five at the time of documented traumatic events. *Journal of the American Academy of Child and Adolescent Psychiatry, 27,* 96–104.

Terr, L., Bloch, D. A., Michel, B. A., Shi, H., Reinhart, J. A., & Metayer, S. A. (1996). Children's memories in the wake of Challenger. *American Journal of Psychiatry, 153,* 618–625.

Tessler, M., & Nelson, K. (1996). Making memories: The influence of joint encoding and later recall by young children. In K. Pezdek & W. P. Banks (Eds.), *The recovered memory/false memory debate* (pp. 101–120). San Diego: Academic.

Wagenaar, W. A., & Groeneweg, J. (1990). The memory of concentration camp survivors. *Applied Cognitive Psychology, 4,* 77–87.

Widom, C. S., & Morris, S. (1997). Accuracy of adult recollections of childhood victimization: Part 2. Childhood sexual abuse. *Psychological Assessment, 9,* 34–46.

Widom, C. S., & Shepard, R. L. (1996). Accuracy of adult recollections of childhood victimization: Part 1. Childhood physical abuse. *Psychological Assessment, 8,* 412–421.

Wiesel, E. (1985). Let him remember. In E. Abrahamson (Ed.), *Against silence: The voice and vision of Elie Wiesel* (Vol. 1, p. 368). New York: Holocaust Library.

Williams, L. M. (1994). Recall of childhood trauma: A prospective study of women's memories of child sexual abuse. *Journal of Consulting and Clinical Psychology, 62,* 1167–1176.

Yuille, J. C., & Cutshall, J. L. (1986). A case study of eyewitness memory for a crime. *Journal of Applied Psychology, 71,* 291–301.

Sources of Fantastic Elements in Allegations of Abuse by Adults and Children

Constance J. Dalenberg
Karen Z. Hyland
Carlos A. Cuevas
California School of Professional Psychology, San Diego

A pretty 9-year-old girl smiles engagingly at her interviewer. Does the social worker know why she is at Children's Hospital today? No, the interviewer has not been briefed. Well, it is because she murdered a baby yesterday, chopped it to pieces with a knife, and put it into a blender, the girl explains calmly, glancing around the room. The room looks familiar, the child says. Maybe she was here before. She thinks perhaps she came to the hospital when her mother poisoned her father, herself, and her dog.

A 5-year-old boy tearfully recounts his encounter with the man who was alleged to have brutally raped him. The man did rape him, the boy says. He also painted the boy's feet with poison, injected his own penis with drugs, and set fire to it.

While waiting for a trial of a man who allegedly assaulted dozens of children, the purported victims gradually disclose more and more serious abuse. Although most children gave credible descriptions initially, the final accusations include animal mutilation, black magic, rape with objects, and torture. The allegations are judged unbelievable in the light of physical evidence, and the charges are dropped.

Researchers and clinicians from many backgrounds have noted, with some dismay, that a bizarre, improbable, or fantastic element within an allegation of child physical or sexual abuse is not a rare event (Everson, 1997). Recently reversed convictions in high-profile day-care center cases (in which an initially charged defendant was released) have almost uniformly included allegations that most would find questionable, with children reporting attacks by sharks, abuse aboard ships and airplanes, stabbings that leave no marks, or multiple child murders (cf. Ceci & Bruck, 1995). A random sample collected by Dalenberg (1996b) yielded an estimate that 3% of initial allegations of severe abuse by children between the ages of 3 and 17 might include a fantastic element. The 800 interviews transcribed to date were chosen from among 6,000 videotapes that constituted the records of a child protection facility. "Gold standard" cases were randomly chosen from among those children whose abuse was verified by confession, and whose injuries were judged medically consistent with the allegations. Additional evidence was available for over 80% of these cases. "Questionable" cases were randomly chosen from among children whose charts indicated a denial by the perpetrator, contradictory physical evidence, and no supportive medical evidence. All tapes were transcribed and evaluated in a three-stage accuracy check process and a six-stage coding of content and demeanor (with interrater reliabilities on coding categories ranging from .77 to .98). Results indicated that fantastic elements were most frequently found in reports from children ages 4 to 9. Fantastic elements were defined by reference to fantasy figures, by impossible or extremely implausible features of the story (as assessed by raters), and by descriptions of extreme abusive acts that should have been (but were not) supported by external evidence.

Several intuitively derived clinical checklists (e.g., Gardner's, 1995, *Protocols*) include the presence of fantastic elements as indicators of the falsity of the full allegations, an understandable point of view if not an empirically defensible one. Early findings from the previously mentioned research (Dalenberg, 1996b; Dalenberg, Hyland, & Cuevas, 1997) indicated that fantastic elements were statistically associated with severity of true allegations rather than with falsity in general, although the results must be replicated in varying conditions before conclusions can be made with certainty. However, it is clear that implausible details are to be expected within some number of true and false cases, although ratios are unknown, leaving scientifically oriented evaluators frustrated with the loss of one more quick and easy way to sort truth from fiction. Based on an n of 104, the rate of fantastic allegations in the severe gold standard cases among 4- to 9-year-olds was 15.38%. Among severe questionable cases, the rate was 3.85%. Rates in the mild cases ($n = 180$) were under 4%. The probability of fantastic allegations was related to age in that the frequency of children younger than 4 years or older than 9 years making such statements was rare. However, the probability of finding external confirmation was not related to age within the fantastic element group.

Forced back into complexity by the destruction of a beautiful theory by an ugly and disagreeable fact, our team of investigators has studied the demographics, sources, purposes, and correlates of fantastic (highly implausible or impossible) elements in abuse reports. Reality monitoring, an empirically based theory of the manner in which individuals discriminate internally generated from externally perceived events, has been the overall guiding structure for our latest conceptualization and research (cf. Foley, Passalacqua, & Ratner, 1993; Hoffman, 1997; Johnson, 1988). This research centers on the development of the process by which individuals identify the source of a memory (dream, fantasy, overheard or witnessed event, or experienced event).

DIMENSIONS OF REALITY MONITORING

The field of reality monitoring is of obvious relevance to the present issue. Not only has the individual with fantastic beliefs failed in the classic reality monitoring task of discerning perception from internally or externally generated fiction, but he or she has done so in a circumstance in which such discrimination should have been quite simple. In examining why failures occur with such frequency within abuse allegations, it is reasonable to examine the relevance of abuse to the dimensions of reality monitoring presented in Table 8.1. That is, turning to Table 8.2, how might the abuse context (either the accusation or the reality) and other individual difference variables impact: (a) the perceived plausibility of a fantastic element, (b) the awareness or meaning of the context cues to reality, and (c) the phenomenological cues of perception and fantasy for children of varying ages? We first consider intrapsychic issues related to these dimensions, and then address external forces such as suggestion (termed here *reality corruption*).

TABLE 8.1
Reality Monitoring Dimensions

A. The plausibility of the event in reported context
  1. Inherent plausibility of the event
  2. Plausibility of time and space details of memory given other remembered memories
  3. Plausibility of event given other remembered contextual cues
B. The phenomenological match of the event to prototypical internally generated and externally perceived events
  1. Vividness of memory
  2. Perceptual detail
  3. Strength of memory trace
  4. Recollections regarding the cognitive operations that may have produced the event

TABLE 8.2
The Effects of Individual-Difference Variables and Abuse
Context on Reality Monitoring Dimensions

A. What individual-difference variables effect judgments of plausibility of an event?
1. Reality-testing skills
(a) Chronic psychotic or delusional disorders
(b) Acute trauma-related deficits
2. Age-related difference variables
(a) Adequate knowledge
B. How does the abuse context impact the plausibility of other events?
1. Change in world view stemming from abuse
2. Dissociativity as a hindrance to assessment of context
3. Confusion of emotionally similar events
C. How might abuse impact the phenomenology of real and fantasized events?
1. Dissociativity as a hindrance to reality monitoring
2. Increased likeness in the phenomenology of real and fantasy worlds
(a) Increase in vivid nightmares
(b) Increased saliency of false memory through repeated imagery or thought
D. How might authorities corrupt reality monitoring?
1. Direct suggestion
2. Interrogatory suggestion

Plausibility of the Event

The use of inherent plausibility as an indicator of whether an internal event should be classified as perception or imagination is one of the best established themes in the reality monitoring literature (Bentall, Baker, & Havers, 1991; Johnson, 1988; Johnson, Kahan, & Raye, 1984). Recent experiments on false memory also confirm this finding, concluding that an attempt to plant a false idea will generally fail if the subject cannot accommodate the information into existing schemata (Hyman & Pentland, 1996; Pezdek, 1995). Schema-biased processing appears to operate for both adults (Hyman & Pentland, 1996) and children (Baker-Ward, Hess, & Flannagan, 1990; Welch-Ross & Schmidt, 1996). This leads to the question addressed in this chapter. Under what conditions will a highly implausible (and false) event slip through this filter and into accepted memory?

The most straightforward answer would be that some individuals, notably those with psychotic disorders, lack reality-testing skills. As a central feature of their disorders, delusional individuals do not seek disconfirmation of their beliefs (cf. Brett-Jones, Garety, & Helmsley, 1987) and make conclusions based on less data than do controls (Dudley, John, Young, & Over, 1997; Huq, Garety, & Helmsley, 1988). Certainly abuse accounts within adult psychiatric populations are not rare events (Briere & Zaidi, 1989), and it would not be surprising to find that some bizarre content was occasionally incorporated (cf. Bernet, 1993) in an allegation from a seriously ill individual.

If the typical reporter of fantastic abuse content was blatantly psychotic, our problems in diagnosis and evaluation might be a bit easier. However, fantastic abuse allegations are quite often made by children and adults whose reality functions appear otherwise intact (cf. Bernet, 1993; Dalenberg, 1996b; Everson, 1997). Little is known about the psychology of such individuals, but the literature regarding the proneness to fantasy provides a basis for further work in the area.

Fantasy-prone individuals, like those with delusional disorders or a predisposition to hallucinations, also appear to have less stringent guidelines for the acceptance of an improbable belief as truth (Rankin & O'Carroll, 1995). Irwin (1990, 1991) reported that fantasy-prone adults are more likely to express belief in most paranormal phenomenon, and Rhue and Lynn (1987a) noted that fantasizers self-report more difficulty in differentiating fantasy and reality. Importantly, one developmental route of fantasy proneness is an aversive and frightening childhood environment (Rhue & Lynn, 1987b) or a particularly sexually or physically abusive one (Lynn & Rhue, 1988).

Clinical trauma literature also suggests that trauma-based hallucinations are a plausible source for fantastic elements. Hallucinations were reportedly a symptom of 9% of abused children in forensic or clinical samples (Famularo, Kinscherff, & Fenton, 1992), and up to 76% of sexual abuse victims in inpatient psychiatric units (Livingston, 1987; Livingston, Lawson, & Jones, 1993). These symptoms reportedly occur in traumatized children and adults without formal thought disorders (Nurcombe et al., 1996), resolve quickly with psychotherapeutic as opposed to psychopharmacological interventions (Hornstein & Putnam, 1992; Kaufman, Birmaher, Clayton, Retano, & Wongchaowart, 1997), and may be refractory to treatment with standard neuroleptics and responsive to medications that affect posttraumatic stress disorder (PTSD; cf. Davidson, 1992; Kaufman et al., 1997).

A first recommendation for forensic or clinical examination of the meaning of a fantastic element, then, is an assessment of the reporter's overall reality-testing skills. This includes assessment of the timing of the appearance of the fantastic element and a formal evaluation of reality-testing abilities and fantasy-proneness. This assessment would be geared toward differentiating the causal theories that have been implicitly and previously referenced. That is, it may be that the patient or participant shows no elevations in fantasy-proneness or deficits in reality-testing, suggesting another route for understanding this phenomenon (see later sections.) If a reality-testing problem is found, however, one then must evaluate the possibility that the reality-testing deficits are the cause of both the abuse allegation and the fantastic element (and thus the allegation is likely to be false) or that the abuse is the cause of the reality-testing problems, and thus the proneness to fantasy (and the allegation is likely to be true).

Specifically, if a fantasy element was due to a misperception resulting from general reality-testing problems or fantasy proneness, and if the abuse itself is part of the fantasy, then it is more likely (but not certain) that the following differentiating features would be present:

1. The fantasy-proneness or reality-testing deficit will be general, rather than specific to abuse issues. This theoretical distinction has been supported empirically in the Wycoff, Dalenberg, Viglione, and Meloy (1998) study described later.

2. The abuse-related fantasy will not show a pattern of acute expression close to the time of the alleged trauma, nor will it resolve quickly. Reality testing difficulties present in acute cases by adult victims of marital violence were not present during follow-up testing (Strauss, 1996). As previously stated, hallucinations by child victims of violence were also time-limited (Hornstein & Putnum, 1992; Kaufman et al., 1997).

3. The hallucinatory forms of fantastic elements will be responsive to neuroleptics in cases of generalized psychosis, less so in trauma-induced psychotic states (Davidson, 1992; Hornstein & Putnam, 1992; Kaufman et al., 1997).

4. With less certainty, it would be predicted that one of the other empirically based routes for fantasy-proneness (e.g., parental encouragement of fantasy and/or a history of immersion in the creative arts) will be present. Less emphasis is placed on the fourth criteria because a subset of fantasy-prone individuals show none of the known developmental risk factors for this personality trait (Rhue & Lynn, 1987a). However, others will show one of the classic nonabuse-related pathways to fantasy-proneness, such as parental encouragement of fantasy combined with an isolated and lonely childhood (Rhue & Lynn, 1987b).

If the fantastic allegation results from reality distortion after trauma, however, one of two patterns is likely to be present. In the acute case, in which the fantastic element is hallucinatory, it is likely that: (a) the abuse event will involve terror or horror (cf. Carlson, 1997; Dalenberg et al., 1997); (b) the fantastic aspects of the story will be highly abuse or perpetrator-related, while other aspects of the individual's life history will not contain such elements (Wycoff et al., 1998), (c) continuing commitment to fantastic elements will respond to medications affecting PTSD and/or psychotherapy (Kaufman et al., 1997), and (d) the fantasy element will emerge over the first few months as opposed to late in psychotherapy (see

Reality Corruption Section). Examples of the acute case are presented in Kaufman et al.'s recent article. In our own laboratory, we have recently documented that battered women show an apparently time-limited problem with reality testing closely following their battering experience, a problem not present in a group of battered women more than 1 year postbattery (Strauss, 1996).

The hypothesis of the fantastic element entering the system due to fantasy-proneness developed through prolonged exposure to abuse (as opposed to acute hallucinatory causal routes) is most difficult to test or describe empirically. We have some optimism among our research team for the potential of the Rorschach in helping to make this distinction in adults. Wycoff et al. (1998) used another psychiatric group known to have difficulty with the reality–fantasy distinction—borderline adults. Patients alleging an abuse history showed a reality-testing deficit on abuse-related Rorschach responses that did not appear in their general protocol, and borderlines without an abuse history showed a more pervasively high X-% (poor conformance of response with blot characteristics). The high X-% statistic is a general measure of the degree to which an individual produced responses that failed to conform to the actual characteristics of the inkblot.

Developmental Issues Related to Plausibility.   Children appear to be underestimated in the eyewitness literature on capacity to make the reality–fantasy distinction. Small and very specific reality-monitoring differences appear in the literature when comparing adult to either children 6 years old and under (Markham, 1991; Parker, 1995) or the very old (McGinnis & Roberts, 1996). Differences between adults and children 9 years or older are almost nonexistent in the literature, and younger children's weaknesses, if any, appear to be in the arena of differentiating between various internal sources (e.g., what they said from what they thought) rather than between internal and external sources (e.g., what they imagined from what they saw: Johnson & Foley, 1984). Children also appear to have a tendency to appropriate the actions of others, that is, state that they had performed an action in fact performed by another person (Foley et al., 1993).

On the other hand, although the most respected experts on reality monitoring agree that the young child has the memory system capacity to make the fantasy–reality distinction and can do so in the laboratory (Johnson, 1988; Johnson, Hashtroudi, & Lindsay, 1993), there is reason to believe that there will be more failures in the application of the distinction within the complex abuse allegation scenario. Both the strategic use of memory qualities to make reality–fantasy decisions (discussed later), and the world knowledge on which reality–fantasy decisions are often based, are in part learned. Children may simply lack the background to label a specific abuse-related event as implausible.

This latter dimension—adequate knowledge or background for making fantasy–reality distinctions—is particularly important for fairly evaluating children's claims. Although a child's belief in Santa Claus has been used in the anecdotal clinical literature as a basis to dismiss a child's fantasy-laden abuse claim as wholly false (Gardner, 1995), it is important to realize that the most important predictor of this belief is not fantasy-proneness, intelligence, or other intrapsychic dimensions, but instead parental encouragement of this belief (Prentice, Manosovitz, & Hubbs, 1978). One is reminded of the famous comment attributed to Thomas Jefferson in commenting on meteors ("It is easier to believe that two Yankee professors would lie than that stones fell from heaven") that implausible theories can at times prove to be true. Our willingness to move such phenomena (e.g., meteors, Santa Claus, or ritual abuse) from the category of pseudoscience to potential truth in our own minds thus depends in part on the biases of our scientific teachers as well as on their persuasive skills. Thus, it is not surprising that belief that one has seen an alien spacecraft (as an adult) rests most reliably on the prior beliefs of these adults in the sources that present UFOs as scientifically plausible (Spanos, Burgess, & Burgess, 1994). Belief in the prevalence of ritual abuse allegations also relates to attendance of workshops by relevant experts (Bucky & Dalenberg, 1993).

For children then, an implausible element in an abuse allegation may bypass the reality monitoring screen quite simply because the element is not regarded as implausible, even after a delay. The child who told us (cf. Dalenberg et al., 1997) that her knife passed easily through a joint as she dismembered a baby, for instance, would not be expected to realize that this should not be so. This point has been made eloquently by Everson (1997), in his thorough categorization of types of fantastic element. Here it will be argued, however, not only that children might be reasonably expected to use a different cultural context to determine plausibility (cf. Wooley. 1997), but that the experience of abuse might change the child's view of the nature of the world, and therefore of plausibility of fantastic abuse elements.

The aforementioned hypothesis is made based on clinical data, a limited pilot study, and the work of Samuels and Taylor (1994). The latter authors, studying the development of the fantasy–reality distinction, included an independent variable that they interpreted as the emotionality of the event. Children ages 3 to 5 rated the possibility that pictures of actual and fantasy events "could happen in real life." The emotionality of the pictures was varied by including frightening and nonfrightening events. As expected, children (particularly the 5-year-olds) were far more likely to state that the actual as opposed to the fantasy pictures contained events that could occur. The result of interest here was that the children were three times more likely to say that the actual events could not happen if they were frightening than if they were neutral. Apparently (and happily), for many young children, violent reality (e.g., a robber threatening a man with a knife) is as unlikely to occur as violent or threatening fantasy (e.g., a giant chasing a child).

These results raise the interesting possibility that experience with violence could change a child's capacity for the fantasy–reality distinction by removing one of the imperfect indicators (scary figures and frightening events are typically fictional) that was previously used. As a 5-year-old boy who had been attacked by a dog in his garage soberly explained to his clinical evaluator (cf. Dalenberg et al., 1997), "I never knowed monsters were real 'til my dog day." After all, if violent assaults can happen to 3-year-olds, with parents either complicit or unable to protect, what is so unbelievable about demons and monsters? Pilot data from our laboratory ($n = 12$) support the hypothesis (using Samuels and Taylor's, 1994, methodology) that children with violent pasts would not show the tendency to differentially label violent imagery as unlikely to occur. If abuse experience makes reality more like fantasy (containing more violence) and fantasy more like reality, the plausibility criteria would be less easily applied by abused children, resulting in more frequent reality-monitoring mistakes.

Findings such as those previously mentioned add new difficulties to the already complex job of forensic evaluation of these cases. The implication is that the presence of violent fantasy, even if clearly identifiable as fantasy, should not at this scientific junction lead the forensic examiner to internally move toward a false allegation hypothesis. Abuse allegations may be a result of violent fantasy, as will be argued later, but here it is argued that abuse may also be a cause of a change in fantasy life.

Context Cues for Fantasy

A second category of reality monitoring cues frequently cited by participants asked to differentiate fantasy and reality is the embeddedness of the element in supporting knowledge. Your classification of your attendance at a jazz festival as a memory might be supported by memories of buying the ticket, parking the car, seeing friends at the event, discussing the music the next day, and so on. Similarly, your memory of seeing Notre Dame in person may be classified as a dream because you have no memories of going to Paris. Thus, again Hyman and Pentland's (1996) findings are relevant: An individual's prior memories and beliefs form a context both for the inherent plausibility of the fantastic element, as previously argued, and for the situation-specific plausibility of the element. That is, prior memories of the self and other not only allow judgments about whether Situation X could have occurred, but also a judgment about whether Situation X could have occurred to Person Y.

Abuse experience may affect the context cues of fantasy by rendering the abuser dangerously or even impossibly omnipotent in the eyes of the victim. Van Dalen and Glasserman's (1997) example of a child who reported that his father's mere presence killed three of his pets may be an example of this phenomenon. The omnipotence of the battering male in the eyes of his battered spouse is another conceptually similar concept (cf. Ewing, 1987). In these cases, it is likely that the fantasy element will be in the form of enhanced abilities or implausible achievements of the perpetrator.

Abuse also may impact the context (and phenomenological) cues of fantasy by affecting dissociative tendencies. Although there is some controversy on the topic, the overwhelming majority of literature on dissociation links its development to abusive experiences in childhood (Braun, 1990; Hornstein & Putnam, 1996). In addition to reducing the clarity of memory, which may in turn modify the phenomenology of perception and imagination (bringing them closer together), the well-known link between dissociation and a variety of memory failures might influence the depth and complexity of the contextual field of childhood memory. It is logical to assume that a less detailed set of memories will contain less information that might be used to contradict a new piece of implausible data.

Although the mechanism for this effect is unclear, growing support is being marshaled for the hypothesis that dissociative individuals are more subject to false memory (Dalenberg, 1996a; Hyman & Billings, 1998; Qin, Goodman, & Barry, 1998). All three studies, using different paradigms, found more memory mistakes committed by dissociative individuals, including false implausible detail (Dalenberg, 1996). It is also interesting to note in this regard that one fantastic element that has received tremendous critical attention, the allegation of satanic ritual abuse conspiracies, appears highly associated with multiple personality disorder, the extreme representative of the dissociative continuum (Swica, Lewis, & Lewis, 1996).

The Qin et al. (1998) data is most directly relevant to the point made here. Using a word-recognition task, Qin et al. asked subjects to recall if items had been presented in earlier trials, using words: (a) that had been presented (old), (b) that had not been presented but were conceptually related to old words, or (c) that represented both new items and new concepts. Importantly, the mistake made by the dissociative group was not confusion between the first and third groups, but between the first and second. Thus, dissociation seems to blur the boundary between perception and imagination in cases where the two are conceptually similar, perhaps when fantasy resonates emotionally (or cognitively) with feelings (or memory traces) created by true events.

The empirical data examining the relationship of dissociativity and propensity to endorse false memories in children have yet to be developed. Clinically, however, the confusion between perception and emotionally similar fantasy appears quite common in abused children who include fantastic elements in their allegations. When assessing children's accounts of abuse immediately after their assaults and several weeks or months thereafter, we have encountered a number of clear recorded examples in which a plausibly reported sensation (a piercing pain during an anal assault or a burning sensation later) became, over time, a concretized implausible detail (he stuck a knife in my behind or set fire to his penis). Forensically, this suggests: (a) that an interviewer in a case involving fantastic allegations should attend to the symbolic connotation of the child's literal statements, and (b) that careful attention should be paid to the timing of the entrance of fantastic elements.

Phenomenological Cues for Fantasy

The final class of cues for reality monitoring of fantasy to be discussed are those cues related to qualitative differences between the internal experience of perception and imagination. Abundant research suggests that internally generated events (as opposed to perceptions of witnessed events) are more likely to be coded together with the cognitive operations that generated them (Durso, Reardon, & Jolly, 1995), have a weaker memory trace (Hoffman, 1997), have less perceptual detail (Johnson et al., 1988, 1994), are recalled with less perceptual clarity (McGinnis & Roberts, 1996), and lack contextual attributes (Johnson et al., 1988; McGinnis & Roberts, 1996). These differences between internally and externally generated representations appear in adults and children, although children are less likely to understand the potential use of these mechanisms for making a fantasy–reality distinction (Markham et al., 1999; Parker, 1995). Further, those individuals who are dissociative or fantasy-prone by constitution or through abuse experience may generally have perceptions that are weaker, and less clear and detailed than individuals without such tendencies. Thus, dissociative or fantasy-prone individuals may have perceptions that are qualitatively more similar to fantasy. It also appears possible that an abuse experience could change the quality of fantasy (most specifically, of nightmares), rendering them more vivid and more phenomenologically similar to reality.

It is well accepted that trauma affects the frequency of nightmares in both adults and children, as well as the phenomenological experience of waking up in fear, temporarily confused as to time and place (Labbate & Snow, 1992; Van Bork, 1982; van der Kolk, 1984). We have seen less discussion, however, about the effect on daily reality of this change in the phenomenology of fantasy. We believe, however, that the increase in frequency and vividness of nightmares makes the fantasy–reality distinction in waking life more difficult, and contributes to the possibility of a fantastic allegation.

Two sources of data support this hypothesized source for fantasy presented as reality. First, we have analyzed our own data on the frequency of nightmares in children who do or do not include fantastic elements in their accounts of abuse. As can be seen in Table 8.3, nightmares are associated with severe (confirmed) abuse in our sample of children (z for proportions = 2.05, $p < .05$).

Second, experimental evidence has supported the contention that repetition of fantasy (or imagery) increases the likeness of the imagined event to other perceived or actual remembered events (Suengas & Johnson, 1988). For instance, Suengas and Johnson found that repetition increases the strength and vividness of the memory. Repeated nightmares, then, could become increasingly difficult to discriminate from reality. The similarity in themes of the nightmares of trauma victims and the fantasy accounts of child victims (cf. Dalenberg et al., 1997)—replications of the trauma in different settings, concretization of a somatic aspect of the trauma, and revenge fantasies—also adds to the plausibility of this mechanism. Fantastic elements in adults may be encouraged in part by the natural decay of the phenomenological saliency of real (as well as nightmare) content, blurring the distinction between traumatic reality and the nightmares that might have followed it in childhood. Reality-monitoring experiments comparing real to imagined adult and childhood events (performed with adult participants) consistently noted smaller phenomenological differences in the childhood comparisons (McGinnis & Roberts, 1996).

TABLE 8.3
Nightmare Report in Children With Documented
Child Abuse Histories, Ages 3 to 17

	Nightmare or Sleep Disturbance Report[a]	
	Negative	Positive
Nonsevere	67%	33%
$n = 90$	($n = 60$)	($n = 30$)
Severe	51%	49%
$n = 71$	($n = 36$)	($n = 35$)
Fantastic element group	42%	58%
$n = 12$	($n = 5$)	($n = 7$)

[a]Includes only children explicitly asked about sleep disturbance. Relationship of fantasy to severity is based on full n of 644 and more in-depth analysis of $n = 284$ children under 10 years old.

The first author recently assessed a former abuse victim diagnosed with dissociative identity disorder who claimed that her abusive father left a heated object inside her for days at a time. Although the truth of her sexual abuse history itself is supported by multiple family sources and some physical evidence, she is extremely fantasy-prone and likely to hallucinate her father's presence. Also, a 9-year-old child victim was recently forensically evaluated who was also a sexual abuse victim making fantastic claims. She reported a fear, which became a reality in her dreams, that her father had left something inside her after the rape. She gave as evidence of this claim the burning sensation and sense of fullness (inflammation) that she experienced. The parallels in the fantastic claims of the adult and the nightmares of the child are quite compelling.

Reality Corruption by Authorities

The reality-corrupting authority, who may be the perpetrator, an accuser, or a well-meaning helper, also must be considered in the development of models of understanding intrusion of fantasy elements in abuse accounts. Such an authority might confuse fantasy and reality for the victim or nonvictim by implicitly addressing any of the reality-monitoring categories listed in Table 8.1. Most directly, the authority might affect the abuse recounter's belief in the plausibility of various explanations of events by using direct suggestion. The powerful wish for a narrative truth (Spence, 1982) would push the client toward acceptance of the explanation, as would the client's wish to win the therapist's interest and approval.

The direct suggestion research has not been extremely successful in producing stable false beliefs of unlikely or implausible features. Stephen Ceci and his associates have thoroughly studied this phenomenon (Ceci & Bruck, 1995; Ceci, Caves, & Howe, 1981; Ceci, Crotteau-Huffman, & Smith, 1994; Ceci, Loftus, Leichtman, & Bruck, 1994), typically making use of paradigms in which an important figure in the child's life strongly argues that the fantasy component is accurate. For instance, children in the Bruck et al. (1995) research were explicitly told many months following a short office visit with a doctor that it was a research assistant (RA), not a nurse, who gave them a shot. They were further told that the RA herself had stated that she remembered giving the child a shot and that it was the RA's job to give the shots. Such claim to personal knowledge is probably rare in the abuse interviewing profession. However, a sizable minority of the children shifted their story (with the surprising finding being that so many children held to their own memories).

In the Sam Stone study, approximately 70% of 3-year-olds and 40% of 5-year-olds were willing to endorse an entirely fantasy-based account of the visit of a stranger to their school. The figures reflect the condition in which children were interviewed with coercive questioning and told that the teacher had previous negative experience with Sam Stone. Even with repeated leading questioning and prior exposure to propaganda regarding Sam Stone's likelihood of misbehavior, mild challenging of the belief led virtually all of the children over the age of 3 to return to their accurate statement that the fantasy events did not occur. Such research tends to suggest that successful "implantation" by repeated exposure to a suggestive interviewer should be quite rare in children over 5 years of age, and that this should be particularly true if the person's existing memories rendered the possibility of the event quite low (Pezdek, 1995). Given the relationship between age and suggestibility in the previously mentioned studies, it is likely that implantation would be more difficult in older children and adults. Further, it is possible that those with childhood experience with abusive authorities might be less suggestible and trusting, a supposition that is in keeping with some research and clinical theory (e.g., Leavitt, 1997). However, it is reasonable to argue that the most effective direct reality corruption should be achieved by an authority with high credibility and relevant experience (Lampinen & Smith, 1995).

Higher rates of false memory and belief in implausible allegations should occur when the authority figure engages in the procedures studied under the rubric of "interrogatory suggestibility" (Brown et al., 1998). Some of these were present in the Sam Stone paradigm mentioned before. Here, the authority figure claimed to know that the false event occurred, repeatedly urged the child or adult to accept the belief, and used social manipulation to encourage acceptance of the suggestions. Social reward for abuse disclosures or punishment for denial of abuse history may be present (Garven et al., 1998). For ethical reasons, this type of interviewing has not been studied within the most relevant abuse-related contexts. However, the well-known Loftus paradigm (Loftus & Pickrell, 1995), and the related Hyman paradigm (Hyman & Billings, 1998), which are used to induce false memories in adults, both achieve false memories in approximately 25% of samples with the claim that the interviewer has knowledge of the truth of the memory received from a reliable source (typically the subject's mother), and the encouragement to remember. Even higher rates of agreement have been obtained with children under these circumstances (Garven et al., 1998). The degree of reality corruption achievable solely through suggestion (simple misinformation without social pressure) of abuse-related events appears to be small in most reports using children older than 3 (Brown et al., 1998). Based on research reviewed earlier on schema and memory, it is reasonable to assume that implausible false memories will be associated with the lowest acceptance rate.

It is easier to support the proposition that reality corruption could occur by the authority's effect on the phenomenological boundary of fantasy and reality. For instance, the therapist's encouragement of repeated fantasy of abuse before memories emerge is likely to increase the perceptual detail and vividness of the story, bringing it closer in quality to perceptual memories. Rehearsal of fantasy in laboratory experiments may have this effect (Suengas & Johnson, 1988), although it may also clarify the difference between the qualitative experience of reality and imagination (Johnson, Raye, & Durso, 1980). Further, encouragement of the patient or participant to concentrate on the emotional valence of the fantasy also appears to produce cases of imagination that simulate memory (Suengas & Johnson, 1988). This too might occur in psychotherapy, and is more likely to be part of the repertoire of a competent clinician than is repeated guided imagery for abusive events that are not currently in memory.

An interaction between authority effects and intrapsychic sources of fantasy could occur when a child victim of serious trauma enters psychotherapy with a clinician who is not aware of the potential roles that fantasy might play in true and false abuse accounts. Such a therapist, particularly during a prolonged court case, might feel an obligation to believe all of the child's statements in an effort to resist pressure to believe none of them. Concerned about undermining both the child's confidence and the strength of the legal case, evaluators may fear that acknowledgment of fantasy elements might brand the child as a liar (as well it might if these complex mechanisms are not understood and explained). The therapist may be further confused by the tendency for actual victims of sexual abuse to also show more bizarre and frequent sexual fantasies of abuse as adults (Briere et al., 1994).

Finally, it is the authors' contention that too little attention has been given to the important role of patient dissimulation in understanding fantasy elements. Two recanters, both of whom successfully filed complaints or suits against their therapists, told the first author that their fantastic claims began as conscious lies (after pressure to "disclose" from their therapists). "Lies are told to those who care," DePaulo and Bell (1996) wrote, and such emotionally charged lies may become remembered truths. As such, the combination of a desperately needy and psychologically vulnerable patient and a therapist who is intrigued with unusual therapeutic accounts might be a risky one.

SUMMARY

This review and theoretical speculation is meant to encourage scholars to use reality monitoring literature to organize further research into the phenomena of fantastic elements within abuse accounts. Increased understanding of such allegations might facilitate several important outcomes, including development of treatment strategies that support rather than undermine patient reality testing. More sophisticated assessment capacity would also decrease the likelihood that fantastic elements could be used to destroy the credibility of children with valid cases of serious child abuse. Additionally, fantastic claims with no basis in reality might be more quickly identified.

As for the children whose accounts begin this chapter, outcomes have been mixed. Alex, the little boy who was raped, was initially disbelieved, but was eventually proven to be telling the truth after medical evidence supported his case. Christine, however, the little girl who reported fantastic stories of satanic abuse and poisoning by her mother, was still being evaluated when I last had contact with her interviewers. Thus far, we have learned that her mother confessed to giving her child poison (although it is not clear that she did so), that her parents claim membership in a cult, and that the child was put to sleep with stories of ritual abuse and satanic circles. We know that psychosis is present in a number of the child's relatives, and that fantasy is encouraged in her family. No physical evidence of Christine's murderous activities has emerged. Our continued frustration with a lack of direction and ability to competently assess such accounts is a personal reminder of the importance of further research.

REFERENCES

Baker-Ward, L., Hess, T., & Flannagan, D. (1990). The effects of involvement on children's memory for events. *Cognitive Development, 5,* 55–69.

Bentall, R., Baker, G., & Havers, S. (1991). Reality monitoring and psychotic hallucinations. *Journal of Clinical Psychology, 30,* 213–222.

Bernet, W. (1993). False statements and the differential diagnosis of abuse allegations. *Journal of the American Academy of Child and Adolescent Psychiatry, 32,* 903–910.

Braun, B. (1990). Dissociative disorders as sequelae to incest. In R. Kluft (Ed.), *Incest-related syndromes of adult psychopathology* (pp. 227–245). Washington, DC: American Psychiatric Press.

Brett-Jones, J., Garety, P., & Helmsley, D. (1987). Measuring delusional experiences: A method and its application. *British Journal of Clinical Psychology, 62,* 355–364.

Briere, J., Smiljanich, K., & Henschel, D. (1994). Sexual fantasies, gender, and molestation history. *Child Abuse and Neglect, 18,* 131–137.

Briere, J., & Zaidi, L. (1989). Sexual abuse histories and sequelae in female psychiatric emergency room patients. *American Journal of Psychiatry, 146,* 1602–1606.

Brown, D., Scheflin, A., & Hammond, D. (1998). *Memory, trauma treatment, and the law.* New York: Norton.

Bruck, M., Ceci, S., Francoeur, E., & Barr, R. (1995). "I hardly cried when I got my shot!" Influencing children's reports about a visit to their pediatrician. *Child Development, 66,* 193–208.

Bucky, S., & Dalenberg, C. (1993). The relationship between training of mental health professionals and the reporting of ritual abuse and multiple personality disorder symptomatology. *Journal of Psychology and Theology, 20,* 233-238.

Carlson, E. (1997). *Trauma assessments: A clinician's guide.* New York: Guilford.

Ceci, S., & Bruck, M. (1995). *Jeopardy in the courtroom: A scientific analysis of children's testimony.* Washington, DC: American Psychological Association.

Ceci, S., Caves, R., & Howe, M. (1981). Children's long-term memory for information that is incongruous with their prior knowledge. *British Journal of Psychology, 72,* 443-450.

Ceci, S., Crotteau-Huffman, M., & Smith, E. (1994). Repeatedly thinking about a non-event: Source misattributions among preschoolers. *Consciousness and Cognition, 3,* 388-407.

Ceci, S., Loftus, E., Leichtman, M., & Bruck, M. (1994). The possible role of source misattributions in the creation of false beliefs among preschoolers. *International Journal of Clinical and Experimental Hypnosis, 42,* 304-320.

Chadwick, P., & Lowe, C. (1990). Measurement and modification of delusional beliefs. *Journal of Consulting and Clinical Psychology, 58,* 225-232.

Cohen, G., & Faulkner, D. (1989). Age differences in source forgetting: Effects on reality monitoring and on eyewitness testimony. *Psychology and Aging, 4,* 10-17.

Dalenberg, C. (1996a). Accuracy, timing and circumstances of disclosure in therapy of recovered and continuous memories of abuse. *Psychiatry and the Law, 24,* 229-275.

Dalenberg, C. (1996b). Fantastic elements in child disclosures of abuse. *APSAC Advisor, 3,* 1-10.

Dalenberg, C., Hyland, K., & Cuevas, C. (1997, January). *Prevalence and nature of fantastic elements in children's descriptions of abuse.* Paper presented at the International Society for the Study of Traumatic Stress, Montreal, Quebec.

Davidson, J. (1992). Drug therapy of post-traumatic stress disorder. *British Journal of Psychiatry, 160,* 309-314.

DePaulo, B., & Bell, K. (1996). Truth and investment: Lies are told to those who care. *Journal of Personality and Social Psychology, 71,* 703-716.

Dudley, R., John, C., Young, A., & Over, D. (1997). Normal and abnormal reasoning in people with delusions. *British Journal of Clinical Psychology, 36,* 243-258.

Durso, F., Reardon, R., & Jolly, E. (1995). Self–nonself-segregation and reality monitoring. *Journal of Personality and Social Psychology, 48,* 447-455.

Everson, M. (1997). Understanding bizarre, improbable and fantastic elements in children's accounts of abuse. *Child Maltreatment, 2,* 134-149.

Ewing, C. (1987). *Battered women who kill.* New York: Free Press.

Famularo, R., Kinscherff, R., & Fenton, T. (1992). Psychiatric diagnoses of maltreated children: Preliminary findings. *Journal of the American Academy of Child and Adolescent Psychiatry, 37,* 863-867.

Foley, M., Durso, F., Wilder, A., & Friedman, R. (1991). Developmental comparisons of explicit versus implicit imagery and reality monitoring. *Journal of Experimental Child Psychology, 51,* 1-13.

Foley, M., Passalacqua, C., & Ratner, H. (1993). Appropriating the actions of another: Implications for children's memory and learning. *Cognitive Development, 8,* 371-401.

Gardner, R. (1995). *Protocols for the sex-abuse evaluation.* Creskill, NJ: Creative Therapeutics.

Garven, S., Wod, J., Malpass, R., & Shaw, J. (1998). More than suggestion: The effect of interviewing techniques from the McMartin Preschool case. *Journal of Applied Psychology, 83,* 347-359.

Hoffman, H. (1997). Role of memory strength in reality monitoring decision: Evidence from source attribution biases. *Journal of Experimental Psychology: Learning, Memory, and Cognition, 23,* 371-383.

Hornstein, N., & Putnam, F. (1992). Clinical phenomenology of child and adolescent dissociative disorders. *Journal of the American Academy of Child and Adolescent Psychiatry, 32,* 1077–1085.

Hornstein, N., & Putnam, F. (1996). Abuse and the development of dissociative symptoms and dissociative identity disorder. In C. Pfeffer (Ed.), *Severe stress and mental disturbance in children* (pp. 449–473). Washington, DC: American Psychiatric Press.

Huq, S., Garety, P., & Helmsley, D. (1988). Probabilistic judgments in deluded and non-deluded subjects. *Quarterly Journal of Experimental Psychology, 40,* 801–812.

Hyman, I., & Billings, F. (1998). Individual differences and the creation of false childhood memories. *Memory, 6,* 1–20.

Hyman, I., Husband, T., & Billings, F. (1995). False memories of childhood experiences. *Applied Cognitive Psychology, 9,* 181–197.

Hyman, I., & Loftus, E. (in press). Memory: Modern conceptions of the vicissitudes of early childhood memories. In D. Halperin (Ed.), *False memory syndrome: Therapeutic and forensic perspectives.* Washington, DC: American Psychiatric Press.

Hyman, I., & Pentland, J. (1996). The role of mental imagery in the creation of false childhood memories. *Journal of Memory and Language, 35,* 101–117.

Irwin, H. (1990). Fantasy proneness and paranormal beliefs. *Psychological Reports, 66,* 655–658.

Irwin, H. (1991). A study of paranormal belief, psychological adjustment, and fantasy proneness. *Journal of the American Society for Psychical Research, 85,* 317–331.

Johnson, M. (1988). Reality monitoring: An experimental phenomenological approach. *Journal of Experimental Psychology: General, 117,* 390–394.

Johnson, M., & Foley, M. (1984). Differentiating fact from fantasy: The reliability of children's memory. *Journal of Social Issues, 40,* 33–50.

Johnson, M., Foley, M., Suengas, A., & Raye, C. (1988). Phenomenal characteristics of memories of perceived and imagined autobiographical events. *Journal of Experimental Psychology: General, 117,* 371–376.

Johnson, M., Hashtroudi, S., & Lindsay, D. S. (1993). Source monitoring. *Psychological Bulletin, 114,* 3–28.

Johnson, M., Kahan, T., & Raye, C. (1984). Dreams and reality monitoring. *Journal of Experimental Psychology: General, 113,* 329–344.

Johnson, M., Kounios, J., & Reeder, J. (1994). Time-course studies of reality monitoring and recognition. *Journal of Experimental Psychology: Learning, Memory and Cognition, 20,* 1409–1419.

Johnson, M., Raye, C., & Durso, F. (1980). Reality monitoring: Second perceptions and thoughts. *Bulletin of the Psychonomic Society, 15,* 402–404.

Johnson, M., & Suengas, A. (1989). Reality monitoring judgements of other people's memories. *Bulletin of the Psychonomic Society, 27,* 107–110.

Kaufman, J., Birmaher, B., Clayton, S., Retano, A., & Wongchaowart, B. (1997). Case study: Trauma-related hallucinations. *Journal of the American Academy of Child and Adolescent Psychiatry, 36,* 1602–1605.

Labbate, L. A., & Snow, M. P. (1992). Posttraumatic stress symptoms among soldiers exposed to combat in the Persian Gulf. *Hospital and Community Psychiatry, 43,* 831–833.

Lampinen, J., & Smith, V. (1995). The incredible (and sometime incredulous) child witness: Child eyewitnesses' sensitivity to source credibility cues. *Journal of Applied Psychology, 80,* 621–627.

Leavitt, F. (1997). False attribution of suggestibility to explain recovered memory of childhood sexual abuse following extended amnesia. *Child Abuse and Neglect, 21,* 265–272.

Livingston, R. (1987). Sexually and physically abused children. *Journal of the American Academy of Child and Adolescent Psychiatry, 26,* 413–415.

Livingston, R., Lawson, L., & Jones, J. (1993). Predictors of self-reported psychopathology in children abused reportedly by a parent. *Journal of the American Academy of Child and Adolescent Psychiatry, 32,* 948–953.

Loftus, E., & Pickrell, J. (1995). The formation of false memories. *Psychiatric Annals, 25,* 720–725.

Lynn, S., & Rhue, J. (1988). Fantasy proneness: Hypnosis, developmental antecedents, and psychopathology. *American Psychologist, 43,* 35–44.

Markham, R. (1991). Development of reality monitoring for performed and imagined actions. *Perceptual and Motor Skills, 72,* 1347–1354.

Markham, R., Howie, P., & Hlavacek, S. (1999). Reality monitoring in auditory and visual modalities: Developmental trends and effects of cross-modal imagery. *Journal of Experimental Child Psychology, 72,* 51–70.

Mather, M., Henkel, L., & Johnson, M. (1997). Evaluating characteristics of false memories: Remember/know judgments and memory characteristics questionnaire compared. *Memory and Cognition, 25,* 826–837.

McGinnis, D., & Roberts, P. (1996). Qualitative characteristics of vivid memories attributed to real and imagined experiences. *American Journal of Psychology, 109,* 59–77.

Nurcombe, B., Mitchell, W., Begtrip, R., Tramontaria, M., LaBasbera, J., & Pruitt, J. (1996). Dissociative hallucinations and allied conditions. In F. Volkmar (Ed.), *Psychoses and pervasive developmental disorders in childhood and adolescence* (pp. 107–128). Washington, DC: American Psychiatric Press.

Parker, J. (1995). Age differences in source monitoring of performed and imagined actions on immediate and delayed tests. *Journal of Experimental Child Psychology, 60,* 84–101.

Pezdek, K. (1995, July). *Childhood memories: What types of memories can be suggestively planted?* Paper presented at the meeting of the Society for Applied Research in Memory and Cognition, Vancouver, British Columbia.

Prentice, N., Manosovitz, M., & Hubbs, L. (1978). Imaginary figures of early childhood: Santa Claus, Easter Bunny, and the Tooth Fairy. *American Journal of Orthopsychiatry, 48,* 618–628.

Qin, J. J., Goodman, G. S., & Barry, S. M. (1998, March). *False childhood memory and false word recognition: Are they related?* Paper presented at the Biennial Conference of American Psychology-Law Society, Redondo Beach, CA.

Rankin, P., & O'Carroll (1995). Reality discrimination, reality monitoring, and disposition toward hallucination. *British Journal of Clinical Psychology, 34,* 517–528.

Rhue, J., & Lynn, S. (1987a). Fantasy proneness and psychopathology. *Journal of Personality and Social Psychology, 53,* 327–337.

Rhue, K., & Lynn, S. (1987b). Fantasy proneness: Developmental antecedents. *Journal of Personality, 55,* 121–137.

Rosenfeld, A., Nadelson, C., & Krieger, M. (1979). Fantasy and reality in patients reports of incest. *Journal of Clinical Psychiatry, 40,* 159–164.

Samuels, A., & Taylor, M. (1994). Children's ability to distinguish fantasy events from real-life events. *British Journal of Developmental Psychology, 12,* 417–427.

Spanos, N., Burgess, C., & Burgess, M. (1994). Past-life identities, UFO abductions, and satanic ritual abuse: The social construction of memories. *Intentional Journal of Clinical and Experimental Hypnosis, 42,* 433–446.

Spence, D. (1982). *Narrative truth and historical truth: Meaning and interpretation in psychoanalysis.* New York: Norton.

Strauss, K. (1996). *Differential diagnosis of battered women through psychological testing: Personality disorder or post traumatic stress disorder?* Unpublished doctoral dissertation, California School of Professional Psychology, San Diego.

Suengas, A., & Johnson, M. (1988). Qualitative effects of rehearsal on memories for perceived and imagined complex events. *Journal of Experimental Psychology: General, 117,* 377–389.

Swica, Y., Lewis, D., & Lewis, M. (1996). Child abuse and dissociative identity disorder/multiple personality disorder: The documentation of childhood maltreatment and the corroboration of symptoms. *Child and Adolescent Psychiatric Clinics of North America, 5,* 431–447.

Van Bork, J. (1982). Symptomes dits psychosomatiques de l'adulte et evenements traumatiques de l'enfance [Psychosomatic symptoms in adults and early psychotrauma]. *Revue de Medecine Psychosomatique et de Psychologie Medicale, 24,* 233–241.

van Dalen, A., & Glasserman, M. (1997). My father, Frankenstein: A child's view of battering parents. *Journal of the American Academy of Child and Adolescent Psychiatry, 36,* 1005–1007.

Welch-Ross, M., & Schmidt, C. (1996). Gender-schema development and children's constructive story memory: Evidence for a developmental model. *Child Development, 67,* 820–835.

Wooley, J. (1997). Thinking about fantasy: Are children fundamentally different thinkers and believers from adults? *Child Development, 68,* 991–1011.

Wycoff, A., Dalenberg, C., Viglione, D., & Meloy, R. (1998). *Sexually abused and nonabused borderlines: Differentiating groups through psychological testing.* Unpublished manuscript.

9

Individual Differences in Adults' Suggestibility and Memory Performance

Mitchell L. Eisen
California State University, Los Angeles

Eugene Winograd
Emory University

Jianjian Qin
Princeton University

Human memory, or at least memory reports, can be distorted in a variety of ways, and in many different situations (see Roediger, 1996, and Schacter, 1995, for reviews). A particular type of memory or report distortion that has attracted much attention in the last several decades is *eyewitness suggestibility*. This term refers to the phenomenon that, as a result of postevent suggestion, people come to remember suggested misinformation as a part of an originally witnessed event (e.g., Lindsay, 1990; Loftus, 1975; Loftus, Miller, & Burns, 1978; Zaragoza & Lane, 1994). Since Loftus and her colleagues demonstrated the phenomenon in laboratory-based experiments in the late 1970s, substantial research effort has been devoted to isolating the underlying mechanisms of eyewitness suggestibility. Early conjectures included the memory impairment hypothesis, according to which eyewitness suggestibility occurs because memories of the original event are irrevocably damaged or erased by postevent misinformation (e.g., Loftus, 1979; Loftus et al., 1978). Later studies have shown, however, that eyewitness suggestibility could arise independently of actual memory impairment (e.g., McCloskey & Zaragoza, 1985). Modern researchers now generally agree that multiple mechanisms, both cognitive and socioemotional, are responsible for eyewitness suggestibility (e.g., Ceci & Bruck, 1993; Schooler & Loftus, 1993).

Modern researchers also agree that not all individuals are equally likely to succumb to the influence of suggestion. Some are more ready to accept misinformation than others. A question that naturally arises is why some individuals are more suggestible than others. To put it more specifically, what factors account for individual differences in eyewitness suggestibility? Answers to this question can be particularly useful in practical settings. In a court of law, for example, such information could potentially help fact-finders evaluate the reliability of witnesses. In addition to its practical significance, research on individual differences may also contribute to theories of memory distortion by placing additional constraints on the ideas developed. As Underwood (1975) pointed out, any theoretical process will necessarily have a predicted tie with performance. Thus, predictions concerning individual differences in eyewitness suggestibility could provide a critical test of a theory of suggestibility. For example, if a particular theory predicts that certain individual differences (e.g., dissociation) are important factors in eyewitness suggestibility (see Brown, Scheflin, & Hammond, 1998), empirical findings regarding the relation between dissociation and eyewitness suggestibility should provide a test of the viability of the theory. If no such relation emerges after extensive search, then the theory would have to be abandoned, or at least significantly modified. As Underwood (1975) put it, "The most important function of the individual-differences approach is that of nipping an inappropriate theoretical assumption in the bud" (p. 133).

The main purpose of this chapter is to provide an updated review of currently available studies on individual differences in eyewitness suggestibility. We begin with a brief discussion of a useful distinction between two types of eyewitness suggestibility, namely delayed versus immediate acceptance of misinformation (Schooler & Loftus, 1993), followed by a description of the most commonly used paradigms in eyewitness suggestibility research. We then review individual-difference factors that relate to eyewitness suggestibility. This review is conducted with an eye toward theory (e.g., source-monitoring theory) of how misinformation leads to distortions in memory reports and/or actual alterations of memory traces.

DELAYED VERSUS IMMEDIATE ACCEPTANCE
OF MISINFORMATION

The term *suggestibility* has been used to explain a wide array of diverse phenomena, from hypnotic responsivity to simple gullibility (see Kirsch, 1997, for a review). Within the area of eyewitness memory research, suggestibility is generally employed to describe one's susceptibility to misleading information (Schooler & Loftus, 1993). Studies that examine eyewitness memory and suggestibility still vary greatly in regard to how this construct is examined and measured. Notwithstanding, most studies investigating eyewitness suggestibility involve a single common element: the presentation of misleading information. The most common designs involve viewing a set of slides, reading a narrative, or watching a staged performance (the "event"), and then being questioned about the event (the "postevent interview") either immediately or after some delay. Misinformation can be presented either prior to a postevent interview or as a part of the postevent questioning.

Schooler and Loftus (1993) proposed a distinction between two general types of susceptibility to misinformation: delayed misinformation retrieval and immediate misinformation acceptance. Schooler and Loftus noted that delayed misinformation retrieval corresponds to whether an individual incorporates suggested misinformation into subsequent memory reports. This type of eyewitness suggestibility is examined in paradigms where the misinformation is presented at some point subsequent to the original event yet prior to the postevent interview. The term *delayed* denotes the fact that the misleading information is presented prior to the interview but its effects on memory reports are detected later at the time of the interview; thus, there is a delay between when the misinformation is presented and the test of its effects. In contrast, immediate misinformation acceptance involves the immediate acceptance of inaccurate presuppositions in misleading questions, and is assessed in paradigms that involve a one-time presentation of misinformation in the form of a misleading question at interview. The term *immediate* refers to the fact that the individual is presented with the misinformation for the first time and is now asked either to accept the inaccurate presuppositions of the questions or reject them. The distinction between delayed retrieval errors and immediate misinformation acceptance can be useful not only in theorizing about the mechanisms of eyewitness suggestibility, but also in making predictions regarding individual differences in suggestibility.

EXPERIMENTAL PARADIGMS IN EYEWITNESS SUGGESTIBILITY RESEARCH

The "Classic" Misinformation Paradigm

Studies designed to create delayed misinformation retrieval errors typically employ a paradigm, based on the work by Loftus and her colleagues in the late 1970s (see Hyman & Loftus, chap. 3, this volume for a review; Loftus, 1975, 1979; Loftus et al., 1978), referred to as the "standard" or "classic" misinformation paradigm. Garry and Loftus (1994) describe these classic misinformation studies as involving three phases. In the first phase, participants witness an original event (e.g., viewing a slide show).

Following a delay that lasts from a few minutes to several days or weeks, misinformation regarding some critical items of the original event is imparted to the participants (e.g., through reading of a prosaic account of the original event presented under some guise or through answering questions in which misinformation is imbedded). This constitutes the second phase. During the third phase, which again takes place after a delay, participants are interviewed about their memories of the original event. A misinformation effect (eyewitness suggestibility) is defined as the difference between performance on critical misled items and nonmisled control items.

One particularly useful way to conceptualize the delayed acceptance of misinformation is to consider the resulting distortion in memory or memory reports as source-monitoring errors. *Source monitoring* refers to the process by which people make attributions about the origins of their mental experiences, such as memories (Johnson, Hashtroudi, & Lindsay, 1993; Johnson & Raye, 1981; Mitchell & Johnson, in press). According to the source-monitoring framework, features of an experienced event (e.g., perceptual characteristics, experimental context) are bound together as the result of encoding processes. When memories are retrieved, some subset of those encoded features is activated. Source attribution involves making decisions based on the activated memorial information, which ranges from a vague sense of familiarity to a vivid sense of such features. Both *heuristic processes* (e.g., making source attributions based on memory features that are, on average, characteristic of a given source) and *systematic processes* (e.g., considering the plausibility of the memory) are involved in source monitoring. Failure in source monitoring could occur for many different reasons. For example, insufficient source diagnosticity of the activated memorial information or using a lax response criterion could lead to increased source-monitoring errors.

In the classic misinformation paradigm, errors could arise if an individual remembers both the information from the original event and from the postevent suggestion, but fails to identify accurately the actual source of his or her memories. Errors could also occur if the individual remembers the information from the postevent suggestion and not from the original event, but mistakes the misinformation as being from the original event. There is growing evidence that source-monitoring failure plays a critical role in delayed acceptance of misinformation (e.g., Lindsay, 1990; Zaragoza & Lane, 1994). For example, participants are sometimes highly confident of their source attributions and claim that they have specifically recalled the source (Zaragoza & Lane, 1994; Zaragoza & Mitchell, 1996).

Paradoxically, Schooler and Loftus (1993) proposed that the delayed acceptance of misinformation is related to better rather than poorer memory abilities. They hypothesized that better memory should lead to more vivid recall of the misinformation, resulting in a confusion of postevent information with details of the original event.

The Immediate Acceptance of Misinformation Paradigm

The *immediate acceptance of misinformation* paradigm is very similar to the classic misinformation paradigm, except that misinformation in this paradigm is imparted to participants at the time of the memory test, often in the form of suggestive misleading questions. Participants in this paradigm experience the original event, and after a delay that varies in length, are interviewed with suggestive questions that contain misinformation.

Studies designed to assess immediate acceptance of misinformation do not necessarily invoke the idea of source confusion and/or memory distortion. Rather, these studies are designed to assess how an individual's memory report might be affected by suggestive questions. The immediate acceptance of misinformation paradigm has been used more frequently in studies of children's than adults' eyewitness suggestibility (e.g., Eisen, Goodman, Qin, & Davis, 1999). However, one type of study that typically involves adults and that fits into this general category concerns interrogative suggestibility, which is "the tendency of an individual's account of events to be altered by misleading information and interpersonal pressure within an interview" (Singh & Gudjonsson, 1992, p. 155). Gudjonsson and his colleagues have developed the Gudjonsson Scale of Interrogative Suggestibility (GSS; Gudjonsson, 1984) as well as a theory of interrogative suggestibility to predict individuals who will be more susceptible to highly suggestive questioning during a police interrogation (e.g., Gudjonsson, 1983, 1984; Gudjonsson & Clarke, 1986).

In contrast to delayed retrieval errors, Schooler and Loftus (1993) proposed that the immediate acceptance of misinformation should be related to poorer memory and lack of attention to details (see also Gudjonsson & Clark, 1986). The authors argue that individuals who have poorer memory for the original details of an event would be less likely to notice when the postevent information is inconsistent or discrepant with the original event than individuals who have better memory for the original details.

Other Paradigms That Lead to Memory Distortion

Although the classic and immediate misinformation paradigms have been most extensively studied in relation to eyewitness suggestibility, in recent years, growing attention has been paid to other misinformation paradigms that can also lead to memory distortion. These paradigms include the *false childhood memory* paradigm (Loftus & Pickrell, 1995) and the *Deese/Roediger and McDermott* (Roediger & McDermott, 1995) paradigm.

Studies based on these paradigms also reveal individual differences in eyewitness suggestibility.

The False Childhood Memory Paradigm.   To demonstrate that an entirely false account of a never-experienced childhood event can be created, Loftus and her colleagues (Loftus, 1993; Loftus & Pickrell, 1995) designed the false childhood memory paradigm. In her original study, Loftus asked the older brother of a 14-year-old boy to suggest a false memory about an event (being lost in a shopping mall) that was supposed to have occurred when the boy was 5 years old. After being told the story by his older brother, the boy was asked to write about his memory of this event (and of three other true events from his childhood) once every day for 5 days. By the end of this process, the boy described the false event in detail and with great confidence. Variations of this procedure have now been used successfully by other investigators (Hyman & Billings, 1998; Hyman, Husband, & Billings, 1995; Hyman & Pentland, 1996; Qin, 1999; see Hyman & Loftus, chap. 3, this volume, for a review).

Studies using the false childhood memory paradigm demonstrate that it is possible for people to incorporate suggestions about false events into their personal autobiographical memory accounts (but see Pezdek, Finger, & Hodge, 1997). Similar to delayed retrieval errors produced in classic misinformation studies, the acceptance of suggested nonevents into one's autobiographical memory involves source-monitoring errors. In this case, the confusion is between what was imagined or some internally generated mental representation and that of an externally experienced event (Johnson & Raye, 1981; Johnson, Raye, Wang, & Taylor, 1979).

An interesting variation of the false childhood memory paradigm involves *imagination inflation* (Garry, Manning, Loftus, & Sherman, 1996). Garry et al. reported that systematically imagining nonevents that could have occurred in childhood significantly increased people's confidence that imagined events actually happened to them (but see Pezdek & Eddy, in press). A similar effect has been replicated by other investigators (Heaps & Nash, in press; Paddock et al., 1998). As is the case with the classic misinformation paradigm and the false childhood memory paradigm, imagination inflation likely involves delayed retrieval errors.

Deese/Roediger-McDermott Paradigm (DRM).   Roediger and McDermott (1995) recently introduced a laboratory-based paradigm to study memory distortion that provides a compelling demonstration of false recognition effects in a list learning task (Deese, 1959). In the DRM paradigm, participants are asked to recall several lists of semantically associated words. This is followed by a recognition test that includes previously presented words, semantically related (i.e., critical) lures that were not presented previously, and unrelated words. Roediger and McDermott (1995) reported high levels of false recognition to semantically related lures. In addition, participants reported high confidence that they actually remembered hearing the critical lures being read aloud during the acquisition. Since this initial study, numerous other studies have replicated the findings (e.g., Mather, Henkel, & Johnson, 1997; McDermott, 1996; Norman & Schacter, 1997; Payne, Elie, Blackwell, & Neuschatz, 1996; Reed, 1996; Robinson & Roediger, 1997; Seamon, Luo, & Gallo, 1998; Tussin & Greene, 1997; Winograd, Peluso, & Glover, 1998).

False recognition of nonpresented critical lures (like delayed acceptance of misinformation) involves failure of source monitoring. To the extent that eyewitness memory and other forms of memory distortion result from souce-monitoring problems, an interesting question is whether recognition errors on the DRM task are related to eyewitness suggestibility and memory distortion. Findings have been somewhat inconsistent so far. For example, Eisen, Lorber, et al. (1999) found a modest positive relation between false recognition errors on the DRM task and errors of commission on misleading questions in a study designed to tap immediate susceptibility to misleading information in adults. Similarly, Platt, Lacey, Iobst, and Finkelman (1998) recently found that false recognition errors on the DRM task were positively correlated with distortions in autobiographical memory. A study by Wilkinson and Hyman (1998), however, failed to reveal such a relation.

INDIVIDUAL-DIFFERENCE FACTORS
IN EYEWITNESS SUGGESTIBILITY

In the remainder of the chapter, we focus on sources of individual-differences in eyewitness suggestibility. We discuss individual-difference factors in relation to delayed misinformation effects, immediate misinformation effects, and other forms of suggestibility, such as those derived from the imagination inflation and DRM paradigms. As is evident in our review and as we argue, it appears that the relations between individual-difference factors and adults' eyewitness suggestibility may well depend on the type of paradigm employed to elicit memory distortions.

Age

Age is perhaps the most extensively examined individual-difference factor in eyewitness suggestibility research. Because of this, there is an enormous database to draw from in examining age-related differences in suggestibility using a wide variety of paradigms. Taken as a whole, the data indicate that there is a clear developmental trend in both delayed and immediate acceptance of misinformation. Although children can be fairly accurate in their memory reports of salient and personally significant events (e.g., Saywitz, Goodman, Nicholas, & Moan, 1991), young children, especially preschoolers, are significantly more suggestible than older children and adults (Ceci, Crotteau-Huffman, Smith, & Loftus, 1994; Ceci, Ross, & Toglia, 1987; Poole & Lindsay, 1994; see Pipe & Salmon, chap. 10, Poole & Lindsay, chap. 15, and Saywitz & Lyon, chap. 4, this volume, for reviews). Once children reach school age, suggestibility appears to decrease, although there is evidence that even adolescents may still be somewhat more suggestible than adults, especially when negative feedback is provided (e.g., Richardson, Gudjonsson, & Kelly, 1995). Consistent with developmental differences in eyewitness suggestibility are the findings that younger children have more difficulties in source-monitoring tasks (e.g., Akil & Zaragoza, 1995).

There is also evidence that suggestibility increases once again when one grows older (e.g., over 60 years of age; Bartlett, Strater, & Fulton, 1991; Dywan & Jacoby, 1990; List, 1986; Loftus, Levidow, & Duensing, 1992; McIntyre & Craik, 1987; Rankin & Kausler, 1979; Tun, Wingfield, Blanchard, & Rosen, 1996). It is well documented in the memory and aging literature that the elderly tend to experience more difficulties in a variety of memory tasks than their younger counterparts. For example, compared to younger adults, elderly adults perform more poorly on tests of free recall (List, 1986) and several categories of event recall (Yarmey & Kent, 1986), are more likely to retrieve misinformation (Loftus, Levidow, & Duensing, 1992) and are more likely to forget the source of facts (McIntyre & Craik, 1987). There is also emerging evidence that older adults appear to make more recognition errors on DRM tasks (Tun, Wingfield, Blanchard, & Rosen, 1996).

Schacter and his colleagues recently proposed that the increased susceptibility to memory distortion in elderly is associated with older adults' impaired source-monitoring ability (see Schacter, Isreal, & Racine, in press; Schacter, Norman, & Koutstaal, 1998, for reviews). These researchers argue that elderly adults encode information in a less distinct manner, which increases their susceptibility to various kinds of memory distortion. More specifically, Schacter and his colleagues propose that older adults have access to less detailed source information, consider less of the source information available to them, and tend to adopt looser criteria in making source decisions. A deficiency in source monitoring would in turn lead to heightened suggestibility. This proposal is supported by studies that demonstrate growing difficulties in the elderly on a variety of source-monitoring tasks. For example, older adults are more likely to claim that nonfamous names or faces they have recently seen are actually famous

(Bartlett, Strater, & Fulton, 1991; Dywan & Jacoby, 1990). Older adults also make more errors in source-monitoring tasks that involve categorized pictures (Koustaal & Schacter, 1997) and combinations of videos and pictures (Schacter, Koutstaal, Gross, Johnson, & Angell, 1997). Moreover, older participants rely more on schematic knowledge in performing source-monitoring tasks, which may lead to more source-monitoring errors when the actual source is inconsistent with their existing schemas (Mather, Johnson, & De Leonardis, 1999).

In summary, it has been well established that age is associated with eyewitness suggestibility. Both younger children and elderly adults appear to be more susceptible to damaging effects of misinformation than young adults. There is also growing evidence that the heightened susceptibility in younger children and the elderly may be due at least partly to increased source-monitoring difficulties in these age groups.

Intellectual Ability

Intellectual ability has been found to be associated with the immediate acceptance of misinformation. For example, Eisen, Goodman, Qin, and Davis (1997) reported that verbal abilities as assessed by the Wechsler scales were inversely related to errors on misleading questions in a group of low-socioeconomic status (SES) children. There is little evidence, however, of significant associations between intelligence and delayed acceptance of misinformation. One early study by Powers, Andricks, and Loftus (1979) found no relation between delayed retrieval errors in a classic misinformation paradigm and scores on several subtests of the Washington Pre-College Test (WPC) designed to tap intellectual ability. However, a search of the PsychInfo database generated no recent study on the issue.

In contrast, a bulk of studies have examined the relation between intelligence and interrogative suggestibility. Early studies on the relations between interrogative suggestibility and intelligence yielded somewhat inconsistent results. Gudjonsson (1983) reported a negative relation between scores on the Gudjonsson Scale of Suggestibility (GSS; Gudjonsson, 1984) and intelligence, as measured by the Wechsler Adult Intelligence Scale (WAIS; Wechsler, 1955). Tully and Cahill (1984) reported a similar finding. Using the National Adult Reading Test in England (NART) as a measure of intelligence, however, Tata (1983) found no relation between scores on the GSS and intellectual abilities.

Faced with these discrepant findings, Gudjonsson (1988) speculated that intelligence might be most clearly related to suggestibility in participants with lower intellectual abilities. In a study designed to examine this possibility, Gudjonsson (1988) administered the GSS and a short form of the Wechsler Adult Intelligence Scale, revised (WAIS–R; Wechsler, 1981) to 160 adults, 90 of whom were from a forensic population (i.e., incarcerated). As predicted, for participants with scores 100 or less on the WAIS–R, with 100 being the population average score, lower intellectual ability was related to high interrogative suggestibility as measured by the GSS. However, for participants with WAIS–R scores of 101 or above (i.e., scores generally considered above average), interrogative suggestibility was unrelated to intellectual ability. Based on these results, Gudjonsson proposed that people with low intellectual ability are more likely to become confused and uncertain when asked misleading questions, which leads to an increased likelihood of acquiescing to the misleading questions.

There is also evidence that interrogative suggestibility may be specifically related to verbal intelligence. Singh and Gudjonsson (1992) examined relations between intellectual ability as measured by the Wechsler Intelligence Scale for Children, Revised (WISC–R; Wechsler, 1974) and suggestibility as measured by the GSS in a group of adolescent boys. A significant relation emerged between scores on the GSS and verbal IQ scores but not between scores on the GSS and performance IQ scores. The lack of a relation between performance IQ and the GSS may not be so surprisingly given the fact that the GSS is based on memory for narrative information, which is likely tied to verbal abilities.

In summary, there is evidence that intellectual abilities are related to immediate acceptance of suggestion, especially in the context of police interrogations. The negative correlation between intelligence and interrogative suggestibility may be more prominent in people with lower intellectual abilities and when verbal IQ is considered. It is unknown, however, as to whether or not intelligence is associated with delayed acceptance of misinformation in a classic misinformation paradigm.

Acquiescence

One personality trait commonly believed to be linked to suggestibility is acquiescence (Gudjonsson, 1986; Tousignant, 1984; also see Loftus & Schooler, 1993, for a review). *Acquiescence* is defined as a person's tendency to answer questions affirmatively regardless of content (Cronbach, 1946). Logically, this type of indiscriminant positive responding should be related to errors of commission on misleading questions.

Tousignant (1984) examined the relation between delayed retrieval errors on a classic misinformation task and acquiescence as measured by performance on the *R* scale (a.k.a. the Edwards Acquiescence Scale; Edwards & Abbott, 1969) of the Minnesota Multiphasic Personality Inventory (MMPI). In this study, 144 undergraduates viewed a slide presentation depicting a purse snatching and then were given a questionnaire about the details of the slides. Half the participants received misinformation imbedded in a question that inaccurately referred to certain items in the slides, while the other half of the participants received no misinformation. Finally, participants were given a true–false recognition test about the slide presentation. Tousignant reported a positive relation between acquiescence and the delayed acceptance of misinformation for the misled participants. Aside from this study by Tousignant (1984), however, no other solid data linking acquiescence to delayed acceptance of misinformation exist. There is also good reason to view the findings from Tousignant's study with caution because the R scale of the MMPI is not highly regarded as a measure of acquiescence.

More empirical evidence is available concerning relations between acquiescence and immediate acceptance of misinformation. In fact, most studies that reported a relation between acquiescence and suggestibility have used the immediate acceptance of misinformation paradigm. In one such study, Gudjonsson (1986) examined the relationship between acquiescence and performance on the GSS. Acquiescence was measured by an individual's tendency to respond affirmatively to opposing items within the same questionnaire. It was predicted that a pattern of indiscriminant agreement with inconsistent items should be positively related to the immediate acceptance of misinformation on the GSS. Consistent with this prediction, Gudjonsson found a modest positive correlation between acquiescence and immediate acceptance of misinformation on the GSS. Furthermore, the relations appeared to be stronger when negative feedback was provided to participants.

In a more recent study, Eisen et al. (1999) examined the relation between acquiescence and the immediate acceptance of misinformation using a slightly different approach. In this study, 112 students took part in a series of events that included the administration of the MMPI-2 (Hathaway & McKinley, 1989), which includes a scale designed to assess indiscriminant affirmative responding to items of opposing content (True Response Inconsistency Scale [TRIN]), that is, a measure of acquiescence (Butcher, Dahlstrom, Graham, Tellegen, & Kaemmer, 1989). One week later, the participants were administered an unannounced memory test that included 24 misleading questions about the events that took place in the previous session. Performance on the misleading questions was used as a measure of suggestibility. Eisen, Lorber, et al. (1999) found that acquiescence, as measured by the tendency to give indiscriminant affirmative responses to items of opposing content on the TRIN scale, was positively related to errors on the misleading questions, $r = .34$, $p < .001$.

In summary, it appears that acquiescence is associated with immediate acceptance of misinformation, including interrogative suggestibility, perhaps because high acquiescent individuals are more likely to consent indiscriminately. The studies by Gudjonsson (1986) and Eisen, Lorber, et al.

(1999) show that acquiescence accounts for a modest yet significant proportion of the variance in individuals' immediate susceptibility to misleading information. As yet, there is little evidence regarding the relation between acquiescence and delayed acceptance of misinformation.

Agreeableness

Two major components of agreeableness are trust and compliance (Costa & McCrea, 1992), making agreeableness closely related to acquiescence. Logically, one would expect that increased levels of trust and compliance would be positively related to the acceptance of misinformation. Eisen et al. (1998) recently explored this possibility in an experiment on immediate susceptibility to misleading information. The study also explored how agreeableness might serve as a moderating factor between susceptibility to misleading information and the mode of questioning employed. It was predicted that agreeableness would be positively related to errors on misleading questions in a closed social interaction between two individuals but to a lesser extent when misleading questions were administered in a paper-and-pencil test. The latter form of questioning was expected to reduce the amount of social pressure. One hundred and forty college students took part in a series of staged events that involved the administration of a variety of individual-difference measures, one of which was the short form of the NEO Personality Inventory, Revised (NEO PI–R; Costa & McCrea, 1992). One week later, the students were administered a structured interview that included both misleading and nonsuggestive specific questions about what happened during the staged events. Half the students were interviewed individually and half were given the same questions via a group-administered paper and pencil survey. As predicted, agreeableness was positively related to errors on misleading questions. Although agreeableness was positively related to errors on misleading questions in a closed social interaction between two individuals, the correlation was nonsignificant in the group administered paper-and-pencil test condition. Perhaps the tendency to be more agreeable is most important when social demands are placed on individuals, such as when they are in face-to-face conversations. Importantly, these findings indicate that individual-difference factors may interact with situational factors to affect memory distortions. Theories of suggestibility should account for these possible complexities.

In summary, there is some evidence that high agreeable individuals are more likely than less agreeable individuals to make errors when answering misleading questions, especially in a test condition where social pressure is high. Although links between agreeableness and delayed acceptance of misinformation have not been explored, one may predict that highly agreeable people would be more likely to accept suggestions from others than would low agreeable people. This could lead to incorporation of suggested information into subsequent memory reports among the highly agreeable people. Thus, the relation between agreeableness and delayed acceptance of misinformation remains an unexamined empirical question.

Field Dependence and Locus of Control

Field Dependence.   Field orientation refers to the extent an individual depends on internally generated versus externally supplied information. Field dependent individuals rely more on externally derived information than do field independent individuals. It is conceivable that an overreliance on externally derived information may lead to heightened suggestibility in both delayed and immediate acceptance of misinformation, and there is indeed some evidence linking field dependence to delayed retrieval errors and source-monitoring difficulties. For example, Durso, Reardon, and Jolly (1993) conducted an experiment to investigate the relation between field dependence and source-monitoring errors. In their Experiment 1, 48 college students were administered the group version of the Embedded Figures Test (EFT; Witkin, Oltman, Raskin, & Karp, 1971). The EFT is a perceptual test that involves locating a previously seen simple figure in a complex background designed to obscure the figure. Field dependence is associated with more difficulty in locating the figure, which presumably stems from a "dependence" on the external cues surrounding the figure. The students then watched a videotape of an actor reading a series of sentences where the last word was quite familiar and predictable (e.g., Humpty dumpty sat on a _____). Half of the sentences were incomplete and the subjects were asked to fill in the final, familiar word. It was hypothesized that field dependent individuals would have more difficulty differentiating internally generated words from externally presented words on a recognition test administered subsequent to the task, and results confirmed this prediction. Field dependent individuals were less accurate on the internal versus external source-monitoring task than field independent individuals. However, field dependent individuals were no worse than their field independent counterparts at discriminating between two external sources of information (Experiment 2) or two internally generated memories (Experiment 3).

Gudjonsson and Clarke (1986) proposed that field dependence would be associated with heightened interrogative suggestibility. Singh and Gudjonsson (1992) tested this hypothesis in a sample of adolescents. Forty adolescent boys completed the GSS and the EFT. Field dependence was related to errors on misleading questions presented before the negative feedback was given on the GSS but not to the likelihood that boys' shifted their answers after negative feedback was given. It appears that field dependent individuals tend to rely more on externally provided information to shape their responses (e.g., to misleading questions), but they are no more likely to acquiesce to social pressures than field independent individuals.

Locus of Control.   Locus of control (LOC) differs from field orientation in that LOC is related to an individual's *expectancy* of reliance on the self versus reliance on outside factors. An early study by Christiaansen, Ochalek, and Sweeney (1984) examined the relation of both field dependence and LOC to eyewitness accuracy. No relations between either one of these variables and remembering the appearance of people were found. In a more recent study, Paddock et al. (1998) examined the relation between LOC and delayed retrieval errors using an imagination inflation paradigm. Paddock et al. (1998) noted that external LOC has been associated with increased susceptibility to interpersonal influence (Lefcourt, 1993) and thus hypothesized that individuals who have an external versus internal LOC would be more vulnerable to the effects of guided imagery and would show increased confidence in the verticality of imagined events. As predicted, their results showed that external LOC was related to enhanced certainty for imagined nonevents.

Summary.   Results indicate that field dependent individuals and individuals with external LOC are more susceptible to external influence and more likely to make faulty source discriminations under certain conditions than are field independent individuals and individuals with internal LOC. Available data also suggest that evident increases in memory errors among field dependent and external LOC individuals are not necessarily due to them having generally poor memory abilities, but rather to their susceptibility to misleading information independent of social pressure. Although more research would be needed to clarify these propositions, difficulties with the constructs (e.g., field independence) have led to a decrease in research on these individual-difference measures.

Hypnotizability

It is often assumed that hypnotizability is strongly related to suggestibility, although data to support this assumption are far from definitive. One possible reason for this assumption is that many investigators use the term *suggestibility* interchangeably with hypnotizability. Another reason is that the data often cited to support this relation come from studies of pseudomemories in which hypnosis is used to facilitate the implantation of false-event memories (see Lynn, Neuschatz, & Fite, chap. 12, this volume). In these pseudomemory studies, direct suggestions of false information are given to participants who are under or not under hypnosis. Participants also complete measures of their general hypnotizability. A consistent finding from these studies is that, compared to low hypnotizable individuals, high hypnotizable individuals are more prone to distortion of memory reports when given direct suggestions during hypnosis (Barnier & McConkey, 1992; Labelle, Laurence, Nadon, & Perry, 1990; McConkey, Labelle, Bibb, & Bryant, 1990; Sheehan, Staltham, & Jamison, 1991a, 1991b). The highest levels of acceptance of misinformation are evident when high hypnotizability (an individual-difference trait) is combined with a hypnotic induction. Interestingly, when studies do not involve a hypnotic induction, hypnotizability per se has not been consistently related to the acceptance of misinformation.

Hypnotizability and Delayed Acceptance of Misinformation. In the early 1980s, Sheehan and colleagues conducted a series of experiments to examine how hypnosis might be related to susceptibility to misleading information using a mix of classic misinformation and false memory paradigms (Sheehan, Grigg, & McCann, 1984; Sheehan & Tilden, 1983, 1984, 1986). These investigations generally yielded null findings regarding the role of hypnotizibility. In more recent studies by Sheehan and his associates, however, highly hypnotizable individuals were found to be more likely to accept false suggestions when the suggestions were offered under hypnosis (Sheehan, Statham, & Jamison, 1991a, 1991b).

Other researchers also found evidence that hypnotizability is positively associated with increased suggestibility in research paradigms designed to tap delayed retrieval errors. For example, Barnier and McConkey (1992) showed a slide sequence of a purse snatching to 30 high- and 30 low-hypnotizable participants. Misinformation about the slide sequence was then presented either during hypnosis or waking conditions. Highly hypnotizable participants were more likely to provide false reports than low hypnotizable participants, both in hypnosis and waking conditions. More recently, Heaps and Nash (2000) examined the relation between hypnotizability as measured by the Waterloo–Stanford Scale of Hypnotic Susceptibility (WSGC; 11-point version; Bowers, 1993), and suggestibility as measured in an imagination inflation task. Student participants were administered the WSGC during regular class times. In a subsequent, unrelated experimental session, students were given a battery of individual-difference tests and took part in imagination inflation procedures. The results indicated that imagination inflation was positively related to hypnotizability.

Heaps and Nash (2000) provide several reasons as to why high hypnotizability is associated with increased suggestibility. For one, hypno-

tizable individuals tend to be better at visualization than low-hypnotizable individuals, and imagery vividness has been implicated as underlying source-monitoring errors (Dobson & Markham, 1993; Markham &
Hynes, 1993). Also, in addition to being better at visualization, hypnotizable individuals tend to be more dissociative (see Whalen & Nash,
1996, for a review) and show increased levels of absorption (Tellegen &
Atkinson, 1974). Each of these factors may lead to increased source confusions and therefore delayed retrieval errors. Further, as discussed later,
both dissociative tendencies and high absorption have been found to be
related to increased susceptibility to misleading information.

Hypnotizability and Immediate Acceptance of Misinformation. Findings regarding the relation between hypnotizability and immediate acceptance of misinformation are somewhat mixed. In a study by Register and
Kihlstrom (1988), the experimenters administered the GSS to high- and
low-hypnotizable individuals, in both hypnotic and waking conditions.
They did not find a significant relation between suggestibility as measured by the GSS and hypnotic responsivity. In a similar study by Linton
and Sheehan (1994), however, a positive correlation was found between
suggestibility as measured by the GSS and hypnotizability as measured
by scores on the Harvard Group Scale of Hypnotic Susceptibility (HGSHS:
A; Shore & Orne, 1962). Spanos, Gwynn, Comer, Baltruweit, and deGroh
(1989) found a similar relation using a different paradigm. Spanos et al.
had participants view a simulated robbery on film. Several days later, participants were interrogated about mug shot identifications in either hypnotic or waking conditions. In a third session 1 week later, participants
were cross-examined about errors they made during the previous interrogation. Interestingly, Spanos et al. found that highly hypnotizable individuals made more misattributions when initially interrogated with highly
suggestive questions, but they were also significantly more likely to reverse these errors during cross examination. Spanos et al. speculated that
highly hypnotizable individuals were not so much more prone to memory
distortion, but were in fact more prone to comply to social pressures (see
also Graham & Green, 1981; Hajek & Spacek, 1987; Shames, 1981).

There is evidence that the relation between hypnotizability and immediate acceptance of misleading information can be complex and may involve interactions between individual-difference and situational factors.
Eisen (1996) investigated the relation between immediate susceptibility to
misleading information and hypnotizability as measured by performance
on the HGSHS: A (Shore & Orne, 1962). Eisen hypothesized that the correlation between hypnotizability and susceptibility to misleading information would be attenuated under conditions where misinformation is con-

veyed in the absence of social pressure, outside of hypnotic context; and when participants were questioned about salient aspects of their own actions as opposed to minor details of a written narrative, slide sequence, or video presentation. Eighty-five college students were administered the HGSHS: A. Several days later, the students were administered a surprise memory test that included nonsuggestive factual questions as well as highly suggestive misleading questions about events that occurred in the previous experimental session. The memory test was administered in the form of a paper-and-pencil test, which was designed to reduce social pressure. Consistent with his prediction, Eisen did not find a significant correlation between hypnotizability and errors on misleading questions for events occurring during hypnosis or for events that occurred prior to the induction. Eisen's finding provided an interesting contrast to those of Spanos et al. (1989) and Linton and Sheehan (1994), who showed that when social pressure is present, highly hypnotizable individuals are more likely to assent to misleading questions.

Summary.   Hypnotizability is a complex multidimensional phenomenon that may be linked to different types of suggestibility. There is evidence that highly hypnotizable individuals are more susceptible to both delayed and immediate acceptance of misinformation. However, different reasons might explain the correlations between hypnotizability and the two types of eyewitness suggestibility. The relation between hypnotizability and delayed acceptance of misinformation may be linked to individual differences in imagery ability, dissociative tendencies, and absorption, which are close correlates of hypnotizability and may lead to increased source-monitoring errors. The correlation between hypnotizability and immediate acceptance of misinformation, on the other hand, can best be explained by compliance to social pressures in memory questioning. It may be that individuals who are more likely to comply with hypnotic suggestions to perform various tasks on measures of hypnotizability are also more likely to comply with suggestions offered in highly suggestive interviews where social pressure is applied.

Imagery Ability

Several studies have reported a positive relation between imagery ability and delayed retrieval errors in a variety of suggestibility paradigms (Hyman & Billings, 1998; Qin, 1999; Tousignant, 1984; Winograd et al., 1998). Delayed retrieval errors in these studies are generally attributed to source-monitoring confusions. Individuals with high-imagery abilities are able to produce relatively vivid memories of suggested misinformation that may closely resemble memories of experienced events. Source-monitoring decisions, which rely largely on average differences between characteristics of memory resulting from different sources, can become more difficult for these individuals. Based on the source-monitoring framework (Johnson, Hashtroudi, & Lindsay, 1993; Johnson & Raye, 1981; Mitchell & Johnson, in press), it is predicted that people with high-imagery abilities are more prone to delayed acceptance of misinformation.

Tousignant (1984) examined the relation between imagery abilities and delayed acceptance of misinformation in a classic misinformation paradigm. Of the five different measures of visualization ability and preference for visual processing, only one, the Vividness Visual Imagery Questionnaire (VVIQ; Marks, 1973), performed as predicted: The VVIQ was positively related to delayed misinformation retrieval errors on a yes–no recognition test, although this correlation only approached significance, $r = .20$, $p < .06$. In a similar study, Dobson and Markham (1993) examined the relation between vividness of visual imagery and source-monitoring performance. After viewing a film, participants read a narrative that included a description of the events in the film along with some new information that was not in the film. A surprise memory test that involved verbal recognition was administered after a delay. Specifically, participants were presented with a series of statements and were asked to distinguish whether the statements contained information from the film only, the narrative only, both, or neither. Participants were classified as either having high- or low-visualization ability based on their VVIQ scores. The results indicated that high visualizers were significantly more likely to report that information contained in the text narrative was actually presented in the film. Dobson and Markham hypothesized that high visualizers created pictorial images in their mind for the verbally presented material, which were more likely to be confused with visual information from the film.

Imagery ability is also implicated in other types of suggestibility-based memory distortions. For example, Hyman and Billings (1998) examined the relation between visual imagery and delayed retrieval errors in a false childhood memory paradigm. In their study, the experimenters suggested that their adult participants had experienced a false event in their childhood that had allegedly been described to the experimenter by the subjects' parents (spilling a bowl of punch at a wedding when they were 5 years old). To make the "cover story" more believable, they also asked the participants about some true events that were actually reported by their parents. When the individuals were unable to recall the event, they were asked to think about self-knowledge related to the event and imagine it. In an unrelated experimental session, the subjects were administered the Creative Imagination Scale (CIS; Wilson & Barber, 1978) as a measure of visual imagery ability. Hyman and Billings hypothesized that adults who report more vivid visual imagery as measured by the CIS will be more likely to produce false memories. As predicted, false memory creation was positively related to CIS scores, $r = .36$.

There is also some evidence to suggest that imagery ability might be related to recognition errors on the DRM task (Roediger & McDermott, 1995). However, findings are somewhat mixed. For example, Winograd et al. (1998) examined the relation between false recognition errors on the DRM task and vividness of visual imagery as measured by the VVIQ and a short form of the CIS. Based on the findings of Hyman and Billings (1998), Winograd and his colleagues predicted that high visualizers would be particularly prone to false recognition errors on the DRM task. Consistent with their prediction, these researchers found that performance on the VVIQ was positively related to the tendency to falsely recognize the nonpresented but semantically associated critical lures. More specifically, vivid imagers were more likely to claim that they remembered the false items being presented in the list. No significant correlations were found, however, between performance on the short form of the CIS and false recognition errors on the DRM task. In a similar study by Platt et al. (1998), the relation between performance on the DRM task and individual differences in visualization as measured by the Imagination and Creative Memories Inventory (ICMI; Wilson & Barber, 1978) was examined. A significant relation between scores on the ICMI and false recognition errors on the DRM task was not found. Two separate studies have also failed to reveal a significant relation between visualization capacity and delayed retrieval errors as assessed in an imagination inflation paradigm (Heaps & Nash, in press; Paddock et al., 1998).

In contrast to the relative abundance of studies concerning the relation between imagery ability and delayed acceptance of misinformation, we could not find studies that examined the relation between visualization and immediate acceptance of misleading information. If immediate acceptance of misinformation is largely due to acquiescence to misinformation, there would be little reason to suspect that vividness of visual imagery would be related to immediate acceptance of misinformation.

In summary, imagery ability appears to be associated with delayed misinformation-retrieval errors. Some inconsistency exists, due at least in part to the way imagery ability and suggestibility are measured. Of the visualization measures used, the VVIQ appears to perform most consistently across studies. The full version of the CIS is also related to delayed retrieval errors in studies using the false childhood memory paradigm (Hyman & Billings, 1998; Qin, 1999). Furthermore, imagery ability appears to be consistently related to delayed retrieval errors in both the classic misinformation paradigm and the false childhood memory paradigm. The data are more mixed, however, regarding the relation between imagery ability and false-recognition errors in the Deese/Roediger–McDermott task.

Dissociation

The construct of dissociation has been closely linked to the false-memory debate in large part because theories of dissociation have been frequently employed to explain lost and recovered memories (see Brown, Sheflin, & Hammond, 1998, for a review). Various definitions of dissociation have been proposed, including "the lack of the normal integration of thoughts, feelings, and experiences into the stream of consciousness and memory" (Bernstein & Putnam, 1986, p. 727), and the "disruption in the usually integrated functions of consciousness, memory, identity, or perception of the environment" (American Psychiatric Association, 1994, p. 477). Dissociation is most commonly assessed with the Dissociative Experiences Scale (Bernstein & Putnam, 1986). Recent developments in the conceptualization and measurement of dissociation suggest that a typological model provides a better fit for the data on how dissociation is displayed by the population at large (Waller, Putnam, & Carlson, 1996). This typological perspective predicts the existence of two groups: (a) pathological dissociators, and (b) nonpathological persons who display some level of dissociative traits ranging from mild experiences of absorption to more profound but nonpathological dissociative tendencies. Pathological dissociation is measured by the DES–T subscale of the DES.

Putnam (1997) noted that source amnesias are common in individuals who suffer from dissociative disorders. Putnam explained that a chronic sense of depersonalization and detachment seen in individuals with pathological dissociation gives a dream-like quality to their autobiographical memories. This makes it difficult for these individuals to determine if a memory for a given event reflects their actual personal experience, someone else's experience, or a dream. As a result, Putnam (1997) has observed that dissociative individuals are less confident of their recollections and that this lack of confidence may make them more vulnerable to the damaging effects of misinformation (Gudjonsson & Clark, 1986). According to Putnam, discontinuities in memory associated with pathological dissociation leave the individual open to plausible suggestions on how to fill the gaps in their autobiographical memory. Nonpathological dissociative tendencies as measured by mild elevations on the DES may also cause individuals to be less confident in their memories and more vulnerable to suggestion. Recently, several investigators have examined the relation between scores on the DES and susceptibility to misleading information.

Dissociation and Delayed Acceptance of Misinformation. If high-dissociative individuals experience more difficulties in source monitoring, they should also be more susceptible to delayed acceptance of misinformation. Surprisingly we could not locate any experimental study that examined the relation between dissociation and eyewitness suggestibility in a classic misinformation paradigm. Other evidence exists, however, that dissociation is related to delayed acceptance of misinformation in other paradigms. Most noticeably, dissociative tendencies have been consistently found to be associated with false childhood memories. In a study by Hyman and Billings (1998), for example, dissociation as measured by the DES was highly correlated with the acceptance of suggested early autobiographical memories. Using the false childhood memory paradigm, the investigators obtained a correlation of .48 between DES scores and endorsement of false childhood memories. Using a similar paradigm, Qin (1999) found a more modest, yet still significant correlation between scores on the DES and the creation of false memories following suggestion, $r = .23$. Furthermore, in Qin's study, five out of six participants who were classified as having a pathological-dissociative condition (Waller et al., 1996) created memories for childhood events that did not actually occur.

In situations where no misinformation is provided, dissociation does not appear to relate to spontaneous memory errors. Platt et al. (1998) examined the relation between dissociation as measured by the DES and autobiographical memory distortion in a paradigm that does not involve misinformation. In this study, participants were contacted the evening of the verdict of the O. J. Simpson trial and completed a questionnaire that asked about the circumstances surrounding their learning of the verdict. Subjects were then contacted either 6, 12, or 18 months later and asked to complete a similar questionnaire and a series of individual-differences measures that included the DES. No significant relation was found between scores on the DES and autobiographical memory distortion. This pattern of data seems to suggest that the heightened suggestibility in high dissociative individuals may be a result of source-monitoring failure, rather than a deficiency in general memorial ability.

There is also some tentative evidence that high dissociation may be related to imagination inflation. Paddock et al. (1998) reported a positive relation between scores on the DES and enhanced certainty for imagined nonevents. Paddock et al. proposed that dissociative individuals seem more prone to interpersonal influence in this type of suggestibility paradigm.

Studies examining relations between dissociation and false recognition errors on the DRM task have provided mixed results. Winograd, Peluso, and Glover (1998) reported that the DES scores were positively related to false recognition errors on the DRM task. However, Eisen et al. (1998) and Qin (1999) both failed to find a similar correlation.

Dissociation and Immediate Acceptance of Misinformation. Few studies have examined the relation between dissociation and immediate acceptance of misinformation. One exception is the study by Eisen and Carlson (1998) described earlier in this chapter. For a group of 130 college students, Eisen and Carlson found that scoring on the DES was significantly related to errors on misleading questions. However, contrary to predictions, DES scores were not related to performance on the specific, nonsuggestive questions designed to assess event memory. In addition, the relation between dissociation and immediate susceptibility to misleading information found in Eisen and Carlson's study was far more modest than those correlations reported in paradigms that involve delayed acceptance of misinformation (Hyman & Billings, 1998; Paddock et al., 1998; Qin, 1999; Winograd et al., 1998). Eisen and Carlson reported that DES and DES-T scores accounted for approximately 3% to 5% of the variance in commission errors on misleading questions. In contrast, two studies have reported fairly robust correlations between DES scores and the immediate acceptance of misinformation as measured by Yield 1 scores on the GSS–2 (Merckelbach, Muris, Rassin, & Herslenberg, 2000; Wolfradt & Meyer, 1998).

Summary. There appears to be a fairly robust relation between dissociation as measured by the DES and delayed misinformation retrieval errors in studies using a variety of different research paradigms. However, data linking dissociation to immediate susceptibility to misleading questions are not as strong.

Absorption

Absorption is defined as an individuals' ability to set ordinary reality aside temporarily while engaging in fantasy (Tellegen & Atkinson, 1974). This construct is generally assessed with the Tellegen Absorption Scale (TAS; Tellegen & Atkinson 1974), which is designed to assess individuals' tendency to become deeply involved (absorbed) in everyday activities. Absorption is considered to be an important factor in both dissociation (Bernstein & Putnam, 1986) and hypnotizability (Tellegen & Atkinson 1974), and has also been found to relate to measures of visual imagery (Lynn & Rhue, 1988). Labelle, Laurence, Nadon, and Perry (1990) reported that absorption was highly related to pseudomemory creation. Given the relations between absorption and these other individual-difference factors, one would also expect that absorption would be associated with delayed acceptance of misinformation.

Although there is some evidence that absorption might be related to spontaneous memory errors (Platt et al., 1998), studies that examined the relation between absorption and suggestibility have turned out largely negative results. Hyman and Pentland (1998) proposed that individuals high in absorption would become more involved in the suggested false events and therefore be more likely to accept false memories. However, a significant relation between scores on the TAS and false memory creation was not found: Although the two variables were positively related, $r = .23$, the correlation did not reach statistical significance.

There is currently no evidence to support a reliable relation between absorption and immediate acceptance of misinformation. Eisen and Carlson (1998) investigated relations between immediate acceptance of misinformation and absorption as measured by the TAS. Contrary to their prediction, scores on the TAS were not related to errors on misleading questions or errors on factual nonsuggestive questions.

In summary, the data linking absorption to suggestibility are weak. Although Platt et al. (1998) found a positive relation between absorption and autobiographical memory errors, Eisen and Carlson (1998) and Hyman and Pentland (1996) both failed to find a significant relation between absorption and either delayed or immediate susceptibility to misleading information.

SUMMARY

In summary, our review of individual differences in eyewitness suggestibility indicates that suggestibility may not be a unified construct. Rather, the literature surveyed points to the notion that there are at least two types of suggestibility: delayed misinformation retrieval errors and immediate acceptance of misleading information (Schooler & Loftus, 1993). Although delayed retrieval errors are likely to be associated with source confusion between what is experienced (i.e., witnessed) and what is suggested, immediate acceptance of misinformation is more likely a result of succumbing to suggestion under social pressure. It follows that different individual-difference factors might be associated with these two types of suggestibility. Our review of the literature is generally consistent with this prediction: Although individual-difference factors such as age, hyponotizability, and dissociation were found to be related to both types of suggestibility, other factors, such as intelligence, acquiescence, and agreeableness were mainly associated with immediate acceptance of misinformation, whereas factors such as imagery ability were associated with delayed acceptance of misinformation.

It is possible that the type of errors seen in memory reports produced by biased interrogators and misleading cross-examination in court (immediate susceptibility to misinformation) may not be the same as false memories resulting from repeated suggestive interviews or memory errors produced through highly suggestive therapeutic techniques, such as hypnosis or guided imagery (delayed misinformation retrieval errors) techniques. This distinction may also be useful in advancing theories of eyewitness suggestibility, which can benefit from the individual-difference approach as advocated by Underwood (1975). Still, much work needs to be done to better specify the underlying mechanisms of memory distortion in general, and of these two types of eyewitness suggestibility in particular. In the meantime, the courts should keep in mind that the individual differences identified by researchers to date are of limited usefulness in predicting the accuracy of an individual's eyewitness memory.

REFERENCES

Akil, J. K., & Zaragoza, M. S. (1995). Developmental differences in eyewitness suggestibility and memory for source. *Journal of Experimental Child Psychology, 60*(1), 57–83.

American Psychiatric Association. (1994). *Diagnostic and statistical manual of mental disorders* (4th ed.). Washington, DC: Author.

Bartlett, J. C., Strater, L., & Fulton, A. (1991). False recency and false fame of faces in young adulthood and old age. *Memory and Cognition, 19,* 177–188.

Barnier, A. J., & McConkey, K. M. (1992). Reports of real and false memories: The relevance of hypnosis, hypnotizability, and context of memory test. *Journal of Abnormal Psychology, 101*(30), 521–527.

Bernstein, E. M., & Putnam, F. W. (1986). Development, reliability, and validity of a dissociation scale. *The Journal of Nervous and Mental Disease, 174,* 727–735.

Bowers, K. S. (1993). The Waterloo-Stanford Group C (WSGC) scale of hypnotic susceptibility: Normative and comparative data. *International Journal of Clinical and Experimental Hypnosis, 41*(1), 35–46.

Brown, D., Scheflin, A. W., & Hammond, D. C. (1998). *Memory, trauma treatment, and the law.* New York: Norton.

Butcher, J. N., Dalhstrom, G. W., Graham, J. R., Tellegen, A., & Kaemmer, B. (1989). *MMPI–2 Minnesota Multiphasic Personality Inventory–2.* Minneapolis: University of Minnesota Press.

Ceci, S. J., & Bruck, M. (1993). The suggestibility of the child witness: A historical review and synthesis. *Psychological Bulletin, 113*(3), 403–439.

Ceci, S. J., Crotteau-Huffman, M., Smith, E., & Loftus, E. F. (1994). Repeatedly thinking about nonevents. *Consciousness & Cognition, 3,* 338–407.

Ceci, S. J., Ross, D. F., & Toglia, M. P. (1987). Suggestibility of children's memory: Psycholegal implications. *Journal of Experimental Psychology, 116,* 39–49.

Christiaanson, R. E., Ochalek, K., & Sweeney, J. D. (1984). Individual differences in eyewitness memory and confidence judgments. *Journal of General Psychology, 110*(1), 47–52.

Costa, P. T., & McCrae, R. R. (1992). *Manual for the NEO PI–R.* Odessa, FL: Psychological Assessment Resources, Inc.

Cronbach, L. J. (1946). Response sets and test validity. *Education and Psychological Measurement 6,* 475–494.

Deese, J. (1959). Influence of inter-item associative strength upon immediate free recall. *Psychological Reports, 5*, 305–312.

Dobson, M., & Markham, R. (1993). Imagery ability and source monitoring: Implications for eyewitness memory. *British Journal of Psychology, 32*, 111–118.

Durso, F. T., Reardon, R., & Jolly, E. J. (1993). Self–nonself-segregation and reality monitoring. *American Psychological Association, 48*, 447–455.

Dywan, J., & Jacoby, L. L. (1990). Effects of aging on source monitoring: Differences in susceptibility to false fame. *Psychology and Aging, 3*, 379–387.

Edwards, A. L., & Abbott, R. D. (1969). Further evidence regarding the R scale of the MMPI as a measure of acquiescence. *Psychological Reports, 24*, 903–906.

Eisen, M. (1996). The relationship between memory, suggestibility and hypnotic responsivity. *American Journal of Hypnosis, 39*(2), 126–137.

Eisen, M., & Carlson, E. B. (1998). Individual differences in suggestibility: Examining the influence of dissociation, absorption, and a history of childhood abuse. *Applied Cognitive Psychology, 12*, 47–61.

Eisen, M. L., Goodman, G. S., Qin, J., & Davis, S. L. (1997, August). Individual difference factors related to maltreated children's memory reports. In M. L. Eisen (Chair), *Suggestibility in children's eyewitness memory reports: New research and Emerging consensus.* Symposium presented at the 105th annual meeting of the American Psychological Association, Chicago.

Eisen, M. L., Goodman, G. S., Qin, J., & Davis, S. L. (1999). Individual differences in maltreated children's memory and suggestibility. In L. Williams & V. L. Banyard (Eds.), *Trauma and memory* (pp. 31–46). Thousand Oaks, CA: Sage.

Eisen, M. L., Lorber, W., Kistorian, R., Morgan, D., Yu, S., Tirtabudi, P., & Cardenas, E. (1999). Individual differences in college students susceptibility to misleading information. In M. Eisen (Chair), *Individual difference in suggestibility in memory distortion.* Symposium presented at the 3rd biennial meeting of the Society for Applied Research in Memory and Cognition, Boulder, CO.

Eisen, M. L., Yu, S., Tirtabudi, P., Nicosia, D., Breitbart, A., Krause, W., Marginian, D., & Knorr, K. (1998). *The relationship between agreeableness and suggestibility.* Paper presented at the 105th annual meeting of the American Psychological Association. San Francisco.

Garry, M., & Loftus, E. F. (1994). Pseudomemories without hypnosis. *International Journal of Clinical and Experimental Hypnosis, 42*(4), 363–378.

Garry, M., Manning, C. G., Loftus, E. F., & Sherman, S. J. (1996). Imagination inflation: Imagining a childhood event inflates confidence that it occurred. *Psychonomic Bulletin and Review, 3*, 208–214.

Graham, K. R., & Green, L. D. (1981). Hypnotic susceptibility related to an independent measure of compliance—alumni annual giving: A brief communication. *International Journal of Clinical and Experimental Hypnosis, 29*, 66–76.

Gudjonsson, G. H. (1983). Suggestibility, intelligence, memory recall and personality: An experimental study. *British Journal of Psychiatry, 142*, 35–37.

Gudjonsson, G. H. (1984). A new scale of interrogative suggestibility. *Personality and Individual Differences, 5*, 303–314.

Gudjonsson, G. H. (1986). The relationship between interrogative suggestibility and acquiescence: Empirical findings and theoretical implications. *Personality and Individual Differences, 7*(2), 195–199.

Gudjonsson, G. H. (1988). The relationship of intelligence and memory to interrogative suggestibility: The importance of range effects. *British Journal of Clinical Psychology, 27*, 185–187.

Gudjonsson, G. H., & Clark, R. (1986). Suggestibility in police interrogation: A social psychological model. *Social Behavior, 1*, 83–104.

Hajek, P., & Spacek, J. (1987). Territory, hypnotic susceptibility, and social influence: A pilot study. *British Journal of Experimental and Clinical Hypnosis, 4*, 115–118.

Hathaway, S. R., & McKinley, J. C. (1989). Manual for the *Minnesota Multiphasic Personality Inventory-2 (MMPI-2)*. Minneapolis: University of Minnesota Press.

Heaps, C., & Nash, M. R. (2000). Individual differences in imagination inflation. *Psychonomic Bulletin and Review, 6*(2), 313–318.

Hyman, I. E., Jr., & Billings, F. J. (1998). Individual differences and the creation of false childhood memories. *Memory, 6*(1), 1–20.

Hyman, I. E., Husband, T. H., & Billings, F. J. (1995). False memories of childhood experiences. *Applied Cognitive Psychology, 9*(3), 181–197.

Hyman, I. E., & Pentland, J. (1996). The role of mental imagery in the creation of false childhood memories. *Journal of Memory and Language, 35*, 101–117.

Hyman, I. E., & Pentland, J. (1996). The role of mental imagery in the creation of false childhood memories. *Journal of Memory and Language, 35*(2), 101–117.

Johnson, M. K., Hashtroudi, S., & Lindsay, D. S. (1993). Source monitoring. *Psychological Bulletin, 114*, 3–28.

Johnson, M. K., & Raye, C. L. (1981). Reality monitoring. *Psychological Review, 88*(1), 67–85.

Johnson, M. K., Raye, C. L., Wang, A., & Taylor, T. (1979). Fact and fantasy: The role of accuracy and variability in confusing imaginations with perceptual experiences. *Journal of Experimental Psychology: Human Learning and Memory, 5*, 229–240.

Kirsch, I. (1997). Suggestibility or hypnosis: What do our scales really measure? *Journal of Clinical and Experimental Hypnosis, 45*(3), 212–225.

Koustaal, W., & Schacter, D. L. (1997). Gist-based false recognition of pictures in older and younger adults. *Journal of Memory and Language, 37*, 555–583.

Labelle, L., Laurence, J. R., Nadon, R., & Perry, C. (1990). Hypnotizability, preference for an imagic cognitive style, and memory creation in hypnosis. *Journal of Abnormal Psychology, 99*, 222–228.

Lefcourt, H. M. (1993). Durability and impact of locus of control construct. *Psychological Bulletin, 112*, 411–414.

Lindsay, D. S. (1990). Misleading suggestions can impair eyewitnesses ability to remember event details. *Journal of Experimental Psychology Learning, Memory and Cognition, 16*, 1077–1083.

Linton, C. P., & Sheehan, P. W. (1994). The relationship between interrogative suggestibility and susceptibility to hypnosis. *Australian Journal of Clinical Hypnosis, 22*(1), 53–64.

List, L. (1986). Age and schematic differences in the reliability of eyewitness testimony. *Development Psychology, 22*, 50–57.

Loftus, E. F. (1975). Leading questions and the eyewitness report. *Cognitive Psychology, 7*, 569–572.

Loftus, E. F. (1979). *Eyewitness testimony*. Cambridge, MA: Harvard University Press.

Loftus, E. F. (1993). The reality of repressed memories. *American Psychologist, 48*, 518–537.

Loftus, E. F., Levidow, B., & Duensing, S. (1992). Who remembers best? Individual differences in memory for events that occurred in a science museum. *Applied Cognitive Psychology, 6*(2), 93–107.

Loftus, E. F., Miller, D. G., & Burns, H. J. (1978). Semantic integration of verbal information into a verbal memory. *Journal of Experimental Psychology: Human Learning and Memory, 4*, 19–31.

Loftus, E. F., & Pickrell, J. E. (1995). The formation of false memories. *Psychiatric Annals, 25*(12), 720–725.

Markham, R., & Hynes, L. (1993). The effect of vividness of imagery on reality monitoring. *Journal of Mental Imagery, 17*(3–4), 159–170.

Marks, D. F. (1973). The vividness of visual imagery questionnaire. *British Journal of Psychology, 64*, 17–24.

Mather, M., Henkel, L. A., & Johnson, M. K. (1997). Evaluating characteristics of false memories: Remember/know judgments and memory characteristics questionnaire compared. *Memory and Cognition, 25,* 826–237.

Mather, M., Johnson, M. K., & De Leonardis, D. M. (1999). Stereotype reliance in source monitoring: Age differences and neuropsychological test correlates. *Cognitive Neuropsychology, 16,* 437–458.

McCloskey, M., & Zaragoza, M. (1985). Misleading postevent information and memory for exams: Arguments and evidence against memory impairment hypotheses. *Journal of Experimental Psychology: General, 114*(1), 1–16.

McConkey, K. M., Labelle, L., Bibb, B. C., & Bryant, R. A. (1990). Hypnosis and Pseudomemory: The relevance of test context. *Australian Journal of Psychology, 42,* 197–205.

McDermott, K. B. (1996). The persistence of false memories in list recall. *Journal of Memory and Language, 35,* 212–230.

McIntyre, J. S., & Craik, F. I. M. (1987). Age differences in memory for item and source information. *Canadian Journal of Psychology, 41,* 175–192.

Merckelbach, H., Muris, P., Rassin, E., & Herslenberg, R. (2000). Dissociative experiences and interrogative suggestibility in college students. *Personality and Individual Differences, 29*(6), 1133–1140.

Mitchell, K. J., & Johnson, M. K. (in press). Source monitoring: Attributing mental experiences. In E. Tulving & F. I. M. Craik (Eds.), *Oxford handbook of memory* (pp. 179–195). New York: Oxford University Press.

Norman, K. A., & Schacter, D. L. (1997). False recognition in young and older adults: Exploring the characteristics of illusory memories. *Memory and Cognition, 25,* 838–848.

Paddock, R. J., Joseph, A. L., Chan, F. M., Terranova, S., Loftus, E. F., & Manning, C. (1998). When guided visualization procedures may backfire: Imagination inflation and predicting individual differences in suggestibility. *Applied Cognitive Psychology, 12,* 63–75.

Payne, D. G., Elie, C. J., Blackwell, J. M., & Neuschatz, J. S. (1996). Memory illusions: Recalling, recognizing, and recollecting events that never occurred. *Journal of Memory and Language, 35,* 261–285.

Pezdek, K., & Eddy, R. (in press). Imagination inflation: A statistical artifact of regression toward the mean. *Applied Cognitive Psychology.*

Pezdek, K., Finger, K., & Hodge, D. (1997). Planting false childhood memories: The role of event plausibility. *Psychological Science, 8,* 437–441.

Platt, R. D., Lacey, S. C., Iobst, A. D., & Finkelman, D. (1998). Absorption, dissociation, and fantasy-proneness as predictors or memory distortion in autobiographical and laboratory-generated memories. *Applied Cognitive Psychology, 12,* 77–89.

Poole, D., & Lindsay, D. S. (1994, March). Interviewing preschoolers: Effects of non-suggestive techniques, parental coaching, and leading questions on reports of non-experienced events. *Paper presented at the biennial meeting of the American Psychology and Law Society,* Santa Fe, NM.

Powers, P. A., Andriks, J. L., & Loftus, E. F. (1979). Eyewitness accounts of females and males. *Journals of Applied Psychiatry, 64,* 339–347.

Putnam, F. W. (1997). *Dissociation in children and adolescents.* New York: Guilford.

Qin, J. J. (1999). *Adults' memories of childhood: True versus false reports.* Unpublished doctoral dissertation, University of California, Davis.

Rankin, J. L., & Kausler, D. H. (1979). Adult age differences in false recognitions. *Journal of Gerontology, 34*(1), 58–65.

Read, J. D. (1996). From a passing thought to a false memory in 2 minutes: Confusing real and illusory events. *Psychonomic Bulletin and Review, 3*(1), 105–111.

Register, P. A., & Kihlstrom, J. F. (1988). Hypnosis and interrogative suggestibility. *Personality and Individual Differences, 9*(3), 549–558.

Richardson, G., Gudjonsson, G. H., & Kelly, T. P. (1995). Interrogative suggestibility in an adolescent forensic population. *Journal of Adolescence, 18,* 211–216.

Robinson, K. J., & Roediger, H. L. III (1997). Associative processes in false recall and false recognition. *Psychological Science, 8,* 231–237.

Roediger, H. L. (1996). Memory illusions. *Journal of Memory and Language, 35*(2), 76–100.

Roediger, H. L., & McDermott, K. B. (1995). Creating false memories: Remembering words not presented in lists. *Journal of Experimental Psychology: Learning, Memory, & Cognition, 21,* 803–814.

Saywitz, K. J., Goodman, G. S., Nicholas, E., & Moan, S. F. (1991). Children's memories of a physical examination involving general touch: Implications for reports of child sexual abuse. *Journal of Consulting and Clinical Psychology, 59*(5), 682–691.

Schacter, D. L. (1995). Memory distortion: History and current status. In D. L. Schacter (Ed.), *Memory distortion: How minds, brains and societies reconstruct the past* (pp. 1–43). Cambridge, MA: Harvard University Press.

Schacter, D. L., Israel, L., & Racine, C. (in press). Suppressing false recognition younger and older adults: The distinctiveness heuristic. *Journal of Memory and Language.*

Schacter, D. L., Koutstaal, W., Gross, M. S., Johnson, M. K., & Angell, K. E. (1997). False recollection induced by photographs: A comparison of older and younger adults. *Psychology and Aging, 12*(2), 203–215.

Schacter, D. L., Norman, K. A., & Koutstaal, W. (1998). The cognitive neuroscience of constructive memory. *Annual Review of Psychology, 49,* 289–318.

Schooler, J. W., & Loftus, E. F. (1993). Multiple mechanisms mediate individual differences in eyewitness accuracy and suggestibility. In J. M. Puckett & H. W. Reese (Eds.), *Mechanisms of everyday cognition* (pp. 177–204). Hillsdale, NJ: Lawrence Erlbaum Associates.

Seamon, J. G., Luo, C. R., & Gallo, D. A. (1998). Creating false memories of words with or without recognition of list items: Evidence for nonconscious processes. *Psychological Science, 9*(1), 20–26.

Shames, M. L. (1981). Hypnotic suggestibility and conformity: On the mediational mechanism of suggestibility. *Psychological Reports, 49,* 563–565.

Sheehan, P. W., Grigg, L., & McCann, T. (1984). Memory distortion following exposure to false information in hypnosis. *Journal of Abnormal Psychology, 93*(3), 259–265.

Sheehan, P. W., Staltham, D., & Jamieson, G. A. (1991a). Pseudomemory effects and their relationship to level of susceptibility to hypnosis and state instruction. *Journal of Personality and Social Psychology, 60,* 130–137.

Sheehan, P. W., Staltham, D., & Jamieson, G. A. (1991b). Pseudomemory effects over time and hypnotic setting. *Journal of Abnormal Psychology, 100,* 39–44.

Sheehan, P. W., & Tilden, J. (1983). Effects of suggestibility and hypnosis on accurate and distorted retrieval from memory. *Journal of Experimental Psychology: Learning Memory and Cognition, 9,* 283–293.

Sheehan, P. W., & Tilden, J. (1984). Real and simulated occurrences of memory distortion in hypnosis. *Journal of Abnormal Psychology, 93*(1), 47–57.

Sheehan, P. W., & Tilden, J. (1986). The consistency of occurrences of memory distortion following hypnotic induction. *The International Journal of Clinical and Experimental Hypnosis, 24*(2), 122–137.

Shore, R. E., & Orne, E. C. (1962). *Havard Group Scale of Hypnotic Susceptibility, Form A.* Palo Alto, CA: Consulting Psychologist Press.

Singh, K. K., & Gudjonsson, G. H. (1992). Interrogative suggestibility among adolescent boys and its relationship with intelligence, memory, and cognitive set. *Journal of Adolescence, 15,* 155–161.

Spanos, N., Gwynn, M., Comer, S., Baltruweit, W., & deGroh, M. (1989). Are hypnotically induced pseudomemories resistant to cross examination? *Law and Human Behavior, 13,* 271–289.

Tata, P. R. (1983). *Some effects of stress and feedback on interrogative suggestibility: An experimental study.* Unpublished master's thesis, University of London.

Tellegen, A., & Atkinson, B. (1974). Openness to absorbing the self-altering experiences ("Absorption"), a trait related to hypnotic suceptibility. *Journal of Abnormal Psychology, 83,* 268–277.

Tousignant, J. P. (1984). *Individual differences in response bias and recall: A characterization of the effects of misleading post-event information.* Unpublished doctoral dissertation, University of Washington, Seattle.

Tully, B., & Cahill, D. (1984). *Police interviewing of mentally handicapped persons: An experimental study.* London: The Police Foundation of Great Britain.

Tun, P. A., Wingfield, A., Blanchard, L., & Rosen, M. J. (1996, April). *Older adults show greater false recognition effects than young adults.* Paper presented at the Cognitive Aging Conference, Atlanta, GA.

Tussin, A. A., & Green, R. L. (1997). False recognition of associates: How robust is the effect? *Psychonomic Bulletin & Review, 4,* 572–576.

Underwood, B. J. (1975). Individual differences as a crucible in theory construction. *American Psychologist, 2,* 128–134.

Waller, N., Putnam, F. W., & Carlson, E. B. (1996). Types of dissociation and dissociative types: A taxometric analysis of dissociative experiences. *Psychological Methods, 1*(3), 300–321.

Wechsler, D. (1955). *Manual for the Wechsler Adult Intelligence Scale (WAIS).* New York: The Psychological Corporation.

Wechsler, D. (1974). *Manual for the Wechsler Intelligence Scale for Children–Revised (WISC-R).* New York: The Psychological Corporation.

Wechsler, D. (1981). *Manual for the Wechsler Adult Intelligence Scale-Revised (WAIS-R).* New York: The Psychological Corporation.

Whalen, J. E., & Nash, M. R. (1996). Hypnosis and dissociation: Theoretical, empirical, and clinical perspectives. In L. K. Michelson, W. J. Ray, et al. (Eds.), *Handbook of dissociation: Theoretical, empirical, and clinical perspectives* (pp. 191–206). New York: Plenum.

Wilkinson, C., & Hyman, I. E. (1998). Individual differences related to two types of memory errors: Word lists may not generalize to autobiographical memory. *Applied Cognitive Psychology, 12,* 529–546.

Wilson, S. C., & Barber, T. X. (1978). The Creative Imagination Scale as a measure of hypnotic responsiveness: Applications to experimental and clinical hypnosis. *American Journal of Clinical Hypnosis, 20,* 235–249.

Winograd, E., Peluso, J. P., & Glover, T. A. (1998). *Individual differences in susceptibility to memory illusions* (Emory Cognition Project Reports, No. 36). Atlanta: Emory University.

Witkin, H. A., Oltman, P. K., Raskin, E., & Karp, S. A. (1971). *A manual for the embedded figures test.* Palo Alto, CA: Consulting Psychologists Press.

Wolfradt, U., & Meyer, T. (1998). Interrogative suggestibility, anxiety, and dissociation among anxious patients and normal controls. *Personality and Individual Differences, 25*(3), 425–432.

Yarmey, A., & Kent, J. (1980). Eyewitness identification by elderly and young adults. *Law and Human Behavior, 4,* 359–371.

Zaragoza, M. S., & Lane, S. M. (1994). Source misattributions and the suggestibility of eyewitness memory. *Journal of Experimental Psychology: Learning, Memory & Cognition, 20*(4), 934–945.

Zaragoza, M. S., & Mitchell, K. J. (1996). Repeated exposure to suggestion and false memories. *Psychological Science, 7,* 294–300.

What Children Bring to the Interview Context: Individual Differences in Children's Event Reports

Margaret-Ellen Pipe
University of Otago, New Zealand

Karen Salmon
University of New South Wales, Australia

> *The emotional cannot be divorced from the cognitive nor the individual from the social.*
>
> —Brown, Bransford, Ferrara, and Campione (1983, p. 150)

Children differ markedly from one another in how well they recall and re-count their past experiences. Whereas some children provide relatively full accounts with only minimal prompting, others say little. Likewise, some children are resistant to suggestions even when faced with strongly misleading questions, and others are less resistant. Age clearly contributes to these differences, but it by no means fully accounts for them. As Ceci, Huffman, Smith, and Loftus (1994) pointed out, "Age is a rather crude variable" and may mask important sources of individual differences. Indeed, there is often considerable variability in the way children of a simi-lar age respond to requests for information. In research on children's memory and testimony, such within age-group variability has typically been treated as simply random variation and largely ignored. It is almost certainly the case, however, that at least some of the differences in the de-tail and accuracy with which children describe their experiences are meaningful and can be accounted for. Children differ with respect to a number of cognitive, social, and personality variables, which are likely to impact on aspects of both their memory and reporting of events. Such in-dividual differences are particularly relevant to forensic investigations, where the ability to predict, for example, if an individual child is likely to be misled, to lie, to be mistaken, or to benefit from a particular method of interviewing, would be of considerable value. Such questions about the role of individual differences in forensic contexts have only begun to be asked, much less answered. Nonetheless, recent studies suggest promising directions for understanding individual differences across children that help place children's testimony in context and provide useful leads as to how we might better accommodate all children giving evidence.

In this chapter, we highlight recent studies and consider theoretical perspectives that lead us to expect individual differences in children's accounts, which, in turn, may have implications in forensic contexts. The search for individual differences is not only a matter of identifying those factors that may impact on children's testimony, but also the conditions under which they are relevant. Many cognitive variables are likely to correlate with age and, as a result, their importance in accounting for differences between children will be limited to the period during which they emerge or undergo dramatic change. Others may be imperfectly correlated with age, and still others may transcend age differences and perhaps be expected to impact on memory and testimony over the life span. Further, the impact of some variables may be restricted to particular kinds of experiences or measures of recall. Thus, the impact of individual-difference variables may be contextually dependent, be specific to particular measures of memory, and/or be relevant only within a particular age range.

We distinguish between individual differences due to cognitive variables and those relating to social-personality variables, following the parameters established by Quas, Qin, Schaaf, and Goodman (1997). In the cognitive domain the primary focus of research on individual differences in relation to memory has been on knowledge and language, although recent studies have also examined individual differences in representational abilities, imagination, source monitoring, and metacognition. In the social-personality domains we focus on the role of temperament, attachment, and coping styles in accounting for individual differences in children's reports. At present, these all appear to be promising areas of research, although others will almost certainly emerge based on the recent interest in this topic.

COGNITIVE VARIABLES

Children's Knowledge and Memory

That children's knowledge impacts their recall and reporting of events is a widely accepted theory (Farrar & Goodman, 1990, 1992; Nelson, 1986). Knowledge may be particularly important in determining what is attended to and how that information is encoded (Bransford, 1979). Orn-

stein (1995) affirmed, "What an individual already knows, and the expectations that are established by this knowledge, can seriously affect how the
world is monitored, how events are interpreted, and thus how incoming information is coded and placed in memory" (pp. 589–590). Stein, Wade, and
Liwag (1997) similarly argue that encoding of the original event is critical,
as it is during encoding that inferences are often made. Stein et al.'s (1997)
perspective highlights the potential benefits of considering a child's reports
in the context of his or her personal history. For example, the functional significance of an event to an individual may affect the focus of attention during encoding, the knowledge brought to bear, the understanding process
and subsequent decision making, and action. In turn, appraisal and understanding influence the content and accuracy of memory. Knowledge may
also influence the recall of information, for example, with schemas serving
as retrieval cues (Reiser, Black, & Abelson, 1985).

There is ample evidence from laboratory-based research with children
that knowledge can impact on memory (Chi & Ceci, 1987; Ornstein,
Baker-Ward, & Naus, 1988; for review, see Schneider & Bjorklund, 1998)
even when in opposition to other factors such as age (Chi, 1978) or learning aptitude (Schneider & Korkel, 1989). Children's knowledge has also
been linked to an ability to recall and recount events. One approach has
been to examine recall of a specific event in relation to what is typically recalled about such events in general, or in relation to typical features of the
event. Clubb, Nida, Merritt, and Ornstein (1993), for example, assessed
children's general knowledge in a particular domain, namely a well-child
doctor visit, and then related this normative knowledge to children's
memory for a specific experience of visiting the doctor. Aspects of the doctor visit that children were generally knowledgeable about corresponded
to aspects another group of children had reported regarding a specific
visit to the doctor. That is, children's recall of the specific episode corresponded to what might be described as a script for a doctor visit. Clubb et
al. (1993) argued against the interpretation of children's descriptions of a
specific event as simply reflecting a script, because the language children
used to describe their general knowledge differed from that used by children to describe the specific doctor visit. For example, in describing what
generally happens, children were more likely to use present or future
tense, which is characteristic of scripts, than when describing the specific
episode. However, consistent with memories becoming more knowledge-
like over time (Bransford, 1979; Myles-Worsley, Cromer, & Dodd, 1986),
Ornstein et al. (1998) found that when 4- and 6-year-old children were interviewed about the doctor visit after a delay of 12 weeks, general knowledge began to have quite an impact on children's recall. During the visit,
typical features that might be expected to occur were omitted from the
event, and other, atypical features were added. At the 12-week delay, the

omitted but typical features were often included in children's spontaneous reports and children were particularly inaccurate when specifically questioned about the omitted features. Even when questioned immediately after the event, a significant proportion of the younger children responded that the omitted feature had been included. After long delays, it may be increasingly difficult for children to recall the details of a specific event as distinct from other similar events or their general knowledge.

A second approach has been to examine the relation between the knowledge of individual children and their subsequent event recall. Children's knowledge can be assessed either directly (e.g., as in Clubb et al., 1993) or indirectly, for example, via parental report (Goodman, Quas, Batterman-Faunce, Riddlesberger, & Kuhn, 1994, 1997). In our laboratory, we examined the relationship between children's knowledge in a particular domain and memory for a specific episode within that same domain (Bennett & Pipe, 2001). Children's knowledge of fire safety was assessed prior to a standard visit to the school by firefighters from the fire department. Knowledge was assessed again following the visit, and children were also asked about the specific event, the visit by the fire fighters, what they did, what the children did, and so on. Knowledge increased as a result of the visit and measures of knowledge at the two interviews were correlated. For the present purposes, the interesting finding was that previsit knowledge did not relate significantly to children's recall of the visit, that is, the specific episode, when they were interviewed a few days later. However, knowledge did relate to recall 6 months later. We speculated that after the 6-month delay, children's recall of the specific event had become more script- or gist-like and reflected their general knowledge rather than their memory of the specific event, whereas soon after the event children were relying on "verbatim" memories (cf. Brainerd, Reyna, Howe, & Kingma, 1990; Myles-Worsley, Cromer, & Dodd, 1986; Ornstein et al., 1998).

Goodman et al. (1994) found that children who were knowledgeable about a painful medical procedure, the Voiding Cystourethrogram (VCUG), answered questions more accurately and were less susceptible to suggestion than less knowledgeable children. Knowledge was assessed through parental report, shortly afterwards. Children who had expectations about the VCUG procedure provided more correct information than children whose parents had not discussed the procedure or who had not had prior VCUGs. Lack of knowledge or prior expectation was not, however, related to errors in recall. Baker-Ward, Burgwyn, and Parish (1994) similarly found that children's knowledge of a dental visit, as assessed from parental report of previous related experiences, was related to children's subsequent recall with more knowledgeable children providing more information.

Although these studies suggest that children's advance knowledge of a procedure may impact their recall, other studies have failed to find such a relation. In a subsequent study of children's recall of the VCUG procedure, Quas et al. (1999) found that although parental preparation was (negatively) related to the degree of stress children experienced during the procedure, it was not related to the amount of information children reported. They suggested that this failure to replicate their earlier finding may be due to parental reports of preparation being retrospective over long time delays of between 1 and 6 years, whereas in Goodman et al. (1994), assessments of parental preparation were made soon after the procedure. Alternatively, it may be that the relation between preparation, a measure of knowledge, and recall does not last over long delays. Even after short delays, differences in knowledge due to preparation have not always had an impact on subsequent recall. In addition to obtaining parental reports of how much their children knew about going to the dentist, Baker-Ward, Burgwyn, and Parrish (1994) attempted to manipulate children's knowledge by showing children a video of a typical dental treatment session prior to the visit. The 3-year-old children who watched the video did not recall more information about their dental visit than children in control conditions who viewed an unrelated video or no video.

Knowledge is not a simple construct, and the term has been used in various ways in discussions of its potential impact on memory. DeMarie-Dreblow (1991) pointed out, knowledge will not always enhance recall, with some levels of knowledge having a greater impact than others. When knowledge is well organized and overlearned it may be most effective in enhancing recall (Pressley & Van Meter, 1994). It is entirely possible that the effects of recently acquired knowledge, for example, as in studies examining the effects of preparing children for upcoming procedures or novel experiences, typically using vicarious sources, may differ in magnitude and/or duration from the effects of an established knowledge base, for example, acquired over time through personal experience.

The foregoing notwithstanding, knowledge may have not only positive effects on children's reports, it can also have negative effects (Bransford, 1979; Ornstein et al., 1998; Quas et al., 1997). Ornstein et al. (1998) found that, following a long delay, children made more general knowledge-based intrusions in their accounts of a specific doctor visit, consistent with the view that children's recall becomes more script-like over time (Myles-Worsely et al., 1986). Moreover, as Quas et al. pointed out, children's existing knowledge may increase their susceptibility to misleading suggestions about a specific experience if the suggestions are consistent with their general knowledge but not with the specific to-be-remembered event. Leichtman and Ceci (1995), for example, found that children accepted more suggestions consistent with their prior knowledge of what a character who visited their preschool was usually like, than when they had no prior knowledge. These findings extended laboratory-based studies by demonstrating that providing a particular prior knowledge framework when children read stories, leads to increased errors consistent with that framework (Brown, Smiley, Day, Townsend, & Lawton, 1977). It remains possible, however, that when events are personally experienced, distinctive, salient, and relatively unique, memories are less vulnerable to such influences.

The forensic implications of the findings relating knowledge and memory are clear. When children provide evidence, knowledge can be like a double-edged sword, both enhancing children's recall and also potentially leading to errors. Knowledge may increase the amount and perhaps also the coherence of children's accounts. Conversely, children may be more likely to make knowledge-based errors, perhaps confusing similar episodes, or, over time, drawing on general knowledge to fill in gaps in their accounts. A child's individual history and knowledge are likely to be particularly important in determining how well and how accurately experiences can be recounted over long time periods.

Language and Conversation

There is enormous potential for language-related factors to contribute to individual differences in children's memory, reporting of events, and for these characteristics to impact on children's testimony. Most obvious for forensic interviews, perhaps, is children's ability to both comprehend and use language. However, the few studies examining a relationship between individual differences in language ability and recall have failed to find strong evidence for a general association (Gordon et al., 1993; Greenhoot, Ornstein, Gordon, & Baker-Ward, 1999; Gross & Hayne, 1999). Quas (1998), for example, found that language ability, as measured by the Peabody Picture Vocabulary Test (PPVT), did not relate to 3- and 5-year-old children's free recall accounts, nor was it a significant predictor of children's ability to resist misleading questions. However, Quas found significant relationships between receptive language and children's responses to specific questions. Children scoring higher on the PPVT were more accurate in answering specific questions about an interaction they had taken part in than children with less advanced receptive language skills. Receptive vocabulary was related to fewer errors for specific questions and more correct responses. It is reasonable to assume that receptive language skills are particularly important when children answer questions. That similar relationships were not also found for misleading questions could reflect an overshadowing of the impact of linguistic factors by additional social factors known to have a marked effect on children's responses to misleading questions (e.g., cf. Ackil & Zaragoza, 1995; Ceci & Bruck, 1993; Greenstock & Pipe, 1996).

Gordon et al. (1993) speculated that linguistically advanced children would provide more information about an event verbally, but that less advanced children would benefit from the provision of nonverbal props and provide additional information through demonstration and reenactment. This prediction was made specifically for the younger (3-year-old) children, given the greater variability in language skills typical of this age group. However, the only effect of language, assessed using the Test of Early Language Development (Hresko, Reid, & Hammill, 1981), was for the older (5-year-old) children in the study, and this was a significant predictor only when considered in combination with one of the measures of temperament (approach–withdrawal), as discussed later.

There are other ways in which language may contribute to individual differences in children's recall. A growing amount of research indicates that children learn how to organize event recall, for example, through their conversations and discussions with their caregivers (Fivush & Fromholf, 1988; McCabe & Peterson, 1991; Reese & Fivush, 1993). These researchers have shown that, regardless of the specific event being discussed, there are general, stable styles for discussing past events, especially in terms of the extent and type of support that parents provide for their children. Some parents elaborate on their children's responses to questions about past experiences and others simply repeat the question until the child provides the correct answer (Fivush, Pipe, Murachver, & Reese, 1997). As Reese and Fivush (1993) recently showed, by the time children are ages 5 or 6 they also have internalized these styles of recounting the past with their parents.

There are several potential implications related to these differences for children's memory of past events (see Fivush et al., 1997, for discussion). Most obvious perhaps, is in the ways that a child may recount their experiences in terms of styles of recall, including how much information children report, the amount of detail, and possibly even the fluency of their accounts. Perhaps more importantly from a forensic perspective, events discussed in greater detail and with greater frequency may result in stronger event representations and be more likely to be retained over time than those not discussed or discussed less fully (Fivush et al., 1997). Internalizing a particular style of remembering may also eventually influence the way in which children encode events. That is, children may learn from their interactions with their parents what is interesting and what is not, what should be encoded about an event, and what information need not be attended to. Individual differences in adult–child talk are generally reflected in the way the child actually remembers and talks about the past, as the different styles are internalized.

How an event is talked about at the time, or before or after it occurs, can directly influence the content of children's reports of the event. Tessler and Nelson (1994) found that how parents and children talk about events as they are occurring influences children's subsequent recall. Aspects of an event discussed by parents and/or children while they were taking part in the event were better recalled than those not discussed. Ornstein, Principe, Hudson, Gordon, and Merritt (1997) similarly reported that the way the VCUG procedure was discussed at the time it was taking place was significantly related to children's subsequent recall of the procedure. That is, children for whom the explanations were more detailed and those who asked more questions recalled more about the procedure than those who had less discussion at the time of the procedure. The way in which events are discussed afterwards may also impact on children recall. For example, in the VCUG study, Goodman et al. (1994) found that in cases where parents reported that they had discussed the procedure and had time to attend to the child's reactions, a decrease in memory errors and reduced suggestibility was observed. Quas et al. (1999) similarly found that parental reports of talking about an event afterwards were related to accuracy in response to specific questions, with those children whose parents reported more postevent communication making fewer errors.

The effects of talking about events are likely to interact with children's knowledge in the domain of the event. For example, narration relating to an event may be less important when the event is transparent, familiar, and the purpose and goals are easy to infer. Narration is also likely to help establish links between experiences, therefore, helping the child to recognize the experience as familiar or to categorize it along with other, similar experiences. In this way, narration may be an important means by which children relate their current experiences to the past, and ultimately construct meaningful representations of their ongoing experiences (see Fivush et al., 1997). The extent to which narration is useful in tapping into a child's prior experience must, of course, depend on prior experience. When children are recalling experiences such as sexual abuse, language-related considerations lead to the prediction of poor recall under many circumstances. Experiences that are poorly understood in the first instance, and that are not discussed at the time or afterwards, may be especially difficult to recall in narrative form. As we have suggested elsewhere, events unspoken may be those least likely to be remembered over time (Fivush et al., 1997).

Source Monitoring and Suggestibility

Several studies have focused on preschool children and the cognitive skills that might underlie the ability to resist misleading suggestions. The issue of children's suggestibility has been the issue of most concern when children enter the courtroom. It has, as a result, been the most controversial topic in the history of research on children's eyewitness memory (see, e.g., Ceci & Bruck, 1993, 1998; Goodman, 1984; Poole & Lindsay, chap. 15, this volume; Saywitz & Goodman, 1996, for reviews). Although the majority of children are not mislead or subject to misinformation effects, a significant minority (from an applied perspective) are susceptible. As Ceci et al. (1994) explained, "Courts want to know whether a particular child in a particular setting is likely to be a reliability risk" (p. 389). As noted at the beginning of this chapter, although such a goal may be important in a forensic context, such precision in prediction has yet to be achieved.

Preschoolers are the most easily misled group in interview situations (Ceci & Bruck, 1993), and the age at which they are particularly susceptible to misleading suggestions corresponds to the time of development of several potentially relevant cognitive abilities. Several researchers have been specifically interested in whether it is possible to predict inaccuracies in children's reports that result, for example, from exposure to misinformation. Welch-Ross, Diecidue, and Miller (1997) argued that if children are going to maintain an original memory in the face of a suggestion that conflicts with it (misinformation), they need to be able to successfully reason about conflicting mental representations. In the Welch-Ross et al. study, children between the ages of 3 and 6 listened to a story and were then presented with conflicting information (i.e., misinformation). When children were interviewed about the story 1 week later and suggestibility was assessed, they also completed a number of tasks assessing their understanding of conflicting mental representations, such as appearance–reality tasks. Welch-Ross et al. found that better performance on the representational tasks was related to reduced suggestibility.

However, using the same measure as used by Welch-Ross et al., Quas failed to find a significant association between representational ability and the susceptibility of 3- and 5-year-old children to suggestions. It is not simply the case that in Quas's study there was an absence of variability in memory performance, because other measures of individual differences, namely language and impulsiveness, were related to measures of memory performance. If, as Welch-Ross et al. suggest, source monitoring mediates the impact of representational ability on suggestibility, these inconsistent results may reflect the different information sources used in the respective studies; in particular, in Quas's study, children had taken part in an event, which is likely to be much more easily discriminated from suggested information than the story used in the Welch-Ross et al. study.

Whereas the emergence of the ability to maintain conflicting representations is likely to be relevant only among a restricted age range, this is not the case for source monitoring ability. Indeed, the suggestibility of not only children, but also of some adults, has been attributed to source misattributions (e.g., Ackil & Zaragoza, 1995), that is, the inability to remember the source of information. Ackil and Zaragoza provided evidence consistent with source-monitoring ability contributing to suggestibility effects in young children, and found school-aged children much less accurate in source monitoring (and more suggestible) than older children and college students. Leitchman and Morse (1997) also assessed children's source-monitoring abilities in relation to children's true and false event memories. The children in the study were between 3 and 5 years old, and were repeatedly asked about true and false events over an 8-week period. Children with poorer source-monitoring skills assessed on independent tasks were more likely to accept the false events as having occurred than children with better source-monitoring skills. This finding suggests a relationship between source-monitoring abilities and suggestibility in young children. However, as Quas et al. (1997) pointed out, the effect of age was not controlled for independently, and it is possible that the correlations between source-monitoring ability and suggestibility reflect changes across age in both. Of course, such correlations are of interest in their own right. Nonetheless, more compelling evidence that source-monitoring ability is critical to individual differences in suggestibility would be the finding of such a relation within age groups as well as across age groups.

Imagination and Fantasy

There is a long history of assuming that younger children are more easily misled and less accurate than older children because, as Stephen explained, "In infancy the strength of the imagination is out of all proportion to the power of the other faculties; and children constantly say what is not true, not from deceitfulness, but simply because they have come to think so, by talking or dreaming what has passed" (Stephen, 1863, cited in Stafford, 1962, p. 309). Such views have been substantially modified since the late 1800s. Nonetheless, the possibility that imagination and fantasy proneness may play a role in accounting for errors in children's reports has recently been explored in the study of individual differences.

Quas et al. (1997) suggested that one reason for expecting imagination to play a role is that imaginative children may be better at visualizing imagined events and details, thus creating a more similar kind of visual image to that created by an actual event. As a consequence, real and imagined events are more difficult to discriminate between. The evidence is conflicting; on the one hand, Shyamalan, Lamb, and Sheldrick (1995) found that children who were more imaginative as indicated by their choice of paired items describing themselves (a subset of items from the Wilson-Barber Inventory; Myers, 1983), were more likely to report that a false event occurred than children who were low on imaginativeness on this measure. Note, however, that Quas (1998) recently failed to replicate this finding with a younger group of children, although it is possible that the measure of imaginativeness was inappropriate for the younger children in Quas' study. In our laboratory, we have also included imaginativeness and "fantasy proneness" as individual-difference measures (Priestley, 1999; Priestley & Pipe, 1999). Imaginativeness was assessed in terms of whether or not the child had imaginary friends (Taylor, Cartwright, & Carlson, 1993), spontaneously engaged in fantasy play when given the opportunity (Taylor et al., 1993), and the manner in which children engaged in tasks involving pretense when asked to do so (Overton & Jackson, 1973). Engagement in the tasks involving pretense was positively correlated with correct recall of information about the event. Further, children who spontaneously engaged in fantasy play were significantly more likely to make errors than children who did not. No other measures of fantasy and imagination related to the accuracy of children's event reports.

It is important to distinguish between the possibility that children have some confusion between things imagined and those that have happened, and an awareness of imaginative activities as representational or symbolic. The means of assessing imaginativeness is likely to be critically important in determining the nature of any relation with memory measures. The positive relationship found in our study (Priestley & Pipe, 1999), with respect to the amount of information reported, may reflect a greater degree of awareness of imaginative activities or descriptions as imaginative for some children. On the other hand, consistent with Shyamalan et al.'s (1995) findings, we also found that children who more readily engaged in fantasy play were more likely to make errors in their memory reports, perhaps reflecting a greater sensitivity to the demands of both the interview and play situations.

Nonverbal Measures of Representation

Interest in other cognitive abilities has developed from the search for ways of enhancing children's accounts using, for example, props or drawings. We were interested in children's use of props such as toys, dolls, models and other methods of enhancing children's event reports (Priestley, 1999; Priestley & Pipe, 1999). We have also been aware that to use such props presupposes that children are able to use the items as representations to talk about the past. We therefore administered DeLoache's "sticker task," a measure of children's ability to use a doll or line drawing as a representation of themselves (DeLoache, Anderson, & Smith, 1995), to 3- and 4-year-old children who had taken part in a contrived medical assessment. Children were interviewed a week later with photos or toys and dolls as prop items, or in a verbal (only) interview. Contrary to our expectations, there were no significant relationships between children's performance on the sticker task and errors in children's accounts with or without the props. We did, however, find that representational ability (as measured by the sticker task) was related to more complete reports.

Children's representational abilities were also examined in the context of understanding the mechanisms underlying the effectiveness of drawing as a means of facilitating children's verbal event reports. Gross, Hayne, and colleagues have, in two papers, reported significant associations between adult rankings of the quality of 3- to 6-year-old children's drawings of a unique event and the amount of information that the children reported (Butler, Gross, & Hayne, 1995; Gross & Hayne, in press). However, Gross and Hayne (1999) also assessed children's general level of drawing skills, using a measure of human figure drawing (the Draw-a-Person [DAP] Quantitative Scoring System; Naglieri, 1988) and found that there was no significant relationship between skill assessed by the DAP test and the amount of information recalled. They suggested that, if drawings served to cue retrieval, this effect appeared to be restricted to the actual production of the drawing itself.

Standard Measures of Memory

A discussion of cognitive-related variables that might underlie individual differences in children's event memory reports would, perhaps, be incomplete without at least raising the question of whether such differences reflect more general differences in memory or even IQ. That is, on the basis of standard memory tests such as digit span, can we make any useful predictions about children's accounts of their experiences? Surprisingly few studies have included other measures of memory. In some studies, digit span was included to ensure that groups of children for whom event memory differences might be expected are similar on other measures of memory. For example, Goodman, Hirschman, Hepps, and Rudy (1991), compared digit span scores of groups of children undergoing stressful and nonstressful medical procedures, to ensure any differences were, indeed, due to stress rather than between-group differences on independent measures of memory. However, they did not examine the relation between digit span and other event memory measures. In two unpublished studies from our laboratory, we failed to find any significant correlations between digit span scores and either verbal or nonverbal measures on 5- to 6-year-old children's recall of the event, Visiting the Pirate (Owens, 1996). In a study involving slightly older children, however, Bennett and Pipe (1999) recently found that digit span correlated with children's recall soon after they had taken part in a similar event, although not when they were reinterviewed 6 months later. It is possible that the differences between studies reflect the different age groups in each, perhaps in interaction with the specific events involved. Suffice to note that in laboratory-based studies, tasks that are structurally dissimilar typically do not show high intercorrelations (see Schneider & Bjorklund, 1998, for review).

A promising approach is suggested by laboratory-based studies examining differences in children's knowledge of memory processes (metamemory) and their recall. Henry and Norman (1996), for example, found that 4- and 5-year-old children's recall of a number of toys was related to their performance on two metamemory tasks. In one metamemory task children were asked to predict their ability to remember, and in the other, they made judgments about two pictures shown in the easier memory task, for example, pictures showing a small number versus those showing a large number of items. Swanson (1987) similarly found free recall to be related to metamemory measures in older (10-year-old) children. Bennett and Pipe (1999) found that metamorial knowledge, including awareness of strategy use, was positively related to children's open-ended event recall. Schneider, Schlagmuller, and Vise (1998), however, found that when they examined the role of knowledge, strategy use, and metamemorial knowledge in mathematical models, metamemorial knowledge had a relatively weak effect.

SOCIAL-PERSONALITY VARIABLES

Some of the most intriguing and promising research examining individual differences has come from what might at first seem an unexpected direction, research designed to examine the influence of attachment relationships and temperament on children's event recall. Yet, underlying each of these factors are cognitive mechanisms that are likely to influence the way that events are encoded and appraised. As reflected in the quotation at the beginning of this chapter, the view that children's performance on cognitive tasks such as memory is integrally connected with their social and emotional functioning is now widely accepted.

Attachment

With respect to attachment, Goodman and colleagues have examined the relation between measures of parental attachment and recall and errors for children undergoing the VCUG procedure. Goodman et al. (1994, 1997) found that stress levels were related to inaccuracies in recall but that parental attachment style was also associated with children's errors and accounted for the relation between stress and memory errors. Children whose parents indicated an avoidant or an anxious–ambivalent attachment style were observed to be more stressed during the VCUG procedure and also to make more errors than children whose parents indicated a secure attachment style. The authors pointed out that one implication of this finding is that when differences in memory are found for high versus low stress groups, rather than reflecting any direct effect of stress on memory, these may reflect personality or parenting variables resulting in both high levels of stress and inaccuracies. Preliminary evidence using the same measures of parental attachment suggests that such relations may be applicable for stressful experiences such as the VCUG, but not for other, less stressful experiences, such as children's memory of the birth of a sibling (Bidrose, 1998).

Other researchers have begun to shed light on possible mechanisms underlying the association between attachment and memory. Farrar, Fasig, and Welch-Ross (1997) investigated the association between attachment and autobiographical memory and, in particular, the relation between preschool children's secure or insecure attachment status, as assessed by the Attachment Q-Sort (Waters, Vaughn, Posada, & Kondo-Ikemura, 1995) and the emotional content of mother–child conversations about past experiences. Their results suggested an influence of both the child's attachment status and gender; insecure mother–daughter dyads engaged in more talk about negative emotions than did secure mother–daughter dyads. Once negative emotion topics had been introduced, however, secure mother–daughter dyads were more open to elaborating on them than were insecure dyads. In contrast, the insecure mother–daughter dyads elaborated only following initiations of positive emotions. Attachment may, therefore, be one factor that influences the extent to which parents and children (especially mothers and daughters) talk about particular kinds of events in the present and the past and, therefore, how they are recalled.

Following the work of Mary Main and her colleagues (Main, Kaplan, & Cassidy, 1985), Goodman and Quas (1996) proposed that one way in which different styles of attachment may influence memory is by determining the encoding and reporting of information about affectively laden situations. They speculated that children of anxious–ambivalent parents may be preoccupied with locating a source of security during stressful events, thereby influencing encoding, whereas children of avoidant parents may attempt to deny their feelings during the recounting of a stressful event. Both strategies are likely to augment the numbers of errors in these children's accounts. In contrast, children of secure parents may have an ability to form coherent representations of positive and negative aspects of their experiences and to regulate their emotions more effectively, thereby aiding not only encoding, but also recall.

Recent laboratory research examined the association between a child's focus of attention during an affectively laden event, his/her attachment status, and memory. Belsky, Spritz, and Crnic (1996) investigated the extent to which the attachment status (secure or insecure) of 3-year-old male children at 12 months as assessed in the "strange situation" was associated with focus of attention and recognition memory. The child's focus of attention was assessed by his propensity to be distracted by a clicker sound during positively and negatively affective-laden information presented in puppet shows. These researchers found that boys with secure attachment histories recognized more positive events than negative events, whereas the reverse was true for boys with insecure attachment histories. There was no interaction between attachment style and distractibility.

A pattern of findings emerged that implicates attachment as influencing both the nature of the information that children attend to and subsequently recall, and also the accuracy of their reports of stressful or affectively laden events. Of course, there are a number of issues that remain outstanding. For example, the processes that mediate the influence of the child's attachment status on memory have yet to be delineated. In real-world stressful situations, do securely attached children recall different types of correct information compared to insecurely attached children, as predicted by Goodman and Quas (1996)? Further, different researchers have used various means of assessing attachment and these may not yield similar classifications (Rutter, 1995; Thompson, 1998). The associations between attachment, gender, and parent–child talk about the past are also potentially noteworthy. Nonetheless, such relationships may, in due course, shed some light on what has been a puzzling relationship between stress and event recall.

Temperament

The influence of *temperament* on children's recall of events has also been a focus of recent investigation in individual differences. Temperament has been construed as involving enduring "individual differences in dispositional emotionality and its regulation," influenced by inheritance, environmental factors that affect an individual's biological status, and by the social context (Eisenberg, 1998), although a number of conceptual and definitional difficulties with temperament as a construct have been noted (Eisenberg, 1998; Goldsmith et al., 1987).

Gordon et al. (1993) reasoned that temperament might be a factor in children's event recall insofar as different types of interview protocols might be best suited to different personality characteristics. In particular, children who are slow to warm up to new situations might perform better when they can respond nonverbally than when they are in a strictly verbal interview situation. These researchers used the Temperament Assessment Battery (TABC; Martin, 1988), in which parents rate, on 7-point scales, the child's behavior on each of 48 items according to the frequency with which the behavior occurs. The scale incorporated six dimensions of temperament and three (approach–withdrawal, emotionality, and adaptability) were found, in initial analyses, to be related to recall. When these three variables were entered into regression analyses, the total amount of information recalled by 5-year-old children was significantly predicted by emotionality. Children rated by their parents as expressing emotions more intensely, particularly negative emotions, reported more correct information than children who were described as expressing their feelings less intensely. Further, 5-year-old children who tended to approach rather than withdraw from new situations (assessed by approach–avoidance), and who had better language skills, provided more verbal elaborations than those who were less able linguistically and less outgoing. For 3-year-old children, the associations between temperament and memory were not as strong as for the older children. However, children who tended to approach new situations provided a greater amount of nonverbal elaboration than children who tended to withdraw in the face of unfamiliar settings. The authors suggested that individual differences in temperament may be associated with differences among children in their style of responding to questions posed by interviewers. It is possible, for example, that children who are at ease in new situations provide more information verbally and nonverbally, whereas other children may respond better in one or the other modality.

Merritt, Ornstein, and Spicker (1994) also investigated the association between temperament and 3- to 7-year-old children's recall of the VCUG, a more stressful experience for most children than a standard doctor visit. Two of the six temperament dimensions on the TABC, *adaptability* (the ease and speed of adjustment to new social circumstances) and approach–avoidance, were related to children's recall and measures of behavioural distress. Children who were rated by their parents as adapting well to new situations were also judged by the technologist as being less fearful during the VCUG than children who were reported to adapt less well to new situations. Not surprisingly, more adaptable children were also more likely to approach, rather than avoid, new situations. Further, children who easily adapted to new situations correctly reported more information in open-ended recall at both an initial test and after a 6-week delay than less adaptable children (Ornstein, Shapiro, Clubb, Follmer, & Baker-Ward, 1997). However, no association between temperament and recall was found by Baker-Ward, Burgwyn, Ornstein, & Gordon (1995) when they investigated children's memory for minor surgery for facial lacerations.

These findings suggest that temperament does have an impact on the amount of information that children recall. As yet, it is unclear whether temperament influences the ways in which information about stressful events is encoded and appraised or how it is retrieved in the interview context (Ornstein et al., 1997) or both. As Ornstein and his colleagues asserted, encoding may be enhanced for children who adapt well to new situations and reduced for those who are less able to adapt and who attempt to avoid the situation in various ways. Children who adapt well to new situations are likely to feel more comfortable and this may enable them to retrieve and perhaps especially, report more correct information than less adaptable children. It may be that children's characteristic style of expressing emotion interacts with the type of event, so that, for example, there are greater observable differences in less stressful than more stressful events. Gordon et al. (1993) suggested, however, that the links between temperament and recall should be interpreted cautiously, particularly in consideration of the different perceptions of a child that may emerge through different methods of measurement.

Coping Styles

The ways in which children cope with stressful situations, both as they unfold and after their occurrence, are also likely to influence what is recalled about an experience. The construct of coping is complex and various classification schemes have been proposed (see Rudolph, Dennig, & Weisz, 1995, for a review in paediatric contexts; Spaccarelli, 1994, for a review of coping in child sexual abuse). In essence, however, effective coping involves the ability to regulate or modulate emotion or arousal, and processes involving the deployment of attention appear to be integral (Krohne, 1993; Saarni, Mumme, & Campos, 1998). Coping is, of course, not independent of temperament; for example, high intensity and frequency of negative feelings can interfere with effective coping (Saarni et al., 1998). Further, the ability to shift and refocus attention is regarded as integral to some conceptualisations of temperament (Derryberry & Rothbart, 1997; Eisenberg, 1998).

The concepts of *attention* (an orientation to the threatening aspects of the situation), also conceptualized as an active coping style, and *avoidance* (removing attention from the threatening aspects of the situation) are of particular importance to understanding of children's responses to a stressful or painful experience (Krohne, 1993; Peterson, 1989; Rudolph et al., 1995). Baker-Ward et al. (1995) investigated the association between coping style and memory for 3- to 7-year-old children undergoing minor surgery for facial lacerations. Children who were rated by the surgeon as keeping their eyes closed to a greater extent during the procedure reported less information in open-ended recall after 6 to 8 weeks than children who were more likely to keep their eyes open. Further, children who were rated as asking more questions during the procedure were less susceptible to misleading questions after the delay. Baker-Ward et al. (1995) suggested that their findings were consistent with the assumption that coping styles such as information-seeking or information-avoiding may mediate the relation between stress and memory.

Findings of Cortez and Bugental (1995) also highlight the potential importance of the focus of attention during an event on what is subsequently recalled. These researchers manipulated 5- to 6-year-old children's perceptions of control when viewing a video of an ambiguous medical examination in which threat cues (conveyed by adult facial expressions) were either present or absent. Perceived control was manipulated by a priming video, viewed before the medical examination. In the priming video, children were either portrayed as having relatively high control (e.g., a child narrator and content depicting children saving their parents from disaster) or low control (e.g., an adult narrator and a mother saving her children). Results showed that adult or child priming and the presence or absence of threat cues in the video were associated with errors in recall. Specifically, children primed for adult control made more errors after witnessing socially threatening cues, whereas those primed for high control showed greater accuracy after witnessing threat cues than in the absence of such cues. Further, visual attention was found to serve as a mediator; children low in control showed visual avoidance in response to socially threatening cues and this predicted errors. Cortez and Bugental (1995) reported that these findings were consistent with data obtained among older children who were dispositionally high on perceived control. Of note, in this context, are findings by Goodman et al. (1994) that mother's ratings of their children's expression of pride for undergoing the VCUG, presumably associated with a sense of perceived control, were positively associated with the amount of information that the children reported in free recall. Cortez and Bugental argued, further, that attentional disengagement as a means of emotion regulation may have both costs and benefits. It may serve to buffer the child against excessive levels of stress but may also limit the opportunity to learn about the stimulus. Alternately, high attentional engagement may increase the child's level of distress but may optimize the opportunity for the acquisition of information (see also Derryberry & Rothbart, 1997; Daleiden & Vasey, 1997, for related perspectives).

More directly relevant to forensic interviews, coping does not occur only during a stressful event but also occurs afterwards, including during the interview when the child is asked to provide an account of a stressful event. This may have significant repercussions for what is remembered and reported. Steward (1993), for example, identified a group of children who, when interviewed 6 months after a painful and invasive medical procedure, did not rate any touch as painful. This group (the "he didn't touch me" group) differed from another group of children who did not report painful touch and had not experienced it (the "no pain/no reason" group) on two characteristics: There were more boys than girls in the "he didn't touch me" group, and they had a relatively more extensive history of medical intervention than the "no pain/no reason" group. Despite their failure to report their painful experiences, the "he didn't touch me" children were more accurate in their descriptions of the people present during their procedure and the clinic room than were the "no pain/no reason" group. Steward comments that strong negative emotions such as helplessness and fear may "drive a wedge between remembering and reporting, and result in what we have begun to term a narrative of omission" (p. 212). This may be especially thé case for boys, with whom parents may talk less about emotions (Fivush & Kuebli, 1997) and for whom the expectation of relative stoicism begins at a young age.

When the research findings concerning the impact of attachment, temperament, and coping style are considered together, several interesting issues arise that have implications for future avenues of research. First, to the extent that children deploy their attention differently depending on factors such as their attachment status, temperament, and coping style, different children might report quite different information about the same event without necessarily being incorrect (Stein et al., 1997). In other words, individual-difference factors such as coping style and attachment influence not only the amount of information that children report and their vulnerability to errors, but also the ways in which events are appraised and the kinds of information that are reported. As Stein et al. (1997) pointed out, "Apparent 'errors' in memory can also result from the fact that two comprehenders have different goals during an interaction, and thus report different details from the event. Although reviews of eyewitness testimony studies give the impression that only one correct interpretation of an event sequence is possible, multiple interpretations can be constructed, each focusing on different information in the event" (p. 26).

This point heralds the importance of incorporating a social information-processing framework in future research in the area. Seminal work by Crick and Dodge (1994), for example, highlights how children with problems in social adjustment display a range of characteristic processing styles, including selectively attending to aggressive or aversive acts and attributing hostile intent in ambiguous situations. Similarly, anxious children have been found to selectively attend to threatening information, to quickly interpret a situation as dangerous, even though a further search would show that it is not, and to subsequently avoid the information

(Daleiden & Vasey, 1997). Such information-processing biases are likely to have a marked impact on what is stored in memory about an event.

The second issue that arises from the research reviewed in this chapter, is an emerging picture suggesting that superior recall is associated with a child's having a sense of control or confidence in a stressful situation. When the findings of the impact of attachment style, temperament, and coping style are considered together, it appears that it is the children who are relatively competent in a range of areas of functioning (e.g., are securely attached, more adaptable, tending to approach rather than avoid new situations and feeling in control) who provide superior accounts of their experiences. The extent to which a child feels in control of the situation she or he is experiencing may influence the way in which attention is deployed during the event and the kind of information that is subsequently reported in accounts of the event or, conversely, omitted. Perhaps of greater importance than the child's sense of control over the situation is the child's sense of control over his or her emotional response; in other words, the extent to which the child can regulate his or her emotional experience. It may be that children who have effective means of regulating their level of emotional response are those who will have superior recall (see also Howe, 1998, for a similar argument).

This finding has important implications within the context of children's evidence: Many of the children who are required to give evidence—those who have experienced various forms of child maltreatment—may be particularly disadvantaged in recounting their experiences. Children who have experienced maltreatment have been shown to have difficulty achieving the tasks of early childhood (Masten & Coatsworth, 1998). In a review of the literature investigating the impact of maltreatment on children, Cicchetti and Lynch (1995) reported findings suggesting that not only are children who have experienced maltreatment likely to have insecure attachment relationships with parents, but they also have difficulty regulating emotion—in other words, their coping skills are less effective, making them particularly vulnerable to both internalizing and externalizing problems. Additionally, both expressive and receptive language, and other representational capacities are relatively impaired in maltreated children, and they tend to perform at a lower level than nonmaltreated children on standardized tests of intellectual functioning. These findings highlight the potential differences between maltreated children and many of the child participants in current studies investigating children's eyewitness testimony and point to the importance of including clinical populations in our research if it is to have appropriate forensic relevance.

Not only is it possible that there are differences between maltreated and nonmaltreated children, but some recent data from Eisen, Goodman,

Qin, and Davis (1999) suggested individual differences within a mal-treated sample of children may be related to measures of psycho-pathology. In this study, a group of children undergoing assessment relat-ing to abuse and neglect were assessed on a number of measures of psychological functioning, including the Global Assessment Functioning (GAF) scale and a measure of dissociation. In addition, their memory for a physical examination, including genital examination and venipuncture, was assessed in free recall and following questioning. Higher GAF scores, indicating lower levels of psychopathology, were associated with better memory of the anogenital exam and increased resistance to misleading in-formation. On the other hand, measures of dissociation were not consis-tently related to memory scores or resistance to suggestibility. These find-ings are preliminary, but clearly raise the importance of looking for individual differences relating to children's history of maltreatment and the consequences that follow from it. Eisen et al. also raise a number of dif-ficulties in assessing dissociation, which in turn raise difficulties for as-sessing the relation between dissociation and memory measures.

CONCLUSIONS

There are important applied implications of a focus on individual differ-ences independent of age, as in the research reviewed in this chapter. A fo-cus on individual differences represents a shift away from thinking of children at a particular age as reliable or unreliable or as likely to be credi-ble or not credible. It also represents a shift away from thinking that some kinds of events are likely to be better remembered than others. Rather, a focus on individual differences highlights the way in which the child's prior history, including knowledge, previous experiences, characteristic ways of reacting and emotional response to the event, as well as their fam-ily context, interact to determine how well a particular event is remem-bered and reported. Thinking about individual differences also alerts us to the specific abilities we may be requiring of children in recalling events from some time ago, distinguishing between different sources of informa-tion, such as what has been witnessed and what has simply been talked about, the representational skills we may be requiring of a child in using a particular interviewing technique, as well as more general characteristics of the child.

We are still a long way from making the kinds of predictions the courts would like us to be able to make concerning the reliability of an individual child. None of the individual-difference variables examined would allow us, with any confidence, to make predictions about the individual child in terms of his or her reliability or accuracy. But, we have made significant progress in taking account of the interaction between contextual and individual characteristics, family relationships, parenting styles, and other variables, and their impact on children's reports of their past experiences. These are the kinds of studies on individual differences that, as Ornstein (1995) described, could potentially "assist clinical and legal professionals in the tailoring of interviews to best meet the needs and capabilities of individual children, so as to maximize estimates of what they have stored in memory while minimizing the extent to which information provided by interviewers disrupts or distorts those memories" (p. 473). Providing testimony about embarrassing, traumatic experiences will always be difficult for children. Understanding that individual children may have particular difficulties may help us better understand and accommodate their needs in the interview context.

REFERENCES

Ackil, J. A., & Zaragoza, M. S. (1995). Developmental differences in eyewitness suggestibility and memory for source. *Journal of Experimental Child Psychology, 60,* 57–83.

Baker-Ward, L., Burgwyn, E. O., Ornstein, P. A., & Gordon, B. N. (1995, April). *Children's reports of a minor medical emergency procedure.* Paper presented at the biennial meeting of the Society for Research in Child Development, Indianapolis, IN.

Baker-Ward, L., Burgwyn, E. O., & Parrish, L. A. (1994, April). *Does knowledge affect young children's memory for a very first dental visit?* Paper presented at the Young Children's Accounts of Medical and Dental Examinations: Remembering and Reporting Personal Experiences Symposium conducted at the biennial meeting of the Conference on Human Development, Pittsburgh.

Belsky, J., Spritz, B., & Crnic, K. (1996). Infant attachment security and affective-cognitive processing at age 3. *Psychological Science, 7*(2), 111–114.

Bennett, H., & Pipe, M.-E. (2001). *The effects of prior knowledge on children's event memory: Evidence from a naturally-occurring event.* Manuscript submitted for publication.

Bidrose, S. (1998). *Recalling stressful and non-stressful events over long delays.* Manuscript in preparation.

Bjorklund, D. F. (1985). The role of conceptual knowledge in the development of organization in children's memory. In C. J. Brainerd & M. Pressley (Eds.), *Basic processes in memory development* (pp. 102–142). New York: Springer-Verlag.

Brainerd, C. J., Reyna, V. F., Howe, M. L., & Kingma, J. (1990). *The development of forgetting and reminiscence.* Chicago: Society for Research in Child Development.

Bransford, J. D. (1979). *Human cognition: Learning, understanding, and remembering.* Belmont, CA: Wadsworth.

Brown, A. L., Bransford, J. D., Ferrara, R. A., & Campione, J. C. (1983). Learning, remembering, and understanding. In P. H. Mussen (Series Ed.), J. H. Flavell & E. M. Markman (Vol. Eds.), *Handbook of child psychology: Vol 3. Cognitive development* (4th ed., pp. 77–166). New York: Wiley.

Brown, A. L., Smiley, S. S., Day, J. D., Townsend, M. A. R., & Lawton, S. C. (1977). Intrusion of a thematic idea in children's comprehension and retention of stories. *Child Development, 48,* 1454–1466.

Butler, S., Gross, J., & Hayne, H. (1995). The effect of drawing on memory performance in young children. *Developmental Psychology, 31,* 597–608.

Ceci, S. J., & Bruck, M. (1993). Suggestibility of the child witness: A historical review and synthesis. *Psychological Bulletin, 113,* 403–439.

Ceci, S. J., & Bruck, M. (1998). Children's testimony: Applied and basic issues. In W. Damon (Ed.-in-Chief), & I. E. Sigel & K. A. Renninger (Vol. Eds.), *Handbook of child psychology: Vol 4. Child psychology in practice* (5th ed., pp. 713–774). New York: Wiley.

Ceci, S. J., Huffman, M. L., Smith, E., & Loftus, E. F. (1994). Repeatedly thinking about a nonevent: Source misattributions among preschoolers. *Consciousness and Cognition, 3,* 388–407.

Chi, M. T. H. (1978). Knowledge structure and memory development. In R. Siegler (Ed.), *Children's thinking: What develops?* Hillsdale, NJ: Lawrence Erlbaum Associates.

Chi, M. T. H., & Ceci, S. J. (1987). Content knowledge: Its role, representation, and restructuring in memory development. In H. W. Reese (Ed.), *Advances in child development and behavior* (Vol. 20). Orlando, FL: Academic.

Cicchetti, D., & Lynch, M. (1995). Failures in the expectable environment and their impact on individual development: The case of child maltreatment. In D. Cicchetti & D. J. Cohen (Eds.), *Developmental psychopathology: Vol 2. Risk, disorder, and adaptation* (pp. 32–71). New York: Wiley.

Clubb, P. A., Nida, R. E., Merritt, K., & Ornstein, P. A. (1993). Visiting the doctor: Children's knowledge and memory. *Cognitive Development, 8,* 361–372.

Cortez, V., & Bugental, D. B., (1995). Priming of perceived control in young children as a buffer against fear-inducing events. *Child Development, 66,* 687–696.

Crick, N. R., & Dodge, K. A. (1994). A review and reformulation of social information-processing mechanisms in children's social adjustment. *Psychological Bulletin, 115,* 74–101.

Daleiden, E. L., & Vasey, M. W. (1997). An information-processing perspective on childhood anxiety. *Clinical Psychology Review, 17,* 407–429.

DeLoache, J., Anderson, K., & Smith, C. (1995, April). *Interviewing children about real-life events.* Paper presented at the biennial meeting of the Society for Research in Child Development, Indianapolis, IN.

DeMarie-Dreblow, D. (1991). Relation between knowledge and memory: A reminder that correlation does not imply causality. *Child Development, 62,* 484–498.

Derryberry, D., & Rothbart, M. K. (1997). Reactive and effortful processes in the organization of temperament. *Development and Psychopathology, 9,* 633–652.

Eisen, M. L., Goodman, G. S., Davis, S. L., & Qin, J. (1999). Individual differences in maltreated children's memory and suggestibility. In L. M. Williams & V. L. Banyard (Eds.), *Trauma and memory* (pp. 31–45). Thousand Oaks, CA: Sage.

Eisenberg, N. (1998). Introduction. In W. Damon (Ed.-in-Chief) & N. Eisenberg (Vol. Ed.), *Handbook of child psychology: Vol 3. Social, emotional and personality development* (5th ed., pp. 1–24). New York: Wiley.

Farrar, M. J., Fasig, L. G., & Welch-Ross, M. (1997). Attachment and emotion in autobiographical memory development. *Journal of Experimental Child Psychology, 67,* 389–408.

Farrar, M. J., & Goodman, G. S. (1990). Developmental differences in the relation between scripts and episodic memory: Do they exist? In R. Fivush & J. A. Hudson (Eds.), *Knowing and remembering in young children* (pp. 30–64). New York: Cambridge University Press.

Farrar, M. J., & Goodman, G. S. (1992). Developmental changes in event memory. *Child Development, 63,* 173–187.

Fivush, R., & Fromhoff, F. (1988). Style and structure in mother–child conversations about the past. *Discourse Processes, 8,* 177–204.

Fivush, R., & Kuebli, J. (1997). Making everyday events emotional: The construal of emotion in parent–child talk about the past. In N. L. Stein, P. A. Ornstein, C. Brainerd, & B.

Tversky (Eds.), *Memory for everyday and emotional events* (pp. 267–294). Mahwah, NJ: Lawrence Erlbaum Associates.

Fivush, R., Pipe, M.-E., Murachver, T., & Reese, E. (1997). Events spoken and unspoken: Implications of language and memory development for the recovered memory debate. In M. Conway (Ed.), *Recovered memories and false memories* (pp. 34–62). Oxford, England: Oxford University Press.

Genevro, J. L., Andreassen, C. J., & Bornstein, M. H. (1996). Young children's understanding of routine medical care and strategies for coping with stressful medical experiences. In M. H. Bornstein & J. L. Genevro (Eds.), *Child development and behavioral pediatrics.* Mahwah, NJ: Lawrence Erlbaum Associates.

Goldsmith, H. H., Buss, A. H., Plomin, R., Rothbart, M. K., Thomas, A., Chess, S., Hinde, R. A., & McCall, R. B. (1987). Roundtable: What is temperament? Four approaches. *Child Development, 58,* 505–529.

Goodman, G. S. (1984). Children's testimony in historical perspective. *Journal of Social Issues, 40,* 9–31.

Goodman, G. S., Hirschman, J. E., Hepps, D., & Rudy, L. (1991). Children's memory for stressful events. *Merrill Palmer Quarterly, 37,* 109–157.

Goodman, G. S., & Quas, J. A. (1996). Trauma and memory: Individual differences in children's recounting of a stressful experience. In N. Stein, P. Ornstein, C. Brainerd, & B. Tversky (Eds.), *Memory for everyday and emotional events* (pp. 267–294). Hillsdale, NJ: Lawrence Erlbaum Associates.

Goodman, G. S., Quas, J. A., Batterman-Faunce, J. M., Riddlesberger, M., & Kuhn, J. (1994). Predictors of accurate and inaccurate memories of traumatic events experienced in childhood. *Consciousness and Cognition, 3,* 269–294.

Goodman, G. S., Quas, J. A., Batterman-Faunce, J. M., Riddlesberger, M. M., & Kuhn, G. (1997). Children's reactions to and memory for a stressful event: Influences of age, anatomical dolls, knowledge, and parental attachment. *Applied Developmental Science, 1,* 54–75.

Gordon, B. N., Ornstein, P. A., Nida, R. E., Follmer, A., Crenshaw, M. C., & Albert, G. (1993). Does the use of dolls facilitate children's memory of visits to the doctor? *Applied Cognitive Psychology, 7,* 459–474.

Greenhoot, A. F., Ornstein, P. A., Gordon, B. N., & Baker-Ward, L. (1999). Acting out the details of a pediatric check-up: The impact of interview condition and behavioral style on children's memory reports. *Child Development, 70*(2), 363–380.

Greenstock, J., & Pipe, M.-E. (1996). Interviewing children about past events: The influence of peer support and misleading questions. *Child Abuse and Neglect, 20,* 69–80.

Gross, J., & Hayne, H. (1999). Drawing facilitates children's verbal reports after long delays. *Journal of Experimental Psychology: Applied, 5,* 265–283.

Henry, L. A., & Norman, T. (1996). The relationships between memory performance, use of simple memory strategies and metamemory in young children. *International Journal of Behavioural Development, 19,* 177–199.

Hresko, W. P., Reid, D. K., & Hammill, D. D. (1981). *The Test of Early Language Development.* Austin, TX: Pro-Ed.

Huffman, M. L. (1998, March). *Individual differences in children's suggestibility for morally charged events.* Poster presented at the American Psychology-Law Society Conference, Redondo Beach, CA.

Izard, C. E., & Harris, P. (1995). Emotional development and developmental psychopathology. In D. Cicchetti & D. J. Cohen, *Developmental psychopathology: Vol 1. Theory and methods* (pp. 467–503). New York: Wiley.

Krohne, H. W. (1993). Vigilence and cognitive avoidance as concepts in coping research. In H. W. Krohne (Ed.), *Attention and avoidance: Strategies in coping with aversiveness* (pp. 19–50). Goettingen, Germany: Hogrefe & Huber.

Leichtman, M. D., & Ceci, S. J. (1995). The effects of stereotypes and suggestions on preschoolers' reports. *Developmental Psychology, 31*, 568–578.

Leitchman, M. D., & Morse, M. B. (1997, April). Individual differences in preschoolers' suggestibility: Identifying the source. Paper presented in J. A. Quas & G. S. Goodman (Chairs), *Individual differences in children's memory and suggestibility: New research findings and directions.* Symposium conducted at the biennial meeting of the Society for Research in Child Development, Washington, DC.

Main, M., Kaplan, N., & Cassidy, J. (1985). Security in infancy, childhood, and adulthood: A move to the level of representation. In I. Bretherton & E. Waters (Eds.), Growing points of attachment theory and research. *Monographs of the Society for Research in Child Development, 50*(1–2, Serial No. 209).

Martin, R. P. (1988). *The Temperament Assessment Battery for Children.* Brandon, VT: Clinical Psychology Publishing.

Masten, A. S., & Coatsworth, J. D. (1998). The development of competence in favorable and unfavorable environments: Lessons from research on successful children. *American Psychologist, 53*(2), 205–220.

McCabe, A., & Peterson, C. (1991). Getting the story: A longitudinal study of parental styles in eliciting narratives and developing narrative skill. In A. McCabe & C. Peterson (Eds.), *Developing narrative structure* (pp. 217–253). Hillsdale, NJ: Lawrence Erlbaum Associates.

Merritt, K. A., Ornstein, P. A., & Spicker, B. (1994). Children's memory for a salient medical procedure: Implications for testimony. *Pediatrics, 94*, 17–23.

Myers, S. A. (1983). The Wilson-Barber inventory of Childhood Memories and Imaginings: Children's form and norms for 1337 children and adolescents. *Journal of Mental Imagery, 7*(1), 83–94.

Myles-Worsley, M., Cromer, C. C., & Dodd, D. H. (1986). Children's preschool script reconstruction: Reliance on general knowledge as memory fades. *Developmental Psychology, 22*(1), 22–30.

Nelson, K. (1986). *Event knowledge: Structure and function in development.* Hillsdale, NJ: Lawrence Erlbaum Associates.

Ornstein, P. A. (1995). Children's long-term retention of salient personal experiences. *Journal of Traumatic Stress, 8*, 581–605.

Ornstein, P. A., Baker-Ward, L., & Naus, M. J. (1988). The development of mnemonic skill. In F. E. Weinert & M. Perlmutter (Eds.), *Memory development: Universal changes and individual differences* (pp. 31–50). Hillsdale, NJ: Lawrence Erlbaum Associates.

Ornstein, P. A., Merritt, K. A., Baker-Ward, L., Furtado, E., Gordon, B. N., & Principe, G. (1998). Children's knowledge, expectation, and long-term retention. *Applied Cognitive Psychology, 12*, 387–405.

Ornstein, P. A., & Naus, M. J. (1985). Effects of the knowledge base on children's memory strategies. In H. W. Reese (Ed.), *Advances in child development and behavior* (Vol. 19, pp. 113–148). Orlando, FL: Academic.

Ornstein, P. A., Principe, G. F., Hudson, A. E., Gordon, B., & Merritt, K. A. (1997, March). Procedural information and stress as mediators of children's long-term recall. Paper presented in J. A. Quas & G. S. Goodman (Chairs), *Individual differences in children's memory and suggestibility: New research findings and directions.* Symposium conducted at the biennial meeting of the Society for Research in Child Development, Washington, DC.

Ornstein, P. A., Shapiro, L., Clubb, P. A., Follmer, A., & Baker-Ward, L. (1997). The influence of prior knowledge on children's memory for salient medical experiences. In N. Stein, P. Ornstein, C. Brainerd, & B. Tversky (Eds.), *Memory for everyday and emotional events* (pp. 267–294). Mahwah, NJ: Lawrence Erlbaum Associates.

Overton, W., & Jackson, J. (1973). The representation of imagined objects in action sequences: A developmental study. *Child Development, 44*, 309–314.

Owens, J. L. (1996). *Cause and effect: The influence of event structure on children's recall.* Unpublished doctoral dissertation, University of Otago, Dunedin, New Zealand.

Pressley, M., & Van Meter, P. (1994). What is memory development the development of? A 1990s theory of memory and cognitive development 'twixt 2 and 20. In P. E. Morris & M. Gruneberg (Eds.), *Theoretical aspects of memory* (2nd ed., pp. 79–129). London: Routledge.

Priestley, G. (1999, April). *Representation, imagination, and children's event reports.* Poster presented at the biennial meeting of the Society for Research in Child Development, Albuquerque, NM.

Priestley, G., & Pipe, M.-E. (1999, September). *Representation, imagination, and young children's event reports.* Paper presented at the New Zealand Psychological Society Conference, Dunedin, New Zealand.

Qin, J. J., Eisen, M. L., Goodman, G. S., Davis, S. L., Hutchings, D., & Tyda, K. S. (1997, March). The impact of trauma and dissociation on children's memory for stressful events in the context of child abuse investigations. In J. A. Quas & G. S. Goodman (Chairs), *Individual differences in children's memory and suggestibility: New research findings and directions.* Symposium conducted at the biennial meeting of the Society for Research in Child Development, Washington, DC.

Quas, J. A. (1998). *Children' memory of experienced and nonexperienced events across repeated interviews.* Unpublished doctoral dissertation, University of California, Davis.

Quas, J. A., Goodman, G. S., Bidrose, S., Pipe, M.-E., Craw, S., & Ablin, D. (1999). Emotion and memory: Children's long-term remembering, forgetting, and suggestibility. *Journal of Experimental Child Psychology, 72,* 235–270.

Quas, J. A., Qin, J. J., Schaaf, J., & Goodman, G. S., (1997). Individual differences in children's and adult's suggestibility and false event memory. *Learning and Individual Differences, 9,* 359–390.

Reese, E., & Fivush, R. (1993). Parental styles of talk about the past. *Developmental Psychology, 29,* 596–606.

Reiser, B. J., Black, J. B., & Abelson, R. P. (1985). Knowledge structures in the organization and retrieval of autobiographical memories. *Cognitive Psychology, 17,* 89–137.

Rudolph, K. D., Dennig, M. D., & Weisz, J. R. (1995). Determinants and consequences of children's coping in the medical setting: Conceptualisation, review, and critique. *Psychological Bulletin, 118*(3), 328–357.

Rutter, M. (1995). Clinical implications of attachment concepts: Retrospect and prospect. *Journal of Child Psychology and Psychiatry, 36*(4), 549–571.

Saarni, C., Mumme, D. L., & Campos, J. J. (1998). Emotional development: Action, communication, and understanding. In W. Damon (Ed.-in-Chief) & N. Eisenberg (Vol. Ed.), *Handbook of child psychology: Vol 3. Social, emotional, and personality development* (5th ed., pp. 237–310). New York: Wiley.

Saywitz, K., & Goodman, G. S. (1996). Interviewing children in and out of court: Current research and practice implications. In J. Briere, L. Berliner, J. A. Buckley, C. Jenny, & T. Reid (Eds.), *The APSAC handbook of child maltreatment* (pp. 297–318). Thousand Oaks, CA: Sage.

Schneider, W., & Bjorklund, D. F. (1998). Memory. In W. Damon (Ed.-in-Chief), D. Kuhn, & R. S. Siegler (Vol. Eds.), *Handbook of child psychology: Vol. 2. Cognition, perception, and language* (5th ed., pp. 467–521). New York: Wiley.

Schneider, W., & Korkel, J. (1989). The knowledge base and text recall: Evidence from a short-term longitudinal study. *Contemporary Educational Psychology, 14,* 382–393.

Schneider, W., Schlagmuller, M., & Vise, M. (1998). The impact of metamemory and domain-specific knowledge on memory performance. *European Journal of Psychology of Education, 13,* 91–103.

Shyamalan, B., Lamb, S., & Sheldrick, R. (1995, August). *The effects of repeated questioning on preschoolers' reports.* Poster presented at the American Psychological Association Annual Convention, New York.

Spaccarelli, S. (1994). Stress, appraisal, and coping in child sexual abuse: A theoretical and empirical review. *Psychological Bulletin, 116,* 340–362.

Stafford, C. F. (1962). The child as a witness. *Washington Law Review, 37,* 303–324.

Stein, N. L., Wade, E., & Liwag, M. D. (1997). A theoretical approach to understanding and remembering emotional events. In N. L. Stein, P. A. Ornstein, B. Tversky, & C. J. Brainerd (Eds.), *Memory for everyday and emotional events* (pp. 15–48). Mahwah, NJ: Lawrence Erlbaum Associates.

Steward, M. S. (1993). Understanding children's memories of medical procedures: "He didn't touch me and it didn't hurt!" In C. A. Nelson (Ed.), *Memory and affect in development* (pp. 171–225). Hillsdale, NJ: Lawrence Erlbaum Associates.

Swanson, H. L. (1987). The influence of verbal ability and metamemory on future recall. *British Journal of Educational Psychology, 57*(2), 179–190.

Taylor, M., Cartwright, B., & Carlson, S. (1993). A developmental investigation of children's imaginary companions. *Developmental Psychology, 29,* 276–285.

Tessler, M., & Nelson, K. (1994). Making memories: The influence of joint encoding on later recall by young children. *Consciousness and Cognition, 3,* 307–326.

Thompson, R. A. (1998). Early sociopersonality development. In W. Damon (Ed.-in-Chief) & N. Eisenberg (Vol. Ed.), *Handbook of child psychology: Vol 3. Social, emotional, and personality development* (5th ed., pp. 25–104). New York: Wiley.

Waters, E., Vaughn, B., Posada, G., & Kondo-Ikemura, K. (Eds.). (1995). Caregiving, cultural and cognitive perspectives on secure-base behavior and working models. *Monographs of the Society for Research in Child Development, 60*(2–3, Serial No. 244).

Welch-Ross, M. K. (1997, March). *Children's understanding of the mind: Implications for suggestibility.* Paper presented at the biennial meeting of the Society for Research in Child Development, Washington, DC.

Welch-Ross, M. K., Diecidue, K., & Miller, S. A. (1997). Young children's understanding of conflicting mental representation predicts suggestibility. *Developmental Psychology, 33,* 43–53.

III

ADULTS IN THE FORENSIC INTERVIEW CONTEXT

The Cognitive Interview Method
to Enhance Eyewitness Recall

Ronald P. Fisher
Kendra H. Brennan
Florida International University

Michelle R. McCauley
Middlebury College

It is taken for granted that eyewitness evidence is critical for police investigations. Indeed, this intuitively obvious belief has been confirmed in several recent surveys of police officers in the United States and the United Kingdom (Kebbell & Milne, 1998; Rand Corporation, 1975; Sanders 1986). For instance, in Kebbell and Milne's survey of British police officers, 86.6% of all respondents indicated that witnesses usually, almost always, or always provide the major leads for an investigation. Despite the stated importance of eyewitness evidence, 52.6% of the respondents claimed that witnesses rarely or never remember as much information as the interviewer wants. Something is amiss.

One possible solution to this problem, the focus of the present chapter, is to improve the method of interviewing to elicit information from witnesses. The interview process is a prime candidate for improvement because (a) it can be controlled strategically, (b) police receive inadequate training in interviewing and hence make avoidable errors, and (c) existing relevant scientific knowledge can be adapted to the task. The specific solution that we examine is the Cognitive Interview (CI) method for interviewing cooperative witnesses (Fisher & Geiselman, 1992).

Several reviews of the CI literature have appeared recently (Bekerian & Dennett, 1993; Fisher, 1995; Geiselman & Fisher, 1997; Memon & Koehnken, 1992). The present chapter adds to this literature by (a) examining the CI's use with children and other unconventional populations, (b) discussing the reliability of CI-elicited testimony, and specifically, the CI's ability to combat suggestibility, and (c) evaluating the CI along forensi-cally relevant criteria.

PSYCHOLOGICAL PRINCIPLES
AND INTERVIEWING TECHNIQUES

The following is a thumbnail description of the core elements of the CI, or-ganized in terms of the three basic psychological processes: memory/gen-eral cognition, social dynamics, and communication. For a more complete description, see Fisher and Geiselman (1992). Each section begins with a global analysis, followed by related principles of psychology, and con-cludes with the specific interviewing techniques recommended by the CI to implement these principles.

Memory/General Cognition

Many crimes occur suddenly and without warning. As a result, witnesses can do little to prepare themselves to encode a crime properly. For cogni-tive theory to be useful in an eyewitness memory task, it must be drawn from either the research on retrieval processes in memory or from general principles of cognition.

Context Reinstatement. Many laboratory experiments have demon-strated that memory retrieval is most efficient when the context of the original event is reinstated at the time of recall (Tulving & Thomson, 1973). Therefore, at the beginning of the interview, witnesses should be in-structed to mentally recreate the external environment, and their affective, physiological, cognitive, and emotional states that existed at the time of the original event.

Limited Mental Resources. People have only limited mental re-sources to process information (Baddeley, 1986; Kahneman, 1973). Thus, performance suffers when we perform several difficult tasks at once. Wit-nesses may conduct superficial searches through memory because they are concurrently listening to the interviewer's questions. Interviewers may fail to record all of the witness's responses because they are concur-rently formulating the next set of questions. Interviewers can minimize these errors by refraining from asking questions while the witness is searching through memory, and by using a tape recorder to record the witness's answers.

Witness-Compatible Questioning.   Each witness's mental representation of an event is unique. Interviewers should therefore tailor their questions to the mental representation of each particular witness instead of asking all witnesses the same set of questions. This rule is often violated by interviewers who use a standardized checklist to guide their questioning (Fisher, Geiselman, & Raymond, 1987).

Varied Retrieval.   Different retrieval cues may access different aspects of a complex event (Anderson & Pichert, 1978). Therefore, witnesses should be asked to think about events in many different ways, for instance, in chronological and reverse order. When using this technique, interviewers must be cautious not to convey that the witness's earlier recollections were incorrect (Poole & White, 1993; Warren, Hulse-Trotter, & Tubbs, 1991).

Multisensory Coding.   Events are represented conceptually and also in terms of their various sensory properties (Paivio, 1971). Access to these sensory codes is facilitated by instructing witnesses to concentrate on these sensory dimensions, for instance, by closing their eyes and visualizing the event (Bekerian & Dennett, 1997).

Social Dynamics

The principal social characteristic marking the police–witness dyad is that the police officer has greater social status and more control than the witness. As a consequence, police often dominate the social interaction within the interview. Although this control may be desirable when interrogating a hostile suspect, it is counterproductive when interviewing cooperative witnesses.

Active Witness Participation.   The witness has extensive firsthand information about the target event, and therefore the witness, not the interviewer, should be doing most of the mental activity during the interview. In practice, however, witnesses — especially children — often sit passively waiting for the interviewer to ask questions (Fisher et al., 1987). Interviewers can induce witnesses to take more active roles by explicitly requesting them to do so, asking open-ended questions, and — especially with children — constructing the social dynamic so that the witnesses perceive themselves to be the "experts" and therefore should dominate the conversation.

Developing Rapport.   Witnesses, and especially victims, are often asked to report in detail about intimate personal experiences to a police officer, who is a complete stranger. To overcome this natural barrier, police interviewers should invest time at the outset of the interview to develop meaningful rapport with the witness (cf. Rogers, 1942), something they rarely do in practice (Fisher et al., 1987).

Communication

For police interviews to be effective, investigators must communicate their unique investigative needs to the witness, and witnesses must communicate their unique knowledge of the target event to the investigator. Improper communication will encourage witnesses to withhold valuable information or to provide irrelevant or imprecise answers.

Promoting Extensive, Detailed Responses.   Police interviews require witnesses to describe people, objects, and events in more detail than they do in casual conversation. Inducing such extraordinary responding mandates that police convey this goal explicitly, which they rarely do. To compound the problem, witnesses often withhold information because they do not know what is relevant for a police investigation. To minimize this editing, interviewers should instruct witnesses to report everything they think about, even if trivial or out of chronological order.

Code-Compatible Output.   Traditionally, interviews are verbal exchanges between the interviewer and the respondent. Some people, however, are more expressive nonverbally, and certainly some events are easier to describe nonverbally (Leibowitz, Guzy, Peterson, & Blake, 1993). Ideally the response format should be compatible with the witness' mental representation of the event, thereby minimizing the transformations required to convert the mental representation into an overt response (cf. ideo-motor theory, Greenwald, 1970). For example, if an event was experienced tactily (e.g., brushing against a fabric) then the witness might respond in a similar tactile mode, by touching various fabrics.

Sequence of the CI

The CI follows a designated order intended to maximize the effectiveness of the individual techniques. The general strategy is to guide the witness to those memory codes richest in relevant information and to facilitate communication when the codes have been activated. The CI is divided into five sections:

Introduction.   The introduction establishes the appropriate psychological states and interpersonal dynamics required to promote efficient memory and communication during the remainder of the interview. The interviewer attempts to (a) develop rapport with the witness; (b) convey his or her investigative needs for extensive, detailed information; and (c) encourage the witness to play an active role by volunteering information.

Open-Ended Narration.   An open-ended narration permits the interviewer to infer the witness's overall representation of the event and to develop an efficient strategy for probing the various memory codes. The interviewer notes which "mental images" the witness has of the perpetrator and significant objects (e.g., weapons) and develops a preliminary plan about which images to probe, in what order, and which questions to ask when each image is evoked.

Probing.   The probing stage is the primary information-gathering phase during which the interviewer guides the witness to the richest sources of knowledge and thoroughly exhausts these sources of their contents. The interviewer might direct the witness to close his or her eyes and to think about the best view he or she has of the perpetrator, and then to describe that image in extensive detail. Follow-up questions related to this image are asked to elicit additional information.

Review.   In the review stage, the interviewer reviews the information already recorded to check its accuracy. This also provides the witness with an additional opportunity to recall the event.

Close.   When closing the interview, the interviewer fulfills any official police requirements and offers suggestions to extend the functional life of the interview by encouraging the witness to contact him or her when she thinks of new information that was not revealed in the interview.

EMPIRICAL TESTS OF THE COGNITIVE INTERVIEW

The CI has been examined in approximately 50 laboratory tests, many of which were conducted by Ron Fisher or Ed Geiselman in the United States, or by Amina Memon, Becky Milne, Ray Bull, and Gunter Koehnken and their colleagues in England and Germany. In these tests, volunteer witnesses (typically college students) observed either a live, nonthreatening event or a film of a simulated crime. Several hours or a few days later, the witnesses participated in a face-to-face interview. The witnesses received either the CI or a control interview. The control was either a "standard" police interview or a "structured interview" that incorporated generally accepted principles of interviewing minus those unique to the CI. The interviews were tape recorded, transcribed, and then scored for the number of correct statements and incorrect statements made by the participants. Across these studies, the CI has typically elicited between 25% to 100% more correct statements than Standard or Structured interviews. The accuracy of the reported statements is high and comparable for both types of interview — see, later in this chapter, different methods of evaluating accuracy (see Bekerian & Dennett, 1993; Fisher & McCauley, 1995, for reviews; and Köhnken, Milne, Memon, & Bull, 1999, for a meta-analysis).

Recent studies have examined the effectiveness of the CI with other, nonstandard populations, notably, young children, the elderly, and people who are intellectually impaired. These groups are particularly important to study because they are overrepresented as victims and because law enforcement personnel and jurors may hold negative biases regarding their credibility as witnesses (Westcott, 1991; Williams, 1995).

Several studies have examined the CI with "normal" children, ages 7 and above. Mirroring the research with adults, these studies either compared the CI with real-world interviewers (social workers experienced in children's interviewing; McCauley & Fisher, 1995) or with a pared-down version of the CI that is similar to commonly accepted recommendations (e.g., the Memorandum of Good Practice; Memon, Wark, Bull, & Koehnken, 1997; Milne, Bull, Koehnken, & Memon, 1995; Saywitz, Geiselman, and Bornstein, 1992). The general pattern of data found with adults also obtains for children: The CI increases correct recall by approximately 25% to 70%, and at equivalent and high levels of accuracy. Furthermore, the accuracy rates in these studies, typically between 80% to 90%, are in the same range as that found with adults, supporting the claim that children's testimony, even if less complete than adults, is equally reliable (e.g., Chi & Ceci, 1986; Marin, Holmes, Guth, & Kovac, 1979; Saywitz, 1987) when nonsuggestive questions have been asked.

We offer a few qualifiers about the research and the use of the CI with "normal" children. First, as with interviewing adults, the CI is merely a set of guidelines, with the expectation that there will be variation to match the individual needs and abilities (cognitive, social, emotional) of the specific respondent. Second, almost all tests of the CI have been with children at least 7 years old. Thus, whereas we are confident that the CI is effective with children 7 years old and older, there is little empirical basis currently for claims about the CI's effectiveness — either supporting or opposing — with younger children. Finally, at least one of the CI components (changing perspective) has been contraindicated by some of the CI research (see the section on Accuracy of Recall for further discussion).

We are aware of three CI studies conducted with intellectually impaired or learning disabled children and adults (Brown & Geiselman, 1990; Milne & Bull, 1996; Milne, Clare, & Bull, 1999). In all of these studies, the CI increased the amount of correct recall (from 25% to 35%) and at equivalent levels of accuracy, similar to the pattern with unimpaired children and adults. Although unimpaired adults and children remembered more than intellectually impaired adults and children, their accuracy rates were high and similar to one another.

Only one study has been conducted with older adults (Mello & Fisher, 1996). Here, too, the CI led to an increase in the amount recalled (146%) in comparison to the control technique, and again at high and similar levels of accuracy (ca. .89). Interestingly, a modified version of the CI, which was developed specifically to meet the information-processing needs of older adults, was no more effective than the "standard" CI.

Three common patterns are observed in all of these studies with "atypical" populations: (a) the CI elicited more correct information than a typical police/social worker interview or one that followed generally recommended interview procedures; (b) the accuracy of recall was almost identical for the CI and control interviews; and (c) although the amount recalled was usually less for the "atypical" populations than for "normal" college-age adults, the accuracy rates were similar across groups, and were usually quite high (mid-.80s). From the police investigator's perspective, more leads can be generated from most witnesses by using the CI; from the juror's or judge's perspective, these various witness pools were equally and highly credible, despite the common bias that these atypical groups are not credible.

One interesting pattern in these studies is that the CI was approximately equally effective with all groups of witnesses even though the technique was not modified to meet the information-processing needs of any particular group. On the one hand, this makes sense, as there are many findings within the cognitive literature suggesting that all of these groups' recollections can be enhanced by providing basic mnemonics strategies (e.g., organization, semantic processing; Geiselman, Saywitz, & Bornstein, 1993; Presley & Levin, 1980). Similarly, within the eyewitness literature, there are general patterns that also hold for many groups, such as the higher accuracy associated with open-ended questions than for forced-choice questions (Dent & Stephenson, 1979; Saywitz, 1987). On the other hand, the finding of a uniform effect goes against the current trend to focus on differences among people. We suspect that this latter finding suggests a reorientation in thinking about intervention procedures, namely, if one wishes to enhance the performance of an atypical person, it is more helpful to know about the cognitive machinery of the typical person than to know what makes the atypical person unique.

In addition to the lab studies, two field studies found the advantage of the CI to hold equally well when interviewing actual victims and witnesses of crime. In one of these studies (Fisher, Geiselman, & Amador,

1989), 16 experienced detectives from the Metro-Dade Police Department tape recorded several interviews, mainly from victims or witnesses of purse snatchings or commercial robbery. The detectives then were divided into two equivalent groups based on their supervisors' evaluations and on their objective performance (number of statements elicited on the tape recorded interviews). One of the two groups received training on the CI, and the other did not. Although the two groups were comparable before training, the trained group of detectives elicited 63% more information than the untrained group after training. Furthermore, the trained detectives elicited 48% more alleged facts after training than before training. Of the seven trained detectives, six improved dramatically (34% to 115%). Only the one detective who did not change his interviewing style did not improve.

In such field studies, accuracy cannot be measured directly. We therefore estimated accuracy by examining those cases in which there was a second witness to determine if the second witness corroborated the experimental witness's testimony. Of the 325 potentially corroborable statements, (a) almost all (94%) were corroborated, and (b) the corroboration rates were as high for the CI-trained interviews (94%) as for the untrained interviews (93%).

A parallel field study was conducted in England by George and Clifford (1992, 1996) in which experienced police investigators tape recorded interviews before and after training (or no training for some). The investigators' questioning styles changed dramatically as a result of CI training. Compared to the untrained group, and also to themselves before training, the CI-trained group (a) asked fewer questions, (b) asked a higher proportion of open-ended questions, (c) asked fewer leading questions, and (d) interjected more pauses. These changes in questioning style were also accompanied by an increase in the amount of information elicited. The CI group elicited 55% more information after than before training, and 14% more information than the untrained group.

The one task in which the CI has not been successful is in identifying people from photoarrays or lineups. In four separate studies conducted in Fisher's lab, the Correct and False Identification rates were virtually identical for the CI and standard interview procedures (Fisher, Quigley, Brock, Chin, & Cutler, 1990). The CI fared somewhat better in a recent study by Gwyer and Clifford (1997), in which there was a slight reduction in False Identifications, but no differences in Hits. But even here, the positive effects did not occur reliably. They were noticeable at short retention intervals (2 days) but not at long retention intervals (4 days). Thus, whereas the CI reliably enhanced performance in tasks that required describing people, it has not been helpful in tasks that required identifying people.

In summary, the CI effect, at least with description tasks (i.e., descriptions of experiences as opposed to identification tasks), has been found repeatedly by different researchers, with different witness populations, and in a variety of settings. Furthermore, the magnitude of the effect is extremely large. In Köhnken et al's (1999) meta-analysis of 55 experiments, the mean effect size was 0.87 (see Cohen, 1988). We suspect that this effect size is actually an underestimate of the CI's effectiveness, as many studies contained in the meta-analysis (a) implemented only a few of the CI's many components (all of the studies using the original version of the CI; e.g., Geiselman et al., 1984); (b) did not train the interviewers properly (e.g., Memon, Holley, Milne, Koehnken, & Bull, 1994); or (c) compared the CI to an unusually good control (structured) interview, which is considerably better than a typical police or social worker interview (Fisher, 1999). Despite these factors, which ought to dilute the CI effect, the magnitude of the effect is still large.

ACCURACY OF RECALL

Although it is generally agreed that the CI elicits considerably more information than conventional interview techniques, there is disagreement about how to interpret these findings. The pivotal question here is whether or not the additional information elicited by the CI is purchased with a concomitant decrease in accuracy. If so, this would trivialize the CI as a memory-enhancing technique, because its benefits might be explained simply as the other side of the quantity–accuracy tradeoff (Koriat & Goldsmith, 1996).

How might an interview procedure affect the accuracy of recollection? We adopt as our conceptual framework that errors of recollection occur because of source confusions (Johnson, Hashtroudi, & Lindsay, 1993) and/or failures of metacognition to edit incorrect recollections. Second, we assume that errors of recollection can either occur naturally or they can be induced artificially by an external agent who introduces misleading information during the investigation.

Naturally Occurring Errors

The first priority is to decide how to measure recall accuracy, as different methods are reported in the literature. Sometimes (in)accuracy is reported as the absolute number of errors that appear in a witness's testimony and sometimes it is reported as the proportion of all responses that are incorrect (i.e., rate of inaccuracy). This distinction is critical, as the CI occasionally increases the absolute number of errors, but it never increases the rate of inaccuracy. We present here a detailed argument about why the absolute number of incorrect statements is not an appropriate measure of inaccuracy, because some researchers have drawn incorrect conclusions based on using this measure.

The concept of recall accuracy refers to the degree to which a witness's recollection corresponds to what actually happened. As such, recall accuracy is conventionally measured as the number of errors (incorrect statements) divided by the total number of statements recalled (Koriat & Goldsmith, 1994). This normalizing procedure, dividing by the total number of responses, is implemented to equate for differences in total amount recalled, which varies across different conditions. Comparable normalizing functions exist in almost all domains. In signal detection theory, for instance, proneness to error is measured as the number of false alarms divided by the total number of catch trials (False Alarm rate). Similarly, a car's efficiency is measured as miles per gallon, and a baseball player's effectiveness is the number of hits per total number of at bats. Assuming that recollection accuracy is no different than these other measures, error rate (number of errors divided by total number of responses) is the appropriate measure.

To reify the argument, imagine that two people witness a crime, and that each can provide 100 facts at 90% accuracy. Interviewing both witnesses will generate more errors (20) than interviewing only one (10). But certainly, no one would refuse to interview the second witness simply because the total number of errors will increase. The second witness's set of 100 facts is just as informative as the first. And it is obviously better to have 200 facts at 90% accuracy than 100 facts at 90% accuracy. The analogy to the CI is apparent: It elicits additional facts, but at the same accuracy rate. Anyone who is concerned about additional (absolute number of) errors when using the CI would have to argue that it is preferable to interview only one of the two witnesses. The logical extension of this argument is not to interview anyone at all for fear of eliciting some incorrect responses. Does anyone, other than the criminal, really endorse this policy? Accuracy rate, and not absolute number of errors, is the appropriate measure.

When we examine accuracy rate, the CI is equivalent or slightly better than Standard or Structured interviews. In Köhnken et al's (1999) meta-analysis of 55 experiments, the accuracy rates for CI and control interviews were .85 and .82, respectively. Therefore, we can safely conclude that there is no cause for concern that the CI generates unduly low accuracy, or at least lower accuracy than any other tested interview method.

Which components of the CI allow witnesses to maintain a relatively high accuracy rate while recalling additional information? It is difficult to isolate specific components of the CI, as they are typically manipulated as a "package." Nevertheless, we speculate that three techniques are critical: (a) Witnesses are told explicitly not to guess or fabricate answers, (b) most of the information is gathered from open-ended questions, and (c) few leading questions are asked. We suspect that these tactics encourage witnesses to maintain a high metacognitive threshold before outputing recollections (Koriat & Goldsmith, 1996) and they introduce few opportunities for source confusions (Johnson et al., 1993). We do not take any special credit for having developed these strategies, as certainly they were known before the CI was developed. Nevertheless, these tactics are observed in practice more so when interviewers are trained to conduct a CI than when either not trained or when trained to conduct more conventional police interviews (Fisher et al., 1987; George & Clifford, 1992, 1996).

It has been suggested by others that various components of the CI should decrease recollection accuracy. The following three CI components have been targeted: visualization, report everything, and change perspective. Roberts (1996) claimed that visualization should lower accuracy, as it has been found to promote errors in studies using the source-monitoring framework (Johnson et al., 1993). Similarly, Loftus and her colleagues have suggested that the use of guided imagery may be responsible for some of the false memories observed when attempting to recover previously inaccessible memories in a clinical setting (Garry, Manning, Loftus, & Sherman, 1996; Loftus, 1998). It is important to distinguish between the visualization procedure as used in source-monitoring experiments or in clinical settings and as used in the CI. Participants in source-monitoring experiments are asked to visualize a scene or event that the experimenter *knows* to be incorrect; in other words, it is a blatantly deceptive (misleading) technique. Alternatively, experimental participants may be asked to imagine an event which they have already claimed did not happen (Garry et al., 1996). Within a clinical setting, the clinician may direct the client to construct an image (the interpretation sought by the clinician) of an event that the client could not previously recall (e.g., Maltz, 1991). By comparison, when visualization is used in the CI, witnesses are asked to visualize an event *they have already described verbally* to the interviewer, and without any suggestion by the interviewer about what should be incorporated into the image. Such a use of visualization, which is known to enhance recollection without decreasing the accuracy rate (Bekerian & Dennett, 1997), is quite different from that used in the source-monitoring or false-memory research.

Milne (1997) suggested that the report everything technique could encourage errors because it asks witnesses "to lower their subjective criterion" for responding (p. 34) and presumably encourages a witness to guess or fabricate (see also Memon, Wark, Bull, & Koehnken, 1997; Memon, Wark, Holley, Bull, & Koehnken, 1997). This is a misreading of the report everything technique as stated in Fisher and Geiselman (1992), where witnesses are asked to report everything, "when [they] think of it, whether it seems trivial, out of place, or inconsistent [with earlier claims]" and that they should not worry about the story being "well organized and systematic" (p. 41). There is no suggestion that witnesses should lower their output criterion to produce unsure responses. Just the opposite, "[The interviewer] must explicitly warn [the witness] not to guess or fabricate" (p. 41). Once again, we suspect that some of the criticism of the CI has been misdirected.

We agree with some of the criticism that has been leveled at the change perspective technique, in which witnesses are encouraged to view the event from another salient person's perspective. This has been shown to be problematic in some tests with young children (Geiselman & Padilla, 1988; Memon, Cronin, Eaves, & Bull, 1993; Saywitz et al., 1992) — although not in all tests (Memon et al., 1993). Given the potential for error, we therefore currently recommend not using the change perspective technique for young children. When adults are tested, the technique does not decrease accuracy (Boon & Noon, 1994; Memon, Cronin, Eaves, & Bull, 1995; Milne, 1997). We suggest that changing perspective might be most valuable with adult witnesses in highly traumatic cases, when witnesses would otherwise find describing the event from their own perspective too disturbing. In such instances, witnesses may be able to overcome their fears by describing the event as if seen through another person's eyes, a technique used periodically by psychiatrists in highly arousing situations (Schacter, 1996; see also Nigro & Neisser, 1983). When the technique is used, it is imperative that the interviewer indicate that the witness should report only those events that he or she actually saw, and not to fabricate a response (see Fisher & Geiselman, 1992, p. 111).

Induced Errors

As suggested earlier, police interviewers who use the CI are less likely to induce errors by asking misleading questions than are conventional police interviewers (George & Clifford, 1992). Police, however, are not the only people who interview or interact with victim/witnesses. Well-meaning parents or friends of the victim/witness may also introduce misleading information, knowingly or unknowingly. It would also not be surprising for attorneys to introduce misleading information. Can the CI circumvent the potentially distorting effects of misleading information introduced by others?

An effective interview procedure might reduce the undesirable effects of misleading questions either by (a) inoculating the witness against later misleading questions, or (b) circumventing the source confusion created by an earlier misleading question. Several laboratory experiments have been conducted in which the misleading questions were given before the interview (CI or control; Geiselman, Fisher, Cohen, Holland, & Surtes, 1986; Hayes & Delamothe, 1997, Milne et al., 1995), after the interview (Geiselman et al., 1986; Milne et al., 1995), or both before and after the interview (Memon, Holley, Wark, Bull, & Koehnken, 1996). In overview, it appears that the CI can reduce somewhat the debilitating effects of misleading questions; however, this occurs only when the CI is conducted before the misleading questions are asked. Once the misleading questions are asked, their influence cannot be reduced by conducting a later CI.

These results are disconcerting, given that many people will have opportunity to alter the witness's memory irrevocably before a proper interview can be conducted. Furthermore, some of these people, especially family and friends of the witness, are outside the boundaries of the law, so that little can be done to prevent them from altering the witness's memory. One implication of this sensitivity to external influence is that it is important to interview the witnesses properly as early as possible after a critical event to inoculate them against later improprieties. Often, police officers who arrive first on the scene only conduct a cursory interview to elicit the basic facts, and then leave the thorough interviewing for later in the investigation. As a final note, the finding that an earlier CI may inoculate witnesses somewhat against ensuing leading questions is particularly important because interviewers are most likely to ask leading questions at the end of the interview, after extracting as much information as possible from nonleading questions. Indeed, the Memorandum of Good Practice (1992) sanctions the use of leading questions as a last resort, after having elicited as much information as possible from nonleading questions.

To summarize the empirical research on the information-gathering capabilities of the CI:

1. The CI elicits more correct information than conventional police interviewing procedures, or procedures based on generally accepted principles of interviewing.
2. The information gathered with the CI is of equivalent or slightly higher accuracy than information gathered with other techniques.
3. The CI has been found to be effective with a wide variety of witnesses, ranging from approximately 7 to 80 years of age, and with those of limited intellectual ability; the CI has not been tested adequately with children less than 7 years old (for the lone study, see Chapman & Perry, 1995).
4. CI interviewers are less likely than conventional police interviewers to ask misleading questions; furthermore, CI interviewers are more likely to use open-ended questions, which are known to elicit more accurate responses than do closed-ended questions.

5. The CI can reduce somewhat the effect of misleading questions, but only when the CI precedes the misleading questions.

LEGAL CHALLENGES

Although the CI has been found reliably to enhance recollection, might it contain other characteristics that render it unacceptable for forensic use? As with any innovative technique, and especially one that is used primarily by the prosecution — although note that the CI could be used by the defense — we expect the CI to be challenged in the courts. On what grounds might it be challenged, and how well does it stand up to these attacks?

There are at least five possible lines of attack against the CI (cf. hypnosis; Wrightsman, 1987): First, the CI may generate unreliable information; second, it may render witnesses hypersuggestible to leading or misleading questions; third, it may alter the witness's confidence; fourth, it may unduly influence the perceptions of decision makers involved in the case; and fifth, it may alter the effectiveness of ensuing interviews or other procedures conducted with the witness.

We can dismiss the first two concerns, as we have already noted that (a) CI-elicited recollections are as accurate or slightly more accurate than those from conventional interviews, and (b) the CI does not render witnesses hypersuggestible to leading questions. We focus now on the remaining arguments and then examine two legal cases in which the CI was at issue.

Witness Confidence

Even if the CI does not directly affect the testimony itself, it may elevate witnesses' confidence in their testimony, which might inflate their influence on various decision makers (Cutler, Penrod, & Dexter, 1989; Cutler, Penrod, & Stuve, 1988; summarized in Cutler & Penrod, 1995). This would be particularly disturbing if witnesses were unduly confident after an incorrect recollection, and especially after an incorrect positive identification (cf. hypnosis; Sheehan & Tilden, 1983). Seven experiments (five description-recall tasks and two identification tasks) have examined the effects of the CI on witness confidence (measured either by self-report scales or as inferred by trained judges). Of the five recall tasks, two experiments found no reliable differences in confidence between the CI and a control interview (McCauley & Fisher, 1995; Mello & Fisher, 1996); one found a slight increase in confidence for the CI, but this was a harmless effect, as it occurred only for correct responses — there was no difference for incorrect responses (Geiselman, et al., 1984); one found a slight increase in confidence (Gwyer & Clifford, 1997); and one found a slight decrease in confidence for the CI (Köhnken, Schimmossek, Aschermann, & Hofer, 1995). Of the two experiments that examined identification (from photo-arrays and videotaped lineups), both found no differences between the CI and control interviews (Fisher, Quigley, Brock, Chin, & Cutler, 1990; Gwyer & Clifford, 1997). On balance, the evidence appears to suggest that the CI does not unduly increase witnesses' confidence in their recollec-tions, either for descriptions or identifications.

Perceptions of Decision Makers

Thus far, all of the studies have examined the effect of conducting a CI on the witness's behavior or on the testimony itself. However, because the ul-timate decision maker is someone other than the witness (e.g., police offi-cer, attorney, juror, or judge), we also need to be concerned with their im-pressions. What are these decision makers' perceptions of the CI and the resulting testimony? Do they assign either greater or lesser credibility to witnesses who have been interviewed with a CI?

Two recent studies examined these issues. Kebbell, Wagstaff, and Preece (in press) presented transcripts to jurors in a mock trial (burglary) and informed them that the witnesses' testimony was elicited either by an innovative technique (original version of CI) or by a procedure typically used by British police (asking the witness to "try again" to recall addi-tional information). The jurors were instructed about the various compo-nents of the CI. After reading the transcripts, the jurors answered several questions about the quality of the interviewing techniques. For our pur-poses, the critical questions focused on whether the techniques increased the likelihood of eliciting incorrect information and whether they should be used by the police. The jurors also made a guilty–not guilty verdict. The results showed that the jurors' evaluations of the CI and control tech-niques were indistinguishable on all dimensions, including verdict.

In a second study, subjects listened to tape recordings (taken from an earlier CI experiment) of witnesses being interviewed with a CI or with a conventional police interview (Fisher, Mello, & McCauley, 1999). The lis-teners then rated the credibility of the witnesses on several dimensions (e.g., accuracy of memory, confidence, intelligence, trustworthiness). In two separate experiments, one in which the witnesses were children and the second in which the witnesses were adults, there were no differences in perceived credibility. These nondifferences were apparently not due to insensitivity of the data, as other differences were observed: Specifically, conventional interviewers were perceived to be more manipulative than were CI interviewers. This was a serendipitous finding, but, with the ben-efit of hindsight, not all that surprising given that CI interviewers ask fewer questions, ask fewer leading questions, and in general play a more passive role in the interview than conventional interviewers. These results suggest that, if anything, the CI should be more acceptable as an interview procedure — assuming, of course, that it is undesirable for an interviewer to manipulate the witness.

Carry-Over to Other Investigative Procedures

Although the information gathered in the CI interview itself is not tainted, the act of conducting a CI may distort or invalidate other procedures that occur later in the investigation. Two possible candidates are (a) a follow-up interview conducted by another investigator, and (b) an analysis of the truthfulness of the witness's testimony.

Three experiments have examined whether there are any carry-over effects of conducting a CI on a later interview. McCauley and Fisher (1995) interviewed young children with either a CI or a Standard interview a few hours after playing a game and then later, after 2 weeks; Brock, Fisher, and Cutler (1999) interviewed young adults within 10 minutes after watching a video of a car accident and then 1 week later; and Memon, Wark, Holley, Bull, and Koehnken (1996) interviewed young children 1 to 2 days after watching a live magic show and then 10 to 13 days later. In all of these studies, the CI enhanced recall at the time it was conducted, but in none of these studies was there a carry-over effect on the follow-up interview. Neither the amount nor the accuracy of recall on the second interview was affected by the type of interview conducted earlier.

A critical component of an investigation, especially of child witnesses who have allegedly been abused, is to evaluate the credibility or truthfulness of the witness's testimony. One method that has been somewhat successful in this task is Statement Validity Assessment, of which Criteria-Based Content Analysis (CBCA) is a core component (Köhnken & Steller, 1988). The issue is whether CBCA can be used effectively in conjunction with a CI, or whether the administration of a CI interferes with using the CBCA. We expected the CI to be helpful — or at least not disruptive — because the child's narrative is an essential part of the CBCA, and the CI facilitates obtaining such narratives. Steller and Wellershaus (1995) interviewed children either with a simplified version of the CI (only context reinstatement and varied retrieval) or with the traditional interview procedure used in such CBCA studies. They found that, although judges (trained adults) rated stories as more truthful (whether actually true or not) when using the CI than a conventional interview, the ability to discriminate between truthful and fabricated statements was equivalent. Köhnken et al. (1995) replicated the experiment with adult respondents, but with the complete CI, and again found that the CBCA discriminated equally well between truthful and fabricated statements whether the CI or the more traditional interview was conducted. Furthermore, when discriminant analyses were conducted with both types of interview, the CI was slightly more discriminating than was the traditional technique. Thus, at least with respect to using the CBCA to evaluate the truthfulness of testimony, the CI can be implemented without any loss of discriminating power.

Court Cases

We know of only two court cases, one in England and one in the United States, in which the CI was at issue. In *R v. Hill* (1995, as described in Milne, 1997, and Ray Bull, personal communication, December 3, 1997), which was heard by the National Court of Appeal in London, a convicted murderer claimed that he did not commit the crime, but that his friend did. The friend was then interviewed with the CI and provided a detailed account of the murder episode. The Court then received a report reviewing the published CI research written by the appellant's expert and found acceptable by the Crown lawyers' (prosecution) expert. Eventually, the court overturned the original conviction, claiming that the (original) eyewitness evidence could have been mistaken. The Court did not mention the CI in its ruling, thus we do not know whether the Court viewed the CI favorably or unfavorably. Its decision, however, was compatible with the information elicited by the CI and incompatible with the original eyewitness testimony.

A second case entailed a pretrial hearing in California, in which the defendant was charged with vehicular homicide (*People v. Tuggle*, 1995). Some of the evidence used by the prosecution had been elicited from witnesses by a police officer trained to use the CI. The defense attorney challenged the use of the CI, claiming that it was similar to hypnosis and that it promoted inaccurate eyewitness testimony. After listening to expert witnesses from both sides testify about the CI, the judge ruled against the defense's objection to the CI and permitted the CI-elicited testimony to stand.

Admittedly, these are only two cases, and we do not know if other cases will bring more potent arguments against the use of the CI. As matters stand now, though, the CI has not been challenged successfully, and CI-elicited testimony has been accepted by the courts.

We expect the CI to be challenged in the future by attorneys, simply because of their obligation to challenge any innovative procedure used by the opposition. In our thinking, such a challenge should be based on the specific components of the CI — a particular instruction given by the interviewer or a specific question — rather than to challenge the entire interview. At some level, the CI is just a collection of individual techniques, and its acceptability should be based on the component techniques, not on whether a label has been given to the collection of component techniques (the "Cognitive Interview"). Furthermore, a proper challenge needs to demonstrate that the offensive instruction or question had actually been implemented during the interview, and not merely that the interviewer was trained to use the technique or that the offensive technique was nominally a component of the CI. This is critical because, in most cases, interviewers use only a fraction of all the CI techniques (George & Clifford, 1992; Kebbell, Milne, & Wagstaff, 1999; Memon, Wark, Holley, Bull, & Koehnken, 1996). Finally, an effective challenge needs to present a compelling reason to believe that a particular CI technique promotes incorrect recollection. Of the techniques that are regularly used by CI-trained police interviewers in actual investigations (see George & Clifford 1992; Kebbell et al., 1999), none are known to promote increased errors. Nevertheless, it will be interesting to see how challenges to the CI materialize in the future.

CONCLUSION

We conclude this chapter with a note of warning. There is currently enough experimental and anecdotal evidence to demonstrate that the CI elicits considerably more information than a conventional police interview. There is no evidence, however, that the information gathered with the CI is more accurate than information gathered with conventional interviews. Across several laboratory and field experiments, recollections elicited by the CI were equivalent to, or only slightly more accurate, than those elicited by conventional interviews. Judges, jurors, police investigators and others who make decisions based on witness testimony should therefore be equally reserved or confident about the testimony's accuracy and should not be influenced by whether it was elicited by a CI or a conventional interview. There is simply more information on which to base the decision.

ACKNOWLEDGMENTS

We wish to thank Ed Geiselman, a valued colleague, for his work to develop the CI; Becky Milne for her contribution to the research and for her valuable comments on an earlier draft of this chapter; and the National Institute of Justice for their support (grants USDJ-83-IJ-CX-0025, USDJ-85-IJ-CX-0053, and USDJ-88-IJ-CX-0033).

REFERENCES

Anderson, R. C., & Pichert, J. W. (1978). Recall of previously unrecallable information following a shift in perspective. *Journal of Verbal Learning and Verbal Behavior, 17,* 1–12.

Baddeley, A. D. (1986). *Working memory.* Oxford, England: Oxford University Press.

Bekerian, D. A., & Dennett, J. L. (1993). The cognitive interview technique: Reviving the issues. *Applied Cognitive Psychology, 7,* 275–298.

Bekerian, D. A., & Dennett, J. L. (1997). Imagery effects in spoken and written recall. In D. Payne & F. Conrad (Eds.), *Intersections in basic and applied memory research* (pp. 279–289). Mahwah, NJ: Lawrence Erlbaum Associates.

Boon, J. C. W., & Noon, E. (1994). Changing perspectives in cognitive interviewing. *Psychology, Crime and Law, 1,* 59–69.

Brock, P., Fisher, R. P., & Cutler, B. L. (1999). Examining the cognitive interview in a double-test paradigm. *Psychology, Crime and Law, 5,* 29–45.

Brown, C. L., & Geiselman, R. E. (1990). Eyewitness testimony of mentally retarded: Effect of the cognitive interview. *Journal of Police and Criminal Psychology, 6,* 14–22.

Chapman, A. J., & Perry, D. J. (1995). Applying the cognitive interview procedure to child and adult eyewitnesses of road accidents. *Applied Psychology: An International Review, 44,* 283–294.

Chi, M. T. H., & Ceci, S. J. (1986). Content knowledge and the reorganization of memory. *Advances in Child Development and Behavior, 20,* 1–37.

Cohen, J. (1988). *Statistical power analysis for the behavioral sciences.* Hillsdale, NJ: Lawrence Erlbaum Associates.

Cutler, B. L., & Penrod, S. D. (1995). *Mistaken identification: The eyewitness, psychology, and the law.* New York: Cambridge University Press.

Cutler, B. L., Penrod, S. D., & Dexter, H. R. (1989). The eyewitness, the expert, and the jury. *Law and Human Behavior, 13,* 311–332.

Cutler, B. L., Penrod, S. D., & Stuve, T. E. (1988). Juror decision making in eyewitness identification cases. *Law and Human Behavior, 12,* 41–55.

Dent, H., & Stephenson, G. (1979). An experimental study of the effectiveness of different techniques of questioning child witnesses. *British Journal of Social and Clinical Psychology, 18,* 41–51.

Fisher, R. P. (1995). Interviewing victims and witnesses of crime. *Psychology, Public Policy, and Law, 1,* 732–764.

Fisher, R. P. (1999). *Exercising control in researching the cognitive interview.* Manuscript in preparation.

Fisher, R. P., & Geiselman, R. E. (1992). *Memory-enhancing techniques in investigative interviewing: The cognitive interview.* Springfield, IL: Thomas.

Fisher, R. P., Geiselman, R. E., & Amador, M (1989). Field test of the cognitive interview: Enhancing the recollection of actual victims and witnesses of crime. *Journal of Applied Psychology, 74,* 722–727.

Fisher, R. P., Geiselman, R. E., & Raymond, D. S. (1987). Critical analysis of police interview techniques. *Journal of Police Science Administration, 15,* 177–185.

Fisher, R. P., & McCauley, M. L. (1995). Information retrieval: Interviewing witnesses. In N. Brewer & C. Wilson (Eds.), *Psychology and policing* (pp. 81–99). Hillsdale, NJ: Lawrence Erlbaum Associates.

Fisher, R. P., Mello, E., & McCauley, M. L. (1999). Are jurors' perceptions of eyewitness credibility affected by the cognitive interview? *Psychology, Crime and Law, 5,* 167–176.

Fisher, R. P., Quigley, K. L., Brock, P., Chin, D., & Cutler, B. L. (1990, March). *The effectiveness of the cognitive interview in description and identification tasks.* Paper presented at the American Psychology and Law Society, Williamsburg, VA.

Garry, M., Manning, C. G., Loftus, E. F., & Sherman, S. J. (1996). Imagination inflation: Imagining a childhood event inflates confidence that it occurred. *Psychonomic Bulletin and Review, 3,* 208–214.

Geiselman, R. E., & Fisher, R. P. (1997). Ten years of cognitive interviewing. In D. G. Payne & R. G. Conrad (Eds.), *A synthesis of basic and applied approaches to human memory* (pp. 291–310). Mahwah, NJ: Lawrence Erlbaum Associates.

Geiselman, R. E., Fisher, R. P., Cohen, G., Holland, H., & Surtes, L. (1986). Eyewitness responses to leading and misleading questions under the cognitive interview. *Journal of Police Science and Administration, 14,* 31–39.

Geiselman, R. E., Fisher, R. P., Firstenberg, I., Hutton, L. A., Sullivan, S. J., Avetissian, I. V., & Prosk, A. L. (1984). Enhancement of eyewitness memory: An empirical evaluation of the cognitive interview. *Journal of Police Science and Administration, 12,* 74–80.

Geiselman, R. E., & Padilla, J. (1988). Cognitive interviewing with child witnesses. *Journal of Police Science and Administration, 16,* 236–242.

Geiselman, R. E., Saywitz, K. J., & Bornstein, G. K. (1993). Effects of cognitive questioning techniques on children's recall performance. In G. S. Goodman & B. L. Bottoms (Eds.), *Child victims, child witnesses: Understanding and improving testimony* (pp. 71–93). New York: Guilford.

George, R., & Clifford, B. R. (1992). Making the most of witnesses. *Policing, 8,* 185–198.

George, R., & Clifford, B. R. (1996). The cognitive interview: Does it work? In G. Davies, S. Lloyd-Bostock, M. McMurran, & C. Wilson (Eds.), *Psychology, law and criminal justice: International developments in research and practice* (pp. 146–154). New York: de Gruyter.

Greenwald, A. G. (1970). Sensory feedback mechanisms in performance control: With special reference to the ideo-motor mechanism. *Psychological Review, 77,* 73–99.

Gwyer, P., & Clifford, B. R. (1997). The effects of the cognitive interview on recall, identification, confidence and the confidence/accuracy relationship. *Applied Cognitive Psychology, 11,* 121–145.

Hayes, B. D., & Delamothe, K. (1997). Cognitive interviewing procedures and suggestibility in children's recall. *Journal of Applied Psychology, 82,* 562–577.

Johnson, M. K., Hashtroudi, S., & Lindsay, D. S. (1993). Source monitoring. *Psychological Bulletin, 114,* 3–28.

Kahneman, D. (1973). *Attention and effort.* Englewood Cliffs, NJ: Prentice-Hall.

Kebbell, M. R., & Milne, R. (1998). Police officers' perception of eyewitness factors in forensic investigations. *Journal of Social Psychology, 138,* 323–330.

Kebbell, M. R., Milne, R., & Wagstaff, G. F. (1999). The cognitive interview: A survey of its effectiveness. *Psychology, Crime and Law, 5,* 101–115.

Kebbell, M. R., Wagstaff, G. F., & Preece, D. (in press). The effect of belief that testimony was elicited with a cognitive interview on jurors' judgments of guilt. *Psychology, Crime and Law.*

Köhnken, G., Milne, R., Memon, A., & Bull, R. (1999). The cognitive interview: A meta-analysis. *Psychology, Crime and Law, 5,* 3–27.

Köhnken, G., Schimossek, E., Aschermann, E., & Hofer, E. (1995). The cognitive interview and the assessment of the credibility of adults' statements. *Journal of Applied Psychology, 80,* 671–684.

Köhnken, G., & Steller, M. (1988). *Issues in criminological and legal psychology* (No. 13). Leicester, England: British Psychological Society.

Koriat, A., & Goldsmith, M. (1994). Memory in naturalistic and laboratory contexts: Distinguishing the accuracy-oriented and quantity-oriented approaches to memory assessment. *Journal of Experimental Psychology: General, 123,* 297–316.

Koriat, A., & Goldsmith, M. (1996). Monitoring and control processes in the strategic regulation of memory accuracy. *Psychological Review, 103,* 490–517.

Leibowitz, H. W., Guzy, L. T., Peterson, E., & Blake, P. T. (1993). Quantitative perceptual esti-mates: Verbal versus nonverbal retrieval techniques. *Perception, 22,* 1051–1060.

Loftus, E. F. (1998, March). *Memory and its discontents.* Paper presented to Florida Conference on Cognition, Miami.

Maltz, W. (1991). *The sexual abuse healing journal.* New York: Harper/Collins.

Marin, V., Holmes, D. L., Guth, M., & Kovac, P. (1979). The potential of children as eyewit-nesses. *Law and Human Behavior, 3,* 295–305.

McCauley, M. R., & Fisher, R. P. (1995). Facilitating children's recall with the revised cogni-tive interview. *Journal of Applied Psychology, 80,* 510–516.

Mello, E. W., & Fisher, R. P. (1996). Enhancing older adult eyewitness memory with the cog-nitive interview. *Applied Cognitive Psychology, 10,* 403–417.

Memon, A., Cronin, O., Eaves, R., & Bull, R. (1993). The cognitive interview and child wit-nesses. In G. M. Stephenson & N. K. Clark (Eds.), *Children, evidence, and procedure: Issues in criminological psychology* (No. 20). Leicester, England: British Psychological Society.

Memon, A., Cronin, O., Eaves, R., & Bull, R. (1995). An empirical test of the mnemonic com-ponents of the cognitive interview. In G. Davies, S. Lloyd-Bostock, M. McMurran, & C. Wilson (Eds.), *Psychology, law and criminal justice: International developments in research and practice* (pp. 135–145). New York: de Gruyter.

Memon, A., Holley, A., Milne, R., Koehnken, G., & Bull, R. (1994). Towards understanding the effects of interviewer training in evaluating the cognitive interview. *Applied Cognitive Psychology, 8,* 641–659.

Memon, A., Holley, A., Wark, L., Bull, R., & Koehnken, G. (1996). Reducing suggestibility in child witness interviews. *Applied Cognitive Psychology, 10,* 503–518.

Memon, A., & Koehnken, G.(1992). Helping witnesses to remember more: The cognitive in-terview. *Expert Evidence, 1,* 39–48.

Memon, A., Wark, L., Bull, R., & Koehnken, G. (1997). Isolating the effects of the cognitive in-terview techniques. *British Journal of Psychology, 88,* 179–197.

Memon, A., Wark, L., Holley, A., Bull, R., & Koehnken, G. (1996). Interviewer behaviour in investigative interviews. *Psychology, Crime and Law, 3,* 135–155.

Memon, A., Wark, L., Holley, A., Bull, R., & Koehnken, G. (1997). Eyewitness performance in cognitive and structured interviews. *Memory, 5,* 639–656.

Memorandum of good practice. (1992). Department of Home and Health. London: Her Maj-esty's Stationery Office.

Milne, R. (1997). *Analysis and application of the cognitive interview: Vol. 3. Discussion, references and appendices.* Unpublished doctoral dissertation, University of Portsmouth, England.

Milne, R., & Bull, R. (1996). Interviewing children with mild learning disability with the cog-nitive interview. In N. Clark & G. Stephenson (Eds.), *Investigative and forensic decision mak-ing* (pp. 44–51). Leicester, England: British Psychological Society.

Milne, R., Bull, R., Koehnken, G., & Memon, A. (1995). The cognitive interview and suggest-ibility. In G. Stephenson & N. Clark (Eds.), *Criminal behaviour: Perceptions, attributions, and rationality* (Division of Criminological and Legal Psychology Occasional Papers, No. 22). Leicester, England: British Psychological Society.

Milne, R., Clare, C. I. W., & Bull, R. (1999). Using the cognitive interview with adults with mild learning disabilities. *Psychology, Crime and Law, 5,* 81–99.

Nigro, G., & Neisser, U. (1983). Point of view in personal memories. *Cognitive Psychology, 15,* 467–482.

Paivio, A. (1971). *Imagery and verbal processes.* New York: Holt, Rinehart & Winston.

People v. Tuggle, 1995.

Poole, D. A., & White, L. T. (1993). Tell me again and again: Stability and change in the re-peated testimonies of children and adults. In M. Zaragoza, J. Graham, G. Hall, R. Hirschman, & Y. Ben-Porath (Eds.), *Memory and testimony in the child witness* (pp. 24–43). Thousand Oaks, CA: Sage.

Pressley, M., & Levin, J. (1980). The development of mental imagery retrieval. *Child Development, 51*, 558–560.

Regina v. Hill, Court of Appeal, London, 1996.

Rand Corporation. (1975). *The criminal investigation process* (vols. 1–3). (Rand Corporation Technical Report R-1777-DOJ). Santa Monica, CA.

Roberts, K. (1996). How research on source monitoring can inform cognitive interview techniques. *Psycholoquy* [Electronic journal]. Available 96.7.44.witness-memory.15.roberts

Rogers, C. R. (1942). *Counselling and psychotherapy: Newer concepts in practice*. Boston: Houghton-Mifflin.

Sanders, G. S. (1986). On increasing the usefulness of eyewitness research. *Law and Human Behavior, 10*, 333–336.

Saywitz, K. J. (1987). Children's memory: Age-related patterns of memory errors. In S. Ceci, M. Toglia, & D. Ross (Eds.), *Children's eyewitness memory* (pp. 36–52). New York: Springer-Verlag.

Saywitz, K. J., Geiselman, R. E., & Bornstein, G. K. (1992). Effects of cognitive interviewing and practice on children's recall performance. *Journal of Applied Psychology, 77*, 744–756.

Schacter, D. L. (1996). *Searching for memory: The brain, the mind, and the past*. New York: Basic Books.

Sheehan, P. W., & Tilden, J. (1983). Effects of suggestibility and hypnosis on accurate and distorted retrieval from memory. *Journal of Experimental Psychology: Learning, Memory, and Cognition, 9*, 283–293.

Steller, M., & Wellershaus, P. (1995). Information enhancement and credibility assessment of child statements: The impact of the cognitive interview technique on criteria-based content analysis. In G. Davies, S. Lloyd-Bostock, M. McMurran, & C. Wilson (Eds.), *Psychology, law, and criminal justice: International developments in research and practice* (pp. 118–126). New York: de Gruyter.

Tulving, E., & Thomson, D. M. (1973). Encoding specificity and retrieval processes in episodic memory. *Psychological Review, 80*, 352–373.

Warren, A., Hulse-Trotter, K., & Tubbs, E. C. (1991). Inducing resistance to suggestibility in children. *Law and Human Behavior, 15*, 273–285.

Westcott, H. L. (1991). The abuse of disabled children: A review of the literature. *Child: Care, Health and Development, 17*, 243–258.

Williams, C. (1995). *Invisible victims. Crimes against people with learning disabilities*. London: Jessica Kingsley.

Wrightsman, L. S. (1987). *Psychology and the legal system*. Monterey, CA: Brooks/Cole.

Hypnosis and Memory: Implications for the Courtroom and Psychotherapy

Steven Jay Lynn
Jeffrey Neuschatz
Rachael Fite
State University of New York at Binghamton

The belief that hypnosis has a special power to retrieve lost memories is as pervasive today as it was when it was endorsed by luminaries such as Janet, Breuer, and Freud. Indeed, many contemporary psychotherapists and individuals in the general population believe that hypnosis can enhance recall far beyond what can be obtained by ordinary means (see Lynn, Myers, & Malinoski, 1997, for surveys). Recently, the American Society of Clinical Hypnosis (ASCH) has sought to advance hypnosis in clinical and forensic contexts by issuing practice guidelines that legitimize the use of hypnosis for memory improvement or recovery (Hammond et al., 1995). Contrary to these optimistic assessments of the value of hypnosis in memory recovery, many academic psychologists have argued against the use of hypnosis for this purpose, instead highlighting the potential of hypnosis to create false memories in psychotherapeutic and forensic contexts.

Just as differences of opinion have divided workers in the field, hypnosis has proven to be a formidable challenge for the courts. In fact, the pendulum of judicial opinion has swung between the extremes of denying the admission of hypnotically elicited testimony to treating hypnotic testimony much like any other type of testimony. In this chapter, we consider representative positions that courts have taken with respect to hypnosis, evaluate these positions against our assessment of the literature on hypnosis and memory, and consider the forensic implications of the use of memory recovery in psychotherapy.

HYPNOSIS IN THE COURTROOM

Historical Positions

Over the years, judicial opinion has shifted on the basis of how hypnosis has been perceived by the academic and broader professional community. In the landmark case of *People v. Ebanks* (1897), it was opined that "The law of the United States does not recognize hypnotism" (p. 1053), and a precedent was established of per se inadmissibility, which rendered any testimony elicited during or after hypnosis inadmissible. This decision was defensible based on the fact that hypnosis was not recognized by any professional organization as a legitimate therapeutic or scientific tool at the time of the ruling. Because of this situation, much expert testimony about hypnotically elicited memories was excluded by the *Frye v. United States* (1923) decision which held that scientific information must be "sufficiently established to have gained general acceptance in the particular field to which it belongs" (p. 1014). As a consequence, hypnotically elicited testimony was virtually eliminated in the courts for many years: From the mid-1800s to the late 1960s, there were fewer than 50 appellate cases involving hypnosis (Scheflin & Shapiro, 1989).

It was not until *Harding v. State* (1968) that certain courts began to soften their position regarding hypnosis, and a variety of approaches were adopted by courts across the country. Contrary to Frye, in the Harding case, the court ruled that hypnotically elicited testimony was acceptable because the hypnotist was a well-trained professional and the procedures were neither leading nor suggestive.

The open or per se admissibility standard became popular during the period from 1968 to 1978 (Brown, Scheflin, & Hammond, 1998) as hypnosis achieved greater respectability. This respectability was abetted by major professional societies' (e.g., American Psychological Association, American Medical Association) recognition of hypnosis as a useful adjunct to psychotherapy, by increasing numbers of professionals using hypnosis in treating problems from anxiety disorders to personality and schizophrenic disorders (Kraft & Rudolfa, 1982), and by police insisting that hypnosis was a valuable investigative tool. Indeed, Perry, Orne, London, and Orne (1996) observed that in certain cases, hypnotically elicited recall was recognized by the courts as more reliable than actual physical evidence.

The per se admissible standard, which treats hypnotically elicited testimony as no different from other testimony, maintains that hypnosis is not invariably biasing and does not render a witness incompetent. Furthermore, this standard implies that triers of fact can distinguish suggested memories from previously held memories. Nevertheless, open admissibility retains the proviso that the adversary witness and expert can be cross-examined. Indeed, in *State v. Brown*, the court stated, "We believe that an attack on credibility is the proper method of determining the value of hypnotically induced testimony."

Open admissibility began to spark controversy and was increasingly challenged in the courtroom as hypnotic testimony was adjudged admissible even when it was elicited by untrained laypersons, and as the pitfalls and perils of hypnotically elicited testimony received due recognition. For instance, Orne, Whitehouse, Dinges, and Orne (1988) wrote: "In *State v. Mack* (1980), a hypnotized person remembered eating a pizza in a restaurant that did not serve pizza, seeing tattoos on someone who had none, and having been stabbed with scissors or a knife where there was no evidence that a weapon was involved" (p. 41).

In *People v. Shirley* (1982), the California Supreme Court adopted a sweeping "per se inadmissible" rule. In this case, the testimony of the victim changed substantially after she was hypnotized the night before she testified. Furthermore, the hypnosis was performed by the deputy district attorney who obviously had a vested interested in the outcome of the case and the woman's testimony. The California Supreme Court was compelled by a review of the literature on hypnosis and memory, and ruled that the testimony was inadmissible and that any case-by-case analysis of hypnotic procedures would be too costly, thereby justifying a per se rule of inadmissibility.

Following the Shirley case, experts increasingly testified that hypnosis was an unreliable recall procedure, that it increased suggestibility and pressures to comply with the hypnotist, that hypnotized persons could not discriminate accurate and false memories, that hypnosis "hardened" or "crystallized" testimony to the point that it rendered the witness immune to cross-examination, and that hypnosis conducted by police and laypersons carried great risks of pseudomemory formation. For purposes of our discussion, *pseudomemories* can be defined as false reports of specific thoughts, feelings, and actions. Pseudomemories may range from inaccurate reports of small details or minutiae of experience to gross distortions of events.

The Tide of Opinion Shifts

Given the many concerns expressed about the reliability of hypnotically elicited testimony, the tide of judicial opinion turned against per se admissibility, so that currently, only a few states (e.g., Wyoming, Tennessee) continue to hold that hypnotically elicited testimony is generally admissible (see *Prime v. State*, 1989; *State v. Brown*, 1983; *State v. Glebock*, 1981).

However, certain state courts have also recognized the problems with a sweeping per se exclusion rule and as a result have allowed certain exceptions. For instance, in *People v. Sorscher* (1986) a dentist was accused of hypnotizing his male patients and making sexual advances towards them while they were hypnotized. A strict interpretation of the per se exclusion rule would indicate that testimony of the victims was inadmissible because the testimony concerns events that occurred while the witnesses were hypnotized. The court, however, refused to apply the Michigan per se exclusion rule to this case and stated that excluding posthypnotic recollections in such cases does not serve the cause of justice.

Similarly, in *Rock v. Arkansas* (1987) the U.S. Supreme Court ruled against per se inadmissibility. Vickie Rock reported that she had partial amnesia for the details of shooting her husband and was hypnotized to enhance her memory. After hypnosis, she remembered the gun had misfired because it was defective. The trial court adopted the per se inadmissibility standard and refused to permit this testimony because it had resulted from hypnosis. The Supreme Court ruled that to preclude the hypnotically refreshed testimony of the defendant in a criminal trial was a violation of constitutional rights.

One way that courts have resolved their seeming ambivalence about hypnotically elicited testimony is to stipulate that such testimony can be admitted only when procedural guidelines and safeguards, elaborated in *State v. Hurd* (1981), are implemented. These so-called "Hurd" or "Orne" rules include the following six procedural rules or safeguards:

1. A psychiatrist or psychologist experienced in the use of hypnosis, who qualifies as an expert, must conduct the session.
2. The professional conducting the session should be independent of and not regularly employed by the prosecutor, investigator, or defense.
3. Any information given to the hypnotist by law enforcement personnel or the defense prior to the hypnotic session must be recorded, either in writing or another suitable form.
4. Before inducing hypnosis, the hypnotist should obtain from the subject a detailed description of the facts as the subject remembers them. The hypnotist should carefully avoid influencing the description by asking structured questions or adding new details.
5. All contacts between the hypnotist and the subject must be recorded.
6. Only the hypnotist and the subject should be present during any phase of the hypnotic session, including the prehypnotic testing and the posthypnotic interview.

Notably, because of the perceived potential for hypnosis to impair recall, Hurd maintains that the burden of establishing admissibility by clear and convincing evidence rests on the party who seeks to introduce hypnotically elicited testimony.

A number of state and federal courts that allow exceptions to the "admissibility with safeguards" rule apply a "totality of circumstances" test. In such instances, the case is judged not so much in terms of compliance with specific guidelines, but rather in terms of the "totality of circumstances" that attended the hypnosis session.

For instance, in *Borawick v. Shay* (1996), a 30-year-old plaintiff accused her aunt and uncle of sexually abusing her when she was in their home. The victim reported that she had no memory of the abuse for 20 years. However, during hypnosis she reported that she recalled her aunt and uncle abused her but she did not remember the event after hypnosis was terminated. Some months after the last hypnotic session, she recalled being sexually abused by her father, and in 1992, as a result she filed suit. In evaluating the "totality of circumstances" attending this case, the district court excluded the testimony, stating that the hypnotist was not qualified.

The Daubert Principle

The totality of circumstances test is consistent with the Daubert principle in that the trial judge is charged with the responsibility of ruling (under Federal Rule 702) whether the expert is testifying to scientific knowledge, after an assessment of whether the "reasoning or methodology underlying the testimony is scientifically valid and of whether that reasoning or methodology properly can be applied to the facts in issue" (*Daubert v. Merrell Dow Pharmaceuticals, Inc.*, 1993, p. 12). This rule extends the Frye test in that whereas general acceptance in the scientific community is still a consideration, other scientific evidence can be entered into testimony that is deemed by the judge to be "scientific." This judgment is not necessarily straightforward, in that it is not always easy to gauge the extent to which testimony meets the criteria for scientific testimony under Daubert. These criteria include falsifiability of the underlying theory, determination of error rate, peer review and publication, and general acceptance in the relevant scientific community (see Fagiman, Kay, Saks, & Sanders, 1995).

Daubert, at least as it was interpreted in the *Borawick v. Shay* (1995) case, leaves the door open to broad judicial interpretations and discretion about what evidence to admit. Perry et al. (1996) and others observed that the Daubert ruling is more liberal than Frye's general acceptance criterion and argued that "It is not clear what will happen to hypnotically elicited testimony under Daubert." One possibility is that it may lead to the gradual erosion of per se exclusions of such testimony. On the other hand, it may mean that hypnosis will continue to be excluded from many courts, not because of "general acceptability grounds, but on Daubert standards of unreliability" (Gianelli, 1995, p. 78). Moreover, as Underwager and Wakefield (1998) note, "Errors by a biased or incompetent judge claiming to consider the totality of the circumstances and admitting evidence with no scientific validity or credibility would be very difficult to reverse" (p. 398). The courts in most of the 40 cases reportable by 1994 used Daubert to reject scientifically unsound evidence, and it is noteworthy that hypnotically elicited testimony has been excluded because of the recognition of suggestibility effects (Underwager & Wakefield, 1998). Because Daubert is a statutory rather than a constitutional case, it is not binding on the states, which have the option to follow Frye (Gianelli, 1994).

Although a sizable minority of states follow the "admissibility with safeguards rule" and the federal courts follow the "totality of circumstances test" (see Brown et al., 1998), most states (25 of 30 state supreme courts that have ruled on admissibility of hypnotically elicited testimony; Perry et al., 1996; see Fagiman et al., 1995, for a list of cases) have rejected the idea of admitting hypnotic testimony on a case-by-case basis and considering the totality of circumstances, and, instead, have opted for a broad per se exclusion rule.

Our review makes it clear that judicial opinion has wavered on the admissibility of hypnotically enhanced testimony. At this point it seems reasonable to examine the literature on hypnosis and memory to determine the appropriateness of judicial decisions that have been tendered in this arena of legal and academic debate.

A REVIEW OF THE EVIDENCE

The available evidence (see Lynn, Lock, Myers, & Payne, 1997; Lynn, Malinoski, & Green, 1997) supports the Shirley decision to the extent that hypnotically elicited testimony is far from reliable. In a meta-analysis involving 34 studies, Erdelyi (1994) concluded that hypnosis does not increase recognition or recall accuracy of nonmeaningful materials (e.g., nonsense syllables). Erdelyi (1994) also reported that although hypnosis increased the amount of meaningful information recalled compared to recall levels achieved by nonhypnotized controls, this increase in recall was accompanied by an increase in the amount of false recollections. When the number of responses was controlled by forcing participants to report a certain number of responses, there was no difference in the amount of accurate information recalled by hypnotized and nonhypnotized subjects.

In a meta-analysis of 24 studies, Steblay and Bothwell (1994) also concluded that there was no reliable difference in the amount recalled by hypnotized and nonhypnotized subjects on structured recall tests including particular questions about the target information. Whereas three studies in Steblay and Bothwell's analysis reported a superiority of recall in hypnotized subjects when recall was measured using unstructured free recall tests, in four more recent studies conducted in our laboratory (see Lynn, Lock, et al., 1997), hypnotized subjects either fared no better or performed worse than nonhypnotized subjects on tests of accurate recall whether the tests were unstructured or structured.

Apart from the yield of accurate information, hypnosis may increase recall errors. Stebaly and Bothwell (1994) reported that five of the studies they reviewed secured evidence that hypnosis increased the number of unprompted (i.e., not specifically elicited by misleading questions) recall errors relative to nonhypnotized control subjects. Research in our laboratory (e.g., Kaltenbach, Lynn, Abrams, Matyi, & Belleza, 1987; Krackow, Payne, & Lynn, 1998) has consistently demonstrated that nonhypnotic motivational instructions that urge participants to "try your best on the recall test" and recall mnemonics (e.g., contextual reinstatement) derived from Geiselman and Fisher's (1997) cognitive interview (CI; see Fisher, Brennan, & McCauley, chap. 11, this volume), yield equivalent or superior recall (i.e., as many accurate memories and equal or fewer inaccurate memories) compared with hypnosis. In short, hypnosis is not a reliable technique for augmenting memory, and alternative techniques are as effective as hypnosis in eliciting a high volume of accurate information and they do not appear to increase false memory risk like hypnosis does. Future research might not only compare confidence in hypnotic versus CI stimulated recollection, but the types of errors produced with hypnosis versus the CI (e.g., bizarre or fantastical errors).

Of great concern in forensic situations is that hypnosis can increase confidence in inaccurate as well as accurate memories (Stebaly & Bothwell, 1994), thereby having the potential to distort testimony. The "overconfidence effect" is not uniformly evident, and in some studies in which overconfidence has been observed, its magnitude has been small (Lynn, Myers, & Malinoski, 1997). Excessive confidence in what is remembered warrants concern in legal settings. After all, the confidence expressed by a witness is the single most important factor in persuading subjects-jurors that a witness correctly identified the culprit (Wells & Branford, 1998). And as Steblay and Bothwell (1994) have concluded, "Hypnosis is not necessarily a source of accurate information; at worst it may be a source of inaccurate information provided with confident testimony" (p. 649). Finally, there are indications that hypnotizable subjects are particularly susceptible to placing undue confidence in inaccurate remembrances (see Lynn, Myers, & Malinoski, 1997).

Traumatic Memories and the Question
of Generalizability

The precise relevance of laboratory-based hypnosis research to everyday
life can be questioned insofar as the materials that are employed in the
laboratory are not as traumatic, complex, or emotionally laden as real-life
events (Yuille & Cutshall, 1986). This argument implies that hypnosis
may, in fact, be useful in augmenting the recall of particularly emotional
or traumatic events. Such an argument was made by Hammond et al.
(1995), who maintained that hypnosis may have particular utility as a
memory recovery technique with traumatized persons because trauma
blocks memory due to the state-dependent nature of memory. That is, retrieving a traumatic memory may depend on the congruence of the current context and mood with the context and mood at the time the event occurred, and hypnosis has the ability to reinstate those original conditions
(Hammond et al., 1995, p. 15).

   This claim is not tenable for several reasons. First, Hammond et al. did
not specify exactly how hypnosis leads to congruence between states. In
fact, hypnosis often involves relaxation suggestions that, by their very nature, do not reinstate the context of a traumatic event (Shobe & Kihlstrom,
1997). Second, research conducted with arousing but not personally
threatening material (e.g., films of shop accidents and fatal stabbing, a
mock "live" assassination, and a murder filmed serendipitously) demonstrate that hypnosis did not increase recall of arousing stimuli (Lynn et al.,
1997). Moreover, if hypnosis were particularly suited to aid recovery of
emotionally arousing memories, then arousal level and recall would be expected to be correlated. However, this is not the case: Arousal level does not
seem to be related to levels of hypnotically facilitated recall (Lynn, Malinoski, & Green, 1997). Third, there is still no consensus among memory researchers as to whether, and to what degree, emotional trauma can block
memory for a single, repeated, or prolonged event (Lindsay & Read, 1995).
Fourth, context effects and mood congruence effects have proven to be difficult to replicate in laboratory settings (Eich, 1995). Fifth, there is no consensus
among memory researchers that emotionally laden memories are encoded,
stored, or retrieved differently from other more mundane memories. In
summary, the available evidence indicates that hypnosis is not particularly
suited for recovering emotionally laden memories.

   Still, it is appropriate to question the generalizability of laboratory research to real traumatic situations, and to exhort researchers to devise creative designs that better approximate real-life situations. It is worth noting
that research that establishes a modicum of ecological validity by studying so-called emotionally laden "flashbulb" memories provides no support for the special advantage of hypnosis in retrieving such memories. To

the contrary, Krackow, Payne, and Lynn's (1998) recent study of flashbulb memories of Princess Diana's death showed that hypnosis produced the least consistent recall over a 3-month follow-up compared with simple task motivation instructions and instructions designed to reinstate the context of original exposure to the news of the tragedy. In short, the available evidence provided no reason to believe that hypnosis holds special promise for enhancing recall of emotionally arousing or traumatic events.

Vulnerability to Suggestive Information

Another important question regarding hypnosis and eyewitness testimony is whether hypnotizability increases vulnerability to suggestive information. In general, people who are either high or medium hynotizable report more false memories in response to misleading information compared to low hypnotizable controls (see Lynn & Nash, 1994). The fact that false memories are reported by high and medium hypnotizable persons, who comprise the majority of the population, and that even low hypnotizable persons occasionally report pseudomemories (E. C. Orne, Whitehouse, Dinges, & M. T. Orne, 1996), implies that many individuals (typically in the range of 20% to 60%; see Lynn et al., 1997) are susceptible to the influence of misleading and suggestive memory recovery techniques. Hypnotizability is an important trait in that it has been linked with pseudomemories in nonhypnotic as well as hypnotic contexts.

Hypnosis and Age Regression

If hypnosis does not enhance recall of events in the relatively recent past, is there any reason to believe that it would be effective in recalling more distal events? The answer is "no." In a review of more than 60 years of research on hypnotic age regression (a technique in which an adult subject is asked to respond to specific hypnotic suggestions to think, feel, or act like a child at a particular age), Nash (1987) found that the behaviors and experiences of age regressed adults were often different from those of actual children. No matter how compelling "age regressed experiences" appear to observers, they reflect participants' fantasies, beliefs, and assumptions about childhood; they rarely, if ever, represent literal reinstatements of childhood experiences, behaviors, and feelings.

In one illustrative study (Nash, Drake, Wiley, Khalsa, & Lynn, 1986) adults age regressed to age 3 years reported the identity of their transitional objects (e.g., blankets, teddy bears). Another set of adults, who previously tested as low hypnotizable, served as controls and were asked to role play the performance of excellent hypnotic subjects, following the nonhypnotic simulation procedures described by Orne (1979). Parents of the 14 hypnotized and 10 role-playing participants were asked to verify the participants' reports of childhood transitional objects. Results showed that hypnotized participants were less accurate than control participants in identifying the specific transitional objects they had used. Hypnotized participants' recollections, for example, matched their parents' reports 21% of the time, whereas role-playing participants' reports were corroborated by their parents 70% of the time.

In another study, Hamel and Lynn (1996) used Naglieri's (1986) Draw-A-Person test, which provides a valid measure of developmental level based on figure drawings. The investigators age regressed hypnotized and simulating adult subjects to the second grade and asked them to draw pictures of a man, a woman, and of themselves. Hypnotized participants gave their age during age regression as 7.1 years, and simulators gave their age as 7.2 years. Furthermore, the participants spelled words in a childlike manner, showing clear changes between their adult and child handwritings. However, the age regressed hypnotized and simulating participants did not perform in a manner consistent with their stated ages on the figure drawing tasks. In order to succeed at the drawing task, that is, to draw pictures like a child who was truly 7 years old, we presumed that the adult participants must have an accurate memorial representation of what they would have drawn at the target age. Our results, however, implied that this was not the case. That is, the age regressed hypnotized and simulating participants did not perform in a manner consistent with their stated ages on the figure tasks. In fact, the hypnotized participants performed in a manner consistent with children who were nearly 9 years old (8.97 years) and the simulating participants performed in a manner consistent with children who were nearly 8 years old (7.98 years). In short, despite their compelling role enactments, hypnotized participants did not perform in a childlike manner on the figure drawing task, raising suspicions that their memories pertinent to the drawing task were inaccurate.

Sivec and Lynn (1996a) compared hypnotized versus alert imagining participants' performance when it was suggested that a person experience a meaningful event at an age that it was possible to verify that the event did not occur. Sivec and Lynn age regressed participants to the age of 5 and suggested that they played with a Cabbage Patch Doll if they were a girl or a He-Man toy if they were a boy. These were the most popular toys released by Mattel Toy Company for a 5-year period. Half of the participants received hypnotic age regression instructions and half of the participants received suggestions to age regress that were not administered in a hypnotic context. However, the toy was not released until 2 or 3 years after the target time of the age regression suggestion. Interestingly, none of the nonhypnotized persons were clearly influenced by the suggestion. They did not rate the memory of the experience as real, nor were they confident that the event occurred at the age they were regressed to. After hypnosis, however, 20% of the hypnotized participants rated the memory of the experience as real and were confident that the event occurred at the age to which they were regressed. Hence, the pseudomemory effect was specific to the hypnosis condition.

Whereas it is not ethical to conduct laboratory studies of the effects of social influence on abuse reports, it is possible to examine the effects of social influence on reports of events that occur before the cutoff for infantile amnesia. Researchers converge in their opinion that memories before age 2 are not likely to be veridical descriptions of actual historical events (see Malinoski, Lynn, & Sivec, 1998). In one such study, Sivec and Lynn (1996b) asked hypnotized and nonhypnotized participants about their earliest memories. Only 3% of the 40 participants in the alert condition recalled a memory earlier than 2 years of age the first time they were asked to report their earliest memory. However, during hypnosis, 23% of the 40 hypnotized participants reported a memory earlier than age 2, 20% reported a memory earlier than 18 months, 18% reported a memory earlier than 1 year, and 8% reported a memory of earlier than 6 months. The second time they were asked for an early memory, only 8% of the nonhypnotized participants reported a memory earlier than 2 years, and only 3% reported memories of 6 months or earlier, statistics consistent with large surveys we have conducted with college students. In contrast, 35% of hypnotized participants reported memories earlier than 18 months, 30% of subjects reported memories earlier than 1 year, and 13% of subjects reported a memory before 6 months.

By merely encouraging participants to concentrate and try hard to recall earlier memories, Marmelstein and Lynn (in press) were able to engender a nearly 1-year decrement in the age of the earliest memory recalled relative to baseline reports preceded by no such motivating instructions. However, after participants were queried again following a brief hypnotic induction, even earlier memories emerged. That is, nearly two thirds of participants reported memories that fell below the cutoff of infantile amnesia (i.e., 2 years of age or younger). Furthermore, during hypnosis, more than half of the participants reported memories from 18 months or younger, more than 40% of the participants' memories dated from age 1 or younger, and more than 20% of the participants recalled memories dating from age 6 months or younger. Even in nonhypnotic trials that followed, in which participants were contacted several days later by telephone by a person not affiliated with the earlier experiment, more than one third of the individuals contacted maintained that their earliest memory was from 2 years of age or younger, and one quarter of the participants continued to claim recall from 18 months or younger.

Nonhypnotic Suggestive Recall Procedures

As impressive as these findings appear to be, it is important not to mini-mize the fact that nonhypnotic suggestive recall procedures can produce dramatic changes in memory reports across trials (Malinoski & Lynn, in press). In Malinoski and Lynn's (in press) study, for example, when par-ticipants were repeatedly encouraged to report increasingly earlier mem-ories, provided with a rationale that it was possible to do so, and verbally rewarded for their early memory reports, more than three fourths of the participants reported memories at age 2 or earlier. Thus, although hypno-sis may increase false memory risk to some extent, a variety of suggestive procedures may do so as well.

Underscoring this conclusion, Bryant and Barnier (in press) recently showed that more than half of high hypnotizable hypnotized individuals and more than half of highly hypnotizable awake persons reported auto-biographical memories of their second birthday, when they received a suggestion to do so, whereas the majority of the low hypnotizable persons did not report memories dating back to their second birthday. However, the hypnotized and awake persons could be distinguished from one an-other in the sense that half the highly hypnotizable individuals in the awake condition but none of the individuals in the hypnosis condition re-tracted their memory reports after they were told that research shows that they cannot have memories of their second birthday. In short, those highly hypnotizable persons who were hypnotized were more likely to maintain their belief in the face of conflicting evidence, indicating that certain hyp-notized individuals developed a compelling belief in the reality of the suggested memories.

PROCEDURAL GUIDELINES AND SAFEGUARDS

Admissibility with safeguards standards implies that the accuracy of memories can be improved by following certain procedural guidelines. As already noted, the Hurd rules (*State v. Hurd*, 1981) require that certain procedural safeguards be implemented before hypnotically elicited testi-mony can be brought to the bar. The idea that the totality of circumstances must be considered prior to adjudging testimony as admissible, like ad-missibility with safeguards, implies that the impact of hypnotic proce-dures on testimony can be evaluated with respect to the guidelines or pro-cedures followed.

In the recent case of *Borawick v. Shay* (1996), in which a totality of cir-cumstances rule was adopted, the following determinants of admissibility were noted: (a) whether hypnosis was used for clinical or forensic pur-

poses, (b) whether the witness received any suggestions from the hypnotist or others prior to or during hypnosis, (c) the presence or absence of a
permanent record such as a videotape, (d) the hypnotist's qualifications, (e)
if corroborating evidence exists to support the reliability of the hypnotically
refreshed memories, (f) the subject's hypnotizability and proneness to confabulate, (g) expert opinion regarding the reliability of the procedures used
in the case, and (h) pretrial testimony. Additionally, the party attempting to
admit the hypnotically enhanced testimony bears the burden of persuading
the district court that the balance tips in favor of admissibility.

Procedural guidelines make a great deal of sense insofar as the recall
expectancies conveyed to the participant, how questions are phrased, and
whether the interviewer uses suggestive procedures or not can have an
appreciable impact on hypnotic and nonhypnotic testimony (see Hirt,
Lynn, Payne, Krackow, & McCrae, in press). For instance, Lynn, Malinoski, and Green (1997) made a simple change in the permissiveness of the
request to recall early memories ("If you don't remember, it's alright," for
a low expectancy condition vs., "Tell me when you get an earlier memory," for a high expectancy condition), and found that it resulted in a difference of average recall of nearly 1 year ($M = 3.45$ years vs. $M = 2.28$ years,
respectively) across groups of participants asked over four recall trials for
their earliest recollections. By the end of the recall interview, 43% of participants in the high expectancy condition reported a memory at or before
the age of 24 months, compared with 20% of the participants in the low expectancy group.

Furthermore, it is known that false memories can be mitigated by mon-
etary incentives for accurate recall, and by a variety of situational demand
characteristics that imply that accurate recall is desirable (see Lynn et al.,
1997, for a review). It would therefore seem that false memories can be
substantially reduced given the establishment of conducive recall procedures. However, despite their apparent face validity and promise, procedural guidelines have not been universally embraced. Critics of the guidelines argue that hynotically elicited testimony is so unreliable that no
array of procedural safeguards can outweigh the inherently biasing effect
of hypnosis. As stated in *People v. Gonzales* (1982), the Hurd guidelines
have the potential to confer an unwarranted "aura of reliability" on hypnotic testimony, thereby raising the specter of a miscarriage of justice.

This criticism can, likewise, be voiced with regard to the guidelines ad-
umbrated by the "federal" model, developed by the Federal Bureau of Investigation (FBI) for use in criminal investigations (Ault, 1979), and
adopted by many federal agencies. The federal model specifies a somewhat more lenient set of guidelines (e.g., contrary to Hurd, the people in
the room during the session may include attorneys, a police artist, a close
friend, and so forth) that can be subjected to the same criticisms as Hurd.

The American Society of Clinical Hypnosis (ASCH; Hammond et al., 1995) has recently proffered a set of guidelines that combined elements of both Hurd and the federal model, yet the ASCH guidelines are arguably more stringent in requiring (a) the objective measurement of hypnotizability, (b) a discussion of the imperfections of memory "in and out of hypnosis," (c) a posthypnotic discussion with investigating officers or attorneys regarding the "potential limitations of additional material that was obtained, and that all of the information must be independently corroborated for it to have credibility" (p. 47), and (d) a written report of the session with salient details noted (e.g., observations, "depth of trance, phenomena elicited, hypnotizability score"). What impact these guidelines will have, or whether they will replace the Hurd guidelines as the field standard is difficult to determine in that there have been few or no court cases involving these guidelines.

Whereas it is possible to speculate about the relative merits of one set of guidelines over another, in actuality, it is difficult to evaluate the strengths and limitations of any of the procedures given the dearth of systematic research. The limited evidence from a number of studies of the effects of prehypnotic "warnings" about the imperfections of hypnotically elicited recall does not inspire a great deal of confidence in their protective effect. In one study (Burgess & Kirsch, in press), warnings mitigated some of the memory distortions associated with hypnosis. However, warnings did not improve recall above and beyond a nonhypnotic condition. In another study (Green, Lynn, & Malinoski, 1998), warnings minimized memory distortions during but not after hypnosis. And, in a third study (Lynn & Neuschatz, 1999), repeated information about hypnosis and memory, or so-called "warnings" (e.g., that hypnotic and nonhypnotic memories are not necessarily accurate), taken directly from those recommended by ASCH and delivered before, during, and after hypnosis, did not improve recall relative to a nonhypnotic condition. Whereas it can be said that leading questions distort recall and should be scrupulously avoided, the value of other procedural guidelines on hypnotic recall have not been well established. Clearly, testimony to this effect ought to be introduced to the triers of fact.

In our opinion, the overriding conclusion warranted by the literature is that, as a general rule, hypnosis should not be used to assist recall in a forensic or any other situation. That said, it may be possible to envision certain exceptions such as desperate (e.g., attempt to recall a license plate in a kidnapping) or "last resort" investigative situations where other recall methods have been tried and have failed to elicit useful material. The one positive finding regarding hypnosis and recall is that hypnosis often produces more recall (with accurate and inaccurate details) than nonhypnotic methods. So, when accurate recall that can be potentially corroborated is a priority, and inaccuracy in detail can be tolerated, then hypnosis may well prove fruitful in criminal investigations. Hypnosis in such situations would be acceptable to the extent that any critical information secured can be corroborated, rendering hypnotically elicited testimony immaterial to the investigation. When hypnosis is contemplated in such instances, it would be advisable to conduct a hearing on the viability of the use of hypnosis, although various exigencies, including time and cost pressures, and problems in determining operative criteria for the use of last resort recall enhancement procedures, may render this option impractical. Additionally, it would be prudent for the judge to instruct the jury about the possibility that hypnosis elicits a degree of unwarranted recall confidence.

We envision few situations in which nonhypnotic, nonsuggestive techniques (e.g., strong motivational instructions, the CI) that have been shown to elicit a comparable or greater volume of memories would not be preferable to hypnosis. Even in those rare situations where hypnosis is deemed acceptable, previous guidelines do not go far enough in that they do not recommend assessing participants' confidence in their initial and posthypnotic recall. Without this information, it is impossible to evaluate fully the potentially biasing effect of hypnosis and hypnotic testimony on the witness.

Although we argue against the use of hypnosis to bolster recall, it does not necessarily follow that all hypnotically elicited testimony is, by its very nature, inaccurate, and that hypnosis inevitably corrupts a person's memory. Accordingly, a broad per se exclusion rule, which completely prohibits a person from testifying even about "nonhypnotic" recollections, seems unduly restrictive and fails to acknowledge that suggestive procedures that are routinely used in preparing witnesses for trial and in police investigations, for example, have the potential to bias and distort memories (Spanos, Quigley, Gwynn, Glatt, & Perlini, 1991). Indeed, the effects of leading or suggestive questions are probably much greater than the effects of the administration of an hypnotic induction. It is unfortunate that nonhypnotic interviews have not been examined as rigorously as hypnotic interviews with regard to the potential of memory contamination following leading questions. What is clear is that extreme caution needs to be exercised in administering hypnotic and nonhypnotic interviews to victims and witnesses to avoid any taint of leading or suggestive procedures.

RECOVERED MEMORIES IN PSYCHOTHERAPY

It is important to underscore the point that clinical and forensic contexts diverge in important respects. In psychotherapy, safeguards comparable to those routinely used in forensic situations are not implemented, there is

no systematic attempt made to examine the influence of hypnotic procedures on memory and recall confidence, there is no cross-examination of
the witness of events, and there is generally no attempt made to corrobo-
rate memories.

In therapies geared toward memory recovery, the use of hypnosis is intended to penetrate barriers in memory and self-awareness, promote insight, and maximize treatment gains. In such therapies, hypnosis is often
used as a special technique to recover allegedly repressed or dissociated
childhood memories of trauma or abuse. Hence, "memory recovery," as
used in the parlance of this chapter, does not pertain to the commonplace
discussion of historical events of typical "talk therapies," but, rather, to
the explicit attempt to uncover supposedly forgotten or unconscious
memories that are hypothesized to lie at the heart of current problems in
living. Survey research (Poole, Lindsay, Memom, & Bull, 1995; Underwager & Wakefield, 1998) indicates that approximately 6% to 7% of clients
who recover memories of child sexual abuse take some legal action
against the alleged perpetrator, and not all of these actions result in courtroom trials. Nevertheless, Underwager and Wakefield (1998) noted that
approximately 200 cases of recovered memories of childhood abuse have
reached the appellate level.

Lindsay and Read (1995) stated that legislative changes made it easier
for memory recovery claims to proceed in the legal system. Interestingly,
many courts have applied a delayed discovery rule tolling the statute of
limitations in cases of recovered memories of child sexual abuse, or have
limited the delayed discovery rule in situations where the memory is
claimed to be completely repressed until it is recovered. In yet other cases,
the plaintiff must only claim that he or she was unaware that current psychological problems were caused by the abuse during the statutory period. Finally, some state legislatures have extended the statutory period
until 2 or 3 years after abuse is remembered or it is claimed the abuse
caused injury (see Underwager & Wakefield, 1998, p. 411). Underwager
and Wakefield (1998) observed that the courts have generally taken one of
the following four postures with respect to recovered memory claims:

1. Discovery rules may not apply to recovered memory claims.
2. Recovered memory claims do not extend the statute of limitations as
   a statutory disability. However, the statute of limitations applies
   when the plaintiff is aware abuse occurred but was unaware of the
   resultant damage.
3. Independent corroboration is required to apply the discovery rule.
4. Determination of the reliability of repressed memory theory, where
   the Daubert standards are applied, must precede any extension of
   the statute of limitations.

Supreme and appellate courts in a variety of states including Alabama, California, Michigan, New Hampshire, Wisconsin, and Texas have been critical of scientific support for repressed memory claims.

Civil malpractice suits against therapists for implanting memories have increased in number and visibility in recent years, as exemplified by the well-publicized Humenansky, Ramona, and Cool cases, in which half a million to multimillion dollar settlements were awarded. In each of these cases, leading and suggestive procedures such as hypnosis and/or sodium amytal were used. In each of these cases, the assumption of "repressed memory" was challenged and the specific role of leading procedures was considered.

Each civil suit must be judged based on its own merits. After all, there is much about memory retrieval that we do not and cannot know. For instance, we do not know how many apparent memories uncovered in therapy are in fact false. It could be almost none, or it could be almost all. Whereas hypnosis confers no particular advantage in recalling emotionally arousing events in the laboratory (see Lynn et al., 1997), we cannot be absolutely sure how hypnosis affects the rates of true and false memories of real-life traumatic events.

Despite certain ambiguities, there is no firm empirical rationale or "good enough" reason to use aggressive procedures in psychotherapy to excavate memories. Listed below are a number of reasons for therapists to eschew these procedures.

1. "Recovered memory therapy . . . is predicated on the trauma-memory argument—that memories of traumatic events have special properties that distinguish them from ordinary memories of the sort usually studied in the laboratory (p. 70). . . . Nothing about the clinical evidence suggests that traumatic memories are special, or that special techniques are required to recover them" (Shobe & Kihlstrom, 1997, p. 74).

2. Most survivors of traumatic abuse past the age of 3 do not forget their abuse. In fact, the literature points to the opposite conclusion: In general, memory following traumatic events is enhanced. Nevertheless, there is still controversy regarding the possibility of a small number of individuals forgetting childhood traumas (see Lynn & McConkey, 1998; Shobe & Kihlstrom, 1997).

3. Even if a certain percentage of accurate memories can be recovered in therapy, it may be pointless to do so. As Lindsay observes, "numerous lines of evidence suggest that only a very small percentage of psychotherapy clients have problems that are caused by non-remembered histories of abuse" (p. 364). Certainly no empirical work reveals a causal connection between nonremembered abuse and psychopathology.

4. There is no demonstrable benefit associated with the straightforward catharsis of emotional events in treatment. To the contrary, a recent

review of the literature (Littrell, 1998) on exposure therapies (which do not rely on memory recovery but the reexperience of already remembered events) reveals that the mere experience and expression of painful memories and emotions, when not grounded in attempts to engender positive coping and mastery, can be harmful.

5. There is no empirical basis to argue that hypnotic or nonhypnotic memory recovery procedures are any more effective than present-centered approaches in treating the presumed sequelae of trauma or psychological problems in general. Indeed, there is no empirically supported psychotherapy or procedure that relies on the recovery of forgotten traumatic events to achieve a positive therapeutic outcome.

One author (Adshead, 1997) has gone so far as to argue that if memory work with trauma patients is not an effective treatment, then "it would therefore be just as unethical to use memory work for patients who could not use it or benefit by it, as it would be to prescribe the wrong medication, or employ a useless surgical technique" (p. 437).

Dour assessments of the usefulness of hypnosis for recovering forgotten memories in psychotherapy, and even prohibitions against its use, have also been voiced by a number of professional societies. For example, the American Psychological Association–Division 17–Counseling Psychology (1995) guidelines state that hypnosis should not be used for memory recovery, a conclusion also reached by the Canadian Psychiatric Association (1996). The American Psychological Association (1996) has recommended that hypnosis not be used for clients who are attempting to retrieve or confirm recollections of histories of abuse, and the American Medical Association (AMA, 1994) has stated that hypnosis should be used only for investigative purposes in forensic contexts.

In conclusion, there is by now a growing consensus that there is little justification for memory recovery therapies. If there is no empirical justification for memory recovery therapy, there is even less justification for using suggestive techniques like hypnosis in psychotherapy. As argued elsewhere (Lynn et al., 1997), "the answer to the question of whether hypnosis should be used to recover historically accurate memories in psychotherapy is 'no' " (p. 82).

REFERENCES

Adshead, G. (1997). Seekers after truth: Ethical issues raised by the discussion of "false" and "recovered" memories. In J. D. Read & D. S. Lindsay (Eds.), *Recollections of trauma: Scientific evidence and clinical practice* (pp. 435–440). New York: Plenum.
American Medical Association, Council on Scientific Affairs. (1994). *Memories of childhood abuse (CSA Report 5-A-94).*

American Psychological Association, Division 17 Committee on Women, Division 42 Trauma and Gender Issues Committee. (1995, July 25). *Psychotherapy guidelines for working with clients who may have an abuse or trauma history.* Washington, DC: Author.

American Psychological Association. (1996, February 14). *Working group on investigation of memories of childhood abuse: Final report.* Washington, DC: Author.

Ault, R. L. (1979). FBI guidelines for use of hypnosis. *International Journal of Clinical and Experimental Hypnosis, 27,* 449–451.

Borawick v. Shay, 68 F.3d 597 607 (2d Cir. 1995) cert. denied, _ U.S. _, 116 S.Ct. 1869, 134 L.Ed.2d 966 (1996).

Brown, D., Scheflin, A. W., & Hammond, D. C. (1998). *Memory, trauma treatment, and the law.* New York: Norton.

Bryant, R. A., & Barnier, A. J. (in press). Eliciting autobiographical pseudomemories: The relevance of hypnosis, hypnotizability, and attribution. *International Journal of Clinical and Experimental Hypnosis.*

Burgess, C. A., & Kirsch, I. (in press). Expectancy information as a moderator of the effects of hypnosis on memory. *Contemporary Hypnosis.*

Canadian Psychiatric Association. (1996). Position statement: Adult recovered memories of childhood sexual abuse. *Canadian Journal of Psychiatry, 41,* 305–306.

Daubert v. Merrell Dow Pharmaceuticals, Inc., 113 S. Ct. 2786 (1983).

Daubert v. Merrell Dow Pharmaceuticals, Inc., 509 U.S. 579, 113 S. Ct. 2786, 125 L. Ed. 2d 469 (1993).

Eich, E. (1995). Searching for mood dependent memory. *Psychological Science, 6,* 67–75.

Erdelyi, M. (1994). Hypnotic hypermnesia: The empty set of hypermnesia. *International Journal of Clinical and Experimental Hypnosis, 42,* 379–390.

Fagiman, D., Kay, D., Saks, M., & Sanders, J. (Eds.). (1995). *Modern scientific evidence: The law and science of expert testimony* (pp. 480–527). St. Paul, MN: West.

Frye v. United States, 293 F. 1013 (D.C. Cir. 1923).

Geiselman, R. E., & Fisher, R. P. (1997). Ten years of cognitive interviewing. In D. G. Payne & F. G. Conrad (Eds.), *Intersections in basic and applied memory research* (pp. 291–310). Mahwah, NJ: Lawrence Erlbaum Associates.

Giannelli, P. C. (1995). The admissibility of hypnotic evidence in U.S. courts. *International Journal of Clinical and Experimental Hypnosis, 43,* 212–233.

Green, J. P., Lynn, S. J., & Malinoski, P. (1998). Hypnotic pseudomemories, prehypnotic warnings, and the malleability of suggested memories. *Applied Cognitive Psychology, 12,* 431–444.

Hamel, J., & Lynn, S. J. (1996). *Figure drawings: A new look at trance logic.* Unpublished manuscript, Ohio University, Athens.

Hammond, D. C., Garver, R. B., Mutter, C. B., Crasilneck, H. B., Frischholz, E., Gravitz, M. A., Hibler, N. S., Olson, J., Scheflin, A., Spiegel, H., & Wester, W. (1995). *Clinical hypnosis and memory: Guidelines for clinicians and for forensic hypnosis.* Des Plaines, IL: American Society of Clinical Hypnosis Press.

Harding v. State, 246 A2d 302 (Md. Ct. Spec. App. 1968) Cert. denied, 395 U.S. 949 (1969).

Hirt, E., Lynn, S. J., Payne, D., Krackow, E., & McCrea, S. (in press). Memory and expectancy: Inferring the past from what we know must have been. In I. Kirsch (Ed.), *Expectancy, experience, and behavior.* Washington, DC: American Psychological Association.

Kaltenbach, P., Lynn, S. J., Abrams, L., Matyi, C. L., & Belleza, F. (1987, May). *Hypnotic and nonhypnotic recall enhancement: The effects of interpretation of events witnessed.* Paper presented at the meeting of the Midwestern Psychological Association, Chicago.

Kraft, W. A., & Rudolfa, E. R. (1982). The use of hypnosis among psychologists. *American Journal of Clinical Hypnosis, 24,* 249–257.

Krakow, E., Payne, D., & Lynn, S. J. (1998). *The death of Princess Diana: Flashbulb memories, hypnosis, and contextual reinstatement.* Unpublished manuscript, Binghamton University, Binghamton, NY.

Lindsay, D. S., & Read, J. D. (1995). "Memory work" and recovered memories of childhood sexual abuse: Scientific evidence and public, professional, and personal issues. *Psychology, Public Policy, and Law, 1,* 846–908.

Littrell, J. (1998). Is the reexperience of a painful event therapeutic? *Clinical Psychology Review, 18,* 71–102.

Lynn, S. J., Lock, T., & Myers, B., & Payne, D. (1997). Recalling the unrecallable: Should hypnosis be used for memory recovery in psychotherapy? *Current Directions in Psychological Science, 6,* 79–83.

Lynn, S. J., Malinoski, P., & Green, J. P. (1997). *The reliability and stability of early memory reports.* Unpublished manuscript, Binghamton University, Binghamton, NY.

Lynn, S. J., & McConkey, K. M. (1998). *Truth in memory.* New York: Guilford.

Lynn, S. J., Myers, B., & Malinoski, P. (1997). Hypnosis, pseudomemories, and clinical guidelines: A sociocognitive perspective. In D. Read & S. Lindsay (Eds.), *Recollections of trauma: Scientific studies and clinical practice* (pp. 305–336). New York: Plenum.

Lynn, S. J., & Nash, M. R. (1994). Truth in memory: Ramifications for psychotherapy and hypnotherapy. *American Journal of Clinical Hypnosis, 36,* 194–208.

Lynn, S. J., & Neuschatz, J. (1999). *Hypnosis, prehypnotic warnings, and ideomotor suggestions.* Unpublished manuscript, Binghamton University, Binghamton, NY.

Malinoski, P., & Lynn, S. J. (in press). The plasticity of very early memory reports: Social pressure, hypnotizability, compliance, and interrogative suggestibility. *International Journal of Clinical and Experimental Hypnosis.*

Malinoski, P., Lynn, S. J., & Sivec, H. (1998). The assessment, validity, and determinants of early memory reports: A critical review. In S. J. Lynn, K. M. McConkey, & N. P. Spanos (Eds.), *Truth in memory* (pp. 109–136). New York: Guilford.

Marmelstein, L., & Lynn, S. J. (in press). Expectancies, group, and hypnotic influences on early autobiographical memory reports. *International Journal of Clinical and Experimental Hypnosis.*

Naglieri, J. A. (1986). *Draw a person: A quantitative scoring system.* San Diego, CA: Harcourt Brace Jovanovich.

Nash, M. R. (1987). What, if anything, is age regressed about hypnotic age regression? A review of the empirical literature. *Psychological Bulletin, 102,* 42–52.

Nash, M. R., Drake, M., Wiley, R., Khalsa, S., & Lynn, S. J. (1986). The accuracy of recall of hypnotically age regressed subjects. *Journal of Abnormal Psychology, 95,* 298–300.

Orne, E. C., Whitehouse, W. G., Dinges, D. F., & Orne, M. T. (1996). Memory liabilities associated with hypnosis: Does low hypnotizability confer immunity? *International Journal of Clinical and Experimental Hypnosis, 44,* 354–369.

Orne, M. T. (1979). The use and misuse of hypnosis in court. *International Journal of Clinical and Experimental Hypnosis, 27,* 311–341.

Orne, M. T., Whitehouse, W. G., Dinges, D. F., & Orne, E. C. (1988). Reconstructing memory through hypnosis: Forensic and clinical applications. In H. M. Pettinati (Ed.), *Hypnosis and memory* (pp. 21–63). New York: Guilford.

People v. Ebanks, 49P 1049 (Cal 1897).

People v. Gonzales, 329 N.W.2d 743 (Mich. 1982), modified on other grounds, 336 N.W.2d 751 (Mich.1983).

People v. Shirley, 641 P.2d 775 (Cal.) cert. denied, 439 U.S. 860 (1982).

People v. Sorscher, 151 Mich. App. 122, 391 N.W. (1986).

People v. Sorscher, 151 Mich. App. 122, 391 N.W. 2d 365 (1996).

Perry, C., Orne, M. T., London, R. W., & Orne, E. C. (1996). Rethinking per se exclusions of hypnotically elicited recall as legal testimony. *International Journal of Clinical and Experimental Hypnosis, 44,* 66–81.

Poole, D. A., Lindsay, D. S., Memon, A., & Bull, R. (1995). Psychotherapy and the recovery of memories of childhood sexual abuse: U.S. and British practitioners' opinions, practices, and experiences. *Journal of Consulting and Clinical Psychology, 68,* 426–437.

Prime v. State, 767 P.2d 149, 153 (Wyo. 1988).

Prime v. State, 767 P.2d 149 (Wyo.Sup.Ct. 1989).

Rock v. Arkansas, 483 U.S. 44 (1987).

Scheflin, A., & Shapiro, L. (1989). *Trance on trial.* New York: Guilford.

Sheehan, P. (1988). Confidence and memory in hypnosis. In H. M. Pettinati (Ed.), *Hypnosis and memory* (pp. 95–127). New York: Guilford.

Shobe, K. K., & Kihlstrom, J. F. (1997). Is traumatic memory special? *Current Directions in Psychological Science, 6,* 70–74.

Sivec, H., & Lynn, S. J. (1996a). *Hypnotic age regression from the cabbage patch: Hypnotic vs. nonhypnotic pseudomemories with a verifiable event.* Unpublished manuscript, Ohio University, Athens.

Sivec, H., & Lynn, S. J. (1996b). *Early life events: Hypnotic vs. nonhypnotic age regression.* Unpublished manuscript, Ohio University, Athens.

Spanos, N. P., Quigley, C. A., Gwynn, R. I., Glatt, R. L., & Perlini, A. H. (1991). Hypnotic interrogation, pretrial preparation, and witness testimony during direct and cross-examination. *Law and Human Behavior, 15,* 639–653.

State v. Brown, 337 N.W.2d 138 (N.D. 1983).

State v. Glebock, 616 S.W. 897, 903-04 (Tenn. Crim. App. 1981).

State v. Hurd, 432 A.2d 86 (N.J. 1981).

State v. Mack, 292 N.W.2d 764 (Minn. 1980).

Steblay, N. M., & Bothwell, R. K. (1994). Evidence for hypnotically refreshed testimony: The view from the laboratory. *Law and Human Behavior, 18,* 635–651.

Underwager, R., & Wakefield, H. (1998). Recovered memories in the courtroom. In S. J. Lynn & K. M. McConkey (Eds.), *Truth in memory* (pp. 394–436). New York: Guilford.

Underwager, R., & Wakefield, H. (1990). *The real world of child interrogations.* Springfield, NY: Thomas.

Wells, G. L., & Bradford, A. L. (1998)."Good you identified the suspect": Feedback to eyewitnesses distorts their reports of the witnessing experience. *Journal of Applied Psychology, 83,* 360–376.

Yapko, M. D. (1994). Suggestibility and repressed memories of abuse: A survey of psychotherapists' beliefs. *American Journal of Clinical Hypnosis, 36,* 194–208.

Yuille, J. C., & Cutshall, J. L. (1986). A case study of eyewitness memory of a crime. *Journal of Applied Psychology, 71,* 291–301.

13

Interrogative Suggestibility and "Memory Work"

Katharine Krause Shobe
Naval Submarine Medical Research Laboratory

John F. Kihlstrom
University of California, Berkeley

In 1982 Patricia Burgus entered therapy for depression. After being diagnosed with multiple personality disorder, Burgus was treated with a variety of techniques that led her to remember being sexually abused as a child and participating in a satanic cult. At one point in her treatment Burgus was committed to an inpatient service for 2 years. She recently won a $10.6 million lawsuit against her therapist and the hospital, claiming that the treatment implanted false memories of the abuse and cult activity (Belluck, 1997). The Burgus case illustrates an important legal and social phenomenon that has emerged over the past decade or so. People, mostly women, entering therapy for various problems, including anxiety, depression, eating disorders, and substance abuse, have recovered memories of incest, other forms of childhood sexual abuse, and even satanic cult activity. What to make of these memories?

It is one thing for a patient to bring into therapy an independently documented history of abuse, or a history of abuse that he or she has always remembered. But it is another thing entirely when a patient enters therapy with no inkling of past abuse, or perhaps only the hypothesis that he or she might have been abused, in the absence of any relevant memories. Under such circumstances, therapists — especially those who believe that childhood abuse and other trauma are salient causal factors in adult maladjustment and psychopathology (e.g., Blume, 1990; Briere, 1992;

309

Kirschner, Kirschner, & Rappaport, 1993; McCann & Pearlman, 1990) —
may employ a variety of techniques, sometimes known collectively as
memory work (McCann & Perlman, 1990), to help patients recover, explore,
and integrate traumatic memories. Some observers of the recovered memory phenomenon have cautioned that some of these procedures are so
suggestive that they may yield memories that are grossly distorted or false
outright (e.g., Loftus & Ketcham, 1992; Ofshe & Watters, 1994; Pendergrast,
1996; Yapko, 1994; see also Kihlstrom, 1996a, 1996b, 1997, 1998).

THE PREVALENCE OF MEMORY WORK

Do clinicians actually use these memory retrieval techniques? Recent surveys suggest that many do. In a random survey of members of certain
clinical divisions of the American Psychological Association, over one
quarter of the respondents reported using specific memory retrieval techniques, such as guided imagery, dream interpretation, and bibliotherapy,
with clients who had no specific memory of childhood sexual abuse
(Polusny & Follette, 1996). The mean percentage of clients believed to
have no memory of their sexual abuse was 22%. Even though only 8% reported this memory retrieval as their primary therapeutic goal, 34% reported that remembering sexual abuse is important in therapy. A survey
with a different population found that most clinicians (71%) reported using memory recovery techniques, such as hypnosis, dream interpretation,
and journaling (Lindsay & Poole, 1998; Poole, Lindsay, Memon, & Bull,
1995).

It is important to note, however, that the survey questions did not ask
specifically about clients who lacked specific memories, so the questions
could have been interpreted to include clients with preexisting memories.
This criticism can be extended to suggest that the results of such surveys
show that the majority of clinicians do not use memory retrieval techniques with clients who present with no memory of abuse — although the
question remains why clinicians would use memory recovery techniques
with clients who already have access to traumatic memories. Even if only
a minority of therapists utilize these techniques, it still the case that a large
number of people seeking therapy may be exposed to these methods.

No one can say for sure whether, and how often, memory work creates
memories of abuse out of whole cloth, because in the absence of independent corroboration no one is able to determine how faithfully a person's
memory represents his or her objective, historical past. However, it is clear
that these techniques increase the risk of distorted or false memory, because they create, and capitalize on, the conditions for interrogative suggestibility to occur in therapy.

INTERROGATIVE SUGGESTIBILITY

The idea of interrogative suggestibility may be defined as "the extent to which, within a closed social interaction, people come to accept messages communicated during formal questioning, as the result of which their subsequent behavioural response is affected" (Gudjonsson & Clark, 1986, p. 84). Actually, the empirical literature reflects two quite different approaches to the study of interrogative suggestibility. The experimental approach is illustrated by the work of Loftus (1975, 1992) and her colleagues on the postevent misinformation effect in eyewitness memory. Although research continues to define the constraints on the effect (e.g., Pezdek, Finger, & Hodge, 1997), and debate continues over its underlying mechanisms (e.g., McCloskey & Zaragoza, 1985), it is clear that a substantial proportion of subjects incorporate into their memories erroneous information contained in leading questions posed by the experimenter. The individual differences approach is exemplified by the work of Gudjonsson (1984, 1987, 1989, 1991) and his colleagues, which documents individual differences in response to postevent misinformation, and their associations with various personality, social, and cognitive variables. Gudjonsson distinguishes between two types of suggestibility that are important in police interviewing: susceptibility to leading questions and response to negative feedback.

According to Gudjonsson (1987, 1992), interrogative suggestibility differs from other types of suggestibility in important ways: (a) The questions are concerned with memory recollection of past experiences and events, (b) the questioning procedure takes place in a closed social interaction, and (c) interrogative suggestibility builds on uncertainty of the individual and involves a stressful situation with major consequences for all involved. However, it is not clear that such a sharp distinction is justified. Certainly interrogative suggestibility differs from the direct suggestions for motor actions and sensory experiences characterized by Hull (1933) as personal heterosuggestion and by Eysenck and Furneaux (1945) as primary suggestibility; it also differs from the placebo response (Evans, 1989) and from hypnotizability (Register & Kihlstrom, 1988). However, interrogative suggestibility shares features with the implied suggestions (albeit for cognitive as opposed to sensory changes) characteristic of impersonal heterosuggestion (Hull, 1933) or secondary suggestibility (Eysenck & Furneaux, 1945). It also seems similar to social suggestibility (Hilgard, 1991), as represented by conformity, gullibility, and persuasibility—the tertiary suggestibility posed, but not empirically documented, by Eysenck (1947). Comprehensive multivariate studies of the relationships among various forms of suggestibility remain on the agenda for future research (Destun & Kuiper, 1996).

The paradigmatic differences between the experimental and individual differences approaches to the study of interrogative suggestibility are reminiscent of the two cultures in scientific psychology, experimental and correlational, outlined by Cronbach (1957). Like Cronbach, Schooler and Loftus (1986) suggested that the two approaches should be viewed as complementary, not competitive or mutually exclusive. In fact, Gudjonsson and Clark (1986) proposed an integrative social-psychological model stating that "interrogative suggestibility is construed as arising through a particular relationship between the person, the environment, and significant others within that environment" (Gudjonsson, 1991, p. 281).

INTERROGATIVE SUGGESTIBILITY IN MEMORY WORK

The model of interrogative suggestibility proposed by Gudjonsson and Clark (1986) consists of five interrelated components: (a) a closed social interaction between interviewer and interviewee, (b) a questioning procedure, (c) a suggestive stimulus, (d) acceptance of the suggestive stimulus, and (e) a behavioral response to the suggestion. Although this model was developed in a forensic context, the question that arises is whether there are other settings in which interrogative suggestibility has important consequences. For example, the situation in which a person enters therapy with no memory of childhood abuse, is exposed to memory retrieval techniques by a therapist who believes that abuse may have occurred, and then comes to believe that she has a sexual abuse history, seems to be one in which interrogative suggestibility may play an important role.

A Social Interaction and Questioning Procedure

In Gudjonsson and Clark's (1986) model, the initial component of interrogative suggestibility involves a questioning procedure within a closed social interaction involving the interviewer and the interviewee. Questions are asked of the interviewee by the interviewer, usually relating to some event that the person has either participated in or witnessed. In other words, recall of episodic memories is important. The interrogation situation sets the stage for the interrogator and respondent to adopt certain cognitive sets that affect the interaction between the two participants. This cognitive set consists of existing general expectations relative to perceiving, thinking, remembering, and social information, which results in either a suggestible or resistant response.

The form and content of the questioning are guided by certain expectations and premises that either party may hold, which may be ill founded and uninformed, and likely make each party's perception of the answers selective. In sum, people see what they expect or desire to see. Interpersonal trust is another important prerequisite for yielding to suggestions. If the person believes that the interrogator's intentions are genuine and is not suspicious of him or her, then the person has already fulfilled a determinant of suggestibility. Interpersonal trust forms the catalyst for leading questions or suggestions to be perceived as plausible, believable, and without deception.

Individual therapy sessions consist solely of the clinician and the client, making the therapeutic encounter an exceptionally close social interaction between two people. Indeed, in the earliest phase or stage of recovery work, as in most forms of psychotherapy, one of the primary goals is to form a collaborative therapeutic alliance (Herman, 1992; Simonds, 1994). Moreover, the relationship between the clinician and the client is not equal; the clinician is assumed to be the authority—or, at least, more knowledgeable than the client. Herman (1992) bluntly stated that "the patient enters therapy in need of help and care. By virtue of this fact, she voluntarily submits herself to an unequal relationship in which the therapist has superior status and power" (p. 134). Brenneis (1994) provided a thoughtful analysis of how the analytic dyad promotes suggestion and how the authority of the clinician increases the probability for suggestions to be accepted. The mere fact that therapy consists of an unequal relationship between therapist and client provides the basis for interrogative suggestibility to develop.

By its nature, all psychotherapy requires the patient to trust the clinician. Specifically, in recovered memory therapy, trust and safety are deemed essential in healing from the effects of trauma (Herman, 1992). When the traumatic childhood history is known, this approach towards recovery is well advised. However, when the client presents with no memory of childhood abuse and is subjected to trauma therapy, trust may enhance the suggestibility inherent in interactions between the clinician and client, particularly when memory retrieval techniques are used. Because a person who believes an interrogator's motives are genuine, honest, and without bias is more suggestible than a person who is suspicious of the intentions, this blind trust of the therapist on the part of the client will further heighten the client's suggestible cognitive set. This situation is not unique to individual therapy—memory recovery can also be an important goal of group therapy as well (Herman & Schatzow, 1984).

A Suggestive Stimulus and Uncertainty

Another component of interrogative suggestibility is the nature of the suggestive stimulus (Gudjonsson & Clark, 1986). In a forensic interview setting, questions can be leading because they contain certain premises and expectations, which would suggest wanted or anticipated answers. Suggestive stimuli such as leading questions will have the most influence on a person who has developed a suggestible cognitive set. In the therapeutic context, this is where memory retrieval techniques play a crucial role in building on suggestibility. Hypnosis, guided imagery, dream interpretation, and journaling are all techniques that encourage reduced source monitoring (Johnson, Hashtroudi, & Lindsay, 1993).

During interrogation, there is a large degree of uncertainty when a person's memory for events is incomplete or nonexistent. Uncertainty refers to the situation when the person does not know the right answer to a question, and relates to the strength of the person's internal frame of reference and knowledge states rather than feelings of confidence. According to Gudjonsson and Clark's (1986) theoretical model of interrogative suggestibility, when the person does not know the answer definitively she is potentially open to suggestion, because the stronger the person's frame of reference, or memory of events, the more likely she will detect being misled.

Typically, the second phase of recovery work, or retrospective incest therapy, involves accessing the traumatic memories (Courtois, 1988). This approach does not depend on whether the client has always remembered the abuse, remembered fragments of the abuse, or has no memory at all. Suggestive stimuli, or techniques, can have the most deleterious effects on clients who have no memory of abuse, but the therapist continues with memory retrieval techniques because the client's symptoms are interpreted as signifying the presence of unconscious memories of trauma.

According to some advocates of memory work, the use of memory retrieval techniques helps in memory recovery because the survivor of childhood abuse develops the ability to dissociate, and this ability is utilized to reach an all-knowing unconscious (Dolan, 1991). This explanation relies on the idea of state-dependency, a notion that an event encoded in one cognitive, emotional, or physiological state is better remembered when that same state is subsequently recapitulated (see Eich, 1989, for a review). So, if a child dissociates while being abused, later the memory will be unavailable to conscious awareness, and can only be retrieved when the person has access to the unconscious through dissociation or trance. Dolan (1991) stated, "The effectiveness of this rather direct approach to the unconscious probably derives in part from the highly developed natural hypnotic abilities characteristic of most survivors of sexual abuse" (p. 109). A similar view is advocated by Maldonado and Spiegel (1995). "Some clients approach memory work with little or no previous recall of traumatic events" (Simonds, 1994, p. 143), and "a traumatic memory may be entirely repressed" (McCann & Pearlman, 1990, p. 28), but retrieval of these forgotten traumatic memories is the catalyst for the integration, assimilation, and resolution of the trauma (Claridge, 1992; Courtois, 1988; Dolan, 1991; McCann & Pearlman, 1990).

Hypnosis.   In trauma therapy, the use of memory retrieval techniques is justified when "both the client and therapist strongly suspect sexual abuse, the client is suffering from symptoms known to be indicative of sexual abuse, and these symptoms have not responded to less intrusive forms of treatment" (Dolan, 1991, p. 141). An example is the case of Nora (Dolan, 1991, p. 157) who entered therapy because of panic attacks, choking feelings, and intense fear. Traditional therapy was not helpful, so hypnosis was used to retrieve the suspected unconscious traumatic material. During hypnosis Nora was told that the therapist was talking directly to her unconscious and that this part of her mind knew what to do and could help in remembering what was necessary for healing. After this session, Nora "found out what I thought I would" (p. 161), that her father had sexually abused her. Fredrickson (1992) wrote about "repressed memory syndrome," describing people who have no memory of abuse but display symptoms that characterize adults who have unconscious memories of trauma. For any unusual reactions a client may have, she is told to ask herself if there is anything about the situation that could be associated with sexual abuse.

A prominent view of trauma therapists is that hypnotic techniques help patients gain access to unconscious memories (Dolan, 1991; Fredrickson, 1992; Maldonado & Spiegel, 1995; McCann & Pearlman, 1990; Simonds, 1994; but see Kihlstrom, 1994). The use of hypnosis to recover memories rests on the idea that the experience of the dissociated state of mind will trigger retrieval of memories associated with a previous state of dissociation. In other words, because the trauma was encoded while the person was dissociating, the only way to get back the memory is through a technique that ostensibly relies on dissociation such as hypnosis. A trance state is induced, and then several techniques may be used to help patients remember. A common approach is to use age regression in which the client is told that she is getting younger and younger, returning to the time of the trauma (Price, 1986). At that point the person becomes a child once again and talks about what she sees. Or screen techniques require the patient to project the traumatic images or thoughts onto an imaginary screen. The images and thoughts do not have to be accurate portrayals of the traumatic event that is to be remembered; they can be whatever the patient chooses. Simonds (1994) proposed that using the screen technique allowed the client to see the events of the past unfold on an imaginary movie screen by distancing the patient from the event.

Guided Imagery.   Another memory retrieval technique, guided imagery, begins with the client picking a focal event or feeling and letting themselves imagine what would have happened next (McCann & Pearlman, 1990). Any images that emerge during this technique are thought to be symbolic representations of the abusive event. Also, guided imagery is thought to rely on the use of "imagistic memory" to retrieve abuse memories by letting the client complete a picture of what happened (Fredrickson, 1992). The truth about whatever the client remembers while imagining what might have happened doesn't have to be decided immediately, but can wait until later. The client can even select the person who she thinks is most likely to have committed the abuse. A similar memory retrieval technique is journal writing, or journaling. This entails the client keeping a journal and writing spontaneously or free-associating to images she has had. As with the other memory retrieval techniques, accuracy of the discovered memories or images is of no importance. The client is instructed to go with whatever comes to mind and seems to feel right.

Dreams. Some clinicians have written that dream content can be interpreted to reveal unconscious memories of childhood events (Fredrickson, 1992; Williams, 1987). The idea is that dreams preserve the traumatic experience in an indelible nature, or that partial memories surface during dreams (Walker, 1994). Fredrickson (1992) suggested that unconscious memories often surface through dreams in fragments or symbols; therefore, examining dream content can be a gateway to unconscious memories. However, there is reason to be skeptical about the veridicality of flashbacks or dreams even in people who have documented trauma (Brenneis, 1997; Frankel, 1994). A study by Berger, Hunter, and Lane (1971) demonstrated with a group of college students in group therapy that dream content was determined by the person's presleep experience. The material that was aroused during the therapy sessions was represented and worked over in the dreams, such that the content of the dreams was related to the material discussed in the preceding group session. Extending this finding to a therapeutic situation that includes memory recovery as the central focus, it is easy to see how and why a client may dream of childhood abuse even if the abuse never happened.

Reality Monitoring. Is there a potential for these techniques to produce false memories? Everything we know points to an affirmative answer. Hypnosis, guided imagery, dream interpretation, and journaling allow the client to suspend reality orientation and lower her critical judgment (see Lindsay & Read, 1994, for a review). These techniques allow the client to rely on imagination and imagery to recreate a plausible scenario of abuse. Ideas and images generated during these techniques have the potential for being perceived as actual events later, mainly due to the person's diminished ability for source monitoring and the increased perceptual detail that accompanies each revisualization. It has been shown that memories of real events have more visual detail, are more vivid, include more information about space and time, while imagined events have fewer of these qualities (Johnson, 1988). Yet, some sources promoting memory retrieval techniques claim that the memories uncovered will be vague, sketchy, and hazy, even after many workings, and moreover, that these qualities signify the authenticity of the memory (Bass & Davis, 1988; Fredrickson, 1992). Another potential for memory creation is when repeated induction of focal images is used to trigger the memory; this results in the image becoming more familiar over time with increasing confidence that it is real.

It is known that people can confuse imagined events, or self-generated thoughts, with real events or internal thoughts (Johnson & Raye, 1981), suggesting that people can remember experiencing events when they were only imagined. Hypnosis and other memory retrieval techniques facilitate the transformation of mental images and vague fragments into compelling memories that are believed with great confidence. Orne, Whitehouse, Orne, and Dinges (1996) state that these effects of hypnosis are not unique to hypnotically susceptible people; increased confidence, increased productivity, and source misattributions are exhibited by low and medium hypnotizables. In their words, "hypnosis provides a license for fantasy" (p. 172). Effects from one retrieval technique can be exacerbated when the result is used to spur more memories using another technique. This is exactly what Fredrickson (1992) suggested for hypnosis – to use a dream fragment or an image received from guided imagery as a focal point. The difficulty in this approach is that the more an inaccurate image or fragment is used, the more likely it will be accepted either by the process of repetition or through source-monitoring difficulties. This is similar to Dywan's (1995) idea of the illusion of familiarity; that is, during hypnosis, when a person attempts to retrieve information, the items remembered are generated more vividly and with greater fluency and are therefore likely to induce the feeling of familiarity.

It can be argued that spontaneously recovered memories of childhood abuse are less likely to be influenced by suggestions, while memories that are retrieved via a long, drawn-out process are more likely to be the result of suggestion. Claridge (1992) suggested that after some memory work is done, the clinician should ask the client, "If these experiences hold the pieces of your memories, what sort of memories do they suggest to you?" (p. 247). This question allows the patient's imagination to take precedence over the accuracy of the recovered images or memory fragments. Moreover, Claridge acknowledges that memory retrieval of childhood abuse proceeds by slow, fragmentary recall and that the abuse can be inferred before the completion of any memories (see also Fredrickson, 1992). Memory recovery therapy continues until the traumatic memories emerge.

Additionally, the social context of hypnosis provides another means for increased suggestibility. Spanos reported that subjects who were told before hypnosis that being hypnotized would increase their ability to remember past lives were more likely to remember past lives, and that the prehypnotic suggestions influenced the type of lives remembered (Spanos, Menary, Gabora, DuBreuil, & Dewhirst, 1991). This position is also argued by Lynn and Kirsch (1996), who state that hypnosis is often conducted in a context that the recovered memories are assumed accurate, which in turn suggests that people adopt a lax standard for distinguishing between reality and fantasy. So, the context in which retrieval techniques are used may be just as important as the techniques themselves in increasing suggestibility.

Making the Implicit Explicit. Some writers have suggested that traumatic memory relies more on state dependency than memory for ordinary events (Briere, 1992; Whitfield, 1995). Traumatic memory is sometimes equated with implicit, rather than explicit memory, in that it is encoded and stored at a somatosensory level and is nonverbal (Hovdestad & Kristiansen, 1996; van der Kolk, 1994; but see Kihlstrom, 1996a; Shobe & Kihlstrom, 1997). According to Hovdestad and Kristiansen (1996), "implicit memories return[ing] during times of extreme arousal suggest that the principles regarding state-dependent learning and memory may also apply" (p. 40), and "memories acquired in one neuropsychophysiological state are accessible mainly in that state" (Whitfield, 1995). Walker (1994) suggested that psychotherapy helps to translate subcortical, traumatic memories into the "cognitive areas of the brain so that they can be more easily communicated to others" (p. 86). Techniques that allow the person to return to the original abuse event will reinstate the original affective state and allow the person to retrieve the state-dependent memories. Does this mean that the person has to recapitulate the internal state of dissociation, or reexperience the state of extreme terror? It is not clear how a stress-related dissociative state is to be induced in therapy, and it is quite clear that any attempt to get the person to reexperience traumatic stress, even in imagination, would compromise another goal of recovered-memory therapy, that of creating a "safe place" for the patient. This appears to be a major ambiguity in the literature.

Another major concern is the claim that memories initially encoded in a somatosensory state can later become accurate verbal narratives, which is the major goal of trauma therapy. Despite an intense implicit emotional memory, if the memory was not encoded explicitly in the first place, it can never become explicit. As LeDoux (1996) stated, "It is completely possible that one might have poor conscious memory of a traumatic experience, but at the same time form very powerful implicit, unconscious emotional memories through amygdala-mediated fear conditioning . . . there is no way for these powerful implicit memories to then be converted into explicit memories. Again, if a conscious memory wasn't formed, it can't be recovered" (p. 245).

As suggested earlier, when a person enters therapy for a host of problems that cannot be tied to any particular diagnosis, a therapist may believe and/or suggest that the person has a history of childhood abuse and has repressed or dissociated the memory, rendering it unconscious.[1] The client would initially have an overwhelming feeling of uncertainty as to the source of her problems and what the best approach to take in therapy would be. After listening to the therapist suggest a history of abuse, and after undergoing memory retrieval techniques to uncover memories, the recovery of memory offers a solution to this uncertainty.

Another way uncertainty can influence suggestibility in memory work is an extension of LeDoux's (1996) comment about forming a conscious memory. If a person conjures up images during hypnosis or guided imagery, and if there are no explicit components accompanying the image, then the uncertainty as to what the image is or represents may cause the person to hypothesize what happened in order to achieve a sense of closure or relief. As a result, this fantasy may later be interpreted as fact. As an example, Fredrickson (1992) stated that unconscious memories do not seem real when they are first recovered, and that the client will not be able to determine whether they are real or not for a year or more. Yet, processing and repeating the information as if it were a real event for 12 months will make it harder later to determine whether the event was imagined or accurate.

Acceptance of the Stimulus and a Behavioral Response

In addition to the use of suggestive stimuli, the person must exhibit some acceptance of the stimuli in order for interrogative suggestibility to continue, according to Gudjonsson and Clark's (1986) model. This doesn't require that the person incorporate the information into his or her memory, but rather that the suggestion is perceived to be plausible and credible. For example, rather then providing answers to questions they remember clearly, people may make responses that seem plausible and consistent within the context in which the suggestions are made.

In addition to interpersonal trust and uncertainty, another prerequisite for interrogative suggestibility is an expectation of success. When these

---

[1]Theoretically, there are important differences between the concepts of repression and dissociation (Kihlstrom & Hoyt, 1990). For example, Janet argued that dissociated mental contents were accessible to conscious awareness under certain conditions (e.g., in hypnosis or naturally occurring somnambulistic states), whereas Freud asserted that repressed material could be known only indirectly, through inference and symbolic interpretation. For Freud, repression is a defense mechanism, employed to counteract anxiety, although dissociation, for Janet, is an inadvertent byproduct of stress. However, in the contemporary literature on traumatic memory, the terms *repression* and *dissociation* are often used interchangeably to refer to hypothetical processes by which memories are rendered inaccessible to conscious awareness. In this chapter, we follow the usage of the particular authors whose work we are discussing.

three factors operate together, the potential for the person to be highly suggestible is compounded. For example, if a person is uncertain about the events that took place, he or she can respond "I don't know" during the interview. However, if it is communicated during the interview that the person should know the answer, and that he or she is expected to know it and provide it, then it is more likely that the person will accept the suggestions imbedded in the context of the interview.

Feedback, especially negative feedback, is important during interrogation. Negative feedback attempting to modify an unwanted response can be either explicit or implicit; it doesn't have to be stated explicitly or verbally. For example, repeating the same question several times is a form of implicit feedback that conveys to the person that the answer is not acceptable. Interrogative suggestibility is also heightened by positive feedback when the interviewer reinforces wanted answers, perhaps by uttering "good," or by showing more interest after that response. It has been shown that negative feedback encourages people to change or shift their answers and heightens their responsiveness to further suggestions (Gudjonsson, 1984). Also, the more often suggestions are repeated, the more potent they become (Zaragoza & Lane, 1994).

The use of memory retrieval techniques in therapy allows the client to conjure up images and fantasies that will be accepted as valid memories if they are congruent with the client's belief system. If the client entered therapy with no memory of childhood abuse, she may come to form this belief merely by the fact that the therapist suggests it and attempts to retrieve the memories. In this circumstance the client's belief in abuse will mesh with the images retrieved during hypnosis or guided imagery, resulting in a pseudomemory.

Many trauma therapists have written that it is important to emphasize the recall of material that is necessary in order to heal or to live a satisfying life (Fredrickson, 1992; Herman, 1992). The client is informed that recovery of traumatic memories will clear the way for their symptoms and problems to recede and disappear. For example, McCann and Pearlman (1990) recommend that "uncovering techniques should be used only after the client and therapist agree that the client is ready to discover the hidden material" (p. 98). Statements like these provide the client with an expectation that memory retrieval techniques will undoubtedly supply the client with unconscious memories. In addition, the mere fact that memory recovery techniques are used implies that there actually are memories of abuse to be uncovered. One therapist suggested that unconscious memories indicate that the abuse happened in the client's own home and couldn't have possibly been done by a stranger (Fredrickson, 1992). If this is communicated to the person before undergoing memory work, it may suggest to the client what is expected. Moreover, if the book that includes this statement is read by the client, it may unduly influence subsequent therapeutic developments.

Clinicians who suspect hidden memories of childhood abuse and use memory retrieval techniques provide a type of negative feedback when the techniques are repeatedly used. Essentially the therapist is conveying that previous attempts to recover memories failed or were not sufficient, and that the client should try again to provide an adequate response. When the client reports memory fragments after undergoing memory work, the therapist will interpret this as confirmation of the initial belief in childhood abuse, and will reinforce the client's behavior. This is analogous to the phenomenon of confirmation bias, in which the clinician may seek evidence that confirms her original belief of childhood abuse and will avoid gathering any conflicting evidence (Evans, 1989). Also, as soon as the person recovers previously unconscious memories of some long-forgotten trauma, then the uncertainty vanishes.

The completion of interrogative suggestibility is achieved when the respondent gives some kind of a behavioral response to the suggestive stimulus (Gudjonsson & Clark, 1986). This means that believing or accepting the suggestion privately is not sufficient; the person must make some kind of verbal or nonverbal indication that he or she accepts the suggestion. This is accomplished in recovered memory therapy when the client confers with either the therapist, a friend, or family about what she believes happened to her. When a person has a traumatic event in her past, and spontaneously recovers it, this approach of talking to someone about it is well advised. Support during recovery is necessary, otherwise the person will feel victimized once again. However, if a person comes to believe she was abused as a child after entering therapy for depression, undergoing many months of memory retrieval techniques, and providing the therapist with memories, acceptance of the suggestion of abuse is only prolonged when the person expresses it as truth to other people. One therapist suggested that when telling others, "avoid being tentative about your repressed memories. Do not just tell them; express them as truth" (Fredrickson, 1992, p. 204). This advice has been taken to heart. As of September 1997, more than 500 recovered memory suits had been filed in criminal and civil courts across the country.

BEYOND SUGGESTIBILITY

Interrogative suggestibility is as important an issue in therapeutic settings as it is in forensic ones. Several techniques used in "memory work" involve highly suggestive situations and interactions, and can lead to various types of memory errors. Furthermore, suggestibility effects may be magnified when a client has a feeling of uncertainty about the source of his or her problems. However, suggestibility is not the only element in therapeutic or forensic situations that can give rise to distorted and false recollections.

Consider, for example, the McMartin Preschool Case ("Dismissal of Buckey charges," 1990; *People v. Buckey*, 1984), in which a number of nursery-school teachers were accused of abusing their pupils. In the end, most charges were dropped before trial, and none of the defendants were ever convicted, despite one of the longest and most expensive trials in California history. The core of the case was provided by a large number of interviews with children who had been enrolled in the school, which many of the jurors in the case criticized as leading. An analysis of these interviews (Wood et al., 1997) revealed that they did, in fact, contain many suggestive questions of the sort implicated in interrogative suggestibility. But they also contained a number of other "social incentive" elements that further increased the risk of error, distortion, and false recollection in the children's reports. For example, the technique of "Other People" informed the child that someone else had already provided a certain piece of information, and then asked the child to affirm it. In "Positive and Negative Consequences," children received, or were promised, praise, criticism, and other rewards and punishments for making certain statements. In the technique of "Asked and Answered," a question was repeated that the child had already unambiguously answered. In "Inviting Speculation," the child was asked to offer opinions, speculations, or fantasies about particular events.

An experimental study, in which young children were interviewed about a classroom visitor, showed that this package of interviewing techniques, administered even in relatively small amounts, led to a substantial increase in false memories and allegations (Garven et al., 1997). Further, the authors noted that the children became more acquiescent as the hour-long interviews progressed. Consistent with the model of Gudjonsson and Clark (1986), which emphasizes the entire situation in which leading and suggestive questions are posed and answered, the entire package of social incentive techniques produced far more errors than suggestive questions alone.

On the basis of these findings, Garven et al. (1997) proposed the SIRR model for eliciting false statements from interview subjects by virtue of Suggestive questions, social Influence, Reinforcement, and Removal from direct experience (including inviting speculation and the use of puppets). Obviously, the same elements are common features of memory work.

THE THERAPIST AND THE DETECTIVE

Why include a chapter on memory work, a clinical practice, in a book on suggestibility in the forensic interview? After all, "I'm not a detective; I'm a psychotherapist. It would be inappropriate for me to act like a detective.

I'm there to help my client heal" (E. Sue Blume, interview with Morley Safer on the CBS program *60 Minutes*, April 17, 1994). And, "As a therapist, your job is not to be a detective; your job is not to be a fact finder" (J. L. Herman, interview with Ofra Bickel on the Public Broadcasting Service program *Frontline*, 1995).

Many clinical practitioners appear to share Blume's and Herman's view of the therapeutic enterprise (Moen, 1995). From their point of view, the job of the therapist is to help patients construct coherent narratives of their lives that explain how they got where they are, and how the patient can recover and heal. This goal, they believe, can only be accomplished when the patient has a place of safety, and creating this safe place entails an attitude of acceptance and unconditional positive regard toward the patient. In therapy, so the claim goes, what is most important is what the patient feels and believes, rather than what actually happened. Even if the patient's narrative is inaccurate in some respects, it contains enough truth for the therapist to work with.

Such a stance may be defensible when therapy is focused exclusively on feelings and fantasies—on narrative truth as opposed to historical truth (Spence, 1984)—though frankly it is not clear that therapies focusing the patient's attention on the past are as effective, or as efficient, as those that emphasize the here and now. Whenever therapy begins, as recovered memory therapy begins, with the assumption that the patient's problems have their origins in historical experience; when the patient's memories, and beliefs about his or her past, spill over to affect his or her relations with parents and other family members, as they must inevitably do in recovered memory therapy; and when these memories and beliefs are presented as evidence in the civil and criminal courtroom, as they often are, then the therapist does become a detective, and the reliability of the fact-finding process becomes a legitimate target of scrutiny. It is under these circumstances that the therapist, no less than the detective, needs to pay attention to the process by which evidence is gathered. In this process, interrogative suggestibility, including the suggestive components of the interview situation as well as the vulnerability of the interviewee to suggestion, becomes a critical consideration.

ACKNOWLEDGMENTS

Preparation supported by Grant #MH-35856 from the National Institute of Mental Health. We thank Lillian Park and Jodi A. Quas for their comments.

REFERENCES

Bass, E., & Davis, L. (1988). *The courage to heal: A guide for women survivors of child sexual abuse.* New York: Harper & Row.

Belluck, P. (1997, November 6). "Memory" therapy leads to a lawsuit and big settlement. *New York Times,* p. A1.

Berger, L., Hunter, I., & Lane, R. (1971). The effect of stress on dreams. *Psychological Issues, 7,* 1–213.

Blume, E. S. (1990). *Secret survivors: Uncovering incest and its aftereffects in women.* New York: Ballantine.

Brenneis, C. B. (1994). Belief and suggestion in the recovery of memories of childhood sexual abuse. *Journal of the American Psychoanalytic Association, 42,* 1027–1053.

Brenneis, C. B. (1997). *Recovered memories of trauma: Transferring the present to the past.* Madison, CT: International Universities Press.

Briere, J. N. (1992). *Child abuse trauma: Theory and treatment of the lasting effects.* Newbury Park, CA: Sage.

Claridge, K. (1992). Reconstructing memories of abuse: A theory-based approach. *Psychotherapy, 29,* 243–252.

Courtois, C. (1988). *Healing the incest wound: Adult survivors in therapy.* New York: Norton.

Cronbach, L. J. (1957). The two disciplines of scientific psychology. *American Psychologist, 12,* 671–684.

Destun, L. M., & Kuiper, N. A. (1996). Autobiographical memory and recovered memory therapy: Integrating cognitive, clinical, and individual difference perspectives. *Clinical Psychology Review, 16,* 421–450.

Dismissal of Buckey charges ends longest case in U.S. (1990, August 2). *New York Times,* p. A18.

Dolan, Y. M. (1991). *Resolving sexual abuse: Solution-focused therapy and Ericksonian hypnosis for adult survivors.* New York: Norton.

Dywan, J. (1995). The illusion of familiarity: An alternative to the report-criterion account of hypnotic recall. *International Journal of Clinical and Experimental Hypnosis, 43,* 194–211.

Eich, E. (1989). Theoretical issues in state dependent memory. In H. L. Roediger & F. I. M. Craik (Eds.), *Varieties of memory and consciousness: Essays in honor of Endel Tulving* (pp. 331–354). Hillsdale, NJ: Lawrence Erlbaum Associates.

Evans, F. J. (1967). Suggestibility in the normal waking state. *Psychological Bulletin, 67,* 114–129.

Evans, J. (1989). *Bias in human reasoning: Causes and consequences.* Hillsdale, NJ: Lawrence Erlbaum Associates.

Eysenck, H. J. (1947). *The dimensions of personality.* London: Routledge & Kegan Paul.

Eysenck, H. J., & Furneaux, W. D. (1945). Primary and secondary suggestibility: An experimental and statistical study. *Journal of Experimental Psychology, 35,* 485–503.

Frankel, F. (1994). The concept of flashbacks in historical perspective. *International Journal of Clinical and Experimental Hypnosis, 42,* 321–336.

Fredrickson, R. (1992). *Repressed memories: A journey to recovery from sexual abuse.* New York: Simon & Schuster.

Garven, S., Wood, J. M., Malpass, R. S., & Shaw, J. S. (1997). More than suggestion: The effect of interviewing techniques from the McMartin Preschool case. *Journal of Applied Psychology, 83,* 347–359.

Gheorghiu, V. A., Netter, P., Eysenck, H. J., & Rosenthal, R. (Eds.). (1989). *Suggestion and suggestibility: Theory and research.* Berlin: Springer-Verlag.

Gudjonsson, G. H. (1984). A new scale of interrogative suggestibility. *Personality and Individual Differences, 5,* 303–314.

Gudjonsson, G. H. (1987). Historical background to suggestibility: How interrogative suggestibility differs from other types of suggestibility. *Personality and Individual Differences, 8,* 347–355.

Gudjonsson, G. H. (1989). Theoretical and empirical aspects of interrogative suggestibility. In V. A. Gheorghiu, P. Netter, H. J. Eysenck, & R. Rosenthal (Eds.), *Suggestion and suggestibility: Theory and research* (pp. 135–143). London: Springer-Verlag.

Gudjonsson, G. H. (1991). The application of interrogative suggestibility to police interviewing. In J. F. Schumaker (Ed.), *Human suggestibility: Advances in theory, research, and application* (pp. 279–288). New York: Routledge.

Gudjonsson, G. H. (1992). *The psychology of interrogations, confessions, and testimony.* Chichester, England: Wiley.

Gudjonsson, G. H., & Clark, N. K. (1986). Suggestibility in police interrogation: A social psychological model. *Social Behaviour, 1,* 83–104.

Herman, J. L. (1992). *Trauma and recovery* (2nd ed.). New York: Basic Books.

Herman, J., & Schatzow, E. (1984). Time-limited group therapy for women with a history of incest. *International Journal of Group Psychotherapy, 34,* 605–616.

Hilgard, E. R. (1991). Suggestibility and suggestions as related to hypnosis. In J. F. Schumaker (Ed.), *Human suggestibility: Advances in theory, research, and application* (pp. 37–58). London: Routledge.

Hovdestad, W., & Kristiansen, C. (1996). Mind meets body: On the nature of recovered memories of trauma. *Women and Therapy, 19,* 31–45.

Hull, C. L. (1933). *Hypnosis and suggestibility: An experimental approach.* New York: Appleton-Century-Crofts.

Johnson, M. K. (1988). Reality monitoring: An experimental phenomenological approach. *Journal of Experimental Psychology: General, 117,* 390–394.

Johnson, M. K., Hashtroudi, S., & Lindsay, D. S. (1993). Source monitoring. *Psychological Bulletin, 114,* 3–28.

Johnson, M. K., & Raye, C. L. (1981). Reality monitoring. *Psychological Review, 88,* 67–85.

Kihlstrom, J. F. (1994). Hypnosis, delayed recall and the principles of memory. *International Journal of Clinical & Experimental Hypnosis, 42,* 337–345.

Kihlstrom, J. F. (1996a). Suffering from reminiscences: Exhumed memory, implicit memory, and the return of the repressed. In M. A. Conway (Ed.), *Recovered memories and false memories* (pp. 100–117). Oxford, England: Oxford University Press.

Kihlstrom, J. F. (1996b). The trauma–memory argument and recovered memory therapy. In K. Pezdek & W. P. Banks (Eds.), *The recovered memory/false memory debate* (pp. 297–311). San Diego, CA: Academic.

Kihlstrom, J. F. (1997). Memory, abuse, and science. *American Psychologist, 52,* 994–995.

Kihlstrom, J. F. (1998). Exhumed memory. In S. J. Lynn & K. M. McConkey (Eds.), *Truth in memory* (pp. 3–31). New York: Guilford.

Kihlstrom, J. F., & Hoyt, I. P. (1990). Repression, dissociation, and hypnosis. In J. L. Singer (Ed.), *Repression and dissociation: Implications for personality theory, psychopathology, and health* (pp. 181–208). Chicago: University of Chicago Press.

Kirschner, S., Kirschner, D. A., & Rappaport, R. L. (1993). *Working with adult incest survivors: The healing journey.* New York: Brunner/Mazel.

LeDoux, J. (1996). *The emotional brain: The mysterious underpinnings of emotional life.* New York: Simon & Schuster.

Lindsay, D. S., & Poole, D. A. (1998). The Poole et al. (1995) surveys of therapists: Misinterpretations by both sides of the recovered memories controversy. *Journal of Psychiatry and Law, 26,* 383–399.

Lindsay, D. S., & Read, J. D. (1994). Psychotherapy and memories of childhood sexual abuse: A cognitive perspective. *Applied Cognitive Psychology, 8,* 281–338.

Loftus, E. F. (1975). Leading questions and eyewitness report. *Cognitive Psychology, 7,* 560–572.

Loftus, E. F. (1992). When a lie becomes memory's truth: Memory distortion after exposure to misinformation. *Current Directions in Psychological Science, 1,* 121–123.

Loftus, E. F., & Ketcham, K. (1992). *The myth of repressed memories: False memories and allegations of abuse.* New York: St. Martin's Press.

Lynn, S. J., & Kirsch, I. I. (1996). Alleged alien abductions: False memories, hypnosis, and fantasy proneness. *Psychological Inquiry, 7,* 151–155.

Maldonado, J. R., & Spiegel, D. (1995). Using hypnosis. In C. Classen (Ed.), *Treating women molested in childhood* (pp. 163–186). San Francisco: Jossey-Bass.

McCann, I. L., & Pearlman, L. A. (1990). *Psychological trauma and the adult survivor: Theory, therapy, and transformation.* New York: Brunner/Mazel.

McCloskey, M., & Zaragoza, M. (1985). Misleading postevent information and memory for events: Arguments and evidence against memory impairment hypotheses. *Journal of Experimental Psychology: General, 114,* 1–16.

Moen, S. P. (1995). Consequences of the therapist's claim "I'm not a detective." *Journal of Psychiatry and Law, 23,* 477–484.

Ofshe, R., & Watters, E. (1994). *Making monsters: False memories, psychotherapy, and sexual hysteria.* New York: Scribner's.

Orne, M., Whitehouse, W., Orne, E., & Dinges, D. (1996). "Memories" of anomalous and traumatic autobiographical experiences: Validation and consolidation of fantasy through hypnosis. *Psychological Inquiry, 7,* 168–172.

Pendergrast, M. (1996). *Victims of memory: Sex abuse accusations and shattered lives* (2nd ed.). Hinesburg, VT: Upper Access Press.

People v. Buckey, No. A750900 (filed Mar. 22, 1984).

Pezdek, K., Finger, K., & Hodge, D. (1997). Planting false childhood memories: The role of event plausibility. *Psychological Science, 8,* 437–441.

Polusny, M. A., & Follette, V. M. (1996). Remembering childhood sexual abuse: A national survey of psychologists' clinical practices, beliefs, and personal experiences. *Professional Psychology: Research and Practice, 27,* 41–52.

Poole, D., Lindsay, D. S., Memon, A., & Bull, R. (1995). Psychotherapy and the recovery of memories of childhood sexual abuse: U.S. and British practitioner's opinions, practices, and experiences. *Journal of Consulting and Clinical Psychology, 63,* 426–437.

Price, R. (1986). Hypnotic age regression and the reparenting of self. *Transactional Analysis Journal, 16,* 120–127.

Register, P. A., & Kihlstrom, J. F. (1988). Hypnosis and interrogative suggestibility. *Personality and Individual Differences, 9,* 549–558.

Schooler, J. W., & Loftus, E. F. (1986). Individual differences and experimentation: Complementary approaches to interrogative suggestibility. *Social Behaviour, 1,* 105–112.

Schumaker, J. F. (1991). *Human suggestibility: Advances in theory, research, and application.* New York: Routledge.

Shobe, K. K., & Kihlstrom, J. F. (1997). Is traumatic memory special? *Current Directions in Psychological Science, 6,* 70–74.

Simonds, S. L. (1994). *Bridging the silence: Nonverbal modalities in the treatment of adult survivors of childhood sexual abuse.* New York: Norton.

Spanos, N. P., Menary, E., Gabora, N. J., DuBreuil, S. C., & Dewhirst, B. (1991). Secondary identity enactments during hypnotic past-life regression: A sociocognitive perspective. *Journal of Personality and Social Psychology, 61,* 308–320.

Spence, D. P. (1984). *Narrative truth and historical truth.* New York: Norton.

van der Kolk, B. A. (1994). The body keeps the score: Memory and the evolving psychobiology of posttraumatic stress. *Harvard Review of Psychiatry, 1,* 253–265.

Walker, L. E. A. (1994). *Abused women and survivor therapy: A practical guide for the psychotherapist*. Washington, DC: American Psychological Association.

Whitfield, C. (1995). The forgotten difference: Ordinary memory versus traumatic memory. *Consciousness and Cognition, 4*, 88–94.

Williams, M. (1987). Reconstruction of early seduction and its aftereffects. *Journal of the American Psychoanalytic Association, 35*, 145–163.

Wood, J. M., Schreiber, N., Martinez, Y., McLaurin, K., Strok, R., Velarde, L., Garven, S., & Malpass, R. S. (1997). *Interviewing techniques in the McMartin Preschool and Kelly Michaels cases: A quantitative analysis*. Manuscript in preparation, University of Texas, El Paso.

Yapko, M. D. (1994). *Suggestions of abuse: True and false memories of childhood sexual trauma*. New York: Simon & Schuster.

Zaragoza, M. S., & Lane, S. M. (1994). Source misattributions and the suggestibility of eyewitness memory. *Journal of Experimental Psychology: Learning, Memory, & Cognition, 20*, 934–945.

IV

CHILDREN IN THE FORENSIC INTERVIEW CONTEXT

Questions and Answers: The Credibility of Child Witnesses in the Context of Specific Questioning Techniques

Robyn Fivush
Emory University

Carole Peterson
Memorial University of Newfoundland

April Schwarzmueller
Eckerd College

Once children enter the legal system, as victims or witnesses, they are interviewed multiple times by multiple people before giving testimony in court (Myers, 1987). Interestingly, "common sense" beliefs about the effects of repeated interviews on children's memories and/or reports of what transpired lead to contradictory conclusions. On the one hand, it is argued that repeatedly recalling an event helps children (and adults) to consolidate their memory of what occurred, leading to a more durable memory. On the other hand, repeatedly recalling an event can lead children (and adults) to begin to reconstruct what happened, adding details that make sense but that may not be accurate. Which position reflects what actually happens over the course of repeated interviews is critical, not only for theoretical reasons, but for interpreting and evaluating children's testimony in applied forensic situations.

Two recent reviews of the literature (Fivush & Schwarzmueller, 1995; Poole & White, 1995) concur that simply asking children to recall an event again and again does not have a detrimental effect on their memory reports, and may even have beneficial effects under certain conditions. Indeed, everything we know about memory from experimental research indicates that repeatedly recalling an event is a form of rehearsal that helps buffer against forgetting (see Brainerd & Ornstein, 1991; Schwartz & Reisberg, 1991, for reviews). However, forensic interviews may not be as benign as most of the interviews conducted in experimental studies. When police, social workers, and lawyers interview children for legal purposes, they must often go beyond asking the child for free recall of what happened, and pose specific, and sometimes leading questions.

In this chapter, we extend the previous reviews of the effects of repeated interviews on children's memories by considering forensic issues more completely. In the first section, we summarize the general effects of repeated questions both within the same interview and across interviews. Because this literature has been reviewed in detail so recently (Fivush & Schwarzmueller, 1995; Poole & White, 1995), we provide only a brief overview here. We then turn to the question of what happens over longer periods of time. Children often testify months or years after the actual event has occurred; it is therefore important to consider how and what young children are able to recall over long delays. The first two sections focus on children's recall in the absence of misleading or suggestive questions. Most of this research examines children's responses to general, open-ended questions, such as "What happened . . . ?" and "Tell me about. . . ." or nonleading questions such as "What did the person look like?" and "What was the person wearing?" In the third section, we consider the effects of repeatedly interviewing children in more suggestive or coercive ways, for example, by providing erroneous information in the question or by cajoling the child to respond. Finally, we examine the effects of specific question types on children's memory reports. In particular, differences between questions that ask the child to recall a specific piece of information, and yes–no questions, questions that only require the child to acquiesce or deny a piece of information are compared. Throughout, we draw implications for forensic interviewing, and at the end, we provide some overall guidelines for forensic interviewing that emerge from the research.

REPEATED QUESTIONS

When children are interviewed for legal purposes, they are often asked the same questions over and over (Myers, 1987). When this occurs within the same interview, it is considered a "check" on the child's accuracy; if the child gives a different answer to the same question asked again during the same interview, it is often assumed that the child's testimony is not accurate. But, as several theorists have pointed out, this may be more a function of the social demands of the situation than of the child's memory. When children are asked the same question again, they may assume that the adult interviewer did not approve of the first answer given (Moston, 1987; Rose & Blank, 1974). Especially in situations in which children may feel uncomfortable, as in being interviewed by a relative stranger about an upsetting event, children may change their answers in order to please the adult (Siegel, Waters, & Dinwiddy, 1988). Thus, it is important to bear in mind when interpreting the literature on suggestibility that children's acceptance of erroneous information may be more a matter of changing their report as a function of the social context, than a change in the underlying memory.

Several studies have found that children are highly likely to change their answer the second time a question is asked within the same interview (Cassel & Bjorkland, 1995; Laumann & Elliot, 1992; Moston, 1987; Poole & White, 1991; Warren, Hulse-Trotter, & Tubbs, 1991). This is especially true for children age 6 and younger. For example, Cassel and Bjorkland (1995) found that 42% of the 6-year-olds in their study changed their responses to a specific question about a video of a bicycle theft (Did the boy have permission to take the bike?) the second time the question was asked, but few of the 8-year-olds changed their answer. It is also important to note here that children may be substantially more likely to change their answer when asked a leading question phrased as a yes–no question (e.g., The bike was stolen by the mother, wasn't it?), than when asked to provide information (e.g., Who stole the bike?), an issue that we discuss at greater length later in this chapter. These results indicate that repeating a question within the same interview as a memory check for young children is often detrimental. Children, especially preschoolers, appear to respond to the repeated question as an indication that the adult was not pleased with their first answer, and are therefore likely to change their answer as a result of the social demands of the situation, not necessarily as a function of poor memory.

In contrast to repeating questions within the same interview, the social situation is quite different when the same question is asked repeatedly across separate interviews. Because time has passed between recall occasions, and often a different person is conducting the interview (e.g., a social worker, a police officer, or a lawyer), children may not think that a repeated question means that the first answer was not acceptable. Moreover, given the general finding in the memory literature that rehearsal buffers against forgetting (see Schwartz & Reisberg, 1991, for a review), there is good reason to predict that recalling an event on multiple occasions will help children report what occurred rather than hinder them.

Research examining the effects of previous interviews on children's subsequent recall provides some support for this prediction, but it seems to be tempered by developmental differences. After examining repeated interviews over relatively brief durations of days or weeks, no study has found detrimental effects of repeated nonsuggestive interviews, in the sense that no study has found an increase in the amount of inaccurate information reported. And, for children aged 7 to 8 years or older, recalling an event even once often leads to better subsequent recall (Flin, Boon, Knox, & Bull, 1992; Memon, Wark, Bull, & Koehnken, 1995). Recalling an event once does not seem to be as beneficial for children younger than age 7, but recalling an event several times is beneficial for subsequent memory at all ages (Baker-Ward, Gordon, Ornstein, Larus, & Clubb, 1993; Baker-Ward, Hess, & Flannagan, 1990; Cassidy & DeLoache, 1995; Gee & Pipe, in press; Goodman, Bottoms, Schwartz-Kenney, & Rudy, 1991; Warren & Swartwood, 1992). Repeated interviews do not compromise children's memory reports, and may even help children to recall more information, at least over short delays. (The way in which recall may change over more substantial delays is discussed in detail later.)

One reason why repeatedly recalling an event may lead to better subsequent memory is that in the process of recall, children reactivate the memory of the experience. Thus, recall may be similar to reexperiencing the event, leading to a stronger memory trace. It is also possible that recalling an event immediately after experiencing it serves to organize and consolidate the memory, and prepares children for subsequent verbal recall. If so, an immediate interview would be particularly beneficial for subsequent memory.

Yet several studies have found no effects of timing of the first recall; in general it does not seem to matter whether the interview occurs immediately or within a couple of weeks after the event for it to have a beneficial effect for older children. For younger children, when the interviews occur seems less important than the number of previous interviews. However, this remains an intriguing developmental question. It may still be the case that the first interview must occur within a specific time window for it to help buffer against forgetting, and this time window may be longer for older children than for younger children.

One line of research in support of this possibility comes from the infant memory literature. This literature obviously focuses on nonverbal memory of an event, and thus any parallels must be drawn with caution. However, for infants, the timing of reactivating a memory through partial reinstatement of the event is critical for subsequent retrieval. Using a conjugate reinforcement paradigm, in which infants learn to kick in order to make an attractive mobile move over their crib, Rovee-Collier and her colleagues (Boller, Rovee-Collier, Borovsky, O'Conner, & Shyi, 1990; Rovee-Collier & Gerhardstein, 1997) demonstrated that the period during which reactivation of a memory is effective follows a clear developmental trajectory, with older infants able to maintain the behavioral response without reinstatement for longer periods of time than younger infants. And Sheffield and Hudson (1994) have shown a similar pattern with toddlers; 1-year-old children need to be reminded of an event sooner than do 2-year-olds in order to be able to reenact the event when returned to the original context.

Evidence of memory through behavioral reenactment is obviously very different from verbal recall. Most important, verbal recall takes place outside of the spatial–temporal context of the original event, and this is not true for behavioral reenactment. Indeed, infants are heavily dependent on being back in the original context in which the event was experienced in order to evidence any memory of the event at all. Moreover, there is no evidence that events occurring before the ability to describe the event in language will ever become accessible for verbal recall (see Fivush, Pipe, Murachver, & Reese, 1997, for a review). Therefore, the data from the infant memory literature can only be taken as suggestive that, just as the timing of behavioral reinstatement is critical in extending the life of a behavioral response in infancy, the timing of verbal reinstatement through recalling an event may be critical for extending the life of a verbally accessible memory. In general, younger children show steeper forgetting curves than older children, at least for word lists, and possibly for complex events as well (see Brainerd, Reyna, Howe, & Kingma, 1990, for an overview). It may be the case that younger children need to verbally rehearse an event sooner after an event's occurrence in order to buffer against long-term forgetting. Although the research indicates that an interview immediately after the event occurs is not critical, the first recall may have to occur within a specified period of time for it to be effective, and this timing may be developmentally sensitive.

Overall, whereas repeating questions within the same interview is usually detrimental especially for younger children, repeating questions across interviews does not have the same effect. In fact, repeated interviews may benefit long-term retention. For children older than about age 7, even one previous recall often leads to better subsequent recall. For children younger than 7, participating in one previous recall may or may not be effective, but participating in several previous recalls seems to be. An important avenue for further research is to examine the effects of the timing of interviews on children's retention, in addition to the number of interviews.

CHILDREN'S RECALL OVER LONG DELAYS

Studies on repeated interviews tend to examine children's memories over a relatively brief period of several weeks or a few months. But, just as children who enter the legal system are interviewed multiple times, it is also

the case that children often testify in court several years after the actual
event occurred (Myers, 1987). What is it that young children can remember about personally experienced events over such long delays? Warren
and Swartwood (1992) asked children to recall how they heard about the
Challenger space shuttle disaster at several time delays up to 2 years after
the event. Whereas children older than age 8 at the time of the disaster
showed better recall if they had previously recalled the event, children
younger than this showed no effects of prior recall at the 2-year delay.
Similarly, Poole and White (1991, 1993) interviewed groups of 4- and 6-
year-olds and adults about a staged argument either immediately and 1
week later, or only 1 week later. All were then interviewed again 2 years
later. Researchers found few effects of prior interviews at either the 1-
week or the 2-year delay on open-ended questions. They also found high
inconsistency between interviews in the youngest children's responses to
specific questions, both at 1 week and at 2 years. Again, however, it is important to note that the specific questions were all yes–no questions. Still,
these results raise the question of stability of memory over long periods of
time. How much information are young children able to remember over
periods of several months or years, and how might the memory change
over time? Perhaps most important from a forensic viewpoint, is there increasing error in memory over long delays?

Somewhat surprisingly, there is now a good deal of evidence that children as young as 3 years of age can recall accurate details about past experiences, and they can retain these memories over delays of several years
(Fivush, Gray, & Fromhoff, 1987; Fivush & Hamond, 1990; Hamond &
Fivush, 1990; Sheingold & Tenney, 1982; Todd & Perlmutter, 1980; see
Fivush, 1993, for a review). For example, Hudson and Fivush (1990) asked
children to recall a kindergarten class trip to an unusual museum of arche-
ology immediately after the experience, 6 weeks later, 1 year later, and 6
years later. Children recalled the event in great detail and quite accurately
up to a year later. Six years later, children were still able to recall the event
but they needed more cues and prompts from the interviewer, and they
recalled less information overall than they had at the 1-year delay. Moreover, whereas there were virtually no errors in children's reports at the 1-
year delay, at the 6-year delay, some children made reconstructive errors,
inferring certain items or actions that had not occurred. Still, memory was
largely accurate even at this long delay, and what children did recall was
recalled in great detail.

Similarly, Fivush and Schwarzmueller (1998) demonstrated that children now 8 years of age are able to recall accurately events they experienced up to 5 years in the past. Children recalled just as much information
at age 8 as they had when they initially recalled these events at either age
3, 4, 5, or 6 years. Two aspects of the results deserve note. First, in this

study, there was no increase in error even over these long delays. This is most likely because the events asked about when the children were 8 were highly distinctive, personally meaningful events in the children's lives, much more so than a class trip to a museum. Second, although children's recall remained highly accurate, the content of their recall changed dramatically; children recalled different aspects of the event at the interview conducted when they were 8 years old than they had at the previous interview. In fact, up to 70% of the information recalled at the age 8 interview was new and different information than recalled at the previous interview, although still accurate according to parental report.

Importantly, several studies have now documented that children's recall of an event changes substantially across recall occasions, whether the recalls are separated by a few weeks (Fivush, Hamond, Harsch, Singer, & Wolf, 1991; Hudson, 1990b) or several years (Fivush & Hamond, 1990; Fivush & Shukat, 1995). The reasons for this high level of inconsistency between children's reports of an event are still not clear. Part of the answer seems to lie in the way in which recall is elicited. Children seem to recall different information when they are recalling the event with someone who was present during the event than when recalling the event with someone who was not present. Children may perceive informed versus naive interviewers as needing different kinds of information. Content of recall also varies as a function of the types of questions children are asked. In situations where children are asked to supply specific types of information they may easily be able to do so, but they may not include this information in a free recall of the event.

We must emphasize that, in these studies, children did not report information that was contradictory; rather, children seemed to focus on different aspects of the event to report. For example, in recalling going to SeaWorld, one young child focused on how they got there, and her mother getting lost and needing to ask directions when she first recalled the event at age 5, but a year later at age 6, she focused on the whale show, and how exciting it was to see Shamu. Although it is still not clear why children choose to focus on different aspects of an event on different recall occasions, it is imperative to point out that inconsistency, in and of itself, is not an indication of inaccuracy.

More experimentally controlled studies of children's memories over long periods of time confirm and extend the findings from the more naturalistic memory research. In the Poole and White (1993) study mentioned earlier, they asked children now aged 6 or 8 years old and adults to recall a brief altercation they witnessed 2 years in the past. The overall amount of accurate information declined over time, but the amount of inaccurate information did not increase. In contrast, Salmon and Pipe (1997) interviewed children about a quasi-medical laboratory event immediately and

1 year later. Again, there was a decrease in amount of accurate information recalled but, in this study, there was also an increase in inaccurate information. Moreover, information reported at the second interview, but not at the first interview, was significantly more likely to be in error than to be accurate. Similarly, Peterson and Bell (1996) reported that 3- through 13-year-old children's memories for minor medical traumas requiring emergency room treatment remained extremely accurate over a 6-month delay, and there was little forgetting over this period of time. However, although accuracy remained quite high, there was a slight increase in errors. After interviewing these same children again 2 years after their injury and treatment, Peterson (1999) reported that children were able to recall as much information about their experiences at this long delay as they had initially, although recall for the injury was more accurate and more exhaustive than was recall of the treatment. Highly distinctive and salient events seem to be extremely well recalled even after substantial delays.

Peterson and Bell also included a group of 2-year-olds who showed a different pattern; because of their limited language skills, they were unable to verbally recall much about their experience at the time of occurrence, they included a considerable amount of error even in their initial reports, and their errors increased over time. In general, research suggests that there may be a qualitative shift in children's abilities to give accurate verbal reports sometime between the ages of 2½ and 3 years of age. Furthermore, Peterson and Rideout (1998) found that children who were under 2 years of age and therefore did not have the language skills to verbally describe their experience at the time it occurred, remained unable to verbally recall it during repeated interviews over the subsequent 18 months. Although it is beyond the scope of this chapter to review this issue in detail, it is important to note that children who are too young to provide a verbal account of an event when it is experienced remain unable to recall that event verbally even as their language skills develop (see Fivush et al., 1996; Fivush, 1998, for reviews). Peterson and Bell's data further indicated that any verbal recall produced in these later interviews by children who were 2 or younger at time of experience included a great deal of error. Once children are able to provide a verbal account at the time of experience, at about 2½ to 3 years of age, they seem to be able to retain these memories over long delays. However, while these reports remain remarkably accurate, there is often a decrease in amount of accurate information reported and a small, but significant increase in amount of inaccurate information included with increasing delays.

In an attempt to disentangle when there will be decreases in amount of accurate information and/or increases in amount of inaccurate information, several aspects of the event should be considered. Most important, events that remain distinctive are less likely to become confused with other events the child experiences, and thus are less likely to suffer from inferences and reconstructions leading to error. Certainly, the quasi-medical event studied by Salmon and Pipe is less distinctive and more confusable with other events than either medical events requiring emergency room treatment or the kinds of unique events studied in the more naturalistic research, such as going to DisneyWorld, or being a flower girl in an aunt's wedding. Thus we would expect increasing error over time for events that are more similar to other experienced events and, in contrast, less increase in error over time for more distinctive events that are not easily confusable with other events.

Note that increasing error for less distinctive events is most often a matter of confusing details among similar experiences rather than reporting details that were never experienced. In general, children's recall changes dramatically as a function of the number of experiences with similar events (see Hudson, Fivush, & Kuebli, 1992, for a full theoretical discussion). Children's reports become more schematic, in that they report more of the component activities that occur across most episodes of a similar event but report these activities in less detail (Fivush & Slackman, 1986), and preschool children often confuse the specific details of one event with the details of another similar event (Farrar & Goodman, 1990; Hudson, 1990a). This becomes important in forensic situations when children are being asked to recall one specific episode of a repeated experience, as often occurs with physical and sexual abuse. Therefore, it is not so much a question of decreasing accuracy, but rather a process of confusing details as repeated experiences begin to be represented and remembered in terms of what "usually happens." Children, and especially preschoolers, may be able to report what usually happens accurately but have difficulty recalling the details of a specific instance of a repeated event.

Related to the issue of distinctiveness is personal significance. Many of the laboratory events studied are not particularly interesting and/or meaningful to the child and therefore are less likely to be remembered over time. One reason for this may be because events that are interesting and meaningful tend to be talked about and thought about more often than other kinds of events. As we have already reviewed, recalling an event multiple times may help buffer against forgetting. Thus, personal significance may be the impetus leading to higher levels of rehearsal for some events over others, rendering these events more memorable over longer periods of time.

In general, the research indicates high levels of accuracy in young children's recall of distinctive events over time and over multiple interviews. However, over long delays, children may report less information overall, and may include more inaccurate information in their verbal reports. This pattern may be especially likely when other similar events have been experienced. When events remain highly distinctive, children may be able to recall as much information, and recall it as accurately, even after long delays. It must be emphasized that the studies reviewed thus far did not include misleading or suggestive questions. If talking about events with others helps buffer against long-term forgetting by essentially reinstating the event through language, what might the effects be when erroneous information is included in these conversations?

REPEATED SUGGESTIVE QUESTIONS

Extensive literature documents that children are susceptible to misleading and suggestive questions (see Ceci & Bruck, 1993, for review). When children are presented with misinformation after an event's occurrence, they may begin to accept that information as having occurred during the event itself. Obviously, this is a complex phenomenon, and several factors influence the extent to which children are likely to be suggestible, including level of active participation in the event (Goodman, Rudy, Bottoms, & Aman, 1990), whether or not bodily touch occurred (Steward, 1993), and the demeanor of the interviewer (Carter, Bottoms, & Levine, 1996; Goodman et al., 1991). In addition, there are developmental differences in suggestibility, such that younger children, especially preschoolers, are more suggestible than older children, and there is intriguing evidence that temperamental factors such as distractibility (Ornstein, 1995), and emotional factors, such as attachment relations (Goodman, Quas, Batterman-Faunce, Riddlesberger, & Kuhn, 1994), may play a role in individual differences in children's susceptibility to suggestion.

Although it is incontrovertible that interviewing children in suggestive and misleading ways compromises their memory reports, it is not clear to what extent misinformation presented after an event's occurrence changes the child's memory of what occurred. Most studies of children's suggestibility rely on children's responses to yes–no questions about the presented misinformation, but as we discuss in detail in the next section, these kinds of questions may be particularly problematical for young children. Little research has examined children's tendencies to incorporate suggested information into their subsequent recall of the event. Cassel and Bjorkland (1995) asked 6- and 8-year-olds and adults to recall a video of a bicycle theft three times across a 1 month interval. Even those participants exposed to misinformation during the first or second interview did not come to recall that information at their final interview. Levels of accuracy of free recall were extremely high at all interviews and ages, although older children and adults recalled more information overall than the younger children. Importantly, however, whereas even the youngest children did not report the misinformation in their recall, they did acquiesce to the misleading questions significantly more often than did the older children and adults. Similarly, Poole and White (1991) found little inclusion of misinformation presented about a witnessed altercation into children's free recall of the event 1 week later, but younger children acquiesced to misleading questions more often than older children.

These results suggest that suggestibility may reflect children's tendencies to acquiesce to authority as much as changes in children's memories of what occurred (see also Ceci, Toglia, & Ross, 1990). Children, and especially preschoolers, may be susceptible to the form of the question and the authority of the interviewer such that they are more likely to acquiesce to a yes–no question, but this does not necessarily mean that their memory of the event has changed, as this information does not seem to corrupt their subsequent recall of the event. From a legal standpoint, whatever the mechanism underlying children's suggestibility, it is still equally detrimental to their credibility as witnesses. Moreover, these studies indicate effects of misleading information after only one intervening interview that includes misinformation. What happens if children are repeatedly questioned in misleading and suggestive ways? When adults were asked the same questions repeatedly during the same interview, and these questions contain misleading information (e.g., "Which door did the young man wearing gloves enter through?" when the man was not wearing gloves), they subsequently claimed that they remembered the presented misinformation ("Yes, the man was wearing gloves.") at substantially higher rates than participants presented with the misinformation only once (Mitchell & Zaragoza, 1996; Zaragoza & Mitchell, 1996).

Ceci and his colleagues have conducted two studies examining young children's reactions to repeated suggestive questioning. In Leichtman and Ceci (1995), a visitor, Sam Stone, came into preschoolers' classrooms during story time, said hello, walked around, and then walked out. In the control condition, children were asked to recall this event four times in a neutral manner. In the stereotype condition, in which the authors tried to bias the children against the visitor, children were told before the visit that Sam Stone would be coming and that he was nice but clumsy; they were then interviewed four times in a neutral manner. In the suggestibility condition, children were interviewed four times after the event in a misleading way suggesting that Sam Stone had been naughty and dirtied a teddy bear and ripped a book. Finally, in the stereotype plus suggestibility condition, children received both the stereotyped information before the visit and the misinformation after the visit. At a final fifth interview, children were asked to recall what happened when Sam Stone visited their classroom and were then asked a series of specific questions. Children in the control condition showed highly accurate recall, again indicating that even young children can recall events accurately over multiple interviews in the absence of misleading and suggestive questions. But children in the other conditions all showed some effects of the misinformation, and of the children in the stereotype plus suggestibility condition, one third to one half of the children spontaneously reported that Sam Stone had performed the naughty deeds. However, these numbers dropped to approximately 20% when asked if they really saw Sam Stone do these things. Still, one fifth of the children in this condition continued to insist that Sam Stone had done these things even when offered a countersuggestion that he had not. Thus it is quite clear that repeated suggestions over multiple interviews are detrimental to children's memory reports.

Ceci, Huffman, Smith, and Loftus (1994) further demonstrated that children can begin to report events that never occurred at all. They asked 3- to 4- and 5- to 6-year-old children a series of open-ended questions about events that they had experienced (e.g., "Did you ever go to the circus?", having confirmed with parents that the child had been to a circus) and questions about events never experienced ("Did you ever get your finger caught in a mousetrap and have to go to the hospital to get it removed?"). Each child was asked these questions between 7 and 10 times approximately 1 week apart. At a final interview 10 weeks later, children were asked to give a narrative about each of the events. All children acknowledged that the true events had happened and gave narratives about these events at the final interview. However, about one third of the children also assented that the false events had occurred and gave a narrative about these events at the final interview, although children's rate of falsely assenting at the last session was almost equal to that at the first session. Ceci et al. argued that simply asking children to think about an event may lead some children to generate a visual image confusable with a real memory. These results demonstrate that, under certain conditions, children will come to report events that did not occur.

The issue of the conditions under which young children are more or less likely to begin to report events that have not occurred is still open to debate. One problem with the Ceci et al. methodology is that it is not clear that the children understood that they were supposed to report only true events. That is, the interviewer may have given the impression that the task was to make up stories. Further, the cues used (e.g., "Did you ever get your hand caught in a mousetrap and have to go to the hospital to get it removed?") already have the bare bones of the story given to the child and the child simply needs to elaborate on it, as opposed to the kinds of open-ended question used to query about true events (e.g., "Did you ever go to the circus?"), which requires children to form the component actions of the event in their narratives. Perhaps more important, events for which children have some background knowledge are more likely to be suggestively induced than less familiar events. Pezdek and Hodge (1998) repeatedly asked children about getting lost in a shopping mall, a highly familiar and highly plausible event, and getting a rectal enema, a less familiar and less plausible event. Although almost 30% of the children reported getting lost in the mall, few children acquiesced to the rectal enema suggestion. These results indicate that children are less likely to acquiesce to events for which they have no background knowledge even under repeated suggestive questioning. Still, the research indicates that repeatedly interviewing young children (and adults; see, e.g., Hyman, Husband, & Billings, 1995) in suggestive and misleading ways can seriously compromise the credibility of their subsequent memory.

In summary, whereas repeated interviews in and of themselves do not seem to decrease accuracy, there are several conditions under which repeatedly questioning children does lead to increasing error. First, repeating the same questions within the same interview often leads young children to change their initial response, most likely due to the social demands inherent in this situation. Second, repeatedly questioning children in misleading or suggestive ways leads to large increases in erroneous memory reports. However, the form of the question and the required memory response must be considered. In most studies of suggestibility, children acquiesce to yes–no questions containing erroneous information. It is possible that yes–no questions pose a special problem for young children. It is to a consideration of how children answer specific types of questions that we now turn.

THE FORM OF THE QUESTIONS

Because it is well established that young children do not provide much information in response to general, open-ended questions and instead require more specific probes, it is odd that the form of the specific questions being directed toward young children has received so little empirical attention. In particular, the syntactic form of these specific questions has been largely ignored. Nevertheless, the syntactic format of the questions may have an important effect on the outcome of any child interview.

The two most commonly used syntactic formats of questions are yes–no questions and questions that use wh- question words, for example, *who*, *where*, *when*, and *what*. More specifically, (a) one can ask a yes–no question in which the particular information of interest is provided by the interviewer and the child is simply asked to affirm or deny its truth, for example, "Were you in the bedroom? Was your father there? Did the man wear a red shirt?"; (b) alternatively, one can ask a wh- format question in which the child is asked to supply a particular detail, for example, "Where were you? Who was there? What did the man wear?" These two question formats are not only different syntactically, they may have different consequences in terms of the veracity of information provided by the child. A wh- format question requires the child to provide the sought after information without the interviewer predetermining what that information consists of. In contrast, in yes–no questions the interviewer predetermines the information and the child simply responds "yes" or "no." In order to do this correctly, the child must understand the underlying assumption of yes–no questions, namely that the truth of the stated proposition must be the sole determiner of the child's response.

The literature on eyewitness memory in preschoolers is rife with confusions about the nature of the questions that the children were asked. In a review of the syntactic form of questions addressed to young children, Peterson and Biggs (1997) found that a number of investigators label yes–no questions as "specific questions" (e.g., Baker-Ward et al., 1993; Baker-Ward, Ornstein, Gordon, Follmer, & Clubb, 1995; Vandermaas, Hess, & Baker-Ward, 1993) or "cued recall" questions (Lepore & Sesco, 1994), whereas others provide children with an unspecified mixture of both yes–no and wh- questions (e.g., Merritt, Ornstein, & Spicker, 1994). This unspecified mixture of yes–no and wh- questions has been given other labels, for example, "direct questions" (Goodman, Hirschman, Hepps, & Rudy, 1991; Goodman et al., 1994), "cued recall" (Flin, Boon, Knox, & Bull, 1992), and "probed recall" (Saywitz & Nathanson, 1993). In such unspecified mixtures of yes–no and wh- questions, it is impossible to separate children's performance on these two types of questions. Most alarmingly, if children responded to these two question formats with different degrees of accuracy, it is possible that the conclusions reached in these studies need to be reevaluated.

The potentially problematic nature of yes–no questions was highlighted in early research by Fay (1975). He asked 3-year-old monolingual speakers of English questions that were clearly nonsense, for example, "El camino real?" These uninterpretable utterances were accompanied by the standard rise in intonation that accompanies English yes–no questions. In spite of the nonsensical nature of the questions, 62% of 3-year-olds nevertheless answered "yes" to them. In other words, young children have a strong bias to respond to yes–no question intonation, even when they do not understand the question's meaning.

More recently, Peterson and Biggs (1997) assessed the accuracy of yes–no questions asked of 2- to 13-year-old children who were recalling injury experiences that had required hospital emergency room treatment, such as breaking bones, requiring stitches, and so on. Both wh- and yes–no questions were asked. Importantly, the accuracy of the children's responses to yes–no questions was highly affected by whether the child said "yes" or "no." This was not true for school-aged children; however, preschoolers who were between 2 and 4 years of age were at chance levels of performance when they replied "no." That is, approximately 50% of the time they said "no," the veridical response should have been "yes." They were more likely to be correct when they responded "yes" to the experimenter's questions (i.e., about 85% of the time).

In the previous study, there was no attempt to systematically vary the questions asked of the children, so a more systematic investigation of question format was conducted by Peterson, Dowden, and Tobin (1999). They recruited 3- to 4-year-olds from a preschool and engaged them individually in various activities. One week later, children were individually questioned about the previous events. Every question asked of the children had three different formats for different children: wh- format, yes–no format for which the veridical response was "yes," and yes–no format for which the veridical response was "no." Findings also indicated that it made a substantial difference if the veridical response to the question was "yes" or "no." When the veridical response was "no," the child's responses were at chance levels. In other words, the children had a bias to say "yes," and if in fact this was the correct response, this bias led to high rates of "accurate" responding; in contrast, if "no" was the correct response, this bias undermined their accuracy rates.

Furthermore, the content about which children were questioned also made a difference. They were asked about the environment of the room they had been in, the characteristics of the two people who had interacted with them, and the nature of the craft activities in which they had engaged. Both "yes" and "no" responses were at chance levels when children were questioned about the environment. When the characteristics and the behavior of the two experimenters were queried, children's responses were at chance levels when the veridical answer should have been "no." Only when queried about the craft activity were children more likely to respond accurately than inaccurately when they should have said "no," and even for this content, one quarter of the time they gave the incorrect response of "yes." In contrast, they were almost always correct when the veridical response about activities should have been "yes."

What does it mean when the accuracy of a child's response is affected by whether the veridical response should have been a "yes" or a "no"? If children understand the questions and answer to the best of their ability, the accuracy of response to both types of questions should be equivalent. The fact that the accuracy of response is so different suggests that there are other factors operating besides whether the proposition queried by the question is true or not. Such factors could include task demands that encourage children to respond "yes" if they don't understand the question (such as in the children described by Fay, 1975). Or, children's responses may be affected by a host of other things such as response habit, the success of certain responses in terminating questioning, because children want to be liked by (and therefore agree with) adults, because of compliance, and so on. Such differences in response accuracy, depending on whether the child says "yes" or "no," or whether the underlying proposition being queried was true or false, are disturbing.

There is another issue explored in the research by Peterson, Dowden, and Tobin (1999). In accordance with some situations in which children are questioned, children were not explicitly told that they could answer "I don't know," and they almost never did so when the question was in yes–no format, regardless of question content. However, they much more frequently replied "I don't know" spontaneously when the question format was wh- in nature. In particular, children did not seem able to recall the characteristics of the environment in which the initial interaction took place. For wh- questions about this content, 70% of the children's responses were "I don't know." (In contrast, less than 10% of the wh- questions about activities elicited an "I don't know" response.) Nevertheless, when given a yes–no question about the characteristics of the environment, children almost never responded "I don't know" — rather, they asserted "yes" or "no," and that answer was as likely to be wrong as right. This pattern of results suggests that yes–no questions are more likely to be responded to than are wh- questions with a facade of certainty, when in fact the child has no idea what the response should be.

Repeated Yes–No Questions

Given that young children have such difficulty with the form of yes–no questions in general, as well as repeated questions within the same interview, how do they respond when asked the same yes–no questions repeatedly? Schwarzmueller (1997) addressed this question by asking 4- and 6-year-old children yes–no questions and wh- questions repeatedly, both within the same interview and across two interviews 1 week apart. Children were first asked for free recall of a structured play activity, visiting the wizard, and were then asked the same set of four yes–no questions and four wh-questions, three times in the same interview. They were then asked again for free recall and the eight specific questions a week later. Another group of children was asked for free recall and the four yes–no questions and the four wh- questions only once during the first interview and again a week later.

First, it is important to point out that, although the older children recalled more than the younger children during free recall, all children were highly accurate at both interviews. Responses to the wh- questions were also highly accurate for the older children; 90% of their responses to these questions were accurate at both interviews. However, 4-year-olds had more difficulty with specific wh-questions. Seventy percent of their responses were accurate at the first interview and 65% were accurate at the second interview. One reason why these young children may have had some difficulty responding to wh- questions is because these questions asked children to supply a specific piece of information (e.g., "What shape was the cookie cutter?") rather than more open-ended wh- questions that allow children to select information to recall (e.g., "What games did you play?"). Interestingly, in contrast to research reviewed earlier in this chapter, when children were asked the same wh- questions repeatedly within the same interview, they did not change their answer. Even if they gave a wrong answer the first time the question was asked, they continued to give the same wrong answer throughout the interview. This suggests that when children are asked the same question repeatedly in a supportive context, in which the interviewer explains he or she wants to make sure to remember what the child said, rather than in a situation in which the child may feel challenged, children are able to maintain their responses over repeated questioning. But importantly, consistency may not necessarily mean accuracy. In this study, children giving an inaccurate response were as consistent in response to repeated questions as were children providing accurate information.

Interestingly, the 4-year-olds responded to 83% of the yes–no questions accurately on the first interview, and to 81% correctly on the second interview. The 6-year-olds were accurate on 98% of the questions in the first interview and 94% in the second interview. But for three of the four yes–no questions, the correct response was "yes," so perhaps it is not surprising that even the 4-year-olds appeared accurate on these questions. As already argued, preschoolers seem to have a yes bias so when the correct answer is yes, their recall appears accurate. Moreover, when asked the same yes–no questions within the same interview, children tended to respond consistently; all of the 6-year-olds and 8 of the twelve 4-year-olds were completely consistent across repeated yes–no questions. However, while the 6-year-olds were near ceiling in accuracy, several of the 4-year-olds were consistent but inaccurate.

Overall, these findings indicate that yes–no questions may be particularly difficult for young children. The form of the question asks for a response even when children do not know the answer. And, there seems to be specific biases such that children are much more likely to respond "yes" to yes–no questions than "no." Overall, it is clear that yes–no questions should be avoided if at all possible in forensic interviewing, and certainly children's responses to these questions should be assessed with caution. Outside of controlled experimental conditions, the interviewer does not know what occurred during the event and therefore questions that ask the child only to confirm what happened are quite likely to lead to erroneous conclusions. Responses to wh- questions in which children must actually supply some information seem to be less prone to error, although there may be differences between different types of wh- questions as well. Not surprisingly, more open-ended wh- questions ("Who was there?", "What did you do?") are responded to more accurately than more specific, closed-ended wh- questions that require a specific piece of information in response (e.g., "What color was the man's shirt?", "What did he touch you with?").

IMPLICATIONS FOR FORENSIC INTERVIEWING

The research reported in this chapter has clear implications for interviewing children in forensic situations. Although it has been reliably demonstrated that even children as young as 3 years of age are able to accurately recall personally experienced events over long delays, there are several circumstances that compromise this accuracy. Whereas it is now generally known and accepted that use of misleading and suggestive questions is detrimental to children's accuracy, two additional findings emerge from this review. First, asking the same question repeatedly within the same interview often compromises young children's memory responding. Repeated questions seem to be especially detrimental when they are leading or suggestive, or asked in a challenging tone of voice. Children younger than about age 7 seem to assume that when an interviewer asks the same question again, it is because the interviewer did not approve of the first answer, and they are quite likely to change their response in order to meet the implied social demands of the situation. Thus, this technique, far from being an effective memory check, undermines young children's credibility.

Second, and much more far-reaching, the research reviewed here clearly demonstrates that young children have considerable difficulty responding appropriately to yes–no questions. Preschoolers especially seem to understand the form of this question as demanding a response and will provide a response even if they have no idea what the correct answer is (indeed, even if no correct answer is possible). Moreover, they are substantially more likely to simply acquiesce to a yes–no question than to deny it. Thus, yes–no questions should be avoided if at all possible.

Young children's difficulties with yes–no questions raise issues about the interpretation of much of the suggestibility literature. Two basic methodologies have been used in this research. In the majority of studies, the child experiences or witnesses some event, and then in the course of being interviewed, she is asked suggestive or misleading questions. These questions are most often phrased as yes–no questions (e.g., "Did he take your clothes off?", "Did he touch your private parts?"). The second methodology also involves the child experiencing or witnessing an event. Then in the course of a first interview, misinformation is presented, and the child is asked about this misinformation in a subsequent interview, again often in the form of a yes–no question. The problem is that yes–no and wh-questions are combined for analyses. Many of the results of the suggestibility literature may be a function of children's difficulty in responding to yes–no questions. Recall that studies generally do not examine whether children incorporate suggested information into their free recall of an event, and those few studies that have looked at this have not found this to be the case. What this pattern indicates is that, although children may acquiesce to yes–no questions, whether misleading or not, their acquiescence may not compromise their subsequent recall. Certainly, the issue of the form of the question must be carefully examined in future studies of suggestibility if we are to gain a full understanding of the mechanisms underlying young children's eyewitness testimony.

This conclusion must be tempered by the studies examining repeated suggestive questioning. In these situations, it is much more likely for children to begin to recall information that was not present during the event. In fact, some children even begin to recall entire events that never occurred. The conditions under which children are most and least likely to report suggested information after multiple interviews need to be explicated in future research. In particular, as Pezdek and her colleagues (Pezdek, Finger, & Hodge, 1997; Pezdek & Hodge, 1998) have argued, the background information available and the plausibility of the suggested event must play a role in whether or not children will report events that never happened. Moreover, individual differences that distinguish children who are most or least likely to be susceptible to suggestive questioning need further specification.

The finding that children's free recall remains reasonably accurate even after minimal exposure to suggestive questions (although it seems to be compromised by multiple suggestive interviews) is further evidence that the best forensic evidence remains what children are able to recall in response to open-ended questions. Unfortunately, young children, although accurate, are also often sparse in the amount of recall. This leads to the issue of how to question young children without compromising accuracy. Fortunately, although yes–no questions undermine accuracy, open-ended wh- questions do not seem to be as problematic. Even preschoolers respond at high levels of accuracy to wh- questions, such as who was there, where were you, what were you doing, and so forth. Forensic interviewers can probe young children's memory with these kinds of general questions with reasonable assurance that they will not be compromising the accuracy of the report.

It is clear that repeated interviews, in and of themselves, do not lead to increasing error in children's reports. As long as the interviews include only open-ended wh- questions, children's recall remains accurate over repeated interviews, and, indeed, repeated interviews may even facilitate amount of recall over long delays by helping to buffer against forgetting. Thus, the issue in forensic interviewing is how are children questioned, not how many times are children questioned.

This needs to be considered in the context of time since the event occurred. In many of the empirical studies, children recalled less information after long delays of a year or more, and there is often a corresponding increase in inaccurate information provided. However, a few studies did not find increasing error with increasing time. One possible explanation for the discrepant finding is the level of distinctiveness of the event being queried. Events that remain highly distinctive in the child's life may remain highly memorable, and little error may be reported even after long delays. The less distinctive the event, the more confusable with other similar events, and the more likely that children will begin to import details from these similar events into their recall. This may be a critical issue in forensic interviewing, as many children who come to the attention of the legal community are victims of repeated abusive experiences.

Surprisingly, there are few studies in the literature assessing children's susceptibility to suggestion for events that have been experienced many times (but see Goodman et al., 1994, for some relevant data). However, there is copious literature on children's ability to report familiar and recurring events that indicates that from age 3 forward, children are able to give accurate, organized accounts of recurring experiences (see Nelson, 1986; Fivush, 1997, for reviews). The problem from a legal standpoint is that these reports are quite general; children recall what usually happens and have great difficulty recalling a specific experience. This appears to be a robust aspect of young children's memory, and it is not clear how to reconcile this with the legal need for specificity.

In sum, this review indicates both strengths and limitations of young children's ability to give credible testimony. Under conditions in which young children are being interviewed about highly distinctive, personally meaningful events and are asked only open-ended questions, their ability to give accurate reports even after long delays is quite impressive. But, when children are interviewed in suggestive and misleading ways, especially if these suggestions are repeated across interviews, and if interviewers rely on yes–no questions, young children's memory cannot be considered at all credible. It is not so much a question of children's memory per se, as the way in which memory is elicited in the interviewing context. The question is not how credible are child witnesses; the question is how careful are forensic interviewers.

REFERENCES

Baker-Ward, L., Gordon, B. N., Ornstein, P. A., Larus, D. M., & Clubb, P. A. (1993). Young children's long-term retention of a pediatric examination. *Child Development, 64,* 1519–1533.

Baker-Ward, L., Hess, T. M., & Flannagan, D. A. (1990). The effects of involvement of children's memory. *Cognitive Development, 5,* 55–69.

Baker-Ward, L., Ornstein, P. A., Gordon, B. N., Follmer, A., & Clubb, P. A. (1995). How shall a thing be coded? In M. S. Zaragoza, J. R. Graham, G. C. N. Hall, R. Hirschman, & Y. S. Ben-Porath (Eds.), *Memory and testimony in the child witness* (pp. 61–85). Thousand Oaks, CA: Sage.

Boller, K., Rovee-Collier, C., Borovsky, D., O'Conner, J., & Shyi, G. (1990). Developmental changes in the time dependent nature of memory retrieval. *Developmental Psychology, 26,* 770–779.

Brainerd, C., & Ornstein, P. A. (1991). Children's memory for witnessed events: The developmental backdrop. In J. Doris (Ed.), *The suggestibility of children's recollections* (pp. 10–20). Washington, DC: American Psychological Association.

Brainerd, C. J., Reyna, V. F., Howe, M. L., & Kingma, J. (1990). The development of forgetting and reminiscence. *Monographs of the Society for Research in Child Development, Serial No. 222, 55.*

Carter, C. A., Bottoms, B. L., & Levine, M. (1996). Linguistic and socioemotional influences on the accuracy of children's reports. *Law and Human Behavior, 20,* 335–358.

Cassel, W. S., & Bjorklund, D. F. (1995). Developmental patterns of eyewitness memory and suggestibility: An ecologically based short-term longitudinal study. *Law and Human Behavior, 19,* 507–532.

Cassidy, D. J., & DeLoache, J. S. (1995). The effects of questioning on young children's memory for an event. *Cognitive Development, 10,* 109–130.

Ceci, S. J., & Bruck, M. (1993). Suggestibility of the child witness: A historical review and synthesis. *Psychological Bulletin, 113,* 403–439.

Ceci, S. J., Huffman, M. L. C., Smith, E., & Loftus, E. F. (1994). Repeatedly thinking about a non-event: Source misattributions among preschoolers. *Consciousness and Cognition, 3,* 388–407.

Ceci, S. J., Toglia, M. P., & Ross, D. F. (1990). The suggestibility of preschooler's recollections: Historical persepctives on current problems. In R. Fivush & J. A. Hudson (Eds.), *Knowing and remembering in young children* (pp. 285–300). New York: Cambridge University Press.

Farrar, M. J., & Goodman, G. S. (1990). Developmental differences in the relation between scripts and episodic memory: Do they exist? In R. Fivush & J. Hudson (Eds.), *Knowing and remembering in young children* (pp. 30–64). Cambridge, England: Cambridge University Press.

Fay, W. H. (1975). Occurrence of children's echoic responses according to interlocutory question types. *Journal of Speech and Hearing Research, 18,* 336–345.

Fivush, R. (1993). Developmental perspectives on autobiographical recall. In G. S. Goodman & B. L. Bottoms (Eds.), *Child victims, child witnesses: Understanding and improving testimony* (pp. 1–24). New York: Guilford.

Fivush, R. (1997). Event memory in childhood. In N. Cowan (Ed.), *The development of memory in childhood* (pp. 139–162). Sussex, England: Psychology Press.

Fivush, R. (1998). Children's memories for traumatic and non-traumatic events. *Development and Psychopathology, 10,* 699–716.

Fivush, R., Gray, J. T., & Fromhoff, F. A. (1987). Two year olds talk about the past. *Cognitive Development, 2,* 393–409.

Fivush, R., & Hamond, N. (1990). Autobiographical memory across the preschool years: To-
    wards reconceptualizing childhood amnesia. In R. Fivush & J. A. Hudson (Eds.), *Knowing
    and remembering in young children* (pp. 223–248). New York: Cambridge University Press.

Fivush, R., Hamond, N. R., Harsch, N., Singer, N., & Wolf, A. (1991). Content and consis-
    tency of young children's autobiographical recall. *Discourse Processes, 14*, 373–388.

Fivush, R., Pipe, M-E., Murachver, T., & Reese, E. (1997). Events spoken and unspoken: Im-
    plications of language and memory development for the recovered memory debate. In
    M. Conway (Ed.), *True and false memories* (pp. 34–62). London, England: Oxford Univer-
    sity Press.

Fivush, R., & Schwarzmueller, A. (1995). Say it once again: Effects of repeated questions on
    children's event recall. *Journal of Traumatic Stress, 8*, 555–580.

Fivush, R., & Schwarzmueller, A. (1998). Children remember childhood: Implications for
    childhood amnesia. *Applied Cognitive Psychology, 12*, 455–473.

Fivush, R., & Shukat, J. (1995). Content, consistency, and coherency of early autobiographical
    recall. In M. S. Zaragoza, J. R. Graham, G. C. N. Hall, R. Hirschman, & Y. S. Ben-Porath
    (Eds.), *Memory and testimony in the child witness children's and adults' eyewitness testimony.*
    Thousand Oaks, CA: Sage.

Fivush, R., & Slackman, E. (1986). The acquisition and development of scripts. In K. Nelson
    (Ed.), *Event knowledge: Structure and function in development* (pp. 71–96). Hillsdale, NJ:
    Lawrence Erlbaum Associates.

Flin, R., Boon, J., Knox, A., & Bull, R. (1992). The effects of a five-month delay on children's
    and adult's eyewitness testimony. *British Journal of Psychology, 83*, 323–336.

Gee, S., & Pipe, M.-E. (in press). Helping children to remember: The influences of object cues
    on children's accounts of a real event. *Developmental Psychology.*

Goodman, G. S., Bottoms. B. L., Schwartz-Kenney, B. M., & Rudy, L. (1991). Children's testi-
    mony about a stressful event: Improving children's reports. *Journal of Narrative and Life
    History, 1*, 69–99.

Goodman, G. S., Hirschman, J. E., Hepps, D., & Rudy, L. (1991). Children's memory for
    stressful events. *Merrill Palmer Quarterly, 37*, 109–158.

Goodman, G. S., Quas, J. A., Batterman-Faunce, J. M., Riddlesberger, M. M., & Kuhn, J.
    (1994). Predictors of accurate and inaccurate memories of traumatic events experienced
    in childhood. *Consciousness and Cognition, 3*, 269–294.

Goodman, G. S., Rudy, L., Bottoms, B. L., & Aman, C. (1990). Children's concerns and mem-
    ory: Issues of ecological validity in the study of children's eyewitness testimony. In R.
    Fivush & J. A. Hudson (Eds.), *Knowing and remembering in young children* (pp. 249–284).
    New York: Cambridge University Press.

Hamond, N. R., & Fivush, R. (1990). Memories of Mickey Mouse: Young children recount
    their trip to DisneyWorld. *Cognitive Development, 6*, 433–448.

Hudson, J. A. (1990a). Constructive processes in children's event memory. *Developmental
    Psychology, 2*, 180–187.

Hudson, J. A. (1990b). The emergence of autobiographic memory in mother–child conversa-
    tion. In R. Fivush & J. A. Hudson (Eds.), *Knowing and remembering in young children* (pp.
    166–196). New York: Cambridge University Press.

Hudson, J. A., & Fivush, R. (1991). As time goes by: Sixth graders recall a kindergarten event.
    Applied Cognitive Psychology, 5, 346–360.

Hudson, J. A., Fivush, R., & Kuebli, J. (1992). Scripts and episodes: The development of event
    memory. *Applied Cognitive Psychology, 6*, 483–505.

Hyman, I. E., Husband, T. H., & Billings, F. J. (1995). False memories of childhood experi-
    ences. *Applied Cognitive Psychology, 9*, 181–197.

Laumann, L. A., & Elliot, R. (1992). Reporting what you have seen: Effects associated with
    age and mode of questioning on eyewitness reports. *Perceptual and Motor Skills, 75*,
    799–818.

Leichtman, M. D., & Ceci, S. J. (1995). The effects of stereotypes and suggestions on pre-schoolers reports. *Developmental Psychology, 31*, 58–578.

Lepore, S. J., & Sesco, B. (1994). Distorting children's reports and interpretations of events through suggestion. *Journal of Applied Psychology, 79*, 108–120.

Memon, A., Wark, L., Bull, R. L., & Koehnken, G. (1995). *Children's event memory: The effects of interview technique and repeated questioning.* Manuscript submitted for publication.

Merritt, K. A., Ornstein, P. A., & Spicker, B. (1994). Children's memory for a salient medical procedure: Implications for testimony. *Pediatrics, 94*, 17–23.

Mitchell, K. J., & Zaragoza, M. S. (1996). Repeated exposure to suggestion and false memory: The role of contextual variability. *Journal of Memory and Language, 35*, 246–260.

Moston, S. (1987). The suggestibility of children in interview studies. *First Language, 7*, 67–78.

Myers, J. E. B. (1987). *Child witness law and practice.* New York: Wiley.

Nelson, K. (1986). *Event knowledge: Structures and function in development.* Hillsdale, NJ: Lawrence Erlbaum Associates.

Ornstein, P. A. (1995). Children's long-term retention of salient personal experiences. *Journal of Traumatic Stress, 8*, 581–606.

Peterson, C. (1999). Children's memories for medical emergencies 2 years later. *Developmental Psychology, 35*, 1493–1506.

Peterson, C., & Bell, M. (1996). Children's memory for traumatic injury. *Child Development, 67*, 3045–3070.

Peterson, C., & Biggs, M. (1997). Interviewing children about trauma: Problems with "specific" questions. *Journal of Traumatic Stress, 10*, 279–290.

Peterson, C., Dowden, C., & Tobin, J. (1999). Interviewing preschoolers: Comparisons of yes/no and wh- questions. *Law and Human Behavior, 23*, 539–555.

Peterson, C., & Rideout, R. (1998). Memory for medical emergencies experienced by 1- to 2-year-olds. *Developmental Psychology, 34*, 1059–1072.

Pezdek, K., Finger, K., & Hodge, D. (1997). Planting false childhood memories: The role of event plausibility. *Psychological Science, 8*, 437–441.

Pezdek, K., & Hodge, D. (1998). *Planting false childhood memories in children: The role of event plausibility.* Manuscript submitted for publication.

Poole, D. A., & White, L. T. (1991). The effects of question repetition on the eyewitness testimony of children and adults. *Developmental Psychology, 27*, 975–986.

Poole, D. A., & White, L. T. (1993). Two years later: Effects of question repetition and retention interval on the eyewitness testimony of children and adults. *Developmental Psychology, 29*, 844–853.

Poole, D. A., & White, L. T. (1995). Tell me again and again: Stability and change in the repeated testimonies of children and adults. In M. S. Zaragoza, J. R. Graham, G. C. N. Hall, R. Hirschman, & Y. S. Ben-Porath (Eds.), *Memory and testimony in the child witness children's and adults' eyewitness testimony* (pp. 24–43). Thousand Oaks, CA: Sage.

Rose, S. A., & Blank, M. (1974). The potency of context in children's cognition: An illustration through conservation. *Child Development, 45*, 499–502.

Rovee-Collier, C., & Gerhardstein, P. (1997). The development of infant memory. In N. Cowan (Ed.), *The development of memory in childhood* (pp. 5–40). Sussex, England: Psychology Press.

Salmon, K., & Pipe, M.-E. (1997). Props and children's event reports: The impact of a 1-year delay. *Journal of Experimental Child Psychology, 65*, 261–292.

Saywitz, K. J., & Nathanson, R. (1993). Children's testimony and their perceptions of stress in and out of the courtroom. *Child Abuse and Neglect, 17*, 613–622.

Schwartz, B., & Reisberg, D. (1991). *Learning and memory.* New York: Norton.

Schwarzmueller, A. (1997). *The effects of repeated questioning on children's recall for an event.* Unpublished doctoral dissertation, Emory University, Atlanta, GA.

Sheffield, E., & Hudson, J. A. (1994). Reactivation of toddlers' event memory. *Memory, 2,* 447–465.

Sheingold, K., & Tenney, Y. J. (1982). Memory for a salient childhood event. In U. Neisser (Ed.), *Memory observed* (pp. 201–212). San Francisco: Freeman.

Siegel, M., Waters, L., & Dinwiddy, L. (1988). Misleading children: Causal attributions for inconsistency under repeated questioning. *Journal of Experimental Child Psychology, 45,* 438–456.

Steward, M. (1993). Understanding children's memories of medical procedures: "He didn't touch me and it didn't hurt." In C. A. Nelson (Ed.), *Memory and affect in development: The Minnesota Symposium on Child Psychology* (Vol. 26, pp. 171–226). Hillsdale, NJ: Lawrence Erlbaum Associates.

Todd, C., & Perlmutter, M. (1980). Reality recalled by preschool children. In M. Perlmutter (Ed.), *New directions for child development: No. 10. Children's memory* (pp. 69–86). San Francisco: Jossey-Bass.

Vandermaas, M. O., Hess, T. M., & Baker-Ward, L. (1993). Does anxiety affect children's reports of memory for a stressful event? *Journal of Applied Psychology, 7,* 109–128.

Warren, A. R., Hulse-Trotter, K., & Tubbs, E. (1991). Inducing resistance to suggestibility in children. *Law and Human Behavior, 15,* 272–285.

Warren, A. R., & Swartwood, J. N. (1992). Developmental issues in flashbulb memory research: Children recall the Challenger event. In E. Winograd & U. Neisser (Eds.), *Affect and accuracy in recall: Studies of "flashbulb" memories* (pp. 95–120). New York: Cambridge University Press.

Zaragoza, M. S., & Mitchell, K. J. (1996). Repeated exposure to suggestion and the creation of false memories. *Psychological Science, 7,* 294–300.

15

Children's Suggestibility in the Forensic Context

Debra Ann Poole
Central Michigan University

D. Stephen Lindsay
University of Victoria, Canada

Research on the suggestibility of children has achieved a far-ranging impact on the evolution of standards for investigative interviewing. Assumptions about the strengths and weaknesses of children as witnesses underlie varied recommendations regarding strategies for raising abuse issues, the types of questions interviewers should ask, what ancillary aids are considered acceptable at various points during the interviewing process, and the number of interviews that are considered appropriate (see Everson & Boat, chap. 16, this volume; Saywitz & Lyon, chap. 4, this volume). Although many research topics help us to understand children's behavior during investigative interviews, including basic research on the development of attention, event memories, language, and concept formation (Poole & Lamb, 1998), controversies about what constitutes best practice in forensic evaluation have hinged predominantly on interpretations of the data on children's suggestibility.

In an award-winning article about the history of research on children's suggestibility, Ceci and Bruck (1993) summarized evidence on the credibility of children's reports from studies conducted during the early 1900s to the "modern period," from 1979 to 1992. Ceci and Bruck attributed the paucity of research in the mid-1900s to the rejection of psychological research by the legal community, which questioned whether studies that resulted in group averages were relevant for judging the reliability of individual witnesses in specific situations. Between 1979 and 1992, however, a variety of social changes increased interest in research on eyewitness testimony, and studies abounded. In addition to an increase in the number of abuse reports, other changes included pressures on social scientists to relate scientific findings to socially relevant issues, a broadening of admissibility of expert psychological testimony in court, and innovations for dealing with child witnesses. Since 1992, studies on children's suggestibility have continued to proliferate, with two priorities dominating the literature: (a) an increased emphasis on testing children's memory for complex and personally salient events, to provide better abuse situation analogs, and (b) renewed interest in laboratory studies using traditional memory stimuli (e.g., word and sentence lists), to permit controlled tests of theoretical models that hold promise for explaining discrepant findings.

Our goal in this chapter is not to provide an exhaustive review of the literature on children's suggestibility, as Ceci and Bruck were able to accomplish in 1993, but rather to discuss selected studies that illustrate how a variety of factors typically relate to children's eyewitness accuracy. In order to organize a body of findings that currently includes hundreds of research reports, we divided our review into three sections that represent stages of thinking about children's suggestibility. Although we do not claim that these stages are distinct or nonoverlapping periods of research from a historical perspective, it is the case that information from earlier stages is necessary to ask the types of questions that characterize later stages. We labeled these sections (a) the search for general principles, (b) understanding exceptions to the general principles, and (c) the integration of eyewitness findings into forensic decision making.

THE SEARCH FOR GENERAL PRINCIPLES

When interest in suggestibility research resurfaced in the 1980s, researchers assembled a body of evidence on children's performance as witnesses. Much of this early research can be characterized as "what if" research: What would children report if we contaminated their memories in this or that way, or pressured them to respond incorrectly with this or that encouragement (see Ceci & Bruck, 1993, for a review)? Often, investigators observed specific interviewer behaviors in transcripts of forensic interviews, then recreated those behaviors in the laboratory to test whether such processes were sufficient to distort children's testimony. The final product was a set of aphorisms that continue to guide professionals today. As we argue later in this review, however, the extent to which these aphorisms hold true across a range of situations has frequently been overstated.

The Architecture of Suggestive Interviews

In various publications, Ceci and Bruck (e.g., Bruck & Ceci, 1997; Ceci & Bruck, 1995) have argued that suggestive interviews share a consistent "architecture," with the central driving force being *interviewer bias*. As described by Bruck and Ceci (1997),

> interviewer bias characterizes an interviewer who holds a priori beliefs about the occurrence of certain events and, as a result, molds the interview to elicit from the interviewee statements that are consistent with these prior beliefs. One hallmark of interviewer bias is the single-minded attempt to gather only confirmatory evidence and to avoid all avenues that may produce disconfirmatory evidence. Thus, a biased interviewer does not ask questions that might provide alternate explanations for the allegations (e.g., "Did your mommy tell you, or did you see it happen?"). Nor does a biased interviewer ask about events that are inconsistent with the interviewer's hypothesis (e.g., "Who else beside your teacher touched your private parts? Did your mommy touch them, too?"). And a biased interviewer does not challenge the authenticity of the child's report when it is consistent with the interviewer's hypothesis. When a child provides inconsistent or bizarre evidence, it is either ignored or interpreted within the framework of the biased interviewer's initial hypothesis. (p. 75)

In their book, *Jeopardy in the Courtroom* (1995), Ceci and Bruck cited numerous examples of interviewer bias from high-profile child sexual abuse cases. Among the potentially suggestive techniques they observed were asking specific rather than open-ended questions; interjecting new information into conversations in the form of leading questions; repeating questions numerous times when the interviewer was not satisfied with the child's initial answer; setting a tone of accusation by suggesting, for example, that the child might be afraid to tell; inducing negative stereotypes of the alleged offender by suggesting that he or she had in fact done bad things; using peer pressure (e.g., informing children that their friends or siblings had already told); reinforcing children for comments related to abuse; and asking children to pretend or think about interactions that they claimed not to remember.

The transcripts cited by Ceci and Bruck are provocative examples of quite blatant interviewer bias. Concerns about suggestive interviewing cannot be dismissed, however, on the grounds that such examples are too atypical to inform us about what occurs in less sensational investigations. On the contrary, recent research has shown that interviewers who are not especially coercive often resort to one or more of the aforementioned techniques. In one informative study, for example, Warren, Woodall, Hunt, and Perry (1996) analyzed 42 transcripts of sexual abuse interviews conducted by child protective services personnel in a single state. Interviewers rarely told children that "I don't know" or "I don't understand" were acceptable responses, the majority of the interviewers relied on specific yes–no questions rather than open-ended questions (even when raising the topic of abuse), and they frequently interjected information into interviews that children had not yet volunteered. Indeed, 94% of the interviewers introduced new, potentially leading information, and this group averaged over seven new pieces of information per interview. Furthermore, this new information often was repeated by the interviewers, as frequently as 60 times during the course of a single conversation.

Interviewers can inadvertently introduce ambiguity or bias into forensic conversations even when they do not have a strong agenda to collect evidence of abuse. Analyses of investigative interviews and inspection of transcripts from laboratory studies of eyewitness testimony reveal that young children are difficult to interview: They often fail to identify which topic is under discussion at the beginning of a conversation (Fivush & Shukat, 1995; Steward & Steward, 1996), they drift off topic without signaling interviewers (Poole & Lamb, 1998), and they are sometimes difficult to understand (Warren et al., 1996). In all of these cases, the children introduced ambiguous information, and interviewers, in their attempts to keep the conversation going, sometimes picked up on this information, embedded their interpretations of it into specific questions, and thereby exerted suggestive influence despite the best of intentions. Consider an example of one such misunderstanding reported by Warren et al.:

Interviewer:	Is it good or bad to tell a lie?
Child:	G.A. touched me.
Interviewer:	Jesus loves me? Is that what you said?
Child:	Yeah. (p. 235)

We found several examples in our laboratory transcripts demonstrating ways in which children might influence interviewers. In one of our studies (Poole & Lindsay, in press), interviewers asked each child four open-ended questions about a series of science demonstrations, followed by a final prompt without any specific reference to the topic: "Think about what you told me. Is there something you didn't tell me that you can tell me now?" Despite the fact that the previous conversation clearly revolved around the science demonstrations, many children drifted off topic when answering this final prompt, providing bizarre responses such as, "Well, I touched Sophie and I thought I could make my cold disappear if I, I thought somebody was dead back there." Evidently, some children construed the open-ended prompt as a request to talk about things other than the science demonstrations. (We know this only because we videotaped the demonstrations: Sophie wasn't part of them, and no one died!) If interviewers constructed follow-up questions based on these responses, they could easily direct conversations in ways that produced unwarranted concerns — easily, that is, if the children acquiesced to specific follow-up questions about things that had not actually occurred, provided narratives for these unusual events, and failed to clarify their intentions when interviewers explicitly asked them to do so. The studies we review in this chapter were designed to explore the consequences of these dynamic interplays between children's memories, their conversational habits and assumptions, and the behavior of interviewers.

Children's Reactions to Suggestion: Specific Questions

Research has clearly shown that children's reports of an event, like those of adults, can be influenced by suggestion. The extent to which children are swayed, however, varies enormously depending on the salience of the target event, whether the misinformation falsified central information or only peripheral details, the timing and type of suggestibility manipulation, and the age of the children. (For a review of another factor, individual differences in children's memory and suggestibility, see Pipe & Salmon, chap. 10, this volume.)

Perhaps the most common yet subtle form of suggestion in forensic interviews is the use of specific questions. Although there is no universally accepted way to categorize questions (Poole & Lamb, 1998), the term "specific question" usually refers to questions that can be answered in a single word or phrase, including questions such as "What color was his car?" and closed questions such as yes–no (e.g., "Was his car white?") and multiple-choice questions (e.g., "Was his car blue or white?"). Specific questions include probes that do not suggest particular answers (although they may encourage speculation) and questions that mention specific response options. In contrast, open-ended invitations/questions generally require multiple word responses, and children have more leeway with these probes to choose which aspect of an event they will describe (e.g., "Tell me what happened today on the playground" or "What happened today on the playground?").

The most ubiquitous finding in eyewitness research is that young children's answers to specific questions are less accurate than their answers to open-ended questions. In studies of 3- to 11-year-olds by Dent (1991) and Goodman, Hirschman, Hepps, and Rudy (1991, Study 1), for example, between 7% and 9% of the information in free recall was erroneous, whereas error rates on specific questions ranged between 19% and 33%. The explanation for these discrepancies in accuracy involves both memory and social processes. Regarding memory, children and adults are less accurate when they answer questions about peripheral details as compared to central details (Goodman, Aman, & Hirschman, 1987; Steward, Bussey, Goodman, & Saywitz, 1993), and specific questions often ask about details that children may not remember well. Regarding social processes, children and adults often try to answer questions that request information they cannot possibly know (Poole & White, 1991, 1993), and they sometimes attempt to answer even ambiguous or bizarre questions (e.g., "Is a cup sadder than an orange?"; Pratt, 1990; Winer, Rasnake, & Smith, 1987). Children learn early in their lives to maintain conversational turns and to be cooperative by offering answers to questions (Warren & McCloskey, 1997), and they may feel even more obligated to respond when they are questioned by an authority figure (Ceci, Ross, & Toglia, 1987; Tobey & Goodman, 1992).

Developmental trends in inappropriate speculation to specific questions vary depending on the topic of the question (i.e., whether it involves unusual or more mundane events) and whether the knowledge base of the witnesses supports speculation. For example, Poole and White (1991) asked research participants a question they could not possibly answer without guessing: "What does the man do for a living—what is his job?" Shortly after witnessing an event involving an unfamiliar man, adults were much more likely to suggest the answer to this question than were 4-, 6-, and 8-year-olds, possibly because the adults had the knowledge base to generate plausible responses (e.g., "He probably works for the university"). Among those participants who were interviewed immediately after the target event, for example, 80% of the adults speculated to the third repetition of this question, compared to only 23% of the children. Two years later, many of these participants were interviewed again, but with different results (Poole & White, 1993). Because debriefing after the first study informed participants that the man was a research assistant, Poole and White did not code responses that related to working on the project or being a student. No adult in this follow-up study generated an irrelevant response to this question, but 21% of the children offered answers such as "lumber company," "worked with my daddy," and "worked on a farm."

Closed questions, such as multiple-choice and yes–no questions, are especially problematic for young children. Walker, Lunning, and Eilts (1996) asked kindergartners, second graders, and fifth graders to watch a videotape and then answer multiple-choice questions such as "Did you see a little girl or a little boy on the video?" The kindergartners were significantly less accurate than the older children, but children in all three age groups were more likely to choose the second alternative in response to this type of multiple-choice question. Furthermore, kindergartners answered correctly only 17.5% of the time when neither option was correct, whereas second and fifth graders more often provided correct "neither" responses (37.5% and 48.3% of the time, respectively). Studies have shown that error rates on yes–no questions are sometimes even higher (Poole & Lindsay, 1995). Research by Brady, Poole, Warren, and Jones (1999) indicates that individual children are not consistent across questions in the extent to which response biases influence their replies, suggesting that it would be difficult to predict which children are particularly at risk of answering yes–no questions unreliably. (For field studies that compared accuracy across various types of question, see Peterson & Bell, 1996; Peterson & Biggs, 1997.)

How prone are children to err by responding "yes" to yes–no questions that mention fictitious events? Fortunately for interviewers, children are less likely to make errors when the questions ask about salient events or events that are unlikely to have occurred given the context of the target event. For example, 5-year-olds who were interviewed about a medical examination falsely acquiesced to 20% of the yes–no questions about details that were typical of medical examinations but that had not actually happened, whereas they acquiesced to only 7% of questions that suggested events that were unlikely to occur in the context of a medical examination (Baker-Ward, Gordon, Ornstein, Larus, & Clubb, 1993). Similarly, out of 114 3- to 8-year-olds in one of our recent studies, only 3 children (all 4 years old) falsely said "yes" to questions about whether a man had put something yucky in their mouths or hurt their tummies when they had not heard about these events from parents or previously been questioned about them (Poole & Lindsay, in press). Saywitz, Goodman, Nicholas, and Moan (1991) found that only 3% of 5- and 7-year-old girls who did not experience a genital examination during a doctor's visit falsely reported vaginal touching when asked directly, and only 6% falsely reported anal touching, although the error rate was higher (22%) for direct questions about a less embarrassing topic (tapping the spine).

Developmental trends in accuracy on yes–no format questions are more consistent than trends for inappropriate speculation: Generally, young children falsely acquiesce more often than older children, but nonetheless they also can be remarkably accurate. A recent study by Steward and Steward (1996) illustrates that young children are both surprisingly accurate and startlingly inaccurate, depending on the interview strategies that adults select. Steward and Steward arranged for children ages 3 to 6 years old to be interviewed three times after a pediatric clinic visit: immediately, after a 1-month delay, and again after a 6-month delay. The children were assigned to one of four interviewing conditions: (a) verbal interviewing only, or verbal interviewing enhanced by (b) anatomically detailed dolls, (c) line drawings, or (d) computer graphics. In the immediate interview, no child who was interviewed without props made a false report of touch to the genitals, buttocks, or anus in free recall. Errors did occur, however, among children who were interviewed with a "double-check" procedure in which the interviewer asked specific yes–no questions about body touch while pointing to the prop: In the initial interview, 8% falsely reported genital touch, 12% reported touching of the buttocks, and 18% reported anal touch. The combination of degraded memory traces (Pezdek & Roe, 1995) and repeated interviewing with suggestive techniques (see Fivush, Peterson, & Schwarzmueller, chap. 14, this volume) is illustrated in this study by comparing initial rates of false reporting with the double-check procedure to rates when children were re-interviewed a month later, when 15%, 12%, and 30% falsely reported touch of the genitals, buttocks, and anus, respectively.

Children's Reactions to Suggestions: Encouraging Speculation

Specific questions are risky not only because children might guess, but also because such questions could produce false memories if the children later believed that their sense of familiarity for these confabulations stemmed from actual experiences. Clearly, there is a greater risk of "source monitoring" errors whenever interviewers repeatedly encourage children to answer specific questions even when they are reluctant to do so.

Ackil and Zaragoza (1998) investigated whether forcing children to confabulate about a witnessed event would lead them to misattribute confabulated details to the witnessed event. First graders, third/fourth graders, and college students watched a video and subsequently answered a series of questions. Some of the questions referred to fairly salient events that occurred in the video (e.g., "Who was the only person who stayed in the boat with the snake in it?"), whereas other questions asked for information that was not in the video (e.g., "Where was Delaney bleeding?" when Delaney clearly did not bleed). Participants in the Free condition were not instructed to guess; in the Forced condition, participants were instructed that they must provide an answer to each question even if they had to guess. One week later, a different experimenter told participants that the other experimenter had asked them about some things that never happened in the video, and the new experimenter administered a memory test to assess whether the participants would report actually having witnessed the confabulated items.

There was evidence that participants in the Forced condition began to believe that they actually saw their confabulated items in the video. That is, they claimed to have seen 35% of the details that they only confabulated compared to 17% for control items. This "forced confabulation effect" was evident among all age groups, but the first graders were more likely to misattribute confabulated details than the third/fourth graders, who in turn were more likely to misattribute details than the college students. These age differences were not due to younger children forgetting that they had discussed the details with the experimenter, however. Most of the time, the children did not deny that they had talked about the false details; instead, they were more likely than adults to claim that the confabulated items were both in the video and discussed with the experimenter. These findings parallel results from our laboratory that young children have difficulty specifying the source of information that is presented in only one of two possible sources (Poole & Lindsay, in press).

How much pressure does it take to encourage children to provide confabulated responses? In Ackil and Zaragoza's study, participants in the Forced condition often had to be persuaded to respond. Despite instructions that they were required to guess, 92% of the first graders, 96% of the third graders, and 69% of the college students had to be probed twice or more by the experimenter on at least one false-event question to elicit a response, as illustrated by this excerpt from their laboratory transcripts of an interview with a third grader:

Experimenter: What did the boy say Sullivan had stolen?
Participant: Ahh, I forget what that was.
Experimenter: Oh, can you just take a guess then?
Participant: Mmm, no, I don't think so.
Experimenter: Well, what to you think would make him really mad if Sullivan had stolen it?
Participant: Ahh, maybe like a radio or something?
Experimenter: O.K.

Thus although a minority of children speculated even when they were not told to do so, many children who were instructed to guess had to be encouraged to make up responses. Similarly, in highly scrutinized interviews such as those related to the Kelly Michaels case, a recurring feature is that some children resisted misleading questioning (at least initially), as in this excerpt from Ceci and Bruck (1995):

Interviewer: Did she drink the pee pee?
Child: Please that sounds just crazy. I don't remember about that. Really don't. (p. 73)

In two studies, we evaluated the consequences of ignoring children's initial "no" responses and encouraging them to provide narrative elaboration (Poole & Lindsay, 1995, in press). Children who had individually participated in a series of science demonstrations were first interviewed with open-ended questions, then leading question pairs each consisting of a yes–no question (e.g., "Did Mr. Science . . . ?") followed by a request to elaborate (e.g., "Tell me about . . . ?" if the child said "yes" and "Can you tell me about . . . ?" if the child said "no"). Among the questions were three "control" questions that asked about science demonstrations or touching events that the children had not experienced or heard about. We were fascinated to find that although most children said "no" when asked a yes–no question about these novel events, some nonetheless were willing to describe the events when we suggested that they might be able to do so. For example, in one study 19% of the 3- to 4-year-olds, 16% of the 5- to 6-year-olds, and 5% of the 7- to 8-year-olds who responded "no" to novel science demonstrations provided at least some relevant narrative information when asked the follow-up question (Poole & Lindsay, 1998). As research with adults shows (see chaps. 3 and 13), children are not uniquely vulnerable to social situations that encourage them to confabulate. Nevertheless, there is considerable evidence indicating that young preschoolers generally have higher rates of false recognitions, confabulations, and source confusions than do older children or adults (Schacter, Kagan, & Leichtman, 1995).

Children's Reactions to Suggestions: Misinformation

In the studies described, some children generated descriptions of nonexperienced events either because interviewers simply asked them about those events or because they were encouraged by the interviewer to provide a description. Because children are more accurate when initial interview instructions warn against yeah-saying or speculation (see chap. 4), such studies demonstrate that the social context of interviews can lead children to assume that they should respond even if their answers are wrong. In more overtly suggestive experimental manipulations, researchers have explicitly presented false information in the form of misleading questions during interviews (e.g., "The woman was carrying a newspaper when she entered the bus, wasn't she?") or by presenting stories or conversations that contained inaccurate stereotypes of individuals and/or descriptions of events that did not occur.

Numerous studies have shown that some children falsely respond "yes" to misleading questions, even when the target event is salient (e.g., stressful medical procedures) and the questions suggest touching experiences or other events that might be related to abuse. Eisen, Goodman, Qin, and Davis (1998), for example, studied 108 children who had been hospitalized for a 5-day inpatient stay for the assessment of abuse. Each child received a physical examination and medical assessment, an anogenital exam, a forensic interview regarding allegations of abuse or neglect, and a psychological consultation. On the final day, the children answered questions about the anogenital exam that included misleading questions. Their data illustrated several recurring findings: (a) preschool children's error rates often are strikingly higher than those of older children; (b) error rates decline gradually with age well into the school-age years; and (c) across age groups, children are less likely to err on questions that involve body touch than on questions about more mundane issues. For example, on misleading questions that did not involve abuse-related issues, the 3- to 5-year-olds erred 32% of the time, compared with 17% errors by the 6- to 10-year-olds and 6% by the 11- to 15-year-olds. In contrast, the average percentage of errors across these three age groups on abuse-analog questions (e.g., "The doctor did not have any clothes on, did he/she?") were 20%, 4%, and 0%.

Although it is typical for only a minority of children to report fictitious touching experiences the first time they are presented misleading information, exposing children to suggestive information before direct or misleading questions dramatically increases reports of nonexperienced events. In one of our "Mr. Science" studies, for example, no 5- to 8-year-olds falsely reported a novel touching experience the first time they were asked direct yes–no questions, but between 33% and 38% falsely reported touching experiences that were described in a story they had previously heard (Poole & Lindsay, in press).

Many studies illustrate how misleading information and leading questions combine to increase false reports. An excellent example is Leichtman and Ceci's (1995) creative "Sam Stone" study, in which preschoolers observed while a stranger visited their classroom and subsequently were interviewed with open-ended and specific questions about his behavior. Children assigned to the stereotype condition were told before the visit that Sam was clumsy and prone to break things, whereas children in the control condition received no specific information about Sam. After Sam's visit, the children were interviewed either suggestively or nonsuggestively on four occasions, followed by a fifth interview that was identical for all children. Thus, data were available from four conditions of information exposure: control (no stereotypes or suggestions), stereotype (but no suggestive interviews), suggestive interviews (but no stereotype), and stereotype plus suggestions. No child in the control or stereotype conditions made false allegations in free recall, and few children in the suggestive interviews condition made accusations in free recall. In contrast, 46% of the younger children and 30% of the older children who had experienced stereotype induction and suggestive interviews reported false accusations during free recall, and the majority of these children accused Sam of at least one misdeed in response to probe questions. Across studies, a pattern of escalating accusations across interviews (i.e., more elaborate narratives by individual children as well as accusations by a higher proportion of children) are characteristic of strong suggestibility manipulations such as telling children that nonevents actually occurred, asking them to think about them repeatedly (Ceci, Loftus, Leichtman, & Bruck, 1994), and using multiple forms of suggestion (e.g., Bruck, Hembrooke, & Ceci, 1997; Garven, Wood, Malpass, & Shaw, 1998). Moreover, there is no compelling evidence that experts can reliably discriminate between narratives of actual events and fictitious narratives that were elicited with such techniques (Bruck et al., 1997; Ceci & Huffman, 1997; Lamb et al., 1997).

A series of interesting studies by Newcombe and Siegal (1996, 1997) illustrates how both social and memory processes might contribute to misinformation effects. In one study, Newcombe and Siegal (1996) read a story to 3- to 5-year-old children about a little girl, Karen, and her first day at school. The next day, an experimenter introduced either biased or unbiased information about two critical details of the story. One week later, interviewers asked the children about the original details using questions that explicitly focused on the target information (e.g., "Do you remember how Karen was sick when you heard her story for the first time?") or questions in a nonexplicit format (e.g., "Do you remember how Karen was sick when you heard her story?"). The children gave many suggested answers when questioned in the nonexplicit format, but fewer when questions clearly marked which event was under discussion. Children's difficulty with nonexplicit questions could be due to a variety of factors, including an assumption that the misinformation is the preferred answer (a "social" mechanism) or a failure to monitor source in the absence of explicit instructions (a "memory" mechanism).

Available data suggest that both social and memory mechanisms often contribute to misinformation effects. In one of our Mr. Science studies (Poole & Lindsay, in press), for example, we introduced misinformation about a complex event by asking parents to read their children a story that described both experienced and nonexperienced "mini-events," including descriptions of science demonstrations and a nonexperienced touching event. We were surprised that even the 8-year-olds reported many nonexperienced events in free recall and in response to direct questions. After instructions to report only from personal experience and not from the story, however, the 5- to 8-year-olds retracted the majority of allegations of nonexperienced touching, indicating that they remembered the source of the misinformation. In contrast, the 3- and 4-year-olds did not benefit significantly from our source monitoring instructions. Other investigators have also found that preschoolers experience particular difficulty with source monitoring (Gopnik & Graf, 1988; Taylor, Esbensen, & Bennitt,

1994). Because preschoolers' source monitoring can be accurate under some conditions (e.g., when the two sources are highly discriminable), it is believed that the age-related deficits observed under other conditions do not reflect a general difficulty with understanding test instructions (Foley, Harris, & Herman, 1994; Foley & Johnson, 1985; Lindsay, Johnson, & Kwon, 1991). Of course, older children and adults, too, sometimes experience source monitoring failures, even when they are explicitly directed to attend to source (see Lindsay, 1990; Lindsay et al., 1995).

Children's Reactions to Suggestions: Other Social Cues and Pressures

Interviewers exacerbate the impact of specific and misleading questions when they combine suggestive questions with other social pressures, such as making statements that create an atmosphere of accusation (e.g., "You'll feel better once you've told," Goodman, Wilson, Hazan, & Reed, 1989, or "He wasn't supposed to do that, that was bad . . . What else did he do?", Lepore & Sesco, 1994), selectively reinforcing or repeating children's comments that support a preconceived hypothesis (Lepore & Sesco, 1994), using peer pressure by telling the child that other children have already told, or using high status interviewers who express concern that "something bad might have happened" (Tobey & Goodman, 1992). Experts generally agree that children's accuracy can be compromised by two extreme styles of interviewing: an accusatory, incriminating style (Goodman, 1993), and a "buddy–buddy" style in which interviewers use reinforcement and praise in a way that selectively shapes specific responses (Garven et al., 1998).

A recent study by Garven et al. (1998) illustrated how social influence and reinforcement can exaggerate the negative effects of suggestive questioning alone. These investigators perused transcripts from the famous McMartin preschool case to identify six potentially error-producing techniques: (a) *suggestive questions* (i.e., questions that mention an event the child had not already mentioned, such as "Did he touch you on the bottom?"), (b) *other people* (telling the child that the interviewer has already received information from another person regarding the topic), (c) *positive consequences* (implying praise or approval by making a statement such as this one from the McMartin interviews: "Can I pat you on the head . . . look at what a good help you can be. You're going to help all these little children just because you're so smart"), (d) *negative consequences* (making negative comments when the child denies an allegation), (e) *already answered* (repeating a question that the child has unambiguously answered), (f) *inviting speculation* (asking the child to offer opinions or speculations about past events or framing the child's task as "pretending" or solving a mystery).

Garven et al. (1998) arranged for children 3 to 6 years of age to attend a special story time led by a male graduate student. One week later, the children were interviewed individually in one of two conditions: the Suggestive Control condition, which involved suggestive questions about things that the student did not do (such as tearing a book and putting a sticker on the child's knee), and the Social Incentives condition, which included the suggestive questions and the other suggestive techniques previously enumerated. The children who were interviewed with Social Incentives made more than three times more false allegations (58% of the possible allegations) than children interviewed with suggestive questions alone (17%). Although the allegations in this study did not involve embarrassing or bizarre touching, it is noteworthy that the children were willing to make these accusations during an interview that exposed them to social incentives for only 5 to 10 minutes. In a subsequent study, Garven, Wood, and Malpass (2000) demonstrated that positive and negative reinforcement were especially powerful techniques for eliciting children's reports of both mundane and fantastic elements.

Summary

Many investigators have found that children can be highly accurate when they are interviewed about salient events, even when they are interviewed after relatively long delays (Goodman et al., 1991). Nonetheless, children are susceptible to various forms of suggestion. Although adults are also susceptible to suggestive influences, it is clear that under many conditions resistance to suggestion increases with age. It is relatively easy to induce children to report erroneous details by asking specific or misleading questions, particularly if the children are young or the questions concern peripheral aspects of the interaction. Furthermore, a surprising minority of children narrate nonexperienced events when interviewers ask them yes–no questions followed by requests to describe the events, and this phenomenon occurs even in school-aged children who have heard the fictitious events described by a parent. When interviewers asked children questions about experienced events with embedded questions about nonexperienced touching or misdeeds, only a minority of even the youngest children in most studies made a false report. A variety of manipulations can increase this percentage dramatically, however, including exposure to narratives that describe touching, conversations that induce negative stereotypes about the individual in question, and repeated suggestive interviews (especially those that contain social pressures and reinforcement). With regard to recent data, the question, "How suggestible are children" seems overly focused on children's behavior, because error rates are influenced so dramatically by interviewers' behaviors (e.g., the preliminary instructions they provide and whether they structure opportunities for children to clarify their responses with explicit source monitoring procedures).

Given the vast variability across studies in the percentages of children who succumb to suggestive influences, it has not been easy for researchers to provide what the general public and the legal community repeatedly demand: thumb-nail summaries that capture general trends. Nonetheless, a few general principles have so frequently been highlighted in the literature on children's eyewitness testimony that they deserve to be revisited. These aphorisms are that (a) information in free recall is generally accurate, (b) children are resistant to suggestion about salient events such as touching experiences, and (c) younger children are more suggestible than older children.

UNDERSTANDING EXCEPTIONS
TO THE GENERAL PRINCIPLES

Debates about whether it is accurate to portray children as highly suggestible or resistant to suggestion are at least partially due to the fact that different authors have focused on data from different types of eyewitness studies. A typical design of early studies involved exposing children to an event and then interviewing them using a step-wise procedure: Interviewers first asked free recall questions, followed by specific and sometimes misleading questions. Although such studies have provided a wealth of information about children's accuracy across various types of questions, they rarely simulated the confluence of influences that incited critics to question the reliability of children's testimonies. Exceptions to widely accepted assumptions about children's eyewitness accuracy became more evident when researchers explored a wider range of suggestibility manipulations, such as those described in this chapter.

The Accuracy of Children's Free Recall

The belief that information reported in free recall is generally accurate stems from dozens of studies that have found that children's free recall reports are often as accurate as (although less complete than) adults' (e.g., Goodman & Reed, 1986). These studies have been cited as evidence that "spontaneity" of a disclosure is diagnostic of accuracy, and that a variety of contextual and emotional features typical of freely recalled statements indicate veracity (e.g., Myers, 1992). Numerous reviews of children's eyewitness testimony have emphasized, as Douglas (1996) concluded, that "in response to free recall [questions], young children remember less information in comparison to older children and rarely recall incorrect information" (par. 2).

Poole and Warren (1995) argued that confidence in the accuracy of children's free-narrative accounts may be ill-founded because it is based on studies that did not simulate characteristics of forensic settings, such as long delays, the presence of multiple suggestive interviews, or the possibility of exposure to misinformation outside the interview setting. Studies that have simulated these conditions have arrived at very different conclusions. Warren and Lane (1995), for example, found that 9-year-olds who had been exposed to an early suggestive interview repeated 21% of the suggested details in subsequent free-recall reports collected a week later. Similarly, we found that 41% of 3- and 4-year-old children reported suggested events in response to open-ended probes such as, "Tell me everything you can about what happened in the science room" (Poole & Lindsay, 1995), and a subsequent study (Poole & Lindsay, in press) documented similar intrusions in children as old as 8 years. Also, recall that when children were exposed to misleading stereotypes and suggestive interviews in Leichtman and Ceci's (1995) "Sam Stone" study, 46% of the youngest children and 30% of the oldest children spontaneously reported in a final interview that Sam had committed fictitious misdeeds.

Together with other data on spontaneous false reports (e.g., Bruck, Ceci, Francoeur, & Barr, 1995), these studies demonstrated that problems associated with children's suggestibility cannot be remedied simply by instructing interviewers to ask only open-ended questions. Rather, interviewers should consider whether there have been opportunities for memory contamination prior to formal interviews, and they should phrase questions to be less ambiguous to children, monitor that children are on-topic, and provide opportunities for children to clarify the sources of their knowledge.

Children's Resistance to Questions About Nonexperienced Touching

Early suggestibility studies were often dismissed by critics who accurately argued that implanting suggestions about trivial event details or neutral events did not prove that children could be swayed to report non-experienced touching. When researchers began including questions about touching in their interviews, it became clear that, in most cases, children were more willing to report fictitious impersonal events than fictitious touching events (e.g., Saywitz et al., 1991). There is no evidence, however, that touching is a special class of event that is immune to memory implantation. As with all events, whether touching is dismissed by children as silly, context-discrepant, or too embarrassing to discuss depends on the nature of their experiences and the interviewing context.

We can speculate about the features associated with false allegations by considering studies that found rather high rates of false reports regarding touch. In a study by Pezdek and Roe (1997), 4- and 10-year-olds individually participated in a 25-minute session with a female experimenter. Each child was assigned to one of two major conditions: touched by the experimenter or not touched. Some children from each of these conditions were not misinformed about their experience (i.e., the control conditions), whereas children in the experimental conditions heard descriptions that falsified the touching experience (i.e., claiming the touch did not occur when it had, that a different touch occurred, or that touching did occur when it had not). Interviewers asked each child a general question about touch, "When I showed you the picture of the flower on the screen and asked if you could see it, did I touch you?" and two more specific target questions (e.g., "When I showed you . . . did I put my hand on your shoulder?"). Pezdek and Roe's primary conclusion was that it was easier to mislead children by substituting one event for a related event than it was to implant a new event or erase an event that actually had occurred. Another intriguing result, however, concerns children's responses to the general question about touch. Across the three experimental conditions, percent correct was only 35% for the 4-year-olds and 46% for the 10-year-olds, and performance was low even in the control conditions (50% and 56% correct, respectively). Moreover, the probability of responding "yes" to this question was the same whether or not participants had been touched, and did not exceed chance. Pezdek and Roe concurred with an earlier conclusion by Goodman and Clarke-Stewart (1991) that children's responses to general, nonspecific questions regarding touch tend to be of limited value.

Of course, falsely reporting a touch to the hand is a far cry from reporting hurtful or genital touch. In our studies, we implanted reports that a man put something yucky in children's mouths or hurt their tummies by framing the suggestions in a socially appropriate way in the misleading narrative (e.g., by saying that the man pushed too hard when trying to apply a reward sticker to the child's tummy). Other studies that elicited false assentions to questions about sexual touching interviewed children who were being evaluated for abuse or were questioned about medical exams, contexts in which touching is not a particularly far-fetched possibility (e.g., Eisen et al., 1998; Steward & Steward, 1996). It is probable, then, that children will be most likely to report false touching when their experiences outside and inside the interview situation serve both to increase the plausibility of such experiences and to disinhibit them from discussing touch.

Developmental Trends in Suggestibility

Preschool children were more suggestible than older children and adults in 83% of the studies reviewed by Ceci and Bruck (1993). Since that review was completed, numerous studies have found that younger children produce more false reports of novel or suggested events than older children, even when children are questioned about highly salient and even stressful events (e.g., Quas et al., 1999). The term *suggestibility*, however, refers to a multifaceted concept that subsumes numerous processes, including acquiescence to yes–no questions and failures to understand that the interviewer only wants information from one of two possible sources. Obviously, the magnitude of misinformation effects will be determined by the joint contribution of various processes, including how well children of various ages remember the target information, how well they remember the misinformation, and how they access and communicate this information when their memories are tested.

Earlier we described an example of more accurate performance by younger children: A study by Poole and White (1991) found that children did not have the knowledge base to speculate on an "impossible" question, leading them to volunteer correct "I don't know" answers more frequently than adults. Similarly, in one of our recent studies (Poole & Lindsay, in press), the number of suggested events reported in free recall did not vary across a broad age range (3 to 8 years), and age trends for leading questions were flatter than we expected. Despite the fact that the older children in our study were better able to clarify that these false reports had not actually occurred (i.e., when interviewers later asked them about the source of their knowledge), their more developed verbal skills and apparent eagerness to talk to the interviewer camouflaged their superior abilities early in the interview. Contrary to the general assumption that suggestibility declines with age, studies also have found that the magnitude of false recognition and misinformation effects sometimes are invariant or increase with age (Brainerd & Reyna, 1998).

Under what circumstances are older children as suggestible, or even more suggestible, than younger children? According to Brainerd and Reyna's (1998) theoretical analysis, processes that make testimony more accurate (e.g., retention of surface forms and other item-specific information about the target events) and factors that make testimony less accurate (e.g., retention of the semantic, relational, and elaborative properties of misinformation) both increase with age. Therefore, developmental trends in testimony accuracy will be influenced by test factors that favor reliance on one type of memory trace versus the other. Regarding the older children in our studies, for example, it is possible that their superior knowledge about science activities promoted better verbatim and gist memories of the misleading story narratives, which involved descriptions of mini-events that were linked thematically. Thus the older children reported more false events than we expected before interviewers cued them to report only from a particular source, but unlike the younger children they were better able to differentiate these false events after explicit source monitoring instructions. (See Brainerd, Reyna, & Poole, 2000, for a discussion of counterintuitive memory findings that have forensic implications.)

THE INTEGRATION OF EYEWITNESS FINDINGS
INTO FORENSIC DECISION MAKING

Although findings from eyewitness studies do not enable us to estimate the likelihood that any particular child was abused, they can help us understand the impact of interventions on groups of children with specified characteristics. For example, research indicates that genital touching is often underreported when interviewers ask only open-ended invitations to "tell what happened," and that specific questions can dramatically increase accuracy for children who have been touched (Saywitz et al., 1991; Steward & Steward, 1996). Furthermore, there is evidence that children are often confused by general yes–no questions about touch, and that they may be more accurate when the nature of the touching is clearly explained (Pezdek & Roe, 1997). Conversely, however, a proportion of young children falsely acquiesce to specific questions, and using props with specific yes–no questions to clarify the nature of the touching experience entails some risk (e.g., Steward & Steward, 1996).

We recently described how a Bayesian approach might help us understand the practical significance of information about a child's interviewing history (Poole & Lindsay, 1998). Specifically, we were interested in how confidence in the accuracy of children's disclosures to direct questions might vary as a function of two variables: if children had previously been exposed to leading interviews, and the base rate of the target event (e.g., sexual abuse) in the group interviewed.

A Bayesian analysis reveals that suggestive interviews decrease the probability that an abuse report is accurate unless those interviews increase the rate of reporting abuse proportionally for both abused and nonabused children (Poole & Lindsay, 1998).[1] More specifically, according to a Bayesian analysis, the probability that a child who reports abuse was in fact abused is the product of two components: prior odds (the base rate of abuse in the group being studied) and a likelihood ratio (the probability of abused children reporting abuse relative to the probability of non-

---

[1]We thank Robyn Dawes for suggesting this point.

abused children reporting abuse). Thus, a determination of the probability of an abuse report being indicative of true abuse (posterior odds) must consider both the prevalence of abuse in the group being assessed, and the relative likelihood that abused and nonabused children will report abuse.

According to a Bayesian approach, suggestive questions are likely to be especially risky whenever the majority of abused children disclose abuse in response to direct, nonsuggestive questions. In such a situation, the potential for suggestive questions to increase false abuse reports from nonabused children is likely to be much greater than the potential that they will increase true reports among abused children. To further understand this analysis, consider the following example, which assumes a base rate of seven abused children for every three nonabused children questioned:

> Assume that 65% of abused children disclose abuse in response to direct questions, but that an additional 25% disclose after leading interviewing. Leading interviewing therefore increases the disclosure rate to 90% (i.e., 25%/65% is a 38% increase in disclosures from using leading questions). Also assume, however, that 5% of nonabused children falsely report abuse in response to direct questions, but that an additional 20% report falsely under conditions of leading questioning, raising the rate of false reporting to 25% (i.e., 20%/5% is a 400% increase in false reports). With a prior odds of 70:30, the posterior odds of abuse given a "yes" response under no leading questioning is 97% (70:30 × 65:5 [prior odds × the likelihood ratio]), but only 89% under leading questioning (70:30 × 90:25 [prior odds × the likelihood ratio]). Bayes's theorem therefore informs us that leading interviewing would most likely *decrease* estimates of the probability of abuse given a "yes" response; leading interviewing would increase confidence in a "yes" response only if it elicited proportionately more accurate "yes" responses than inaccurate "yes" responses. (Poole & Lindsay, 1998, p. 18)

Rates of accurate and inaccurate "yes" responses from eyewitness studies can be used to illustrate how leading interviews might alter estimates of the probability of abuse in groups of children with various base rates of abuse. To provide illustrative examples, we selected percentages from studies that questioned children aged 7 and under. We began by assuming that the a priori probability of abuse in a particular jurisdiction was 7:3, or seven accurate allegations for every three invalid suspicions. Furthermore, we assumed that when nontouched preschoolers are asked directly about touch, only 5% falsely assent (e.g., Leichtman & Ceci, 1995), but that when touched children are directly questioned, about 74% acknowledge those experiences (Saywitz et al., 1991; Steward & Steward, 1996). Table 15.1a illustrates the results based on this set of assumptions: Given a positive report of abuse, there is a 97% chance that the child was

TABLE 15.1

Hypothetical Probabilities of Abuse Given Assent to a Direct
Abuse Question, as a Function of the A Priori Probability
of Abuse and the Child's Interviewing History

a: A Priori Probability of Abuse = 70%

	Abused *n = 700*	*Nonabused* *n = 300*	
"Yes" responses, no leading interviews	518	15	P(abuse|yes) = 97%
"Yes" responses, leading interviews	665	120	P(abuse|yes) = 85%

b: A Priori Probability of Abuse = 50%

	Abused *n = 500*	*Nonabused* *n = 500*	
"Yes" responses, no leading interviews	370	25	P(abuse|yes) = 94%
"Yes" responses, leading interviews	475	200	P(abuse|yes) = 70%

c: A Priori Probability of Abuse = 10%

	Abused *n = 100*	*Nonabused* *n = 900*	
"Yes" responses, no leading interviews	74	45	P(abuse|yes) = 62%
"Yes" responses, leading interviews	95	360	P(abuse|yes) = 21%

Note. Examples assume that abused children correctly assent to 74% of direct questions
with no prior leading interviews and 95% of direct questions with leading interviews;
nonabused children falsely assent to 5% of direct questions with no prior leading interviews
and 40% of direct questions with leading interviews.

From "Assessing the Accuracy of Young Children's Reports: Lessons From the Investigation
of Child Sexual Abuse" by D. A. Poole and D. S. Lindsay, 1998, *Applied and Preventive Psychology,*
7, p. 19. Copyright © 1998 by Cambridge University Press. Reprinted with permission.

in fact abused. Table 15.1a evaluates this percentage for children exposed
to leading questioning. For this age range, assume that 40% of nonabused children acquiesce to abuse allegations (between the 20% figure in
Eisen et al., 1998, and the over 70% figure from Leichtman & Ceci, 1995),[2]

---

[2]The 70% false assent rate observed in Leichtman and Ceci's study corresponded to the 3-
and 4-year-olds' performance following the induction of a false stereotypes about the alleged
events and following repeated leading interviews. Preschoolers' false report rates following
a single leading interview are typically lower, as are older children's (e.g., 5- and 6-year-olds)
false report rates following multiple interviews.

but that asking leading questions increases correct assentions to direct abuse questions to 95% of abused children. As shown in Table 15.1a, there is an 85% chance of abuse given a positive response. Although confidence in the reliability of a "yes" response decreases, there is still a high probability of abuse. In other words, suggestibility manipulations would need to be strong to substantially increase doubt when the base rate of abuse among those children interviewed is believed to be moderate to high.

Tables 15.1b and 15.1c report the (hypothetical) probabilities of abuse given a "yes" response when the base rates of abuse are 50% (Table 15.1b) and 10% (Table 15.1c). Although we do not know the actual base rate of abuse among various groups, the declining base rates in Table 15.1 simulate situations in which, for example, we move from cases in which children have disclosed abuse to cases in which adults merely suspect abuse on the basis of weak evidence. Confidence in the accuracy of a "yes" response declines dramatically when there has been a history of leading interviews, especially when the base rate of abuse is low.

One can also look at the flip side of Table 15.1: the probability of abuse given that the child answers "no," or the probability of a false negative. With a 70% a priori probability of abuse, 39% of children who respond "no" to a direct question after no leading interviews were abused, compared to only 16% after leading interviews. Thus, leading interviews dramatically decrease the number of false "no" responses when the base rate of abuse is high. However, the benefit from leading interviews declines as a function of decreases in the base rate of abuse: With a 50% a priori probability of abuse, these values are 21% versus 8%; with a 10% a priori probability of abuse, these values are 3% versus 1%.

How can this analysis inform forensic decisions? One of the conflicting issues in interviewing is when (if ever) it is justified to encourage disclosures with leading interviews. From the current analysis (based on studies that tested children aged 7 and younger), it is clear that leading interviewing of young children cannot be justified for situations in which the a priori probability of abuse is assumed to be low, the majority of abused children disclose without leading interviews, and the leading interviews are suggestive enough to encourage false responses among nonabused children. Many professionals would argue that leading interviewing may be justified when base rates of abuse are high, however, particularly if it can be shown that interviewers can further decrease the rate of false positives by using clarifying instructions or procedures. As Poole and Lindsay (1998) concluded, "It makes sense that professionals who work in environments with a high base rate of abuse would favor leading interviewing techniques and downplay the risks from those procedures. Professionals who primarily analyze cases with lower base rates of abuse should have heightened concerns about the dangers of leading interviews, however" (p. 19).

CONCLUSIONS

During the 1990s, researchers have made considerable progress toward understanding children's suggestibility. Studies have mapped the circumstances associated with more or less accurate reports and proposed a number of mechanisms that can lead children to report erroneous details or fictitious events. Converging results have popularized a number of generalizations regarding children's testimonies, and exceptions to these generalizations are being identified and explained.

Many gaps remain in our understanding of suggestibility, however, that hamper efforts to develop protocols for forensic settings. To date, researchers have focused on two age groups: children under 8 years of age and adults. Such research does not provide a basis for predicting the accuracy and completeness of school-age children's reports. Changes in knowledge base, perceptions of authority, and memory source monitoring that occur during the transition to the school years make it inappropriate to speculate about how school-age children will respond to the myriad social and cognitive demands imposed by various interviewing strategies. Although even adults can be led to report fictitious events from their childhood (see Hyman & Loftus, chap. 3, this volume), such demonstrations do not help us predict the circumstances under which school-age children would be swayed about the true state of affairs regarding salient and relatively recent events. By expanding the database to document how children across all stages of development react to a wide variety of suggestibility manipulations, and developing more complete theoretical accounts of the interviewing process, researchers will contribute to the development of improved interview techniques that maximize disclosures while minimizing false reports. Future research and theory should also improve experts' position to postdict the reliability of allegations that emerge under particular conditions. Finally, developments in the empirical and theoretical knowledge base may help reduce distressing abuses of the findings summarized in this chapter (e.g., at one extreme, claims to the effect that one must always "believe the child," and at the other, attempts to discredit child victims/witnesses by invoking findings from studies that do not simulate the conditions of the cases in question).

REFERENCES

Ackil, J. K., & Zaragoza, M. S. (1998). The memorial consequences of forced confabulation: Age differences in susceptibility to false memories. *Developmental Psychology, 34,* 1358–1372.

Baker-Ward, L., Gordon, B. N., Ornstein, P. A., Larus, D. M., & Clubb, P. A. (1993). Young children's long-term retention of a pediatric examination. *Child Development, 64,* 1519-1533.

Bjorklund, B. R., Douglas, R. N., Park, C. L., Nelson, L., Sanders, L., Graché, J., Cassel, W. S., & Bjorklund, D. F. (1997, April). When does misleading questioning cause children to change their minds as well as their answers? Paper presented in D. F. Bjorklund (Chair), *Factors influencing children's suggestibility to repeated questions: How misinformation changes children's answers and their minds.* Symposium presented at the biennial meeting of the Society for Research in Child Development, Washington, DC.

Brady, M. S., Poole, D. A., Warren, A. R., & Jones, H. R. (1999). Young children's responses to yes–no questions: Patterns and problems. *Applied Developmental Science, 3,* 47–57.

Brainerd, C. J., & Reyna, V. F. (1998). Fuzzy-trace theory and children's false memories. *Journal of Experimental Child Psychology, 71,* 81–129.

Brainerd, C. J., Reyna, V. F., & Poole, D. A. (2000). Fuzzy-trace theory and false memory: Memory theory in the courtroom. In D. F. Bjorklund (Ed.), *False memory creation in children and adults: Theory, research, and implications* (pp. 93–127). Mahwah, NJ: Lawrence Erlbaum Associates.

Bruck, M., & Ceci, S. J. (1997). The suggestibility of young children. *Current Directions in Psychological Science, 6,* 75–79.

Bruck, M., Ceci, S. J., Francoeur, E., & Barr, R. (1995). "I hardly cried when I got my shot!" Influencing children's reports about a visit to their pediatrician. *Child Development, 66,* 193–208.

Bruck, M., Hembrooke, H., & Ceci, S. (1997). Children's reports of pleasant and unpleasant events. In J. D. Read & D. S. Lindsay (Eds.), *Recollections of trauma: Scientific evidence and clinical practice* (pp. 199–213). New York: Plenum.

Ceci, S. J., & Bruck, M. (1993). Suggestibility of the child witness: A historical review and synthesis. *Psychological Bulletin, 113,* 403–439.

Ceci, S. J., & Bruck, M. (1995). *Jeopardy in the courtroom: A scientific analysis of children's testimony.* Washington, DC: American Psychological Association.

Ceci, S. J., & Huffman, M. L. C. (1997). How suggestible are preschool children? Cognitive and social factors. *Journal of the American Academy of Child and Adolescent Psychiatry, 36,* 948–958.

Ceci, S. J., Loftus, E. F., Leichtman, M. D., & Bruck, M. (1994). The possible role of source misattributions in the creation of false beliefs among preschoolers. *International Journal of Clinical and Experimental Hypnosis, 42,* 304–320.

Ceci, S. J., Ross, D. F., & Toglia, M. P. (1987). Suggestibility of children's memory: Psycholegal implications. *Journal of Experimental Psychology: General, 116,* 38–49.

Dent, H. R. (1991). Experimental studies of interviewing child witnesses. In J. Doris (Ed.), *The suggestibility of children's recollections* (pp. 138–146). Washington, DC: American Psychological Association.

Douglas, R. N. (1996). Considering the witness in interviews. *Psycoloquy, 7*(21), witness-memory.7.douglas.

Eisen, M. L., Goodman, G. S., Qin, J., & Davis, S. (1998). Memory and suggestibility in maltreated children: New research relevant to evaluating allegations of abuse. In S. L. Lynn & K. McConkey (Eds.), *Truth in memory* (pp. 163–189). New York: Guilford.

Fivush, R., & Shukat, J. (1995). What young children recall: Issues of content, consistency and coherence of early autobiographical recall. In M. S. Zaragoza, J. R. Graham, G. C. N. Hall, R. Hirschman, & Y. S. Ben-Porath (Eds.), *Memory and testimony in the child witness* (pp. 5–23). Thousand Oaks, CA: Sage.

Foley, M. A., Harris, J. F., & Hermann, S. (1994). Developmental comparisons of the ability to discriminate between memories for symbolic play enactments. *Developmental Psychology, 30,* 206–217.

Foley, M. A., & Johnson, M. K. (1985). Confusions between memories for performed and imagined actions: A developmental comparison. *Child Development, 56,* 1145–1155.

Garven, S., Wood, J. M., & Malpass, R. S. (2000). Allegations of wrongdoing: The effects of reinforcement on children's mundane and fantastic claims. *Journal of Applied Psychology, 85,* 38–49.

Garven, S., Wood, J. M., Malpass, R. S., & Shaw, J. S. (1998). More than suggestion: The effect of interviewing techniques from the McMartin Preschool case. *Journal of Applied Psychology, 83,* 347–359.

Goodman, G. S. (1993). Understanding and improving children's testimony. *Children Today, 22,* 13–15.

Goodman, G. S., Aman, C., & Hirschman, J. (1987). Child sexual and physical abuse: Children's testimony. In S. J. Ceci, M. P. Toglia, & D. F. Ross (Eds.), *Children's eyewitness memory* (pp. 1–23). New York: Springer-Verlag.

Goodman, G. S., & Clarke-Stewart, A. (1991). Suggestibility in children's testimony: Implications for sexual abuse investigations. In J. Doris (Ed.), *The suggestibility of children's recollections* (pp. 92–105). Washington, DC: American Psychological Association.

Goodman, G. S., Hirschman, J. E., Hepps, D., & Rudy, L. (1991). Children's memory for stressful events. *Merrill-Palmer Quarterly, 37,* 109–158.

Goodman, G. S., Quas, J. A., Batterman-Faunce, J. M., Riddlesberger, M. M., & Kuhn, J. (1994). Predictors of accurate and inaccurate memories of traumatic events experienced in childhood. *Consciousness and Cognition, 3,* 269–294.

Goodman, G. S., & Reed, R. S. (1986). Age differences in eyewitness testimony. *Law and Human Behavior, 10,* 317–332.

Goodman, G. S., Wilson, M. E., Hazan, C., & Reed, R. S. (1989, April). *Children's testimony nearly four years after an event.* Paper presented at the annual meeting of the Eastern Psychological Association, Boston.

Gopnik, A., & Graf, P. (1988). Knowing how you know: Young children's ability to identify and remember the sources of their beliefs. *Child Development, 59,* 1366–1371.

Lamb, M. E., Sternberg, K. J., Esplin, P. W., Hershkowitz, I., Orbach, Y., & Hovav, M. (1997). Criterion-based content analysis: A field validation study. *Child Abuse and Neglect, 21,* 255–264.

Leichtman, M. D., & Ceci, S. J. (1995). The effects of stereotypes and suggestions on preschoolers' reports. *Developmental Psychology, 31,* 568–578.

Lepore, S. J., & Sesco, B. (1994). Distorting children's reports and interpretations of events through suggestion. *Journal of Applied Psychology, 79,* 108–120.

Lindsay, D. S. (1990). Misleading suggestions can impair eyewitnesses' ability to remember event details. *Journal of Experimental Psychology: Learning, Memory, and Cognition, 16,* 1077–1083.

Lindsay, D. S., Gonzales, V., & Eso, K. (1995). Aware and unaware uses of memories of postevent suggestions. In M. S. Zaragoza, J. R. Graham, G. C. N. Hall, R. Hirschman, & Y. S. Ben-Porath (Eds.), *Memory and testimony in the child witness* (pp. 86–108). Thousand Oaks, CA: Sage.

Lindsay, D. S., Johnson, M. K., & Kwon, P. (1991). Developmental changes in memory source monitoring. *Journal of Experimental Child Psychology, 52,* 297–318.

Myers, J. E. B. (1992). *Legal issues in child abuse and neglect.* Newbury Park, CA: Sage.

Newcombe, P. A., & Siegal, M. (1996). Where to look first for suggestibility in young children. *Cognition, 59,* 337–356.

Newcombe, P. A., & Siegal, M. (1997). Explicitly questioning the nature of suggestibility in preschoolers' memory and retention. *Journal of Experimental Child Psychology, 67,* 185–203.

Peterson, C., & Bell, M. (1996). Children's memory for traumatic injury. *Child Development, 67,* 3045–3070.

Peterson, C., & Biggs, M. (1997). Interviewing children about trauma: Problems with "specific" questions. *Journal of Traumatic Stress, 10*, 279-290.

Pezdek, K., & Roe, C. (1995). The effect of memory trace strength on suggestibility. *Journal of Experimental Child Psychology, 60*, 116-128.

Pezdek, K., & Roe, C. (1997). The suggestibility of children's memory for being touched: Planting, erasing, and changing memories. *Law and Human Behavior, 21*, 95-106.

Poole, D. A., & Lamb, M. E. (1998). *Investigative interviews of children: A guide for helping professionals.* Washington, DC: American Psychological Association.

Poole, D. A., & Lindsay, D. S. (1995). Interviewing preschoolers: Effects of nonsuggestive techniques, parental coaching, and leading questions on reports of nonexperienced events. *Journal of Experimental Child Psychology, 60*, 129-154.

Poole, D. A., & Lindsay, D. S. (in press).Children's eyewitness reports after exposure to misinformation from parents. *Journal of Experimental Psychology: Applied.*

Poole, D. A., & Lindsay, D. S. (1998). Assessing the accuracy of young children's reports: Lessons from the investigation of child sexual abuse. *Applied and Preventive Psychology, 7*, 1-26.

Poole, D. A., & Warren, A. (1995, March). Recent challenges to three commonly held assumptions about children's eyewitness testimony. In D. Peters (Chair), *Children as witnesses: New research, new issues.* Symposium conducted at the biennial meeting of the Society for Research in Child Development, Indianapolis, IN.

Poole, D. A., & White, L. T. (1991). Effects of question repetition on the eyewitness testimony of children and adults. *Developmental Psychology, 27*, 975-986.

Poole, D. A., & White, L. T. (1993). Two years later: Effects of question repetition and retention interval on the eyewitness testimony of children and adults. *Developmental Psychology, 29*, 844-853.

Pratt, C. (1990). On asking children—and adults—bizarre questions. *First Language, 10*, 167-175.

Quas, J. A., Goodman, G. S., Bidrose, S., Pipe, M-E., Craw, S., & Ablin, D. S. (1999). Emotion and memory: Children's long-term remembering, forgetting, and suggestibility. *Journal of Experimental Child Psychology, 72*, 235-270.

Saywitz, K. J., Goodman, G. S., Nicholas, E., & Moan, S. F. (1991). Children's memories of a physical examination involving genital touch: Implications for reports of child sexual abuse. *Journal of Consulting and Clinical Psychology, 59*, 682-691.

Schacter, D. L., Kagan, J., & Leichtman, M. D. (1995). True and false memories in children and adults: A cognitive neuroscience perspective. *Psychology, Public Policy, and Law, 1*, 411-428.

Steward, M. S., Bussey, K., Goodman, G. S., & Saywitz, K. J. (1993). Implications of developmental research for interviewing children. *Child Abuse and Neglect, 17*, 25-37.

Steward, M. S., & Steward, D. S. (with L. Farquhar, J. E. B. Myers, M. Reinhart, J. Welker, N. Joye, J. Driskill, & J. Morgan). (1996). Interviewing young children about body touch and handling. *Monograph of the Society for Research in Child Development, 61*(4-5, Serial No. 248).

Taylor, M., Esbensen, B. M., & Bennitt, R. T. (1994). Children's understanding of knowledge acquisition: The tendency for children to report that they have always known what they have just learned. *Child Development, 65*, 1581-1604.

Tobey, A. E., & Goodman, G. S. (1992). Children's eyewitness memory: Effects of participation and forensic context. *Child Abuse and Neglect, 16*, 779-796.

Walker, N. E., Lunning, S. M., & Eilts, J. L. (1996, June). *Do children respond accurately to forced choice questions?: Yes or no.* Paper presented at Recollections of Trauma: Scientific Research and Clinical Practice, NATO Advanced Study Institute, Port de Bourgenay, France.

Warren, A. R., & Lane, P. (1995). Effects of timing and type of questioning on eyewitness accuracy and suggestibility. In M. S. Zaragoza, J. R. Graham, G. C. N. Hall, R. Hirschman, & Y. S. Ben-Porath (Eds.), *Memory and testimony in the child witness* (pp. 44-60). Thousand Oaks, CA: Sage.

Warren, A. R., & McCloskey, L. A. (1997). Language in social contexts. In J. B. Gleason (Ed.), *The development of language* (4th ed., pp. 210-258). New York: Allyn & Bacon.

Warren, A. R., Woodall, C. E., Hunt, J. S., & Perry, N. W. (1996). "It sounds good in theory, but . . .": Do investigative interviewers follow guidelines based on memory research? *Child Maltreatment, 1,* 231-245.

Winer, G. A., Rasnake, L. K., & Smith, D. A. (1987). Language versus logic: Responses to misleading classificatory questions. *Journal of Psycholinguistic Research, 16,* 311-327.

16

The Utility of Anatomical Dolls and Drawings in Child Forensic Interviews

Mark D. Everson
University of North Carolina–Chapel Hill

Barbara W. Boat
University of Cincinnati

In child sexual abuse investigations, the scarcity of eyewitnesses and physical evidence focuses extraordinary forensic attention on the child (Everson & Boat, 1989; Steward & Steward, 1996). Helping young children talk about possibly difficult and sensitive topics is an enormous challenge as abuse is often a complex event that children are ill-prepared to describe. Although a number of factors and types of evidence must be considered, the capacity of the legal system to protect children and find the truth too often relies heavily on the words of young children. The purpose of the investigative interview is to help determine if an alleged abusive event occurred by eliciting as accurate and as complete a report as possible. The challenge to professionals is to determine the most effective means of getting an accurate, complete report.

Since the 1990s, concerns about the use of props, especially the utility of anatomical dolls in forensic interviews with children, have occupied a prominent place among investigators and researchers. Should we or should we not employ the dolls, anatomical drawings, or any kind of props? What are the possible positive and negative outcomes of our choices? What can we say definitively about the utility of the dolls or other props? What research support is needed to help us with our decisions?

These questions continue to be timely, although our speculation, based on informal surveys of colleagues, is that doll use has decreased substantially in the last several years in response to recent attacks on their utility (e.g., Bruck, Ceci, Francoeur, & Renick, 1995; Ceci & Bruck, 1995).

The central tenet of this chapter is that more than a decade of research of the dolls has failed to provide clear and meaningful answers to questions about the efficacy and suggestibility of anatomical props like dolls as interview aids. This is due, we believe, to the fact that much of the research has failed to make proper distinctions between different doll functions in the interview process, between the impact of the dolls versus the impact of question type, between the impact of the dolls versus the impact of other props, and lastly, between acceptable and unacceptable interview practice with the dolls. As a result, much of the research is limited in its usefulness for guiding forensic practice.

Nonetheless, we believe the following conclusions, to be elucidated later in this chapter, are warranted given the current state of our knowledge:

1. Anatomical dolls can serve several distinct functions in the forensic interview process (Everson & Boat, 1994). Blanket endorsements or condemnations of the dolls without regard to specific function are therefore unwarranted.

2. There is growing evidence that the use of anatomical dolls as demonstration aids or as anatomical models (when paired with yes–no questions) enhances children's recall of private parts touching (especially for children 5 years and older) in comparison to unaided free recall or a purely verbal interview (Goodman, Quas, Batterman-Faunce, Riddlesberger, & Kuhn, 1997; Katz, Schonfeld, Carter, Leventhal, & Cicchetti, 1995; Saywitz, Goodman, Nicholas, & Moan, 1991; Steward & Steward, 1996).

3. There is substantial evidence that asking leading, misleading, suggestive, or highly specific yes–no questions about private parts touching in conjunction with anatomical dolls can lead to significant false reports of genital or anal touching in young children (Bruck et al., 1995; Saywitz et al., 1991; Steward & Steward, 1996). It is unclear how much the presence of anatomical dolls contributes to this result over and above the impact of the problematic questions (e.g., misleading questions).

4. There is growing evidence that the use of props (especially toy-like medical props) in conjunction with anatomical dolls can lead to distortions and inaccuracies in children's recall (Bruck et al., 1995; Goodman et al., 1997; Steward & Steward, 1996).

5. An anatomical doll or drawing to focus the child's attention and to serve as a body map may be essential in interviewing young children about genital and anal touching. However, anatomical dolls may not be superior to anatomical drawings for this purpose (Steward & Steward, 1996).

ANATOMICAL DOLL USE IN FORENSIC INTERVIEWS

The starting point in any discussion of the utility of anatomical dolls must include an examination of how the dolls are used in the forensic interview process. Distinguishing among various uses of the dolls can be important because frequently the dolls are described only as being "used" or "not used" in an interview setting. To develop a comprehensive list of the various uses of anatomical dolls, we conducted an extensive literature search to find written guidelines or protocols for interviewing children in sexual abuse evaluations that included directions for using anatomical dolls (Everson & Boat, 1994). The 20 written guidelines we identified represented a number of professional organizations (e.g., American Academy of Child and Adolescent Psychiatry, 1988; American Psychological Association [APA], 1991; American Professional Society on the Abuse of Children [APSAC], 1990) as well as a range of forensic perspectives (e.g., Boat & Everson, 1988; Gardner, 1989; White, Strom, Santilli, & Quinn, 1987) but were primarily clinical, as opposed to research, based. From a review of these guidelines, we identified five recommended or accepted functions the dolls can serve in sexual abuse assessments: Comforter, Icebreaker, Anatomical Model, Demonstration Aid, and Screening Tool/ Memory Stimulus (Table 16.1). The functions are described next.

Comforter.   The dolls can be used as "cuddly toys" in place of teddy bears, and so on, to provide tactile comfort for the child. Typically, a single, clothed doll is given to the child to hold while the interviewer models or verbally encourages the child to use the doll for comfort, support, or companionship: "Can my doll sit in your lap while we talk?" The interviewer refrains from focusing attention on the doll's sexual body parts and does not initiate or suggest that the doll be undressed. This is a rela-

TABLE 16.1
Review of Recommended Uses in Guidelines
for Anatomical Dolls in Forensic Interviews

Use	Guidelines (N = 20)
Comforter	2
Icebreaker	5
Anatomical model	16
Demonstration aid	18
Screening tool/memory stimulus	11

Note.   N = number of guidelines reviewed recommending or endorsing particular use.

tively rare use of anatomical dolls and one that does not rely on any of their anatomical features. Only two of the written guidelines reviewed described this use of the dolls.

Icebreaker.   The dolls can serve as a conversation starter on the topic of sexuality by focusing the child's attention in a nonthreatening, non-leading manner on sexual issues and sexual body parts. This may be especially important in the case of younger children and children with less developed language skills who may require direct cueing to understand what, from the universe of possibilities, the interviewer wants the child to talk about (Steward & Steward, 1996). Dolls can also be used to convey tacit permission for the child to describe or demonstrate sexual knowledge and experience. In practice, the icebreaker use is often paired with a survey of body part labels (i.e., anatomical model use).

Anatomical Model.   The dolls can function as anatomical models for assessing a child's labels for parts of the body, understanding of bodily functions, and possible precocious knowledge of the mechanics of sexual acts. The interviewer may point to sexual and nonsexual body parts and ask questions like, "What do you call this part?", "What is it for?," and "Is it for anything else?" The dolls can also serve as visual aids for direct inquiries about the child's personal experiences with private parts. This may include questions such as "Do you have one (vagina)?", "Has anything ever happened to yours?", and "Has it ever been hurt?" Similarly, the dolls can serve as a body map for identifying location on the body. Although such direct questions about genital touch might be viewed as leading in many contexts, a number of experts in the field of forensic interviewing have endorsed their limited use, especially later in the interview process after more open-ended techniques have been attempted (e.g., APSAC, 1990; White et al., 1986; Yuille, 1996). Specific problems with pairing direct questions with anatomical props are discussed later (Steward & Steward, 1996).

Demonstration Aid.   The dolls can serve as props to enable children to "show" rather than "tell" what happened, especially when limited verbal skills or emotional issues, such as fear of telling or embarrassment about discussing sexual activities, interfere with direct verbal description. The interviewer typically directs the child to use the dolls to reenact what the child has experienced or observed, usually after the child has described or suggested that a specific event has occurred. Whether or not a child experiences difficulty communicating verbally, dolls are sometimes useful to confirm an interviewer's understanding of a child's description of abuse and to reduce the likelihood of miscommunication between the child and the interviewer. Demonstration aid is one of the most common uses of the dolls with 18 out of the 20 doll guidelines reviewed endorsing this use.

Memory Stimulus/Screening Tool. Exposure to the dolls, and especially to such features as secondary sexual characteristics, genitalia, and articles of clothing, may be useful in stimulating or triggering a child's recall of specific events of a sexual nature. Supporting this use is research suggesting that props and concrete cues may be more effective in prompting memories in young children than are verbal cues or questions (e.g., Nelson & Ross, 1980). To encourage recall, the interviewer might ask questions such as, "Have you seen one (penis)?" or "Do the dolls help you remember anything else that happened?" The degree to which this use of the dolls may lead to problems in confabulation and fantasy has not been well-researched.

The screening tool function is based on the premise that exposure to the dolls in a nonthreatening setting may provide an opportunity for the child to spontaneously reveal his or her sexual interests, concerns, or knowledge. Typically, the child is given the opportunity to examine and manipulate the dolls freely while the interviewer observes the child's play, reaction, and remarks. The interviewer can be either present or absent (observing through a one-way mirror) during this time, although children are likely to be less inhibited in their manipulations of the dolls without an adult present (Everson & Boat, 1990). After a period of uninterrupted manipulation and exploration of the dolls, the interviewer asks follow-up questions about the child's behavior with, or reaction to, the dolls (e.g., "What were the dolls doing?", "Where did you learn about that?"). Graphic sexual behavior, unusual emotional responses, as well as spontaneous "suspicious" statements made by the child (e.g., "Daddy's pee-pee gets big sometimes") are the focus of follow-up questions to the child. The memory stimulus and screening tool uses regularly overlap and are often difficult to distinguish in practice or in written guidelines. As a result, these two uses were combined in the survey of guidelines summarized in Table 16.1.

Following the identification of accepted doll uses in forensic interviews, we conducted a study to determine how closely practice in the field conforms to the recommendations of the written guidelines (Boat & Everson, 1996). Specifically, we were interested in examining the extent to which these functional uses of anatomical dolls were employed by Child Protective Services (CPS) workers in their investigative interviews. Participants were investigators from county CPS agencies in a mid-south state that regularly videotaped their investigative interviews. Approximately equal numbers of taped interviews of children in the 2 to 5 and 6 to 12 year age ranges were solicited with no selection criteria based on gender, race, or ethnicity. No mention was made of a focus on anatomical dolls. To achieve a wider representation of interviewers, no interviewer could be depicted in more than two tapes, one at each age range.

A total of 97 videotaped interviews were available for analysis, representing approximately 60% of the county CPS agencies that videotaped their interviews in this state. Anatomical dolls were by far the most common interview prop, with a frequency of use at 80% or higher among both age groups. In contrast, anatomical drawings were used in only about 10% of the interviews. Among interviews in which anatomical dolls were employed, the particular doll use was reliably coded into one of the categories described previously (refer to Everson, Boat, & Sanfilippo, 1994, for specific written coding criteria).

The most frequent uses of the dolls were as anatomical models and demonstration aids (see Table 16.2). These were also the two uses most frequently described in the 20 guidelines we had reviewed. It is noteworthy that the dolls were used as demonstration aids in 71% of the interviews with children in the younger age group, including in 4 out of 6 interviews with 2-year-olds, raising concerns about the possible inappropriate use of the dolls among children with limited representational abilities. Interviewers were somewhat more likely to use the dolls as an icebreaker to introduce the topic of body parts and sexuality among younger children (36%) than they were among older children (14%). The diagnostic screen use (in which a child freely interacts with the dolls, and the interviewer follows up on graphic behavior or statements) was also more common in interviews with the younger children (27%) than in those in the older age range (6%). We observed no use of the anatomical dolls in these front-line investigative interviews that did not fit within one of the five functional uses under study. Knowing that various uses of the dolls may differ in the extent to which suggestibility is a concern, any research describing doll use, or anatomical drawing use, should clearly note the specific function(s) the dolls are serving (Everson & Boat, 1994).

TABLE 16.2
Frequency of Functional Uses by Age

Types of Use	2–5 Years (N = 45)	6–12 Years (N = 36)
Comforter	4%	3%
Icebreaker	36%	14%
Anatomical model	93%	92%
Demonstration aid	71%	89%
Screening tool/memory stimulus	27%	6%

MAJOR CRITICISMS OF ANATOMICAL DOLLS

The dolls have been a mixed blessing. Although they have become a cata-lyst for developmentally focused research on children's suggestibility, they also have been the focus of intense, sometimes acrimonious clinical and legal debate (Boat & Everson, 1993; Ceci & Bruck, 1995; Wescott, Davies, & Clifford, 1989). The extreme reactions of some critics of the dolls have been surprising, with the dolls described as "dirty" and "ugly" (Tyl-den, 1987), and "monstrosities" (Gardner, 1992). Their use has been char-acterized as "an affront to common decency" and "a form of child abuse" (Naumann, 1985). Professionals who use the dolls have been labeled "in-competent" (Gardner 1992) and accused of being "guilty of medical mal-practice and unethical conduct" (McIver & Wakefield, 1987).

Some of the negative reactions toward the dolls do not appear to reflect legitimate clinical or scientific concerns. However, two concerns that have been raised about the use of the dolls in sexual abuse evaluations warrant reasoned consideration (Everson & Boat, 1994). The most common criti-cism of the dolls is that they are inherently suggestive and sexually stimu-lating. As a result, the dolls are said to stimulate sexual fantasy and sexual play in children that is likely to be misinterpreted as evidence of sex-ual abuse. A second argument against the use of anatomical dolls in sex-ual abuse assessments is the claim that there is little or no evidence for the efficacy of the dolls as interview tools. Until such scientific evidence ex-ists, the argument goes, interviewers should refrain from using the dolls. These criticisms are addressed in the remainder of the chapter within the context of information available to us from forensically relevant research.

DEFINING FORENSICALLY RELEVANT RESEARCH

Research studies differ substantially in the generalizability of their find-ings to actual forensic practice and in their utility for informing appropri-ate practice. Everson and Boat (1997) suggested that at least eight design features should be considered in assessing the forensic relevance of re-search on anatomical dolls:

> *Salience and memorability of the to-be-remembered (TBR) event:* Genital and anal touch during medical procedures is a useful analogue for some types of sexual abuse. Not all touch to a child's private parts, however, is equally salient and memorable. To increase comparability to sexual abuse, the touching should be conspicuous and noteworthy to the child.

Memorability of TBR event established: It is essential that the memorability of the TBR event be established through demonstration of above chance memory of the event in at least one of the recall conditions of the study.

Distinct doll use(s) tested: Ideally, the impact on memory performance of one or more of the accepted functional uses of the dolls in forensic interviewing should be the focus of study.

Confounding of dolls with other props avoided: To obtain a more valid assessment of doll impact, the use of anatomical dolls should not be confounded with the use of other props, especially those that may be distracting, or that may trigger memory intrusions from other experiences (e.g., medical procedures) the child has had.

Confounding of dolls with leading or suggestive questions avoided: The design of the study should provide for an assessment of the impact of the dolls separate from the impact of leading or suggestive questions, and especially deliberately misleading questions. It is also important to distinguish among at least five types of leading and suggestive questions that may produce substantially different effects on children's recall (Everson, 1999): (a) *direct suggestive questions* regarding genital touching (e.g., "Were you touched there?" or "Did the doctor touch you here?"); (b) *presumptive questions* (e.g., to child who has experienced genital touching by doctor, but has not already mentioned the touching to interviewer: "Show me how the doctor touched you here"); (c) *erroneously presumptive questions* (To child who has neither experienced genital touching by doctor nor suggested such touching to interviewer: "Show me how the doctor touched you here."); (d) *persuasive questions* (e.g., "Didn't they take your socks off before the doctor checked you?"); and (e) *speculative questions* (e.g., "What could the doctor do with a spoon? Show me on the dolls."). These questions are likely to have different levels of acceptability in forensic practice.

Use of realistic, forensic-type questioning: Ideally, the questions to elicit recall should conform at least somewhat to the format recommended for forensic interviewing (e.g., Poole & Lamb, 1998; Yuille, Hunter, Joffe, & Zaparniuk, 1993). This involves the use of free recall followed by more specific questioning. Because a young child's affirmation of genital touch in response to a single direct yes–no question would seldom be considered a credible report of sexual abuse (cf. Faller, 1994), the trained forensic interviewer would also attempt to elicit a detailed description of what occurred through flexible, open-ended, follow-up questioning.

Realistic interval between event and recall: It is extremely rare that a child is interviewed immediately after an abusive episode. Delays of days to months are common. In research, an interval of 1 week to 1 month be-tween the TBR and recall test may be a realistic compromise.

Focus on occurrence and description of private parts touch: To parallel the critical concerns in forensic interviewing, the accuracy of reports and/ or denials of private parts touching should be the primary focus of in-quiry, followed by the accuracy and completeness of the child's de-scription of the nature, extent, and "perpetrator" of such touching.

These specific design features were chosen, from the many features on which the studies could be compared, because of their relevance in ensur-ing the generalizability, validity, and utility of study findings for inform-ing appropriate forensic practice.

THE SUGGESTIVENESS DEBATE I: SEXUALLY NAIVE VERSUS SEXUALLY KNOWLEDGEABLE CHILDREN

The most common criticism of anatomical dolls in sexual abuse evalua-tions, that the dolls are inherently suggestive and sexually stimulating, has several aspects that must be considered (Everson & Boat, 1997). First, many young children are exposed to substantial nudity during their ev-eryday lives, viewing their own nude bodies at various times as well as the bodies of siblings during diapering and bath time. They see peers un-dressed during toileting activities in day care. They may be exposed to pa-rental nudity at home during mutual bathing, dressing, and so on (Rosen-feld, Bailey, Siegel, & Bailey, 1986). If observing real genitalia on real bodies does not appear to evoke significant sexual acting out or other un-toward effects, it is unclear why one would expect the cloth genitalia on dolls to do so. It also seems likely that young children may not associate nudity, and especially doll nudity, with sex, as adults are more likely to do. For example, a 4-year-old's reaction to seeing his mother emerging nude from the shower would likely be quite different from the reaction of his father, his teenage brother, or the telephone repairman.

It is also critical to differentiate between the impact of the dolls on sexu-ally naive versus sexually experienced or knowledgeable children. At least three uses of the dolls (screening tool, memory stimulus, and ana-tomical model) actually depend on the dolls being "suggestive" to the sex-ually experienced or knowledgeable child, if by "suggestive" it is meant that the dolls encourage, stimulate, disinhibit, and provide an easy vehicle for such children to reveal their sexual knowledge during the evaluation process. In none of these three uses should the interviewer infer that abuse has occurred based solely on behavior with the dolls or on sexual knowl-edge displayed (APSAC, 1995). Rather, the dolls provide the impetus for

the interviewer to explore, through follow-up questioning, the source of
the child's knowledge. The underlying assumption is that sexual knowledge in the young child results not from doll-induced fantasy but from
prior sexual exposure or experience.

The critical concern in the suggestiveness debate, therefore, focuses on
the impact of anatomical dolls on nonabused, sexually naive children. Do
anatomical dolls induce nonabused, sexually naive children to engage in
behavior with the dolls (either verbal or nonverbal) that is likely to be misinterpreted as evidence of abuse?

At least two bodies of research with the dolls bear upon this issue. The
first body of research includes 11 studies in which nonreferred, presumably nonabused, children were observed with anatomical dolls (refer to
Everson & Boat, 1990; Koocher et al., 1995, for reviews). The studies included: August and Forman (1989); Everson and Boat (1990); Cohn (1991);
Dawson and Geddie (1991); Dawson, Vaughn, and Wagner (1992); Gabriel (1985); Glaser and Collins (1989); Geddie, Dawson, and Weunsch
(1998); Jampole and Weber (1987); Sivan, Schor, Koeppl, and Noble (1988);
and White, Strom, Santilli, and Halpin (1986). Although they varied somewhat in format, the studies focused on spontaneous and directed play
with the dolls among 2- to 8-year-old children, analyzing the children's
behavior for evidence of sexualized play. Although most of these studies
found that inspecting and touching sexual body parts was fairly common
among these nonreferred samples, play demonstrating explicit sexual activity such as intercourse or oral–genital contact was rare. Summarizing
across the 11 studies, such explicit sexual interaction with the dolls occurred in only approximately 4% of the combined sample of more than
550 children. However, there was evidence that the frequency of explicit
sexual positioning of the dolls may vary by gender, ethnicity, and socioeconomic status (SES), with 20% or more of low-SES African American
male 5-year-olds in the Everson and Boat sample displaying sexual intercourse with the dolls, especially after prompts such as "Show me what the
dolls can do together" (Boat & Everson, 1994; Everson & Boat, 1990).
Geddie et al. (1998) also found that low-SES African American children
were more likely to demonstrate sexualized behaviors with the dolls than
low-SES White children.

Consistent in all these normative research studies on nonreferred, allegedly nonabused children is that sources of sexual exposure for the
nonnaive children (children who demonstrated sexualized behaviors with
the dolls) were available for almost all the children displaying explicit
knowledge of sexual intercourse. These sources included exposure to pornography and observations of sexual activity in the home or elsewhere
(Boat, Everson, & Amaya-Jackson, 1996; Everson & Boat, 1990; Geddie et
al., 1998; Glaser & Collins, 1989). Taken as a whole, therefore, the litera-

ture on children's normative behavior with anatomical dolls fails to support the claim that the dolls stimulate sexual play in sexually naive children or that explicit sexual play with the dolls arises from innate factors independent of sexual exposure and experience.

THE SUGGESTIVENESS DEBATE II: EFFICACY
OF ANATOMICAL DOLLS TO ENHANCE RECALL

The second body of research that directly addresses the suggestiveness debate includes studies investigating the use of anatomical dolls to interview children after they have experienced a known event. This research is also relevant to questions about the efficacy of the dolls in aiding or enhancing recall completeness and accuracy. Everson and Boat (1997) reviewed the subset of this research that uses genital touch as the target event to be remembered (TBR). Their review is summarized later.

The ambiguous and sometimes conflicting findings that characterize much of the research on the efficacy of anatomical dolls is likely attributable in part to limitations in research design. These limitations include confounding the use of anatomical dolls with the introduction of other props, and with the use of leading or suggestive questioning. As a result, in several studies one cannot differentiate the effect of the dolls on recall versus the impact of other possibly distracting props or the impact of leading or suggestive questions that are paired with the dolls. Such props and leading questions may be especially deleterious to the recall accuracy of 2½- to 3½-year-olds (Bruck et al., 1995) and even 4-year-olds (Bruck, Ceci, & Francoeur, 1998).

Researchers began using genital/anal touch during medical procedures as a more ecologically valid analogue for sexual molestation. Such medically oriented touching has several obvious advantages over other target events including its physical parallel to sexual fondling and its likely salience. In addition, as is true in the case of sexual abuse, the child may experience genital touching during medical procedures as painful, distressing, or embarrassing, yet is expected to comply with an adult's request. On the other hand, sexual abuse often involves a number of features that the medical analogue fails to replicate including: genital/anal contact by someone well known if not psychologically close to the child, repeated acts over time, in an atmosphere of secrecy that may be maintained by threats and manipulation, and activities that may be intended to sexually stimulate the child and may involve active rather than passive participation by the child.

Five anatomical doll studies using private parts touch in medical procedures as an analogue for sexual abuse have been published. These studies were examined for each of the eight design features previously mentioned, features that contributed to the forensic relevance of the data obtained. A brief description of each study and its forensically relevant features is provided next. (These studies are discussed alphabetically.)

STUDIES USING MEDICAL ANALOGUE
PROCEDURES AND ANATOMICAL DOLLS

Bruck et al. (1995) investigated the usefulness of anatomical dolls and other props as interview aids among forty 2½- to 3½-year-olds ($M = 35$ months) who had experienced a routine medical examination. Half of the children had been "lightly touched" on the genital area and on the buttocks during this exam and half had not. (Unfortunately, it is unclear whether this aspect of the physical exam involved only a brief cursory look at the "private parts," perhaps in the midst of other distracting activities, or whether it included a comprehensive examination of the genital and anal areas with manual separation of the labial lips, e.g., as well as direct touching of the anus.) Within minutes of the exam, the children were interviewed by a research assistant about their experience. The children were first asked to name the body parts on an anatomical doll depicting their age and gender. They were then asked direct, yes–no (i.e., suggestive) questions as the interviewer pointed to the genital area and buttocks of the doll: "Did Dr. F. touch you here?" Each child was also offered the anatomical doll and other props (e.g., stethoscope, earscope, stick) and asked to demonstrate how the doctor had touched the child's body, then specifically the child's genitals and buttocks (e.g., "Show me on the doll how Dr. F. touched your penis"), an even more strongly leading (i.e., presumptive) question and misleading (i.e., erroneously presumptive) for children in the nongenital exam condition. The children were then shown a small plastic spoon and asked whether the doctor had done something with it (the doctor had not). If the child said "no," this was followed by a speculative question ("What could he do with the spoon. Show me on the doll."), another form of potentially highly leading questioning. Finally, the children in the genital exam condition were asked to demonstrate on their own bodies how the doctor had touched them.

Approximately 50% of the children in both the genital exam and the nongenital exam conditions answered affirmatively when asked directly whether the doctor had touched their genitals or buttocks. Thus, even though the interview occurred within 5 minutes of the TBR event, the accuracy of recall reached only chance levels. This suggested that the private parts examination the children experienced may have been somewhat cursory and not particularly salient or memorable. The fact that 50% of the children who had not had their private parts touched reported such touching in response to suggestive questioning with the dolls is concerning, but the research design does not enable us to distinguish the impact of question form from the impact of the dolls per se. It is noteworthy that warnings against the use in anatomical doll interviews of the form of suggestive question employed by Bruck and her colleagues first appeared in the late 1980s (Boat & Everson, 1988).

During the second phase of the interview when children were asked to use dolls and props to show how they were touched under even more leading questioning, again about half of the children in the nongenital exam condition erred and demonstrated some form of private parts touching. For children who had actually experienced the genital exam, the error rate reached as high as 75% under the researchers' somewhat strict criteria for scoring errors, which included rubbing or inserting a finger in the genital or anal openings and touching the buttocks when asked to show genital touching. This scoring system may have demanded an unrealistic level of precision from such young children, given that the children may not have been able to see exactly where and how the doctor had touched them, especially if they had been lying in a prone position during that part of the exam. Unexpectedly, the accuracy of the children did not significantly improve when asked to use their own bodies instead of the dolls for demonstration purposes, a finding that is discrepant with the findings of DeLoache (1995) on the comparative representational abilities of young children using dolls versus their own bodies.

Bruck and her colleagues recently added a group of 4-year-olds and reanalyzed these data (Bruck et al., 1998) with essentially the same findings. Surprisingly, however, the 4-year-old sample ($M = 49$ months) did not have better recall of genital or buttock touching than the 3-year-old cohort ($M = 35$ months). In fact, a visual comparison of subgroup means revealed that among the children experiencing the genital exam, the 3-year-olds outperformed the 4-year-olds in six out of six subgroups.

Table 16.3 presents a summary of the rating of the Bruck et al. (1995) and Bruck et al. (1998) studies on the eight design features proposed earlier for assessing forensic relevance. The studies received an acceptable rating on two of the eight criteria. The researchers examined the effectiveness of two recommended uses of anatomical dolls (anatomical model and demonstration aid) and focused on the accuracy of children's reports and demonstrations of private parts touching. However, forensic relevance was limited by the fact that the TBR event was characterized by questionable salience; memorability was not established; the use of anatomical dolls was confounded with the use of other props and with at least four different types of leading or suggestive questions; the interview format did not represent realistic, appropriate forensic standards; and the

TABLE 16.3

Comparison of Forensic Relevance of Anatomical Doll Studies

	Salient TBR Event	Memorability Established	Distinct Doll Uses Tested	Confounding of Dolls/Props Avoided	Confounding of Dolls/Leading Questions Avoided	Realistic Forensic Questioning	Credibility Check	Realistic Delay Between Event and Interview	Recall of Private Parts Touch as Focus
Bruck et al. (1995) Bruck et al. (1998)	No	No	Demonstration aid Anatomical model	No	No	No	Yes	No	Yes
Goodman et al. (1997)	Yes	Yes	Demonstration aid Anatomical model	No	No	Somewhat	No	Yes	Yes
Katz et al. (1995)	Yes	Yes	Demonstration aid Anatomical model	Yes	No	Somewhat	No	Yes	No
Saywitz et al. (1995)	Yes	Yes	Demonstration aid Anatomical model	No	No	Yes	No	Yes	Yes
Steward & Steward (1996)	Variable	Variable	Icebreaker Anatomical model	No	Yes	Somewhat	Yes	Yes	Yes

interval between target event and interview was unrealistically short. In addition, many of the children in the sample may have been under the age and developmental level (36 months) at which one can typically conduct a formal forensic interview (Hewitt, 1998; Yuille, 1996). Therefore, conclusions that are useful for practice by front-line investigators are limited.

We believe that further caution is warranted in interpreting the Bruck et al. (1995, 1998) studies because of three anomalous findings. These anomalies include:

1. the recall at only chance levels of the TBR, despite only a 5-minute delay for both age groups in the genital exam condition;
2. the failure of the 4-year-olds to outperform their 3-year-old counterparts in such a straightforward memory task, as would be expected from much of the developmental literature;
3. the failure of the children in either age group to have more accurate recall when using their own bodies for demonstration purposes versus the dolls.

These unexpected findings in concert raise questions about inherent design or procedural flaws that could overshadow any light these studies might cast on the utility of the dolls in forensic interviews.

Goodman et al. (1997) examined the effectiveness of anatomical dolls and other props in aiding children's reports of a painful medical procedure involving urethral catheterization called voiding cystourethrogram fluoroscopy. Forty-six children, ages 3 to 10 years ($M = 5.5$ years), were interviewed 1 to 4 weeks after the procedure. First, a series of prompts that became increasingly more specific were given to elicit a free recall description of the experience. Next, children were given an anatomical doll, a toy doctor kit, and a plastic tube, "to show and tell what happened." Finally, after the dolls were removed, a series of suggestive, leading, and misleading questions were asked (e.g., "Did the nurse touch you down there?").

Relatively few children (20%) mentioned during free recall that their genitals had been touched. However, during the doll/prop demonstration phase, the frequency of such reports jumped to 70%. The 3- to 4-year-olds provided somewhat more correct units of information with the dolls and props than during free recall, but they also provided more incorrect information, much of which was associated with the distracter props (e.g., tongue depressor). In contrast, the dolls and props aided the 5- to 6- and 7- to 10-year-olds in providing additional correct information without a significant increase in error. The 3- to 4-year-olds were less accurate in responding to the direct and leading questions than the two older groups, but the 5- to 6-year-olds were no less accurate than the 7- to 10-year-olds.

As seen in Table 16.3, the Goodman et al. (1997) study received acceptable ratings in five of eight categories assessing forensic relevance, but confounded doll use with other props and with leading suggestive questions in one of the phases of the interview. The interview format approximated forensic standards but apparently did not include follow-up questions for eliciting a more detailed statement from children affirming genital touch to direct, yes–no questions as a check on their credibility.

The next study in the Everson and Boat (1997) review involved 21 children ages 3 to 7 years ($M = 5.1$ years) who were seen in a child sexual abuse clinic for a forensic medical exam to assess suspected child sexual abuse (Katz, Schonfeld, Carter, Leventhal, & Cicchetti, 1995; this study differs from Bruck et al., 1998, Goodman et al., 1997, and Saywitz et al., 1991, because it utilized a sample of children referred for possible sexual abuse rather than normative samples but still used a medical procedure as an analogue for abuse). As a part of the forensic medical examination, the children underwent a series of procedures varying in painfulness and invasiveness that potentially included any or all of the following: full physical exam; external inspection of the genitalia and rectum; internal inspection of the genitalia and rectum; colposcopy; collection of cultures from the vagina, penis, throat, and/or rectum; and blood drawing. One to 2 weeks later, the children were interviewed about the medical exam using an interview format that the researchers modeled somewhat after a forensic interview protocol. First, the children were asked a series of open-ended questions designed to elicit free recall (e.g., "What happened during the visit?", "What did the doctor/nurse do?"). Next, the children were given anatomical dolls and again asked, through open-ended questions, to describe and show what happened during the medical examination. Finally, the children were asked six direct, suggestive questions, three of which addressed genital/rectal procedures (e.g., "Did the doctor touch you in your private parts?"). During this phase of questioning, the dolls were apparently available as a visual aid.

All the children underwent an external inspection of their genital/rectal areas, but the other procedures they experienced varied considerably. The analysis focused on the number of procedures correctly reported. Out of a mean number of 8.8 procedures experienced, during free recall children correctly reported only 1.4; during free recall with the dolls, 2.1; and during direct, suggestive questioning, 5.2. The number of procedures accurately reported during the last condition was significantly greater than those reported under the two free-recall conditions that did not quite differ significantly from one another ($p < .09$). There was a slight, though nonsignificant increase in the number of false reports of procedures under direct questioning with the dolls, but these false reports all involved aspects of the routine rather than private parts exam that the child may have experienced in earlier medical visits. One limitation of this study, in addition to the small sample size with limited statistical power, was the failure to report the accuracy of reports of genital/rectal procedures for each interview condition, separate from other medical procedures.

The Katz et al. (1995) study received acceptable ratings for five categories, but confounded the use of dolls and suggestive questions about genital touch. As noted earlier, the main dependent measure was the total number of medical procedures accurately recalled rather than procedures specifically involving private parts touching. Although the interview approximated a forensic format, follow-up questions were not included to assess the recall of children affirming genital touch to direct, yes–no questions.

Saywitz et al. (1991) conducted the first study of anatomical dolls using the medical procedure analogue. The participants were 72 girls, ages 5 and 7 years old, who underwent physical exams. Half of the children received a comprehensive genital/anal exam that involved visually inspecting the external genitalia and vaginal area, touching the labia, and visually inspecting and touching the anal area, while the other half received a scoliosis examination in place of the genital exam. After 1 week or 1 month, the children's memories of the physical were solicited first through free recall. Then, in the demonstration phase, the child was given several anatomical dolls (one of which had been undressed) as well as toys from a doctor's kit, and asked to show and tell what had happened. Next, the child was asked a series of erroneously presumptive questions about events known not to have happened (e.g., "How many times did the doctor kiss you?"). Finally, a doll-aided, direct questioning phase was introduced. In this phase, the interviewer held up an undressed anatomical doll, pointed to a series of body parts and asked, "Did the doctor touch you here?"

In free recall, only 22% of the children who experienced the anogenital touching reported that their genitals had been touched during the exam, and only 11% reported anal touching. In the doll/prop demonstration phase, there was no increase in the reports of genital or anal touching, but a significant increase in other details reported. This was accompanied by a minor increase in inaccurate information, most of which involved falsely reporting the use of a tongue depressor during the physical exam. Only when the children were asked direct, suggestive questions with the dolls, did the majority of children in the genital exam condition report touching of their private parts. At that point, 92% of the children affirmed genital touching and 82%, anal touching.

Of the 36 children who had not experienced genital or anal touch as part of the checkup, no children falsely reported genital/anal contact in free recall or in doll/props reenactment. However, 3 children (8%) falsely affirmed such contact when suggestive questions were paired with the dolls. Follow-up questions were used in an attempt to elicit descriptions of this reputed touching and 1 of the 3 children supplied details to support her account. This 8% error rate must be interpreted in light of the 22% of children in the genital condition falsely reporting spinal tapping (i.e., the scoliosis exam). Thus, the more common reporting errors did not involve the private parts at all as one would expect if the dolls per se, and especially exposure to their genitalia, lead children to make false reports of genital touching. It seems likely that the reporting errors obtained were more likely due to question form rather than exposure to doll genitalia.

The Saywitz et al. (1991) study addressed forensically relevant concerns in six of the eight categories. The two limitations included confounding the use of dolls with other props and confounding the use of dolls with suggestive questions in the second doll phase. It is noteworthy that this study is the only one of the six medical analogue studies reviewed that followed recommended forensic practice by beginning with open-ended questions, progressing to more specific questions including direct questions about private parts touching, and asking children follow-up questions who affirmed genital contact in response to a direct, suggestive question.

Steward and Steward (1996) conducted the only study to date using the medical analogue to examine the impact of a range of anatomically detailed materials on recall. This study is also unique in employing a more rigorous between-subjects design to assess the impact of anatomical dolls versus no dolls. The sample was composed of 130 children, ages 3 to 6, who had experienced a variety of medical procedures (including forensic medical exams for possible sexual abuse) during outpatient clinic visits in a hospital setting. The children were assigned to one of the four interview conditions, a verbal interview or one of three "enhanced" interview formats: anatomical dolls with medical props, anatomical drawings, or computer-assisted interview with anatomical drawing graphics. The children were interviewed using their assigned interview format immediately after the clinic visit, 1 month later, and 6 months later. The verbal interview format was modeled somewhat after forensic protocols and included a series of broad, open-ended questions (e.g., "What happened to you today?"), that progressed to more specific questions along with free recall prompts (e.g., "Did the doctor touch you?", "Where were you touched?") to highly suggestive questions about body touch (e.g., "Did your clothes get taken off?", "Did anybody put anything inside your body?").

The enhanced interviews closely paralleled the verbal interview with two exceptions. Early in the interview, the children in the enhanced interviews were shown an anatomical doll or drawing and asked to label body parts, including the genitalia (icebreaker use). The doll (along with a box of medical and other toy props) or drawing was available to the child for reference throughout the rest of the interview but was not referred to by the interviewer until the end. At the end of the interview, the interviewer initiated a "double check" by pointing to four body parts (ear, belly button, genitals, and buttocks/anus) on the doll or drawing and asked a direct, suggestive question, "Were you touched there?"

The three enhanced interviews were comparable in their impact on recall accuracy and were combined for most analyses. At the initial interview, among the children whose genitals had been touched during the clinic visits, only 27% in the verbal interview reported such touching while 62% in the enhanced interviews did so spontaneously during free recall, and 73% in the enhanced interviews when asked a direct, suggestive question with the doll or drawing. On the other hand, there were no false reports of genital touching in the purely verbal interview, 3% in the enhanced interview with open-ended and free-recall questions and an additional 5% when the direct, suggestive question was asked in the enhanced interview. A somewhat similar pattern of results was obtained for reports of touching of the buttocks, with only 6% accurately reporting such touching in the verbal interview and only 39% in both the enhanced and enhanced with the direct, yes–no question. Such low reports, even when asked a direct yes–no question, raise questions about the salience and memorability of the touching of the buttocks that occurred during at least some of the medical procedures under study. (Drawings, but not dolls, were used to assess touching of the buttocks, although only the dolls were used to assess anal touching.)

At the 1 month and 6 month interviews, a somewhat similar pattern emerged with substantially higher accurate reports of genital and buttock touching in the enhanced interviews and in the enhanced interviews that included direct questions about touching. However, the use of anatomically detailed interview materials resulted in an approximately 5% to 8% frequency of free-recall false reports of genital/buttock touching with an additional 5% to 10% of false reports when direct, suggestive questions were paired with the anatomical materials.

Anatomical dolls were not associated with any false reports of genital touching during free recall at either the initial or 1 month interview and only 1 at 6 months. When asked directly about genital touching with dolls or drawings, it is also noteworthy that only 1 of approximately twenty 3-year-olds in the three enhanced conditions falsely reported genital touching, and this child was not in the doll group. This finding appears to be in marked contrast with the combined (genital and buttock) false report rate of 50%+ among 3-year-olds in the Bruck et al. (1995) study. However, the dolls inexplicably elicited spontaneous erroneous reports of anal touch at all three interviews with rates ranging from 7 to 22%. At the 6-month assessment, the combined commission error rate for free recall and direct questioning about anal touch reached 36% for doll interviews. It is unclear why there was a differential impact of the dolls on reports of genital versus anal touching in this sample. Further research is needed to attempt to replicate and understand this finding, but an error rate of 22% or higher would be unacceptably high in forensic contexts.

At least two explanations seem feasible. The first relates to the impact of repeated questioning on children's recall. Anal touching, unlike many forms of genital touching, cannot be directly observed on one's body. It is possible that repeated questioning over three interviews, about a rather unusual activity during a doctor's visit, led some children to doubt their earlier memories, especially when they could not observe the affected parts during the alleged touching. In the vernacular, maybe their thinking went something like this: "The adult keeps asking me this weird question. She won't take no for an answer. Maybe she knows something I don't know. Maybe the doctor really did touch me there and I just couldn't see." Alternatively, young children are quite familiar with having their bottoms wiped after toileting. Through a type of source-monitoring error (Ceci & Bruck, 1995), perhaps some children mistakenly attributed such wiping/ touching to the doctor, especially after a delay of 6 months and repeated questioning.

As shown in Table 16.3, the Steward and Steward study scored as forensically relevant in four categories, including being the only study reviewed to examine the impact of the icebreaker doll use. The salience of the target events seemed to be variable and the memorability of certain aspects of touching was not clearly established. The use of anatomical dolls and other possibly distracting props was also confounded. Although the interview format included several realistic features of recommended practice, it did not include follow-up questioning to elicit descriptions from the children who affirmed private parts touching to the direct, suggestive questions. It is noteworthy that this is the only study of the five medical analogue studies to pair suggestive or leading questions with not only anatomical dolls but with other interview aids as well so that the impact of such questions separate from the dolls can be assessed.

Although the Steward and Steward study was in several ways the most sophisticated of the five studies, it is not without its limitations. Not the least of these is the fact that the TBR event, while all involving some form of touch, differed substantially across subjects (see critiques by Bruck & Ceci, 1996; McGough, 1996; and Ornstein, 1996).

THE NEED FOR A BODY MAP

One of the leading arguments against the use of anatomical dolls in sexual abuse assessments is the claim that there is little or no evidence for the efficacy of the dolls as interview aids. Until such scientific evidence exists, the argument goes, interviewers should refrain from using the dolls (Ceci & Bruck, 1995; Wolfner, Faust, & Dawes, 1993).

There are several points to be made about this line of reasoning. First, it is well known that the completeness and consistency of a child's autobiographical or event recall is facilitated by the availability of cues (Fivush, 1993). The younger the child, and/or the more distant the event to be remembered, the more reliant the child may be on external and, often, very specific cues (Baker-Ward, Gordon, Ornstein, Larus, & Club, 1993; Ornstein, Gordon & Larus, 1992). Visual cues and concrete props have also been shown to be more effective in evoking recall in young children than verbal cues or questions (e.g., Jones, Swift, & Johnson, 1988; Nelson & Ross, 1980; Price & Goodman, 1990; but see Salmon, Bidrose, & Pipe, 1995, and Salmon & Pipe, 1997).

It stands to reason, therefore, that visual cues (e.g., to serve as a body map) or concrete props (e.g., for reenactment) would also be helpful in child forensic interviews. Whereas anatomical dolls, regular dolls, puppets, and various types of drawings have been used in forensic interviews, none have received the research attention that anatomical dolls have received. In fact, there is growing evidence that the use of anatomical dolls as interview aids enhances children's recall (especially for children 5 years old and up) when compared to purely verbal interviews (e.g., Goodman & Aman, 1990; Goodman, Quas, Batterman-Faunce, Riddlesberger, & Kuhn, 1997; Leventhal, Hamilton, Rekedol, Tebanao-Micci, & Eyster, 1989; Steward & Steward, 1996).

DRAWINGS AS INTERVIEWING AIDS

Recently, several researchers have become interested in the utility of drawings instead of dolls and props as interviewing aids (e.g., Butler, Gross, & Hayne, 1995; Melnyk & Bruck, 1999; Steward & Steward, 1996). Two directions have been taken in the use of drawings: One involves presenting children with drawings done by others, such as drawings of anatomically correct characters, and asking children to indicate on the drawings what happened during an event (for example, where they were touched). The other direction involves having children draw what happened during an event.

There has been speculation that anatomical drawings are less suggestive than anatomical dolls because the former do not invite exploration of orifices from curious children as the latter can do (Koocher et al., 1995; Steward et al., 1996). Indeed, the use of anatomical drawings is becoming preferred to doll use by some investigative interviewers (e.g., at some of California's Multi-Disciplinary Interview Centers). As mentioned, in Steward and Steward's (1996) study of children's memory for medical procedures, one of the enhanced interview conditions involved the use of anatomical drawings to facilitate children's recall. Findings revealed that the drawings, like the dolls, were often effective in eliciting slightly more information from children about body touch when compared to non-assisted or verbal techniques only. In terms of accuracy and completeness, however, children's performance with the drawings did not differ from children's performance with the dolls. Importantly, Melnyk and Bruck (1999), recently demonstrated that, under some interview conditions, presenting children with interviewer-provided drawings can lead to errors in children's accounts when the drawings depict false events and are coupled with suggestive interviews. Thus, much research is needed to determine the efficacy of presenting dolls versus drawings.

A different approach has involved children drawing what happened during a particular event, instead of, or in addition to, describing the event (Butler, Gross, & Hayne, 1995; Melnyk & Bruck, 1999; Wilhelmy & Bull, 1999). Although children's drawings are often difficult to interpret, children's narratives about their drawings, combined with spontaneous narratives while they are drawing, have been associated with increases in children's recall performance (e.g., Butler et al., 1995; Drucker, Greco-Vigorito, Moore-Russell, & Avaltroni, 1997; Gross & Hayne, 1998). For instance, Butler et al. gave 3- to 6-year-olds a tour of a fire station and later questioned children about what happened during the tour either by asking them what happened or asking them to draw what happened. Five- and 6-year-olds who drew what happened provided more correct information than 5- and 6-year-olds who only verbally recounted what occurred. Further, no increased errors were evident in children's responses when they drew what they remembered. Note that similar beneficial effects of drawing were not evident among 3- and 4-year-olds. In two subsequent studies, Gross and Hayne (1998, 1999) extended these findings. Specifically, they found beneficial effects of drawing on children's memory up to 6 months after experiencing an event and beneficial effects of drawing on children's memory for positive as well as negative experiences. However, as with the use of interviewer-provided drawings as interview aids, the utility of children's drawings may be dependent on a child's age. Bruck et al. (1999) found that repeatedly telling young children to draw false events can induce errors and false reports in a subsequent interview. Thus, further research on the use of drawings as interview aids is needed.

THE RESEARCH CHALLENGE

In conclusion, we concur with the findings of the APA Anatomical Doll Task Force (Koocher et al., 1995) that a careful analysis of the empirical literature supports the continued use of anatomical dolls in forensic evaluations of child sexual abuse. However, many issues that bear directly on forensic practice remain unresolved. Some of these issues include the comparative impact of anatomical dolls, anatomical drawings, and regular dolls as interview aids; the relative efficacy of the various doll uses across the developmental range; the appropriate use of different types of questions with interview props like the dolls; and the possible role of interview props like the dolls in encouraging fantasy and confabulation in young children (see Everson, 1997). The medical analogue is clearly a research paradigm with substantial potential for addressing these issues. The challenge lies in designing research that is empirically sound, but forensically relevant.

REFERENCES

American Academy of Child & Adolescent Psychiatry. (1988). Guidelines for the clinical evaluation of child and adolescent sexual abuse. *Journal of the American Academy of Child and Adolescent Psychiatry, 27*(5), 655–657.

American Professional Society of the Abuse of Children. (1990). *Guidelines for psychosocial evaluation of suspected sexual abuse in young children.* Chicago: Author.

American Professional Society of the Abuse of Children. (1995). *Practice guidelines: Use of anatomical dolls in child sexual abuse assessment.* Chicago: Author.

American Psychological Association. (1991). *Statement on the use of anatomically detailed dolls in forensic evaluations.* Unpublished manuscript, APA Council of Representatives.

August, R. L., & Forman, B. D. (1989). A comparison of sexually and nonsexually abused children's behavioral responses to anatomically correct dolls. *Child Psychiatry and Human Development, 20,* 39–47.

Baker-Ward, L., Gordon, B. N., Ornstein, P. A., Larus, D. M., & Clubb, P. A. (1993). Young children's long-term retention of a pediatric examination. *Child Development, 64,* 1519–1533.

Boat, B. W., & Everson, M. D. (1986). *Using anatomical dolls: Guidelines for interviewing young children in sexual abuse investigations.* Chapel Hill: University of North Carolina, Department of Psychiatry.

Boat, B. W., & Everson, M. D. (1988). Interviewing young children with anatomical dolls. *Child Welfare, 68*(4), 337–352.

Boat, B. W., & Everson, M. D. (1993). The use of anatomical dolls in sexual abuse evaluations: Current research and practice. In G. S. Goodman & B. L. Bottoms (Eds.), *Child victims, child witnesses: Understanding and improving testimony* (pp. 47–70). New York: Guilford.

Boat, B. W., & Everson, M. D. (1994). Exploration of anatomical dolls by nonreferred preschool-aged children: Comparisons by age, gender, race, and socioeconomic status. *Child Abuse and Neglect, 18*(2), 139–153.

Boat, B. W., & Everson, M. D. (1996). Concerning practices of interviewers when using anatomical dolls in child protective services investigations. *Child Maltreatment, 1*(2), 96–104.

Boat, B. W., Everson, M. D., & Amaya-Jackson, L. (1996). Consistency of children's sexualized or avoidant reactions to anatomical dolls: A pilot study. *Journal of Child Sexual Abuse, 5*(1), 89–104.

Boat, B. W., Everson, M. D., & Holland, J. (1990). Maternal perceptions of nonabused young children's behavior after the children's exposure to anatomical dolls. *Child Welfare, 59*(5), 389–400.

Bruck, M., & Ceci, S. J. (1996). Issues in the scientific validation of interviews with young children. Commentary on Steward & Steward (1996): Interviewing young children about body touch and handling. *Monograph Series for the Research in Child Development*, 204–213.

Bruck, M., Ceci, S. J., Francoeur, E., & Renick, A. (1995). Anatomically detailed dolls do not facilitate preschooler's reports of a pediatric examination involving genital touching. *Journal of Applied Experimental Psychology, 1*, 95–109.

Bruck, M., Ceci, S. J., & Francoeur, E. (1998). A comparison of 3- and 4-year-old children's use of anatomically detailed dolls to report genital touching in a medical examination. *Journal of Applied Experimental Psychology*.

Bruck, M., Melnyk, L., & Ceci, S. J. (1999). *Draw it again Sam: The effect of drawing on children's memory and source monitoring ability*. Manuscript submitted for publication.

Butler, S., Gross, J., & Hayne, H. (1995). The effect of drawing on memory performance in young children. *Developmental Psychology, 31*, 597–608.

Ceci, S. J., & Bruck, M. (1995). *Jeopardy in the courtroom*. Washington, DC: American Psychological Association.

Cohn, D. (1991). Anatomical doll play of preschoolers referred for sexual abuse and those not referred. *Child Abuse and Neglect, 15*, 455–466.

Dawson, B., & Geddie, L. (1991). *Low income, minority preschoolers' behavior with sexually anatomically detailed dolls*. Unpublished manuscript.

Dawson, B., Vaughn, A. R., & Wagner, W. F. (1992). Normal responses to sexually anatomically detailed dolls. *Journal of Family Violence, 7*(2), 135–152.

DeLoache, J. (1995). The use of dolls in interviewing young children. In M. S. Zaragoza, J. R. Graham, G. H. Hall, R. Hirshman, & Y. S. Ben-Porath (Eds.), *Memory and testimony in the child witness*. Newbury Park, CA: Sage.

Drucker, P. M., Greco-Vigorito, C., Moore-Russell, M., & Alvatroni, J. (1997, April). *Drawing facilitates recall of traumatic past events in young children of substance abusers*. Poster presented at the biennial meeting of the Society for Research in Child Development, Washington, DC.

Everson, M. D. (1997). Understanding bizarre, improbable, and fantastic elements in children's accounts of abuse. *Child Maltreatment, 2*(2), 134–149.

Everson, M. D. (1999). *Leading and suggestive questions in the child forensic interview*. Manuscript submitted for publication.

Everson, M. D., & Boat, B. W. (1989). False allegations of abuse by children and adolescents. *Journal of the Academy of Child and Adolescent Psychiatry, 28*(2), 230–235.

Everson, M. D., & Boat, B. W. (1990). Sexualized doll play among young children: Implications for the use of anatomical dolls in sexual abuse evaluations. *Journal of the American Academy of Child and Adolescent Psychiatry, 29*, 736–742.

Everson, M. D., & Boat, B. W. (1994). Putting the anatomical doll controversy in perspective: An examination of major doll uses and related criticisms. *Child Abuse and Neglect, 18*, 113–129.

Everson, M. D., & Boat, B. W. (1997). Anatomical dolls in child sexual abuse assessments: A call for forensically relevant research. *Applied Cognitive Psychology, 11*, 55–74.

Everson, M. D., Boat, B. W., & Sanfilippo, M. (1994). *Functional uses of anatomical dolls in sexual abuse evaluations*. Unpublished manuscript.

Faller, K. (1994). Child sexual abuse allegations: How to decide when they are true. *Violence Update, 4*(6), 1–11.

Faller, K., & Corwin, D. L. (1994). Children's interview statements and behaviors: Role in identifying sexually abused children. *Child Abuse and Neglect, 19*(1), 71–82.

Fivush, R. (1993). Developmental perspectives on autobiographical recall. In G. S. Goodman & B. L. Bottoms (Eds.), *Child victims, child witnesses: Understanding and improving testimony* (pp. 1–24). New York: Guilford.

Gabriel, R. M. (1985). Anatomically correct dolls in the diagnosis of sexual abuse of children. *Journal of the Melanie Klein Society, 3*, 40–50.

Gardner, R. A. (1989). *The parent alienation syndrome and the differentiation between fabricated and genuine child sexual abuse.* Cresskill, NJ: Creative Therapeutics.

Gardner, R. A. (1992). *True and false accusations of child sexual abuse.* Cresskill, NJ: Creative Therapeutics.

Geddie, L., Dawson, B., & Wenunsch, K. (1998). Socioeconomic status and ethnic differences in preschoolers' interactions with anatomically detailed dolls. *Child Maltreatment, 3*(1), 43–52.

Glaser, D., & Collins, C. (1989). The response of young, non-sexually abused children to anatomically correct dolls. *Journal of Child Psychology and Psychiatry, 30*, 547–560.

Goodman, G. S., & Aman, C. (1990). Children's use of anatomically detailed dolls to recount an event. *Child Development, 61*, 1859–1871.

Goodman, G. S., Quas, J. A., Batterman-Faunce, J. M., Riddlesberger, M. M., & Kuhn, J. (1994). Predictors of accurate and inaccurate memories of traumatic events experienced in childhood. *Consciousness and Cognition, 3*, 269–294.

Goodman, G. S., Quas, J. A., Batterman-Faunce, J. M., Riddlesberger, M. M., & Kuhn, J. (1997). Children's reactions to and memory for a stressful event: Influences of age, anatomical dolls, knowledge, and parental attachment. *Applied Developmental Sciences*, 54–75.

Gross, J., & Hayne, H. (1998). Drawing facilitates children's verbal reports of emotionally laden events. *Journal of Experimental Psychology: Applied, 4*, 163–179.

Gross, J., & Hayne, H. (1999). Drawing facilitates children's verbal reports after long delays. *Journal of Experimental Psychology: Applied, 5*, 265–283.

Hewitt, S. K. (1998). *Assessing allegations of sexual abuse in preschool children: Understanding small voices.* Thousand Oaks, CA: Sage.

Jampole, L., & Weber, M. K. (1987). An assessment of the behavior of sexually abused and non-sexually abused children with anatomically correct dolls. *Child Abuse and Neglect, 11*, 187–192.

Jones, D. C., Swift, D. J., & Johnson, M. S. (1988). Nondeliberate memory for a novel event among preschoolers. *Developmental Psychology, 24*, 641–645.

Katz, S., Schonfeld, D. J., Carter, A. S., Leventhal, J. M., & Cicchetti, D. V. (1995). The accuracy of children's reports with anatomically correct dolls. *Developmental and Behavioral Pediatrics, 16*(2), 71–76.

Koocher, G. P., Goodman, G. S., White, C. S., Friedrich, W. N., Sivan, A. B., & Reynolds, C. R. (1995). Psychological science and the use of anatomically detailed dolls in child sexual abuse assessments. *Psychological Bulletin, 118*, 199–122.

Leventhal, J. M., Hamilton, J., Rekedal, S., Tebano-Micci, A., & Eyster, D. (1989). Anatomically correct dolls used in interviews of young children suspected of having been sexually abused. *Pediatrics, 84*(5), 900–906.

McGough, L. S. (1996). Achieving real reform: The case for American interview protocols. Commentary on Steward & Steward (1996), Interviewing young children about body touch and handling. *Monograph Series for the Research in Child Development*, 188–203.

McIver, W., & Wakefield, H. (1987). *Behavior of abused and nonabused children with anatomically correct dolls.* Unpublished manuscript.

Melnyk, L., & Bruck, M. (1999, March). *Why does drawing increase children's suggestibility?* Poster presented at the biennial meeting of the Society for Research in Child Development, Albuquerque, NM.

Naumann, R. (1985). *The case of the indecent dolls or can voodoo be professional?* Unpublished manuscript.

Nelson, K., & Ross, G. (1980). The generalities and specifics of long-term memory in infants and young children. In M. Perlmutter (Ed.), *New directions for child development: Vol. 10. Children's memory* (pp. 87–101). San Francisco: Jossey-Bass.

Ornstein, P. A. (1996). To interview a child: Implications of research on children's memory. Commentary on Steward & Steward (1996), Interviewing young children about body touch and handling. *Monograph Series for the Research in Child Development*, 215–221.

Ornstein, P. A., Follmer, A., & Gordon, B. N. (1995, April). The influence of dolls and props on young children's recall of pediatric examinations. In M. Bruck & S. J. Ceci (Chairs), *The use of props in eliciting children's reports of past events: Theoretical and forensic perspectives*. Biennial meeting of the Society for Research in Child Development, Indianapolis, IN.

Ornstein, P. A., Gordon, B. N., & Larus, D. M. (1992). Children's memory for a personally experienced event: Implications for testimony. *Applied Cognitive Psychology, 6*, 49–60.

Poole, D. A., & Lamb, M. E. (1998). *Investigative interviews of children: A guide for helping professionals*. Washington, DC: American Psychological Association.

Price, D. W. W., & Goodman, G. S. (1990). Visiting the wizard: Children's memory for a recurring event. *Child Development, 61*, 664–680.

Raskin, D. (1990, September 6). Sworn deposition in case of State of Florida vs. Bobby Finjnje, Eleventh Judicial Circuit Court, Dade County, Florida.

Rosenfeld, A. A., Bailey, R. R., Siegel, B., & Bailey, G. (1986). Determining incestuous contact between parent and child: Frequency of children touching parent's genitals in a nonclinical population. *Journal of the American Academy of Child and Adolescent Psychiatry, 25*, 481–484.

Salmon, K., Bidrose, S., & Pipe, M.-E. (1995). Providing props to facilitate children's event reports: A comparison of toys and real items. *Journal of Experimental Child Psychology, 60*, 174–194.

Salmon, K., & Pipe, M.-E. (1997). Props and children's event reports: The impact of a 1-year delay. *Journal of Experimental Child Psychology, 65*, 261–292.

Saywitz, K., Goodman, G., Nicholas, G., & Moan, S. (1991). Children's memory of a physical examination involving genital touch: Implications for reports of child sexual abuse. *Journal of Consulting and Clinical Psychology, 5*, 682–691.

Sivan, A. B., Schor, D. P., Koeppl, G. K., & Noble, L. D. (1988). Interaction of normal children with anatomical dolls. *Child Abuse and Neglect, 12*, 295–304.

Steward, M., & Steward, D. (1996). Interviewing young children about body touch and handling. *Monograph Series for the Society for Research in Child Development, 61*(4–5, Serial No. 248).

Terr, L. (1988). Anatomically correct dolls: Should they be used as a basis for expert testimony? *Journal of the American Academy of Child and Adolescent Psychiatry, 27*, 254–257.

Tylden, E. (1987). Child sexual abuse. *The Lancet, 2*, 1017.

Wescott, H., Davies, G., & Clifford, B. (1989). The use of anatomical dolls in child witness interviews. *Adoption and Fostering, 13*, 6–14.

White, S., Strom, G. A., Santilli, G., & Halpin, G. (1986). Interviewing young children with anatomically correct dolls. *Child Abuse and Neglect, 10*, 519–529.

White, S., Strom, G. A., Santilli, G., & Quinn, K. M. (1987). *Clinical guidelines for interviewing young children with anatomically correct dolls*. Unpublished manuscript, Case Western Reserve University School of Medicine, Cleveland, OH.

Wilhelmy, R., & Bull, R. (1999). *Drawing to remember: Using visual aids to interview child witnesses*. Manuscript submitted for publication.

Wolfner, G., Faust, D., & Dawes, R. (1993). The use of anatomical dolls in sexual abuse evaluations: The state of the science. *Applied and Preventative Psychology, 2*, 1–11.

Yuille, J. (1996). *Investigating allegations of child abuse: An interview protocol*. Training workshop at the 12th Annual Midwest Conference on Child Sexual Abuse and Incest, Madison, WI.

Yuille, J. C., Hunter, R., Joffe, R., & Zaparniuk, J. (1993). Interviewing children in sexual abuse cases. In G. Goodman & B. Bottoms (Eds.), *Understanding and improving children's testimony: Clinical, developmental and legal implications* (pp. 95–115). New York: Guilford.

17

Using a Structured Interview Protocol to Improve the Quality of Investigative Interviews

Kathleen J. Sternberg
Michael E. Lamb
National Institute of Child Health and Human Development

Phillip W. Esplin
Private Practice, Phoenix, AZ

Yael Orbach
National Institute of Child Health and Human Development

Irit Hershkowitz
University of Haifa, Israel

As other chapters of this book have highlighted, there remains considerable controversy concerning the extent to which children and adults are susceptible to suggestion in laboratory and forensic contexts. This controversy notwithstanding, most researchers agree that the manner in which children are questioned can profoundly affect the quality and extent of children's reports (Brainerd & Ornstein, 1991; Foley & Johnson, 1985; Lamb, Sternberg, Esplin, Hershkowitz, & Orbach, 1999; Poole & Lamb, 1998; Saywitz, 1987). In this chapter, we discuss interview methods that enhance children's ability to report experienced events accurately by relying primarily on questions that access their memory using free-recall prompts. Although children, like adults, can be affected by suggestive interviewing techniques, we demonstrate how the use of structured interview protocols can maximize the quality of information obtained from children and avoid inadvertent suggestion and thus its possible effects. We cannot change the characteristics and abilities of the children being interviewed, but we can dramatically affect the quality of children's reports by altering interviewers' styles and strategies. In this chapter, we describe the pragmatic and conceptual factors that led us to develop structured interview protocols and then illustrate how such protocols enhance the quality of information obtained from children in investigative interviews. We begin with a brief overview of expert recommendations regarding investigative interview practices, and then discuss attempts to improve the quality of investigative interviews by providing intensive training. Finally, we discuss a series of studies designed to assess the utility of increasingly detailed and complete interview guidelines.

THE PROBLEM

Since the mid-1980s, professional and public awareness of child sexual abuse has increased dramatically. This increased awareness has fostered numerous controversies concerning the best means of obtaining information from children about their experiences. In spite of improved medical technologies and other sophisticated forensic techniques, child victims' accounts of their experiences are of paramount importance to investigators because most perpetrators deny accusations of abuse and sex crimes are rarely witnessed by others. The crucial importance of information obtained from children poses unique challenges for police officers, social workers, and the family and criminal court systems, all of whom are unaccustomed to relying on children so heavily. The forensic interview is also a unique psychological context for the child witness. Children are unaccustomed to being treated as meaningful informants about important events, and everyday conversations with parents and teachers are characterized by different communicative rules than investigative interviews. In many conversations with adults, for example, children are expected to provide brief and superficial responses to questions like "How was school today?" or "Do you have much homework?" On other occasions, adults "test" children by asking questions to which the adults already know the answers. In contrast, investigative interviewers have no first hand knowledge of the alleged events under discussion. Interviewers must therefore communicate to children the importance of providing complete, detailed, and accurate accounts of their experiences.

HOW SHOULD CHILDREN BE INTERVIEWED?

A review of the literature suggests substantial consensus among researchers regarding the most desirable investigative interview techniques (American Professional Society on the Abuse of Children [APSAC] Guidelines, 1990/1997; Bull, 1992, 1995; Fisher & Geiselman, 1992; Jones, 1992; Lamb, Sternberg, & Esplin, 1998; Lamb, Sternberg, Orbach, Hershkowitz,

& Esplin, 1999; Memorandum of Good Practice, 1992; Poole & Lamb, 1998; Raskin & Esplin, 1991; Raskin & Yuille, 1989; Warren & McGough, 1996; Yuille, Hunter, Joffe, & Zaparniuk, 1993). There is universal agreement concerning the need to develop rapport with children before questioning them about the alleged criminal incidents, and it is further recommended that interviewers allow children to practice narrative elaboration techniques and have an opportunity to correct interviewers in the introductory phase of the interview (Geiselman, Saywitz, & Bornstein, 1993; Warren & McGough, 1996). Most professionals also agree that investigative interviews should be conducted using a "funnel" approach, with interviewers beginning with open-ended questions (e.g., "Tell me what happened."), using focused but not suggestive questions as little and as late in the interviews as possible. It is further accepted that responses to many focused questions (such as "Did he or she touch you?") should be followed by open-ended probes designed to elicit free-narrative accounts (e.g., "Tell me everything about that."). These recommendations are supported by findings obtained in laboratory and field studies of memory development suggesting that open-ended questions are preferable because they access recall memory processes, whereas focused questions tend to engage recognition memory processes that are more prone to error and narrow the retrieval of information considerably. When recall memory is probed using open-ended prompts, respondents attempt to provide as much relevant information as they "remember," whereas focused questions often require children to select options or confirm or reject information provided by the interviewer and exert pressure to respond, whether or not the respondent is sure of the response. In laboratory contexts, *errors of commission* (reporting details that did not happen) are much more likely to occur when recognition memory is probed using focused questions, whereas *errors of omission* (failing to report details that happened) are more likely when recall memory is probed using open-ended questions (Dent, 1982, 1986; Dent & Stephenson, 1979; Oates & Shrimpton, 1991).

Are Best Practice Guidelines Followed in Actual Investigative Interviews?

Unfortunately, actual forensic interviews are not always conducted in compliance with these expert professional guidelines, as we learned when we began closely analyzing investigative interviews. For the purposes of our research, we distinguished among four central types of interviewer utterances or prompts. *Invitations* were defined as open-ended or free recall prompts (e.g., "Tell me about that."). *Direct* prompts focused the child's attention on details that he or she has already mentioned (e.g., when the child says, "I fell off my bike," the interviewer might say,

"Where did you fall?"), whereas *option-posing* questions or prompts focused the child's attention on details that he or she had not mentioned
(e.g., "Did you fall off your bike?"). *Suggestive* questions assumed information that had not been provided by the child or implied that certain responses were expected (such as "What did he or she say?" when the child
has not mentioned that he or she spoke.). What we call suggestive
prompts are most similar to the prompts defined as "leading" in forensic
contexts. To minimize confusion, the utterances we formerly labeled
"leading" are referred to as *option-posing utterances* in this chapter because
the majority of them involved the presentation of options from which the
child had to select. When the word "leading" appears here, it has its conventional meaning. The label "focused" is used here to refer collectively to
direct, option-posing, and suggestive prompts or questions. The terms
"prompts" and "utterances" are used interchangeably in this chapter.

   Despite warnings concerning the risks of asking leading and suggestive questions, analyses of investigative interviews conducted at sites in
the United States, United Kingdom, Sweden, and Israel all revealed that
over half of the information is typically elicited from children using focused questions (e.g., Aldridge & Cameron, 1999; Cederborg, Orbach,
Sternberg, & Lamb, 2000; Craig, Scheibe, Kircher, Raskin, & Dodd, 1999;
Davies, Westcott, & Horan, 2000; Davies & Wilson, 1997; Lamb, Hershkowitz, Sternberg, Boat, & Everson, 1996; Lamb et al., 1996; Lamb, Sternberg, & Esplin, 2000; Sternberg et al., 1996; Walker & Hunt, 1998). The
overreliance on focused questions is evident regardless of the children's
age, the nature of the offense, the professional background of the interviewers, or the utilization of props and toys like anatomical dolls. A detailed analysis of 42 interviews conducted by child protection workers, for
example, revealed that interviewers "failed to allow the children to provide spontaneous narratives at their own pace without interruptions and
specific questioning. Further, they frequently introduced new, potentially
leading information during the interviews and failed to clarify the sources
of new information introduced by themselves or the children" (Warren,
Woodall, Hunt, & Perry, 1996, pp. 243). Davies and Wilson (1997) described similar problems with interviews conducted in the United Kingdom following implementation of the *Memorandum of Good Practice* (1992).
In 28% of the cases reviewed, interviewers did not attempt to elicit free-
narrative responses from children, and in an additional 43% of the cases,
interviewers allowed less than 2 minutes to obtain information from free
recall. The interviewers also asked many yes–no questions that can lead
children to confirm the interviewers' hypotheses.

   Evidence of widespread failures to implement recommended interview practices have prompted the development of numerous training
programs designed to improve the quality of investigative interviews.

Unfortunately, however, attempts to evaluate these training programs raise many doubts about their effectiveness. In her evaluation of a 3-day training program for police officers and social workers in the United Kingdom, for example, Aldridge (1992; Aldridge & Cameron, 1999) reported that training had little effect on interviewing skills. A group of experienced police officers and social workers attended lectures and seminars and were also given opportunities to practice using the new information they had learned. Following the training program, however, interviewers did not do an adequate job of rapport building and continued to ask many leading and suggestive questions, leading Aldridge (1992, p. 237) to conclude: "In order that the strategies improve and become dependably useful there must be a number of experiences of interviewing with different children in different types of situations. Such learning experience is not possible in a three-day course."

Likewise, Warren and her colleagues (1999) evaluated the impact on questioning techniques of the intensive *What Kids Can Tell Us Institute* at Cornell University. The comprehensive 10-day seminar covered a variety of related topics, including: research methods, language development, introduction to memory, cognitive and social development, and legal issues related to interviewing. In addition, the seminar fostered in depth discussions and provided opportunities to practice the skills being recommended. Although interviewers improved their understanding of the principles of good investigative interviews, they were unable to apply these principles in actual interviews, and thus their interview styles changed remarkably little. Although interviewers used fewer props and did a better job of reviewing the "ground rules" after the training than before, for example, most of the information was still obtained from children using focused questions with only one quarter of the information obtained using more general questions.

Unfortunately, our training sessions in Israel and the United States were similarly ineffective. Experienced investigators participated in intensive training seminars (approximately 40 hours in length) that began with discussions of memory processes, children's linguistic and memory capacities, factors influencing suggestibility, and step-wise interview principles. We reviewed videotaped interviews that illustrated the appropriate and inappropriate use of both open-ended and focused questions. In an attempt to personalize the learning experience, we also reviewed interviews conducted by the participants themselves, highlighting positive techniques as well as areas needing improvement. Participants were encouraged to ask questions and a considerable amount of time was devoted to discussions. In addition, we described the conceptual basis of Statement Validity Analysis (SVA) and Criterion-Based Content Analysis (CBCA) on the assumption that familiarity with these techniques might improve interview quality, as suggested by Undeutsch (1982, 1989) and Raskin and Yuille (1989).

In spite of our consistent emphasis on the importance of obtaining information using free-recall memory prompts, and numerous demonstrations of the superiority of open-ended questions, posttraining evaluations suggested that interviewers continued to rely primarily on focused questions to elicit information from children. An evaluation of interviews completed after our training in Israel ($n = 22$ interviews) revealed that only 2% of the interviewers' utterances were invitations, whereas 34% were option-posing and suggestive utterances (Lamb et al., 1996). Five percent of the information was elicited using invitations, whereas 33% was elicited using option-posing and suggestive questions. A training session in the United States was similarly ineffective (Sternberg et al., 1996). Analyses of the types of questions asked by interviewers ($n = 45$ interviews) revealed that invitations accounted for 5% of the interviewers' utterances whereas option-posing and suggestive questions comprised 49% of their utterances. Children provided 18% of the details in response to invitations and 39% in response to option-posing and suggestive questions.

These findings suggested that interviewers continued to obtain a great deal of information using option-posing and even suggestive questions after intensive training. Although the interviewers internalized the concepts and recommendations presented in the training sessions, their interviews were often disorganized and they failed to obtain narrative accounts from the children. These findings underscored how difficult it is for interviewers to implement interviewing guidelines during actual interviews and prompted us to conduct our first study using a detailed interview protocol or script.

"SCRIPTING" THE INTRODUCTORY PHASE OF THE INTERVIEW

In our first experiment, we focused on improving the organization and quality of the introductory phase of the interview (Sternberg et al., 1997). In the study, 14 Israeli youth investigators conducted a total of 51 investigative interviews of alleged victims ranging from 4.5 to 12.9 years of age. Each investigator used both of the investigative "scripts" we created. The partially scripted introductory protocols, designed to guide interviewers through the introduction and "truth and lie ceremony," both began with hypothetical questions concerning the color of the interviewer's shoes and whether he or she was sitting or standing. Thereafter, the procedures diverged as the interviewers attempted to build rapport using either focused questions or open-ended prompts. Although the questioning style differed, children in both conditions were asked about the same topics (home, school, and a recent holiday), and both scripts required approximately 7 minutes to complete. On completion of the scripted section, all children were asked the same open-ended question to initiate the substantive phase of the interview: "Now that we know each other a little bit better, I want to talk to you about the reason we are here today. I understand that something may have happened to you. I want you to tell me about it from the very beginning to the very end, as best you can remember." We hoped to determine how practicing a response style in the presubstantive phase of the interview affected the amount and quality of information provided by children in its substantive phase.

In the open-ended condition, the rapport building phase of the interview was designed to "train" the child to respond to the types of questions he or she should be asked in the substantive phase of the interview. Not only were children allowed to rehearse "narrative elaboration techniques," but they were also given opportunities to practice retrieving information from autobiographical memory, and providing additional information about aspects of events they had already mentioned. In the "direct" condition, a series of focused questions was used to develop rapport with the children. Children were denied the opportunity to practice responding to open-ended questions. In both conditions, children were given multiple opportunities to correct mistakes made by the investigators.

Prior to this study, the interviewers elicited narrative allegations that averaged 25.1 words and 7.1 details, whereas children in both conditions provided much longer and richer responses. Children in the open condition provided 2½ times as many words ($M = 250$) and details ($M = 91$) in response to the first substantive question as did children who were interviewed using direct questions ($Ms = 103$ words, 38 details). Seventy-five percent of the children in both conditions mentioned the core details of the incident in their responses to the first substantive question and a further 20% mentioned core details more vaguely. These results suggested that when children are given an opportunity to provide narrative accounts, many are indeed able to do so.

Children in the open-ended condition continued to provide more details in response to invitations than children in the direct condition. Although the open-ended training influenced the response style of the children, it had little effect on the interviewers' style of questioning, however. As soon as they had asked the first substantive question (which was the last scripted utterance), the interviewers reverted to their usual more focused style of questioning. In other words, even when children provided lengthy responses to the first open-ended substantive question, interviewers did not continue to ask open-ended questions but rather shifted to more focused questions.

The results of this experiment thus suggested that adherence to a structured interview protocol improved the organization of the interview and ensured that interviewers introduced the substantive topic (abuse) in a nonsuggestive fashion. In addition, because the structured protocol prescribed how the investigators introduced themselves, encouraged children to tell the truth and to correct the investigators' mistakes, and built rapport, these issues were always addressed whenever the interviewers followed the detailed guidelines. Because the results were so promising, we decided to conduct a study in which we expanded the "script" beyond the first substantive question.

THE PARTIALLY SCRIPTED INVESTIGATIVE PROTOCOL

Our next study was designed to determine if structuring a portion of the substantive phase of the interview would further improve the organization and quality of information obtained (see Sternberg, Lamb, Esplin, & Baradaran, 1999, for complete details). Our review of earlier interviews by the investigators who participated in the second study revealed that these interviewers, like those included in the other studies, had great difficulty following general interview guidelines. The introductory phases of their interviews were disorganized and interviewers seldom introduced themselves or the purposes of the interview comprehensibly. The children's understanding of truthfulness and the consequences of deception were probed using inappropriately complex language and the children's responses were often uninterpretable. The quality of rapport building varied greatly, and many interviewers began the substantive phase of the interview prematurely, without a clear transition from their discussion of nonsubstantive issues. Most of the information obtained from the children was elicited using option-posing and suggestive questions. Questions about the frequency of abuse were developmentally inappropriate (e.g., "How many times did it happen?") and often elicited absurd responses (e.g., "a million"), which led to counterproductive interactions between the child and the interviewer ("Oh, it couldn't have happened a million times! Remember, you need to tell me the truth."). Such responses from children raised questions about their credibility and created unnecessary tension in the interview.

Through the introductory phases, the guidelines we introduced in this study were similar to those used in the previous study. Interviewers then proceeded to ask a series of four nonleading questions to introduce the substantive issue under investigation. These four questions followed a general request for information, "Tell me the reason you came to talk with me today," to increasingly focused options if the child failed to understand the interviewers' intent. If a disclosure occurred, interviewers were instructed to say: "Tell me all about that" or "Then what happened." If a narrative allegation was elicited, the interviewers were instructed to ask, "Did that happen one time, or more than one time?" Beyond that, interviewers were free to probe for further information as necessary although all were encouraged to use open-ended prompts whenever possible.

In this study, investigative interviews with alleged victims of child sexual abuse (n = 15) were collected from seven experienced police officers prior to the implementation of the protocol. The preprotocol interviews were comparable to the protocol interviews with respect to the victims' age, relationships with the perpetrators, and offense severity. Children ranged in age from 4 to 11 years of age (M = 7.13, SD = 2.39) and reported a wide range of sexual offenses—including anal or genital penetration, fondling under or over the clothes, and sexual exposure. On completion of a week-long interview training session, these seven investigators were asked to alternate using either the Direct or Open-ended rapport-building protocols when conducting investigative interviews. Twenty-nine interviews (15 Direct Protocol, 14 Open Protocol) were included in the protocol-phase of the study.

Use of the structured protocol markedly improved the interviewers' questioning style. Compared to preprotocol interviews, in which interviewers asked an average of 4 invitations in the substantive phase of the interview, an average of 6 and 8 invitations were asked in the substantive phase of the protocol interviews for the direct and open protocols, respectively. The increased use of open-ended questions was accompanied by a decrease in the use of option-posing questions (preprotocol M = 35; postprotocol, direct M = 16, open M = 16). In addition, children in the protocol interviews provided more information from free-recall memory (direct M = 23%, open M = 36%) than children who were interviewed before investigators began using the protocol (M = 9%). Children in the open-ended condition provided more details (M = 23.5) in response to the first substantive question than children in the direct condition (M = 8.71) and children in the baseline condition (M = 1.07).

Again, these findings suggested that the use of detailed interview guidelines improved the quality of interviewers' questions and the quality of information obtained from children. Unfortunately, the protocols used in this study left extensive leeway for interviewers to continue asking other kinds of questions. Because interviewers frequently asked option-posing and suggestive questions, interviewers did not take advantage of the children's ability to recall their experiences. We therefore went one step further and developed a fully structured protocol to see whether its implementation might further improve the quality of investigative interviews in the field.

THE FULLY STRUCTURED INTERVIEW PROTOCOL

As before, the goal of the fully structured protocol was to operationalize interview guidelines based on research findings and to maximize interviewers' adherence to these guidelines. Like its predecessors, the protocol was designed to facilitate the retrieval of rich and accurate information about alleged incidents of abuse experienced by children. In the fully structured interview, we sought to maximize the amount of information obtained using free-recall prompts by exhausting open-ended questioning techniques and using option-posing questions only at the end of the interview in order to minimize the risks of contamination. The data obtained in this study are still being analyzed, but we illustrate the protocol in this section using excerpts from transcribed interviews of 4- to 12-year-old children. The quoted excerpts come from a variety of interviews to minimize the possibility that the interviewers, children, or alleged perpetrators might be recognized, but no efforts have been made to "clean up" the actual dialogue. As a result, many of the quoted utterances are not those that we recommended.

The protocol begins with the interviewer introducing him/herself to the child. This is followed by a "truth and lie ceremony" designed to establish that the child understands what it means to be truthful and to motivate the child to be truthful in the interview.

Interviewer:	My name's X and it's my job to talk to kids about things that have happened to them, okay? And one of the things that we're going to talk about here first is what's true and what's not true. Okay? And it's very, very important that we only talk about what is true, okay? When you and I are talking here in this room, okay? Just so I know that you know, I'm going to ask you a couple questions about what's true and what's not.
Child:	Okay.
Interviewer:	If I said that my shoes were green, is that true or not true?
Child:	Not true.
Interviewer:	Very good. If I said that you were standing, instead of sitting?
Child:	Not true.
Interviewer:	Very good. I can see you understand that all, huh? Good.

Following the "truth and lie ceremony," the ground rules for the interview are explained and practiced. The research described earlier in this chapter suggested that interviewers have a difficult time implementing good interview techniques even when they understand them, so we thought it was important to practice these strategies in the presubstantive phase of the interview.

Interviewer: If you don't understand or if you don't know the answer, just say, "I don't know," or "I don't understand." So if I were to ask you what's my dog's name. What would you say?

Child: I don't know.

Interviewer: That's exactly right. You don't know, do you, because you've never met my dog. So you should know that it's okay for you not to know the answer or to correct me if I say something that's wrong. Okay? So if I said that you were a 2-year-old boy, what would you say?

Child: Girl.

Interviewer: Girl, that's right, because you are a 4-year-old girl, huh? So you should know that you can correct me if I make a mistake or say something that's wrong. So if I said that you were standing up, what would you say?

Child: I'm sitting down.

Interviewer: That's exactly right because you are, you're sitting down.

After establishing that the child is allowed to correct the interviewer, the interviewer poses an open-ended question to familiarize him/herself with the child, and allow the child to provide a narrative response.

Interviewer: Well, tell me all about things you like to do at home.

Child: Pick on my sisters and brothers.

To encourage the child to provide detailed information, the interviewer asks the child to elaborate her response.

Interviewer: You do? Tell me about that.

Child: Well, they get in my stuff and I get really mad so I just pick on them.

The interviewer then asks the child to talk about school.

Interviewer: Now you told me about home, tell me all about school.

Child: I like to study Math.

Interviewer:	Tell me all about that.
Child:	I like to use a calculator to solve word problems and to be the first to get the answer.
Interviewer:	It sounds like your really like math. Now, tell me all about what you don't like about school.
Child:	Spelling.
Interviewer:	Uh-huh.
Child:	I hate spelling.
Interviewer:	Tell me about that.
Child:	Because every like week, we get like really hard words and if I miss like five, it's an F or a B.
Interviewer:	Uh-huh.
Child:	And I just don't like, like it because my teacher, because I'm with him. It's dumb.

After gently prompting for elaborated accounts of positive and negative events at school, the protocol guides the interviewer to help the child practice narrative elaboration skills. To practice the retrieval of information from episodic memory, the child is asked to describe in detail a recent holiday and again to elaborate upon that description.

Interviewer:	Tell me about Christmas day.
Child:	Christmas day?
Interviewer:	Uh-huh.
Child:	I woke up because I heard the coffee going on, because my mom, she, every morning on Christmas day, she has to have a cookie.
Interviewer:	Uh-huh.
Child:	And cup of coffee, and then we opened presents. And then I got dressed. And then I went to my grandma's, opened more presents then went to my other grandma's, opened more presents, had lunch, and then we went home. The kids took a nap. I watched, I stayed up and watched us, movies with my mom and dad and my second older sister. And then, we went to the store to get dinner. And that's it.

After obtaining a brief narrative account like this, the interviewer is encouraged to use a time segmentation technique to elicit more information about the event ("Tell me everything that happened from the time you went home until you went to the store."). Although other techniques can be used to encourage narrative elaboration (e.g., location cues like "Tell me what happened in the bedroom.") time segmentation is the most generic because every event has a beginning and an end. Accounts of events like birthday parties, the last day of school, and Easter, can be segmented into smaller units and probed for more detail.

Interviewer:	Uh-huh. Good. I want you to think really hard and tell me everything that happened from the time you went to your first grandma's to the time you went to your second grandma's on Christmas day.
Child:	Um . . . I can't remember.
Interviewer:	You can't? I want you to try really hard.
Child:	Okay. Oh yeah, we went to my first grandma's and then we had to wait for some cousins to get there and then us, waited for my aunt to get there, then everyone sat around the Christmas tree and we, my grandma passed out the presents, and we opened them. And I tried on my new clothes my grandma got me. And then we was eating the snacks and then we left and went to my other grandma's and then we opened, we had to wait for my other cousins and aunts to get there. We sat around the TV until they got there and watched *Little Rascals*. Then they got there and then we opened presents.
Interviewer:	Hmm. Then what happened?
Child:	Then we went home and the kids took and nap and then us, we, when they woke up, us we went to X to get pizza.

Because it is essential that children provide as much information as possible from episodic memory in the course of investigative interviews, children are given a second opportunity to practice describing a nonabuse-related event.

Interviewer:	All right. Well, tell me what you have been doing today from the time you got up this morning until you ate lunch.
Child:	Okay. This morning?
Interviewer:	Uh-huh.
Child:	I took my socks from my sister and then I got dressed, got my baby sister dressed, brushed my hair, gave my mom a kiss and hug, and then went off to school, ate breakfast and then after breakfast me and the new kid, her name's X.

Interviewer: Uh-huh.

Child: We went on the swings and we held hands and then, un-
               til the bell rang we done that. And then I went to reading
               and then, we had a spelling test and library. And then I
               left to go to science. And then, us we went to uh, lunch.

This interviewer again used the time segmentation technique to encourage the child to elaborate upon the account.

Interviewer: Hmm, very good. Tell me everything you did from
               lunchtime until you got here today. I don't want you to
               leave anything out.

Child: Okay. I was at recess, after lunch and then the bell just
               rang and I, some of my friends, well ex-friends, they told
               me the office wanted me. And I go, whatever. And then,
               I walked in and then I heard X, "Come to the office
               please." So I went to the office, and my teacher, us, she
               told my mom that I've been wandering the halls because
               my brother got beat up.

Interviewer: Uh-huh.

Child: He has a black eye. And I was trying to tell his teacher
               and Mr. X, the principal. And, my teacher thought I was
               wandering the halls, and she made me stand against the
               wall. And then my mom came and got me, and she left
               again to go back in the school and tell them something.
               And then we left and we kept stopping at the stop light
               and then I asked my mom for a piece of gum and she
               said, "Just a minute," and then we stopped a couple
               more times at the stop lights and I asked her again, and
               she said, "You can you wait until we get there," and I
               said, "Yes," and then we got there, out here, and then, I
               met you and then I got to color and then draw.

When interviews follow the fully structured protocol, the introductory
section of the interview requires approximately ten minutes to complete.
By the time this phase is complete, the interviewer has used partially
scripted prompts to introduce him or herself, reviewed the ground rules
of the interview, allowed the child to practice reporting two events from
episodic memory, and made him or her familiar with time segmentation
techniques for eliciting elaborated responses. The child has been given an
opportunity to describe an unpleasant event (although this is not illustrated here) and the interviewer has had an opportunity to familiarize him

or herself with the child's linguistic style and developmental capacities and develop a sense of how willing the child is to cooperate. A transition is then made into the substantive portion of the interview.

Because of uncertainties about children's developmental level, their motivation to disclose abuse, and their understanding of why they are being interviewed, the investigator must be ready with multiple nonleading options to facilitate communication. The series of questions in the structured protocol begins with an open-ended prompt, includes a variety of techniques to shift attention to the alleged events, and proceeds to more focused and, ultimately, somewhat leading questions to use when the child "fails to disclose" in response to the more open-ended probes. The substantive section of the interview begins as follows:

Now that I know you a little better, I want to talk about why you are here today. Tell me why you came to talk to me. (General open-ended question designed for the child who understands why he or she is being interviewed and is ready and willing to disclose.)

If the child does not make an allegation of abuse, the interviewer says:

It is important for me to understand why you came to talk to me. (Similar to the previous question but emphasizes the importance of understanding as a way of motivating the child.)

If no allegation is made, the interviewer asks the following questions in the order they are presented here, until the child refers to the alleged abuse:

I heard that you saw a policeman (social worker, doctor, etc.) last week (yesterday). Tell me what you talked about. (Cues children, when relevant, about recent conversations they have had with professionals. Designed to motivate reluctant witnesses by signaling that the interviewer knows that s/he has talked about the alleged incident(s) before and/or to cue the child in a nonsuggestive fashion if s/he is not sure why s/he is being interviewed.)

As I told you, my job is to talk to kids about things that might have happened to them. It's very important that I understand why you are here. Tell me why you think your mom (your dad, etc.) brought you here today. (Designed to cue children for whom parental concern is a salient feature, whether or not the children share their parents' concerns.)

Is your mom (dad, etc.) worried that something may have happened to you? (Wait for a response; if it is affirmative say:) *Tell me what they are worried about.* (Designed to cue more strongly children for whom parental concern is a salient feature.)

I heard that someone has been bothering you. Tell me everything about the bothering. (Designed to cue children who are concerned about something. The word "bother" appeared to be the least suggestive cue to focus the attention of a child who was not aware of the interviewer's purpose.)

I heard that someone may have done something to you that wasn't right. Tell me everything about that, everything you can remember. (Designed to cue children who believe or have been told that a moral transgression has occurred.)

Note that, although these questions adopt a variety of techniques to establish a shared frame of reference, none involve mentioning the alleged actions, the alleged perpetrator, the alleged location, and so on. The investigator's goal is to elicit such information from the child, even if he or she "knows" or has a hypothesis about the alleged incidents. By asking the questions as formulated in the protocol, the interviewer avoids inadvertently interjecting assumptions or biases about what might have happened.

The following example is excerpted from an interview with a 9-year-old child. It illustrates how the interviewer makes a transition to the substantive phase of the interview:

Interviewer: Okay. So tell me about why your parents brought you up here today.

Child: Because of the things that CA did to me.

The child's response suggests he is "on the same track" as the interviewer. Any disclosure, even a general disclosure like this would be followed (as it was in this interview) by the following open-ended probe:

Interviewer: Tell me everything about that, everything you can remember.

This prompt is designed to elicit a detailed account of the event using a free-recall prompt.

Child: He did things that were wrong and against the law.

This child is being cooperative but not providing specific information. The interviewer must therefore communicate the extent and richness of detail needed by encouraging the child to provide a narrative account of the reported event.

Interviewer: Tell me all about the things that were wrong and against the law.

Child: Well he started showing me stuff from books. And then he told me to come into my mom and dad's room with him and look at pictures on the Internet and, first I didn't want to but then he would kind of, made me. So he said I'll tell something about you if you like don't come or something, something like that.

The interviewer follows up with additional open-ended prompts (e.g., "And then what happened") until he or she has a general understanding of what happened.

Interviewer: And then what happened?

Child: And then my mom and dad got home so we went to bed.

Although most children recognize the purpose of the interview and disclose abuse in response to one of the nonleading questions we have formulated, some children do not. In such cases, interviewers may need to employ a more focused prompt to establish the topic of the interview. We were initially reluctant to "recommend" such prompts, but our earlier research on interviews conducted at multiple sites in the United States, United Kingdom, and Israel suggested that, when children failed to make allegations, interviewers almost always asked leading and suggestive questions. We decided, therefore, that it was valuable to formulate minimally leading or suggestive questions to give interviewers the "security" they needed should the open-ended questions "fail."

I heard that something may have happened to you at (location or time of alleged incident). (This prompt is designed for the child who either doesn't know why she or he is being interviewed or is unwilling to disclose. Focusing on the location could cue the child and perhaps reinstate the context of the alleged event. For the reluctant witness, the interviewer's "knowledge about the event" may serve as a catalyst for a disclosure.)

If the child makes a disclosure in response to this prompt, the interviewer offers an open-ended prompt for a narrative elaboration of the event, thereby minimizing the potential for inadvertent contamination of the child's account.

Tell me everything about that, everything you can remember.

If the first leading prompt fails, the interviewer may choose to ask an even more specific question that involves providing a brief (partial) description of the alleged event without mentioning the identity of the perpetrator.

I heard that someone may have (brief summary of allegation without mention of perpetrator).

Any disclosure made by the child in response to this question would be followed by an open-ended probe:

Tell me everything about that, everything you can remember.

The use of leading or suggestive questions to initiate the substantive discussion may contaminate the child's response or even foster a false allegation. As a result we urge interviewers to examine carefully the risks associated with leading questions against the importance of obtaining information from possible victims at this stage of the investigation, given the amount of forensic information already available and the extent of their concerns about protection. Even risky questions are sometimes necessary, but interviewers should also consider terminating the interviews and resuming on another occasion.

When leading or suggestive prompts elicit allegations, the interviewer proceeds to obtain further information as we have suggested, using nonleading open-ended prompts as extensively as possible. Following a focused question with an open-ended question in this way is referred to by our research team as "pairing." Although we encourage interviewers to remain open to the possibility that the child did not experience abuse and therefore has nothing to disclose, interviewers are often concerned that children who fail to disclose will be pressured to disclose by other professionals in subsequent interviews. If they deem it necessary to use leading or suggestive question, the protocol provides them with less damaging options than are typically generated and instructs them to follow up with open-ended prompts.

To maximize the amount of information obtained, it is crucial to obtain information about specific events, particularly if multiple incidents have taken place and the child's initial account is drawn from a more skeletal script memory. Because children's initial accounts are often somewhat generic and do not make clear whether the children were abused on one or more occasions, the protocol instructs interviewers to address this issue early in the substantive phase of the interview. Although interviewers need to probe children for additional information about the first event mentioned, it is important for interviewers to determine whether one or more incidents were experienced before proceeding.

Interviewer: Did that happen one time or more than one time?

Child: It happened bunches of times, well different things happened. It happened every Tuesday which is about a period of a week, 'cause my mom and dad were gone all night. It didn't happen every Tuesday 'cause sometimes he was gone. It happened most of the time.

This child's response indicates that there were multiple events and that they differed from one another. Although most children are capable of providing detailed information about distinct events, interviewers often fail to convey they are interested in specific descriptions of each (or, at least, many) events. The structured protocol guides interviewers to communicate clearly the need for accounts of specific events, directing the child to describe the most accessible events in greatest detail. At this stage, therefore, the interviewer should focus the child's attention on the most recent event:

Interviewer: Okay. Tell me about the last time something happened.

Child: The very, very last time?

The last event experienced by the child is most likely to be remembered well because it involves the shortest time delay (Flin, Boon, Knox, & Bull, 1992; Lamb et al., 1998). Furthermore, for younger children in particular, the most recent event is least likely to be contaminated by postevent influences (Poole & White, 1993).

Interviewer: The very, very last time.

Child: He tried to get in my bottom and he did once but nothing happened.

Interviewer: Okay. Tell me about the time that he tried to stick you in your bottom.

Child: He just asked me to move up and down so his penis would go in and out.

Once it is clear that the child is focused on a specific event, the interviewer probes the child for more information about that event using open-ended prompts, including the time segmentation procedures that were practiced in the rapport-building phase of the interview.

Interviewer:	Tell me all about how that time got started.
Child:	We were in the bathroom because he thought no one would see him there 'cause it was in the bathroom.
Interviewer:	Okay. So you're in the bathroom and tell me about what happens after you guys get in the bathroom. What's the very first thing that happens?
Child:	Nothing. We just, he just sticks it up my bottom and then he did that like two times and that was all.
Interviewer:	Where were your clothes?
Child:	I still had my shirt on and he took off my pants.

After the interviewer has obtained as much forensically valuable information as possible about the last event, he or she then turns attention to another event using the same series of prompts illustrated here. On occasion, children provide some details about the diverse incidents in their initial response (e.g., "Well, it happened in the bathroom, when we were camping, and while I was watching a scary movie with him."). In such cases, the interviewer can use these details, rather than temporal cues ("first time," "last time") to reference specific incidents, asking for example, about "the time in the bathroom," or "the time when you were camping."

Interviewer:	Okay, you told me about the time you looked at pictures on the internet, the time in the bathroom. Tell me about another time.
Child:	Well, he'd just tell me to do some gross stuff to him.
Interviewer:	(Pause) It's really important for me to understand exactly what happened.
Child:	Well, he would like tell me to get Vaseline and rub it on his private and then we'd go into there and watch pictures. . . . And that was really all we did for the first few times.
Interviewer:	So he would have you rub that Vaseline on his private?
Child:	Right here.
Interviewer:	Okay. So you're motioning to kind of your front region. So, tell me about, you said that he asked you to get Vaseline and then rub it on his private. Tell me about how that would happen.
Child:	I would get some out of the thing and just rub it on it.
Interviewer:	What would you rub it on it with?
Children:	Just my hands.
Interviewer:	. . . Where were his clothes?

Child: He had his shirt on and his pants were just pulled down.

Note that, after exhausting the time segmentation ("before," "after," "then what") prompts, interviewers use cue-questions (references to salient details already mentioned by the child) to prompt the child for additional narrative accounts of some aspects of the event. Location prompts (e.g., "You mentioned that something happened in the kitchen. Tell me about that time.") and material prompts ("You said he put some cream on his finger. Tell me all about that.") are often used to obtain more details about some aspect of the event.

After obtaining as much information as possible using open-ended questions and prompts, interviewers may need to ask leading questions to address forensically important issues not mentioned by the child. The potential risk of contamination posed by an option-posing question can be minimized if it is "paired" with an open-ended prompt.

Interviewer: Were your clothes on or off?
Child: Off.
Interviewer: Tell me everything about how they got off.

After obtaining as much information as the children seem able to provide, the script suggests that interviewers ask children if there is additional information they would like to provide and subsequently move to the final phase of the interview, discussing neutral events before closing.

Interviewer: Okay. Um, so what are you guys gonna do later on today? You don't have school.
Child: I'm practicing, do jobs and go play.
Interviewer: What do you practice? You talked about practicing before.
Child: I practice the piano.
Interviewer: Ah, you're a pianist. So do you take lessons or are you just teaching yourself?
Child: Well we're out of lessons for the summer.
Interviewer: Uh, huh (affirmative).
Child: So, and then, we usually have to practice a half an hour and 45 minutes cause the older ones have to practice 45 minutes because my mom (unclear) the piano. And now J. starting to be playing 45 minutes and so they split it like not in half but, you know.
Interviewer: Uh, huh (affirmative).

Child:	So I have to only practice 15 minutes and they only have to practice 20 cause it's summer. But my brother, he likes to practice, he likes the piano a lot. And so he just practices like an hour a day. He doesn't really care.
Interviewer:	Which brother's that?
Child:	L. He's my oldest brother.
Interviewer:	Oh. He likes playing the piano. Well that's cool. So you guys have a piano at your house so you can practice while you're at home.
Child:	Uh, huh (affirmative).

Summary

In sum, the purpose of the structured protocol is to translate empirically based research guidelines into a practical interview tool that can be used by investigators conducting forensic interviews. Our own experiences, and several systematic analyses, demonstrated that interviewers have difficulty translating guidelines into practice, and the structured protocol provides an alternative means of ensuring that investigators benefit from the most recent research findings when conducting investigative interviews.

The structured protocol is designed to improve the quality of information obtained in investigative interviews in several ways. By providing a clear road map of the structure of the interview, first of all, the protocol should yield more organized interviews. Interviewers who follow the protocol will not suddenly realize that they have forgotten to motivate the child to tell the truth, and when confronted by reluctant or confused children, interviewers can follow carefully considered routes instead of trying to formulate nonleading questions on the spot. The structure imposed by the protocol frees up the interviewer to focus on unique aspects and special challenges of the interviews. Second, practice following the order and wording of the questions should help interviewers operationalize general principles, such as the need to obtain narrative accounts from free-recall memory before using focused prompts. Third, by introducing open-ended questions and prompts for detail in the introductory phase of the interview, the protocol trains children to be informative and should thus maximize the quality of information obtained from children about their alleged experiences of abuse. In actual forensic interviews, of course, it is seldom possible to determine the accuracy of children's statements. The protocol is designed to maximize the amount of information elicited using recall-memory prompts, because information elicited in this way is more likely to be accurate (see Lamb et al., 1999, for a review). In addition, the structured interview minimizes opportunities for contamination of the children's accounts. In the next section, we use illustrative data from two ongoing research projects to show how the structured protocol helped to bridge the gap between theory and practice.

EVALUATING THE STRUCTURED PROTOCOL IN ACTUAL FORENSIC INVESTIGATIONS

The first fully structured protocol was implemented by the Israeli Youth Investigative Service in a study designed to examine how visiting the scene of the alleged sexual abuse would stimulate the recall of information from children (see Hershkowitz et al., 1998, for an analysis of some of the data obtained in this study). Fifty-one 4- to 13-year-old children ($M = 9.5$ years) who had reported being victims of sexual abuse, including anal and oral penetration ($n = 7$), fondling under ($n = 18$) or over ($n = 11$) their clothes, and sexual exposure ($n = 15$), were interviewed using a structured protocol (similar to the protocol described in the previous section) in an investigator's office and then at the scene of the alleged abuse. Only cases involving extrafamilial perpetrators of abuse that allegedly occurred outside the home were included in the study.

To evaluate the extent to which the structured protocol improved the quality of interviews conducted by investigators, we compared 55 interviews conducted using the protocol with 50 similar forensic interviews conducted by the same investigators before the protocol was implemented. Interviewers in the protocol condition were also provided with individual and group supervision every 2 weeks. In the individual sessions, supervisors familiar with the protocol provided detailed feedback on transcripts of interviews conducted by the investigators. In group sessions, transcribed interviews were used to illustrate and foster discussion about more general topics (e.g., motivating reluctant witnesses; developmental differences in response patterns).

Analyses revealed drastic improvements in the organization of the interview, the quality of questions asked by interviewers, and the quality of information provided by children (see also Orbach et al., 2000). Fifty-three of the fifty-five 4- to 13-year-old children interviewed using the structured protocol made a disclosure in response to the first transitional utterance ("Do you know why you came here today"), 1 disclosed in response to the next prompt ("I understand you told X that something may have happened to you"), and 1 disclosed in response to a suggestive prompt. Ten of the children not only disclosed but spontaneously provided a narrative account of their experiences in response to the first substantive prompt, 46 children provided a narrative account either then or in response to the first invitation, "Tell me everything about that from the beginning to the end as best you can remember," and 9 children provided a narrative account later in the interview. Children provided an average of 51 spontaneous details in their first narrative response, and the interviewers asked more than five times as many open-ended invitations ($M = 30\%$) as they did in comparable interviews conducted before the structured protocol was introduced ($M = 6\%$). The number of option-posing questions dropped by almost 50% as well (Preprotocol $M = 33\%$, Protocol $M = 18\%$), and much more of the information was obtained using free recall rather than investigator-directed recognition probes. In addition, the interviewers became better critics of their own and their colleagues' interviews.

In another study, we examined investigative interviews conducted by police officers in a large city in the Western United States (Sternberg, Lamb, Orbach, Esplin, & Mitchell, in press). For purposes of the preliminary comparisons described here, 45 interviews conducted using a structured protocol ("Protocol Interviews") were compared with 45 interviews ("Baseline Interviews") that were conducted from 1994 to 1998, before the agency began participating in the research project. Four experienced police officers interviewed children who averaged 8.2 years of age. The offenses alleged by the children included exhibitionism ($n = 3$), touching over the clothes ($n = 15$), touching under the clothes ($n = 57$), and penetration ($n = 17$). Thirty-four of the allegations involved perpetrators who were immediate or extended family members, 54 involved familiar perpetrators who were not family members, and 2 cases involved unfamiliar perpetrators. The Protocol and Baseline interviews were matched with respect to the child's age. In addition to a 3-day-long training seminar in which the structured protocol was introduced, interviewers attended both individual and group training sessions every 6 weeks. Between these sessions, they received written comments on their interviews.

Preliminary analyses suggest a substantial improvement in the quality of interviews being conducted using the structured protocol. In addition to being better organized, interviewers used more open-ended prompts and fewer option-posing and suggestive questions than in the comparison (baseline) interviews. In the baseline condition, only 10% of the interviewers' questions were invitations, whereas in the protocol interviews 35% of the interviewers' questions were invitations. The total amount of information elicited from free-recall memory also increased dramatically; whereas only 16% of the information ($M = 32$ details) was elicited using free recall in the preprotocol interviews, 49% of the information ($M = 94$ details) was obtained using free recall in the protocol interviews. Use of the protocol also reduced the use of directive (baseline $M = 44\%$, protocol $M = 35\%$), option-posing (baseline $M = 35\%$; protocol $M = 23\%$), and suggestive (baseline $M = 11\%$; protocol $M = 7\%$) prompts. In the baseline interviews, 41% of the information was obtained using option-posing and suggestive questions compared with 24% in the protocol interviews. Interestingly and importantly, this pattern of results was similar regardless of the children's age. Although younger children provided shorter and less detailed responses than older children, analyses of interviews with 4- to 6-year-old children revealed that the interviewers relied heavily on invitations (34% of their questions) and succeeded in eliciting a substantial amount of information (49%) using free-recall prompts. These findings are encouraging in light of the difficulties interviewers encounter when interviewing young children.

Together, the results of these two studies suggest that use of a structured interview protocol, in conjunction with detailed feedback and intensive training sessions, enhanced the quality of the interviews conducted in these research sites. The structured protocol provided investigative interviewers with an effective tool for interviewing children ranging from 4 to 14 years of age about a wide range of alleged sexual offenses by a variety of different perpetrators. In our experience, with both partially and extensively structured interview protocols, we have found that the more structured the protocol, the higher the quality of the interviews.

Some researchers and practitioners have expressed the concern that structured protocols might interfere with the interviewers' individual styles. A review of the excerpts we have included here illustrates that the structured protocol leaves room for interviewer spontaneity and does not lead to a monotonous recitation of scripted questions. On the contrary, our data suggest that, when interviewers follow a protocol that structures the interview and standardizes the wording of some major prompts, they can pay more attention to what the children are saying.

CONCLUSION

Several recent high profile cases have illustrated that inappropriate questioning techniques by investigative interviewers interfere with the investigation and resolution of child abuse cases. Because sex crimes are rarely witnessed by others and often leave no clear physical evidence, children's accounts of their experiences are central to the investigative process, and the responsibility for obtaining an accurate and complete account rests with investigative interviewers who are often overburdened and undertrained. Although there is widespread consensus about how children should be interviewed, a review of the interviews conducted in several countries suggests that interviewers have difficulty adhering to the recommended guidelines. Although many appear to understand proper interview techniques, they have difficulty translating these concepts into practice. Even after intensive training, interviewers continue to rely primarily on focused questions (including many option-posing and suggestive questions) instead of exhausting more open-ended questioning strategies first. This reliance on inadequate questioning techniques compromises the quality of investigative interviews, impedes the fact-finding process, and makes it difficult to protect victimized children and innocent adults.

In this chapter, we have illustrated how the use of a structured protocol can facilitate the interviewer's task and improve the quality of information obtained. Using data from several studies, we have shown how use of a structured protocol, in conjunction with individual and group feedback, helps interviewers implement interview guidelines and conduct more organized and less risky interviews.

Although the structured interview protocol described in this chapter is a promising tool for improving the quality of interviews, we view it as an evolving product and plan to incorporate and empirically evaluate new research findings as they emerge. Much remains to be learned about the specific components of the protocol, and about the extent to which it addresses the needs of young children, reluctant witnesses, and children who have disabilities or other handicaps.

ACKNOWLEDGMENT

The authors are grateful to Ann Graffam Walker for helpful comments on an earlier draft of this chapter.

REFERENCES

Aldridge, J. (1992). The further training of professionals dealing with child witnesses. In H. Dent & R. Flin (Eds.), *Children as witnesses* (pp. 231–244). Chichester, England: Wiley.

Aldridge, J., & Cameron, S. (1999). Interviewing child witnesses: Questioning strategies and the effectiveness of training. *Applied Developmental Science, 3,* 136–147.

American Professional Society on the Abuse of Children. (1990, revised 1997). *Guidelines for psychosocial evaluation of suspected sexual abuse in young children.* Chicago: Author.

Brainerd, C. J., & Ornstein, P. A. (1991). Children's memory for witnessed events: The developmental backdrop. In J. Doris (Ed.), *The suggestibility of children's recollections* (pp. 10–20). Washington, DC: American Psychological Association.

Bull, R. (1992). Obtaining evidence expertly: The reliability of interviews with child witnesses. *Expert Evidence, 1,* 5–12.

Bull, R. (1995). Innovative techniques for the questioning of child witnesses, especially those who are young and those with a learning disability. In M. Zaragoza, J. R. Graham, G. C. N. Hall, R. Hirschman, & Y. S. Ben-Porath (Eds.), *Memory and testimony in the child witness* (pp. 179–194). Thousand Oaks, CA: Sage.

Cederborg, A. C., Orbach, Y., Sternberg, K. J., & Lamb, M. E. (2000). Investigative interviews of child witnesses in Sweden. *Child Abuse and Neglect, 24,* 1355–1361.

Craig, R. A., Sheibe, R., Kircher, J., Raskin, D. C., & Dodd, D. (1999). Effects of interviewer questions on children's statements of sexual abuse. *Applied Developmental Science, 3,* 77–85.

Davies, G. M., Westcott, H. L., & Horan, N. (2000). The impact of questioning style on the content of investigative interviews with suspected child sexual abuse victims. *Psychology, Crime, and Law, 6,* 81–97.

Davies, G. M., & Wilson, C. (1997). Implementation of the *Memorandum*: An overview. In H. Westcott & J. Jones (Eds.), *Perspectives on the Memorandum: Policy, practice and research in investigative interviewing* (pp. 1–12). Aldershot, England: Arena.

Dent, H. R. (1982). The effects of interviewing strategies on the results of interviews with child witnesses. In A. Trankell (Ed.), *Reconstructing the past: The role of psychologists in criminal trials* (pp. 279–297). Stockholm: Norstedt.

Dent, H. R. (1986). Experimental study of the effectiveness of different techniques of questioning mentally handicapped child witnesses. *British Journal of Clinical Psychology, 25,* 13–17.

Dent, H. R., & Stephenson, G. M. (1979). An experimental study of the effectiveness of different techniques of questioning child witnesses. *British Journal of Social and Clinical Psychology, 18,* 41–51.

Fisher, R. P., & Geiselman, R. E. (1992). *Memory-enhancing techniques for investigating interviewing: The cognitive interview.* Springfield, IL: Thomas.

Flin, R., Boon, J., Knox, A., & Bull, R. (1992). The effect of a five month delay on children's and adult's eyewitness memory. *British Journal of Psychology, 83,* 323–336.

Foley, M. A., & Johnson, M. K. (1985). Confusions between memories for performed and imagined actions: A developmental comparison. *Child Development, 56,* 1145–1155.

Geiselman, R. E., Saywitz, K. J., & Bornstein, G. K. (1993). Effects of cognitive questioning techniques on children's recall performance. In G. S. Goodman & B. L. Bottoms (Eds.), *Child victims, child witnesses: Understanding and improving testimony* (pp. 71–93). New York: Guilford.

Hershkowitz, I., Orbach, Y., Lamb, M. E., Sternberg, K. J., Horowitz, D., & Hovav, M. (1998). Visiting the scene of the crime: Effects on children's recall of alleged abuse. *Legal and Criminological Psychology, 3,* 195–207.

Jones, D. P. H. (1992). *Interviewing the sexually abused child.* Oxford: Gaskell.

Lamb, M. E., Hershkowitz, I., Sternberg, K. J., Boat, B., & Everson, M. D. (1996). Investigative interviews of alleged sexual abuse victims with and without anatomical dolls. *Child Abuse and Neglect, 20,* 1239–1247.

Lamb, M. E., Hershkowitz, I., Sternberg, K. J., Esplin, P. W., Hovav, M. Manor, T., & Yudilevitch, L. (1996). Effects of investigative style on Israeli children's responses. *International Journal of Behavioral Development, 19,* 627–637.

Lamb, M. E., Sternberg, K. J., & Esplin, P. W. (1998). Conducting investigative interviews of alleged sexual abuse victims. *Child Abuse and Neglect, 22,* 813–823.

Lamb, M. E., Sternberg, K. J., & Esplin, P. W. (2000). Effect of age and delay on the amount of information provided by alleged sex abuse victims in investigative interviews. *Child Development, 71,* 1586–1596.

Lamb, M. E., Sternberg, K. J., Orbach, Y., Hershkowitz, I., & Esplin, P. W. (1999). Forensic interviews of children. In A. Memon & R. A. Bull (Eds.), *Handbook of the psychology of interviewing* (pp. 253–277). Chichester, England: Wiley.

Memorandum of good practice. (1992). London, England: Her Majesty's Stationery Office.

Oates, K., & Shrimpton, S. (1991). Children's memories for stressful and non-stressful events. *Medical Science and Law, 31,* 4–10.

Orbach, Y., Hershkowitz, I., Lamb, M. E., Sternberg, K. J., Esplin, P. W., & Horowitz, D. (2000). Assessing the value of structured protocols for forensic interviews of alleged child abuse victims. *Child Abuse and Neglect, 24,* 733–752.

Poole, D. A., & Lamb, M. E. (1998). *Investigative interviews of children: A guide for helping professionals*. Washington, DC: American Psychological Association.

Poole, D. A., & White, L. T. (1993). Two years later: Effects of question repetition and retention intervals on the eyewitness testimony of children and adults. *Developmental Psychology, 29*, 844–853.

Raskin, D. C., & Esplin, P. W. (1991). Statement validity assessments: Interview procedures and content analyses of children's statements of sexual abuse. *Behavioral Assessment, 13*, 265–291.

Raskin, D., & Yuille, J. (1989). Problems of evaluating interviews of children in sexual abuse cases. In S. J. Ceci, M. P. Toglia, & D. F. Ross (Eds.), *Perspectives on children's testimony* (pp. 184–207). New York: Springer-Verlag.

Saywitz, K. J. (1987). Children's testimony: Age-related patterns of memory errors. In S. J. Ceci, M. P. Toglia, & D. F. Ross (Eds.), *Children's eyewitness memory* (pp. 36–52). New York: Springer-Verlag.

Stellar, M., & Boychuk, T. (1992). Children as witnesses in sexual abuse cases: Investigative interview and assessment techniques. In H. Dent & R. Flin (Eds.), *Children as witnesses* (pp. 47–71). Chichester, England: Wiley.

Sternberg, K., Lamb, M. E., Esplin, P. W., & Baradaran, L. (1999). Using a scripted protocol to guide investigative interviews: A pilot study. *Applied Developmental Science, 3*, 70–76.

Sternberg, K. J., Lamb, M. E., Hershkowitz, I., Esplin, P. W., Redlich, A., & Sunshine, N. (1996). The relationship between investigative utterance types and the informativeness of child witnesses. *Journal of Applied Developmental Psychology, 17*, 439–451.

Sternberg, K. J., Lamb, M. E., Hershkowitz, I., Yudilevitch, L., Orbach, Y., Esplin, P. W., & Hovav, M. (1997). Effects of introductory style on children's abilities to describe experiences of sexual abuse. *Child Abuse and Neglect, 21*, 1133–1146.

Sternberg, K. J., Lamb, M. E., Orbach, Y., Esplin, P. W., & Mitchell, S. (in press). Use of a structured investigative protocol enhances young children's reponses to free recall prompts in the course of forensic interviews. *Journal of Applied Psychology*.

Undeutsch, U. (1982). Statement reality analysis. In A. Trankell (Ed.), *Reconstructing the past: The role of psychologists in criminal trials* (pp. 27–56). Stockholm, Sweden: Norstedt & Sons.

Undeutsch, U. (1989). The development of statement reality analysis. In J. C. Yuille (Ed.), *Credibility assessment* (pp. 101–120). Dordrecht, The Netherlands: Kluwer.

Walker, N., & Hunt, J. S. (1998). Interviewing child victim–witnesses: How you ask is what you get. In C. R. Thompson, D. Herrman, J. D., Read, D. Bruce, D. Payne, & M. P. Toglia (Eds.), *Eyewitness memory: Theoretical and applied perspectives* (pp. 55–87). Mahwah, NJ: Lawrence Erlbaum Associates.

Warren, A. R., & McGough, L. S. (1996). Research on children's suggestibility: Implications for the investigative interview. *Criminal Justice and Behavior, 23*, 269–303.

Warren, A. R., Woodall, C. E., Hunt, J. S., & Perry, N. W. (1996). "It sounds good in theory, But. . . .": Do investigative interviewers follow guidelines based on memory research? *Child Maltreatment, 1*, 231–245.

Warren, A. R., Woodall, C. E., Thomas, M., Nunno, M., Keeney, J., Larson, S., & Stadfeld, J. (1999). Assessing the effectiveness of a training program for interviewing child witnesses. *Applied Developmental Science, 3*, 128–135.

Yuille, J. C., Hunter, R., Joffe, R., & Zaparniuk, J. (1993). Interviewing children in sexual abuse cases. In G. S. Goodman & B. L. Bottoms (Eds.), *Child victims, child witnesses: Understanding and improving testimony* (pp. 95–115). New York: Guilford.

18

The Effects of Social Support on the Accuracy of Children's Reports: Implications for the Forensic Interview

Suzanne L. Davis
Decision Quest, Inc.

Bette L. Bottoms
University of Illinois at Chicago

Over the past two decades, child abuse has steadily gained recognition as a major societal and legal problem. This deserved recognition has brought increasing numbers of children into contact with the legal system (Goodman, Emery, & Haugaard, 1998; Myers, 1992). When children enter our legal system, a system that was designed for adults, alarming issues are raised. One particularly troubling issue is the reliability of children's testimony. Given the inherently private nature of an act of child abuse, especially child sexual abuse, there is often no evidence of abuse other than a child's report (Myers, 1992, 1998). Thus, a child's word is central to investigation and prosecution efforts. But can it be trusted? There are few topics these days that are as emotionally charged or hotly debated within public, private, and professional circles as the accuracy of children's testimony. And with good reason—children's reports can prompt investigations that lead to the discovery and prosecution of actual child abuse, or investigations that target innocent adults for abuse they did not commit. In any legal case that is built primarily on eyewitness testimony—adult or child testimony—there is the potential for justice or injustice, depending on the accuracy of the testimony.

To approach the ultimate goals of uncovering truth and reaching just outcomes in child abuse cases, we can turn to social science for help. There we find a growing body of research that is well represented in this volume and aimed at understanding children's capabilities and discovering techniques for maximizing the accuracy of children's testimony. In typical child testimony studies, children witness or participate in an event; then they are given a mock forensic interview during which they are asked to report what happened. During this interview, child participants are asked various types of questions that differ along a continuum of suggestibility, ranging from the least suggestive, most open-ended free-recall questions (e.g., "What happened when you were here last time?") to more focused, cued-recall questions that usually take two forms: "misleading" questions, which are the most suggestive (e.g., "When you were here, you played with toys, didn't you?" when no such playing occurred) and "specific" questions, which are focused but less suggestive or coercive ("When you were here, did you play with toys?"). Because child witness researchers wish to generalize their results to the context of actual sexual abuse investigations, interview questions are sometimes misleading about "abuse-relevant" events (e.g., "When you were here, the babysitter kissed you, didn't he?"). The degree to which nonabused children give accurate accounts about past events, particularly the degree to which they can resist interviewers' misleading suggestions about things that did not happen, is of primary concern.

Using this paradigm, researchers have studied a variety of factors that affect the accuracy of children's eyewitness reports (for reviews, see Ceci & Bruck, 1993; Davis, 1998b; Goodman et al., 1998; Warren & McGough, 1996). One such factor is social support, a situational, socioemotional variable. In this chapter, we discuss the psychological construct of social support, review literature examining the effect of social support on children's eyewitness accuracy and suggestibility, and present findings from our own research investigating the psychological mechanism that may account for some of the effects of social support.

SOCIAL SUPPORT AND CHILDREN'S TESTIMONY: A REVIEW OF PREVIOUS RESEARCH

Social support has been of interest to researchers across disciplines such as psychology, sociology, and communications. In these disciplines, *social support* is conceptualized as a form of interaction or communication that fosters a feeling of well-being in the target (e.g., Burleson, Albrecht, Goldsmith, & Sarason, 1994). Social support has been operationally defined in various ways, such as informational support (i.e., providing advice), emotional support (i.e., providing affection and nurturance), network support (i.e., being a part of a common group), and esteem support (i.e., the bolstering of self-esteem over time by others; Burleson et al., 1994; Cutrona & Russell, 1990; Tardy, 1994; Zelkowitz, 1989). Perceived social support generally leads to better physical and emotional health, and more fulfilling social relationships (e.g., Sarason, Sarason, & Pierce, 1990).

There is growing interest in the effect of social support on children's eyewitness reports, because the settings that child witnesses encounter (e.g., pretrial forensic interviews, the courtroom) can be either socially supportive or intimidating. For example, children may be questioned by a cold, intimidating interviewer or by a friendly, warm person. Children may be left alone during an interview or on the witness stand, or they may be allowed to have a supportive person by their side (Myers, 1996). Conventional wisdom about the effects of social support is mixed: Some professionals argue for child-friendly interview techniques (e.g., Wood, McClure, & Birch, 1996) and for the presence of support persons, reasoning that social support will be emotionally calming and therefore conducive to children giving accurate reports of past events. Others argue that nearby support persons may be distracting at best and suggestive at worst, and that children who are interviewed in a socially supportive manner may want to give answers that will please their friendly interrogator rather than answers that are accurate (for discussion, see Bull, 1998).

Psychological research and theory provide compelling reasons to expect beneficial effects of social support on children's eyewitness reports. Developmental research demonstrates that young children are sensitive to social context cues, and in particular, children respond to social support. For example, children have been found to regulate their emotional expression to receive social support (e.g., Zeman & Shipman, 1996). Perceived social support has been found to enhance adolescents' and adults' psychological well-being and perceived ability to cope with life stress (for reviews, see Cohen & Wills, 1985; Wolchick, Sandler, & Braver, 1990), grade-school students' academic performance (Harris & Rosenthal, 1985; Rosenthal & Jacobson, 1968), and the accuracy of students' short-term recall (Kelley & Gorham, 1988). The latter findings would be predicted by current developmental theories that stress the importance of environmental support for children to reach their maximum levels of cognitive performance (e.g., Fischer, 1980; Vygotsky, 1978), in contrast to more strictly age- or stage-bound developmental theories (Inhelder & Piaget, 1958).

In light of such research and theory, psychological researchers interested in children's eyewitness testimony have theorized that social support will help, not hinder, report accuracy. Researchers have investigated the effect of social support on children's eyewitness reports in two lines of research. In both, social support has been conceptualized as the provision of emotional support during a mock forensic interview, but the source of the support has differed, as it does in actual forensic settings. Specifically, in empirical studies, support has been provided by either the presence of child peers or by the actions or identity of an interviewer. Next, we review the studies from each of these lines of research. In all of the studies we review, researchers have examined the effects of social support on the accu-

racy of children's eyewitness reports. In some, researchers have also theorized about potential psychological mechanisms underlying the effects;
however, as will be illustrated, these studies provided little empirical evidence about this critical issue.

Peer-Provided Social Support

Researchers who operationalize social support as the presence of a supportive person have studied the effects of children interviewed alone versus in the presence of a same-aged peer. The first researchers to do so were
Moston and Engelberg (1992). They suggested that forensic interviews are
often anxiety-provoking for young children, pointing to evidence from
child witness studies that included a few children who appeared so distressed during the interview that the experiment was either terminated or
a child's parent had to accompany the child during the interview (e.g.,
Goodman & Reed, 1986; Marin, Holmes, Guth, & Kovac, 1979). Because of
the stress, Moston and Engelberg argued, children would prefer to be
with a same-aged peer than by themselves during a forensic interview.
(Such a preference is consistent with social psychological research demonstrating that people generally prefer to be with others rather than alone in
anxiety-provoking situations; Rofe, 1984; Schachter, 1959.) Moston and
Engelberg reasoned that the presence of a peer would provide emotional
support, reduce children's anxiety, and in turn, increase children's ability
to answer interview questions accurately.

Moston conducted several studies to test these ideas. In the first (Moston, 1992, Experiment 1), 7- to 10-year-olds watched a staged classroom
demonstration, and then they were individually asked to freely report
what they had witnessed. The amount of correct information reported
was similar whether children were interviewed alone or in the presence of
a peer who neither witnessed the demonstration nor was allowed to discuss the event with the participant. In subsequent studies (Experiments 2
& 3), 7- to 10-year-olds and peers were allowed to discuss what they had
witnessed before the participants were interviewed (whether or not the
peers had witnessed the demonstration). These child participants reported more correct information than children who were interviewed
alone or children interviewed in the presence of peers with whom they
had not discussed the demonstration. Moston maintained that peers did
not contribute information to the children's reports. Even so, rehearsal or
memory cuing resulting from the discussion—not the emotionally supportive presence of peers—may have accounted for the increase in correct
information. It is also possible that social facilitation occurred (Zajonc,
1965). That is, children interviewed with a peer may have tried harder
than children interviewed alone because they were motivated to appear

smart in front of the peer. Moston failed to measure children's level of anxiety during the interview, so the theorized mediational effect of anxiety could not be tested.

Greenstock and Pipe (1996) replicated and extended Moston's work. In a group, 5- to 10-year-old children experienced an interactive teaching session with an unfamiliar adult. Three days later, children were individually queried about the event with free-recall and more focused cued-recall questions, some that were misleading and some that were specific, or less leading. Children were interviewed either alone or in the presence of a peer who had not participated in the session and who did not discuss the event with participants. Children's interview anxiety was assessed with a modified version of the state anxiety scale of the State–Trait Anxiety Inventory for Children (STAIC, Spielberger, 1979) and with a heart rate measure. Consistent with Moston's initial findings, children who were interviewed in the presence of a peer were no more accurate than were children interviewed alone. They were also no more or less suggestible or anxious.

In a similar study with 5- to 7-year-olds (Greenstock & Pipe, 1997, Experiment 2), a condition was added in which children were allowed to discuss the event with a peer prior to the interview and the peer was allowed to make comments during the interview. The peer was either informed (had participated in the target event) or uninformed (had not participated in the event). Failing to replicate Moston's (1992) results, the study revealed no main effects of peer support on the amount of correct information child participants recalled in response to free-recall, specific, or misleading questions. Greenstock and Pipe also examined the number of correct items reported together by the child participant and the peer during their preinterview discussion and during free recall. Participant–peer pairs in the informed peer-support condition reported more correct information than participant–peer pairs in the uninformed peer-support condition or participants interviewed without a peer. Further, support condition did not affect children's level of anxiety during the interview. Thus, neither these results nor Moston's provide direct evidence that peer presence increases children's report accuracy by increasing perceived emotional support and decreasing anxiety. Instead, these data suggest that increased accuracy associated with peer presence may be purely informational or cognitive in nature—the result of information pooling, cuing, or rehearsal.

Two other peer-support studies, however, have found some evidence for an effect of peer presence that may extend beyond cuing or informational effects. Greenstock and Pipe (1997, Experiment 1) studied children's recall of a naturally occurring stressful event: a dentist visit. Five- to 6-year-olds and 7- to 10-year-olds were interviewed 2 to 4 days after a dentist visit. Children were interviewed either alone, with an informed peer (i.e., a child who had recently visited the dentist) or an uninformed peer (i.e., a child who had not visited the dentist). Children and peers were allowed to discuss the event before the interview, but the peer was not allowed to speak during the interview. Older children's suggestibility was not affected by peer presence, but young children interviewed alone were less accurate in response to misleading questions than young children interviewed in the presence of a peer, even if the peer was uninformed. Again, however, neither younger nor older children's level of self-reported anxiety was affected by support condition.

Finally, in a study by Cornah and Memon (1996), 6- to 7-year-olds participated in a science demonstration with an unfamiliar adult. Two days later their classroom teacher suggested unexperienced details about that demonstration. After 3 more days, children were individually asked specific questions about the demonstration either alone, with an uninformed peer, or with a presumably informed peer (i.e., a peer the child believed had also participated in the demonstration, but who had not). Children and peers did not discuss the event. In contrast to Moston's (1992, Experiment 1) and Greenstock and Pipe's (1996, Experiment 1) results, when peers were present (uninformed or presumably informed), children's responses were more accurate (less suggestible) than when they were interviewed alone. Further, when presumably informed peers were present, children were less suggestible about the unexperienced details than when interviewed with an uninformed peer or alone. Children's interview anxiety was not assessed.

Several observations can be made about these studies. Although mixed, the results demonstrate that peer presence can improve the accuracy of children's reports during forensic interviews when children and peers are allowed to discuss the event in question (Greenstock & Pipe, 1997, Experiment 2; Moston, 1992, Experiments 2 & 3). Importantly, peer presence may reduce children's suggestibility (Cornah & Memon, 1996; Greenstock & Pipe, 1997, Experiment 1). Yet none of these studies definitively explained why, aside from possible cuing and rehearsal resulting from discussion, peer support did or did not improve children's eyewitness accuracy. None demonstrated that social support reduces anxiety during interviews, the main tenet of Moston and Engelberg's (1992) theory. In fact, Greenstock and Pipe's (1996, 1997) failure to find between-condition differences in children's anxiety weighs in against the theorized anxiety-reduction process.

How relevant are the results of peer support studies for understanding how children respond during actual forensic interviews? It is important to note that children are rarely given pretrial forensic interviews with peers or siblings present, although in some states victims may have a support person present. Instead, a child and an interviewer usually interact in a closed social situation, and children rarely have the opportunity to discuss events with peers. When children give testimony in court, however, they are sometimes allowed to take comforting items to the witness stand (e.g., a favorite blanket or a stuffed animal) or to request that support persons accompany them (Myers, 1996). Thus, the results of these peer support studies may be more generalizable to courtroom interviews than pretrial forensic interviews, although it is unknown whether or not peers in fact serve as support persons. However, this generalizability is somewhat limited by the fact that courtroom interviews are likely to be perceived as more stressful than the interviews in these studies. That is, some (though not all) actual child witnesses (Goodman et al., 1992) and child participants who recount events in real courtrooms during realistic mock trial experiments (Saywitz & Nathanson, 1993) perceive the experience to be unpleasant and anxiety provoking.

Interviewer-Provided Social Support

Research examining the effects of interviewer-provided social support are particularly relevant for understanding children's capabilities in a forensic context. In the context of a forensic interview, social support is best understood as defined by Burleson et al. (1994): an interactional or communicative process occurring between people. Social support (or the lack thereof) may be communicated to a witness through an interviewer's verbal or nonverbal behavior. Research examining adults' noneyewitness task performance reveals positive effects of experimenter-provided support. For example, Sarason and Sarason (1986) and Tardy (1992, 1994) found that experimenter-provided support (e.g., offers to help if the participants wanted assistance) led to more accurate performance on anagram-solving tasks relative to when support was withheld. In addition, communication research demonstrates that short-term recall for noneyewitness tasks is improved when experimenters display supportive behaviors (e.g., reduction in physical distance, forward leaning of the body, head nods, and eye contact, Anderson, 1985; Mehrabian, 1969) than when such immediacy behaviors are withheld from research participants (Kelley & Gorham, 1988). However, one eyewitness testimony study with adult men participants found no benefits of interviewer-provided support in the form of head nods, smiles, forward leans, and periodic compliments (Marquis, Marshall, & Oskamp, 1972).

There have been several investigations of interviewer-provided support on the accuracy of children's reports. In some of these studies, interviewer support has been operationally defined in terms of interviewer identity (mother vs. stranger). In other studies, social support has been operationalized in terms of the behaviors exhibited by unfamiliar inter-

viewers. A study conducted by Goodman, Sharma, Thomas, and Constadine (1995) included 4-year-olds who were interviewed by their mothers
or by strangers about an earlier play session with an unfamiliar adult.
Compared to children interviewed by strangers, children interviewed by
their mothers were more accurate in response to specific (nonleading)
questions and more resistant to misleading suggestions that the play-
person had abused them. Assuming that mothers are more supportive
than strangers, Goodman and colleagues' findings suggest that supportive interviewers are more likely than nonsupportive interviewers to obtain accurate information from children. (Aside from supportiveness,
mothers are, of course, more "familiar" than strange interviewers. Some
recent evidence suggests that familiarity alone may increase resistance to
false suggestions; Bjorklund et al., 2000; Quas & Schaaf, 1998.)

Research by Ricci, Beal, and Dekle (1996) presents a somewhat mixed
picture. In their first experiment, 5-year-olds were interviewed by strangers or by their mother about a staged theft the children watched in a slide
presentation. Compared to children interviewed by their mother, children
interviewed by the stranger were less accurate in response to specific
questions, but more accurate in response to a single misleading question.
We hesitate to interpret these results as directly contrasting Goodman et
al.'s because of several important differences in methodology, differences
that have implications for ecological validity. Specifically, Ricci et al.'s
stimulus event was witnessed via a slide show rather than directly experienced, and there was only one misleading question that was not about a
personally significant event. Further, results must be interpreted cautiously because the interview questions were not standardized across interviewer conditions: Although all interviewers were given a prepared list
of interview questions, they were allowed to embellish or repeat the questions at will. This might be a more ecologically valid approach, but it also
allowed for loss of the experimental control necessary for direct comparisons between the two interviewer conditions. In fact, in a follow-up study
in which interviewers were not allowed to deviate from prepared questions (Ricci et al., 1996, Experiment 2), 5-year-olds who were interviewed
by strangers were no more or less accurate than those interviewed by their
mother. Interestingly, children interviewed by strangers appeared less relaxed to independent raters than children interviewed by their mother.

Tobey and Goodman (1992) varied interviewer identity in a study of 4-
year-olds' memory for a play session with an unfamiliar adult "babysitter." After an 11-day delay, children were interviewed about the play
session with free-recall, specific, and misleading questions. Before the
interview, half of the children were approached by a uniformed police officer (actually a university security officer) who explained that the babysitter "may have done some bad things," and that his partner (the inter-

viewer, who was dressed similarly) needed to ask the children some questions. The remaining children were not approached by the police officer and were not led to believe that the interviewer was also a police officer. Results were mixed, but suggested some benefits for the presumably more supportive "civilian" interview condition. Compared to children in the police condition, children in the civilian condition reported more correct and incorrect information in response to free-recall questions, they were no different in terms of general resistance to misleading questions (but they spontaneously volunteered less incorrect information during the misleading questioning), and they were more accurate in identifying the babysitter from a photo lineup. The policeman's identity — an intimidating figure — may have led to the children's decreased accuracy. Alternatively, the negative implications that the policeman suggested (aside from his presumably nonsupportive identity) could have caused children's errors.

Although these studies are informative about ecologically valid concerns (the impact of questioning by parents and police investigators), definitive conclusions about the effects of social support per se cannot be drawn from these results because interviewer identity, or other characteristics, was confounded with supportiveness in each study. Three studies were conducted without this confound, studies that directly tested the effects of interviewer-provided support on children's reports. In the first study, Goodman, Bottoms, Rudy, and Schwartz-Kenney (1991) tracked 3- to 4-year-olds and 5- to 7-year-olds who received routine inoculations at a medical clinic (a naturally occurring stressful situation). Children were interviewed about their clinic visit with free-recall, specific, and misleading questions. For half of the children, the interviewer acted in a supportive manner by giving the children a snack, smiling frequently, and complimenting them periodically without regard for accuracy. The remaining children were interviewed without these supportive behaviors. Citing developmental theories that stress the importance of environmental support for children to perform at their "optimal level" (e.g., Fischer, 1980), Goodman and colleagues theorized that children would be most accurate overall when interview techniques were supportive. They also predicted that interviewer-provided support would decrease children's intimidation, and in turn, decrease their suggestibility. Their study revealed sporadic effects of interviewer-provided support that were generally in the direction of increasing children's accuracy. For example, social support reduced the number of inaccuracies in all children's free recall. After a 4-week delay, social support also reduced younger children's errors in response to misleading questions and questions that incorrectly suggested that abuse had occurred at the clinic. Even so, support increased younger children's omission errors to misleading questions concerning peripheral characteristics of the clinic setting.

In the second interviewer-support study, Carter, Bottoms, and Levine (1996) investigated the effect of linguistically complicated interview questions and social support on 5- to 7-year-olds' reports. Children played with an unfamiliar adult, then were immediately interviewed. Social support and intimidation were operationalized in terms of specific behaviors noted in the clinical literature to convey emotional warmth or the lack thereof (Kelley & Gorham, 1988; Mehrabian, 1969). For example, in the supportive condition, the interviewer built rapport with the child, used a warm and friendly voice, gazed and smiled at the child often, and assumed a relaxed body position. In the nonsupportive condition, the interviewer withheld these behaviors. This manipulation produced more consistent and specific effects than those reported by Goodman et al. (1991), perhaps because the nonsupportive condition was operationalized as more "intimidating" than "neutral" (Goodman et al.'s nonsupportive condition was more accurately described as "neutral"). Results indicated that children in the supportive condition were more resistant to misleading questions than children in the nonsupportive condition. Support had no effect on children's responses to specific questions or to free recall questions. The researchers theorized that interviewer-provided support increased children's resistance to misleading information by decreasing children's anxiety, lessening intimidation, and increasing feelings of empowerment. They collected no data bearing on this theorized mechanism, however.

A third study (Imhoff & Baker-Ward, 1999) replicated Carter et al.'s (1996) methodology with younger children, but found no effects of interviewer support on children's accuracy. Specifically, 3- and 4-year-olds witnessed a classroom demonstration in small groups and were individually interviewed about it 2 weeks later. Interviewer support had no effect on children's responses to specific or misleading questions about the event. The inconsistency between Imhoff and Baker-Ward's and Carter et al.'s results may be attributable to important differences in the support manipulation in each study. Imhoff and Baker-Ward characterized their nonsupportive condition as neutral, during which interviewers sometimes smiled at the children and complimented them on their performance. Thus, Imhoff and Baker-Ward's manipulation may not have been strong enough to produce significant differences in children's suggestibility.

NEW DIRECTIONS FOR SOCIAL SUPPORT RESEARCH

The research we have reviewed represents an excellent start in investigating social support, an important situational factor that may influence children's accuracy in forensically relevant interview situations. Based on this body of work, we believe that researchers can make some tentative recommendations to professionals who conduct child forensic interviews, including the suggestion that interviewers behave in a socially supportive rather than an intimidating manner during forensic interviews, a suggestion others have made (e.g., Wood et al., 1996). More research is necessary, however, before we fully understand the effects of peer- and interviewer-provided social support and, in turn, before we can make other policy recommendations with confidence. Next, we discuss some of the issues that we believe should be priorities for future research. Specifically, we suggest that researchers should (a) identify the psychological mechanism responsible for the effects of social support, (b) investigate possible individual difference factors that might moderate the effects of social support, and (c) explore the limits of social support's benefits. We end by summarizing our own research program, in which we are currently addressing some of these issues.

Understanding the Mechanism Underlying the Effects of Social Support

Studies of social support and children's testimony have been designed to test the extent to which peer- or interviewer-provided social support influences children's reports. In our view, it is time for researchers to identify the underlying mechanisms responsible for those effects (an effort also called for by Carter and colleagues, 1996). Although we know that peer presence can sometimes help children (particularly younger children) report events accurately, we do not understand the underlying reasons for this effect. Do children perceive a same-aged peer as a source of emotional support? Does this in turn allow the children to be less anxious and more effective as they search their memory for the answers to interview questions? Or can other competing explanations (e.g., information pooling, rehearsal, cuing, social facilitation) account for the effects? In directly testing Moston and Engelberg's (1992) theory, Greenstock and Pipe (1996) found no evidence that anxiety mediates the effect of peer-provided support on children's accuracy. Thus, there may be some other mechanism underlying the effect in studies that uncovered benefits of peer support. Before Moston and Engelberg's theory is completely dismissed, however, it is fair to say that anxiety may be a mediator under other circumstances. That is, Greenstock and Pipe may not have tested the mediation of anxiety effectively, because it is doubtful that their child participants were anxious in the first place. The possible mediation of anxiety cannot be fully tested unless a peer-support study includes somewhat stressful conditions, an ethically difficult, but not impossible, situation to arrange or to find outside the laboratory. Identifying the psychological mechanism by which peer support affects children's reports may help us understand discrepancies in the existing literature (i.e., some studies found positive effects and others found no effects of peer support).

Similarly, how does interviewer-provided support help children resist an interviewer's misleading questions? Does interviewer-provided support affect a child's testimony via a different mechanism than peer-provided social support? Both Goodman et al. (1991) and Carter et al. (1996) offered explanations for their effects, but their explanations have not been empirically validated. Recall that Goodman et al. suggested that interviewer-provided support would decrease children's suggestibility by lowering their intimidation. Carter et al. (1996) were somewhat more specific, theorizing that interviewer support reduces children's anxiety and intimidation, increases their feelings of empowerment, and in turn, increases their resistance to misinformation. In support, they cited Sarason and Sarason's (1986) finding that participants completing a complex cognitive task were more self-confident and less anxious when they were given social support than when they were not. Carter and colleagues' (1996) findings of increased accuracy only in response to misleading questions support their argument that the effect of social support is specific to suggestibility resistance. (Goodman et al.'s findings of increased free-recall accuracy do not fit with this specific explanation, however.)

We have interpreted these explanations to mean that interviewer-provided support makes children feel better able to resist the interviewer, which in turn leads to increased resistance to misleading questions. We believe that such an interpretation clearly indicates the social psychological construct of perceived *self-efficacy* (Davis & Bottoms, 1998). Self-efficacy is a personal cognition about one's ability to perform a task in a given situation, or "people's judgments of their capabilities to organize and execute courses of action required to attain designated types of performances" (Bandura, 1986, p. 391). Unlike judgments about one's stable dispositions or competencies, efficacy judgments are transient and altered by social contexts. According to Bandura (1982, 1997), people base their efficacy judgments on cognitive appraisals of information derived from a variety of sources including self-performance, suggestion or exhortation from others, and physiological indices (e.g., heart rate, perspiration). Research with children has shown that efficacy judgments are good predictors of academic and achievement-oriented behavior (e.g., Schunk, 1989, 1991) and that interventions that increase children's appraisals of their ability to complete academic tasks increase their performance.

We propose that the psychological mediator between interviewer-provided social support and decreased suggestibility is a psychological construct we term "resistance efficacy": children's perceived self-efficacy for resisting an interviewer's suggestions. We theorize that social support increases children's perceived resistance efficacy, which in turn increases their resistance to misleading questions. That is, when an interviewer is supportive, children feel more empowered and able to directly contradict an interviewer's misleading suggestions. In contrast, when an interviewer is not supportive, children may feel intimidated and less able to resist an interviewer's suggestions, and in turn, may be more suggestible.

Identifying Individual Differences in Responsiveness to Social Support

Another imperative for future research is the study of individual differences in children's responsiveness to social support manipulations. Several researchers have noted the importance of individual differences in explaining between-subjects variability in children's testimony (e.g., Eisen, Goodman, Davis, & Qin, in press; Goodman & Quas, 1996; Merrit, Ornstein, & Spicker, 1994; Quas et al., 1999). We think there is good reason to expect interactions between individual differences and situational variables such as the social supportiveness of an interview. For example, Carter et al. (1996) theorized that social support reserves (i.e., the amount of social support already existing in one's life) will moderate the effects of interviewer-provided support on children's suggestibility. That is, children who are high in support reserves are already predisposed to feel empowered, but children low in support reserves are not and may be more sensitive to variations of supportiveness in their environment. Children low in support reserves may experience particularly striking increases in resistance to misinformation under supportive interview conditions relative to children high in support reserves. In fact, there is support for this reasoning in a study with adult participants (Sarason & Sarason, 1986): Compared to participants who were high in social support reserves, participants low in support reserves exhibited greater gains in performance on an anagram task when they were offered help from an experimenter.

Social support might also be particularly effective in increasing interview accuracy in children who are dispositionally shy or those who suffer from low self-esteem. Children who are low in self-esteem may doubt their abilities more than children who are high in self-esteem (Harter & Pike, 1984), and thus, may be more sensitive to interviewer-provided social support. Social support may help such children to relax and answer questions to their maximum capability, when they might otherwise be intimidated and withdrawn. Given that abused children — many of the same children who undergo forensic interviews — often suffer from low self-esteem and general withdrawal (e.g., Kaufman & Cicchetti, 1989), it is worthwhile to determine whether temperamentally shy children or those with low self-esteem benefit from social support more than others.

Finally, another individual difference variable that may determine a child's responsiveness to social support is emotional quality of attachment to significant others. Goodman and her colleagues (Goodman, Quas, Batterman-Faunce, Riddlesberger, & Kuhn, 1997; see also Goodman & Quas, 1996) suggested that attachment style, or the manner in which children have formed relationships with primary caregivers (Bowlby, 1969), may be related to children's memory and suggestibility. In line with predictions from attachment theory (Bowlby, 1969), Goodman et al. (1997) found that children's reactions to a stressful medical procedure were related to their parents' romantic attachment style. (Parental attachment style was measured because there are theoretical reasons to expect that parents' attachment may be related to children's interpretations of and communications about distressing events; Bartholomew, 1990; Shaver & Hazan, 1993). Specifically, children whose parents reported insecure attachment (i.e., avoidant and anxious–ambivalent attachments) were more distressed during a stressful medical procedure and made more errors in response to specific and misleading interview questions about the procedure than children whose parents reported secure attachment. The emotional quality of a forensic interview (supportive or nonsupportive) may make attachment issues salient. In particular, insecurely attached children, who are generally more apprehensive and less trusting of others during social interactions, may be more sensitive to interviewer supportiveness than securely attached children who are generally at ease during social interactions.

We have highlighted only a few dispositional factors that might cause children to be more or less sensitive to manipulations of social support. Of course, there may be numerous others. Identifying individual difference variables and controlling for them in social support studies should allow for more specific examinations of the effects of social support. Identification may also have direct practical benefits for forensic interviewing: It may bring us closer to the goal of targeting children who are particularly at risk for suggestibility and who might benefit the most from special supportive interventions.

Exploring the Limits of Social Support Benefits

A third challenge for future research is to determine the potential limits of the positive effects of social support. The studies we have reviewed demonstrate that social support given without regard for children's actual accuracy improves the accuracy of children's reports. In none of the studies, however, were children given social support contingent upon expected or desired answers. Social support used as a positive reinforcer for certain types of answers may have detrimental effects on children's accuracy, as shown by Garven, Wood, Malpass, and Shaw (1998). Specifically, Garven et al. demonstrated that 3- to 6-year-olds can be suggestible in response to misleading questions when persuaded by a friendly, but persistent, coercive interviewer.

There may be other limitations to the benefits of social support. For example, Carter and colleagues (1996) characterized their results as tentative without replication "under conditions that are sometimes encountered in actual abuse cases . . . multiple interviews or long delays" (p. 351). The advent of organized, multidisciplinary responses to child abuse allegations (like those coordinated at children's advocacy centers; Sorenson, Bottoms, & Perona, 1997) has reduced the number of interviews children undergo and the delay between alleged incidents and forensic interviews. Even so, some alleged victims are still questioned repeatedly in forensic settings, sometimes after a significant delay (Gray, 1993; Steward & Steward, 1996). In addition, suspected child abuse victims may participate in multiple therapy sessions in which a therapist will ask them about alleged abuse in a warm and supportive manner. Will repeated exposure to socially supportive interviews be beneficial or have detrimental effects? What is the impact of social support after a significant delay?

We know of no studies investigating the effects of multiple exposures to peer-provided support. Goodman et al. (1991) conducted the only examination of repeated exposure to interviewer-provided support. Children in that study received either one or two interviews (which were either both supportive or both neutral). Effects of support were sporadic across the two interviews, and there was no interaction of the support variable and the number of interviews (which would indicate either a positive or negative effect of repeated exposure to support). The effects of social support over the course of more interviews is not known. Critics and courts (e.g., State v. Michaels, 1993) have voiced concern that multiple supportive interviews will increase suggestibility. In light of the psychological research and theory we have reviewed, however, we would expect a positive effect across multiple interviews, perhaps even an additive effect as repeated exposure to a supportive interviewer builds a child's resistance efficacy.

Regarding the variable of delay, we would expect social support to have its strongest effect after a significant delay, when children doubt their own memory (suggestibility increases for adults and children after memory decays; Gudjonsson, 1992; Loftus, 1979). In fact, Goodman and colleagues (1991) found the strongest effects of support after a 4-week delay as compared to a 2-week delay. But no one has investigated the effects of interviewer-provided or peer-provided support over a longer delay.

OUR CURRENT RESEARCH PROGRAM

We are currently conducting studies to address some of the issues we previously outlined. Next, we briefly summarize an experiment in which our primary goals were to (a) replicate prior research demonstrating the benefits of interviewer-provided support on children's eyewitness reports, (b) explore the relative abilities of anxiety and resistance efficacy to explain the effects of social support on children's suggestibility, and (c) explore individual difference factors as potential moderators of the effects of social support.

In our study (Davis, 1998a; Davis & Bottoms, 1998), which was modeled after Carter et al. (1996), eighty-one 6- and 7-year-olds individually played with a female research assistant who was introduced to each child as a babysitter. Some of the play activities involved innocuous touching (e.g., the babysitter traced the child's body with a crayon and asked the child to tickle her). Immediately afterwards, each child was given a mock forensic interview by a male research assistant, who explained that he was the babysitter's boss and that he wanted to find out if the babysitter was doing a good job. The interview consisted of free recall, specific, and misleading questions, and was administered under either supportive or intimidating conditions. As in Carter et al.'s study, the supportive condition was designed to be child-friendly; that is, the interviewer displayed behaviors found by clinical research to convey emotional warmth (e.g., rapport-building, supportive eye contact, smiles). In contrast, in the nonsupportive condition, the interviewer did not display any supportive behaviors, and, in fact, behaved in an intimidating manner by actively avoiding eye contact, smiles, and so forth.

After the interview, children were greeted by a third adult who administered a shortened version of the state anxiety scale of the STAIC (Papay & Spielberger, 1986; Spielberger, 1979) so that we could test previous assertions that anxiety mediates the effect of support on children's suggestibility (Carter et al., 1996; Moston & Engelberg, 1992). To test our own competing theory regarding resistance efficacy as the mediator, children were also given a specially constructed Resistance Efficacy Scale for children (RES). The RES items were designed to tap children's perceived ability to resist the interviewer (e.g., "How easy or hard it would be to tell the interviewer he was wrong about something, if you know he's wrong?"). Items were accompanied by age-appropriate response scales and orienting practice trials.

As expected, preliminary analyses of our data revealed a replication of Carter et al.'s results: Interviewer-provided support enhanced the accuracy of children's reports by significantly increasing their resistance to misleading questions. Support did not affect children's answers to specific questions. In addition, for the first time, we found that social support influences children's anxiety during a mock forensic interview. Children in the nonsupportive condition rated themselves as significantly more anxious than children in the supportive condition (Ms were 1.6 and 1.4, respectively, on the STAIC, which ranges from 1, indicating low levels of anxiety, to 3, indicating high levels of anxiety). Contrary to others' predictions, however, anxiety did not mediate the effect of interviewer support on children's suggestibility. Instead, our analyses revealed that children's feelings of resistance efficacy were enhanced by social support, and that resistance efficacy mediated the effect of interviewer support on children's accuracy in response to misleading questions (especially for the oldest children in our sample). Specifically, interviewer support increased older children's feelings of resistance efficacy, which in turn increased their resistance to misleading questions.

Thus, ours is the third study to reveal the benefits of interviewer-provided social support on children's suggestibility. It is the first study to demonstrate that a lack of emotional support from an interviewer can have a detrimental effect on children's well-being by increasing their anxiety, and a negative effect on children's accuracy by decreasing their resistance efficacy. We are currently examining our data for the answers to other critical questions such as whether the impact of social support is mediated by individual differences in such domains as social support reserves, attachment style, temperamental shyness, and self-esteem. We are also in the midst of a follow-up study investigating the effects of repeated exposure to social support after more than a year's delay.

CONCLUSION

In this chapter, we have shown that empirical evidence generally disputes speculation that "child-friendly" interviewing methods will lead children to fabricate details or entire abuse allegations to please interviewers. Rather, studies investigating peer-provided support have yielded mixed results, but none has revealed detrimental effects on children's accuracy. Studies investigating interviewer-provided support revealed more solid benefits. Perhaps future research will examine the effectiveness of different modes of communicating social support to children. In light of the evidence we have reviewed, we are confident in our recommendation that forensic interviewers should guard against false reports by interviewing children in a socially supportive, nonintimidating manner. Of course, avoidance of misleading questions is also advised, but because children's responses to open-ended and specific questions are often brief, and because forensic interviewers do not know what really happened during target events, it would be impossible for interviewers to avoid all detailed, even misleading questions.

We hope that researchers will continue research on social support, a variable that is of significant theoretical interest to psychology, but also of applied importance because it is an easily implemented intervention that may have measurable effects on the accuracy of actual child witnesses.

ACKNOWLEDGMENTS

Financial support for our research was provided by grants to Suzanne L. Davis from the American Psychological Foundation/Council of Graduate Departments of Psychology, the American Psychology-Law Society, Sigma Xi, and the Society for the Psychological Study of Social Issues. Toys for families in our study were provided by Chuck E. Cheese, Chicago International Children's Film Festival, Cineplex Odeon, Little Caesar's, McDonald's, Organic Touchstone Company, and Taco Bell. We extend special thanks to the families who participated in the study; to Patrick K. Ackles for assistance with participant recruitment; and to Rosalie B. Guerrero, Andrea L. Krebel, Richard T. Reyes, Jason P. Rohacs, Elaine A. Shreder, and Alon Stein for invaluable research assistance.

REFERENCES

Andersen, P. A. (1985). Nonverbal immediacy in interpersonal communication. In A. W. Siegman & S. Feldstein (Eds.), *Multichannel integrations of nonverbal behavior* (pp. 1–36). Hillsdale, NJ: Lawrence Erlbaum Associates.

Bandura, A. (1982). Self-efficacy mechanism in human agency. *American Psychologist, 37,* 122–147.

Bandura, A. (1986). *Social foundations of thought and action: A social cognitive theory.* Englewood Cliffs, NJ: Prentice-Hall.

Bandura, A. (1997). *Self efficacy: The exercise of control.* New York: Freeman.

Bartholomew, K. (1990). Avoidance of intimacy: An attachment perspective. *Journal of Social and Personal Relationships, 7,* 147–178.

Bjorklund, D. F., Cassel, W. S., Bjorklund, B. R., Brown, R. D., Park, C. L., Ernst, K., & Owen, F. A. (2000). Social demand characteristics in children's eyewitness memory and suggestibility: The effects of different interviewers. *Applied Cognitive Psychology, 14,* 421–433.

Bowlby, J. (1969). *Attachment and loss: Vol. 1. Attachment.* New York: Basic Books.

Bull, R. (1998). Obtaining information from child witnesses. In A. Memon, A. Vrij, & R. Bull (Eds.), *Psychology and law: Truthfulness, accuracy, and credibility* (pp. 188–209). London: McGraw-Hill.

Burleson, B. R., Albrecht, T. L., Goldsmith, D. J., & Sarason, I. G. (1994). Introduction: The communication of social support. In B. R. Burleson, T. L. Albrecht, & I. G. Sarason (Eds.), *Communication of social support* (pp. xi–xxx). Thousand Oaks, CA: Sage.

Carter, C. A., Bottoms, B. L., & Levine, M. (1996). Linguistic and socioemotional influences on the accuracy of children's reports. *Law and Human Behavior, 20,* 335–358.

Ceci, S. J., & Bruck, M. (1993). Suggestibility of the child witness: A historical review and synthesis. *Psychological Bulletin, 113,* 403–439.

Cohen, S., & Wills, T. (1985). Stress, social support, and the buffering hypothesis. *Psychological Bulletin, 98,* 310–357.

Cornah, D., & Memon, A. (1996, March). *Improving children's testimony: The effects of social support.* Paper presented at the biennial meeting of the American Psychology-Law Society, Hilton Head, SC.

Cutrona, C. E., & Russell, D. W. (1990). Type of social support and specific stress: Toward a theory of optimal matching. In S. R. Sarason, I. G. Sarason, & G. R. Pierce (Eds.), *Social support: An interactional view* (pp. 319–366). New York: Wiley.

Davis, S. L. (1998a). *Effects of social support on children's eyewitness reports: A test of the underlying mechanism.* Unpublished doctoral dissertation, University of Illinois, Chicago.

Davis, S. L. (1998b). Social and scientific influences on the study of children's suggestibility: A historical perspective. *Child Maltreatment, 3,* 186–194.

Davis, S. L., & Bottoms, B. L. (1998, April). Effects of social support on children's eyewitness reports. In B. L. Bottoms & J. A. Quas (Chairs), *Situational and individual sources of variability in children's suggestibility an·l false memories.* Symposium conducted at the biennial meeting of the American Psychology-Law Society, Redondo Beach, CA.

Eisen, M. E., Goodman, G. S., Davis, S. L., & Qin, J. (1998). Individual differences in maltreated children's memory and suggestibility. In L. M. Williams (Ed.), *Trauma and memory.* Thousand Oaks, CA: Sage.

Fischer, K. W. (1980). A theory of cognitive development: The control and construction of hierarchies of skills. *Psychological Review, 87,* 477–531.

Garven, S., Wood, J. M., Malpass, R. S., & Shaw, J. S. (1998). More than suggestion: The effect of interviewing techniques from the McMartin Preschool case. *Journal of Applied Psychology, 83,* 347–359.

Goodman, G. S., Bottoms, B. L., Rudy, L., & Schwartz-Kenney, B. M. (1991). Children's testimony about a stressful event: Improving children's reports. *Journal of Narrative and Life History, 1,* 69–99.

Goodman, G. S., Emery, R. E., & Haugaard, J. J. (1998). Developmental psychology and law: Divorce, child maltreatment, foster care, and adoption. In I. Siegel & A. Renninger (Eds.), *Child psychology in practice.* In W. Damon (Series Ed.), *Handbook of Child Psychology* (Vol. 4). New York: Wiley.

Goodman, G. S., & Quas, J. A. (1996). Trauma and memory: Individual differences in children's recounting of a stressful experience. In N. L. Stein, C. Brainerd, P. A. Ornstein, & B. Tversky (Eds.), *Memory for everyday and emotional events* (pp. 267–294). Mahwah, NJ: Lawrence Erlbaum Associates.

Goodman, G. S., Quas, J. A., Batterman-Faunce, J. M., Riddlesberger, M. M., & Kuhn, G. (1997). Children's reactions to and memory for a stressful event: Influences of age, anatomical dolls, knowledge, and parental attachment. *Applied Developmental Science, 1,* 54–75.

Goodman, G. S., & Reed, R. S. (1986). Age differences in eyewitness testimony. *Law and Human Behavior, 10,* 317–332.

Goodman, G. S., Sharma, A., Thomas, S. F., & Constadine, M. G. (1995). Mother knows best: Effects of relationship status and interviewer bias on children's memory. *Journal of Experimental Child Psychology, 60,* 195–228.

Goodman, G. S., Taub, E. P., Jones, D. P. H., England, P., Port, L. K., Rudy, L., & Prado, L. (1992). Testifying in criminal court. *Monographs of the Society for Research in Child Development, 57*(5, Serial No. 229).

Gray, E. (1993). *Unequal justice: The prosecution of child sexual abuse.* New York: Free Press.

Greenstock, J., & Pipe, M. E. (1996). Interviewing children about past events: The influence of peer support and misleading questions. *Child Abuse and Neglect, 20,* 69–80.

Greenstock, J., & Pipe, M. E. (1997). Are two heads better than one? Peer support and children's eyewitness reports. *Applied Cognitive Psychology, 11,* 461–483.

Gudjonsson, G. (1992). *The psychology of interrogations, confessions, and testimony.* Chichester, England: Wiley.

Harris, M. J., & Rosenthal, R. (1985). Mediation of interpersonal expectancy effects: Thirty-one meta-analyses. *Psychological Bulletin, 97,* 363–386.

Harter, S., & Pike, R. (1984). The pictorial scale of perceived competence and social acceptance for young children. *Child Development, 55,* 1969-1982.

Imhoff, M. C., & Baker-Ward, L. (1999). Preschoolers' suggestibility: Effects of developmentally appropriate language and interviewer supportiveness. *Journal of Applied Developmental Psychology, 20,* 407–429.

Inhelder, B., & Piaget, J. (1958). *The growth of logical thinking from childhood to adolescence.* New York: Basic Books.

Kaufman, J., & Cicchetti, D. (1989). Effects of maltreatment on school-age children's socioemotional development: Assessments in a day-camp setting. *Developmental Psychology, 25,* 516–524.

Kelley, D. H., & Gorham, H. (1988). Effects of immediacy on recall of information. *Communication Education, 37,* 198–207.

Loftus, E. F. (1979). *Eyewitness testimony.* Cambridge, MA: Harvard University Press.

Marin, B. V., Holmes, D. L., Guth, M., & Kovac, P. (1979). The potential of children as witnesses. *Law and Human Behavior, 3,* 295–306.

Marquis, K. H., Marshall, J., & Oskamp, S. (1972). Testimony validity as a function of question form, atmosphere, and item difficulty. *Journal of Applied Social Psychology, 2,* 167–186.

Mehrabian, D. (1969). Some referents and measures of nonverbal behavior. *Behavioral Research Methods and Instruments, 1,* 213–217.

Merrit, K. A., Ornstein, P. A., & Spicker, B. (1994). Children's memory for a salient medical procedure: Implications for testimony. *Pediatrics, 94,* 17–23.

Moston, S. (1992). Social support and children's eyewitness testimony. In H. Dent & R. Flin (Eds.), *Children as witnesses* (pp. 33–46). Chichester, England: Wiley.

Moston, S., & Engelberg, T. (1992). The effects of social support on children's eyewitness testimony. *Applied Cognitive Psychology, 6,* 61–75.

Myers, J. E. B. (1992). *Evidence in child abuse and neglect cases.* New York: Wiley.

Myers, J. E. B. (1996). A decade of international reform to accommodate child witnesses: Steps toward a child witness code. In B. L. Bottoms & G. S. Goodman (Eds.), *International perspectives on child abuse and children's testimony: Psychological research and law* (pp. 221–265). Thousand Oaks, CA: Sage.

Myers, J. E. B. (1998). *Legal issues in child abuse and neglect practice.* Thousand Oaks, CA: Sage.

Papay, J. P., & Spielberger, C. D. (1986). Assessment of anxiety and achievement in kindergarten and first- and second-grade children. *Journal of Abnormal Child Psychology, 14,* 279–286.

Quas, J. A., Goodman, G. S., Bidrose, S., Pipe, M. E., Craw, S., & Ablin, D. S. (1999). Emotion and memory: Children's long-term remembering, forgetting, and suggestibility. *Journal of Experimental Child Psychology, 72,* 235–270.

Quas, J. A., & Schaaf, J. (1998). Children's true and false reports of a play interaction. In J. A. Quas & J. Qin (Chairs), *Accurate, inaccurate, and false memories of childhood events.* Symposium conducted at the Sixth National Colloquium of the American Professional Society on the Abuse of Children, Chicago.

Ricci, C. M., Beal, C. R., & Dekle, D. J. (1996). The effect of parent versus unfamiliar interviewers on children's eyewitness memory and identification accuracy. *Law and Human Behavior, 20,* 483–500.

Rofe, Y. (1984). Stress and affiliation: A utility theory. *Psychological Review, 91,* 235–250.

Rosenthal, R., & Jacobson, L. (1968). *Pygmalion in the classroom: Teacher expectation and student intellectual development*. New York: Holt, Rinehart, & Winston.

Sarason, I. G., & Sarason, B. R. (1986). Experimentally provided social support. *Journal of Personality and Social Psychology, 50*, 1222–1225.

Sarason, B. R., Sarason, I. G., & Pierce, G. R. (Eds.). (1990). *Social support: An interactional view*. New York: Wiley.

Saywitz, K. J., & Nathanson, R. (1993). Children's testimony and their perceptions of stress in and out of the courtroom. *Child Abuse and Neglect, 17*, 613–622.

Schachter, S. (1959). *The psychology of affiliation*. Stanford, CA: Stanford University Press.

Schunk, D. H. (1989). Self-efficacy and achievement behaviors. *Educational Psychology Review, 1*, 173–208.

Schunk, D. H. (1991). Self-efficacy and academic motivation. *Educational Psychologist, 26*, 207–231.

Shaver, P. R., & Hazan, C. (1993). Adult romantic attachment: Theory and evidence. In D. Perlman & W. H. Jones (Eds.), *Advances in personal relationships* (Vol. 4, pp. 29–70). London: Kingsley.

Sorenson, E., Bottoms, B. L., & Perona, A. (1997). *Intake and forensic interviewing in the children's advocacy center setting: A handbook*. Washington, DC: National Network of Children's Advocacy Centers.

Spielberger, C. D. (1979). *State-trait anxiety inventory for children*. Palo Alto, CA: Consulting Psychologists Press.

State v. Michaels, 264 N. J. Super 579, 625 A. D. 2d 489 (N. J. Super ad, 1993).

Steward, M. S., & Steward, D. S. (1996). Interviewing young children about body touch and handling. *Monographs of the Society for Research in Child Development, 61*(4–5, Serial No. 248).

Tardy, C. H. (1992). Assessing the functions of supportive messages: Experimental studies of social support. *Communication Research, 19*, 175–192.

Tardy, C. H. (1994). Counteracting task-induced stress: Studies of instrumental and emotional support in problem-solving contexts. In B. R. Burleson, T. L. Albrecht, & I. G. Sarason (Eds.), *Communication of social support: Messages, interactions, relationships, and community* (pp. 71–87). Thousand Oaks, CA: Sage.

Tobey, A. E., & Goodman, G. S. (1992). Children's eyewitness memory: Effects of participation and forensic context. *Child Abuse and Neglect, 16*, 779–796.

Vygotsky, L. (1978). *Mind in society: The development of higher psychological processes*. Cambridge, MA: Harvard University Press. (Original work published 1934)

Warren, A. R., & McGough, L. S. (1996). Research on children's suggestibility: Implications for the investigative interview. In B. L. Bottoms & G. S. Goodman (Eds.), *International perspectives on child abuse and children's testimony: Psychological research and law* (pp. 12–44). Thousand Oaks, CA: Sage.

Wolchik, S. A., Sandler, I. N., & Braver, S. L. (1990). Social support: Its assessment and relation to children's adjustment. In N. Eisenberg (Ed.), *Contemporary topics in developmental psychology* (pp. 319–349). New York: Wiley.

Wood, J. M., McClure, K. A., & Birch, R. A. (1996). Suggestions for improving interviews in child protection agencies. *Child Maltreatment, 1*, 233–230.

Zajonc, R. B. (1965). Social facilitation. *Science, 149*, 269–274.

Zelkowitz, P. (1989). Parents and children as informants concerning children's social networks. In D. Belle (Ed.), *Children's social networks and social supports* (pp. 221–237). New York: Wiley.

Zeman, J., & Shipman, K. (1996). Children's expression of negative affect: Reasons and methods. *Developmental Psychology, 32*, 842–849.

Author Index

Subject Index

A

Adult eyewitness memory, ix–xiii, 14–18, 37, 48, 63–81, 143–159, 177–181, 205–227, 265–282, 287–304, 309–323
  confidence, 278–282
  individual differences, 205–227
  suggestibility, 64, 67, 205–228, 295, 298–299, 312–322
Age differences in memory, 30, 86, 89–90, 179, 195, 211–213, 331–350, 359–362, 391–393
Age regression, see Hypnosis
Amnesia, 6, 178
  anterograde, 15
  childhood, 6
  infantile, 6, 297
  psychogenic, 150–151, 165
  retrograde, 15, 165
Anatomical dolls, see interviewing techniques
Attachment, 247–249, 254
Attachment Q-Sort, 248

B

Bayesian approach, 374
Beck Depression Inventory, 144

C

Child eyewitness memory, ix–xiii, 29–61, 85–113, 116–126, 166–181, 185–200, 211–212, 235–256, 331–350, 355–377, 384–388, 393–402, 409–434, 437–454
  developmental framework, 30–37
  individual differences, 235–256
  suggestibility, 85–113, 166–169, 340–343, 355–377, 393–402, 412, 426, 444–453
Coercive questioning, see Interviewer effect
Cognitive interview, 23–24, 104, 127, 155, 265–282
  empirical tests, 269–273
Configural processing, see Encoding
Context reinstatement, 104, 266
Conversational Interactions, 43, 240–242
  joint-talk, 46–47
Coping with crisis, see Stress
Coping styles, see Personality variables
Creative Imagination Scale (CIS), 222
Criteria-Based Content Analysis (CBCA), 280, 413
Cross-racial identification 128–133
Cued recall, see Recall

D

Daubert principle, 291–292

Made in the USA
Las Vegas, NV
02 October 2021